The Art of Compassionate Business

There are several well-ingrained assumptions regarding the dynamics of work and business activities, which can be refuted. Some examples of these widespread assumptions in the business and work environments are employees being viewed as commodities, competitors perceived as threats, companies' resources seen as limited, and customers perceived as scarce and difficult. All this leads to the question "Is there a way to perform business activities more humanely?"

The second edition of this book challenges the reader to change the way they perform in business situations and become more focused on the human aspects of business activities. The users of this knowledge and those affected by them will undergo a profound transformation in the way they perform business activities. They will benefit from gradually testing and implementing the guidelines conveyed in this book, both in the business environment and in the workplace. When readers put these principles into practice, positive ripple effects are bound to affect other stakeholders of the organisation they work for or own.

The author has refreshed all the concepts and examples introduced in the first edition which includes aspects related to mission and vision, passion, business mindset, organisational learning, improvement of business conversations, use of constructive criticism, and betterment of relationships with the most relevant stakeholders (customers, suppliers, intermediaries, community, employees, etc.). The author also includes a discussion of creativity and the innovation process as well as other relevant aspects related to a healthy business environment and provides various real-life examples of companies which have adopted a loving attitude towards their stakeholders – which has become so important in the current business environment.

The Art of Compassionate Business

Main Principles for the Human-Oriented Enterprise

Second Edition

Dr. Bruno R. Cignacco

Routledge
Taylor & Francis Group

A PRODUCTIVITY PRESS BOOK

Second edition 2024
by Routledge
605 Third Avenue, New York, NY 10158

and by Routledge
4 Park Square, Milton Park, Abingdon, Oxon, OX14 4RN

Routledge is an imprint of the Taylor & Francis Group, an informa business

First edition published in 2019 by Routledge

ISBN: 978-1-032-44543-4 (hbk)
ISBN: 978-1-032-44542-7 (pbk)
ISBN: 978-1-003-37268-4 (ebk)

DOI: 10.4324/9781003372684

Typeset in Adobe Garamond
by KnowledgeWorks Global Ltd.

Contents

SECTION II GENERAL ASPECTS OF LOVE AND BUSINESS

SECTION IV MAIN ASPECTS OF LOVE AND CREATIVITY

SECTION V   APPENDICES

Acknowledgements

This book is dedicated to the memory of my mother, who was the person who first introduced me to the principles which have deeply influenced this book. This text is also dedicated to the memory of my uncle Hugo Francesconi, for his continuous support and faith in me.

I am also deeply grateful to:

- Fayola Saunders, a very sweet and special person in my life who showed great enthusiasm in reviewing the manuscript.
- My son, my father, my sister, my niece, and my godson.
- My friends.
- My clients.
- The educational institutions I have taught at over my career.
- The people working for the publisher for their significant support during the publishing process.

Dr. Bruno R. Cignacco, PhD, is an international business consultant, TEDx speaker, and business coach. For over 30 years, he has advised and trained hundreds of companies on international trade activities and international marketing. He teaches business modules, both at undergraduate and at postgraduate levels, at various universities in the UK. He is a Senior Fellow of the Higher Education Academy (HEA), UK. He is also a Master Life Coach and Master NLP practitioner. He has studied disciplines related to personal development for more than 30 years. He has delivered countless talks, seminars, and conferences in several countries. He is the author of business books, such as *Fundamentals of International Marketing for SMEs* (Atlantic Publishers, 2010) which has been published in several languages, like English (Atlantic Publishers, 2010), Spanish (Macchi Publishers, 2004), and Portuguese (Saraiva Publisher, 2009). His other business book is *Techniques of International Negotiation* (Macchi Publishers, 2014). He is also the author of personal development books published in different languages. His website is www.brunocignacco. com.

Prologue

A human being is a part of the whole called by us universe, a part limited in time and space. He experiences himself, his thoughts and feeling as something separated from the rest, a kind of optical delusion of his consciousness. This delusion is a kind of prison for us, restricting us to our personal desires and to affection for a few persons nearest to us. Our task must be to free ourselves from this prison by widening our circle of compassion to embrace all living creatures and the whole of nature in its beauty.

Albert Einstein

Origins of This Book

In hindsight, I realise the germ of an idea for this book has been dormant in my mind for several years. The topics it contains are the natural development of several books I have written about business and personal development over more than a decade. This book also includes golden insights from my lengthy career as an international business consultant. These topics have been integrated to create a unique text for readers.

There are excellent business books, general texts or specialised ones (on marketing, human resources, business economics, strategy, accounting, management, entrepreneurship and other topics). Most texts indeed offer relevant advice to avid readers who set up, work for, or lead business organisations.

These business texts have a clear focus on specific organisational objectives (e.g., increasing profits, obtaining a bigger market share, improving quality levels, etc.). These books also assume that businesses are operating in an unpredictable and threatening environment, continually facing several challenges, which must be dealt with efficiently. Most traditional business authors make several assumptions regarding the dynamics of business activities, for example:

a. Zero-Sum Game

   All businesses are inserted into a competitive environment, where all participants, with no exception, try to outpace one another. In this "game," each "player" seeks to win at the expense of the others. Mutually beneficial agreements for all parties involved and co-operative bonds between organisations tend to be uncommon, or the exception to this rule.

b. Competitors as Threats

   Other companies are usually perceived as threatening adversaries, which must be outsmarted whenever possible. Companies tend to focus on the external (e.g., allocating resources to beat competitors), rather than on the internal (e.g., developing their own distinct capabilities to stand out in the market). Other organisations can never be perceived as valuable sources of inspiration and feedback, but as threats.

c. Imperative Innovation

Organisations run an endless race to improve their products, services, and processes. Their constant innovation stems from market trends (social, economic, technological, etc.), customers' needs, and the companies' capabilities. Most companies perceive customers as overly demanding and fuelled by a continuous search for the latest novelties (better design, improved performance, etc.). In this frantic race, companies that dare to take a rest risk being tossed out of the market by more innovative competitors.

d. Limited Resources

Another relevant tenet in the business world asserts that all companies count on limited resources, which restrains what they do, as well as how and when. Consequently, companies tend to efficiently co-ordinate and utilise their scarce resources, through strategies and other tools. New resources are generally perceived as difficult to generate because they take extensive time and effort.

e. Difficult Customers

There is a widespread assumption that finding new customers and retaining current ones is always difficult. Gaining customers' loyalty tends to be a troublesome issue because they are perceived as fickle. Customer behaviour is deemed to be difficult to predict. Consequently, many companies perform manipulative activities to seduce customers and prospects by, for instance, using misleading information in adverts, making exaggerated promises regarding products and services, and carefully hiding products' weaknesses, among others.

f. Believing in the Might of Technology

In this fast-paced era, many companies consider that technological devices allow them to achieve their objectives more efficiently. Nonetheless, the excessive use of technology also decreases the direct interaction with people, thus damaging the human connection between businesses and their most relevant stakeholders (customers, employees, suppliers, etc.). In extreme cases, technology can even replace the human resources, such as in the case of automated machines or robots.

g. Unloving Work Environment

In many companies, their work environments are affected by internal politics, for instance, one-upmanship, backbiting, and gatekeeping, among others. These aspects do not contribute to strengthening relationships between workmates and instead prevent them from co-operating with one another. Many of these tactics are driven by an egotistic attitude, which creates a distrust among employees. These political factors often hold people back from adopting a loving attitude with one another.

h. Commoditised People

Figuratively speaking, some companies treat employees as cogs of the organisational machine which can be replaced easily by others. Employees are considered as a "means" to achieve organisational objectives, instead of human beings with needs, emotions, and dreams which must be acknowledged and valued. Employees tend to be entangled in a web of rules, regulations, and procedures which leave them no leeway for taking initiative or being creative. Oftentimes, employees are heartlessly pushed by companies to the limits in order to achieve the goals of the latter. This continuous pressure pushes employees towards stress or burnout.

i. Widespread Conflicts

All organisations are affected by internal and external conflicts. Often, conflicts tend to be solved in an adversarial manner where one party wins at the expense of the other. These win–lose solutions also affect the relationships between the participants in a negative manner. Many companies are more interested in obtaining all the gains from conflictive situations with others than in preserving the relationships with them.

My Background and Expectations for This Book

I have been teaching business modules at several universities at an undergraduate and postgraduate level across the world and acting as a consultant to countless organisations for more than 30 years. I recognised the aforementioned assumptions in all types of organisations both in my professional experience and in most traditional business books. At several points, I asked myself, "Is there a way to perform business activities more humanely?" After years of dwelling on this thought-provoking idea, the answer to this paramount question can finally be found in this book.

In the following chapters, I will elaborate on relevant aspects of business which have been dismissed in most relevant business bibliographies. As an inquisitive cartographer, I will map out the main principles which drive authentic success in businesses that at the same time generate benefits for all parties involved.

How to Reap the Most Benefits from This Book

All principles included in this book are based on a deep awareness of our essence as human beings. Nonetheless, many organisations are oblivious to these principles, despite their enormous benefits. It is not the purpose of this text to deliver law-like generalisations. Nonetheless, the paradigms exposed in this book can certainly be applied to any type of organisational environment and cultural background, for example:

- Small, medium-sized, and big organisations.
- Local, national, regional, and global organisations.
- Organisations related to different sectors, such as primary (extractive, such as agriculture), secondary (transformative or productive), and tertiary (provider of services).
- Non-profit and profit-making organisations, as well as governmental bodies.

This book delivers a heart-warming and hopeful message to organisations. These down-to-earth ideas will help them become more valuable, genuine, and meaningful. The advice provided in this book is timeless.

This text does not provide intricate strategic perspectives, but people-centred principles. Even though some guidelines enclosed in this book are often based on common sense and others counterintuitive, all of them are backed by profuse scientific research and professional experiences. Some of the relevant points explored throughout the book are:

- How to define a business mission with a positive impact on the world.
- How to be more passionate with business activities.
- How to adopt a prosperity mindset in business.
- How to have more loving relationships with stakeholders.
- How to create more connected conversations.
- How to create a warmer work environment.

- How to serve customers in a loving manner.
- How to develop more innovative and impactful ideas.

It is suggested that readers gradually test and implement the guidelines conveyed in this book, both in the business environment and the workplace. When these principles are put into practice, positive ripple effects are bound to affect other stakeholders. The users of this knowledge and those affected by them will undergo a profound internal transformation, which will change the way they perceive business situations.

This book provides guidelines to contribute to more loving work and business environments. This text also shows the obstacles on the way to achieving that objective. There are organisations that will need to change their well-ingrained attitudes and practices to implement the beneficial perspectives suggested in this book.

Brief Notes to the Second Edition

We live in a time when science is validating what humans have known throughout the ages: that compassion is not a luxury; it is a necessity for our well-being, resilience and survival.

Joan Halifax

In its second edition, this book includes a myriad of impactful cases of companies which are both economically successful and human-oriented. These organisations are truly awe-inspiring, as their business projects pursue not only economic results (profits, etc.), but also bring about a positive environmental and social impact. These companies truly aim to bring about a better world for all.

In these organisations, the most important assets are the human beings (employees, customers, suppliers, community members, etc.), not technology, funds, or other resources. Therefore, these organisations purposefully foster robust long-lasting relationships with various stakeholders, as these businesses understand that the main Key Performance Indicators (profitability, etc.) are reliant on the strength of these relationships. These organisations discourage any attitude of unkindness and self-centredness, but instead foster lofty values like compassion, supportiveness, and care.

I hope that readers could take these outstanding examples as valuable models to emulate, both on an individual and on an organisational level. These businesses truly generate positive ripple effects in society and on the planet, as they purposefully care for all their stakeholders, not only their owners.

These businesses cast a powerful beam of light, which shows the right trail to be followed by other organisations, especially those which are only centred on profits. The human-oriented organisations discussed all over this book embrace lofty principles like honesty, transparency, integrity, trust, benevolence, and others, and embody these very principles throughout their daily business practices.

I hope that you enjoy this book as much as I have enjoyed developing it. Thank you for your kind attention.

Dr. Bruno R. Cignacco

MISSION, PASSION, AND PROSPERITY MINDSET

Chapter 1

Importance of a Meaningful Mission

Only when we truly love our work will we put in the time, and take the care, to do it to the best of our ability.

Mark McGuinness

1.1 Importance of a Business Mission

I slept and dreamt that life was joy. I awoke and saw that life was service. I acted and behold, service was joy.

Rabindranath Tagore

It is one of the most beautiful compensations of this life that you cannot sincerely try to help another without helping yourself.

Ralph Waldo Emerson

The terms "mission" and "purpose" will be used interchangeably. A mission is an organisation's main reason for existence in the marketplace. A compelling purpose is one of the most relevant success factors for any organisation. Some organisations' websites have distinctive links to their mission statements.

Kotler et al. (2009) highlighted that a mission should include a very narrow set of objectives and other aspects (the company's industrial sector, its unique qualities, its products and services, specific groups of customers served, and the benefits obtained by them). These authors also observed that a business mission is closely linked to its vision, which includes the company's objectives or intentions for the future. In other words, the vision is the image of what the organisation wants to be in the future.

According to Price and Price (2013), the mission is what the company aspires to do with their daily activities; instead, the vision is what the company intends to become in the future. A well-defined

DOI: 10.4324/9781003372684-2

mission always assists a company in the achievement of its vision. The vision can be reformulated once attained, while the mission is more prone to remain relatively unchanged over time.

Collins and Lazier (2020) observed that a company's vision unleashes outstanding human effort, prompts strategic and tactical decisions, brings about communion and integration of human resources, and prevents the company from depending on specific individuals. These authors also stated that some world-class organisations like HP (a company that sells computers, printers, and accessories), IBM (a company that offers Artificial Intelligence, and cloud and enterprise software), and McKinsey (a company that provides management consulting services) have taken up significant time and effort to set up their clear visions when they were still relatively small-sized.

Both vision and mission should be widely communicated to the organisation's main internal stakeholders (e.g., employees) and external ones (e.g., customers). This communication can be through reports, websites, etc. When an organisation follows its purpose, it attempts to answer the following questions:

■ Why are we here in the marketplace?
■ Who do we want to serve?
■ Why do stakeholders (including customers) prefer our company?
■ What is the general direction of our company?
■ What makes us unique and distinct?
■ What valuable things do we want to create for our stakeholders?
■ What positive changes can we introduce in the marketplace?
■ What is the best way to improve people's lives?
■ How can we add the highest value to others?
■ How can we use our resources (skills, talents, information, etc.) to positively impact the world?

A well-defined business mission will also try to answer some less obvious questions, on an individual level, such as:

■ What is our authentic path in life?
■ Who do we want to be in this world?
■ How can we create more love, joy, and peace around us?
■ What activities give us a sense of fulfilment?
■ How can we use our time productively to help others?
■ What is our future legacy or contribution for others to enjoy?
■ What is our true place in the world?

All organisations can become valuable instruments or catalysts through which people can introduce positive change into the world. The organisation's mission can also be defined as:

■ A project aligned with an organisation's distinct potential and strengths.
■ A significant quest which drives all business endeavours.
■ A wholehearted cause the organisation stays true to.
■ A wellspring of passion the company's contributors are committed to.
■ A generator of shared expectations regarding the business venture.
■ A valuable endeavour to make the world a better place.
■ A motivator which prompts the organisation to endure challenging circumstances.

In the following points, some characteristics of a meaningful mission will be explained. Some tips to discover or rediscover a business mission will also be enumerated. As an example, the company Twice as Warm, which sells high-quality scarves, hats, and other items of clothing, has a very meaningful mission. This business gives an item of clothing to people in need for every product purchased by a customer. These donations are made to local shelters, as well as other organisations which need winter items of clothing (Twice as Warm, 2023).

1.2 Impact of a Well-Defined Mission

1.2.1 A Mission Is Intrinsically Loving

> Everyone has been made for some particular work, and the desire for this work has been put in his heart.

> **Rumi**

Many companies wrongly define their business mission by considering their products or services, or their specific business activities, instead of focusing on how they are of assistance to others. A company's contribution to others should always be at the centre of all business activities. To put it simply, a well-defined mission is focused on serving others in the best manner. Edelman (1993) observed that "Service is the rent each of us pays for living."

A mission-driven company serves others in a unique manner because each organisation has its own set of distinct talents and capabilities. A well-designed purpose is expansive; it brings more good to the world. An authentic mission is always based on lofty values, such as integrity, transparency, fairness, and honesty, among others. The company mission should be aligned with these moral "lighthouses" in order to be authentically meaningful and widely impactful.

An organisation which pursues its mission shows its best side. Figuratively speaking, a mission-centred organisation becomes a wellspring of love; its activities spread love within the company and outside it. A purpose-driven company is prone to recognise the interconnectedness and interdependence with all significant stakeholders in the business environment. This is congruent with both principles of quantum physics and ancient spiritual traditions, which state that everything in the universe is interconnected.

A mission resembles a solid platform from which fruitful relationships with the organisation's stakeholders can develop. The purpose is like a bridge which links a company's internal stakeholders (management, employees) and its external ones (customers, suppliers, community members). A clear mission always has a positive intention, which is to help people feel better (more joy, peace, love, etc.) or to reduce their negative states (anger, sadness, despair, etc.).

A clearly defined purpose is selfless because it helps an organisation generate positive change both internally and externally. A mission is heart-driven because a company's actions to pursue it tend to be driven by its employees' hearts. When a company follows its mission, all its strategies (marketing, production, financial, etc.) tend to be aligned with this purpose, which, in turn, causes a company's activities to be congruent with these strategies.

An example of a loving mission can be seen in the company Sweetgreen, which provides customers with healthy food (fresh, plant-based products) and focuses on sustainable activities. This company's mission is "building healthier communities by connecting people to real food" (Sweetgreen, 2022). This organisation also observed that their plant-based menu makes this company on an average 30% less carbon-intensive, as compared with the average American meal

(Sweetgreen, 2022). In other words, as a consequence of the products offered by this company, this organisation has a positive impact on customers (by providing them with healthy food), but also on the environment (by reducing pollution).

1.2.2 A Mission Generates Engagement and Commitment

> All men dream; but not equally. Those who dream by night in the dusty recesses of their minds wake in the day to find that it was vanity: but the dreamers of the day are dangerous men, for they might act on their dreams with the eyes open, to make it possible.
>
> **T. E. Lawrence**

A company which pursues a well-defined mission makes all its people feel valuable. Employees are more prone to feel uncompromisingly engaged to a company's mission when:

- The organisation regularly demonstrates to employees the importance of pursuing its mission.
- The company explains to employees the relationship between their tasks and its mission and its impact on the world.
- The organisation prompts employees to feel that they worthily contribute to that mission.
- The organisation frequently acknowledges and thanks employees for their valuable contribution to this purpose.
- The organisation allows employees to take ownership and initiative regarding their specific work tasks.
- The company is open to employees' ideas to attain its mission more effectively.
- The company has an attitude of service, which prompts employees to behave in an obliging manner.
- The organisation enables employees to fully use their distinct talents to pursue its mission.
- The organisation makes employees feel that products and services supplied to customers are of real worth.
- The company sets quality standards related to its purpose, to which employees adhere.
- The company activities create a positive impact not only on customers, but also on its other stakeholders, such as suppliers, intermediaries, partners, and the community as a whole.
- The company allows employees to participate in the (re)definition of its purpose.

When employees' contributions are regularly acknowledged with thanks, they are more prone to go the extra mile to support the company's mission. Bridges (2017) observed that "people will follow you if they see you are not just about the money but also about meaning." In some organisations, not only are employees committed to the company's purpose, but they are also proud to work for that organisation.

When the company's mission is relevant to its employees, they tend to feel an unbounded amount of energy and passion to make it come true. Even small routine tasks can become meaningful if they are linked to a meaningful mission (Maslow, 1965). When employees perform their work tasks, they feel that they are not wasting their time but contributing to changing the world on a small or large scale. The mission represents a valuable catalyst to perform their actions. These employees are also more resilient when the company goes through challenging times; in that sense, the company's mission provides these staff members with emotional reassurance.

According to Cameron (2012), when employees perform tasks connected to a meaningful business mission, on the one hand, absenteeism, turnover, and stress are decreased; on the other hand, commitment, engagement, and satisfaction among employees are increased. This specialist pinpointed the main characteristics of meaningful work: it brings about a positive impact on others (e.g., community members); it strengthens relationships with them; it is related to positive values (support, care, etc.); and it generates beneficial long-term effects. Employees are more prone to feel intrinsically motivated when they become aware of how their own work brings about a beneficial impact on others (e.g., customers, community members).

The following is an interesting example of an organisation whose employees do meaningful work. Numotion is a company that offers wheelchairs and equipment for people with mobility problems. This organisation has a large number of staff members. This company's employees engage with customers to provide them with continuous assistance. These staff members straightforwardly experience the positive impact they bring about on these customers' lives (Barczak, 2022).

A company like My Saint My Hero sells handcrafted jewellery products which are produced by Ugandan women who live under very poor economic conditions. The income obtained by the women from selling these products helps them sustain their families and support their children's education. Employees working for My Saint My Hero become inspired by going through stories, photos, and movies regarding these women (My Saint My Hero, 2023; Porath, 2016).

Some employees can feel honoured because their activities at work contribute to leaving a legacy in the world, something bigger than them. Sometimes, a company's mission is totally aligned with the personal objectives of its staff members, which makes their commitment seem effortless and spontaneous. In those cases, they feel compelled to take continuous action towards this purpose.

Besides employees, a meaningful company's mission also prompts other individuals and organisations to contribute to this purpose. When a company's mission is pursued wholeheartedly, people and companies around tend to be naturally drawn to this purpose, creating a strong emotional connection with them. Stakeholders that relate to a mission-oriented company feel comfortable and willing to support it. In those cases, the company should continually remind these stakeholders of the positive outcomes that stem from achieving its mission. An interesting question a company should regularly pose is "Does our purpose connect us with people more deeply?"

An example of a company with a people-oriented purpose is American Express, a well-known organisation which offers various types of credit cards. In relation to its mission, this company states: "Our mission is to become essential to our customers by providing differentiated products and services to help them achieve their aspirations" (American Express, 2022a). This organisation has been recently considered one of the most preferred companies to work for (Great Place to Work, 2022a). For instance, they also give employees free access to their own leadership programmes and to all LinkedIn training courses. This organisation also offers its staff members free access to its onsite wellness centres (American Express, 2022b).

Two Blind Brothers was founded by two blind brothers. This organisation sells high-quality soft items of clothing and donates 100% of its profits to the Foundation Fighting Blindness, whose researchers seek for a cure for blindness. The products offered by Two Blind Brothers are partly made by suppliers which contract blind employees (Te, 2021; Two Blind Brothers, 2023). One of the brothers observed that when this organisation was founded, they had no experience in the fashion sector, just the willingness to bring about a positive impact (MacDonald, 2021).

1.2.3 A Mission Makes People More Proactive and Creative

The only true happiness comes from squandering ourselves for a purpose.

William Cowper

Webb (2016) states that there are two types of goals: "approach objectives," which are goals where people focus on what they want, and "avoidance goals," which are objectives where people seem to avoid what they do not want. Approach goals are set "for" specific things; avoidance goals are set "against" specific issues. From this perspective, when people pursue approach goals, they tend to act in a proactive fashion. When people focus on avoidance objectives instead, they are prone to act in a reactive manner. A well-defined mission is worded as an approach objective; it always states what the organisation is for, not against. The paramount question a company should ask itself is "What are we for?" As seen previously, American Express uses approach goals in its mission, as it aims to become indispensable to customers by providing them with unique products and services (American Express, 2022a).

Fritz (1984) stated that there are two types of perspectives a company can adopt: a problem-solving approach, when it tries to eliminate its difficulties, and a creative perspective, when it focuses on creating something new. This author observed that the creative approach is superior to the problem-solving approach.

As a consequence, when a company defines its mission, it should always use the creative approach, not the problem-solving one. When a company's mission is defined as something new to create, people are more prone to adopt a proactive attitude towards it. A relevant question an organisation should pose to define its mission is "What do we want to create?" As seen previously, the company Sweetgreen uses the creative approach. This organisation wants to build healthier communities by offering them real food (Sweetgreen, 2022).

All activities performed by the company should be congruent with the achievement of its purpose. Companies should always prioritise those tasks and projects which contribute to its mission. The mission constitutes the guiding light against which all company activities are judged and assessed, either as relevant tasks or as irrelevant ones. A company which performs activities contributing to its purpose nurtures it, in the same way as the mother who loves her child. An organisation can keep its mission alive by devoting its time and energy to it.

The company Whole Foods offers a wide range of healthy food products. This company includes noble principles (high-quality standards, environmental stewardship, and giving to communities) as relevant aspects of its business purpose. In relation to environmental stewardship, some activities performed by this company include using packaging made of recycled materials and reducing food waste by donating thousands of food items to food banks, among others (Whole Foods, 2022). In this example, this company prioritises these activities over those unrelated to its purpose like using packaging made of unrecycled materials.

1.2.4 A Mission Balances Short-Term and Long-Term

Success without contribution is hollow and unsatisfying.

Norman Drummond

The majority of businesses commonly devote most of their time to activities which are necessary, for example, paying the bills and obtaining more sales. These activities are primarily focused on the short-term. Nonetheless, a company with a well-defined mission tends to articulate the short-term and long-term in a harmonious manner.

A business mission has a long-term perspective because the company's activities performed to pursue that mission tend to contribute to a valuable legacy for posterity. A well-defined purpose is also transformational and humanistic because it aims to add impactful value to all the company's relevant stakeholders. Conner (2010) observed that a purpose-driven organisation always generates "a wake of positive influence on all constituencies it touches."

The purpose is also holistic because it tends to produce a positive change in humankind as a whole, to a small or great extent. A company which pursues its mission wants to create a beneficial impact on present communities and also on future ones. Csikszentmihalyi (2003) observed that a good business pursues profits, but also contributes to human well-being and happiness, and makes the world a better place. In order to do so, a company utilises its own unique resources, such as relationships, information, technology, and talents. Companies with meaningful missions realise that their profits are not the only outcomes to look for; these profits facilitate the development of projects with a social and environmental impact (Stubbs and Cocklin, 2008). In other words, a meaningful business purpose is always centred on real people as well as their authentic needs (MacCallum et al., 2019).

An example of a good business is Patagonia. This is a very well-known company which sells items of clothing. As part of its mission, this company is in a business to save the planet because it is the only company's shareholder. This organisation recently declared that it transferred all its voting stock to the Patagonia Purpose Trust, whose aim is to preserve Patagonia's values, which are developing products of excellence, acting with integrity, protecting the environment, acting in a just, equitable, and antiracist manner, and exploring unconventional ways of doing things (Patagonia, 2022a, 2022b).

In addition, all the company's nonvoting stock was given to the Holdfast Collective, a not-for-profit organisation whose main aim is to protect nature. According to this decision, Patagonia will pay dividends, after reinvesting in its own development, to help support the environment. Over the last few decades, this company also created a long-term impact by providing environmental organisations worldwide with 1% of its sales (Patagonia, 2022a, 2022b).

When a company is aligned with its purpose, it is less likely that one stakeholder wins at the expense of others. A mission-driven company aims at the so-called "triple bottom line," which includes looking for incremental profits, but also caring for people (e.g., employees, customers, suppliers, community members), and supporting the planet (e.g., producing environmentally friendly products, using recyclable materials) (Elkington, 1999, 2018). Companies with this long-term orientation tend to bring about other positive effects, for example:

- An increase in employees' engagement and morale.
- A lower turnover of employees.
- A higher customer satisfaction.
- A friendlier work environment.
- Loftier quality levels.
- More innovative products and services.
- Outstanding levels of productivity.
- A reinforced brand image.
- A higher reputation.

Fombrun (1996) observed that well-regarded companies "build their reputations by developing practices that integrate economic and social considerations into their competitive strategies."

According to this specialist, each action these companies take makes them appear to be good citizens; not only do they do things correctly, but they also do the correct things. This scholar concluded that a company with an outstanding reputation attracts more customers to its products, employees to its positions, and investors to its shares, which brings about a positive effect on this company's profits.

On the one hand, companies without a clear mission cannot see themselves creating a positive change in the world. They have a narrow view of their activities, which is constrained by well-ingrained limiting assumptions such as "The most important thing is to survive, not to contribute to others," "It is not possible to follow our purpose and obtain profits," "We will never be able to create any significant impact on the world," and similar ones. On the other hand, mission-oriented companies know that it is worth pursuing a meaningful purpose to create a positive effect on the wider community. These companies are willing to improve people's lives and play their relevant part in transforming the world.

A company with a meaningful mission will also foster strong, long-lasting, and mutually beneficial relationships with all its stakeholders (employees, customers, community members, etc.). Post et al. (2002) observed that developing these relationships represents a paramount factor that allows a company to bring about more wealth and success.

In that sense, a company with a meaningful mission should avoid making any decision where a stakeholder wins at the expense of others. For example, the company will avoid selling products that are of low prices and high quality, but pollute the environment. In this case, a stakeholder (customers) is winning at the expense of another (community members). To put it differently, a company should make decisions which take into account all stakeholders' well-being, instead of considering these stakeholders as mere means to the company's end (Freeman and McVea, 2001).

However, some scholars like Bebchuk and Tallarita (2022) observed that, in practice, some factors prevent companies from effectively making discretional decisions that protect all stakeholders, such as the difficulty of dealing with trade-offs between stakeholders. These specialists suggest that the enforcement of regulations and policies that duly consider the interests of different stakeholders can be a more effective way to protect them.

Business Roundtable is a non-profit association and its members are the CEOs of various large-scale American companies. In its "Statement on the Purpose of a Corporation," this organisation observed that "While each of our individual companies serves its own corporate purpose, we share a fundamental commitment to *all* of our stakeholders… Each of our stakeholders is essential. We commit to deliver value to all of them" (Business Roundtable, 2019).

The World Economic Forum is an influential and independent international organisation that fosters co-operation between the public and private sectors. This institution gathers leaders from different areas (e.g., business, culture). In one of its manifestos, this organisation stated that "The purpose of a company is to engage all its stakeholders in shared and sustained value creation. In creating such value, a company serves not only its shareholders, but all its stakeholders – employees, customers, suppliers, local communities and society at large" (Schwab, 2019).

A mission is also related to the short-term. When employees are fully engaged in activities which contribute to a company's mission, they are naturally rooted in the now and are fully present. These employees harness their unique capabilities fully, and their actions tend to be more effortless and flowing. They are less prone to be diverted by worries and fears (which are related to the future) or regrets and guilt (which are linked to the past). According to Csikszentmihalyi (2003), when employees pursue a company's mission, they tend to enter a state of flow – also called "the zone" – and are more prone to focus on the present, namely on the task at hand.

1.2.5 A Mission Produces Economic and Non-Economic Rewards

Put money first, and you'll probably stay poor. Put purpose first, and you're headed toward riches.

David Schwartz

Mission-oriented companies try to answer the question "Why are we in the marketplace?" in order to discover the real motivation behind their purpose. Some entrepreneurs will easily offer an answer to this question, like "to make more money." It is true that companies seek to thrive in the business environment to gain profits. However, these sought-after economic benefits, which are the result of pursuing the company's mission, only represent a small part of the benefits available. As seen previously, Whole Foods, according to its business mission, undertakes projects that support the environment (non-economic aspects).

Nowadays, more organisations understand that being in business is not only about making more money; a well-defined mission implies other reasons for being in the marketplace. By following its mission, a company also brings about other benefits, namely, creating a positive impact on the environment and the community as a whole.

Collins and Porras (2005) recognise two main objectives in any company: "pragmatic pursuit of profits" and "purpose beyond profit." These authors observed that profits represent the oxygen for any company, without which it cannot live. They also stated that profits are never a company's main goal, but only a valuable means to achieve loftier objectives, such as creating a positive impact on society.

According to Maslow (1954), these higher objectives are related to the concept of self-actualisation, which implies finding meaning and fulfilment by accomplishing one's dreams and harnessing one's full potential. The mission can also be related (according to Maslow, 1954) to the need for self-transcendence, which implies helping others in a selfless manner and contributing to an objective bigger than oneself.

This prestigious scholar became well-known for his pyramid of needs, which includes basic needs on the bottom (physiological and safety needs); on an upper level, more advanced needs (socialisation and esteem needs); and on the top, the most advanced needs (self-realisation and self-transcendence).

A mission-driven company understands that its activities never occur in a vacuum because the organisation is inserted in a community affected directly or indirectly by the company's activities. A company which pursues its mission has a very tangible impact on its external environment, for example:

■ Generation of economic benefits for all partners involved related to the company (suppliers, intermediaries, etc.).

■ Development of discoveries (new materials, innovative product designs, etc.) through the company's research and product development projects, which benefit the marketplace and humankind as a whole.

■ Protection of environmental resources (land, air, etc.) as a result of green activities (recycling, use of renewable energies, etc.) performed by the company.

■ Increase in taxes collected by government from the company, which can be used for social purposes (education, infrastructure, etc.).

■ Generation of employment, which gives rise to a decent living for the members of a community.

- Support to communities through the company's social initiatives (sponsoring, donations, etc.).
- Increase in customers' satisfaction through the company's offering of high-quality products and services.

As previously mentioned, Sweetgreen aims for non-economic rewards, by providing customers with food products with a positive impact on their health. In the case of Patagonia, this company also aims for non-economic rewards, by supporting organisations which care for the environment.

De Botton (2016a) observed that companies can also bring about a positive impact on customers by creating "good demand," which is "consumer's choice that is in line with fruitful needs" and contributes to improving their life from the long-term perspective. Some companies' purpose is focused on supplying products and services which positively contribute to their customers' development. Some examples are companies which sell products and services like healthcare services (which contribute to customers' better health conditions) and educational courses (which enhance customers' skills), among others.

An example of a company which creates "good demand" is an educational institution like Khan Academy. This is an organisation whose mission is to "to provide a free, world-class education for anyone, anywhere." This organisation offers thousands of free high-quality trusted online courses on various themes (finance, economics, mathematics, etc.) in various languages, impacting on millions of students. This institution offers learners practice exercises and also instructional videos, providing these learners with a personalised dashboard so that they can learn at their own pace. As they state on their website, 90% of teachers and students using these courses have said that this training is a more effective way of learning than any other online curriculum resources (Khan Academy, 2023).

The founder of this organisation was publicly recognised with the prestigious Heinz Award – which is given to outstanding contributions to the arts, the economy, as well as the environment – (Heinz Awards, 2014). This organisation fosters education activities which are clearly related to "good demand."

Therefore, companies should avoid pursuing a mission related to goods and services which creates "bad demand" in customers, such as junk food and weapons, which have demonstrated their detrimental effects on a society. The mission pursued by a company should always aim to make people's lives better, from the short-term perspective (instant gratification), but also from the long-term viewpoint (better health, thriving careers, increased knowledge, outstanding relationships, etc.).

To sum up, a well-defined mission has a significant transformative power because it challenges the status quo and produces a positive change in the world. When a company defines its own mission, it recognises that the relevant needs of customers and other stakeholders (employees, communities, etc.) can be satisfied more effectively. A company's mission is always bigger than the organisation itself and goes beyond the company's self-interest, in order to positively trickle down into wider society.

There is another important point to highlight. In the business environment, there are various companies which are not really concerned with doing good. These companies tend to focus only on economic indicators (e.g., profits, productivity, market share). There are several reasons often adduced by these companies which do not aim to bring a positive social and environmental impact:

- These companies observe that any social and environmental impact should be brought about by government agencies and non-profit organisations (e.g., charitable institutions, foundations), and not by businesses.

- These companies argue that there are many organisations in the business environment, some of them very successful, which are only focused on profits.
- These companies state that the problems in the world (hunger, injustice, etc.) are so huge that no organisation's contribution will make any significant difference.
- These companies observe that there are always urgent aspects of business (e.g., meeting deadlines) which need to be prioritised over seemingly less urgent ones (e.g., caring for the environment).
- These companies also state that bringing about a social and environmental impact can often be costlier for them (e.g., implementing green manufacturing processes), which can affect their profits negatively.

In addition, behaving in a socially and environmentally impactful manner is often not enforced by law. If this is not obligatory, any activities bringing about a social and environmental impact is solely dependent on the willingness of the company to undertake them. In relation to this, Crane et al. (2019) pinpointed several advantages of businesses acting in a socially and environmentally impactful manner, as follows:

- Enhancement of long-term revenues, which stem from highly satisfied customers and overly engaged employees.
- Reduction of costs stemming from energy saving, decrease in inefficiencies, and less waste.
- Support from different stakeholders, which are positively impacted by the company's activities.

These authors also observed that companies which proactively undertake business projects with a social and environmental impact often pre-empt more stringent legislation that could regulate relevant issues. A well-known negative example is the collapse of Rana Hotel in Bangladesh, where more than a thousand low-wage garment employees died and a few thousands were gravely injured when working in a building already considered unsafe.

After this tragic incident, many brands and retailers of items of clothing, alongside workers in Bangladesh, signed The Accord on Fire and Building Safety in Bangladesh. This legally binding agreement aims to ensure sensible health and safety measures, while preventing fire, construction collapses, and other incidents, in the textile and garment sector (Bangladesh Accord, 2023).

There is another important point to mention. Throughout this book, it will thoroughly be discussed that, in business, being socially and environmentally oriented is never incompatible with being profitable. Successful organisations with a social and environmental impact will be analysed.

There is one more point to highlight. Sisodia et al. (2015) have thoroughly researched on the so-called "firms of endearment" which are purpose-driven companies that take into account the interests of all their stakeholders, meet these stakeholders' innermost needs, while avoiding benefiting any stakeholder at the expense of others; some examples of these companies are Whole Foods, Starbucks, and Southwest Airlines, among others. Some of these companies are discussed throughout this book. According to these authors, in the case of U.S. firms of endearment, over a period of 15 years, these companies had a superior cumulative return of 1,681%, as compared with the cumulative return of 122% of companies related to S&P 500 Index (Sisodia et al., 2023). S&P 500 is an index which includes the 500 top American public companies; this index is based on the stock prices regarding these organisations.

1.2.6 A Business Mission Represents a Company's Map of the World

The man without a purpose is like a ship without a rudder, a waif, a nothing, a no man.

Thomas Carlyle

Human perception is intrinsically limited; people can never perceive the millions of stimuli present in the environment. Besides, people's perceptive systems are guided by their distinct beliefs and values. For example, if a person believes in the abundance of opportunities, he is more likely to find them regularly, as compared with those who do not believe so. This phenomenon, called "confirmation bias," implies that people tend to focus on specific stimuli from the environment which are consistent with their beliefs, dismissing the rest.

The world is intrinsically complex and dynamic. According to the discipline called neuro-linguistic programming (NLP), every person has a distinctive mental map of the world which helps them go through it in a unique manner. These maps are simplified representations of reality. From this perspective, a mission is a shared map which guides the company's people in the performance of their business activities on a continuous basis. In some of the aforementioned examples, such as in the case of Whole Foods and Sweetgreen, these companies' missions represent a paramount compass which guides their business activities.

From the psychological perspective, people use personal stories which help them as guidelines for their lives. These manufactured personal tales can be related to the person itself, other people, and the world in general. These narratives are not necessarily truthful, but credible and meaningful to the creator. People make sense of circumstances in a narrative manner, through their stories. In a similar vein, Zander and Zander (2002) observed that the stories that people hold in their minds help them represent and interpret the world around them. Moreover, these stories *limit* the way they "see" reality.

A company's mission has shared stories embedded in it, especially the ones related to the questions, "Why are we in the marketplace?" and "What is our relevant contribution to others?" These stories are continuous reminders which help a company pursue its mission in a more effective manner. These stories gather the company's people around the purpose and make them feel more optimistic about achieving this purpose.

A well-designed mission is always story-based, which is emotionally compelling. When a mission has an enticing narrative, it lulls people into pursuing it. Some story-telling aspects are implicit in the verbal definition of the mission. Other aspects are fully expressed when the mission is conveyed to others. Very significant narrative aspects related to the mission unfold when the company takes specific actions to pursue it. A mission tends to be pursued more effectively if its narrative is congruent with the personal stories of the people (e.g., employees) contributing to it.

Sackcloth & Ashes has a story which is very compelling. This company sells blankets woven mostly from recycled material. When a customer buys a blanket, this company donates a blanket to the customer's local homeless shelter. The company's founder was compelled to assist homeless shelters because his mother was homeless in the past. Moved by his mother's story, this entrepreneur contacted various homeless shelters to find out about their main needs. These places unanimously told him that the most needed items were blankets, which inspired him to found Sackcloth & Ashes (Sackcloth and Ashes, 2022a, 2022b).

1.2.7 A Business Mission Is an Overarching Goal

The mission is the company's major guideline which is duly considered in any action performed by the organisation. A company's objectives must always be aligned with this general purpose. In the human brain, there is a set of neurons called the "reticular activating system" (RAS). When people set specific goals, their own RAS helps them encounter people, things, and circumstances related to these very objectives. The RAS acts like a filter which sifts through all the stimuli in the environment to concentrate on those significant to the person's objectives.

When people in a company share a mission, which in practice is an overarching goal, their RAS helps them pursue this purpose, in the same way as for minor objectives. Committed employees continually have the organisation's mission on their minds, and their RAS guides them towards situations, circumstances, and people closely related to this very purpose. The company's purpose "moulds" their employees' perceptions, leading them to situations related to this mission. There is a well-known quotation which goes, "What you focus on, grows; what you dismiss, dwindles." When a company follows its mission in a continuous manner, its employees concentrate their attention on this purpose in a single-minded manner.

The following example will clarify this point. As seen previously, in the case of Sweetgreen, mission is "building healthier communities by connecting people to real food." Due to its employees continually having this purpose on their minds, they are more prone to relate to people and circumstances congruent with this very purpose (Sweetgreen, 2022). In this example, staff members are prone to interact with suppliers of ingredients which are suitable for the healthy products offered by this company. These employees are also more prone to attend events that are congruent with the company's mission, for instance, healthy food trade shows.

There is another relevant point to mention. According to the renowned thought leader Fritz (1984, 1999), the primary purpose is the general aim or direction which all other purposes (called secondary ones) are subordinate to. This author stated that the primary purpose is the "organization's most meaningful organizing principle" (Fritz, 1999). From this perspective, the business mission can be considered the company's primary purpose to which all secondary goals (such as corporate objectives, marketing goals, production objectives, etc.) need to be aligned. In other words, the company's purpose is an overall guideline with which all strategies and tactics must be congruent.

A company's mission also dictates which business opportunities will be harnessed and which ones discarded. From this perspective, a company's mission eliminates the uncertainty regarding how to act before different courses of action, avoiding situations of paralysis from excessive analysis. Consequently, a company will choose only those courses of actions aligned with their mission.

A mission pervades each and every of the company's activities. Therefore, when employees pursue the company's mission, they tend to prioritise activities closely related to it. They avoid dissipating their energy on unrelated chores. Seemingly big challenges do not seem so overwhelming to the company because it goes towards what it cares about the most. In the case of Sweetgreen, its mission clearly impacts on the products the company offers to its customers: environmentally friendly, fresh food products which are made from plants. In other words, this set of products is fully aligned with the company's purpose (Sweetgreen, 2022).

There is another significant topic to discuss. According to Kaplan and Mikes (2012), when a company abides by its meaningful mission, this can help the organisation reduce some risks related to their business activities, such as "risks from employees' and managers' unauthorized, illegal, unethical, incorrect, or inappropriate actions." For instance, in companies like Whole Foods whose mission includes values like "environmental stewardship," employees who are committed to this mission purpose will be less inclined to be involved in projects that bring about a negative impact on the environment (e.g., wasting resources, polluting the environment).

Sometimes, an organisation aims to introduce different types of change (e.g., launching of certain innovative products, using new technology) which are not congruent with their own missions. In these situations, change is likely to encounter resistance, especially from people who are truly committed to the company's purpose. In these cases, the organisation should make sure that the change being introduced is consistent with the company's mission, and introduce adjustments to this very change, when necessary.

1.2.8 A Mission Is Inspirational and Meaningful

> People are physically moved to a person who is vulnerable enough to make visible the deep essence of what their heart is giving.
>
> **Mark Silver**

A well-defined mission is meaningful because it clarifies why the company wants to achieve this purpose. The answer to the question "Why is our company in the marketplace?" is reflected in the business mission. A true mission is related to the concept of togetherness because it is truly inspirational to others. Most people realise when a company wants to make a difference to the world, and tend to be more willing to assist the organisation in that process. Mission-driven companies are also perceived as models to emulate.

People tend to feel enthusiasm when they do things they love. A well-designed mission elicits positive emotional states in people, which prompts them to pursue it. These people feel emboldened to take action. Therefore, inspired employees tend to contribute to the mission in a continuous and loving manner, even during challenging times. These employees experience good feelings by using their unique talents to add value to other people. These employees also know that their actions are leaving a positive mark on the world, which represents a good reason to go to work and do their best.

Many people feel that their lives are without meaning. Contrary to this, employees engaged with the company's mission find their lives motivating and meaningful because they are pursuing a purpose related to lofty values such as fairness, benevolence, care, and others. By contributing to that well-meaning purpose, these employees feel useful because their contribution is of real value to others. Frankl (2006) observed that what drives people is their meaning and purpose in life, which implies following their mission and carrying out the tasks necessary for its fulfilment.

Honest Tea has a meaningful and inspiring mission that aims "… to create and promote great-tasting, healthy, organic beverages …" and "… to grow our business with the same honesty and integrity we use to craft our recipes, with sustainability and great taste for all" (Honest Tea, 2022). This organisation offers products that have fair trade and organic certifications. These products are made from the purest ingredients which contribute to enhancing customer wellness. This company sources the ingredients for its products in a responsible way and adopts a fair attitude towards farmers, by providing them with an equitable pay for their inputs. In short, this company brings a positive impact on customers and communities (Honest Tea, 2020).

There is another interesting topic to discuss. A company which follows its mission radiates positive energy which not only animates employees but also its external environment. Mackey and Sisodia (2014) called the purpose a "magnet" which attracts the right human resources to the company. People can sense when a company focuses on worthwhile causes and tend to support it. According to Goleman (1996, 1998), emotional contagion implies that intense emotions tend to be naturally contagious. Therefore, employees who pursue the company's purpose in a whole-hearted manner positively "infect" others around them, who are more prone to provide support.

Lastly, it has been stated that when people follow their calling, a decent livelihood tends to follow. Likewise, when a company follows its purpose and serves others in a genuine and valuable manner, their success is more prone to occur.

1.2.9 A Mission Is Socially Caring

Does this path have a heart? If it does, the path is good; if it doesn't, it's of no use.

Carlos Castaneda

A true mission is defined in a conscientious manner. A well-defined purpose considers the positive impact on all relevant stakeholders and avoids trade-offs among them. Companies which are not mission-oriented are instead more prone to benefit some stakeholders (e.g., customers) at the expense of others (for instance, employees). An authentic mission is holistic because it takes into consideration all the company's relevant stakeholders, even those with little power in relation to the organisation.

As seen previously, a company which pursues a clearly defined mission goes beyond profit-oriented goals. An authentic business mission is related to the concept of corporate social responsibility (CSR). This perspective implies caring for the social environment the company acts within. From this standpoint, the company's activities tend to have a deliberate beneficial impact on the members of its community. Right from its onset, this type of company intends to make a better world.

Some examples of CSR activities are leading foundations, organising charitable events, and donating resources to social causes, among others. This CSR perspective implies the adoption of a generous attitude. In a traditional (and non-generous) approach, a company mostly aims to *obtain* something (more customers, more profits, more sales, etc.). The generous perspective, instead, means that the company is willing to *give* valuable things (funds, technical support, etc.) to the wider community. A company that adopts this selfless perspective becomes more closely connected and integrated to the environment where it is doing business.

For ages, many maladies, such as wars, global warming, sexual exploitation, child labour, and others, have been affecting the world. A true business mission connected to the CSR perspective is aimed at producing a positive shift on the planet, and also brings some support, hope, and solace to people suffering from these global predicaments. As seen previously, in the past, Patagonia has been donating a percentage of its sales to support environmental causes.

In that sense, a meaningful purpose is related to the idea of sustainability. A company that pursues a meaningful mission will aim to undertake business projects that produce a positive impact on current communities, but also on future generations. In a similar vein, sustainable development can be defined as "a development that meets the needs of the present without compromising the ability of future generations to meet their own needs" (WCED, 1987).

This type of organisation will continually adopt an attitude of service to all its stakeholders, providing them with the highest value, with the application of the company's unique skills, capabilities, and resources. A good example of a sustainable company is Whole Foods. As seen previously, this company performs activities that support the environment (using recycled materials, reducing food waste, etc.) and purposefully aims to leave a better planet for future generations.

A company like Humana, one of the biggest health insurance providers, is linked to Humana Foundation, which performs philanthropic activities, like investing in local community projects which bolster financial security and food security, and assisting communities which are affected by natural disasters. In addition, Humana gives its staff members paid time off to volunteer for social causes, providing these employees with a strong sense of purpose (Humana, 2022).

Seventh Generation is a company which sells baby care and home care products. This organisation offers products that are both effective and safe, but also bio-based and toxin-free, which brings about a positive impact on families and the environment. These products are made from biodegradable ingredients coming from plants (instead of petroleum) and have packaging which includes recycled and recyclable materials. The CEO observed that "We believe that business can and *should* be a force for good. And we are on a mission to create a more healthy, sustainable and equitable world for the generations to come" (Seventh Generation, 2023).

There is another relevant topic to discuss. There is a set of sustainability goals developed by the United Nations which include no poverty, zero hunger, good health and well-being, quality education, gender equality, clean water and sanitation, affordable and clean energy, decent work and economic growth, industry alongside innovation and infrastructure, reducing inequalities, sustainable cities and communities, responsible consumption and production, climate action, life below water, life on land, peace alongside justice and strong institutions, and partnerships for the goals. These goals represent a "shared blueprint for peace and prosperity for people and the planet, now and into the future" (SDGS UN, 2023).

Some companies like Jaipur Rugs, which offers high-quality rugs, develop projects with a social impact which are congruent with some of the United Nations sustainability goals. In that sense, this company through its foundation undertakes projects aligned with following sustainability goals: No Poverty (by providing thousands of artisans with skills training and a sustainable way of living), Good Health and Well-Being (by providing these artisans and their communities with frequent health check-ups), and Gender Equality (by providing women with an education course which encourages them to take leadership positions in their own communities), among other goals (Jaipur Rugs, 2023).

1.3 Tips to Discover (and Rediscover) the Business Mission

People without a purpose go nowhere, accomplish little, and enjoy less.

David Schwartz

A company's mission is connected to its meaningful contribution to others, not related to fashions, fads, or trends. Some companies mistakenly believe that they have to play small in the business environment. These companies must stretch themselves and set ambitious purposes. Companies should also avoid being short-sighted due to short-term urgencies and set meaningful purposes with a positive long-term impact on others. Each company has a unique mission, which will help the organisation utilise its own distinct resources, talents, and capabilities. Therefore, there is no "competition" among the missions pursued by different companies.

Some business people have serious difficulties discovering their purpose. They have hectic daily activities which prevent them from reflecting on their mission. It is important that these entrepreneurs set time aside and listen to their inner voice more attentively to discover their true purpose. They should think beyond self-interest and survival needs (which entail the development of a profitable company) and include a long-term perspective (which implies generating a positive impact on all the company's stakeholders).

Hillman (2006) developed the "acorn theory," which states that a person's mission is inborn. From this perspective, people's unique potential and possibilities are already inside themselves, prompting these individuals to fulfil them. Using a relevant analogy, an acorn always has the blueprint of the mighty oak contained within it.

The aforementioned author also observed that people came to this world to fulfil their mission, which includes a particular way of harnessing their distinctive potential through their work and also a unique way of being themselves in the world. From this perspective, a very important question to pose related to one's own mission is, "How can I be of value to other people?" It is interesting to note that the acorn theory can be applied both to individuals and to organisations. Business people can pose other questions to (re)discover and define their mission:

- Who do I admire for their passion and purpose?
- What is my main reason for being in business?
- What are my essential qualities and how I can share them?
- What activities give me joy, fulfilment, or peace and why?
- What activities make me lose track of the time when I am engrossed in them?
- How can I use my unique talents to serve others and solve their problems?
- How can I create an authentic and loving connection with people around me?
- What endeavours connect me to my essence and allow me to give my best to the world?
- What do I want to be remembered for?

Business people should dwell on these questions on a regular basis to obtain insights and define their mission in a more accurate manner. A business mission is never written in stone; a company can always reformulate, update, and rediscover it over time. Nonetheless, according to Duckworth (2017), entrepreneurs cannot discover their mission only by insights; they have to interact with the world to streamline their purpose.

Questions for Self-Reflection

- How can our business mission improve the lives of other people?
- How can I communicate our business mission in a more meaningful way?
- How can I co-operate with others to fulfil the company's purpose?
- How can our company's mission inspire others?

Chapter 2

Relentless Passion

Even the best business plan will not produce any result if it is not backed with passion.

Howard Schultz

2.1 Passion and Business

You cannot push a business you do not love. You cannot push a business in which you put no heart ... Love for a business brings continually new thoughts, plans, ideas, and devices for so improving it. Love for a business brings new force ever to push that business.

Prentice Mulford

In different business meetings and entrepreneurial conferences, when business people were asked the question, "What drives your authentic passion to run your business?", the most frequent answers were:

- I want total financial independence.
- I want to increase the level of profits.
- I want to deliver the best products or services in the market.
- I want to deliver innovative products and services.
- I want to enter new markets.
- I want to solve people's problems in an effective manner.
- I want to satisfy customer needs.
- I want to have more loyal customers.
- I want to beat my competitors.
- I want to improve quality and productivity levels.

However, in all these answers underlie some hidden reasons for making a company thrive. Some usual unmentioned reasons motivating many business people's activities are:

- To do what they are passionate about.
- To utilise their talents and skills openly.

DOI: 10.4324/9781003372684-3

- To make people's lives more fulfilling.
- To create better relationships with others.
- To successfully surmount challenges.
- To learn new capabilities.
- To become a better person.
- To feel recognised by others.
- To make the world a better place.

In this chapter and the following ones, these valuable reasons will be explored in a more thorough manner. As a relevant example of a passionate business leader, it is worth mentioning Anita Roddick, who is the founder of the company The Body Shop. This organisation provides cosmetic products made up of natural ingredients which are sourced in an ethical manner worldwide. This passionate entrepreneur observed that "Businesses have the power to do good." This company has organised campaigns against animal testing, implemented an in-store recycling scheme, and encouraged its employees to volunteer for social causes, among other impactful initiatives (The Body Shop, 2022a).

This company is a B Corp-certified organisation, which means that it has thoroughly met stringent standards regarding its positive environmental and social impact (The Body Shop, 2022a). This makes this company stand out as an example to be emulated by others.

2.2 Main Aspects of Passion

> Visionary companies focus primarily on beating themselves.
>
> **James Collins and Jerry Porras**

Many business people lack passion; they view their activities as a chore. In an almost predictable manner, entrepreneurs with no passion have the following characteristics:

- They dabble with their business activities, not making them a major priority.
- They are prone to give up when they face relevant challenges in their business endeavours.
- They do not remain true to themselves; they perform activities opposite to their values.
- They tend not to harness their distinct skills, and to underperform.
- They are worried about business problems, instead of focusing on their solutions.
- They experience a large amount of resistance to taking unusual actions or considering new ideas.
- They get easily distracted by trivial activities.
- They are not fully committed to what they do.
- They do not feel vigorous and energetic when performing their daily tasks.
- They feel uncomfortable with uncertain and uncontrollable business scenarios.

Passion is the fuel which helps companies pursue their mission. Without passion, business objectives are less likely to be attained. There is no general agreement on an academic definition of the word "passion." Passion is an expression of love; passionate people lovingly give the best of their time, effort, and talents to pursue their mission. They truly love their purpose and pursue it with enthusiasm and single-mindedness. Passionate people's loving attitude towards their mission helps them endure tough situations during their business journey. A passionate person is fully connected to a task – which is perceived as meaningful – and experiences vitality, joy, and aliveness (Perttula and Cardon, 2012).

Therefore, passion represents a continuous heightened emotional state which drives people to follow their mission with tenacity. However, the emotional aspect is only a part of the passion equation. It also includes rational and pragmatic components. All these aspects are interrelated and will be explained in the following points.

2.2.1 Rational Aspect

> If you sit and calculate all the risks before you do something you feel inspired to do, you will throw your highest dream away.
>
> **Jason Chan and Jane Robert**

> He who has a why to live for can bear almost any how.
>
> **Friedrich Nietzsche**

The rational aspect is linked to a meaningful purpose a company wants to achieve. When a company's people are passionate about the organisation's purpose, they always have this purpose on their minds. All their business strategies and tactics are developed to achieve this mission. In relation to this, Blackburn and Epel (2017) observed that people who pursue their purpose are more resilient regarding stress and have better psychological health. Besides, when these individuals have a strong conviction that their purpose can be attained, they are often open to innovative perspectives in order to pursue their mission.

Passionate business people are also more prone to organise and utilise company resources (funds, technology, information, personnel, etc.) in the most effective way to achieve the organisation's purpose. These people adopt an attitude of self-control and discipline in order to avoid being distracted or diverted by any activity not conducive to the mission. Assagioli (1974) observed that discipline does not mean suppression or repression of one's expression, but its regulation so that one's biological and psychological energies are used in a productive manner. In other words, passionate people will regulate their expression so that they only perform activities related to their purpose, and avoid superfluous actions.

From the rational perspective, passionate people learn from their mistakes and setbacks to take necessary corrective actions on their way to the mission. According to Dweck (2012), these people have a growth mentality, which implies willingness to obtain useful feedback for their continuous improvement and development. When appropriate, these people can vary their approaches in order to choose activities more congruent with their mission. Passionate people are more prone to frame any circumstance, including seemingly challenging ones, in a positive manner. From this perspective, failures are interpreted as springboards to do things better next time.

This way of framing issues allows people to switch from a difficulty-focused way of thinking ("I do not know how to do this") to a solution-focused orientation ("I will examine different alternatives to do this") (Cottrell, 2015). The former approach tends to be draining, reactive, immobilising, and uncreative; the latter approach tends to be more proactive, energetic, dynamic, and creative (Oakley and Kroug, 1994).

A well-known example of persistence and discipline is the case of the insightful British inventor and philanthropist Sir James Dyson, who is the owner of the renowned Dyson company. This company sells vacuum cleaners, hand driers, and other products. In the past, this tenacious designer developed more than 5,000 prototypes over several years before ending up with a model of bagless vacuum that worked successfully, which was the first of its kind in the world (Dyson, 2022; Goodman, 2012). In an interview, this passionate business leader stated that every time he failed, he was willing to adopt a different perspective to solve the issues. He wisely quipped, "You never learn from success, but you do learn from failure" (Dyson, 2022; Goodman, 2012).

Sir Richard Branson is the founder of Virgin Group, which comprises an overarching series of business units like trains, airlines, and mortgages, among others. This successful entrepreneur observed that people should not feel bad about their mistakes when doing business because setbacks and errors are a relevant part of the DNA of any business person (Schwantes, 2017). In the past, this business group had several endeavours which failed, such as Virgin Cola, Virgin Vodka, and Virgin Brides, among others (Topham, 2014). Despite these setbacks, this group has grown over time, and it has become very successful worldwide.

These people also understand that a great number of the circumstances they will encounter during their business journey are beyond their control. They understand that they are always dealing with a myriad of uncertain, unpredictable, and uncontrollable factors; therefore, adopting a flexible attitude is key to their success. They therefore avoid resisting these situations or becoming negative about them.

Passionate people realise that they can truly control the way they perceive each circumstance in order to do their best. For example, these individuals tend to perceive troublesome situations as "challenges," instead of "problems." Moreover, in uncertain situations, these people use research to make more informed decisions, but they also adopt an exploratory attitude as they take action. These individuals realise that many aspects of the business process will be discovered by acting towards their purpose.

Some passionate individuals have an unshakeable conviction that circumstances affecting their business projects always unfold in the best way possible. They perceive these situations as part of a bigger picture which cannot be fully known in advance. Some entrepreneurs, like Steve Jobs, the co-founder of Apple, the global company which offers computers, mobile phones, and other products, observed that people can make sense in hindsight of how different situations are linked to one another (Jobs, 2008).

Passionate people tend to avoid overanalysing each action to be taken. Instead, they are empowered to take continuous action and understand that there are no perfect ways to act and no ideal circumstances. Passionate people are willing to fine-tune their activities as they act. These individuals perceive their business endeavours as a learning process; their skills, talents, and actions are continually perfected as they pursue their purpose. In this process, feedback always provides invaluable lessons which help them evolve. Some entrepreneurs, like Sir James Dyson and Sir Richard Branson, have a daring spirit and are willing to take on a new endeavour in an adventurous manner, while learning and fine-tuning their actions over the process. In that sense, Sir James Dyson wisely quipped, "It's a matter of having the right attitude - humble, curious, determined, willing to fail and try … Business is constantly changing, constantly evolving. You've got to try things out" (Goodman, 2012). In a similar vein, Sir Richard Branson clearly observed that "Virgin is an adventurous company because I am an adventurer as well as an entrepreneur" (Entis, 2014).

2.2.2 Emotional Aspect

> Necessity is always the first stimulus to industry; and those who conduct it with prudence, perseverance, and energy, will rarely fail … Attention, application, accuracy, method, punctuality, and dispatch, are the principal qualities required for the efficient conduct of business of any sort.

> **Samuel Smiles**

> Desire is behind all purpose. Civilization rests upon it.

> **Orison Marden**

Passionate people are tirelessly and obstinately committed to taking continuous actions to fulfil their purpose. Their sustained interest and unsated appetite for their purpose prompt these people to bring about positive change in the world, benefitting their company and others (customers, community members, suppliers, etc.). Their sparkling emotional energy is fully focused on their purpose. Their clout and tenacity assist them on a continuous basis to do their best and use every fibre of their beings. In relation to this, Wiest (2013) observed that, "passion is the spark that lights the fire; purpose is the kindling that keeps the flame burning all night." Entrepreneurs previously mentioned, like Anita Roddick, over many years have adopted a relentless attitude towards developing and delivering environmental and ethical products.

Passionate individuals are truly convinced that their purpose is worth achieving, which leads to them performing their tasks in a zealous and unwavering manner. Their steady resolve and temperance prevent them from giving up in challenging circumstances. They continually move forward and do not feel disappointed when failure strikes them.

Passionate people understand that oftentimes valuable opportunities lie within difficult circumstances. Every time these people are pushed down, they tend to come back even stronger and with the benefit of insights. Figuratively speaking, setbacks have the same effect on these people as the wind on a thistle plant, temporarily bending, but never breaking it. As seen previously, James Dyson did not become defeated every time one of his prototypes for a bagless vacuum cleaner failed; on the contrary, these failures were learning opportunities which prompted this business leader to test new prototypes.

There is another important trait of passionate people. Their focus is always narrowed down to what is contributory to their purpose. Passionate people have inexhaustible energy, and love learning from the challenges related to their endeavours. These people enthusiastically share their purpose with others (customers, business partners, etc.), inspiring them and gathering their support.

Passionate people are more prone to respond to difficulties in a proactive and fruitful manner, instead of reacting negatively to them. These individuals also avoid blaming, criticising, or complaining because these actions are energy drainers which prevent them from going towards their purpose. Their positive attitude helps them discover the positive side of each circumstance they face, even negative ones. Their unremitting focus on their purpose helps them to perceive predicaments as learning experiences.

The well-known company 3M is a conglomerate which produces adhesives, among other products. This company turned a seeming predicament into a learning opportunity. In the past, this company was looking for strong adhesives, but this organisation developed a product which did not stick well on surfaces, only in a light manner. This company tried to find a valuable use for this weak adhesive for several years. This apparent failure was later seen as a new product which could add value to customers in a different way. This product became the renowned adhesive notes branded as Post-it (Post It, 2022).

Passionate people are aware of their fears and realise that these fearful states have an instinctive and protective function. However, they always face these fears, feel them, and boldly do what must be done to achieve their purpose anyway. These people also face the ambiguous and the unknown, and are sometimes even comfortable with it, prompted by the momentum of their continuous actions. These individuals are capable of stretching themselves beyond their comfort zone to take actions they have not taken before.

People who pursue their mission are prone to do what they truly love; therefore, they tend to be naturally positive and adopt a loving attitude towards others. Their enthusiasm and joy infect others, as people tend to replicate the emotional states of others around them. This phenomenon is called "emotional contagion."

A company which exudes passion and enthusiasm is Ella's Kitchen. This organisation produces and delivers organic baby and toddler food products. This organisation's mission is "to improve children's lives through developing healthy relationships with food" (Ella's Kitchen, 2022). The company's founder observed: "Like me, everyone at Ella's Kitchen is ethically and passionately driven and commercially directed - I believe this approach has driven our success" (Rigby, 2014).

This passionate organisation also aims to have a positive social impact; this company has donated thousands of pouches of children food to different organisations across the UK (Ella's Kitchen, 2022). This organisation's passionate spirit drove it beyond its home country to a myriad of international markets, continually engaging with various communities of customers in a very enthusiastic manner.

There is another point to highlight. Hawkins (2012, 2013) stated that individuals can access different states of consciousness: high ones (gratitude, peacefulness, love, etc.) and lower ones (shame, grief, fear, etc.). This scientist observed that when people experience high states of consciousness, they counteract the lower states of consciousness of a massive group of people around them. Therefore, with their enthusiastic attitude, passionate people tend to experience a higher state of consciousness which tends to positively transform individuals around them.

Sometimes, despite countless efforts, business people don't see any tangible outcomes from their actions. Leonard (1992) called this phase "plateau," and it is a critical time where most people become disheartened and are prone to give up. Nonetheless, passionate people never become disappointed; they know that the plateau is a necessary stage to fulfil their mission and they are willing to continually work towards it wholeheartedly. Moreover, passionate people tend to show appreciation during the plateau. A company like Amazon, the giant online retailer, obtained its first profits after nine years of being founded (Hendricks, 2004).

From the emotional perspective, passionate people enjoy pursuing their purpose, which is not considered to be "work," but something fun and rewarding. They do not feel obligated to pursue their mission, but they feel compelled to do so because they love it. Sometimes, these people are so obsessed with their mission that they end up creating an imbalance in other areas of their lives (family, health, etc.).

Lastly, Fritz (2003) observed that passion does not necessarily have to be an emotional experience of excitement, which he considers a temporary state. Instead, this author observed that passion can be considered to be "the desire to bring a work into completion," which tends to be a more permanent state. In other words, passionate business people have the continuous desire to achieve the organisation's purpose.

2.2.3 Pragmatic Aspect

> The best time to move ahead is just before you are ready to move ahead.
>
> **Robert Fritz**

Passionate people doggedly wrap their minds around their purpose and take continuous deliberate action towards it. According to Fritz (1991, 2003), people should always focus outwardly, more specifically on their main purpose, and take actions accordingly, instead of centring inwardly (on their emotions, thoughts, and self-image).

Oftentimes, passionate people regularly visualise the main aspects related to their mission; this envisioning process helps them not to lose sight of their purpose. According to research, visualised actions activate the same brain cells as when the real actions are performed. Research also showed that, with every visualisation, the respective neural pathways are strengthened. Continuous visualisation of the purpose represents a simple way to gain motivation towards it.

Dr. Balcetis, a renowned scientist, observed that people should have a narrow focus of attention on the end goal in order to improve its achievement. This scholar also stated that people should visualise the things that might go wrong in their future endeavours and the potential ways of resolving these issues; in this way, people become more motivated with these undertakings (Huberman, 2023). In addition, some researchers like Pham and Taylor (1999) stated that people who visualise the steps to take towards a specific desired future outcome are more prone to be successful, as compared with those who envision the specific end outcome.

Jack Canfield is an outstanding entrepreneur, a world-class motivational speaker, and the co-author of the series "Chicken Soup for the Soul" books, which is a collection that sold more than 500 million copies worldwide (Chicken Soup, 2022). This business leader, with very humble beginnings, has attributed his business phenomenal success to the habit of continually visualising his goals on a regular basis (Canfield, 2005, 2022).

Passionate people avoid making excuses regarding why things might not work out. In addition, passionate people are determined but also flexible; their actions change over time when circumstances require it. They understand that there is no such thing as the perfect strategy to be applied to any situation. When taking action, these people tend to harness their innermost skills and capabilities.

These people are willing to perform unpleasant tasks which contribute to the purpose. All their actions are performed in a wholehearted manner. Tasks that would seem unachievable for people with no passion look doable to passionate individuals. Passionate business people are prone to perform tasks related to their purpose with gust and zest.

Passionate people know the value of small steps; each step sets the foundation for the following ones. Their frequent resolute actions get them nearer to their very purpose. These people realise that taking action generates more motivation and develops a virtuous cycle. They know that the greatest ideas have no value, if not properly implemented. Oftentimes, passionate people are disciplined and form positive habits supportive to the achievement of their purpose. Their disciplined attitude helps these people avoid short-term gratification in order to achieve their mission. The aforementioned entrepreneur Jack Canfield also observed the importance of taking continuous small steps and using feedback to fine-tune future actions (Canfield, 2005).

When passionate people are hit by setbacks, they avoid feeling disheartened and quickly stand up to keep on moving forward; setbacks are always perceived as temporary. These people know that the journey to their purpose is a series of small sprints. They realise that persistent action always pays off; every single action counts. They understand that, oftentimes, companies improve in a progressive manner, not by quantum leaps. Consequently, these individuals are willing to take actions with all their heart, even when the circumstances are not the ideal ones. They know that their actions can be improved on the way, as they get some feedback on the actions taken. They also know that to succeed in the achievement of their mission, their actions, thoughts, and emotions must be aligned with it.

Fox (2010) distinguished two types of actions: true ones and false ones. On the one hand, true action shifts things significantly and always comes from inside out. Genuine actions tend to be lively, graceful, and self-energising; they provide the performers with unbounded vitality. Passionate people tend to perform this type of action on a regular basis. In relation to this, Goleman et al. (1995) called passion "intrinsic motivation," and observed that passionate people feel internally driven to follow their purpose, without relying on any external incentive.

On the other hand, false actions start outside in; these actions are externally driven and often disconnected from one's own interests and desires. In false actions, external factors (other people's opinions, ingrained social assumptions, etc.) have more relevance than one's innermost desires. This type of action is more connected to what must or should be done, instead of being related to one's genuine desires. These actions tend to be more mechanical and less inspired. Passionate people are less prone to perform this type of action.

As seen previously, in the case of Anita Roddick, this entrepreneur started with The Body Shop's ethical activities, while most companies selling cosmetic products in the marketplace were not interested in performing ethical and environmental activities. Nonetheless, she was driven by her authentic motivation to deliver products which could have a positive impact on customers, the community, and the environment (inside-out approach), instead of been driven by what was dictated by the business environment (outside-in approach).

Besides, passionate people tend to concentrate on the relevant business tasks at hand and avoid ruminating on past experiences (for example, through regret, guilt) or future ones (for instance, through fear, trepidation). These people pursue their purpose in a determined manner and avoid being sidetracked by trivial tasks which do not contribute to their mission because they are fully centred on relevant business activities related to their purpose. Such people are prone to enter a state of flow (also called "the zone") which allows them to achieve higher performance levels.

Csikszentmihalyi (2002, 2003) observed that in the flow state, people are less self-conscious, more immersed in the present task, and open to immediate feedback on their performance. As a consequence, their activities seem almost effortless, which allows them to work for extended periods of time without getting tired or distracted. The aforementioned author also mentioned other characteristics of the flow state, like clarity of objectives, control of the situation at hand, achievability of tasks in relation to one's capabilities, and challenges with some degree of complexity and richness.

Lastly, passionate people are resolute with their actions, but not stubborn. It is important to differentiate "determination" from "stubbornness." Passionate people are determined; they are mindful of their mistakes and make adjustments to their future actions and keep on pursuing their purpose. Stubborn people are unwilling to learn from their mistakes and continue acting in the same way again and again.

Questions for Self-Reflection

- Which activities make me feel more passionate?
- How does my passion contribute to the achievement of the company's business purpose?
- How does my passionate attitude help me face dire business circumstances?
- How does my passion help me distinguish relevant tasks from trivial ones?

Chapter 3

Prosperity Mindset

> When you are oriented to abundance, you care less about being in control, and you take more risks.
>
> **Rosamund Stone Zander and Benjamin Zander**

3.1 Business Mindset

3.1.1 General Aspects of Mindset

> You can get everything in life if you will just help others to get what they want.
>
> **Zig Ziglar**

Some define mentality or mindset as "mental perspective," "thought processes," "way to view the world," "personal paradigm," or "mental attitude." A mindset prompts a person to act in a specific way. Most psychologists observe that a person's mindset is affected by three important elements: beliefs, values, and emotional states. A mindset is related to an "inside-out" approach; one's internal resources bring about one's circumstances.

As seen previously, a mindset is related to beliefs. People's beliefs are subconscious rules governing what is true for them, even when not supported by evidence from reality. A person's beliefs stem from different sources: upbringing, relevant personal experiences, training received, communication with other people, and media messages, among others.

Beliefs dictate how people act, think, feel, and perceive reality, as well as how they see themselves (self-image). Beliefs always generate expectations consistent with them. These beliefs can be positive or negative; they are selective and self-confirming because they only allow a person to perceive things congruent with them and dismiss anything that contradicts this individual's beliefs. In the case of Jeff Bezos, the founder of the huge online platform Amazon, some paramount beliefs like "put customers first," "innovate," and "be patient" have been positive pillars which helped him achieve his extraordinary success (Ziems, 2017).

IBM is a company which offers AI, cloud services, and software products. One of its previous chairmen, Thomas Watson Jr., observed that, "any organization, in order to survive and

DOI: 10.4324/9781003372684-4

achieve success, must have a sound set of beliefs on which it premises all its policies and actions." He also stated that the most critical factor in a company's success is the strict adherence to this set of beliefs, and that, in a changing and challenging business environment, a company should be willing to change anything, except its own beliefs (Palmisano, 2023).

Dilts (1994) stated that, on a lower level, beliefs are related to capabilities (which are specific strategies on how to act), behaviour (the actions that people take), and the environment (the external context the individual acts in). This author also observed that, on a higher level, beliefs are related to people's identity, which is, in turn, connected to their purpose or mission. The main aspects of mission have been analysed in Chapter 1.

Some examples of these levels can be observed in the following sentences: "We are one of the main companies worldwide helping people communicate better online" (identity), "Communication is necessary to develop a better world" (belief), "We have excellent technological skills" (capabilities), "We develop highly advanced online platforms" (behaviour), and "We will launch a new interactive multimedia platform for the Chinese market" (environment). Dilts (1994) also observed that identity relates to the question "Who?", beliefs and values answer the question "Why?", capabilities answer the question "How?", behaviour answers the question "What?", and the environment answers the questions "Where?" and "When?"

An example of the importance of beliefs is seen in Spotify, the renowned music streaming company. In this organisation, it is strongly believed that people are happier and their productivity levels are increased when they can decide where to work. Based on this main belief, this organisation provides its staff members with various options on where to work (specific location), as well as work modality (at the office, from home, etc.) (Spotify, 2022).

Tom's of Maine is a company which offers various products, such as oral care items, bath and body products, and deodorant and antiperspirant. On its online platform, this company displays its Statement of Beliefs, which include beliefs like "We believe that we have a responsibility to cultivate the best relationships possible with our coworkers, customers, owners, agents, suppliers and community," and "We believe our company can be financially successful while behaving in a socially responsible and environmentally sensitive manner," among others (Tom's of Maine, 2023).

In relation to this last belief, this company offers products made from ingredients sourced and derived from nature, with no artificial ingredients. These products do not include any animal ingredients, and they are not animal tested. The preparation processes used by the company are supportive of people's health and the environment. This company donates 10% of its profits (in cash and products) to non-profit organisations that support various noble causes (environmental care, health and well-being, as well as disaster relief). The organisation's staff members are prompted to devote up to 12 full days per year of their paid time to support social causes of their choice. For instance, employees have supported various social projects like animal shelters, coaching children's teams, and beach clean-ups, among others. As seen previously, this company brings about a positive social and environmental impact, in accordance with one of its core beliefs (Tom's of Maine, 2023).

A mindset is also related to values. Values are specific beliefs about what is important for a person (fun, stability, happiness, love, generosity, etc.). Values can act as personal moral guidelines, and help people assess what is right and wrong for them. In other words, value is what a person actually stands for, and what this individual rejects. Values are ordered in a hierarchical manner; some values are more important than others.

People tend to make decisions consistent with their highest values. In the case of a company, its most relevant values will affect its activities. The ideal situation for a company is that its employees' values are congruent or aligned with the company's values. Barrett (2017) has observed that what a company stands for (its core values) is as relevant as the quality of the products and services sold by this organisation.

According to Robbins (2001), there are "moving-toward values," which prompt people to take action towards pleasurable outcomes (success, comfort, wealth, etc.), and "moving-away-from values," which are those values which people tend to avoid (scarcity, failure, etc.), as they are painful. In relation to this, Scott Goodson, co-founder of StrawberryFrog, a renowned marketing and communication company, suggests an insightful question, "What do we stand for - and what are we against?" (Buchanan, 2014; StrawberryFrog, 2023).

For instance, Microsoft, a well-known company that produces personal computers, software, and other related products and services, has "moving toward values" such as "respect," "integrity," and "accountability" (Microsoft, 2022). For instance, in the case of the value "integrity," this company does not tolerate the utilisation of forced labour in the production of their goods and services in its own workplace, but also in its suppliers' work environments. This company also shares its workplace practices regarding safety, based on directions set up by the World Health Organization, with its suppliers (Robertson, 2020).

IBM is a company which was previously mentioned. This company's main values are "Dedication to every client's success," "Innovation that matters—for our company and for the world," and "Trust and responsibility in all relationships" (Palmisano, 2023). In this company, employee training tends to be focused more on the company's values, rather than on managerial capabilities (Collins and Blazier, 2020).

Figuratively speaking, a company's values are like the foundations of a house, or like the roots of the tree. In that sense, a house needs solid foundations in order to be built in a successful manner. Similarly, the roots of a tree need to be strong enough, so that its trunk and branches can develop in a thriving manner. Following these analogies, when a company sets up noble values, this organisation can build up more successful strategies, policies, and processes onto these very values.

There is another relevant point to discuss. A mindset is also related to emotions, which are states which people experience, like fear, anger, sadness, happiness, and others. These states bring about physiological changes (quick breathing, pupils' dilation, etc.) as well as interpretations and actions related to them. Emotional states are also reflected in body language (gestures, facial expressions, etc.). Dalmasio (2012) observed that emotions are "complex, largely automated programs of actions" performed by one's body which are complemented by "some ideas and modes of cognition." Besides, emotions continually interact with thoughts and "colour" how a person interprets circumstances.

According to Ellis and Harper (1997), emotions follow this sequence: a person goes through a specific experience, which, in turn, activates specific beliefs and thoughts, which bring about certain emotions and behaviours. These authors noticed that emotions are the result of a biased assessment of specific thoughts. Likewise, the Stoic philosophical school of thought observed that people are not upset by circumstances, but by their interpretation of them.

It is important to pinpoint that thoughts prompt specific emotions closely related to them (a person with negative thoughts is prone to experience negative emotional states). This aspect also works the other way around; certain emotional states are more conducive to specific thoughts: for example, happiness is more likely to trigger positive thinking. On a different note, Wiseman (2013) observed that emotions are mental interpretations of one's physiological sensations (like tension and accelerated heartbeats).

Emotions help people make decisions; through their emotional states, people value positively or negatively different potential courses of action, setting preferences among them (Ben-Ze'ev, 2000). Some emotions (e.g., happiness) can contribute to the development of co-operative ties with others; other emotions (e.g., anger) can bring about distance among people (Fischer and Manstead, 2008). In addition, emotions enhance the expressiveness of the words people convey to others, adding nuances, depth, as well as texture to these words.

Lastly, mindset is a concept which can be related to individuals and companies. In the case of a company, its actions, strategies, and business activities will be driven by the prevalent mindset of its people. These aspects will be explained more thoroughly in the following points.

3.1.2 Mindset and Business Activities

> We cannot choose the things that will happen to us. But we can choose the attitude we will take toward anything that happens.

Alfred Montapert

In business, a positive mindset is the most important resource a company can count on. Every single activity performed by a company is dictated by the predominant mindset in this organisation. From this perspective, the prevailing mindset in a company will help it decide on certain aspects, such as:

- How to discover and harness business opportunities.
- How to allocate the company's unique resources.
- What goals to set for the business activities.
- How to utilise the company's strengths and talents.
- How to add more value to others.
- How to define the business the company is in.
- How to present a unique offering to the market.
- How to invest, save, and spend money.
- What type of business strategy to develop.
- How to develop new products and services.
- How to be motivated by specific objectives.
- How to handle customer service.
- What type of technology to use in business.
- How to recruit and empower employees.
- What business model to follow.
- What productivity and quality levels to set.
- How to grow business activities.
- How to leverage others' capabilities.
- How to relate to other organisations.
- What information to consider for decision-making.
- How to interact with internal and external stakeholders.
- How to tackle obstacles during the business journey.
- How to learn and recover from business setbacks.
- How to deal with uncertain or dire business scenarios.
- How to solve problems in a creative manner.

As previously seen, a mindset is related to beliefs, values, and emotions which, in turn, bring about a distinctive interpretation of reality and prompt actions related to it. In other words, every single action a company takes stems from ideas coming from the prevailing mindset of people working for this company. In a similar vein, Covey (1992) observed that things are always created twice; firstly, in the mind, and secondly, in real practice, in the physical environment. For example, a company's strategy is first thought out thoroughly (mental creation) and then implemented by taking concrete actions to achieve its objectives (physical creation). This obvious idea is frequently forgotten by some entrepreneurs.

A very good example of the power of ideas in business can be seen in the case of the well-known entrepreneur Walt Disney, when mentally designing his future project Disneyland. This entrepreneur stated that the idea of this endeavour came up when he saw his daughters having fun at a carrousel. At that moment, this insightful business leader started giving birth to the idea of safe place where all family members could enjoy a fun time. Moreover, in the development of the idea of this park, he was also assisted by a set of artists he named Imagineers (which integrates the terms "imagination" and "engineering") (The Henry Ford, 2020).

There is another important point to highlight. The concepts of "scarcity mindset" and "prosperity mindset" were used by Covey (1992). On the one hand, a company where there is a prevalent abundance mindset is more likely to generate ideas which bring about positive activities and outcomes. Uber's successful business model for transport services, based on a network that connects drivers and riders, is a good example of the immense power of a brilliant idea (Uber, 2022).

On the other hand, a company with a prevailing scarcity mindset is more prone to generate ideas which lead to detrimental actions and results. It is important to pinpoint that mindsets are never carved in stone; they can be changed. Companies should be aware of the main characteristics of their predominant mindsets in order to reflect on them and change them when necessary.

Yeager (quoted in Dilts et al., 2012) stated that a change in a mindset tends to occur when there is enough motivation, adequate knowledge about a strategy to produce change, and a clear opportunity to bring about this change. In this chapter, some recommendations on how to change the prevailing mindset in an organisation will be given.

3.2 Scarcity Mindset

> The greatest discovery of my generation is that a human being can change his life by altering his attitude.
>
> **William James**

3.2.1 The Looming Threat of Scarcity and Competition

> Life is not about having good cards, but of playing a poor hand well.
>
> **Robert Louis Stevenson**

In the business environment, a scarcity mindset supports the idea of the existence of scarce resources. Business people with a scarcity mindset believe in the threatening power of other companies offering similar products or services, known as "competitors." These two aspects will be analysed in the following points.

Traditional economic theory observes that in the business environment, all resources (capital, technology, land, etc.) are intrinsically limited. From a wider perspective, some economists assert that the main world maladies (poverty, crime, wars, deforestation, etc.) stem from a natural lack of resources worldwide.

Most organisations believe that resources are scarce. Some companies, for instance, claim that there are not enough funds to perform business activities. Other companies complain about the lack of ideas, talent, technology, and time. Some entrepreneurs state that there are insufficient opportunities in the markets and that customers are scarce.

When resources are perceived as limited, organisations tend to continually seek these prized resources, driven by egotism and greed. The concept of "competitors" is closely related to the idea of scarcity of resources. A company "competes" with others because there is not enough (customers, funds, etc.) for all of them. In fact, most companies' strategies take into consideration their competitors as one of their main factors.

The word "competition" is also commonly used in the professional sports environment. In any sport, one team (or player, in individual sports) aims to win at the expense of others. In these cases, the winner gets the sought-after prize and the loser gets nothing (or just a consolation reward). Winners also receive praise and recognition because of their skills, talents, or strategies. In sports, winning is associated with a state of superiority and high achievement. This is also relatable to the business environment. Some examples of these sport events are the World Cup, the Olympic Games, and the Wimbledon Tennis Championships, among others.

From the social perspective, individuals are faced with the idea of "competition" in their early years. Several social institutions, starting firstly with the family, support the concept of "competition," encouraging their children to do better than others. Many families compare themselves with the neighbours next door and try to outpace them.

Schools are other social institutions which foster competition. At most of these institutions, children are encouraged to compete with one another. In most educational systems, students' academic performance is measured with grades; students with "better performance" are rewarded with higher marks than others, which implies competition between them. This grading system continues even when students enter high school and university.

Besides, media news is constantly feeding society with ideas of scarcity of resources and competition. For example, news about unemployment is widely promoted, suggesting that there are not enough jobs for everybody willing to work. Similarly, popular television contests prompt participants to compete with others for a prize. Some examples of TV programmes which foster competition among the participants are "Britain's Got Talent" and "Strictly Come Dancing," where participants compete with each other, and the winners take it all. Most people are impressionable to these media messages, which contribute to the development of a scarcity mindset in them.

In all the aforementioned examples, there is a common framework known as a "zero-sum game," or "win–lose." This is an adversarial model where two or more participants compete for specific scarce resources, and one *always* wins at the expense of others and obtains all resources at stake. Some conflict-resolution methods – for example, lawsuits – are also based on the zero-sum game. These ideas are related to a scarcity mindset in business.

3.2.2 Competition and Scarcity of Resources in the Business World

A mind when stretched by a new idea, never regains its original dimensions.

Oliver Wendell Holmes

As seen previously, most companies continually relate their activities to the concepts of scarcity and competition. Consequently, these companies are prone to use countless tools to deal with their perceived scarcity of resources, for example, business plans, budgets, cost projections, and others.

These tools have two main objectives: firstly, to reduce uncertainty levels regarding future business scenarios, and secondly, to use companies' limited resources (funds, technology, human resources, etc.) more efficiently.

In relation to the concept of "competitors," the majority of companies tend to act in a reactive way. In other words, these companies' activities are driven by their competitors. In these cases, a relevant objective of these companies' business strategies is to outsmart rival organisations. Only a small part of these companies' actions is proactive, which means acting without considering other organisations.

The concepts of "scarcity of resources" and "competition" are fundamental parts of the mindset predominant in most companies. These concepts prime companies' perception of the business environment and prompt them to act accordingly. In other words, companies with a prevalent scarcity mindset tend to perceive a lack of opportunities and resources in the marketplace, which prompts these organisations to "fight" over them.

These companies adopt a "warmongering attitude" because they perceive other organisations as "adversaries" to be defeated. These companies participate in carefully planned "market battles" with rival organisations. In this "battlefield," they use different "weapons" (strategies, tactics, etc.) to beat their "enemies." Most of the well-used business tools have obvious belligerent connotations.

The following example will illustrate this point. In several sectors like the supermarket industry, the "fight" between companies is very conspicuous. For example, in the past, the massive supermarket chain Sainsbury's cut the prices of its products in response to price reductions offered by one of its main competitors, the supermarket chain Aldi (Read, 2021). These price wars are quite common in other industries as well.

3.2.3 Fear, Competition, and Scarcity of Resources

The concepts of "competition" and "scarcity of resources" are fundamentally based on fear. As mentioned previously (in Chapter 2), the scientist Dr Hawkins (2012, 2013) observed that there is a scale of states of consciousness, where fear is one of its lowest states, and love is the highest of this spectrum. From this perspective, business people who are fearful of other companies and of scarcity of resources have a very limited view of the business environment. These organisations cannot tune into a higher state of consciousness, such as love. In the business environment, fear is commonly observed in different ways, for example:

- Fear of being beaten by other companies.
- Fear of not achieving the company's objectives.
- Fear of taking certain business actions.
- Fear of not surviving in the marketplace.
- Fear of navigating uncertain business scenarios.

A company's people can show their fear in various ways, oftentimes very subtle ones, such as doubts, worries, procrastination, complacency, stagnation, distrust, and aggressiveness, among others. Any state of fear is constrictive and limiting for business activities. A company driven by fear-based concepts such as "competition" and "scarcity" tends to be reactive. This type of company tends to have a very narrow view of their business environment, which affects their relevant activities (mentioned in Section 2.2). Companies which make their decisions based on fear are less prone to harness their full potential and embrace their uniqueness.

A company with a predominant scarcity mindset tends to take actions which are driven by fear. This type of organisation tends to act against perceived threats (e.g., competitors and scarcity of resources). From the psychological perspective, this reactive behaviour is related to the so-called fight-freeze-flight response. Therefore, an organisation with a prevalent scarcity mindset is prone to act in three possible ways:

- ■ *Fight:* for example, a company takes specific actions in order to outwit its competitors.
- ■ *Freeze:* for instance, a company remains passive before its competitors' actions.
- ■ *Flight:* for example, a company abandons the marketplace where other companies act, to avoid confronting them.

In the above cases, companies' actions are prompted by an external threatening factor (i.e., competitors). In none of these cases is the company intrinsically motivated, which means acting in a spontaneous and proactive manner. When a company's employees act in a fight-freeze-flight mode, their highest mental skills (analysis, synthesis, creativity, etc.) are temporarily impaired; these individuals cannot access their innermost resources fully. The topic of fear in business activities will be explored thoroughly in Chapter 5. James Dyson is an example of a person who seems to act in a determined and fearless manner. As seen in a previous chapter, this inventor did not have any fear of failure. He tirelessly tried thousands of prototypes and failed, until he developed a functional model of his bagless vacuum cleaner.

As mentioned in the previous chapter, Fox (2010) distinguished two types of actions: unauthentic actions (generated by external factors) and real actions (motivated intrinsically). When a company is driven by competitors or scarcity of resources, it tends to take actions which are reactive. From this standpoint, this type of organisation performs inauthentic activities.

These fear-driven companies cannot fully tap into their valuable resources (talents, technology, information, etc.). This type of company cannot provide its stakeholders (customers, employees, suppliers, community, etc.) with distinctive value either. Employees working for these companies are also less prone to enter a flow state (explained in Chapter 2) where peak performance can be achieved. These companies bring about other negative effects, as follows:

Avoidance of potential beneficial partnerships: A company continually focused on its competitors cannot fathom the possibility of developing partnerships with them. This type of company has an adversarial attitude towards other organisations because it perceives them as opponents, instead of potential collaborators. Potential opportunities stemming from alliances with these companies are missed: for example, sharing or complementing resources (technology, business information, etc.), reducing costs, and assuming joint risks, among others.

Focus on negative factors: The scarcity mindset is intrinsically limited and prompts companies to focus on obstacles, instead of helping these organisations to pursue their mission. These companies are more concerned about threatening factors (other companies in the markets, negative economic situations, more challenging legislation affecting the sector, etc.) than on seizing and creating business opportunities. This type of company is also more worried about fixing their own weaknesses, rather than harnessing their strengths. These companies are more afraid of potential losses than interested in looking for probable gains stemming from their business activities. In short, in any given situation, these companies are centred more on the limitations affecting them than on the possible choices available. This limiting way of thinking does not allow companies to focus on what is really important, which is continuously pursuing their business purpose.

Insufficient development of internal resources: A company mostly centred on external factors (e.g., competitors) is less likely to develop its own internal aspects properly. For example, this type of company might not train their human resources adequately or develop unique products, services, and technology because the company mostly focuses on outpacing its competitors. These companies tend to develop a very small number of creative ideas because they act defensively, which stifles their employees' creative skills.

Impossibility of obtaining valuable feedback: A company which only perceives other companies as threats cannot consider them as valuable sources of information or feedback. The products, services, business models, processes, and strategies related to these organisations cannot be taken as references to emulate, adapt, or improve, either.

Reduction of spontaneity: A company which mostly acts in response to other companies is less likely to act according to its innermost goals and show its uniqueness and originality in the marketplace. As mentioned, this type of company is prone to act reactively, for instance, counteracting or neutralising competitors' moves. Consequently, this organisation is less likely to act proactively, for example, by developing new products or services. Oftentimes, this type of company is more prone to act against its distinct essence and spirit in order to respond to its rivals. Competition-driven companies are not totally free to be themselves because they are slavish to others.

On the contrary, companies like Virgin Group have always acted in a fearless manner. This thriving business group, through its foundation Virgin Unite, has developed a series of joint projects with individuals and organisations to foster relevant themes, such as low-carbon projects, entrepreneurship, and care for human rights, among others. For example, in relation to the entrepreneurship, the Branson Centre of Entrepreneurship Caribbean was created to train individuals on relevant business topics, such as developing business projects for growth and harnessing investment opportunities (Virgin Unite, 2023).

3.2.4 Other Characteristics of a Scarcity Mindset

Scarcity is a lie. Independent of any actual amount of resources, it is an unexamined and false system of assumptions, opinions, and beliefs from which we view the world as a place where we are in constant danger of having our needs unmet.

Lynne Twist

The scarcity mindset is based on fear. As seen previously, a mindset is not only affected by emotions, but also by beliefs and values. A scarcity mindset has specific beliefs, which are generally very limited and rigid, for example:

■ It cannot be done because we do not have enough resources.
■ Other companies have more experience than us regarding this issue.
■ If only we had the right information, we could make the right decision.
■ We cannot offer customers anything different from other companies.
■ We do not have the minimum capabilities to develop this project.
■ We will be defeated by competitors if we go ahead with this.
■ It is not the right time to undertake this project.
■ This new idea is unlikely to succeed; it is better not to take the risk.

■ Let's do things as usual; it is not time to rock the boat.
■ We must take actions to counteract competitors' moves.

As observed, the scarcity mindset does not only include beliefs about limited resources and competition. The previous examples of constraining beliefs are also related to an inability to perform certain actions, incapability of offering something different from other companies, opposition to taking risks, and resistance to change, among other aspects.

Some limiting beliefs are based on the assumption that the company cannot offer distinct value to the marketplace. This type of company is usually convinced that it does not have any unique talents and capabilities as compared with other companies, so it cannot stand out in the eyes of customers.

All these limiting beliefs act as real obstacles to developing new ideas, products, services, or taking alternative courses of action in the business arena. These negative beliefs represent "mental cages" which restrain a company's performance within the limits of these very beliefs. In relation to this, Dilts et al. (2012) observed that there are three main types of beliefs:

■ **Beliefs related to objectives:** This type of belief is related to the attainability of one's objectives. Companies with a prevalent scarcity mindset have negative expectations regarding the achievement of their objectives. An example of this type of belief for a company with a prevailing scarcity mindset can be: "An annual increase in sales of 10% cannot be achieved."
■ **Beliefs related to self-efficacy:** This belief is related to one's *capability* of achieving a certain objective. A company with a predominant scarcity mindset is not confident that it is equipped with the right resources to attain its objectives. An example of a belief which limits a company's self-efficacy can be: "Our company lacks a trained customer service team, therefore we will struggle to attain a 10% annual increase in sales." Some authors like Cash (2013) observed that positive self-efficacy beliefs, alongside optimism, a sense of control, and support from close people make individuals and organisations more resilient. Consequently, there is a direct relationship between one's self-efficacy and the perception of one's resourcefulness. These beliefs can be affected by the influence of other people (e.g., a mentor who encourages their mentees to act in a specific way), or past experiences (e.g., successful performance of an activity), among other factors.
■ **Beliefs related to outcomes:** This type of belief is based on the link between a *cause* (for instance, an action) and an *effect* (a specific result). A company with a scarcity mindset believes that its actions will not produce specific results. An example of a negative belief could be "The actions of our customer service will not produce an increase of 10% annual sales."

All the previous examples of negative beliefs are related to the concept of "scarcity." With these limiting beliefs, the company is convinced that it lacks specific resources (experience, time, distinctive products, valuable information, qualified personnel, etc.) to thrive in its projects.

An example of beliefs which are *not* based on a scarcity mindset can be observed in Anita Roddick, the founder of The Body Shop, a company that produces natural cosmetic products. This entrepreneur insightfully said: "My passionate belief is that business can be fun, it can be conducted with love and (be) a powerful force for good" (Pasha, 2017). This is a good example of a belief related to objectives, which is aiming to do business in a fun, loving, and impactful way.

Another outstanding example of beliefs *not* linked to a scarcity mindset is Bill Gates. He is the co-founder of the giant software and computer company Microsoft. This business leader has wisely quipped: "I believe that if you show people the problems and you show them the solutions, they will be moved to act…" (Medrut, 2022). In this example, there is a belief related to the outcomes. In that sense, in this entrepreneur's belief, there is a cause (showing people the problems and solutions), but also an effect (they will be moved to act).

A mindset is also affected by one's values. A company's values drive its main activities on a regular basis. In other words, the main decisions made by an organisation are based on its upmost values. These values are regularly communicated in different ways (the company's website, etc.) but also through each action the company takes (launching a new product, hiring people, etc.). Oftentimes, these values underpin (and are embedded into) a company's mission and vision; however, sometimes, these values are conveyed in a separate manner, for example, in a values statement.

Companies with a predominant scarcity mindset tend to have values such as stability, safety, survival, risk-aversion, tradition, and control, which make these organisations less willing to take significant risks or explore new ideas. These companies prefer to stick to what is known and avoid highly uncertain scenarios. Oftentimes, these companies have "away-from values" (scarcity, failure) instead of "moving-toward values" (recognition, wealth, etc.).

The scarcity mindset is also related to the concept of "fixed mindset," originally developed by Dweck (2012). From this perspective, companies with fixed mindset consider that they have a given set of capabilities which cannot be changed or improved over time. Therefore, for these companies, it is not worth committing resources or making any effort to develop new capabilities. These organisations tend to avoid activities bringing about potential failures (and learning), and instead, they play it safe.

The aforementioned author observed that these companies are generally uncomfortable with criticism from internal and external stakeholders, and are closed to feedback. People working for these organisations cannot enhance their self-efficacy and improve their capabilities. Besides, these companies are less likely to learn from their own mistakes, which prevents them from taking corrective actions to improve their future performance. People working for these companies tend to be envious of other companies' achievements. A company with a prosperity mindset like Dell, the computer giant, offers its in-house manufacturing team members some training courses on how to develop a growth mindset, among other topics (creativity, critical thinking, etc.) in order to enhance their personal and interpersonal capabilities (Dell, 2022).

As seen previously, companies with a prevailing scarcity mindset tend to focus mostly on their difficulties, incapacities, and constraints. These companies use most of their energy to solve problems, dwelling on them on a continuous basis, for example, worrying, catastrophising, or becoming paralysed by these challenges. These organisations are prone to magnify the negative aspects of each situation and sometimes jump to negative conclusions without a thorough analysis of the relevant issues.

The opposite happens with an entrepreneur with a prosperity mindset, like Jack Ma, the co-founder of Alibaba which is one of the biggest e-commerce platforms worldwide. This entrepreneur was born in China with very modest economic conditions. In his youth, he failed to enter college two times, but then he was accepted. He also was rejected from countless jobs, and ten times from Harvard. At first, he did not have any knowledge of programming or computing. A few decades ago, he realised the potential of online platforms for buying and selling products. Some business ventures he developed tanked. An Internet company he launched, known as Alibaba, became profitable after a few years of its launch (Stone and Hartmans, 2021). This businessman is an example of grit, patience, and determination; he was not overwhelmed by a myriad of obstacles in his way, but instead he found the way around them.

This entrepreneur observed that leaders should always have a positive attitude and avoid moaning. He also stated that, if entrepreneurs are not positive, they have a big problem. In addition, he wisely quipped that, "Today is difficult, tomorrow is much more difficult, but the day after tomorrow is beautiful" (Frost, 2019).

Companies with a scarcity mindset have "no" mentality which is intrinsically narrow-focused and negative. They have multiple excuses and explanations of why things will not work out. This way of thinking tends to bring about a self-fulfilling prophecy; the results obtained by these organisations generally match their negative expectations. Companies with a prevalent scarcity mindset tend to have a restricted perception of the business environment, which prevents them from discovering opportunities around them. These organisations are mostly centred on threatening aspects of the business environment, such as competitors and scarcity of resources, which makes them less willing to play big in their endeavours.

By focusing on negative issues, these companies are less inclined to take full responsibility for their actions. These organisations are less likely to challenge their perceived internal or external limitations with questions like "What really impedes …?" or "What would happen if …?"

Research has shown that people have a natural tendency to adopt a mindset more biased towards the negative. Some researchers like Baumeister et al. (2001) observed a greater impact, duration, and pervasiveness of negative experiences (detrimental circumstances, undesirable people, harsh criticism, adverse impressions, unpleasant sensations, negative places, unloving attitudes from other people, harmful emotions, etc.) on people's lives, as compared with positive experiences. In other words, people's response to negative situations tends to be more intense than to that of positive ones.

These researchers also concluded that people are more inclined to avoid negative experiences than to seek positive ones. From the scientific perspective, this phenomenon is named positive-negative asymmetry effect. Research has also found that this phenomenon has an evolutionary function, which means that primarily focusing on negative situations increases the likelihood of survival. Likewise, Kahneman and Tversky (1984) observed that negative emotions that people experience when they lose a certain amount of money are far more significant than the happy feelings they experience when they gain the same amount.

3.3 A Prosperity Mindset

What lies behind us and what lies before us are tiny matters compared with what lies within us.

William James

3.3.1 Importance of a Prosperity Mindset

People are always blaming their circumstances for what they are. I don't believe in circumstances. The people who get on in this world are the people who get up and look for the circumstances they want, and, if they can't find them, make them.

George Bernard Shaw

In this book, the terms "abundance mindset" and "prosperity mindset" will be used interchangeably with the same meaning. As mentioned previously, people working for a company with a prevailing scarcity mindset are prone to be afraid of competitors which can take customers from them. By contrast, a company with a predominant prosperity mindset realises that there are always countless opportunities in the marketplace for every organisation. This type of organisation is not worried about other companies, and can even wish them well.

These companies never compare themselves with other organisations because they trust their own distinctive talents and capabilities, and embrace them to attain their business purpose. This type of company understands that every organisation can thrive by offering its distinct products and services, and harnessing its unique talents and skills.

Companies with a prevalent abundance mindset know that everything in the business environment is intrinsically dynamic; they are inclined to explore new possibilities ("What it could be") instead of focusing on how things are ("What it is"). These organisations continually ask themselves questions like "What if …?", "What else …?", or "What other ways …?" For example, an insightful inventor like James Dyson, who was discussed previously, asks himself a relevant question like "What if vacuum cleaners can use no bags?" before developing his innovative bagless model. The founders of Uber, the well-known ride sharing app, asked themselves this insightful question "What if people were able to ask for a ride from their phones?", before starting up this company (Blystone et al. 2022).

Companies with an abundance mentality assume that there is a solution for each business challenge and know that it is a matter of time and dedication to find the best solution to any problem. These organisations know that creative ideas generate countless resources (information, technology, funds, etc.), which can be valuable for their business mission. Besides, these companies understand that creative thinking is the most important resource an organisation counts on.

Companies with a prosperity mindset know that there are always opportunities for growth and development, even in the most challenging business scenarios. Wickham (2004) observed that an opportunity is "the gap left in a market by those who serve it" and "a landscape representing possibilities open to us" which is teeming with potential. This author also observed that opportunities give companies the chance to do things in a different and better manner (for instance, developing new products, innovative services, new practices, superior ways of managing information and relationships, etc.).

Companies with a predominant prosperity mindset have an entrepreneurial approach in relation to business activities. Drucker (2007) observed that "the entrepreneur always searches for change, responds to it, and exploits it as an opportunity." Consequently, companies with a prevalent abundance mindset are able to identify, assess, and capitalise valuable opportunities. They avoid complaining about factors affecting their businesses (inflation, taxes, etc.), but they are centred on increasing the value offered to their customers.

Airbnb is a clear example of an organisation with prosperity mindset that was capable of harnessing opportunities in the accommodation sector. This company developed a distinctive business model based on a network which connects owners of properties offered for rent (houses, flats, etc.), and people who want to stay at the properties (or rooms) for a short time. These guests enter some relevant information (destination place to stay, number of people, dates to stay, etc.) on this platform, and it will show various potential hosts for guests to assess the best option.

This platform allows hosts to have additional income from renting their spare properties (or rooms) for a short time; it also allows guests to have access to a wide range of affordable accommodation – often cheaper than other options like hotels – with some relevant benefits (kitchen, etc.) which makes their stay more practical and economical. Airbnb charges a commission to hosts and guests when a booking is made. In addition, hosts can leave reviews on the guests and vice versa.

With this innovative model, this company has disrupted the accommodation industry, as this organisation competes with other companies in this sector (hotels, hostels, etc.), but without the need to own any property. As a consequence, this company has grown significantly, and it is currently present in more than 190 countries (Airbnb, 2022).

There is another point to highlight. People working for organisations with a predominant prosperity mindset do not waste time dwelling on external uncontrollable factors (e.g., conditions of the economy), but they take full responsibility regarding what they can actually manage (their thoughts, emotions, and actions). In this way, they free themselves from reacting to these external factors and also free themselves to make meaningful choices regarding what they think and do. These companies take full responsibility for what they can actually control, which makes them experience a sense of empowerment regarding their business activities.

People working for these companies have a positive mental attitude; they are not "delusionary dreamers." They know that their only limits in their business activities are their minds. In other words, they realise that oftentimes the hindrances they encounter are self-imposed. They also understand that the development of creative ideas and fresh perspectives can help them work around these constraints.

Companies with a prevalent abundance mindset never set goals which are "too realistic," but instead set big objectives, which can motivate these organisations to work on them with passion and determination. In practice, goals which are "too sensible" tend to limit a company's development and growth. Instead, big objectives help the company push its limitations away and widen its perception of the business environment. Headspace, a company that offers mindfulness and meditation programmes, has set a very ambitious mission: "to improve the health and happiness of the world" (Headspace, 2023).

Besides, companies with a prevailing abundance mindset are continually centred on their mission, and are not overwhelmed by obstacles, which they perceive as temporary and surmountable. These organisations never ignore problems affecting them; they just deal with them as soon as these difficulties come up. Their mission is the steady guideline or horizon these companies always aim at.

As a priority, these companies focus on their unique capabilities, strengths, and talents. In the case of the company Google, one of its outstanding core competencies is the management of information online. Consequently, this company has become very successful in products that have fully utilised this core competency, such as Google search engine, Google Translate, Google Maps, Google Scholar, and other information-based platforms.

Companies with an abundance mindset do not deny or neglect their weaknesses. Sometimes, these organisations try to convert their weakness into strengths. However, this usually takes time and implies a medium- to long-term approach. For example, if a company does not have a good customer service call centre, the organisation can train its employees to serve customers in a better manner.

Other times, these companies outsource activities related to their weaknesses. On these occasions, they can use external companies specialised in the areas they are not good at. Following the previous example, the company can contract the service of an external "call centre" to serve customers on the phone. This is a quicker approach and allows companies to focus on what they are really good at, what many authors call "core competencies."

Cisco, a company which offers telecommunication products, hardware, software, and other technological products, outsources its sourcing and manufacturing activities to a myriad of suppliers. In addition, these suppliers should comply with the Responsible Business Alliance Code of Conduct, which was adopted by Cisco (Cisco, 2022). This code prompts Cisco's suppliers to behave in a socially responsible manner (humane treatment of workers, occupational safety and industrial hygiene, greenhouse gas emissions reduction, etc.) (Responsible Business Alliance, 2021).

Companies mostly centred on their strong traits are more prone to offer distinct products and services, and implement unique processes and systems. These companies also tend to add differentiated and significant value to their main stakeholders and are more prone to stand out in the marketplace. Besides, these companies are genuinely concerned about the strengthening of the relationships with their main stakeholders. These organisations are also keen on expanding their business activities, for example, by entering new markets and innovating their products and services. To that effect, Mulford (2015) observed:

> You cannot succeed in a business unless in mind you are ever increasing and expand-ing that business. All great enterprises are thought over and lived over and over again in thought by their projectors, long before the material results are seen. The thought or plan in advance is the real construction of unseen element … The man or woman who succeeds in any business is always in mind living ahead of their business of today.

According to Dr Maltz (2015), a company's people should frequently and empathically delve into the positives, while peripherally glancing at the negatives. From this perspective, people should look at negative circumstances and situations only when it is necessary to make adjust-ments and corrections.

Companies with a prevalent abundance mindset tend to avoid binary alternatives, which uses words such as "or" or "but." An example of binary thinking is when a company provides custom-ers with high-quality products, but its manufacturing process pollutes the environment. In this example, customers benefit, but at the expense of the community. Instead, companies with a predominant prosperity mindset use inclusive approaches, which relate to words such as "and" and "besides." Following the previous example, this type of company can think of offering a high-quality product (which benefits customers) and which is produced with a clean manufacturing process (which supports the community).

The Body Shop is an example of an organisation that avoids a binary approach ("or," "but") and adopts a more inclusive business approach ("and"). In that sense, this organisation offers prod-ucts which are good for customers (natural ingredients) and the environment (environmentally friendly products). These products also bring about a positive impact on animals, as this company is against animal testing.

Companies with a prevailing prosperity mindset adopt a broad outlook on their business activ-ities, which helps them assess traditional and innovative options to handle their challenges. This open attitude also allows these organisations to learn from their setbacks. These business people are prone to count on other relevant characteristics:

- Discerning skills to make the best decisions on any occasion.
- Emotional stability and resilience to endure challenges.
- Increased awareness to discover new opportunities.
- Confidence in themselves and others.
- Respect and care when relating to others.
- Clarity to perceive circumstances in the best way.
- Faith in things always working out well.
- Continuous focus on what is meaningful or adds value.
- Courage to take daring actions beyond their comfort zone.

- Persistence to follow their mission despite setbacks.
- Flexibility to change their course of action when required.

The aforementioned skills are not the privilege of a few organisations; any company can develop them over time when they intend to do so. To that effect, companies with a prevalent prosperity mindset are more prone to develop these capabilities. These organisations have other distinct characteristics, such as positive thinking patterns, ongoing learning attitude, tolerance to ambiguity and uncertainty, and orientation towards action. Each of these characteristics will be explained in a thorough manner in this chapter and the following one. In the examples given in this book (Jack Canfield, Richard Branson, Jack Ma, Anita Roddick, etc.), these characteristics can be observed.

3.3.2 Positive Thinking Patterns

All that we are is the result of what we have thought. The mind is everything. What we think we become.

Buddha

Watch your thoughts, because they become your words; watch your words, because they become your habits; watch your habits, because they become your character; watch your character, because it becomes your destiny.

Plato

3.3.2.1 Awareness of Regular Thinking Patterns

In the province of the mind, what one believes to be true either is true or becomes true.

John Lilly

Some business people consider "positivity" as a topic related to New Age literature. However, this is not true at all. Moreover, from the scientific perspective, there is a relatively recent discipline named "positive psychology," which has formally studied the impact of positivity on relationships, business, career, health, and other areas. According to this standpoint, entrepreneurs are not only successful due to the actions they take and the knowledge they possess and apply, but also because of the conditions of their minds.

Many people realise that their thoughts are the most significant resources they count on. Thoughts generate ideas which help people create what they want. In relation to this, Siebold (2010) observed that prosperous people "understand that money flows from ideas, it is an inside job, and since ideas are limitless, money is limitless." The aforementioned author also stated that the use of strategic thinking to outstandingly solve problems for other people is one of the main characteristics of people with a prosperity mindset.

Likewise, Neill (2013) observed that "we create our individual experience of reality via the vehicle of thought." This author also highlighted that "without thought, there would not be delineation in our world – no perception, no distinction, no variety of experience." Besides, this specialist stated that all people's experiences in life are created from their thoughts; reality is indeed an inside-out series of experiences. All innovative business models, like the ones developed by popular companies like Uber and Airbnb, started as simple but insightful thoughts in their founders' minds.

It is interesting to pinpoint that people have thousands of thoughts a day, but most individuals have the tendency to ruminate negative thoughts. Negative thinking also includes criticising, blaming, insulting, catastrophising, complaining, moaning, etc. Research has demonstrated that the human brain has a negativity bias; it is prone to easily focus on bad experiences over positive ones.

Authors like Lieberman (1997) observed that many people dwell on negative thinking to avoid potential disappointments in case that negative news does arise, or to punish themselves because they feel undeserving. This author also observed that people tend to have negative thoughts when they lack a purpose and their minds wander aimlessly.

Therefore, people must be aware of their thoughts on a regular basis. Oftentimes, people cannot prevent negative thoughts from entering their minds, but they are free either to linger on them or to let them go. Every time their thoughts wander aimlessly into negative topics, they can redirect them towards positive ones. Thinking negatively is a habit and, like all habits, it can be changed with patience and determination.

When people continually focus on positive thoughts, they create a positive loop which prompts them to keep on thinking positively. Positive thoughts feed the subconscious mind, which is the warehouse of a person's knowledge, skills, and automatic behaviour. Some specialists observed that a great part of all actions a person performs during a day are driven by the subconscious mind. In that sense, Wood et al. (2002) observed that 43% of the time, people's actions are habitual.

Some psychologists suggest that people should say to themselves the words "stop" or "cancel" when a negative thought pops up and quickly replace it with a more positive one. People cannot dwell on negative and positive things at the same time; when they dwell on the positive, the negative automatically dissipates. Another way people can replace negative thoughts is to evoke positive past circumstances or to be mindful of things they are grateful for.

When people have negative thoughts, they are more prone to experience negative emotional states. These people tend to become more demotivated, unproductive, and less creative. Their emotional states make them act more reactively, and oftentimes respond in a fight-freeze-flight mode. People who experience negative emotions are less inclined to learn new information or skills in a deep manner.

Positive thinking has several benefits for business activities. Liu and Noppe-Brandon (2009) observed that people who think positively are more open to analysing different circumstances affecting them. These authors highlight that when people think positively, they tend to infect others, who, in turn, start thinking alike, creating a virtuous circle. A person who is positive also tends to be more agreeable with others, which prompts them to act more co-operatively.

The famous entrepreneur Howard Schultz is a good example of a person with positive thinking. This is the businessman behind the great success of Starbucks, one of the biggest coffee shop chains in the world. In the past, this business leader wisely said, "I dreamed big dreams. I dreamed the type of dreams that other people said will not be possible... but it is possible" (Schultz, 2012). After a trip to Italy, this entrepreneur envisioned bringing the Italian coffee experience and tradition to America. This positive entrepreneur contributed with his dream and determined action to the growth and international expansion of Starbucks. This company went from a single store in its beginning, to over 32,000 outlets spread over 80 countries (Starbucks, 2022).

In addition, this company is linked to Starbucks Foundation, which provides non-profit organisations with grants to support communities. These grants support various projects related to relevant themes, such as "youth empowerment, inclusion & diversity, social services, hunger relief, economic opportunity, and coffee-, tea- and cocoa-growing communities" (Stories Starbucks, 2022).

People with positive thoughts tend to be more inquisitive and naturally perceive the positive side of any circumstances, including challenging ones. Research has also shown that when people think positively, they can handle stressful situations more effectively. History has shown countless examples of people facing the most unfavourable conditions and triumphing against all odds because of their positive mindsets. Therefore, it is important that a company's people are mindful of their detrimental thoughts; for example:

Our company is going through a dire financial situation.
It is difficult to obtain new customers.
We are continually beaten by competitors' offerings.
These suppliers are trying to rip us off.
We are incapable of increasing our sales.

Oftentimes, people say that the previous expressions just "describe" the circumstances their companies face. Nonetheless, situations never have a meaning *per se*; the person experiencing them assigns specific meaning to them, which can be positive or negative. In the previous statements, the focus is placed on the negative aspects of each situation. The same sentences can be reframed in a more positive manner; for instance:

Our company is capable of improving the current financial situation.
We aim to satisfy customers' needs more effectively.
We can deliver a unique offering which stands out in the marketplace.
It is important to obtain win-win agreements with these suppliers.
We can develop new products which can boost our sales.

Seligman (2006) called the way specific events are explained by people "explanatory style." In the previous examples, the same events are framed in two different ways: firstly, negatively, and secondly, in a positive manner. This specialist observed that when events are explained in a negative fashion, the person is prone to feel helpless. Instead, when an event is explained in a positive manner, the person tends to feel more energised, confident, motivated, and can have a higher level of performance. These positive statements are more empowering and prompt people to feel more hopeful and in control, in order to take specific actions to improve their situation. Achor (2011) observed that "brains are literally hardwired to perform at their best not when they are negative or even neutral but when they are positive."

As mentioned previously in this book, Jack Canfield is a very successful entrepreneur. Not only is he a best-selling author, but also a very requested and thriving trainer who has led more than 2,500 training events worldwide in the areas of success and personal development. This positive thought leader wisely quipped, "If you can dream it, you can do it" (Canfield, 2022).

Research has also shown that when people frame events more positively, they are less prone to become stressed about them. People with an abundance mindset know that constructive thoughts and emotions make it easier to obtain the necessary resources (people, funds, technology, etc.) to pursue their business mission. Consequently, these individuals tend to be less fearful and hesitant; they also brood less over their setbacks but instead learn from them.

Some decades ago, Anita Roddick observed that some companies in the cosmetics sector were testing their products on animals, which is known as an example of animal cruelty. This business leader positively framed this situation as an opportunity to set up a company like The Body Shop and offer cruelty-free natural products.

There is another important point to highlight. According to Covey (1992), every time people are affected by an external factor (or stimulus), they are able to choose how to respond to it; there is always a gap between stimulus and response. Every time people are aware of this gap and respond with positive thoughts and actions, these individuals become more empowered. Therefore, the small gap connecting stimulus and response is one's real point of power. However, as seen previously, people have the tendency to react negatively to threatening stimuli, which can be very challenging to them. In the previous example, Anita Roddick responded to that stimulus (companies related to animal cruelty), with clear and positive action (setting up a company offering cruelty-free products).

3.3.2.2 Other Relevant Aspects Regarding Thinking Patterns

People with frequent positive thoughts have a "for" mindset, instead of an "against" one. These individuals tend to focus more on what they want to create, instead of centring on what they want to eliminate. These people focus on solutions and things they want to create, instead of dwelling on troublesome situations. Besides, these people also have faith and a sterling conviction that things will work out well in their business activities, which propels them to take continuous actions forward towards their purpose.

These people do not have naïve or passive faith in their goals; these individuals know that they are more likely to achieve their objectives when they perform the necessary activities to do so. Their unwavering confidence and positive expectations help them cast away fear or hesitation, and provide them with enthusiasm and grit to face challenging situations on their way to their mission. When new opportunities or innovative ideas arise, these individuals tend to ask themselves "What if this can be done?", instead of endlessly doubting themselves.

The self-made tycoon John Paul DeJoria, well-known entrepreneur and philanthropist, is a person with a positive mindset. In the past, this businessman with humble origins had serious difficulties catering for his basic needs. In addition, he was homeless twice, had various jobs, and was laid off by some companies, as well. These setbacks did not discourage him, but instead empowered him. These were precious learning opportunities to him. With a tiny loan and a friend, he co-founded John Paul Mitchell Systems, a manufacturer of high-quality hair products for salons. Even though this company struggled at first, it then became a massive world-class organisation (Bilyeu, 2017; Enterprise World, 2022). This entrepreneur's relentless determination, passion, and grit helped him overcome past challenges and thrive in the business arena.

Besides, positive business people believe in their skills, capabilities, and talents, and in all the actions they take. These people are strongly convinced that they can offer something unique and valuable to the work and business environments. These individuals always think of giving their best to others, instead of being continually focused on getting something from them.

As seen previously, Google is a thriving company which generously offers its main high-quality products (Google search engine, Google Translate, etc.) to people for free. In this example, the company is focusing on giving its products away generously, instead of trying to get something from others.

As seen before, negative thinking is usually based on a negative belief system. As mentioned previously, beliefs are one of the cornerstones of a person's attitude, which helps them navigate any situation they encounter. According to Bailes (2004), people's distinct beliefs constitute their main thought atmosphere. It is interesting to pinpoint that many people carry the same beliefs they formed a long time ago, without questioning them. Therefore, people should analyse their beliefs in a detached and continuous manner. Oftentimes, these internal "guidelines" are outdated or not supported by any real facts.

A company's people with negative thoughts can ask themselves questions like "What is the detrimental belief underpinning this thought?", "Is there any relevant evidence that backs this belief?", "What are the consequences of holding this belief?", "Is there any evidence which contradicts this belief?", and "What positive belief can replace this unproductive one?", among others. These individuals can also jot down the insights into these questions. The objective of this introspective exercise is to challenge any useless beliefs and replace them with positive ones.

There is a well-known principle called the Pareto Law (also named the 80/20 principle), which observes that a very minimal set of factors have a paramount importance in any situation; this principle also states that the majority of factors has the minimum relevance. From this perspective, a company's people tend to have a few disempowering beliefs which create the majority of havoc in their business activities. These few detrimental beliefs should be discovered and replaced with positive ones. It is important for people to discover the few negative beliefs limiting them in order to replace them with more positive ones.

Besides, a company's people can gradually change their limiting beliefs by acknowledging their achievements in the business arena, small or big ones, on a regular basis. They can also reflect on the lessons they obtained from their business setbacks. The frequent reflection on their achievements and learning experiences helps people enhance their self-efficacy skills to face future challenges more confidently. In this exercise, besides reflecting on external achievements (more sales, increased productivity, etc.), individuals can also reflect on more internal attainments (calm, patience, joy, kindness, etc.) experienced during their business journey. Wiest (2013) observed that individuals can also change their belief system when they seek and navigate new real experiences.

Some business people take the time to openly celebrate their successful outcomes, for example, with the organisation of social events. These positive habits prevent people from minimising or taking their achievements for granted. In this way, these people's belief systems gradually become more positive.

As previously mentioned, beliefs are formed with information from various sources, for example, other people's opinions, media news, and personal experiences. Therefore, business people should be very watchful of information coming from their environment. For example, naysayers are intrinsically discouraging and infectious and can affect one's belief systems negatively. These negative individuals should therefore be avoided, whenever possible, or time with them should be kept to a minimum.

In relation to this, Howard Schultz observed that there will always be people who will discourage your projects, by saying that they are not possible. This thriving entrepreneur wisely said that it is important to prevent anybody from telling you that what you dream is not possible (Schultz, 2012). As seen, this businessman is behind the success of Starbucks.

As a consequence, a company's people should interact with positive people, when possible. They should also talk to people with different perspectives, from whom they can learn new things. Individuals with a prevalent abundance mindset like motivated, thriving, and positive people to discuss relevant topics, but tend to avoid people keen on gossiping, moaning, and complaining.

A company's people should also be careful with media because their messages are mostly negative and sometimes catastrophic. This does not mean that a company should be uninformed; instead, it should avoid dwelling excessively on media negativity. Many websites, newspapers, magazines, and TV programmes convey only negative business news (bankruptcies, shutdowns, frauds, economic crises, stocks crashes, etc.).

This type of media shows negative news in an exaggerated and sensationalistic way, as part of their core strategy to grab the attention of a bigger audience. The media's insidious outlook on reality prompts most people to worry, which negatively affects their belief systems. As a consequence, people with an abundance mindset tend to critically analyse different sources of information in order to stay in the know; these individuals use their own discernment and experience and avoid continually delving into negative news.

3.3.2.3 Thoughts and Emotions

As seen previously, thoughts are always linked to emotions. Negative thoughts tend to bring about negative emotional states, and positive thinking is prone to generate positive emotions. According to rational emotive behaviour theory and cognitive behavioural therapy, when people face an event, they think about it in a specific way, which brings about related feelings, which, in turn, prompt certain behaviour.

For example, when entrepreneurs face an event (they read negative economic news), this prompts specific beliefs and thoughts (e.g., "My company cannot survive in the current negative circumstances"), which generates an emotional state (these individuals start feeling overwhelmed). In turn, this emotional state prompts these business people to take action (for instance, they decide to shut down their companies). From this perspective, people can question or dispute the belief or thought which triggers their negative emotions. In this example, entrepreneurs can ask themselves "Is it true that this negative situation will affect my business?" to find more balanced thoughts.

By reappraising these thoughts, emotional states can be modified accordingly. Therefore, when people have negative emotions, they should focus on the disturbing thoughts which bring about these emotions, and positively reassess these thoughts, instead of trying to directly act on their emotions. In other words, people should reflect on their own thoughts. The skill of thinking about one's thinking is called metacognition. Some metacognitive questions about thoughts are "How does this thought make me feel?", "What is the evidence for this?", or "Are there alternative ways to think about this?"

Body language (gestures, posture, etc.) is also linked to emotions (and related thoughts). There is a continuous body–mind connection. Specific emotional states bring about their distinct aspects of body language. For instance, sadness is often shown through some signs like droopy eyes and mouth corners pointing downwards. This also works the other way around; research has shown that specific body language can bring about related emotional states. For example, if people purposefully have a positive body language (e.g., they walk with aplomb, stand up confidently, move in a relaxed and assertive manner, and use open gestures), consequently they will tend to have positive emotions and thoughts. A scientist like Wiseman (2013) observed that the intentional use of positive body language like smiling affects emotions (and related thoughts) positively. The famous entrepreneur and thriving motivational speaker Anthony Robbins stated that a positive posture changes a person's state of mind, prompting this individual to bring about positive thoughts and emotions (Robbins, 2001). There is a continuous body–mind connection; when people intentionally use positive body language, they can bring about positive emotions and thoughts.

Besides, a company's people with a prosperity mindset tend to naturally dwell on positive emotional states, such as gratitude, peacefulness, and others. These individuals realise that concentrating on positive emotions brings about more positive thoughts, which helps them make more meaningful and discerning decisions. Likewise, Forgas et al. (1984) have observed that people in a positive mood are prone to make more positive assessments of situations affecting them.

When people experience positive emotions, their thoughts tend to be sharper, as compared with negative emotions like fear, which trigger a defensive response (fight-freeze-flight mode) that narrows their discerning capabilities. Likewise, Goleman (1996, 1998) observed that positivity widens a person's attention; this scholar also observed that positive people tend to be more persistent, motivated, and flexible, which contributes to improving their performance. Miller (2009) observed that positive people tend to become more resilient, overcome challenging circumstances more effectively, develop more fruitful relationships, enjoy their activities more, and experience an overall sense of well-being.

According to Isen (2008), people who experience positive emotions tend to behave in a more empathic manner with others, develop social bonds with them, and also solve conflicts in a friendly manner. When people experience these emotional states, their view of situations around them becomes wider, and these individuals are capable of seeing beyond their own differences with other people (e.g., different beliefs and perspectives), and instead dwell on the common aspects they share with them (Fredrickson, 2011). Research has also shown that positive emotions have the capability to "undo" negative ones (Fredrickson, 2003).

Achor (2011) also observed that when people experience positive emotional states, their brains are inundated with chemicals which foster a good mood (serotonin and dopamine), which, in turn prompt the learning areas of their brains to perform in a heightened way. According to the aforementioned author, this helps these individuals organise, incorporate, and retrieve information more effectively, prompting them to develop more neural connections. As a consequence, these individuals tend to have creative thoughts, make better decisions, and develop a more thorough analysis.

The entrepreneur Sir Richard Branson pinpointed the importance of positive emotions for business activities. This business leader encourages his employees to have fun, to smile, and to enjoy their work; he observed that this will spontaneously happen when the organisation offers good value for customers, and they are satisfied (Branson, 2014).

Some schools of thought suggest that negative emotions can be replaced by positive ones in a very simple way. For instance, if people experience fear, they can focus their attention on experiences, people, or things they are appreciative for. In this example, these two emotional states, fear (negative) and gratitude (positive), are incompatible, which means they cannot be experienced simultaneously. In addition, in order to lessen the impact of disturbing emotions, people can purposefully identify and categorise these emotional states, which means putting them into specific words ("I feel…"). Other schools of thought recommend that when people experience negative emotions, they should observe them, as an external witness, and let them go. This is a simple but effective way to avoid repressing, suppressing, or dwelling on negative emotional states.

The HeartMath Institute, a very prestigious scientific organisation based in the United States, observed that from the energetic viewpoint, negative thoughts and emotional states (so-called "energy deficits") reduce the body's energy. This renowned institution also stated that positive thoughts and emotions (so-called "energy assets") increase body energy, which improves the person's overall performance. This organisation also advises people to keep a journal with their daily energy deficits and gains in order to purposefully reduce the former and increase the latter (Childre et al., 2000).

Lastly, Seligman (2006) also observed that the best perspective any person can adopt is the so-called "realistic optimism." This perspective implies the use of positive explanatory style of events, but oftentimes, a pessimistic view is also admitted so that people can connect to a sense of reality. In other words, realistic optimism implies positive thinking, but it also includes a critical analysis of circumstances, which brings about a more balanced perspective.

In relation to this, Goleman (1996) observed that positive thoughts accompanied by a realistic view of reality protect people from experiencing states of hopelessness, apathy, and depression. This approach proves very valuable, especially when people face tough circumstances or when they navigate turbulent situations.

Sir Richard Branson often combines an optimistic attitude with a down-to-earth approach. When this entrepreneur decided to set up his airline Virgin Atlantic, he thought that customer service offered by other aeroplanes' crews was not good enough (lack of entertainment onboard, uncomfortable seats, airhostesses not smiling, etc.). This entrepreneur was optimistic that his own airline could improve customer service significantly. However, when making the decision to start up Virgin Atlantic airline, he carefully looked into the "downside" of this business endeavour as well. Therefore, when the company bought the first plane from Boeing, this entrepreneur agreed to give that aeroplane back to the producer if his instinct was wrong and the endeavour did not succeed, which did not happen in practice (Branson, 2016).

3.3.3 *Frequent Use of Positive Words*

3.3.3.1 *Importance of Using Positive Language*

Sharp words make more wounds than a surgeon can heal.

Vern McLellan

Letterman (1962) observed that words can be considered the fuel of the mind. Many business people tend to use negative language. It is important to pinpoint that words are the external expression of thoughts; therefore, when people use negative words, their thoughts are not positive. People tend to use negative words when they are overwhelmed, stressed, frustrated, or angry. For example, a company's people might use negative vocabulary when they complain about a lost business deal or when their customers switch to other organisations. It is important that a company's people use positive language on a continuous basis.

As mentioned before, thoughts are connected to emotions on a continuous basis. As a consequence, when people use positive vocabulary, they are prone to experience positive emotional states, which, in turn, generate even more positive thoughts, creating a virtuous cycle. People with positive thoughts and emotions are more prone to effectively use their ability to discern.

Covey (1992) suggested that entrepreneurs should always use "proactive language" in their business activities. Examples of proactive language include sentences like "I choose …," "I prefer …," and "I will." This type of language makes people feel more in control of their responses, especially when they face threatening factors. Likewise, Wiseman (2013) highlighted that when people talk in a positive manner, their words are prone to influence their mood positively. As seen previously, prosperous entrepreneurs like Howard Schultz, from Starbucks, and Jack Ma, from Alibaba, emphasise the need to use positive words, such as "possible."

According to Covey (1992), proactive language is different from reactive language; the latter includes sentences such as "I can't …," "I must …," and "I have to." When a company's people use reactive language, they tend to feel that they have little or no control over their responses. The use of these reactive words also prompts a company's people to have rigid patterns of thinking, which prevents them from exploring alternative approaches in relation to relevant business topics. Oftentimes, the use of reactive words is based on an underlying state of fear.

Consequently, business people should avoid, when possible, the use of self-defeating vocabulary, such as "difficult," "struggle," "cannot," "limitation," "impossible," or similar words. These negative words prompt people to experience negative emotions and bring about more negative thoughts, which prevents people from analysing important topics clearly and taking effective actions.

According to Robbins (2001), business people should always magnify the positive words they use and minimise negative ones in order to increase their positive emotions and reduce the intensity of their negative ones, respectively. For example, if a business person wants to say "I obtained a good business deal," this individual should exaggerate this statement by saying "I obtained an amazing business deal." This last sentence not only enlivens the previous expression but also prompts this person to feel better.

On the contrary, when a person wants to say, for instance, "I feel very angry about losing this customer," this individual should minimise this with a sentence like "I feel slightly frustrated about losing this customer." The use of the latter sentence prompts this person to feel less negative. In relation to this, Letterman (1962) wisely observed that words are the fuses of emotional states. This author observed that the words people use to frame their experiences actually become their experiences.

As mentioned previously, people can find different ways to explain events affecting them. Lieberman (2001) observed that negative situations could be explained more positively when they are shown as temporary, one-off, and unimportant, instead of them being perceived as permanent, continuous, and relevant. When people word negative circumstances in a more positive manner (these experiences are seen as temporary, one-off, and unimportant), their negative emotional reactions towards these circumstances are also decreased or even eliminated, which helps them adopt a more discerning perspective to tackle these situations effectively.

In relation to this, Seligman (2006) added that a negative event can be explained in a personalised manner, which means that the person affected is a "failure," or the cause of this very event. This is an unproductive way to explain negative events. On the contrary, a negative event can be explained in an impersonal manner, which means the person affected by the event did not cause it; this event was brought about by external factors. This second perspective implies a more positive explanation of events. Seligman (2006) also observed that negative events can be perceived and explained as general or universal, which means that they always happen. Besides, negative events can also be interpreted as specific ones (not universal), which is always a more productive interpretation of these situations.

Two entrepreneurs mentioned in this book, for instance, Jack Ma, the co-founder of Alibaba, and John Paul DeJoria, the co-founder of John Paul Mitchell Systems, perceived the setbacks they encountered as temporary. Besides, for these business leaders, these challenges were valuable opportunities to learn and do better.

3.3.3.2 *Other Aspects of Positive Language*

The words a person frequently uses with others are very powerful; these words can strengthen or weaken a relationship. For example, when a company uses words of recognition, gratitude, encouragement, and support with its stakeholders (employees, customers, etc.), these words strengthen relationships with these very stakeholders. The opposite happens when the company uses words which imply manipulation, harsh criticism, and resentment.

Schwartz (1979) suggested that a company's people should talk to other people in a positive manner and encourage them to take action. Moreover, when a person communicates with others positively, they are more prone to co-operate. This author also observed that positive vocabulary is useful when a person (e.g., a manager) sets a plan for another (e.g., an employee) to implement. In this example, the manager can present the plan as an "opportunity for expansion," not only for the company but for the employee on a professional level.

Oftentimes, a company's people do not say negative words overtly, but as part of their unproductive self-talk. These people should adopt a wary attitude towards their internal dialogue, and regularly ask themselves, "Is this internal dialogue constructive or destructive?" If they discover ongoing negative self-talk, they should apply the tips previously explained to improve their thinking patterns.

It is important that people have a positive mental dialogue with themselves and become their best friends. This means frequently talking to themselves in a kind and loving manner. People with positive self-talk become their best coaches, continually encouraging themselves to harness their innermost skills and talents. When people improve their inner conversation, they are more prone to explore non-traditional approaches and possibilities, which were previously stifled by their negative inner dialogue. As seen previously, prosperous entrepreneurs like Howard Schultz from Starbucks, and Richard Branson from Virgin, seem to have a positive mental dialogue, which is a fundamental factor for their business success.

People with a prosperity mindset also tend to use positive metaphors. Authors like Haidt (2006) observed that "human thinking depends on metaphor." A metaphor is a suggested but implicit comparison, in which one thing is used to designate a second one. Metaphors are always meaningful and easily understandable.

From the psychological perspective, metaphors are very powerful because they synthesise a large amount of information in a terse sentence; besides, metaphors act directly on a subconscious level. It is important that entrepreneurs use more positive metaphors. Many people believe that metaphors are only used in prose and poetry; nonetheless, metaphors are regularly used by people in all areas, including business activities.

A negative metaphor commonly used in business is "The marketplace is a battlefield," which uses a war concept to refer to the marketplace. This metaphor is negative because it presupposes that companies act like enemy bands, which try to outpace one another. In this example, a more positive metaphor to be used is "The marketplace is a playground." In this case, a company can adopt a more experimental and explorative attitude towards its external environment, which can help this organisation develop more innovative approaches regarding its business activities.

In relation to this, Morgan (1997) observed that metaphors are like lenses which help organisations perceive themselves and their business issues in different ways. This specialist also stated that metaphors are different ways to relate to reality which can help companies gain new insights about specific situations and develop new strategies to implement. This author has insightfully proposed various metaphors to be used for an organisation: an organisation is a machine, an organisation is a brain, an organisation is a living organism, an organisation is a culture, an organisation is a psychic prison, an organisation is a system of politics, an organisation is transformation or flux, and an organisation is a tool for domination (Morgan, 1986). These metaphors are relevant as they clearly pinpoint various facets of an organisation (Tohidian and Rahimian, 2019).

Lobel (2014) observed that people tend to embody the metaphors they frequently use, and act them out. For example, if a person says "This problem is weighing me down," this individual will tend to *feel* physically and emotionally drained and tired. In other words, the metaphors people use have a concrete impact on their thoughts, emotions, and actions.

Therefore, a company's people should always choose positive metaphors; they should regularly ask themselves questions like "What positive metaphors can we use to define our company and business activities?", "What constructive metaphors can be used to define the marketplace?", and "What other metaphors can we utilise to define other companies in the marketplace?", among others. Patagonia, an attire company which was analysed in a previous chapter, observed that the planet is the only company's shareholder. With this metaphor, this organisation wants to show its unconditional support to support projects which care for the environment.

3.3.4 Positive Perception

Life affords no higher pleasure than that of surmounting difficulties, passing from one step of success to another, forming new wishes and seeing them gratified.

Samuel Johnson

As seen previously, each business situation can be perceived in different ways. When people adopt a grateful attitude, they tend to focus on the positive aspects of circumstances affecting them. Appreciative people tend not to adopt a defensive attitude (or a fight-freeze-flight mode), and consequently, they can access their discerning and creative capabilities more easily. For example, companies can be grateful to employees (for their co-operation in business projects) or to customers (for their loyalty). According to Novak (2016), giving recognition to staff members in the workplace can bolster their morale. The successful business leader John Paul DeJoria wisely observed that, if employees do things correctly, they should be praised loudly in front of others, to make them feel appreciated and acknowledged (Bilyeu, 2017). Companies can even be appreciative for the lessons obtained from their setbacks. The topic of gratitude is analysed thoroughly in Chapter 7.

Business people can also participate in playful activities in order to have a more positive perception of reality. These events put people in a good mood and help them release stress and tension. When people have frequent enjoyable time off, they are less prone to burnout. From the neurobiological standpoint, research stated that, through play, people can explore various potential results in safe environments, which enhances their brain capability, improves their performance, and develops neuroplasticity (Huberman, 2022). The term "neuroplasticity" refers to the nervous system's capacity to change in relation to new situations. Playful events prompt people to experience positive emotions and contribute to their overall well-being. This topic will be dissected later in Chapter 7.

A third way to have a more positive perception is by being more generous with others. Generous people do not focus on scarcity; they give because there is more than enough to share with others. When people give to others, they tend to become more positive. Research has shown that when an individual is generous with others, specific areas of this person's brain become activated, as if this person were receiving economic rewards (Moll et al., 2006). For example, managers can give employees material things (e.g., a salary increase) or non-material ones (e.g., recognition for their contribution to the company).

A company's people can also be generous with other stakeholders (suppliers, customers, etc.). Companies with a prevailing scarcity mindset are unable to be generous because they are continually focused on *getting* something from others (more profits, more revenue, more market share, more customers, etc.). Their greed-driven mentality prevents them from *giving*. This topic will be explored in Chapter 7. As seen previously in this chapter, socially oriented projects like those undertaken by Starbucks Foundation (organisation linked to Starbucks company) and Virgin Unite (organisation related to Virgin Group) are clear examples of organisations with a generous attitude in business.

There is another important point to discuss. Companies with a predominant prosperity mindset avoid perceiving factors of the business environment (changes in the economic conditions, other organisations with similar products, new regulations, etc.) as threatening. In other words, these organisations avoid adopting a defensive attitude towards these factors. Instead, these external factors are perceived as opportunities to grow and evolve.

These companies frequently pose questions like "How can we perceive this factor in a more positive manner?", "What are the opportunities hidden behind these factors?", or "How can this factor affect our company more constructively?" With this positive perspective, companies are more equipped to explore these factors more constructively and find beneficial aspects related to them.

Companies with a prosperity mindset also perceive their setbacks in a positive manner. From this perspective, "failures" become opportunities to do things differently in the future. These organisations can ask themselves questions such as "What can we learn from this?" and "How can we act differently next time?" In other words, these setbacks are considered to be learning experiences which can help these organisations avoid similar mistakes in the future.

In a similar vein, Hill (1928) observed that "every failure brings with it the seed of an equivalent advantage." From this standpoint, each time these companies fail, they are confident in their own capabilities to work things around for the better in future situations. These organisations do not expect their past failures to be repeated in the future or allow these failures to condition them in any way.

Besides, companies with a prevalent abundance mindset tend to focus on the positive qualities of every person they interact with. When they meet a person for the first time, they are prone to have positive assumptions about this individual. These organisations also value their relationships with different stakeholders, acknowledging and respecting their distinct views. Furthermore, these companies tend to express their gratitude to their stakeholders for their contribution to the business activities.

These companies continually connect with people in an honest, supportive, and friendly manner. These organisations also tend to solve all conflicts with them in an amicable manner, without attacking or threatening them. Besides, these companies are prone to develop win-win agreements with all relevant stakeholders, which fairly consider the interests of all parts involved. These organisations always believe that it is possible to develop co-operation bonds with any relevant stakeholder. They understand that their business activities are built on a network of meaningful relationships, which must be preserved and strengthened over time. As seen, companies like The Body Shop, Whole Foods, Tom's of Maine, and Honest Tea, purposefully develop co-operative bonds with stakeholders.

Companies with a prevailing prosperity mindset try to avoid win–lose situations, where a party wins at the expense of others, which are more related to a scarcity mindset. To that effect, these organisations perceive every business situation involving their stakeholders (suppliers, customers, employees, etc.) as a valuable opportunity to develop win-win agreements, in which all participants have their needs duly satisfied. These organisations know that win-win agreements also strengthen their relationships with their stakeholders over time.

Lastly, a company's people with a prosperous mindset are always aware of their own distinct positive values (kindness, honesty, respect, wisdom, etc.). Their noble values act like a compass for their activities. Besides, these people tend to review their list of values on a frequent basis, and change them in order of importance, when necessary. These people regularly remind themselves of their most important values and prioritise those business projects aligned with these relevant principles. As a consequence, they do not waste time with activities which do not honour their main values.

The Body Shop, the company which offers natural cosmetic products, has very noble core values, such as "empowering women and girls," "hard-working natural ingredients," "growing partnerships and supporting communities," "championing sustainability," and "vegetarian and vegan friendly." For example, in relation to the value "championing sustainability," this company uses bottles for their products that are made from recycled materials, and also fully recyclable, contributing positively to the environment. This company also encourages customers to use refillable bottles, which also has a positive environmental impact (The Body Shop, 2022b).

Questions for Self-Reflection

- What are the main fears hindering our company's activities?
- How can I develop a more positive business mindset?
- What are my positive and negative beliefs regarding our company's activities?
- How can I frame a negative business circumstance more positively?

Chapter 4

Additional Aspects of a Prosperity Mindset

4.1 Ongoing Learning Attitude

There are few human beings who receive the truth, complete and staggering, by instant illumination. Most of them acquire it fragment by fragment, on a small scale, by successive developments, cellularly, like a laborious mosaic.

Anaïs Nin

4.1.1 Knowledge and Learning

Tapscott (1996) observed that the current economy is knowledge- and innovation-based, which implies that the most significant value will be added by brain, not brawn. In other words, the creative skills which add value to others in a non-traditional way are appreciated in this economy. The know-how regarding research, development, production, and marketing of products and services is one of the most important assets companies can count on.

Covey (1992) observed that learning and training represent non-urgent but significant activities which all companies should prioritise. Most business people tend to give a lot of importance to learning and self-learning; these people are pragmatic, which means they know that knowledge put into action is power. Likewise, Hill (1928) stated that power is "organized knowledge, expressed through intelligent efforts."

There are different types of knowledge. Polanyi (1967) differentiated tacit knowledge from codified knowledge. The former is developed through specific experiences and practices that a company's people go through, and it is context-specific and difficult to transfer to other environments. The latter is systematised (video courses, books, etc.) which makes it more general and transferable.

The following is a good example of codified knowledge. Leon is a chain of restaurants which sells healthy fast food. In this company, the specific ways in which employees prepare the various dishes shown in the company's menu are clearly set up in a systematised manner. For instance, the specific way to prepare one of its main dishes, the Pear & Ginger Seasonal Porridge with Organic Dairy Milk, is clearly standardised (Leon, 2022). In other words, any of the Leon's employees will

DOI: 10.4324/9781003372684-5

prepare this specific dish in the same way, every single time. Instead, the unique ways in which each of the Leon's employees uses their verbal language (words) and body language (gestures, tone of voice, etc.) to interact with customers are an example of tacit knowledge. This tacit knowledge (how each employee communicates with different customers) will vary from employee to employee to different extents.

Fromm (1976) differentiated "having knowledge" (possessing available knowledge) from "knowing" (which is related to thinking productively). He also observed that "knowing" always implies going beyond the surface of things, to arrive at its core roots, so as "to 'see' reality in its nakedness," and "to strive critically and actively in order to approach truth more closely." Therefore, knowing implies a higher level of awareness; when people are more knowledgeable about a topic, their beliefs and values tend to be affected by it.

Lundvall and Johnson (1994) suggested that there are different types of knowledge: know-how (procedures on how to do things, for example, managerial, manufacturing, and design procedures), know-who (knowledge on who has a specific expertise), know-why (general principles which explain why things are done a certain way, for example, why products must be tested before being launched), and know-what (explicit codified content which includes concepts, facts, frameworks, techniques, tools, etc.).

It is possible to add to this typology "know-when" (knowledge about when to perform specific actions, for instance, when to hire new personnel or develop new products) and know-where (specific knowledge about places, for instance, which markets to enter, which countries to obtain supplies from, etc.). Collison and Parcell (2004) use another classification of knowledge, which includes the knowledge obtained before, during, and after performing an activity.

For example, in the case of Google, the "know what" includes the general knowledge regarding concepts and techniques on coding, which is possessed by Google's engineers. Instead, the "know how" is the specific technical knowledge about coding to be used by these employees to develop the company's main products like Google search engine and Google Maps. Following this example, the "know who" could refer to the specific engineers working for this company who perform coding activities.

In this example, the "know why" is the knowledge about reasons Google's engineers use certain types of coding and specific algorithms instead of others, to develop the company's products. In Google, the "know when" could be related to the timing regarding the development (or launch) of a new product. Lastly, the "know where" could refer to the different markets (countries, areas, etc.) in the world where the company chooses to test or introduce its new products.

4.1.2 Prosperity Mindset and Knowledge

People with a prosperity mindset do not believe that they know everything. They have a humble attitude towards learning. Oftentimes, these people are less reliant on formal training and more confident in self-education. They tend to be self-educated and teachable; therefore, their capabilities can be developed.

These people are interested in a variety of topics, even those seemingly unrelated to their company and sector. For them, learning is pleasurable; they are intrinsically driven to become more knowledgeable. In order to do so, they are willing to tread the path of self-discovery and self-knowledge. These people look for any type of knowledge which could potentially improve their business activities and enhance their capabilities and talents.

These individuals are more keen on practical and specialised knowledge, rather than theoretical and general knowledge. However, they are willing to learn not only conceptual knowledge (facts, models, terms, etc.), but also soft skills: for example, creativity techniques, tools for rapport in business relationships, effective uses of body language, and team-playing capabilities. They realise that these skills help them make better choices in the business arena. Every potentially valuable piece of knowledge is researched deeply and intently. Oftentimes, these people do not apply the knowledge they acquire literally, but instead adapt it to the distinctive reality of their business activities.

People with an abundance mindset adopt an open and curious attitude towards knowledge; they are keen to be continually updated. A frequent question these people ask themselves is "What do I need to learn to achieve the business mission?" and reflect on insights thoroughly. They really understand that knowledge is a meta-resource, a resource of higher order which generates many other resources (capital, technology, etc.). They also understand that the business environment is complex and dynamic, and it can only be clearly understood through continuous learning. They also know that knowledge is power, providing it is applied in a specific way. Warren Buffett, one of the wisest and wealthiest investors in the world, is aware that knowledge, when applied, is power. This business leader is well-known for devoting several hours a day to reading and self-education, and he applied his increasing knowledge to his various investment projects.

People with an abundance mindset know that they must first become more knowledgeable in order to become more successful. Therefore, continuous learning is always a priority goal for these individuals, and is as important as other business objectives (productivity, increasing sales, improving quality, etc.). Moreover, practical knowledge will facilitate the achievement of these other objectives.

Individuals with an abundance mindset also have what some oriental traditions call "beginner's mind": they are always willing to learn. According to Bunting (2016), people with a beginner's mind are capable of seeing the world with fresh eyes; they adopt a curious and receptive attitude, without expectations or judgements.

Autry and Mitchell (1998) observed that the beginner's mind is not hindered by fixed ideas, but instead open to countless possibilities. People with a beginner's mind are hungry for useful knowledge and act like relentless scavengers. The usefulness and impact of the knowledge they obtain are valued from the short- and long-term perspectives. Oftentimes, the validity of this knowledge for specific financial, productive, administrative, and marketing purposes is also considered. Bill Gates, the co-founder of the global company Microsoft, is a business leader with a beginner's mind. In an interview, this entrepreneur confessed that he is always keen to attend college courses to learn more (Rubenstein, 2016).

The consideration of different perspectives makes these people more adaptive to changes in the business environment. These individuals are willing to let go of conservative or previously defended ideas in order to explore others. Their intrepid, passionate, and inquisitive spirit prompts them to look for valuable insights in a myriad of sources, even seemingly trivial ones, for example:

- Past mistakes and setbacks.
- Business reports and comments from opinion leaders.
- Insightful questions posed by themselves or others.
- Activities performed by other companies.
- Traditional media (books, magazines, newspapers, etc.) and non-traditional media (websites, blogs, social networks, etc.) with diverse viewpoints.
- Any type of training (workshops, conferences, seminars, etc.).
- Other external references (successful entrepreneurs, great men and women, artists, humanitarians, philosophers, scientists, etc.) to model or emulate their outstanding aspects.
- Non-traditional sources (contact with nature, family or friends' meetings, etc.).

For example, the Director of Content and Media at Recreational Equipment, Inc. (REI), which is a company that offers quality gear, apparel, and other products for outdoor experiences, is an example of a leader with a learning attitude. This businessman observed that he regularly listens to podcasts regarding various business topics to obtain more valuable insights (Schawbel, 2018).

People with an abundance mindset also gather insights from formal or informal feedback from interactions with different company stakeholders (customers, employees, suppliers, intermediaries, etc.). Individuals with a prosperity mentality are even open to obtaining insights from people who do not think like them, whose beliefs systems and preferences are different. The variety and diversity of viewpoints always enrich their own mental databank. Their circle of influence and mutually beneficial relationships are greatly valued as sources of knowledge, insight, and support.

As seen, Richard Branson is the entrepreneur behind Virgin Atlantic airline. This curious businessman is very keen on gathering insights from various stakeholders. For example, this business leader stated that, when he is on one of his company's planes, he always tries to purposefully talk to customers and employees, and take note on their insights on his notebook. Then he looks into these notes and addresses them, by taking specific actions on this feedback, whenever possible (Krapivin, 2018).

People with an abundance mindset are also dedicated observers of the current and potential trends in the marketplace. Their analysis of the business environment is multidimensional and includes its economic, socio-cultural, legal, and technological aspects, and their complex interrelationships. Companies like Honest Tea, The Body Shop, and Whole Foods, which were analysed previously in this book, are valuable examples of organisations that are aligned with the increasing trend regarding natural products. To that effect, these companies offer products which are congruent with this trend: organic tea drinks, natural cosmetic products, and healthy food products, respectively.

Individuals with an abundance mindset are even willing to look out for valuable ideas in different or unrelated contexts. For instance, if their company belongs to the food sector, they might seek valuable ideas from other sectors (car manufacturing sector, education sector, etc.). Sometimes, they are even open to exploring other fields (arts, sport, politics, etc.) to look for new ideas to be applied to their organisation.

According to Hendricks and Ludeman (1996), prosperous business people usually learn from three main sources: the messages conveyed by their own emotions, the reflection on their past experiences, and the analysis of feedback provided by others. In a similar vein, Rogers (1961) observed that an individual's own experience has the highest validity of all sources of learning, even over opinions, guidance, and guidelines delivered by others. This scholar also stated that "Experience, for me, is the highest authority … no other person's ideas, and none of my own ideas, are as authoritative as my experience."

An example of a business which learns from past experiences, especially failures, is the Tata group, a massive conglomerate which includes several business units (drinks, hotels, consultancy services, etc.). Several years ago, in this group, the business leader and philanthropist, Ratan Tata, implemented a prize given to best failed ideas. This prize aims to foster innovative and explorative attitude among employees. This renowned businessman cleverly said, "To spark innovation, the prize is intended to communicate how important trying and failing can be. Failure is a gold mine for a company" (Parikh, 2021).

As mentioned, people with a prosperity mentality also look for role models, contemporary or past ones, to emulate. These models can include business luminaries, artists, politicians, spiritual masters, and others. Information about these models can be found in articles, books, biographies, etc. People with an abundance mindset tend to dissect the main positive traits of these models and try to replicate and apply them to their own activities.

Lastly, these people are also willing to participate in mastermind groups, which are composed of individuals who want to support each other. These inspirational groups hold regular meetings where each participant expresses their challenges and receives feedback from the rest.

4.1.3 Relevant Aspects of the Learning Process

Learning never exhausts the mind.

David DeSteno

From the neuro-linguistic programming perspective, the learning process generally goes through four stages: unconscious incompetence (people do not know that they do not know a skill), conscious incompetence (people start practising a skill, but they are not good at it yet), conscious competence (people have the skill, but they have to concentrate to use it), and unconscious competence (the skill is used automatically, freeing people's energy for additional activities). A company's people who are very good at certain business activities are prone to perform these tasks at the level of unconscious competence, while when people carry out specific business activities for the first time, they are more prone to be at the stage of conscious incompetence.

Several years ago, Richard Branson started up his new project of an airline, Virgin Atlantic. At the beginning of this business endeavour, this entrepreneur had no experience in the airline sector (except his experience as a customer) and he acknowledged this. This is a clear example of conscious incompetence: at that moment, this business leader clearly knew that he did not have any knowledge about the airline sector.

However, over time, this entrepreneur took action (hiring qualified people, learning from other companies in the sector, interacting with knowledgeable advisors, etc.) and went through the stage of conscious competence, and then the stage of unconscious competence. Over the years, this airline has received several awards, such as Airline Excellence Awards Winner, Best Premium Economy Class Airlines, and Top 20 Airlines in the World (Virgin Atlantic, 2022).

There is another relevant topic to pinpoint. Kolb (1973) observed that the learning process comprises four stages: reflective observation (which includes research and collection of data), developing hypothesis (which implies conceptualisation, conjecturing, speculation, etc.), testing (which includes active experimentation and trial), and audit (which encloses activities such as verification, scrutiny, etc.). This series of stages is circular and allows continuous improvement of the learning experience based on the results obtained from practical application of the knowledge. As seen previously in this book, in the case of the company Dyson, his owner went through this iterative process every time he researched, designed, tested, and analysed each of the thousands of prototypes, which eventually led to a working bagless vacuum cleaner.

Dixon (2000) observed that there is a learning cycle that any organisation goes through, composed of several stages. Firstly, the organisation produces relevant information from internal sources (R+D, past achievements, unsuccessful results, etc.) and external ones (suppliers, customers, etc.). Secondly, this data is disseminated and integrated within the organisation. Thirdly, people in the organisation collectively interpret that information, through inclusive conversations and respectful debates. Oftentimes, these interactions aim to challenge ingrained assumptions in the organisation.

Lastly, people working for the company are ready to take action based on the agreed meaning of the data analysed in the previous stage. Most organisations go through these stages, but oftentimes the stages overlap with one another. In relation to this, Chaston (2004) observed that this organisational knowledge represents a valuable asset and a core competency for a company, which can be disseminated through systems, platforms, and networks created for that purpose.

O'Connor and McDermott (1997) observed that there are two types of learning processes: simple learning and generative learning. In simple learning, a person considers feedback stemming from the learning process and makes adequate adjustments. These authors mention some examples of simple learning, such as trial and error approach, and learning of new capabilities, among others. Simple learning does not produce any change in the learner's mental attitude.

According to these specialists, in generative learning, people receive feedback that transforms their mental attitudes and challenges their beliefs and assumptions, which helps them expand their future experiences and courses of action. These authors give some examples of generative learning, like learning to learn, analysing situations from different perspectives, or questioning one's own beliefs.

People with a prosperity mindset are prone to go though both simple and generative learning. From this perspective, some questions generative learners are prone to ask themselves are: "What are other contexts or areas where this knowledge is useful or meaningful?", "What are other viewpoints on this knowledge?", "What are other possible connotations of this knowledge?", "How does this piece of knowledge relate to others?", and "What are the assumptions to be challenged by this knowledge?", among others. These people are also open to considering feedback delivered by others (employees, suppliers, business partners, etc.). The topic of constructive feedback is analysed in Chapter 9.

As previously mentioned, Sir James Dyson, in his search for an innovative version of vacuum cleaner, has received valuable feedback every single time a prototype failed. The feedback from each setback has brought generative learning which helped this inventor develop more effective prototypes, and eventually a successful bagless vacuum cleaner.

People with an abundance mindset never accept new knowledge at face value; instead, they critically assess it. When they get in contact with new knowledge, they analyse it with an open and receptive mind, temporarily leaving their individual and collective assumptions aside. They often sift the knowledge learned with their critical discernment skills. Sometimes, they contrast and compare information from different sources to test its feasibility, meaningfulness, validity, and truthfulness.

Every time these individuals obtain relevant pieces of knowledge, they are prone to dissect and break them down into their main parts to analyse their main interrelationships. These people can also consider a specific piece of knowledge in a wider context. For example, the analysis of specific customers' behaviours can be analysed within the cultural context that customers are in. People with prosperous mindsets also tend to relate each piece of knowledge to others, even with those not overtly interrelated. They are also willing to share this knowledge with other people in the company in order to discuss it or apply it, when necessary.

The process of learning implies assessing various types of information in a critical and thorough manner. Business people with an abundance mindset often look for diverse views on any relevant business topic (online advertising, use of social media, etc.), and then compare and contrast these perspectives in a discerning manner. These individuals are capable of distinguishing significant pieces of information from trivial ones. Oftentimes, these individuals also look for insights from others, which could challenge their own views and ingrained assumptions. In those cases, these individuals are open to dropping their own views when the insights from others seem more soundly justified.

People with an abundance mindset are also willing to unlearn, which means reflecting on past knowledge in order to discard those pieces which are not relevant or valuable any longer. Not only do these individuals reflect on knowledge obtained from different sources (books, events, etc.) to obtain insight into it, but they also reflect on their own past actions and experiences. Therefore, these people are prone to ask themselves questions like "What were the main obstacles I faced?" and "How could I have done things differently?" In other words, people with a prosperity mindset see everything that occurs to them as a learning experience. As seen in this book, some of the entrepreneurs mentioned in this book, from James Dyson (Dyson) to Sir Richard Branson (Virgin Group), have pinpointed the need to analyse setbacks in order to improve future actions.

During their learning process, people with an abundance mindset are open to going beyond their comfort zone and trying new approaches and challenges, which oftentimes enhances their self-efficacy skills and contributes to their business mission. With a deliberate attitude towards learning, they realise that they can only grow in proportion to their mental expansion. Csikszentmihalyi (2003) observed that entrepreneurs who learn new skills tend to become more confident and empowered to go through more complex business challenges.

4.1.4 Other Aspects of the Learning Process

People with a prosperity mindset know that all circumstances, negative and positive, are stepping stones on their learning journey; therefore, they are willing to reflect on their own mistakes in order to avoid them in the future. However, they never feel stuck, ashamed, or frustrated because of their failures, but receive them with a collected attitude. People with a prosperity mindset consider their setbacks as valuable feedback in the overall process, dissecting their setbacks to obtain insights into them. Every time they make mistakes, they frame them in a constructive manner and ask themselves questions, such as "What can I learn from this setback?" Research has shown that people who are willing to make mistakes are more prone to gather new knowledge and develop novel capabilities (Lee et al., 2003).

In relation to this, Baumeister et al. (2001) observed that people are prone to learn much more quickly from negative events (which implies a certain degree of punishment) than from positive experiences (which entails reward). Sometimes, people with a prosperity mindset can even learn from mistakes made by others (customers, suppliers, etc.). They are keen on "borrowing" lessons learned by other people or organisations in order to apply them to their own business activities.

A company which learned from other organisations is Google. In its origins, this company observed that other portal sites, like Yahoo! and MSN, were crowded with too much information. As a consequence, this company decided to develop a webpage with a distinctive but uncluttered design, with no information overload (Rosenberg, 1998). As it is known, over time, this webpage became the most famous and well-used search engine worldwide.

People with an abundance mindset realise that oftentimes, in order to learn more effectively, they have to do the very things they want to learn. Race (1995) called this type of process "learning by doing." From this perspective, mistakes can never be avoided, and they are an important part of the business journey. According to Rogers (1961, 1969), the main characteristics of this empirical way of learning are proactive and direct involvement and self-evaluation.

People with an abundance mindset do not make excuses (such as insufficient time and other priorities) to avoid learning regularly. Instead, these individuals take their time to invest in increasing their own knowledge on a regular basis because they value a lifelong education. Their ongoing learning process makes them more resourceful in order to achieve their mission. These people are also keen on simplification: they like to summarise complex ideas in simple terms, which requires thorough and deep comprehension of various data. These business people act, as it is known in sociology, as symbolic analysts, the ones who manage knowledge and creative ideas as relevant strategic assets. Albretcht (1979) observed that these knowledge workers are in charge of producing, processing, as well as handling valuable information.

People with an abundance mindset realise that their business ventures are not destinations themselves, but instead valuable development processes. These people choose a learning process which is self-directed and their learning is intrinsically motivated (to enhance their mental skills, to generate new ideas and perspectives, etc.), but also extrinsically driven (for instance, to achieve specific business objectives). They also consider the learning process to be a relevant catalyst to loosen their own self-restricting beliefs and widen their awareness.

Business people with a prosperity mindset follow their own learning and development path. Sometimes, their learning path is structured, systematic, and methodical, which implies setting clear learning objectives and positive learning habits. Oftentimes, their learning process is intuitive and they are open to unplanned learning, for example, valuable lessons stemming from adverse situations affecting their company. These unexpected learning sources are welcomed and fully embraced. For example, Mark Cuban is the owner of the professional basketball team NBA's Dallas Mavericks. This famous entrepreneur and investor stated that his early success is a consequence of him reading three hours every day. He was very keen on learning mostly about the sectors he was interested in (Mashore, 2022). This is a good example of a methodical learning process.

Individuals with a prosperity mindset have a patient attitude towards their learning process. Research has shown that proficiency always takes time; there is no such thing as instant mastery. These people also have an explorative attitude, which makes them resemble curious toddlers eager to discover the wonders of their environment. These people are willing to ask various questions, even the most obvious ones, about any relevant topic, in order to open paths to new perspectives. Asking frequent questions helps them never take things for granted, even when everything seems to be working well.

These people enjoy the learning process because it contributes to their personal and professional development. Their continuous learning path creates new neural pathways in their brains, which broadens their perspective of their activities and the business environment. These individuals consider the process of learning as expansive because it provides them with a more enhanced and refined perception. New knowledge always helps them "read" various situations in a clearer and more through manner. These learning people are more prone to "see" new aspects of the business environment they could not have perceived otherwise. In other words, the learning process helps them make meaningful and valuable, and often subtle, distinctions of different aspects of the business context. By the process of gathering more knowledge, people can deal more effectively with challenging business scenarios.

Warren Buffett is a businessman with a learning attitude. This insightful business leader is behind Berkshire Hathaway, the massive world-class investment organisation. When making any investment decisions, this renowned investor is keen on learning more about the target companies, such as their current and past valuations, their competitive advantages, qualities of its management teams, as well as general economic conditions affecting these companies' sectors, among other aspects. This investor only seeks companies he understands well, with positive long-term economic indicators, reliable and honest management, and an attractive price tag (Bevelin, 2019). This investor also analyses if the owner of the company he intends to invest loves the business or not (Buffett, 2012). His thorough analysis of this information allows him to "read" the potential investment projects in a clearer manner.

In a similar way, in a company like The Body Shop, which sells natural cosmetic products, there is a continuous analysis of naturalness of the ingredients used in the company's products, as well as their positive impact on the environment. This type of assessment allows this company to offer natural high-quality products.

There is a last point to highlight. People with a prosperity mindset know that they don't have to learn everything to run their business efficiently. They generally look for expert advice and professional support when necessary. These people also understand that the knowledge needed for their company's success is multidisciplinary, involving many areas of expertise (legal, marketing, finances, etc.) which are required to support thriving business activities. Some business leaders like James Dyson or Richard Branson have access to various specialists in different areas (marketing, legal aspects, etc.) who can answer questions they might have regarding their business endeavours.

4.1.5 Other Relevant Aspects of a Learning Attitude

People with a prosperity mentality have a "growth mindset," a term coined by Dweck (2012). According to this author, these people can improve their skills over time with effort and commitment. Their perseverant attitude prompts them to engage in challenging activities, instead of avoiding them. Whenever these individuals face setbacks, they keep on acting resiliently and use the feedback stemming from failure to improve their future performance. Consequently, these people are more prone to have higher achievements over time.

Many of these people become even more enduring and resilient after having overcome their failures. Cyrulnik (2009) observed that resilience is one's ability to cope with one's adverse circumstances, while realising that negative events don't inevitably determine one's destiny. According to this author, resilient people are prone to ask themselves "What am I going to do with the adverse situation?" in order to get valuable insights to help them to bounce back and move forward. Reivich and Shatté (2002) observed that "resilient people are able to derive meaning from failure, and they use this knowledge to climb higher than otherwise they would." These authors also observed that resilient people tend to transform setbacks into success. In other words, their setbacks prompt them to develop wiser comebacks. This approach is consistent with cognitive behavioural therapy which states that people's feelings and related behaviour are not generated by events affecting them, but by their personal interpretation (beliefs and related thoughts) of these very events. In the previous chapter, it was mentioned that Jack Ma, the founder of Alibaba, faced several setbacks but bounced back in a resilient way until this entrepreneur became successful with his business endeavour Alibaba. From an organisational perspective, a resilient company has the capability to adapt to internal adverse factors (e.g., bad leaders) or external ones (e.g., economic crisis) in an effective manner, while brightening its capabilities for future adaptations (Sutcliffe and Vogus, 2003).

There is another important topic to pinpoint. Business people generally learn and apply different business models or frameworks to improve their performance. These instruments help companies analyse business circumstances more simply. These instruments integrate different pieces of information and assist companies in their business decisions. For instance, SWOT is a tool most companies use to assess their own strengths and weaknesses, and opportunities and threats in their environment.

However, companies must bear in mind that all these models are like simplified maps. None of these models consider every single factor of a business situation; valuable aspects are always left aside. Companies should also understand that a model is always a means to aid business decisions, but is never an end in itself. Even when some companies are keen on the use of certain models, these organisations should avoid forcing business circumstances to fit into models, but instead keep in contact with real business circumstances.

Cohen and Prusak (2001) observed that "ground truth" is "the complex reality of authentic experiences" which is different from theoretical models and generalities. It is important that companies realise that there is always a gap between these frameworks and the real circumstances. Companies can only bridge this gap through practice, which means navigating real-life business circumstances.

A company like Sony, the giant that offers electronic products on a global level, is keen on knowing the truth on the ground. This renowned organisation acts with total authenticity and transparency in all its business projects. This organisation, which has been recognised as one of the "World's Most Ethical Companies," has core values like "Fairness, Integrity, Honesty, Respect and Responsibility" (Sony, 2021).

4.2 Tolerance to Ambiguity and Uncertainty

4.2.1 General Aspects of Uncertainty

> Only those who will risk going too far can possibly find out how far one can go.
>
> **T.S. Eliot**

The business environment becomes increasingly complex, which always entails dynamism and unpredictability. This environment is affected by several actors (customers, other organisations, communities, etc.) and macro factors (economic aspects, technological discoveries, cultural factors, environmental issues, and political and legal aspects). These actors and factors are interrelated in a very intricate and dynamic manner.

Oftentimes, a company is uncertain about potential changes in external factors (for example, advances in technology or modification of the regulations in force). It is impossible for any company to fully "predict" what is about to occur in future scenarios. Some organisations even profit from the intrinsic uncertainty of the business environment, for instance, insurance companies, economic researchers, financial advisors, and others. Some companies are often uncertain about the occurrence of internal circumstances (for instance, changes in employees' behaviour).

Lorenz (1993) observed that tiny changes in an environment can potentially create unpredictable massive outcomes, which is known as the "butterfly effect." A very well-known metaphor stated that a butterfly flapping its wings could affect the conditions of a tornado that later develops far away. Therefore, business people should view all their actions as important, even those that seem to be insignificant. It is difficult to estimate the long-term effect of a company's actions, both small and large ones.

An example of the butterfly effect can be observed in the organisation Mary Kay Ash. This cosmetics company started up with a minimal investment of only $5,000. In this company, managers have been empowered to make all the company's stakeholders (employees, suppliers, customers, etc.) feel that they count. At this company, all stakeholders – without any exception – are treated in a caring and considerate manner because people really like to be acknowledged and praised. As a consequence of this simple but meaningful approach, this company grew exponentially and became a multi-billion organisation (Sangeeth, 2010).

There is another relevant topic to discuss. Many business people feel anxious and doubtful when dealing with uncertain scenarios; these people are prone to devise plausible explanations for uncertain factors. Other people tend to over-analyse uncertain situations by gathering as much information as possible. Most companies try their best to eliminate, or at least mitigate uncertainty levels affecting their activities. De Mello (1990) wisely quipped that people are not fearful of the uncertain, but afraid of losing what is certain, their current circumstances.

Weick (1995) observed that there are three types of uncertainty: (a) state uncertainty, which means that companies do not know how specific factors are changing; (b) effect uncertainty, which includes the ignorance of the impact of specific factors on the company; and (c) response uncertainty, which implies not knowing the possible ways to respond to change. Similarly, Simon (2016) observed that, when making decisions, people might have uncertainty about the number of options available, and the consequences and usefulness of their choices. This author also stated that in uncertain situations, people tend to decide based on several factors: handy information, things they are acquainted with, or opinions from specialists.

Klein (2003) observed that "the five types of uncertainty are missing information, unreliable information, conflicting information, noisy information and confusing information." From this perspective, noisy information is when relevant data is mixed up with irrelevant data. In all these cases, it is difficult for companies to make effective business decisions. During the Covid-19 pandemic, there were high levels of uncertainty, driven by missing, unreliable, conflicting, noisy, and confusing information. This high uncertainty detrimentally affected companies in various relevant sectors (e.g., airline industry, hotel industry, restaurant sector, etc.), making their decisions more challenging. These high levels of uncertainty varied significantly from country to country.

4.2.2 Companies' Attitude before Uncertainty

> Uncertainty is the only certainty there is; and knowing how to live with insecurity is the only security.
>
> **John Allen Paulos**

Most companies perform a series of activities to handle their "fear of the unknown." According to Meares and Freeston (2008), companies deal with uncertainty in different ways, for example, being over-vigilant regarding future scenarios, becoming endlessly indecisive, avoiding commitments, procrastinating, looking for reassurance from experts, and shunning tasks via delegation, among others. These authors observed that some business people are inclined to worry about uncertain scenarios because this behaviour motivates them and helps them prevent problems or protects them against them.

Klein (2003) observed that people tend to face uncertainty in different ways, for instance, by deferring their decisions, looking for additional information, increasing their attention on the available information, making assumptions on information gaps, making up possible interpretations of the available information, and taking actions despite uncertainty. The aforementioned author observed that people also deal with uncertainty by projecting future scenarios, making simpler and more flexible plans, planning for the worst-case scenarios, taking incremental steps, taking preventive actions, and embracing uncertain scenarios.

Cialdini (2009) commented that oftentimes, in uncertain circumstances, people see how others act and tend to take them as external valid references and imitate them, which is called the "social proof principle." Oftentimes, other people are incorrect; therefore when taking others as references as to how to act, some relevant questions like "Is there any evidence that these people are acting in the best way?" and "Are there better ways of acting in this situation?" should be asked to avoid being misguided by social proof.

Some people tend to become immobilised before uncertain situations; thus, they avoid taking any action. They feel comfortable with the known and fret over new experiences or unfamiliar projects. In order to reduce the uncertainty levels associated with future scenarios, some companies use different tools, such as:

- Setting the business mission and vision.
- Developing various strategies and tactics.
- Setting clear policies, procedures, and systems.
- Preparing budgets and business projects.
- Conducting or contracting research studies.
- Analysing, comparing, and extrapolating information about trends.
- Writing meticulous contracts.
- Using well-proven techniques and tools.
- Assessing and managing potential risks.
- Pre-testing the feasibility of potential processes, products, and services.
- Depicting hypothetical scenarios about future events.
- Contracting insurance policies.

These well-used tools are valid instruments to deal with uncertainty related to business activities. These tools help companies handle their "fear of the unknown." Nevertheless, none of these strategies completely eliminates the uncertainty of future scenarios. These tools have a common factor: they are used to attempt to control what will happen. In other words, their users are fearful of losing control in uncertain scenarios. From the perspective of social psychology, most people experience the so-called "illusion of control" because they believe that they have more control over their own world than they actually have.

In business activities, risk is often related to the outcomes stemming from future scenarios. Valtonen (2016) observed that companies facing risky scenarios can adopt four courses of action: tolerating potential risky scenarios (especially when there are business opportunities in a business project), taking specific actions to reduce their risk (e.g., asking a customer with bad credit score for a collateral), transferring this risk to other companies (getting an insurance policy which covers goods subject to risk), and terminating business projects to avoid risk. Most companies will assess the potential impact of future circumstances and try to take appropriate preventive measures. To that effect, there is profuse literature, as well as professional qualifications, concerning risk management techniques which help people analyse this topic more thoroughly.

Infosys is a company based in India with a big number of employees which specialises in technology consulting and digital services. This company has clearly acknowledged the risk of water shortages affecting its premises in that market. This organisation also understands that these shortages can disrupt some of the company's basic activities (cooling, drinking, cleaning, etc.). This company's teams have undertaken risk assessment activities, and, consequently, took specific actions to deal with that risk (use of smart meters, water recycling, collection of rainwater, use of water reservoirs, etc.). In addition, the organisation regularly assesses water consumption and also the availability of water, among other parameters. As a result of all these measures, there was a significant drop in the water consumption per employee, keeping Infosys fully functional during water shortages (Marker, 2021).

There is another point to highlight. Some entrepreneurs believe that they are capable of predicting future scenarios. There is no such thing as "foreseeing" future scenarios because companies are affected by so many interrelated variables which cannot be fathomed in an accurate manner.

Therefore, business predictions should be put into perspective; these formalised forms of guess-work are always subject to errors.

Even though no entrepreneur has the gift of predicting the future, some business people do use their intuitive insights and reflections on past circumstances to expand their vision of uncertain scenarios. This type of person is prone to imagine the future continuation of some current trends, and even intuit the emergence of new patterns in the marketplace.

Some business people can see the bigger picture, which includes unobvious linkages between current circumstances, and past and future ones. These individuals tend to become leaders because they do not wait for the future to come, but create, shape, and mould it in their minds and with their actions. This foresightedness also includes the "prediction" of the potential consequences of present business activities. Some decades ago, Jeff Bezos, the founder of Amazon, the online retail giant, was able to "foresee" the exponential growth of online sales, which prompted him to start up this company.

4.2.3 *Mental Biases, Uncertainty, and Complexity*

When analysing information about future scenarios, business people are prone to misinterpret available data. Their interpretation of facts tends to be clouded by numerous cognitive distortions, called cognitive errors or mental biases. These mental distortions are prone to modify the information from the environment, eliminate it, generalise it, or even avoid it.

Dobelli (2014) observed that these biases represent deviations from logic and prevent people from thinking optimally about a given situation. These defective patterns of thinking are generally subconscious. These mental biases help business people interpret circumstances more simply and quickly. Nonetheless, these cognitive distortions commonly prompt people to come to incorrect or unfounded conclusions regarding uncertain scenarios.

Copious research has demonstrated numerous examples of cognitive distortions which affect the analysis of uncertain scenarios, for instance, minimising or exaggerating the importance of certain factors, selecting specific pieces of information and discarding others, seeking confirmation of one's beliefs, using stereotypes, confusing typical factors for likely ones and over- or underestimating the likelihood of the occurrence of events. Other distortions are blindly trusting a group's opinion or an expert, linking unrelated factors, confusing cause for correlation, personalising impersonal events, relying exclusively on recent or available information, misevaluating current resources, believing in the repetition of past events, and generalising unique or random factors, among others.

As seen previously, one of the main mental biases is the use of stereotypes. Dove, which is one of the leading brands in the cosmetics industry, goes against this type of bias. In many adverts, companies in the cosmetics sector show idealistic images of women (female models with slim and flawless figures, etc.). In response to this, Dove stands for the idea that every woman is beautiful. This brand wholeheartedly welcomes women's natural beauty, which includes all sizes, shapes, ages, races, hair colour, or styles. Moreover, Dove fosters diversity by using for their promotion activities (adverts, etc.) real women as they actually are (different sizes, shapes, ages, races, etc.), instead of using professional models (Dove, 2022).

There are other factors which prevent people from analysing uncertain situations in an effective manner, like their own beliefs and values. This topic was thoroughly analysed in the previous chapter. Another constraining factor is people's access to limited (incomplete) information when analysing these uncertain scenarios. Some authors like Simon (1971) add up to these limiting factors people's natural restrictions in their span of attention and data processing. All these factors often lead to decisions which are suboptimal because of people's bounded rationality.

As previously explained, the business environment is so complex that no company can take into account all its factors. Therefore, companies tend to perceive situations in a partial manner, ignoring some factors, oftentimes relevant ones. Any organisation counts on incomplete information; they can never gather all the possible data surrounding the business environment because of its complexity and dynamism. In other words, all "educated" decisions a company makes about their future are based on incomplete information. Many of the missing pieces of information are prone to pop out as the company takes action.

Consequently, no company should avoid acting in uncertain scenarios because they do not have all the information needed. Moreover, companies can never be fully ready for the uncertain. When in doubt, a company should take the most positive course of action for all involved. Oftentimes, an organisation realises how to deal with specific situations as they unfold, not in advance.

In order to avoid complacency and continually thrive, a company should be willing to navigate uncertain scenarios. Companies with a predominant prosperity mindset tend to fully embrace uncertainty and imagine future scenarios in a flexible and open-minded manner. These companies use a multidimensional analysis which includes as many relevant factors as possible. Some of these organisations are even keen on uncertain scenarios because these environments are considered fertile ground to develop creative ideas and projects. During a very uncertain scenario like the Covid-19 pandemic, several distilleries went through very challenging economic times. Some of these companies decided to start producing hand sanitiser, a product with a very high demand during the pandemic.

4.2.4 Abundance Mindset and Uncertainty

A company with a prevalent abundance mindset tends to analyse uncertain scenarios in a provisional or tentative manner. This type of company prefers general plausibility over precision. Therefore, for these companies, plans or projects related to uncertain scenarios are never carved in stone, but subject to continuous changes and fine-tuning as actions are taken.

Oftentimes, people with a prosperity mindset tend to make tentative decisions, moved by approximation. These individuals adjust their actions along the way, based on feedback which prompts them to confirm or correct their course of action. These people realise that each business circumstance is affected by a myriad of mostly unknown factors. For example, companies in the airline sector (Easyjet, Virgin Atlantic, British Airways, etc.) are often affected by numerous uncontrollable factors, like upswings and downswings of oil price, and critical weather conditions (hurricanes, etc.), among others. Oftentimes, these factors vary significantly from sector to sector.

Moreover, individuals with a prosperity mindset understand that many factors affecting their future business activities are beyond their control. Therefore, when business circumstances do not play out well, these people avoid interpreting them negatively. Their plans tend to be flexible because many future events affecting them cannot be predicted. Consequently, these companies never set goals in a rigid manner, but as references or guidelines which can be changed over time.

People with an abundance mindset tend to adopt a more explorative and curious attitude regarding future business scenarios. Instead of looking for security and certainty, they develop a sense of wonder and discovery as circumstances unfold, casting away rigid approaches and adapting to changing circumstances. Instead of resisting the "wave" of change, they are prone to "surf" it.

Besides, people with a prosperous mindset perceive their business endeavours as adventures into the unknown and recognise that their main point of power is the present moment. By knowing that no future scenarios can be accurately predicted, they are empowered to take full responsibility and act in the best way possible each moment according to the available information and resources. These people tend to feel less anxious and worried about the uncontrollable future because they focus on what is actually under their control: the now. Because future circumstances cannot be fully foreseen, they also avoid having negative expectations about these situations.

Covey (1992) observed that there are situations when a company does not have total control called "circle of concern." From this perspective, in any situation involving others (organisations, government, etc.), a company has limited influence and never total control over the circumstances. This author also highlighted that there are areas where a company can respond effectively, called its "circle of influence," such as its own actions at each moment. Likewise, the ancient Stoic philosophical school of thought also observed that people can only fully control their thoughts, emotions, and actions; all the rest is beyond their control.

As seen previously, no company has all the information to make the perfect decision about future business scenarios. Therefore, the information gathered by the company should be reasonable, avoiding excessive information gathering. It is better to obtain a sensible amount of information and update and adjust it on a regular basis. In the same way, companies should avoid over-analysis of data in an attempt to predict future possibilities.

Business people with a prosperous mindset never give up or get stopped by uncertain scenarios. These people act in a determined and daring manner, focusing on their purpose in a continuous and wholehearted manner. These individuals are less likely to be concerned about uncertainty affecting their activities. They know that the next steps to take are often discovered as they walk their talk. Small actions contribute to their mission and generate positive momentum which drives these people forward.

When people are at ease with uncertainty, they continually stretch their comfort zone. The zone of comfort is safe, known, and certain, while exploring new business activities, developing new products and services, and entering new markets imply a certain degree of uncertainty and risk. Business people with a prosperity mindset are prone to tread unconventional paths and undertake non-traditional endeavours. These people know that not taking any risks represents a very risky business perspective.

These people take action in a faithful manner. They make the mental choice to believe that if they are doing their best, then things are likely to work out. Even though they do not have the complete picture of how things will unfold, they are willing to take one step at a time towards the achievement of their purpose. As seen previously, in the past, when Richard Branson started up Virgin Atlantic airline, he was not sure that this new business project would succeed; for this reason, he carefully analysed this business endeavour's downside. However, at the same time, this business leader was also hopeful and convinced that this new airline could provide customers with more outstanding service, as compared with other companies in the sector.

4.3 Orientation to Action

> Knowing is not enough, we must apply. Willing is not enough, we must do.
>
> **Goethe**

4.3.1 Importance of an Action-Oriented Attitude

In a previous point, the importance of continuous learning was explained. Nonetheless, even the most relevant knowledge is useless without taking any action on it. People with a prosperity mindset consider their actions as fundamental parts of their business journey. They know that even though their actions cannot guarantee success, their inaction tends to bring about failure. Some business people have great ideas that never come to fruition, as they are reluctant to take effective action. Ideas tend to be forgotten if they are not nailed down by putting them into practice. Individuals with an abundance mindset know that being inactive is prone to making them restless, anxious, hesitant, fearful, or insecure. They realise that their actions can add value to their organisations and also society as a whole.

Most business books profusely highlight the importance of any organisation having a big vision and clear goals to achieve, but only a few authors analyse the significance of taking continuous actions. In that sense, Fritz (1984, 2003) observed that actions are paramount to create anything in the business environment because they close the gap between a company's current reality (the status quo) and its vision (where the company wants to go). From this perspective, no creation can be brought to life without any action. This author also suggested that oftentimes, actions should be taken before one feels completely ready to take them.

Action-oriented people are more vital because they are always taking charge; they go beyond survival and security mode to focus on their growth and development. They know that the best action has not been taken yet because there is always room for improvement. Not only do they take action, but they also follow through on actions taken previously.

People oriented to action avoid being perfectionist. They always choose the most plausible action. Perfectionists are instead prone to get stuck in negative behaviour, such as:

- Comparing their performance with others.
- Finding negative traits in their actions.
- Becoming anxious about their performance.
- Fretting over setbacks.
- Over-controlling their tasks.
- Planning excessively.
- Procrastinating or making excuses.
- Waiting for the ideal circumstances.
- Setting unachievable standards.
- Harshly criticising themselves.

Paradoxically, the aforementioned behaviours prevent perfectionistic people from taking due action. It is important to pinpoint that taking action always creates momentum and motivation, which defeats people's complacency and inertia. Ellis and Harper (1997) observed that "inertia has a tendency to feed on itself." When people take action, their energy is in motion, which prompts them to take even more action. Instead, when people are not used to taking continuous action, it seems harder for them.

The successful entrepreneur and writer Jack Canfield observed that, when people take action, they are more prone to become successful. This business leader also stated that, as people start taking action, things become much easier. This entrepreneur coached a myriad of people, and realised that one of the main differences between losers and winners is that the latter take action continuously (Canfield, 2005).

Successful business people have a ruthless can-do attitude. They do not stop at the level of intention; they actually take action. They know that they will be judged by others for their actions, not their promises or resolutions. They take continuous action, which expands their beliefs about what is possible. They realise that each day is a brand-new opportunity to take action and they are willing to roll their sleeves up to make it happen; they also understand that small commitments create a virtuous cycle, which bring about bigger commitments. As their actions build up gradually, their persistence and discipline eventually pay off.

Bandura (cited in Egan, 1994) states that people are more prone to take action when they expect that their behaviour will lead them to the desired outcomes (also called outcome expectations) and when they feel that their capabilities are adequate for that action (also called self-efficacy). When people take continuous action, their expectations tend to improve and they feel more self-efficacious.

Continuous action helps people overcome any feelings of incompetence and inadequacy. From the psychological perspective, people improve their self-efficacy through the feedback they obtain from their previous actions. Figuratively speaking, people continually adjust their trajectory, like a rocket heading to outer space. A company was mentioned previously, Two Blind Brothers, which sells quality soft items of clothing online. As seen previously, these founders – who are visually impaired brothers – mentioned that they did not have any knowledge or experience regarding fashion or items of clothing. This fact did not prevent them from taking action and setting up this company which successfully offers quality items of clothing to a wide audience.

4.3.2 Traits of Action-Focused Business People

Action-prone people are more enduring and tolerant to frustration. They are willing to go the extra mile without giving up, even during challenging circumstances. Their actions give these people an edge and staying power to navigate dire situations more effectively. They delay instant gratification stemming from the natural comfort and ease of not acting in order to take valuable actions to pursue their purpose.

People with an abundance mindset are continually coaching themselves into action because they do not settle for mediocrity; they know that their present actions contribute to their business future outcomes. These individuals are willing to harness their innermost greatness, which makes them unstoppable. People with an abundance mindset are also willing to step into the unknown and act differently. Sometimes, these people are perceived as slightly naïve or childlike because of their experimental ways of doing things.

Richard Branson, the founder of Virgin Group, is a good example of an action-oriented business leader. As mentioned, with his action-prone attitude, this entrepreneur developed an overarching range of business endeavours for his group, such as Virgin Gyms, Virgin Atlantic, Virgin Trains, and Virgin Media.

Siebold (2010) observed that people with an abundance mindset are "comfortable being uncomfortable." Successful business people are always willing to take action, even when they feel demotivated or moody. Their feelings never prevent them from taking action. They know that as soon as the first step is taken, the following actions get easier and more manageable.

Whenever possible, these people take actions while remaining positive and calm. They avoid having negative expectations, which never contribute to their success. Their emotional stability and continuous focus on their purpose sharpen their discerning and creative skills and improve their performance.

According to Miller (2009), there are four main types of mood people can experience: action mood, calm mood, anxiety mood, and depression mood. This author observed that people in the action mood become positive, experience high energy, and tend to adopt a can-do attitude. This author stated that, in this mood, people tend to be more confident, communicate more openly, and are more likely to analyse new alternatives.

From this perspective, people should strive for balance between the action mood and the calm mood. The calm mood helps people replenish their energy, reflect on their actions, learn from their mistakes, and plan to act differently in the future.

People do not have to wait to be in an action mood in order to act. To that effect, when people start taking action, these activities prompt them to experience the action mood. In other words, when people take action, their mood is boosted accordingly.

According to Robbins (2017), people should force themselves into action because they are never going to feel like acting. This author presents a case for people continually parenting themselves and taking action. Likewise, Schwartz (1979) observed that people should crank up their mental engine in a mechanical manner and take action at the moment, avoiding waiting for their spirit to move them. Some people trick themselves into action, for example, by setting tight deadlines.

People with an abundance mindset take full responsibility. According to Rosenberg (2005), some people tend to avoid responsibility in different ways, such as abiding by the opinions of others, reacting to external forces (e.g., economic factors), blaming others for their faulty character (lazy, indecisive, etc.), complying with external rules, and being driven by their own impulses. Anita Roddick, the founder of The Body Shop, is an example of an entrepreneur who takes full responsibility and is driven by her passion. When she started up this company, this business was fully committed to offering natural, cruelty-free cosmetic products, regardless of what other companies in the sector were doing at that moment.

People who take full responsibility do not pay attention to harsh criticism from others, nor do they retreat before these comments. These people take action without looking for approval from others. After they have taken action, they never feel regret, shame, or guilt. When their actions produce negative outcomes, they are open to learning from them.

Some business people mistakenly wait for the ideal circumstances in order to take action. They use sentences like "I will take action when …" or "I will take action if there is …," and similar ones. These individuals take a long time getting themselves ready to take action. It is important to pinpoint that there is no "perfect" situation or time to take action. A company's people with an abundance mindset harness the present circumstances and take the best action possible at that moment. They take action, even when they do not feel completely ready, and make adjustments on their way.

Action-oriented people search for new opportunities and challenges they can act on. These individuals never refrain from taking risks if these actions might lead them closer to their mission. Their courage and grit prompt them to act whenever it is necessary. Oftentimes, their actions challenge the status quo and what is considered possible in the business environment.

Business people with a prosperity mindset take action to harness their unique strengths and capabilities (and the ones from their company) to add distinct value to the company's stakeholders. These individuals avoid copying other companies' offerings by highlighting their own perspective through every action they take.

As seen previously, when Google originally launched its own search engine, this company aimed to make this platform unique and distinctive (no information clutter, etc.), as compared with the other search engines which existed in the marketplace. This company harnessed its own capabilities (information management skills, etc.) to develop a remarkable product.

4.3.3 Continuous Action, Fear, and Growth

Cuddy (2016) observed that taking action always reinforces future action because each time people take action, they tend to recall their previous experiences of acting, which makes it easier for them to take action again. These people also realise that they are the most important obstacle holding them back from acting. Action-oriented people progressively expand their comfort zone because they abhor becoming stagnant. These people often seem to move beyond what is considered reasonable by the average person. These individuals dare to perform activities most people do not even dare ponder.

By taking continuous actions, people with abundance mindset are empowered to set higher goals over time. These people believe that big objectives can be achieved with determination and flexibility. These individuals know that their true potential is limitless; they realise that extraordinary results can be brought about if they adopt an attitude of commitment. Wattles (2013) observed that business people should take action with the impression of increase, which means having the intention to advance themselves and the people around them. This author also stated that this intention has very tangible effects. Likewise, Schwartz (1979) expressed that actions should always add value to oneself and others.

Some business people are fearful of taking some actions. Ferriss (2017) opines that these people should ask themselves about the worst possible outcomes if actions are taken, the different ways to prevent these potential negative outcomes, and their solutions in case they occur. This author also suggests estimating the benefits of taking action, as well as the cost of not taking these very actions.

This fear of taking action can have a very negative impact on business activities. For example, in a poll undertaken by the business consulting company McKinsey & Company, 85% of the executives enquired have concluded that fear often or always prevents their companies from developing innovative projects (Furstenthal et al., 2022).

Wiest (2013) observed that when a person feels fear of doing something, this task tends to be frightening, but also worthwhile to this individual; in other words, fear often indicates what is worth doing. This author wisely stated that, "Fear means you're trying toward something you love, but your old beliefs, or unhealed experiences are getting in the way."

In order to keep fear of action at bay, Robbins (2017) suggests a simple technique called the "five-second rule." From this perspective, when people feel the need to act, in that moment, they should mentally count down from 5 to 0 and immediately take action without second-guessing. This technique proves to be efficient to overcome negative states people experience when they are about to take action, such as hesitation, lack of confidence, indecisiveness, immobility, and over-analysis.

Thompson (1995) observed that when people act despite their fears, their bodies release adrenalin which provides their actions with more vigour. When people are dominated by fear, their bodies instead release *excessive* adrenalin which renders them inactive and overwhelmed.

There is a technique some psychologists use with some patients (with phobias, compulsive behaviour, and anxiety problems) called progressive exposure. The technique requires gradually exposing oneself to the factors which prompt one to feel fearful, without reacting in any way. This increasing exposure makes one more habituated to the seemingly threatening factors. As a consequence, all negative reactive responses towards the perceived threats eventually get extinguished.

For example, if salespeople feel fearful of making phone calls to customers, they can progressively expose themselves to this situation, by making a few calls, despite their original discomfort and uneasiness. Then they can progressively increase the number of calls over time because they will feel more at ease and less threatened by that situation.

Action-oriented people are proactive and less prone to react to external circumstances (for instance, changes in the economic conditions, new legislation, etc.). These individuals preferably use sentences in active voice ("I do …," "I choose …," etc.) rather than phrases in passive voice ("I am affected by …," "I am defeated by …," etc.). Their proactive orientation prompts them to explore different alternatives around the circumstances they face. They are also willing to harness valuable opportunities which appear in the marketplace. These people reveal how they truly are through their action; their true essence is shown through the steps they take.

When people take action, they tend to feel more empowered, not more helpless, because they focus on what they can control (their behaviour) instead of being centred on the uncontrollable (external circumstances). Action-oriented people are in the driver's seat; they are not victims of circumstances. Psychologically speaking, their locus of control is internal, not external. Walter (2005) observed that all behaviour can be placed on a spectrum, which has a "reactive attitude" on one extreme, and "active attitude" on the other. This author stated that people can gradually move from being reactive to becoming more active, by taking little but consistent steps.

IBM is a company previously analysed in this book. Canon is a renowned company which sells cameras, lenses, and medical equipment, among other products. These two companies (IBM and Canon) are valuable examples of action-oriented organisations. These companies are granted a myriad of patents for their inventions every year because these organisations take continuous actions regarding research and development of new products (England, 2015)

When people with an abundance attitude take action and achieve their objectives, they give sufficient credit to people who supported them during that path. They know that the achievement of goals is always the result of co-operative teamwork. Therefore, these people encourage assistance from others, and they are explicitly grateful for their co-operation.

Action-oriented people are keen on flexible planning. As seen previously, most companies commonly use plans as tools to co-ordinate their resources and deal with uncertainty. Even though plans have a future-orientation, they can never predict forthcoming situations precisely. Besides, plans are always based on imperfect information which is gradually completed, amended, or updated when actions regarding these plans are taken. Consequently, their plans are flexible and can be changed over time as these individuals take action.

Sometimes, action-oriented people visualise themselves taking a specific action before actually performing a certain activity. In other words, these individuals form vivid mental images of them performing an activity in an effective manner and also experiencing positive emotions while doing so. Many athletes and other sports people use visualisation techniques to improve their performance levels in their competitive field. Besides, some research studies corroborate that when people visualise themselves taking action, the same areas of their brains are activated as if they were taking real action. The main aspects of visualisation are explored in Appendix G.

4.3.4 Tips to Become More Action-Oriented

Some companies spend excessive time developing their plans because they tend to over-analyse information, which brings about "paralysis by analysis." Therefore, planning should be done in a reasonable time in order to take timely action. No plan will ever be perfect; a company can always make adjustments as it takes action. Besides, the factors of the business environment (legislation, technology, economy, etc.) are dynamic, so oftentimes a company takes unplanned actions. Action-oriented organisations also take into account these aspects:

■ When these organisations face setbacks, they never remain passive; these companies see failures in perspective and gain insights in order to come back and act more intelligently. Failures only imply that these organisations have not attained their aims yet. Every action taken, even failed ones, gets these companies closer to their business purpose. Each business project can be considered as a work in progress, and obstacles are perceived as opportunities for improvement. An entrepreneur like Jack Ma, who was analysed in this book, is a good example of a business leader that has overcome setbacks.

■ Action-oriented businesses also learn from their achievements. When this type of company attains its goals, it thoroughly analyses what worked well in order to repeat and improve it in future projects. These companies build up momentum on their past successes so as to foster their future successes. As seen previously, an entrepreneur like James Dyson learned from his setbacks and improved his actions over time.

■ Action-prone organisations with a prosperity mindset give their best each time they take action. In other words, they never make tentative moves or halfway effort. Their actions are wholehearted and passionate. When these companies face failure, their people remain calm because they have given their best.

■ Action-oriented companies know when to discontinue overtly inviable projects, even when they have invested sufficient time and effort. Psychologically speaking, most people are affected by a phenomenon called self-justification, which implies justifying their previous assessments of ongoing projects to continue them, even when these projects have not produced tangible results for a significant time. As seen in this book, Virgin Group discontinued some business projects which were unsuccessful (e.g., Virgin Cola, Virgin Vodka, and Virgin Brides).

■ People working for action-oriented organisations take their time to recharge their batteries after having taken action. Therefore, these individuals take time to do some fun things, such as hobbies, travelling, and parties. These activities revitalise them and help them think in a more insightful manner when they resume taking action. A company like McKinsey & Company, which is a renowned consultancy company, introduced meditation into its HR programmes; in this organisation, they are convinced that this type of practice makes employees healthier and more content, which affects positively the profitability levels (Duffy, 2020).

■ Action-oriented organisations take action based on high-quality information, whenever possible. In that sense, these companies look for the most up-to-date and accurate information. Oftentimes, this business information quickly becomes outdated, making it irrelevant if not replaced by more current information. As seen previously, one of the world most insightful investors, Warren Buffett, reads several hours a day to keep himself up-to-date with the most relevant information regarding current or potential investing projects.

■ Action-oriented organisations set clear and reasonable deadlines for actions to be completed over time. Deadlines represent valuable constraints which prompt the companies' people to do their best in order to meet these signposts and prevent them from procrastinating indefinitely. These companies are prone to extend these deadlines, if more time is needed. Companies like Acme Whistles, which is a well-known organisation which manufactures whistles (sport whistles, police force whistles, etc.), set the goal of developing a specific number of new products over a period of time (Acme Whistles, 2022; Blythe, 2012).

■ People working for action-oriented companies prefer to work smart rather than hard. Therefore, these individuals avoid taking mindless actions. These people tend to analyse situations before acting on them. They assess the risks and implications of their actions, without over-analysing these aspects. As seen previously, the company Twice as Warm, which sells quality items of clothing, takes into account the implications of its actions and has a very meaningful mission. For every product purchased by a customer, this company donates one to local shelters, bringing about a positive social impact. However, sometimes, action-oriented people also take some actions on the spur of the moment. These seemingly erratic actions are based on gut instinct, hunches, or intuition. The topic of intuitive insights will be thoroughly analysed in Chapter 15.

- When taking action, action-oriented organisations are focused on their mission and objectives. Therefore, these companies avoid being distracted by other organisations, nor do they compare themselves with them. Action-prone businesses know that the best way to succeed in the business environment is to continually compete with themselves and become better every day. Before taking any action, individuals working for these organisations often ask themselves, "Is this action aligned with our business mission?" If the answer is affirmative, the action is taken; if negative, the action is fully discarded. As seen in Chapter 1, companies like Sweetgreen, Whole Foods, and others only undertake projects which are aligned with their meaningful business purpose.

- Action-prone organisations divide complex business projects, including various actions, into smaller and more actionable "chunks." By doing so, these projects become more manageable and less overwhelming. Individuals working for these companies become more capable when dealing with smaller steps contributing to an overall project. They also believe in the power of small wins which create valuable momentum for future wins. The company Into the AM develops premium handcrafted apparel products. At this organisation, there are clear and measurable objectives for each employee; these goals are detailed both annually and quarterly. As a consequence, every employee can get a series of small wins (Williams, 2022).

- Action-oriented organisations know that not all actions are equal. Therefore, these companies take their time to prioritise actions. Actions which contribute to the achievement of business mission and those which strengthen business relationships with stakeholders are given priority over the rest, when possible. As seen previously, the company The Body Shop, which sells natural cosmetic products, gives priority to activities like using packaging made of recycled material and uses natural high-quality ingredients as these actions are aligned with the organisation's values and purpose.

- Action-prone companies encourage their employees to take one action at a time and focus their energy on the action at hand, but also take consistent steps over time. In that sense, multitasking is strongly discouraged due to its intrinsic ineffectiveness; this is backed by profuse scientific research. These organisations also empower their employees to balance their work tasks with other relevant areas of their lives. These individuals do not exclusively devote their time to business activities, but they try to look for equilibrium with other areas, such as health and family. The7Stars is a renowned independent media agency. This company focuses on its employees' work-life balance, as it offers its staff members a paid gym membership, and regular mindfulness and yoga sessions, as well as unlimited holiday allowance. In addition, employees have no contractually assigned working hours; they work if they need to in order to have things done. This organisation was recognised as one of the best workplaces (Bishop, 2019; The7stars, 2022).

- Action-oriented organisations always take the most suitable actions at each moment. If these actions proved them wrong, these companies are always willing to try other courses of action. To that effect, these companies are flexible and feel comfortable with change; they are open to adapting their actions according to dynamic scenarios. These organisations also know that there is not one way to approach every business situation. These companies, according to Kay (2011), tend to achieve their objectives indirectly. From this standpoint, companies are prone to go through a lot of exploration, iteration, and continuous adjustments of their actions on their way to achieving their goals. As seen previously, in the past, the company 3M was looking for strong adhesives, but this organisation developed a product which did not stick well on surfaces, but lightly. This company tried for several years to find a valuable use for this weak adhesive, which eventually became the well-known Post It sticky notes.

■ Action-prone organisations take action from a perspective of service to all their relevant stakeholders. Their actions represent effective ways to connect to these stakeholders and strengthen the relationship with them. For example, by improving customer service activities, a company is more capable of satisfying customers' innermost needs effectively and thus adding more value to them. The Ecolaundry is a company which offers one-of-a-kind laundering services both for corporate customers and for individuals. This company made a great investment in green technology (water borehole, biomass, and solar) and uses washing machines which are energy-efficient. To that effect, these machines are powered by renewable energy. For their laundering services, the company also utilises environmentally friendly detergents. As a consequence, this company's action brings about a positive impact on customers, but also communities and the environment (The Ecolaundry, 2023).

■ Action-oriented organisations continually assess the outcomes of their actions. They regularly ask themselves this question: "Are our actions taking our company towards where we want to be?" and take corrective actions when necessary. As seen previously, when the inventor James Dyson was testing thousands for prototypes for his bagless vacuum cleaner, he was implicitly asking himself this question.

■ Action-prone companies allow people to delegate activities to others, when possible. Employees do not have to be directly responsible for every single relevant action. Each employee takes certain actions, preferably those they are actually outstanding at, and delegate the rest. The remaining actions will be performed by other employees or external advisors.

■ Action-oriented organisations frequently celebrate their achievements, small and large; they never take these accomplishments for granted. These companies show gratitude to those people whose actions contributed to those successful outcomes. Aisle Planner, which offers project management software for events, allows its team members to open a bottle of champagne to celebrate every time the company obtains 100 new customers. On those occasions, staff members stop what they are currently doing and gather to celebrate this special achievement. This company has a very insignificant churn rate (Williams, 2022).

Action-oriented individuals know that, with continuous repetition and reinforcement, most actions become automatic over time (habits). Habitual activities, either negative or positive, simplify people's decision-making process, and these tasks are performed effortlessly. However, habitual behaviour is often resistant to change. Consequently, action-oriented people thoroughly evaluate their current habits in order to keep the ones which contribute, directly or indirectly, to the company's mission and discard the rest. Oftentimes, these individuals tend to discard certain detrimental habits, such as over-analysing information before taking any action.

Action-prone individuals are prone to form new positive habits. Wiest (2013) observed that, when people develop a positive habit, this is constructive because it gives these individuals a sense of purpose and provides them with emotional stability and predictability. This author also stated that each new positive habit formed by people is beneficial because it affirms their previous decisions, validates their capabilities to take specific actions, and encourages self-regulation of their actions. Habitual behaviour is also less stressful as it requires less attention than non-habitual activities (Wood et al., 2002).

There are different ways to create habits. People can link the specific activities regarding habits they want to take to positive rewards. This will make these individuals more prone to repeat these activities over time, contributing to the development of new habits (Thorndike, 1898). This use of rewards prompts people to perform the rewarded action in a repetitive and more intense way, also making them experience positive emotional states, which reinforces their behaviour (Schultz, 1999). This knowledge can also be applied to detrimental habits; by linking negative habits to unpleasant experiences, these habits are more likely to be broken.

In addition, it is suggested that people should keep record of their new habits, when they are in progress of development (e.g., indicating in a notebook the number of days a new habit is repeated). The recording of these activities makes the whole habituation process more conspicuous and pleasurable (Clear, 2018). Some activities are more prone to become habitual by stacking (or attaching) them to existing habits. In addition, it is also advisable to start taking small habits, instead of significant ones, in order to reduce opposition (Dean, 2013).

Here are some examples of habits in successful companies. Warby Parker, a successful company that sells eyeglasses, has the positive habit of donating a pair of eyeglasses to people in need for every pair this organisation sells (Warby Parker, 2022). This company has a philanthropic approach tied to its business model. In the case of Netflix, employees have the habit of delivering constructive feedback to others (Hastings and Meyer, 2020). In the case of The Ecolaundry, previously mentioned, this company has the positive habits of using green technology, energy-efficient washing machines, and environmentally friendly detergents. As a consequence, this company's action brings about a positive impact on customers, but also on communities and the environment.

According to Wattles (2013), companies with an abundance mindset take actions which are always focused on creating value for others; their actions are never based on fear of other organisations. A company which creates high value is Whole Foods. As previously seen in this book, this company takes regular action to provide customers with great value, by offering them healthy products which also bring about a positive impact on the environment.

In addition, action-oriented people adopt a creative attitude that will help the company harness business opportunities, which are always abundant in the marketplace. The topic of creativity will be explored in Chapters 14 and 15.

Questions for Self-Reflection

- How can I harness uncertainty in a more productive manner?
- What type of knowledge is necessary for my organisation to succeed in the marketplace?
- What type of actions is necessary to pursue the company's mission?
- What is preventing me from taking the next obvious step?

GENERAL ASPECTS OF LOVE AND BUSINESS

Chapter 5

Love and Business Activities

There is something peculiar about human beings. We are loving animals. I know that we kill each other and do all these horrible things, but if you look at any story of corporate transformation where everything begins to go well, innovation appears, and people are happy to be there, you will see it is a story of love.

Humberto Maturana Romesin and Gerda Verden-Zoller

5.1 Main Meanings of Love

Listen, my friend. He who loves, understands.

Kabir

In the world, the lack of love is observed through countless examples: terrorism, racism, human trafficking, wars, corruption, pollution, and other excruciating problems. In the business environment, companies with an unloving attitude display countless examples of misbehaviour: exploiting employees, ripping customers off, acting without integrity with intermediaries and suppliers, using misleading advertising, polluting the environment, using non-renewable resources, and bribing governments, among others. Within most companies, some employees also adopt an unloving attitude towards others, for instance: backbiting, one-upmanship, power struggles, stealing other people's credit, and bullying, among others.

Hamilton (2010) observed that people are naturally hardwired to behave in a loving manner with others. Likewise, Griffith (2016) stated that human beings have an instinctive orientation to behave "in an unconditionally selfless, all-loving, co-operative moral way." Nonetheless, many people tend to frequently act with others in a selfish and uncaring manner. Some negative values (egocentrism, carelessness, manipulation, defensiveness, etc.) present in most social contexts reinforce people's selfish attitude.

Montagu (1957) observed that love is intrinsically social and it is a basic emotional need, as relevant as food. This author also stated that love for others implies active interest, caring support, and involvement regarding their well-being and their development as human beings. A person with a loving attitude towards others is keen to support them in their innermost needs and interests.

DOI: 10.4324/9781003372684-7

Loving people care for others, even when the latter do not request the support from the former. This type of person acknowledges, accepts, and appreciates others as unique human beings. Loving people never judge others, but treat them tenderly. These people develop a profound sense of connectedness with others.

Maturana Romesin and Verden-Zoller (1996, 2008) observed that, from the biological perspective, each emotion is a bodily disposition of what a person can or cannot do in relation to others, and "love is the domain of those behaviours or bodily dispositions in which another arises as a legitimate other in coexistence with ourselves." Moreover, these authors stated that love is "a biological phenomenon ... through which social life arises and is conserved." They concluded that "love is our natural condition, and *it is the denial of love that requires effort*" (emphasis added) (Maturana Romesin and Verden-Zoller, 1996). In a similar vein, Kukk (2017) observed that, when people act selfishly, their brains tend to exert more effort than when they act selflessly, as their brains seem to be naturally hardwired for empathy and compassion.

There is an interesting example of the importance of love in business. The philanthropist and entrepreneur John Paul DeJoria is the co-founder of one of the biggest and most successful hair products companies in the world: John Paul Mitchell Systems. This insightful business leader observed that, in this company, they treat people the way they would like to be treated. "You walk in our company. It's love," he wholeheartedly quipped. As a consequence of this loving environment, he stated that employees truly love what they do. In addition, he has mentioned that this company has one of the lowest turnover rates, which means that a very tiny number of staff members have left this organisation over the years (Bilyeu, 2017).

Research has corroborated that a loving attitude towards others brings about countless positive effects. Hamilton (2010) observed that the brains of people with a loving attitude release opiates, serotonin and dopamine, which lift their mood and make them feel more optimistic. This specialist also stated that adopting a loving attitude towards others generates oxytocin, which is a substance that prods people to behave kindly and selflessly, co-operate, share, and trust others. This author also stated that when a loving person is near another, the latter gets "infected" by the kindness of the former and is prone to act alike.

Sunderland (2007) observed that loving people are less willing to behave aggressively and more inclined to hold lofty values, like kindness, compassion, and altruism. This author stated that, "Loving in peace means that your moment-to-moment stream of consciousness, your thoughts and feelings take you to a warm world inside your head."

Some entrepreneurs purposefully introduce the term "love" in their business projects. The founder of company Kammok, which produces camping products, observed that all decisions made by this organisation, like the choice of its logo and brand, and the selection of the types of materials used in the products to be offered, are all based on love. This business leader defines love as being primarily centred on others, with small or no regard for oneself; in his view, love brings about the greater good (Kammok, 2022; McEvilly, 2012).

Warren Buffett also talks about the importance of love in business. In an interview, this renowned investor has observed that when the company he leads, Berkshire Hathaway, acquires other companies, almost always people who sell these organisations will run them. So, whenever buying a company, Mr Buffett looks at the CEO in their eyes, to see if this person loves the business, because he only wants to rely on people who love the business (Buffett, 2012).

There is another relevant point to highlight. Maturana and Bunnel (1998) observed that, when people adopt a loving attitude, their discerning and creative skills are enhanced. The HeartMath Institute concluded that when people experience loving feelings in the area of their hearts, they enter a state of coherence, where all their body systems act in sync (Childre et al., 2000). As seen previously, Hawkins (2012) concludes that love is one of the highest states of consciousness that exists.

The word "love" cannot easily be defined; there are different possible "definitions" of this term. The list below is not exhaustive, but only exemplificative.

- Love is the link which connects everything that exists.
- Love is the straightener of negative thoughts and emotions.
- Love is continuous care for oneself and others.
- Love is a gentle opener of all possibilities.
- Love is a torch providing clarity in confusing situations.
- Love is the most valuable capital of a human being.
- Love is the main engine of progress and positive change.
- Love is an alchemic shortcut to contentment and peacefulness.
- Love is an internal motivator in challenging situations.
- Love is an enabler of inclusiveness and diversity.
- Love is the silent positive observer of everybody and everything.
- Love is the bridge which shortens any distance between people.
- Love is the overt demonstration of support and affection.
- Love is the facilitator of a more meaningful communication.
- Love is a natural pacifier for any conflictive situation.
- Love is service to others, not servitude nor slavery.
- Love is the true connector of each individual with others.
- Love is the origin of every creative endeavour.
- Love is pure authentic essence, beyond distracting appearances.
- Love is the core element of all fruitful relationships.
- Love is the most powerful antidote to fear.
- Love is the smoothest way to overcome others' defensive behaviour.
- Love is the enlivening principle pervading everything in the universe.
- Love is the truth beyond any type of speculation.
- Love is an open standpoint which welcomes diverse perspectives.
- Love is pure kindness and respect for others.
- Love is the beautiful side in everything that exists.
- Love is the most comforting respite in dire times.
- Love is the state which melts any resistance away.
- Love is the most precious energy needed for triumph.
- Love is the preventer of control and manipulation.
- Love is the balm which enlivens organisational environments.
- Love is the most significant fuel for passion and action.
- Love is a sense of togetherness and integration.
- Love is the uniting substance of all relationships.
- Love is the main driver to attain an authentic mission.

In addition, love also fosters a cycle of mutual respect regarding others. An example of an entrepreneur who fosters love in business is Jack Ma. He is the co-founder of Alibaba, the e-commerce giant which was mentioned previously in this book. This business leader insightfully observed: "If a person wants to be successful, he should have a high EQ. If he doesn't want to lose quickly, he should have a high IQ, but if he wants to be respected, he should have a high LQ, the Q of love" (Frost, 2019).

It is important to clarify that emotional quotient (EQ) is one's set of skills related to emotional intelligence (recognising one's emotions and others', expressing one's emotions wisely, being empathetic to others, etc.) Instead, intellectual quotient (IQ) is one's set of intellectual skills (problem solving, planning, comprehension, learning, etc.). There are various tests that measure these types of skills. From this entrepreneur's perspective, love quotient (LQ) includes the ability to connect to others in a loving way.

There is another point to highlight. On the one hand, love is the natural heightener of people's human qualities. In other words, when people adopt a loving attitude, their positive human side is gracefully enhanced. On the other hand, when people adopt an unloving attitude, even their greatest human qualities are degraded. According to Scheffer (1990), without love, some relevant human virtues become negative qualities. From this author's perspective:

- When people are righteous but lack love, they become intolerant.
- When faithful people have no love, they become fanatical.
- When powerful people are unloving, they become brutal.
- When committed people act without love, they become peevish.
- When orderly people experience no love, they become centred on petty things.

A similar perspective was observed by some ancient Greek philosophers. From their perspective, love naturally lights up all natural human attributes and humanises their rough edges. Besides, with love, all human interactions are smoother, deeper, and more meaningful. It is also possible to define love by its opposite, which means that love is never:

- Being indifferent or nonchalant with others.
- Neglecting other people's valuable needs.
- Dismissing the unique attributes of other people.
- Condemning people overtly or covertly.
- Dismissing people's contribution to a project.
- Threatening people or guilt-tripping them.
- Being dishonest or untruthful to others.
- Controlling or manipulating people.
- Willingly hurting others.

There is also an alternative view of this topic. Bevelin (2017) observed that people are more prone to act based on their self-interest. This author also stated that when people act in a loving or kind manner with others, their behaviour can be explained from a perspective of self-benefit. To that effect, this author stated that "social recognition, prestige, fear of social disapproval, relief from distress, avoidance of guilt, a better after-life or social expectation are some reasons behind 'altruistic' behaviour" (Bevelin, 2017). In a similar vein, De Mello (1990) observed that loving and supportive individuals give themselves the pleasure of helping others, which is based on selfishness.

5.2 The Absence of Love in Business Activities

One who loves is always right.

Peter Deunov

Many terms commonly used in the business world come from the military disciplines. Words such as "strategy," "tactics," and others are related to a defensive and non-loving attitude. As seen previously in this book, the widespread use of these terms implies that there are external threatening forces, which a company should guard itself from. This terminology prompts companies to adopt actions primarily based on fear, not love. In a similar vein, Engelberg and Aaronson (2019) observed that some companies use predatory language in business such as "hunting down customers," "capturing competitors," "stealing buyers from competitors," or "attacking the market," and similar ones. This type of unloving language is fear-based, and bolsters the adoption of a violent and adversarial attitude towards stakeholders.

Another great wealth of words commonly used in the business world comes directly from the industrial field, such as rationalisation, quality levels, and Key Performance Indicators (productivity, etc.), among others. The majority of these relevant terms are quantitative by nature, related to figures to be precisely monitored and measured. Most companies are keen on measurement tools, such as budgets, estimated costs, and plans. Nonetheless, love cannot be measured; it is qualitative by nature. Even though love cannot be quantified, its impact on relationships with stakeholders, productivity levels, customer service, amount of sales, and the bottom line is very tangible.

There is an interesting company named Panera Bread. This is a well-known chain of bakery-café restaurants with thousands of outlets which are based in America. This organisation makes daily donations of its unsold baked products to non-profit organisations to combat food insecurity and hunger. This company developed partnerships with a myriad of charitable organisations, like food pantries and shelters for youngsters, to provide them with baked goods for their needs. This company issues a responsibility report, which includes relevant information regarding this organisation's socially and environmentally oriented projects (development of healthy food products, donations, more efficient use of energy, reduction of carbon dioxide emissions, increasing use of reusable, recyclable and compostable packaging, etc.) (Panera Bread, 2023, 2021).

There is another interesting topic to pinpoint. Some oriental philosophical schools of thought imbue love with feminine traits, such as compassion, care, integration, and nourishment, among others. In the business environment, most organisations are prone to focus more on masculine characteristics, such as productivity, effectiveness, efficiency, and others. Here, the terms "feminine" and "masculine" do not refer to genders; these terms are related to complementary forces or principles which, for example, are shown in the concept of yin and yang.

The Body Shop is a company which sells natural cosmetic products. This organisation was mentioned previously in this book. This company is an outstanding example of an organisation with "feminine values," such as care, nourishment, and others. For instance, one of the company's main values is "growing partnerships & supporting communities." Several decades ago, this company started a fair-trade programme, which is aimed at supporting communities. This programme is the company's "way of sourcing ethical, high-quality ingredients and accessories from around the world, while trading fairly with suppliers." For example, this company buys handcrafted Shea butter from hundreds of women in villages in Ghana, providing these women with beneficial trading terms, and paying these individuals a premium price, which gives them access to a valuable income and supports their communities (The Body Shop, 2022b, 2022c).

There is another relevant point to highlight. Manby (2012) observed that most organisations tend to set "do goals," instead of "be goals." From this perspective, "do goals" are about what the company wants to achieve, and "be goals" are how objectives will be achieved. For instance, a company sets the following "do goal": "to obtain an X level of profit in a specific period of time." In this example, the respective "be goal" could be "by being caring with the community."

In this example, the "do goal" is as important as the "be goal." In this example, the company wants to attain an X level of profit (do goal), not by any means but by creating a positive impact on the community (be goal). Most organisations tend only to measure and reward the achievement of "do objectives," but they dismiss or do not even consider "be goals" for their business activities. A company should always set "be goals" which imply loving traits (compassion, kindness, generosity, gratefulness, benevolence, etc.) towards its stakeholders.

For instance, a company previously mentioned, Kammok, includes among its main values: adventure, community, but also love. This organisation stated that love is "the invisible thread binding each of us together" and "the giving of yourself for the betterment of others." In relation to this, the company truly adopts a loving attitude by donating 1% of its topline revenue to non-profit organisations (Kammok, 2022). This is a good example of a company with an important "be goal." This company adopts a loving attitude towards non-profit organisations.

5.3 Love Is the Opposite to Fear

> There is no difficulty that enough love will not conquer ... No door enough love will not open ... No gulf that enough love will not bridge ... No wall that enough love will not throw down ...
>
> **Emmet Fox**

Some spiritual schools of thought consider love as the opposite to fear, not to hatred, as many people tend to think. As seen previously, fear is a powerful negative emotional state expressed in different ways in the business environment. McBride-Walker (n.d.) observed that fear is the "lived experience of a defensive state constructed with the purpose of self-preservation," which includes a cognitive and emotional response towards a perceived threat. Fear can be considered a natural response human beings inherited from their ancestors, whose survival was threatened by predators, shortages of food, and other dangerous factors.

Every time people are fearful, they do not feel capable of effectively responding to a perceived threat. It is interesting to pinpoint that what is considered threatening tends to vary from person to person, depending on their past experiences, personal assumptions, and even genetic aspects, among other factors. Fredrickson (2013) observed that, when people are scared, they cannot behave lovingly because their survival defences override any possible loving attitude.

The bodies of fearful people release two powerful hormones called cortisol and adrenaline, which, in turn, prompts their focus to narrow down to the menacing factor. Goleman (1996, 1998) observed that fear has physiological aspects (blood rushes to the legs, the face becomes blanched, heart rate speeds up, etc.) which are opposite to the traits observed in a person who demonstrates love to another.

When fear is widespread in a company, people working for it tend to adopt a defensive attitude towards real or perceived threats (for instance, rival companies). These threatening factors are often perceived in a magnified or exaggerated manner. As a consequence, when a company's environment is teeming with fear, people are less inclined to adopt a loving attitude towards others. To put it simply, fear is utterly intimidating and immobilising for most people; it does not bring about any positive change within a company.

Fear is intrinsically protective and restrictive. According to Jeffers (1991), when people feel fear, they feel less capable of handling situations they face at present or in the future. Fearful people's typical behaviour includes, for instance, procrastination, avoiding problematic situations, reluctance to team-play with others, maintenance of a negative status quo, and drawing catastrophic conclusions about future scenarios, among others. When people are fearful, they often feel helpless or unsafe, and they are more prone to adopt a distrusting attitude towards others.

An example of a company which is *not* fear-centred, but love-based is John Paul Mitchell Systems. This company, which offers hair salon products and styling tools, has donated hefty amounts of money to a myriad of social causes, such as the protection of the environment, human rights, and children care, among others (Paul Mitchell, 2022a). An example of an organisation supported by John Paul Mitchell Systems is Baby2Baby, which sends items of clothing, diapers, formula, and cribs to children who need these products. Another example is Reforest Action, an environmentally oriented organisation which undertakes various forestry endeavours, like planting trees in various areas of the world (Baby2Baby, 2022; Reforest Action, 2022).

5.4 Business People's Default Response

Take away love and our Earth is a tomb.

Robert Browning

Most business people tend to experience fearful states which prompt them to perceive the business environment as dangerous. As explained before, fear is the opposite of love and prevents business people from adopting a loving attitude towards others. This defensive mode makes business people focus on potential threats and prevents them from adopting a more proactive and creative attitude. This fear-based perspective prompts organisations to act in specific ways to navigate the business environment. Some common fears most companies face regarding their endeavours are, for example:

■ **Fear of not achieving the company's objectives:** This is related to the so-called fear of failure. These objectives can include goals related to increased productivity, increment of sales and profits, cutting costs, development of new products and services, increase of market share, entry to new markets, improvement of quality levels, training of staff, betterment of customer relationships, widespread public recognition, and internal restructuring of the organisation, among others. For example, in an organisation with this type of fear, the company's objectives might only be related to its current products and markets, while avoiding the exploration of new ones. Organisations where fear of failure is prevalent only aim to set "realistic" objectives according to their own capabilities and resources. These companies avoid setting objectives that stretch them too much because they are fearful of not attaining them. As previously seen, Headspace is a company which offers science-based mindfulness and meditation programmes. This organisation does not seem to have any fear related to achieving its big objectives. In its business mission, this company ambitiously states that it aims "to improve the health and happiness *of the world*" (emphasis added). This company developed partnerships with hundreds of businesses as well as health plans, so that their employees and members can have access to these programmes, and health care can become widespread all over the world. The company's products are currently used by millions of people in a myriad of countries (Headspace, 2023). Research has concluded that the use of this application prompts users to experience more positive emotions, as well as a reduction of depressive symptoms (Howells et al., 2015).

■ **Fear of being out of business:** This is an extreme expression of the fear mentioned in the previous point. This is the fear of not surviving, for example, by not obtaining enough profits, shutting down, or filing for bankruptcy. Many entrepreneurs have continuous gnawing ruminations preventing them from taking "excessive" risks which could take them out of business. These business people tend to adopt an overly conservative attitude and take the well-trodden business path. These people's defensive attitude prompts them to focus mostly on how not to be wiped out of the market. An example of a company which does *not* seem to have any fear of being out of business is Mind Gym. This company offers psychology-based training on various areas (performance management, leadership, diversity, equity, inclusion, etc.). This company is growing exponentially in their activities and delivering these training services in a myriad of countries (The Mind Gym, 2023).

■ **Fear of innovating:** This fear is also related to the penultimate point. Some companies tend to avoid any change by all means; change implies developing new products or markets, introducing innovative administrative systems, trying out new suppliers, and contracting new employees, among others. This type of company is prone to adopt a cautious attitude towards activities with uncertain results. These conservative companies tend to avoid courses of action that do not guarantee success. These organisations prefer to play safe by focusing on well-known scenarios; they fear uncertain situations they cannot fully control. They avoid rocking the boat, even when new ideas might potentially be more beneficial than traditional ones. For example, a company keeps on focusing on the national market, instead of going international, because the internationalisation process, albeit potentially more profitable, is perceived as a riskier endeavour. When facing uncertain scenarios, these organisations become over-reliant on data to "predict" scenarios, such as updated reports, expert advice, and economic news. The following is an interesting topic to analyse. According to the Food and Agriculture Organization (FAO) of the United Nations, above one-third part of all food which is produced ends up as waste. In relation to this, an important example of a great innovation is upcycled food products, which are made from ingredients which normally would not have been utilised to be consumed by people (Sritharan, 2022). In that sense, there is a company which does *not* fear innovation known as The Ugly Company. This company offers upcycled food products, namely sustainable natural snacks made from ugly fruit. This class of fruit is visually imperfect (too big, wrong colour, etc.) and it is generally discarded, even though this fruit is totally adequate to be eaten. By utilising this type of fruit for the development of its healthy dried fruit snacks, this company prevents an immense amount of fruit from going to waste (The Ugly Company, 2022).

■ **Fear of inadequacy:** This fear is related to the perceived lack of the necessary resources to undertake business endeavours. This fear can be related to a lack of tangible resources (capital, technology, human resources, etc.) or intangible ones (specific capabilities, knowledge, time, experience, etc.). Some companies feel continually threatened by business challenges (financial shortages, technological changes, manufacturing hold-ups, etc.) because they do not know how to handle them effectively. An example of company which does *not* have any fear of inadequacy is Google. As known, over the years, this company fully harnesses its core capabilities (management of information, etc.) to develop countless valuable products, like Google Docs, Google Maps, and Google Scholar.

■ **Fear of being deceived:** This fear relates to potential swindling stratagems undertaken by internal or external company stakeholders. In other words, an organisation fears possible deceptive behaviour from others, such as disloyal employees, unreliable suppliers, and delusory retailers, among others. This can also include the fear of the company's innovative ideas being stolen by other organisations. These companies thoroughly analyse trustworthiness of people (employees, suppliers, etc.) related to them. For these organisations, trust tends to be gained gradually; these companies are untrusting by default. These companies take special care to have their own interests fully covered, for instance, through the widespread use of thorough contracts and forms, and utilisation of various passwords, among others. Their distrusting attitude also prompts them to set varying policies and procedures to regulate different company activities (cash management, working time, purchases and sales, etc.). Companies should be cautious with people related to them, but oftentimes, organisations become excessively zealous and protective, which prevents them from harnessing their valuable resources effectively. The following are examples of trusting companies. The first example is Humana, one of the biggest health insurance providers. This company offers some positions for remote workers and it is considered one of the top organisations regarding remote work (Humana Careers, 2022; Humana News, 2020). The use of regular remote work implies a high level of trust within a company. Another good example of a trusting company is FAVI, a company that produces car parts. In this company, one of its previous leaders decided to eliminate the time-clocking system all together, but also to unlock all storage place (rooms, cupboards, and cabinets), as a clear display of trust towards its employees (Minaar, 2017). In this organisation, employees can use the company's vehicles (without the need for approval) to go to a customer or supplier. The stock room is kept unlocked and staff members can take the tools and supplies they need for work (Laloux, 2014).

- **Fear of being outpaced by competitors:** This common fear shows up as a reactive response to other organisations perceived as rivals. A fearful organisation does not want its products and services to be outsmarted by other companies' offerings. This type of company implements strategies that are mostly focused on what other companies do, reacting to their moves instead of adopting a proactive attitude. The following is an interesting story regarding Jaipur Rugs, a company which offers world-class carpets previously discussed in this book (Sisodia and Gelb, 2019). Its business leader stated that a rival company contacted one of Jaipur Rugs' partners which sells the company's rugs. This competitor offered to develop a copy of the Jaipur Rugs' carpets and sell it to this retailer at a reduced price, which was plainly rejected by the retailer. Jaipur Rugs' leader observed that this unethical competitor acted in this way out of fear. Some companies like John Paul Mitchell Systems, The Body Shop, Whole Foods, and Patagonia are examples of companies which are *not* fearful of competitors. These companies are continually focused on developing higher quality products which add more value to customers but also to other stakeholders, regardless of what competing organisations do.
- **Fear of using their resources ineffectively:** Most companies have the assumption that all their resources are limited. These organisations spend significant time coordinating these scarce resources in the most effective manner, to avoid their wastage. These companies utilise an arsenal of tools, like budgets, strategies, planning spreadsheets, schedules, and control of resources. Nevertheless, these organisations do not take into account that some resources, for instance, staff's creative skills, cannot be depleted; these resources can always generate more resources. An example of an organisation which does *not* have any fear of using their resources ineffectively is The Ugly Company. As seen previously, this organisation uses visually unappealing fruit – which is often wasted by other companies – to produce its natural snacks. In other words, this organisation utilises these resources (imperfect fruit) effectively and avoids waste.
- **Fear of not satisfying customers:** All companies know that their customers are their most significant source of income; customers are the organisations' paramount "assets." Some

companies adopt an attitude of customer "retention," which is based on fear of losing them. These organisations have an all-pervading fear of losing their customers because of not satisfying their customers properly. Oftentimes, these organisations are afraid of receiving complaints or objections from customers. These companies also dread negative word of mouth (for example, negative online reviews). An example of a company which is *not* fearful of satisfying its customers is Zappos, the renowned online retailer. At its call centres, employees are trained for an extensive period of time so that these staff members can provide customers with a meaningful and personalised service. For instance, sometimes, customer service officers engage with customers in lengthy phone conversations (which can take hours) to sort out their problems (Mechlinski, 2021). This standard of excellence in customer service is aligned with one of the company's main values "Deliver WOW through services." Through this value, Zappos' employees are encouraged to deliver outstanding services, which exceed others' expectations (Zappos Insights, 2023).

- **Fear of being rejected by other stakeholders:** Some organisations fear that potential customers will reject their products or services. Their fear of not meeting prospects' expectations is related to their perceived lack of originality and distinctiveness of products and services offered. Companies that launch new products have an underlying fear that innovative items will not be accepted by the market, especially when they have not been duly tested beforehand. These organisations also fear being rejected by other stakeholders, for example, other organisations for potential business partnerships, financial institutions for possible loans, media companies for publicity, and the wider community for acceptance and support, among others. As seen previously, companies like The Body Shop and Tom's of Maine offer high-quality products adding high value to customers; consequently, these companies are *not* fearful of their products being rejected by customers.

- **Fear of developing relationships with stakeholders:** Many companies tend to interact with their stakeholders in a goal-oriented manner, which oftentimes fails to consider the human side of the latter. Relationships with stakeholders are often so formal that they are devoid of real substance; countless conventions and rules override any potential meaningful connection with these stakeholders. These meaningless relationships are called "empty forms" by Fritz (2007). Consequently, some companies recognise the need for more meaningful human contact in order to deepen relationships with their main stakeholders. An example of a company which does *not* have any fear of developing partnerships is Ella's Kitchen. This company offers healthy food for children. This outstanding company partnered up with Flavour School, a not-for-profit organisation that assists nurseries and schools with food education and prompts children at nurseries and schools to have more positive relationships with food products (Ella's Kitchen, 2022).

- **Fear of conflicts with stakeholders:** Some companies fear any conflicts with their stakeholders. Conflicts are a natural part of business dynamics. Other organisations, when interacting with their stakeholders (government, employees, customers, suppliers, etc.), try to avoid conflicts with them when possible. Sometimes companies try to solve these conflictive issues in the best way possible. As a consequence, these companies are prone to use a wealth of tools, such as conflict prevention, negotiation, and conciliation. A company which does have a wise approach regarding conflicts with its stakeholders is The Body Shop. As seen previously, this organisation offers fair-trade conditions to its suppliers, which eliminates any potential conflict with them.

- **Fear of success:** Williamson (1996) observed that people's greatest fear is not to be inadequate, but instead they fear that they are powerful in an unbounded manner. As they become bigger, some companies become more concerned about the increasing complexity and investment required to go ahead with their business activities. As a company grows, more suppliers, customers, and employees are needed. Some big companies are also prone to offer a wider range of products. Successful companies tend to have more resources at stake. If business goes well, rewards are significant; if not, losses become overwhelming. Bigger companies also tend to be perceived as more difficult to manage. For this reason, most companies are inclined to adopt a cautious and conservative attitude, as their activities grow over time. These organisations often limit their growth rate by taking only reasonable risks. An excellent example of a company with *no* fear of success is John Paul Mitchell Systems, which was mentioned previously. This company was started up by two friends with a meagre initial investment of 700 dollars. Nowadays, this very successful company performs its business activities all over the world. This company has several millions of dollars in revenues from its products (Paul Mitchell, 2022c).

There is another important point to highlight. Even though all business people aim to be successful in their endeavours, in the depth of their hearts, some tend to experience a straining feeling of not deserving the best outcomes. This is observed in some unintentional self-sabotaging actions, such as promoting their products and services inadequately, misinforming customers, and firing talented people. These incongruent actions are prone to become more common when a company is doing well in the market.

5.5 Love Can Improve Business Activities

Genuine love is volitional rather than emotional. The person who truly loves does so because of a decision to love. This person has made a commitment to be loving whether or not the loving feeling is present.

M. Scott Peck

Love is not primarily a relationship with a specific person; it is an attitude, an orientation of character which determines the relatedness of a person to the world as a whole, not toward an "object" of love.

Erich Fromm

I have delivered countless talks and seminars worldwide and oftentimes my audience is composed of business people; some of them lead the destiny of hundreds of employees. When I engage with entrepreneurs, I regularly say to them, "It is necessary to introduce more love into your business activities." Some of them are confused and astonished by this statement.

Many entrepreneurs have told me that love has nothing to do with their business activities. These business individuals clearly believe that the most relevant objective for their companies is to offer good products and services and increase their revenues and profits over time. Love does not appear among their priority business objectives.

However, the company John Paul Mitchell Systems mentioned previously is a good example of an organisation which does *not* care only for profits. This thriving company also has other objectives, for example, supporting the environment. In that sense, this company increasingly uses more packaging made of materials that are recycled or stem from sustainable sources, which has a positive impact on the environment. This company also develops hair products by avoiding animal cruelty. In that sense, they have been a leading organisation in using a cruelty-free approach (Paul Mitchell, 2022b). As can be seen, this company has very noble objectives beyond its economic goals: caring for animals and protecting the environment as a whole.

There is another interesting point to highlight. Sanders (mentioned in Holden, 2008) observed, "The most powerful source in business isn't greed, fear or even the raw energy of unbridled competition. The most powerful force in business is love." Kevin Roberts, former CEO of one of the most famous advertising agency in the world, Saatchi & Saatchi, stated that this organisation is in the pursuit of love and what that means for its business activities. This global company agrees that people cannot live without love (Roberts, 2004).

As seen previously, love is wishing others the best, and supporting and recognising them as human beings. Most business people tend to link love with non-business environments, for example, close relationships with partners, relatives, friends, and acquaintances. Nonetheless, this sentimental view of love is very limited.

Love is related to qualities such as connection, closeness, affinity, sympathy, care, support, gratitude, generosity, compassion, and others which can be applied to any type of relationships, even business ones. Relationships are a key component of any business; without them, no company can thrive, regardless of the unique traits of its products and services and the deftness of its marketing strategy.

A loving attitude is the foundation of fruitful relationships, both business and non-business ones. According to Lowell and Joyce (2007), relationships are one of the most important intangibles in any company because they add value to the company's products and services through the development of valuable networks.

Rogers (1961) concluded that some people are fearful of having a warm, loving, and caring attitude towards others, and tend to act in an impersonal, distant, or "professional" manner. Oftentimes, this type of attitude is detrimental to the development of thriving relationships with others. In relation to this, Fromm (1956) observed that people who adopt a loving attitude towards others want to bridge the state of separateness between them, while also keeping their own individuality.

Manby (2012) stated that "treating someone with love regardless of how you feel is a very powerful principle," and also observed that "this type of love is the basis for all healthy relationships, bringing out the best in ourselves and others." The Greeks called this type of love "agape," and it can be defined as an affectionate and caring treatment towards others. According to Abrams (2017), this love is "of a higher order" because it requires an act of will and a continuous commitment.

A valuable example of a company which treats others in an affectionate manner is Warby Parker. This organisation sells quality eyeglasses. This company has the "Buy a Pair, Give a Pair" programme. Through this programme, and in partnership with various organisations, this company gives a pair of eyeglasses to people with impaired vision for every pair of eyeglasses bought by customers. Since its onset, this company has given away millions of pairs of eyeglasses (Warby Parker, 2022).

There is another important point to highlight. When a person adopts a loving attitude towards others, there is no reservation towards them. This attitude is non-judgemental and stems from one's deliberate choice. A loving person is naturally kind with others and does not expect reciprocal treatment from them. A person with this attitude treats others in a loving manner, just because they are unique and valuable human beings.

According to Von Hildebrand (2009), a loving person tends to be warm-hearted and generous with others and also assumes the best of people, even when they have not shown any benevolent qualities. To put it simply, people with a loving attitude towards others tend to have positive assumptions regarding them. Schein (2009) observed that assumptions about others are a relevant factor of any organisation's corporate culture. Moreover, corporate culture includes shared and implicit assumptions which set specific ways of thinking, feeling, and perceiving in relation to the company's adaptation to the external environment and their integration within the organisation.

Therefore, when people working for a company have positive assumptions about others inside the organisation (personnel) and outside (suppliers, customers, etc.), this company's culture and its overall performance are affected in a beneficial way. Besides, people with a loving attitude towards others naturally generate more rapport with them and their relationships with them are strengthened.

Drucker (1999) observed that, "Manners are the lubricating oil of an organization." This scholar concluded that saying "thank you" and "please" to others, calling them by their name, and asking about their families help people relate to one another in a better way. These are just a few examples related to a loving attitude towards others. Loving people are always easier to deal with because they tend to shorten the distance between themselves and others and seek mutually beneficial agreements with them. When there is a widespread loving attitude towards others in an organisation, this company is prone to act as follows:

- This organisation does not attempt to deceive customers or manipulate them. Instead, this company continually cares for its customers and guides them to make their best buying decisions. One of the values of the renowned hotel chain Marriott International is "We put people first" (Marriott, 2023a). There is an interesting example on how this relevant value is implemented in practice by this company. Carlos Duque works as a bartender at one of the hotels related to this chain. This kind staff member recalls the names, faces, as well as the preferences of his guests, which helps him develop closer and more trusting bonds with these customers. Several guests even send this bartender a text message to check if he is available to prepare his signature drink for them (Marriott, 2023b). As already seen in this book, there are other organisations which truly care for customers. For instance, The Body Shop (natural cosmetic products), Honest Tea (organic drink products), Leon (healthy meals), and The Ugly Company (natural dry fruit snacks) are valuable examples of companies that offer high-value products to their customers.

- A company with a loving attitude does not consider other organisations as enemies to defeat. Instead, these companies are considered valuable sources of information, and oftentimes potential partners. Ella's Kitchen has developed a partnership with Terracycle, which is an organisation specialising in recycling, in order to develop a recycling project for baby food packaging. As a consequence of this partnership, Ella's Kitchen prevented millions of food pouches from going to landfill. This company also raised funds for socially oriented projects (Ella's Kitchen, 2022). The company Warby Parker, recently mentioned, created a programme called Pupils Project, in partnership with various local government agencies and other organisations in order to provide children at school with free eye testing and eyeglasses (Warby Parker, 2022).

- An organisation with a loving attitude does not de-skill its employees with monotonous and repetitive work. Instead, the company allocates diversified tasks to its employees and encourages them to learn new valuable skills continuously. The organisation tends to assign its employees tasks aligned with their talents and capabilities. Dell, the computer company, committed to upskilling its employees. For instance, this company regularly provides its in-house teams in charge of manufacturing activities with relevant training. These employees receive training in significant topics, such as developing a growth mindset, critical thinking, communication, innovation, decision-making, and digital skills, among others (Dell, 2022). A company like Chipotle, the Mexican grill restaurant chain, provides its staff members with training on diversity and inclusion. This company also provides its staff members with keynote talks as well as thousands of online courses on a myriad of topics (business, wellness, technology, etc.). This company also provides mentoring programmes for minority staff (Bloomberg, 2021; D'Sa-Wilson, 2022).

- A company with a loving attitude does not have high profits as its sole objective, but also sets relevant social and environmental goals, such as supporting communities, caring for the environment, and contributing to a better world, among others. These companies are less calculating and more generous than others. Kay (2011) observed these purpose-driven organisations tend to be more successful than other organisations. A company previously mentioned, Ella's Kitchen, does not have profits as its only objective. This renowned company has developed a partnership with the conservation organisation the World Land Trust, so that this non-profit organisation can assist Ella's Kitchen with the offsetting of carbon emission stemming from its manufacturing process. In addition, through this partnership, Ella's Kitchen purposefully assists with the protection of Ecuador's rainforest, which has been largely destroyed (Ella's Kitchen, 2022). The main objective of this alliance is not economic, but to bring about a positive impact on the environment. Another example of a company whose objectives go beyond economic ones is Dell, the computer giant. This company is continually committed to progressively reducing the carbon emissions and increasing the use of renewable or recyclable material, to bring about a positive impact on the environment (Dell, 2022).

- An organisation with a loving attitude avoids exploiting employees or just paying them enough to get by. Instead, this organisation is proud of paying its employees fairly, which, in turn, increases their employees' satisfaction and productivity. This type of company makes sure that all their personnel's significant needs are covered, so they can live with dignity. Dell is also a good example of a company which treats its employees (and other stakeholders) with dignity and respect. This company fosters a supportive, collaborative, and inclusive work environment. In that sense, the organisation has a myriad of policies in place to deal with potential risks in the workplace (discrimination, child labour and forced labour, health and safety, etc.). This company is also considered one of the best places to work worldwide (Dell, 2022).

- An organisation with a loving attitude does not treat employees as a means to an end to achieve company objectives. In other words, employees are never considered replaceable cogs in the company's machinery, but instead as valuable resources to be appreciated for their individual distinctiveness. As seen recently, a company like Dell fosters an inclusive workplace, where the individual traits of each employee are not only respected, but also appreciated. Another good example of a company with a loving attitude towards its employees is Nvidia. This well-known company develops AI and computer graphics. In this company's workplace, some paramount values like disability inclusion, gender equality, and pay parity are fostered. In addition, the company has developed policies which actively support its LGBTQ+ staff members (Nvidia, 2022a). This organisation is also considered one of the best places to work (Great Place to Work, 2022b).

- A company with a loving attitude looks for more natural, hearty, and personal ways to communicate with its main stakeholders. Therefore, this organisation avoids the exclusive use of technology (emailing, phone, etc.) to get in contact with its stakeholders. Formal ways of communication (meetings, protocols, appointments, etc.) are used alongside informal channels (for instance, casual chats, social events) in order to develop deeper bonds with stakeholders. For example, Monzo, a company which provides online money-management services, organises frequent social events for its staff members like samba sessions, go-karting, and even board-game nights (Bishop, 2019).

A company with a loving attitude tends to use quality data (research studies, focus groups, etc.) to make decisions, but is also open to acting on intuitive insights, instinct, or inspiration. This company sets in force rules and procedures to act in specific ways, but is also open to acting in an adaptive and innovative manner, especially in changing circumstances.

A company's people should not wait for others to start adopting a loving attitude. They should start themselves with this change and observe the ripple effects pervading the rest of the organisation and its external stakeholders. A company's people should frequently ask themselves a very relevant question: "Is love present in the business environment?"

Questions for Self-Reflection

- How does love relate to our organisation's activities?
- How can we be more loving towards our stakeholders?
- Which fears are hindering our organisation's performance?
- How can love improve our business activities?

Chapter 6

Stakeholders and Love

The essence of love is not what we think or do or provide for others, but how much we give of ourselves.

Rick Warren

6.1 How to Treat Different Stakeholders with Love

Darkness cannot drive out darkness; only light can do that. Hate cannot drive out hate; only love can do that.

Martin Luther King, Jr.

In the business environment, love is commonly seen as a feeling totally alien to the cultures of most organisations. Some renowned authors have even observed that love could undermine important business variables or Key Performance Indicators (productivity, quality levels, competitiveness, efficiency, etc.). Most companies focus on improving these indicators, instead of centring on love. It is important to pinpoint that these indicators are always the result of the interactions of an organisation and its internal and external stakeholders. Therefore, when a company adopts a loving attitude towards its stakeholders, these indicators tend to improve naturally.

An organisation with a loving attitude develops continuous goodwill and mutually beneficial relationships with all its relevant stakeholders; this company is more likely to succeed in the business arena. Stakeholders are individuals and organisations with an interest in the company; they can be external (suppliers, intermediaries, competitors, communities, media, government, etc.) or internal (management and the rest of the employees). All stakeholders have their distinctive objectives and agendas.

A company which develops beneficial relationships with its stakeholders is more likely to be supported by them when needed. When a company acts in a considerate manner with stakeholders, they tend to respond in a reciprocal fashion. In order to strengthen its bonds with its stakeholders, an organisation should identify their distinct needs and expectations in order to cater for them in the most effective way.

DOI: 10.4324/9781003372684-8

An example of a company that develops strong relationships with its stakeholders is UPS, the global courier company. This company is linked to UPS Foundation which undertakes projects related to health and humanitarian support, engagement with local communities, and environmental protection. For example, this organisation has participated in the delivery of humanitarian supplies (vaccines) to various communities in need, especially in less developed countries. This organisation also granted funds to communities stricken by natural disasters (e.g., earthquake victims in Haiti). They also provided educational institutions in Colombia with grants for instructional material, furniture, and books to develop new libraries in that country (UPS, 2022a).

There is another important point to discuss. A company can use specific tools (meetings, open telephone lines, emails, surveys, focus groups, etc.) to discover its stakeholders' specific interests. A company should always take into account stakeholders' unique needs when it develops its strategies and makes relevant business decisions. When a company continually cares for its stakeholders, its public image tends to improve significantly.

There are several aspects to consider in relation to a company's image. Butterick (2011) observed that reputation is the representation of various assessments of a company by its stakeholders. According to this specialist, the high reputation of a company stems from various factors, such as delivery of high-quality products, treating customers in a kind and supportive manner, keeping its promises (e.g., delivering the items on time), transparent communication, good image of leadership team, and sound financial results, among others. In addition, Fombrun (1996) observed that reputable companies purposefully look for the welfare of each of its stakeholders.

There are various ways to identify reputable companies, such as the ranking known as Fortune Magazine's World Most Admired Companies, where business people (directors, corporate executives, and analysts) vote for these companies. Companies like Amazon (the retail giant), Microsoft (the software and computer company), and Walt Disney (the global entertainment company) are ranked in the top-ten list of Fortune Magazine's World Most Admired Companies (Fortune, 2023).

There is another important point to highlight. Sometimes, the company discovers that its employees must be trained in order to meet its stakeholders' expectations properly. Oftentimes, the participation of employees from different departments (marketing, finance, etc.) is necessary to meet stakeholders' expectations.

With some stakeholders, a company has formal bonds (for example, suppliers); with other stakeholders, the organisation could have more informal ties (for instance, the community). In some cases, the company can engage stakeholders, by consulting them or deciding with them, before taking specific actions, especially in situations with a potential significant impact on these stakeholders. In other cases, the company makes decisions and then informs or educates stakeholders about the actions taken. In all cases, actions performed by the company should take into consideration the plurality of interests of its stakeholders.

When a company adopts a loving attitude, all its activities (e.g., buying, selling, developing, and launching new products) are based on the development of mutually beneficial relationships with internal and external stakeholders. Strong relationships with stakeholders are always a relevant source of power, which gives an organisation an edge in the marketplace.

A company with a loving attitude performs business activities which do not benefit some stakeholders at the expense of others. This type of organisation, for instance, offers quality products to customers, pays good salaries to employees, develops fair agreements with suppliers, and also adopts a caring attitude for the environment. In this case, the company cares for the well-being of all its stakeholders (customers, employees, suppliers, and community); no stakeholder is considered more valuable than the others.

According to Freeman and McVea (2001), when a company analyses the impact of its actions on various stakeholders, this organisation should consider real "names and faces" regarding these stakeholders and the specific situations they are involved in, rather than simply assessing generic stakeholders' roles. Each of these stakeholders (suppliers, community members, etc.) are living human beings the company needs to treat in a kind and supportive manner; and their needs should be addressed and satisfied (Freeman, 2009a).

For example, if the company wants to set up a potentially polluting new factory near a small town, this organisation should analyse how actual members of that community (specific people living there) will respond to this new business endeavour. This company should also be aware of these people's main preferences, and their concerns, doubts, and fears in relation to this project, among other aspects. In this example, the same type of analysis should be undertaken regarding the other stakeholders (suppliers, employees, customers, etc.).

There is another interesting topic to discuss. Kofman (2013) observed that there are three dimensions to be considered by any organisation regarding its endeavours: the "I" dimension, whose focus is on a personal or individual level; the "We" dimension, which is focused on relationships between a person (or organisation) and others; and the "It" dimension, which takes into account the organisation as a whole. Therefore, when a company nurtures its relationships with its stakeholders, it is adopting the "We" dimension. This author also stated that companies which develop the "We" dimension tend to adopt an attitude of solidarity and connectedness with their most relevant stakeholders.

Salesforce, which offers various types of software to organisations, is a good example of a company which adopts the "We" dimension. In partnership with various educational institutions, this company has provided grants of millions of dollars to support students in school, to unleash their full potential. In addition, this company has also given grants to various organisations to assist youngsters in their career development (skills training courses, mentoring, etc.). Lastly, this company has also made donations to support underrepresented entrepreneurs and underserved communities (Salesforce, 2022a).

6.2 Towards a Wider Definition of Love

As seen previously, outside the business environment, people naturally feel love towards others (friends, relatives, partners, etc.). Many people also effortlessly experience love towards animals, plants, things, places, objects, ideas, and experiences. This type of love does not *exist a priori*; people are prompted to feel love *in response* to a specific target (person, thing, place, etc.).

In this book, the definition of love is wider; it includes the general attitude of connection and genuine care for others. In a company, it implies that people adopt a deliberate and *a priori* loving attitude towards *all* individuals in the business environment. This standpoint is based on the assumption that all people deserve to be loved; they are intrinsically loveable. A person who adopts this loving attitude towards everyone relates to them in a more meaningful and deeper manner.

This proactive and non-judgemental type of love is called "unconditional love," or "love for no reason." People with this loving attitude towards others do not expect anything in return from them. This is love towards anyone, without any motive, regardless of who they are and what they do. Fromm (1956) observed that, "To love one's flesh and blood is no achievement … only in the love of those who do not serve a purpose, love begins to unfold." Metaphorically speaking, this type of love is like a rose which spreads its fragrance to be enjoyed by everyone around it, regardless of their condition or attitude.

A person with this loving attitude focuses mostly on the good qualities of others. This love is kind, forgiving, inclusive, grateful, generous, compassionate, caring, and supportive. This love is also trusting, non-judgemental, and undemanding. People with a loving attitude towards others can connect to the human side of each person inside and outside an organisation. When people working for a company adopt this loving attitude towards all stakeholders, the latter are more prone to feel acknowledged, recognised, and appreciated. Consequently, a loving attitude creates an atmosphere of deeper communion among people, which, in turn, improves business activities in a more effortless fashion.

The following is an example of company with a loving attitude towards its stakeholders. Jaipur Rugs is a successful organisation, which offers fine rugs. This company was already mentioned in this book. This company, through the Jaipur Rugs Foundation, fosters strong bonds with various Indian rural communities, so that thousands of their members can weave rugs and obtain a sustainable and decent income. These community members also receive relevant skills training (Jaipur Rugs, 2022; Jaipur Rugs Foundation, 2022).

Besides, this socially oriented company makes sure that no child labour is involved in the production of rugs it offers. In addition, the company ensures that the rugs offered do not contain any component harmful to health. They also reduce their environmental impact by using low-impact dyes and recycled yarn in their rugs. As it can be seen, this company and its foundation bring about a positive impact on various stakeholders (Jaipur Rugs, 2022).

There is another relevant topic to pinpoint. A very important aspect of a loving attitude is affection. When people are truly affectionate with others, they relate to them in a respectful and caring manner. A loving person avoids making any negative comments to others (slandering, gossiping, criticising, guilt-tripping, etc.), but makes continuous and supportive comments to them, especially when they go through challenging times. A loving person makes others feel at peace with themselves and in their own skins, which also makes them more co-operative and easier to deal with. On the contrary, when people are not treated lovingly, they are very prone to behave in an anxious, restless, scared, and even aggressive manner.

In relation to this, Baumeister et al. (2001) observed that a person's positive (loving) behaviour towards others (smiling, listening to them, etc.) will not affect the relationships with them as much as when this individual decreases negative (unloving) behaviour towards others (e.g., stopping frowning at them or avoiding insulting them). Gottman (1994) also concluded that a relationship can only succeed when the participants' positive interactions outnumber the negative ones by at least 5 to 1.

When a company adopts a loving attitude towards others, its conflicts with them are handled in a more peaceful and conciliatory fashion. A loving attitude helps people consider the interests of everyone involved in a conflicting situation. Loving people are more open to considering diverse perspectives on a topic, as these views enrich its discussion and understanding.

Walt Disney Company, the global entertainment giant, is a company which supports diverse perspectives. This company stated that "the more our consumers worldwide are reflected in our workforce, the better we're able to serve them authentically." This company fosters a diverse and inclusive environment, which encloses various groups such as Hispanic, Asian, Black, and Native American, among others. This company also fosters LGBTQ+ inclusion and supports staff members with disabilities in the workplace. The company's Chief Diversity Officer insightfully observed that "we amplify underrepresented voices … and champion a multitude of perspectives" (Walt Disney Company, 2022a).

A loving attitude is the great pacifier and harmoniser of a company's relationships with its stakeholders. Moreover, when a company's people adopt a continuous loving attitude, they will try to prevent any potential disagreements with other stakeholders. According to their research study, Barsade and O'Neill (2014) have observed that the adoption of a loving attitude in the workplace brings about very tangible positive results such as increased customer satisfaction, higher employee satisfaction, lower absenteeism and turnover, and decreased stress levels, among others. All these indicators tend to impact positively on the bottom line.

Research has concluded that people are prone to underestimate the positive impact of their loving acts on others. In simple words, individuals tend to think that their loving actions towards others are less valuable than the way these very actions are actually perceived by these recipients. Consequently, this underestimation can prevent people from regularly acting in a kind way with others (Kumar and Epley, 2022).

There is an important topic to discuss. Another relevant characteristic of this loving attitude is authenticity. In a company, when people adopt a loving attitude, they become more credible and trustworthy in the eyes of others. A true loving attitude always comes from the heart, and it makes interactions with others smoother and more truthful.

In an organisation, people with a loving attitude communicate with others more deeply, going beyond rigid social masks, business personas, or work roles. A person with a loving attitude encourages others to show themselves as they truly are, with their strengths and talents and their insecurities and vulnerabilities. In a loving environment, people can communicate their needs and viewpoints more openly without the fear of being criticised. Loving people understand that relationships can only prosper when all parts have their needs fulfilled.

The development of loving relationships is never a one-off attempt, but a continuous process. In other words, all of a company's relationships should be continually nurtured and strengthened; they are like plants that must be regularly watered to grow stronger. In a company, people with a loving attitude continually ask themselves, "Does our attitude towards others contribute to a more loving relationship with them?" and "Are we infusing more love into people related to us?", among others.

As previously mentioned, the Walt Disney Company continually fosters strong loving relationships with various stakeholders. This company stated that its main aim is to bring joy and comfort to its communities, and also foster hope, with a special focus on children. Over the years, this company has provided millions of employee volunteering hours and millions of dollars, to support several charitable causes. This company participates in projects that support youngsters. For example, the company offers scholarships and training programmes regarding storytelling and creative skills for youngsters (Walt Disney Company, 2022b). In addition, the company also provides low-resources elementary schools with free performance rights regarding some Disney musicals, free materials, and artistic guidance to teachers in order to foster theatre training in those schools (Disney Musicals in Schools, 2022).

There is another point to highlight. A company's people with a loving attitude are more emotionally intelligent. According to Goleman (1996, 1998), emotional intelligence not only includes the awareness and regulation of one's own emotions, but also management of relationships and social awareness or empathy. According to Gardner (2006), the capability to relate to others in a loving manner can be included as a relevant skill related to interpersonal intelligence, which implies the capabilities to relate to others effectively. This author observed that this type of intelligence "builds on a core capacity to notice distinctions among others – in particular, contrasts in their moods, temperament and motivations" which allows people to "read the intentions and desires of others, even when they have been hidden."

Lastly, in the business world, there is a well-known classification of skills: hard skills and soft skills. From this perspective, on the one hand, hard skills are the specific knowledge (tools, techniques, concepts, frameworks, skills) necessary to be effective in a certain discipline (marketing, logistics, management, etc.). On the other hand, soft skills are the set of personal qualities and capabilities necessary to relate to other people in a better manner.

These soft skills include, among others, flexibility, integrity, commitment, communication, leadership, teamwork, and work ethic. From this standpoint, the capability of adopting a loving attitude towards others can be included in the group of soft skills. Both types of skills (soft and hard skills) are necessary to be successful in the work and business environments.

As seen in this book, companies like Dell, the global computer company, offers its manufacturing team training to develop various soft skills such as creativity, critical thinking, and development of a growth mindset, among others (Dell, 2022). At Google, the most relevant traits of success are soft skills (good communication and listening, empathy towards others, critical thinking, etc.). At this organisation, the most outstanding teams display valuable soft skills, such as emotional intelligence, curiosity regarding others' insights, and equality, among others (Strauss, 2017).

6.3 Main Reasons to Be More Loving with Stakeholders

To love one person with a private love is poor and miserable; to love all is glorious.

Thomas Traherne

People might find it challenging to adopt a loving attitude towards others, especially when others behave in a deceptive or manipulative manner. The default response towards these behaviours is prone to be a defensive one, instead of a loving one. Some psychological schools of thought opine that adopting a loving attitude towards others can always be learned. It can be mastered like any other life skill, with continuous practice and commitment in order to become a positive habit.

In relation to this, Assagioli (1974) observed that people can master a loving attitude towards others in the same way as in any artistic expression: love needs patience, persistence, and discipline. According to this author, when people adopt a loving attitude, they are intervening actively and committing themselves to treating others lovingly.

Bodian (2006) observed that people might find it more difficult adopting a loving attitude towards others, especially when the former regularly behave in a reactive manner towards the latter. Some examples of this reactive behaviour are being resentful, jealous, suspicious, fearful, or angry with other people. All these reactive responses tend to preclude all possible love being given to others.

According to Salzberg (2014), some individuals have difficulties to adopt a loving attitude towards others because they tend to be continually self-centred and preoccupied, which prompts them to interact with others only using a "veneer of civility." Instead, when people behave in a generous, understanding, co-operative, and thankful way with others, the former tends to find it easier to adopt a loving attitude towards the latter (Salzberg, 1995).

Some spiritual perspectives also state that all people, beyond their outer appearances, are living expressions of love. All people are full of love to give to themselves and others; moreover, people have the need to express their love to others. The expression of love is applicable to any context, including the business environment. In a company, there are several reasons for adopting a loving attitude towards its stakeholders:

- ■ **Reciprocal response:** In social psychology, the principle of reciprocity affects all social interactions. According to this principle, if a person adopts a loving attitude to others, the latter tend to feel compelled to respond to the former in a loving manner. The opposite also applies; if a person relates to others in a harsh and uncaring manner, they are prone to adopt an unloving attitude towards this individual. For example, Trader Joe's, a renowned grocery chain, is a company which treats customers in a caring manner. As a consequence, this company's customers respond to this company in a reciprocal manner. To that effect, millions of customers support this company and its products on various social media platforms (Instagram, etc.) (Esbenshade, 2019; Smith, 2020).

■ **Positive colouring:** When people experience positive emotions towards others, such as the ones stemming from a loving attitude, the thoughts and actions of the former tend to be affected positively. People with a loving attitude tend to have a wider, more lively, and vibrant perception of the circumstances affecting them. These individuals are more inclined to connect to others because any defensive behaviour of the former tends to be cast aside. In this book, several examples of companies with a loving attitude with their stakeholders were analysed. It is worth mentioning again the case of The Body Shop which develops strong bonds with its suppliers, through agreements which offer them a fair price for their inputs.

■ **Like attracts like:** Another well-known principle states that "what you focus on, becomes augmented." In practical terms, when a person adopts a loving attitude towards others, this individual tends to attract loving circumstances, people, and situations. The opposite happens when a person has an unloving attitude towards other people. Dr Hawkins (2012) observed that feelings are in fact energy which send out a vibration – "we are sending and receiving stations" – therefore, "the more we love, the more we find ourselves surrounded by love." As mentioned previously, Honest Tea is a company which sells tea drink products, which are healthy and organic. This company naturally attracts conscious customers who want to consume products which are good for their health and the environment.

■ **Heightening of consciousness:** The aforementioned scientist stated that love represents one of the highest states of consciousness, above fear, greed, anger, or any other lower states. This scholar also observed that when people express their love to others, this high state can effortlessly transform lower consciousness states (e.g., fear) in a myriad of people around them.

■ **Interconnectedness:** Some spiritual standpoints have observed that all people are interconnected; seeming separation from one another is an egoic illusion. From a systemic perspective, people are naturally interdependent, like components or parts of the same system. A system is made up of components which relate to one another. From this perspective, every time people adopt a loving attitude towards others, they end up experiencing this very love themselves. The systemic perspective of relationships will be explored more thoroughly later on in this chapter. Some companies that support social and environmental causes (Ella's Kitchen, Patagonia, John Paul Mitchell Systems, and Whole Foods) were previously mentioned in this book. These organisations are very aware of the concept of interdependence in business. These companies clearly understand the impact that their positive business activities have on various stakeholders.

■ **Acknowledgement of others:** A loving attitude towards others is a fundamental way of recognising them as valuable human beings, with special and unique qualities. Likewise, Maturana and Bunnel (1998) observed that "love is the domain of those relational behaviours through which another (a person, being, or thing) arises as a legitimate other in coexistence with oneself." Instead, when a person is unloving with others, this individual is negating them as valid individuals. As seen previously, there are some companies which foster diversity and inclusion in the workplace, like Nvidia and Walt Disney Company, among others. These companies recognise their employees as valuable human beings, with distinctive traits which need to be acknowledged, respected, and welcomed.

- **Enhanced mental capabilities:** Research backs the fact that love constitutes a generative and expansive energy, which helps people harness their innermost mental capabilities (analysis, synthesis, combining, comparing, and contrasting). The aforementioned scholars also concluded that the majority of problems experienced by companies can be sorted out through love because when people experience this enabling state, their intelligence and creativity are naturally expanded. As seen previously, a company like Dell lovingly offers relevant training (growth mindset, creative skills, etc.) to its employees to enhance their core capabilities.

- **Increased trust and co-operation:** Many people are naturally cautious with others, especially when they do not know each other well, or the actions of one can affect the former on a personal level. A person with an unloving attitude tends to behave in a deceptive, disrespectful, unfair, or manipulative manner with others, which makes this individual appear untrustworthy. In those cases, these people might even perceive that the unloving person aims to harm them, which makes them behave in a less co-operative manner with this individual. The opposite happens when a person adopts a loving attitude; in this case, others are more willing to co-operate with this individual. The aforementioned companies (Dell, Nvidia, Walt Disney Company, etc.) foster respect among their employees, which brings about more supportive and co-operative workplaces.

- **Contagious effect:** Goleman (1996, 1998) stated that all emotions a person feels when interacting with others are likely to be mimicked by them. This transference of emotional states is due to the existence of the so-called "mirror neurons" in the human brain (Goleman, 2006). The main function of these neural cells is to replicate the emotions experienced by others in social interactions. As a consequence, when a person adopts a loving attitude towards others, they tend to naturally experience the same emotional state (love) as this individual because of their mirror neurons. In other words, a loving attitude is contagious and contributes to improving the work and business environments. Hatfield et al. (2011) stated that emotional contagion originates in people's mimicry of the others' body language (facial expression, etc.), which prompts their emotions to converge. Research has concluded that contagion of positive emotions brings about more co-operation and also reduces conflict with others (Barsade, 2002).

Likewise, Fredrickson (2013) observed that people who adopt a loving attitude towards others bring positive resonance, which means not only that the former share their positive emotions with the latter, but also that the behaviour and biochemistry of the former become in sync with the behaviour and biochemistry of the latter. From the physiological perspective, people with a loving attitude towards others are also prone to experience a state of warmth, calm, ease, and openness in the area of their chests.

6.4 Main Aspects of a Loving Attitude to Stakeholders

Love is not a problem, not an answer to a question. Love knows no question. It is the ground of all, and questions arise only insofar as we are divided, absent, estranged, alienated from that ground.

Thomas Merton

6.4.1 *Mutual Satisfaction of Needs*

Thriving relationships are always based on the mutual and continual satisfaction of each party's needs. Unilateral gain, unfair agreements, opportunism, and manipulation prevent relationships from prospering and oftentimes lead to a relationship breakup. In any relationship, including business and work ones, members must be continually aware of each other's needs to satisfy them properly. Consequently, each party should be encouraged to communicate their needs to the other.

An organisation should attempt to find a balance between its own needs (achieving a certain level of revenues and profits, reducing costs, improving quality levels, eliciting employees' engagement, etc.) and the needs of its main stakeholders, both external (suppliers, intermediaries, community, etc.) and internal (employees, management). Oftentimes, the alignment of these two types of needs (company's needs and stakeholders') can be challenging.

For example, as an employer, an organisation can satisfy the needs of its employees in different ways, such as paying them a fair salary and providing them with decent work conditions. When workers' needs are duly satisfied, these employees are more prone to satisfy the needs of the employer, for instance, by co-operating at the workplace and giving their best performance. Instead, when employees' needs are not properly satisfied (e.g., employees are not compensated fairly, or they are not being cared for by the employer), they tend to avoid satisfying the needs of the organisation (e.g., they become purposely unproductive or uncollaborative).

In most circumstances, things are not as simple as the previous example. Individuals are multidimensional beings, with a multitude of needs to be satisfied. Maslow (1954) observed that all individuals have different types of needs: basic physiological needs (such as hunger, thirst, and sleep), and more advanced needs related to safety (which includes physical protection, financial security, and health and well-being). From this author's perspective, individuals also have social or belonging needs (e.g., relating to others) and esteem needs (which imply self-respect and validation from others).

From this standpoint, there are also self-actualisation needs (which include accomplishing personal dreams and harnessing one's full potential). This author also related this last category of needs to self-transcendence, which implies assisting others altruistically and contributing to a goal bigger than oneself. From this perspective, people cannot satisfy their higher-level needs (for instance, self-actualisation needs) if their lower-level needs are unmet (for instance, safety and security needs). Maslow (1968) observed that when an individual adopts an unloving attitude towards others, it is generally because some of this person's relevant needs have not been met.

In a company, employees tend to satisfy several of the needs in Maslow's model. For example, the paying of economic compensation (salary, etc.) is prone to satisfy employees' physiological needs (such as hunger and thirst). When employees work in a safe and secure workplace, their safety needs are likely to be met. The existence of a friendly, warm, and co-operative work environment tends to satisfy employees' social and belonging needs.

In this example, when employees are praised and thanked for their contribution to the company, their esteem needs can be met. When employees are offered opportunities to thrive in the company, for example, through job promotions, their need for self-actualisation may be catered for. When people feel that they are contributing to the company's mission in a meaningful manner, their needs for self-transcendence are met. These are just examples relating to employees, but a company must apply the same perspective for all the rest of its main stakeholders (suppliers, customers, suppliers, community, etc.).

Zappos, which is a company that sells shoes and items of clothing online, provides its staff members with free food (Zappos, 2022). This company caters for the physiological needs (hunger) of its employees. Another company, Nvidia, an organisation previously analysed, is ranked as one of the safest places to work regarding some aspects like safety practices and absence of safety fines (Ethos Esg, 2020). This organisation aims to develop a safe and sustainable environment, not only for its employees, but also for other stakeholders (contractors, communities, etc.). This company has a policy which covers all relevant aspects regarding environmental factors, health, safety, and energy (Nvidia, 2022b). This company clearly caters for these stakeholders' safety needs.

As seen previously, an organisation like Walt Disney Company fosters a diverse and inclusive workplace, and caters for its employees' belonging and social needs. As discussed previously, Dell offers its employees with a wide range of training activities (developing a growth mindset, innovation, critical skills, etc.). This set of training events are aimed at satisfying its employees' self-esteem needs.

Whole Foods is a company already analysed. At this company, through its foundation and the Whole Planet Volunteer Program, employees can apply to visit the communities where this company sources its products in order to learn more about these suppliers and their communities, and provide these communities with valuable services, among other activities (Whole Planet Foundation, 2022). Through this programme, Whole Foods caters for its employees' self-realisation and self-transcendence needs.

Alderfer (1972) developed a model called ERG to classify Maslow needs into three categories, and it includes needs, such as existence, relatedness, and growth. From this perspective, the existence needs include safety and physiological needs; the relatedness needs include social needs and certain esteem needs, especially the need to develop relationships with others; and growth needs include self-esteem and self-actualisation needs (McKenna, 2012a). This author observed that none of these types of needs takes precedence over the other, and that an activity (e.g., working for a company) can satisfy many needs at the same time (Alderfer, 1972).

Some authors like Sirgy and Lee (2018) observed that, in general, people always look for a balanced satisfaction of all their needs. These authors also observed that individuals are more prone to achieve life balance and an overall state of well-being when they obtain satisfaction from different life domains (work tasks, family life, community activities, etc.) in an equilibrated manner.

Herzberg (mentioned in De Board, 1978) observed that all individuals have two main needs, which are avoiding discomfort and pain, and developing and growing from the psychological perspective. For example, a company should prevent its employees from experiencing pain and discomfort by setting up a safe and secure workplace, and providing these employees with job security. If the company does not do that, it will bring about employee dissatisfaction.

In this example, organisations can go further and allocate tasks to employees which harness their innermost skills to foster workers' growth and development. Employees can also be acknowledged and praised for their performance for the same purpose. When these factors are present in the workplace, they will bring about employee satisfaction. These factors which support employees' development and growth tend to be more motivating than those preventing workers from pain and discomfort.

6.4.2 Other Aspects Regarding Needs' Satisfaction

Some authors like Schwartz et al. (2010) state that all individuals have a wide range of needs related to different aspects: material (related to survival), physical (e.g., health and fitness), emotional (feeling valued and cared of, etc.), mental (for instance, expression of capabilities), and spiritual (for instance, search for meaning). It is possible to include two more types of needs: social (which implies the development of relationships with others) and environmental (which implies relating to the environment and protecting it).

Employees' material needs can be addressed by setting up a canteen at the workplace where they can have some food to eat during work time. Employees can have their physical needs satisfied, for instance, through working reasonable hours. Employees' mental needs can be met, for instance, through the performance of stimulating and challenging tasks prompting them to use their mental skills. Employees' emotional needs can be met when they are appreciated by the company, for example, through thank-you notes. Employees' spiritual needs can be met by making them feel that they are making a meaningful contribution to a relevant social cause with their work.

Following this example, employees can meet their social needs with a warm and friendly work environment where they can relate to others, such as colleagues and management. In relation to employees' environmental needs, employees can perform tasks contributing to a more sustainable world, for instance, when they perform environmentally friendly activities (recycling, use of "green" packaging, etc.) for the company they work for. Some examples of companies catering for some of these needs have already been included in Section 6.4.1 and in other parts of this book.

Some authors like Robbins (2014) argue that all individuals have six specific types of needs which are search for certainty (or stability), quest for change (or uncertainty), search for one's growth, quest for one's uniqueness and specialness, the need for connection with others, and the quest for making a relevant contribution. From this perspective, employees might find that their needs for stability are met with their monthly pay cheque, and their need for change can be met when they are continually assigned varying and novel tasks, not repetitive ones. Employees can meet their needs for growth when they are offered the chance to be promoted, or work on more advanced tasks. Employees' need for uniqueness can be met when they are being rewarded for their distinctive attributes and contribution to the company they work for.

Employees' need for connection can be satisfied when they develop more meaningful relationships with their colleagues in their company. Lastly, employees can satisfy their need for contribution when they feel that their work activities meaningfully create a significant change for society in a direct or indirect manner. Management, when possible, should explain to employees about the relevant value the latter add to society. Some examples of companies catering for some of these needs have already been included in Section 6.4.1 and in other parts of this book.

Other schools of thought include other needs, for example, the need for expression, the need for autonomy, and the need for physical possession of material goods. Some research has observed that individuals also have a need for power, which means influencing or persuading others, which can be used in a benevolent or manipulative manner; this need is closely related to the need for respect and recognition from others. This need is also closely related to the concept of organisational politics, which will be discussed in Chapter 10.

In most cases, these additional needs can be subsumed in the previous categories. In the previous example, employees' need for expression can be met when they have a voice in some of the company's relevant work projects. Employees' need for autonomy can be satisfied when they are empowered to make significant decisions at work without any superior's authorisation. Employees' need for possession of material goods might be met when they have their own desks in the workplace where they can work at ease. Employees' need for power and recognition can be satisfied when an employee is promoted to a higher position.

Lastly, some scholars observed that there are only two types of needs: the need for material things (e.g., in the case of employees, their need for economic compensation, their need for a safe and secure workplace) and the need for immaterial things (in the example of employees, their need for frequent recognition, their need for improving their skills, their need for contribution to a bigger cause, their need for social bonding, etc.). Nonetheless, it is argued that all needs for material things also have an underlying intangible aspect. For example, in the example of the material need for economic compensation, there is an intangible need to feel financially secure and economically confident, which is evidently intangible.

6.4.3 The Overarching Need for Love

> Love is an incurable disease. No one who catches it wants to recover and all its victims refuse a cure.
>
> **Ibn Hazim**

6.4.3.1 Love Underpins All Other Needs

Stakeholders have a myriad of needs, which must be met in order to develop long-term and mutually beneficial relationships with them. All their main needs (not just some of them) must be satisfied in order for relationships with these stakeholders to prosper. For example, if employees are only offered economic compensation for their work (salary, bonus, etc.), but their other needs (such as feeling understood, heard and respected, etc.) are not properly met, the relationships with these stakeholders are unlikely to thrive. A company should use the same approach with other stakeholders; each stakeholder's needs must be met adequately, while pursuing the organisation's objectives.

There is an overarching need that most needs directly or indirectly relate to, which is the need for love. This need includes the need to love others and the need to be loved by them. Montagu (1957) observed that all "needs must be satisfied in a particular manner, in a manner which is emotionally and physical satisfying" and that "the basis of all social life has its roots in this integral of all basic needs which is the need for security, and the only way it can be satisfied is by love." The term "love" is used here from a wider perspective, which includes appreciation, recognition, keenness, preference, collaboration, care, support, and other similar connotations.

Sometimes, this need is overtly expressed as such, but it is often subtler. For example, when employees look for recognition and appreciation from their superiors, the former look for expressions of love from the latter. In that sense, recognition and appreciation are qualities directly derived from love.

A company which offers products and services to its customers in the marketplace always looks for the acceptance of these offerings by these customers. In other words, this company desires that customers love its products and services. At the same time, every time customers buy any product or service from an organisation over others, they do so because they love this very product or service. To put it differently, their custom is the way that customers express their love for certain goods and services, and, in turn, for the organisation offering them.

Each time an organisation searches for a mutually profitable agreement (win-win) with others (customers, suppliers, intermediaries, etc.), this company aims to fairly consider the other party's needs, not only its own ones. The recognition and discussion of the other party's needs imply adopting a loving attitude towards this very party.

Another example of this is when a company donates funds for a relevant social cause, this generous and supportive attitude is a way for this organisation to express its love to the community. Lastly, when salespeople provide customers with the best advice according to the needs of the latter, the supportive and sympathetic attitude of these salespeople towards customers is a way to express love to these customers.

As mentioned, a company should aim to adopt a win-win approach with all its stakeholders, which means that both the company's needs and the stakeholders' needs are met. An example of the application of the win-win approach is seen in companies like The Body Shop. This company offers ethical natural cosmetic products to customers (win for customers), and these products have not been tested on animals (win for animals). In addition, this company offers fair compensation to its suppliers (win for suppliers), and it also reduces greenhouse emissions (win for the environment). This company applies its Open Hire programme in various markets, and hires its staff members by centring on their potential and avoiding irrelevant interview questions and background checks. Besides, surveys have clearly indicated high employee satisfaction in this company (win for employees) (The Body Shop, 2021).

As seen previously, this company adopts a loving attitude towards internal and external stakeholders. Consequently, the need for love is extremely relevant not only inside a company, but also outside it. In a similar vein, Wiest (2013) observed that through most of their actions, people aim to earn love from others. Several scientific studies corroborated that babies without love are prone to die or suffer from serious illnesses. This need to be loved is not exclusive to babies, but applies to everyone. To sum up, all people, without exception, have the basic need to be loved by others and to love them, which is covertly or overtly related to other needs.

Some specialists observed that love is also closely related to the enhancement of mental skills. To that effect, Buzan (2000) concluded that the human brain's needs are biological nutrition, oxygen, and information, but also love. Consequently, when people have loving relationships with others, this will impact on their mental capabilities in a positive manner.

6.4.3.2 Love Is Developing Affinity Bonds with Others

> No company or institution can amount to anything without the people who make it what it is.
>
> **Max De Pree**

People are naturally gregarious, which means that they are intrinsically social. Affinity is the drive to develop connections with others. Nardi (2005) observed that "affinity is achieved through activities of social bonding in which people come to feel connected with one another, readying them for further communication." Ornish (1999) observed that lonely people have a chance of disease and premature death up to 500% higher as compared with people who regularly relate to others. The need to relate to others is directly related to love.

Montagu (1957) stated that love "is the principal developer of qualities for being human, it is the chief stimulus to the development of social competence." This author also observed that love is "the only quality of the world capable of producing a sense of belonging and relatedness to the world of humanity that every human being desires and develops."

People satisfy their affinity need by joining groups and collective projects. Social psychologists observed that when people belong to a group, they feel acknowledged, understood, validated, and supported by this group. Their personal identities are connected to the group they belong to. A group can also give meaning to its members' lives, especially when the group undertakes activities that have a positive social impact.

In a similar vein, Baumeister and Leary (1995) suggested that people have a need of belongingness that implies looking for regular, positive, and stable relationships with others, in which they show mutual affective concern, support, and care for the welfare of one another. These authors also stated that the development of these relationships tends to be related to positive emotional states (peacefulness, happiness, etc.), whereas the deprivation of these relationships or threats against them could bring about stress and anxiety, as well as other physical and mental problems. A renowned research study has concluded that the development of robust relationships has a positive effect on health conditions (House et al., 1988). Some research has concluded that when people isolate from others, their mental skills (decision-making, time estimation, etc.) tend to be impaired (Ingram et al., 2021).

As seen in this book, The Body Shop develops strong long-lasting relationships with its stakeholders. For example, this company develops robust bonds with its suppliers all over the world; some live in rural communities which have limited employment levels. As a consequence, these suppliers can have access to a fair and decent income in order to support their communities (The Body Shop, 2022b, 2022c).

There is another relevant point to highlight. Hamilton (2010) concluded that the need to belong is purely biological; there is a hormone called oxytocin which prompts human beings to gather together and develop relationships with others. This author further observed that this hormone is also responsible for people's tendency to behave in a compassionate and caring manner with others.

Fredrickson (2013) stated that oxytocin also creates a "calm-and-connect response." Zak (2013) called oxytocin the "moral molecule"; its release makes people experience positive emotional states and reinforces their prosocial behaviour (such as caring for others and collaborating with them). This scientist also said that when a person is being trusted by others, this individual has a rush of oxytocin, which makes this individual feel good. This prompts this person to respond to others in a reciprocal manner.

In a company, employees can satisfy their need for affinity, for example, by participating in collective team projects. Employees who perform these collective activities tend to develop stronger bonds with the other participants. Another way of meeting the affinity need is by inviting employees to company meetings so that they can give their opinions on relevant projects regarding the company's destiny. For instance, Acme Whistles, is a company which manufactures whistles. For the development of its new models of whistles, this organisation fosters the participation and engagement of staff members who work for each of its departments (Acme Whistles, 2022).

A company can satisfy the affinity need of its suppliers and intermediaries (wholesalers, retailers, etc.), when this organisation is in continuous contact with them and makes them feel that they are valuable contributors to the process of adding significant value to customers. For example, a company can satisfy its suppliers' affinity need when it praises them for the quality of the raw material they provide. Sometimes, these suppliers' needs can also be satisfied when a company gives them kind advice on how to improve their quality levels. For instance, Toyota, the renowned car manufacturer, regularly assists its suppliers in the improvement of their operational aspects (Kalkofen et al. 2007).

In the case of retailers, a company can satisfy their affinity needs by being thankful with them for their contribution to the promotion of its products. Oftentimes, the affinity need of these retail outlets can be met when the company offers them recommendations on how to show its products to customers in a more attractive manner.

A company also satisfies customers' belonging needs when they are offered products with the highest value possible and also when they are given valuable suggestions regarding products and services meeting their specific preferences. Customers who bought a product from a company that met their expectations form part of the group of satisfied buyers; these customers tend to be proud of being connected to the company and its products. These customers are more inclined to support the company, and, in turn, promote its products to potential customers, prompting them to try these very products.

Satisfied customers are in love with the company's offerings and they want to share this love with others: friends, colleagues, acquaintances, etc. These customers, for example, might even write positive reviews online about a company's products; their unsolicited endorsement is called "word of mouth," and it is more credible than other forms of promotion, such as advertising or promotional discounts. Solomon et al. (2006) observed that nowadays word of mouth becomes more relevant due to "the decline in people's faith in institutions."

An example of satisfied customers can be found at Trader Joe's, an American grocery chain. This organisation was mentioned previously. In this company, amicable employees continually engage with its customers and provide them with outstanding customer experience. In that sense, this organisation offers customers a selected choice of low-price quality products and makes their shopping experience fun (e.g., using in-store humorous banners to promote its products). This company also allows customers to try the products offered in its stores. As mentioned, this successful chain relies on word of mouth, having a myriad of unpaid but craving fans that unconditionally support the company on social media platforms and recommend its products (Clifford, 2020).

6.4.3.3 Love Is Harmonising Relationships with Others

> Love has a warming effect even on the coldest of hearts.
>
> **Bernie Siegel**

Love is a natural harmoniser of relationships, even business ones. A person with a loving attitude towards others prompts them to put any defensive response aside. This makes the person's interactions with others smoother and more graceful, and the relationships with them tend to become stronger. According to a very lengthy longitudinal research study, the major factor for contentment in people is the development of strong bonds with others (Waldinger and Schultz, 2023). Some research also concluded that when people have a more harmonious and loving relationship with others, their creative skills are enhanced, and their productivity and co-operation increased. However, an unloving person tends to make others feel unappreciated, undervalued, and even disrespected, which weakens the relationships with them over time.

Sometimes, a company adopts an unloving attitude towards its stakeholders by being careless, ungrateful, or manipulative. In these cases, the company's relationships with these stakeholders deteriorate, even when their economic needs (for instance, fair compensation) are duly satisfied by the company. If stakeholders' non-economic needs (for example, feeling acknowledged and appreciated by the company) are not met, these stakeholders tend to experience negative emotions (fear, resentment, etc.), which negatively affects their relationships with this organisation.

Oftentimes, a company's non-loving attitude towards its main stakeholders is a negative habit, which can be changed. Most companies tend to focus excessively on solving short-term problems (paying the bills, dealing with suppliers, obtaining more customers, etc.) and do not take the time to develop long-term loving relationships with their stakeholders. These companies tend to be so overwhelmed with the urgent matters that it prevents them from adopting a loving attitude towards others.

Therefore, people working for a company should frequently ask themselves "How can I be more loving in this relationship?" and "How can I make this relationship closer for both parties?" This type of question raises people's awareness and provides them with insights into how to develop more loving relationships with other stakeholders. The insights garnered from these questions can also help people to connect to the human side of others more deeply. Most business and work relationships only scratch the surface of their potential purposefulness and meaningfulness.

When people adopt a loving attitude towards others, their relationships are harmonised because these people can feel comfortable and at ease. A person working for a company who adopts a loving attitude towards others tends to avoid, when possible, confrontations or disputes with them. If any conflict with these stakeholders arises, the issue tends to be resolved in the most amicable manner; any adversarial ways to tackle this conflict (lawsuits, etc.) are avoided. The use of aggressive approaches, such as threats and ultimatums, to handle the conflicting situations is also put aside.

A conflict between people always implies that their needs are not fully satisfied. From this perspective, the most effective way to solve any conflictive situation for the parties involved is to work out an agreement which duly contemplates their needs. These agreements – called win-win, where no party wins at the expense of the other – are only possible when the parties adopt a loving attitude to one another. This type of agreement makes both parties feel at ease and more connected with each other, which strengthens their relationship over time.

In order to develop win-win solutions to conflicts with others, people working for a company should ask themselves questions like "What are my needs in relation to this stakeholder?", "What are this stakeholder's needs in relation to me?", and "How can the needs of both parties be duly satisfied?" Sometimes, a person really does not know the needs of a stakeholder. In those cases, one can ask this stakeholder questions such as "What are your relevant needs that are not being met in this situation?" and "What solutions do you suggest in order to have your needs satisfied?", among others.

The following example will illustrate the topic of win-win solutions, A company previously mentioned, Honest Tea, which offers natural tea drink products, aims to cater for the needs of its different stakeholders. According to the information provided by this company, these drink products are only made from certified organic ingredients, which means that have been grown without any genetically modified organisms (GMO), unauthorised chemical pesticides or fertilisers, sewage sludge, and irradiation. In addition, these products do not contain any allergens; these drinks are also produced with equipment which is also allergen-free (Honest Tea, 2022).

In this example, the company wins, as it obtains profits from the sales of these products. In addition, its customers also win, as they have access to these healthy products, which are organic and allergen-free. Lastly, the environment also wins, as the production of organic products brings about a more positive environmental impact, as compared with non-organic products.

6.4.3.4 Love Is Recognising and Validating Others

> When you are socially intelligent, you understand and appreciate the very different personalities you meet, as well as what motivates them, what their personal needs are, and how you as an individual can make them comfortable and pleased with you.
>
> **Tony Buzan**

A person with a loving attitude shows interest in others. When a person displays interest in others, this individual is not self-centred, but focused on them. Honest interest in other people implies wishing the best for them and trying to meet their unique innermost needs in the best way possible.

In other words, when people adopt a loving attitude towards others, they are naturally more selfless and also more generous to them. Genuine concern and care for others impacts positively on their sense of self-worth. This loving attitude also contributes to making relationships with others stronger over time. A significant question that people should regularly ask themselves is "How can I be more interested in this person?"

For example, an employer can become more interested in their employees by holding frequent meetings with them in order to know their unique values, interests, dreams, and aspirations. In these interactions, employees can also be asked to express their fears and challenges, as well as their recommendations regarding aspects of the company that need improvement. These encounters also help an employer connect to the human side of its employees, which makes them feel more valued by the company. When duly acknowledged, these employees are more inclined to engage with a company's undertakings and projects in a more co-operative manner.

All people need to feel that they are relevant to others, and that their unique traits and capabilities really count. Employers can satisfy this relevant need by regularly telling their employees that their contribution to the company's success is fundamental. An employer can even explain the specific reasons as to why an employee's activities are valuable for the company. This is a significant way to express love to the company's employees and validate them as worthy human beings. This loving perspective can be applied to any of the company's stakeholders (suppliers, intermediaries, etc.).

In order to validate stakeholders on a frequent basis, a company's people should ask themselves "What do I appreciate in relation to this stakeholder?" This type of question prompts people to focus on the positive aspects of others around them, instead of being self-centred. This question is useful to gather insights into how to relate to others in a kinder, more appreciative, and more humane manner. These insights usually prompt people to overtly express their appreciation to others, which, in turn, contributes to the development of more meaningful and purposeful relationships with them.

SnackNation, which offers healthy snack products for offices, is a good example of company which really appreciates its own employees. In this company, the CEO devotes time to prepare personalised hand-written thank-you letters to its staff members, appreciating their commitment and hard work, and pinpointing their recent accomplishments (Bonusly, 2022).

6.4.3.5 Love Is Exploring Commonalities with Others

> The human side is the interesting thing ... People aren't interested in "cold" facts. They want to know you are human.
>
> **David Schwartz**

Research shows that when two individuals discover that they have some aspects in common (country of origin, preferences, hobbies, values, etc.), these commonalities naturally create a stronger bond between them. Therefore, a very effective way to develop stronger relationships with others is to explore and look for shared aspects with them.

Most people, by default, tend to focus on distinct aspects regarding others (for instance, different opinions, diverse preferences, etc.), instead of looking for similar aspects with them. When a person focuses on dissimilarities regarding others, these differences tend to separate this individual from these very people instead of creating stronger bonds with them. This perspective of separation (and its close neighbours, discrimination and segregation) is always detrimental to the development of fruitful relationships.

When an individual finds common aspects (experiences, beliefs, values, preferences, etc.), even seemingly trivial ones, with another, a sense of communion and belongingness is spontaneously developed. It is important to pinpoint that a person who looks for commonalities with other people when interacting with them does not have to forsake his unique views and qualities.

The search for commonalities with other people has the objective of setting a foundation which enhances the sense of togetherness and rapport between these individuals. These shared aspects help people shorten the distance between themselves and others, especially when they have different social façades (roles, economic position, etc.). According to social psychology research, when people have similar attitudes and values, they tend to develop more robust affinity bonds.

When people find common ground, they are also more likely to drop any defensive mental responses towards one another; their conversations also tend to flow more gracefully and flowingly. Consequently, every time people interact with others, they should mentally ask themselves questions like "What do I have in common with this individual?", "How can these commonalities bring about a closer and deeper relationship between us?", and similar ones.

From a wider perspective, all human beings share their human side or humanness with others. For example, all individuals, with no exceptions, are affected by both positive and negative thoughts and emotions. Likewise, all people have dreams and expectations, but also fears and moments of tribulation. With no exceptions, all people feel confident about certain tasks, and doubtful about others.

As part of their humanness, all individuals have weaknesses and strengths; people are "a work in progress" on their way to improve and develop their potential. Psychologically speaking, all individuals try to do their best, according to the knowledge available to them at each moment, the specific circumstances affecting them, and their past experiences.

All people are continually learning, knowingly or unwittingly, how to become better human beings, and they do so *by living*, through their varying attainments and failings. When people bear in mind the aforementioned aspects when relating to others, they will find it easier to find common ground with them and also be more loving to them.

6.4.3.6 Love Is Praising Others

> Assume that everyone prefers to feel important, needed, useful, successful, proud, respected, rather than unimportant, interchangeable, anonymous, wasted, unused, expendable, disrespected.
>
> **Abraham H. Maslow**

Many companies reward their stakeholders in tangible or material ways, for example, offering discounts to retailers or bonuses to employees. However, there is a more meaningful way to recognise and validate others: giving them compliments. Compliments can be defined as the positive evaluation a person explicitly makes of other people, but praising can also be considered an expression of love for others. Oftentimes, these psychological rewards bring more satisfaction to the receiver than tangible rewards.

According to Leech (1983), an important maxim for conversations states that people should increase comments which imply the approval of others (praises) and also decrease comments implying their disapproval (dispraise). Likewise, Schwartz (1979) observed that "people do more for you when you make them feel important." In a similar vein, Lieberman (2001) observed that when a person compliments others, the receivers of the compliments tend to like and respect this individual more and their connection becomes stronger.

People love to receive honest praise from others because these compliments make them feel good about themselves and boost their self-esteem. Moreover, research has concluded that praises to others can improve their performance. Figuratively speaking, compliments are keys opening the doors to any relationship, even those that have been slammed shut.

When a person does not praise others, this individual is generally taking them for granted. The easiest way to take up the positive habit of praising others is to notice anything interesting in them, even minimal. Compliments to others should always be authentic; people should avoid complimenting others out of duty or political correctness. Consequently, formal compliments to ingratiate oneself with others should be avoided.

Whenever possible, praising should be specific. Some ways to deliver kudos to people are: "Thank you for ... (explaining the reasons this person is thanked for)," "I am very delighted because you ...," and "Our company is pleased that you ...." A person should say these sentences in a warm and friendly tone. In some cases, the compliments can be implied or more indirect, for example, "You seem to be doing a very good job because ...."

Some psychologists suggest that the person delivering the compliment should not be included in it. For example, the compliment "You contributed to ..." is preferable to the compliment "I love that you contributed to ..." to place the focus on the person receiving the kudos. Nonetheless, other specialists observed that when the person delivering the compliment is included in it, the kudos is valid and it has a more appreciative tone. From the perspective of this book, the last option is more advisable because it indirectly highlights the current relationship between the sender and receiver of the compliment.

Some specialists have observed that kudos to others, when expressed publicly, is more impactful than when it is delivered privately. The entrepreneur and philanthropist John Paul DeJoria, the co-founder of the hair products company John Paul Mitchell Systems, wisely quipped, "If someone does something good, praise them loudly and in front of as many people as you can, even if it's one person. It makes them feel good" (Bilyeu, 2017). Novak and Bourg (2016) observed that a company should frequently acknowledge and praise their people for their good ideas, which encourages them to generate more of them. These authors also observed that praising people for their achievements represents an important catalyst for better company's results.

Murray (1964) observed that people have the need for achievement, which implies accomplishing challenging tasks and overcoming problems. Consequently, when a person praises the achievement of others, this individual satisfies this important need. This author also stated that people have the need of succourance, which means being supported, guided, sustained, and loved by others. Therefore, compliments given to others are ways of supporting them, which caters to their succourance need.

Mirivel (2014) observed that altercasting is the process through which a person, by expressing their observations about others, shapes their identities in two possible ways, either positive (strengthening them) or negative (weakening them). From this perspective, praising others has a positive impact on the identities of the recipients of these compliments.

A person can deliver a compliment to another, even when the former wants to raise the issue of a mistake made by the latter. In this case, the person should start the contact with the person who made the mistake with some compliments, and later comment on the blunder. When praise is harmoniously dovetailed with constructive criticism, people tend to be more receptive to it.

For example, if an employee made a mistake, the manager can tell this person, "You always ... (highlighting positive aspects of the recipient's past performance) and I would like for you to be more attentive to ... (kindly explaining the mistake made by the recipient) and try to ... (suggestions on how to avoid similar mistakes in the future)."

Dweck (2012) observed that a person should avoid complimenting personal qualities of others (punctuality, tidiness, etc.), but instead praise the process they go through (which includes effort, time, and commitment) to achieve their goals. This approach is related to the so-called "growth mindset." People with a growth mindset believe that they can always better themselves; they know that their attributes and capacities are not fixed.

From the perspective of a growth mindset, all activities performed by a person are valuable regardless of their results because their disciplined and continual action contributes to the development of their capabilities. Likewise, Dyer (1976) observed that with sufficient effort and time, people can develop any skill, but to do so, they must make the choice to develop that capability.

For example, sometimes managers want to compliment their employees for their valuable participation in a successful work project. In this case, the manager should never say to the subordinate "You are very capable …" or "You are very co-operative." This type of praise is inappropriate because it highlights the personal qualities of this employee.

Instead, a more appropriate compliment for this situation will be, for example, "You did your boot, fully committing your time and giving your best efforts to achieve the results for this project." This praise is not centred on the employee's personal qualities, but on the process of growth and development that this individual went through to contribute to this work project. This type of compliment tends to pinpoint relevant aspects of that process, such as zest, passion, commitment, effort, and discipline.

Lastly, Dweck (2012) observed that a person who delivers praise to another should also pinpoint the specific positive impact of the actions of the latter during the process. In the previous example, the manager can say to the employee things like "Your continuous effort produced a complete change in the company's system of sales."

Companies should make a habit of acknowledging the precious value of others and their relevant contribution to business activities. Consequently, the frequent use of sentences like "Our company is very pleased we have you because …" helps organisations relate to their stakeholders in a more humanised way.

A company previously mentioned, Zappos, encourages its employees to acknowledge and reward one another for their effort and outstanding job. These employees can appreciate and reward their workmates by giving them a monetary bonus (50 dollars) to value their work. Every employee can only give one bonus per month, but they are able to receive more than one bonus from different staff members. However, managers, team leads, and supervisors cannot give these rewards to their direct reports and vice versa (Zappos Insights, 2022).

6.4.3.7 Love Is Acknowledging the Emotional Side of Others

All people have positive and negative emotions which are a relevant part of themselves. Consequently, people need to be acknowledged as sensitive human beings by others. According to Ben-Ze'ev (2000), people tend to experience emotional states, when they perceive relevant changes in their own circumstances, or changes in the situations of others linked to them. In business, some changes that might elicit intense emotional states in people are employee layoffs, launching of an innovative product, downsizing, etc. The way people express themselves on an emotional level as a result of these changes varies from person to person.

Many companies tend to focus primarily on the rational aspects of their stakeholders, dismissing their emotional traits. Most business people are naturally goal-oriented, which implies the active and continuous use of their analytical skills. In most workplaces, people are expected to behave in an emotionless manner. Therefore, emotional aspects tend to be considered hindrances which disrupt levels of performance, productivity, and growth. Consequently, the free expression of emotions is discouraged by most companies.

According to Hochschild (1983), some companies set up rules that foster the expression of positive emotions, but dishearten the expression of negative emotional states. This specialist gave the examples of an airline which strongly encouraged (and trained) its employees to only show positive emotions to passengers (e.g., by smiling at them), especially when they were serving these customers. According to the aforementioned author, this is an example of emotional labour, which means purposefully managing the expression of one's emotional states, in order to perform tasks related to a specific work position in an effective manner. This specialist also observed that, in the case of the airline sector, the smiles that cabin crew members are prompted to display at work alongside the uniform they wear, the ambience music, the distinctive traits of the aeroplane decor, and the drinks offered on board jointly contribute to the way passengers feel on board. Those employees whose positions prompt them to be in contact with customers (customer service officers, etc.) are more prone to be affected by emotional labour.

Companies must realise that human beings are multidimensional, which includes physical, mental, spiritual, and emotional aspects. For instance, many companies tend to exclusively focus on the talents and capabilities brought to work by employees, but only few organisations consider and care for other valuable aspects, such as the various emotional states of these individuals.

In the business environment, most people are reluctant to openly express their feelings to others. As mentioned, in business, there are situations which often elicit negative emotions in people, for instance, conflicts with colleagues, negative customer reviews, etc. When people have unexpressed negative emotions, their perception of reality tends to be detrimentally coloured by these very emotional stakes, which affects their thoughts and actions in a non-constructive manner. Oftentimes, people do not notice the effect of their undisclosed emotions on their perception and interpretation of circumstances and reactions to them. In other words, every time people are not fully aware of their emotional states, these emotions are more prone to control these people's lives.

When a person adopts a loving attitude towards others, this individual encourages them to express their emotional aspects. By acknowledging and understanding these very emotional aspects, people can develop a deeper connection and more meaningful communication with others.

When interacting with others, a person can ask them, for example, "Would you like to tell me how you feel about …?", or more directly "How do you feel about …?" These questions welcome emotional aspects of experiences of these people, making them feel more whole as human beings. When people are allowed to express themselves on an emotional level, they can comment on their setbacks, successful events, opinions, concerns, and aspirations in a more overt manner.

In a research study which included staff members in the healthcare sector, nurses who acknowledged the negative emotions of patients developed stronger and more trusting bonds with them (Yu et al., 2021). An example of a sentence that can be used for this emotional acknowledgement can be: "You look frustrated about… How do you feel about this?" (Kinni, 2021).

The regular use of this type of question also cleans up any "emotional debris" and makes the interactions between both parties more authentic and livelier. These questions empower people to express their feelings in a safe and non-judgemental environment, which makes them feel duly acknowledged as valuable beings who deserve to be understood and cared for.

In the company Ubiquity Retirement + Savings, which helps employees make contributions to their retirement, when its own staff members leave work, they press a button to record their emotions; for example, they click a smiley face if they are happy, or one of the other four options for other emotional states (sadness, etc.). The main objective is to know more about these employees' motivation (Barsade and O'Neill, 2016).

6.4.3.8 Love Is Respecting Others

Kindness is a language which the deaf can hear and the blind can read.

Mark Twain

All individuals want to be respected when they interact with others. Murray (1964) observed that people have a relevant social need called "infavoidance": they tend to avoid any embarrassing, disrespectful, or humiliating circumstances. Consequently, people should always intend to relate to others in a kind, warm, and friendly manner. Maturana and Bunnel (1998) observed that an individual who has a loving attitude towards another accepts and recognises the latter as a legitimate human being.

Any type of condemnatory comments to others like harsh criticism, offensive comments, and snide remarks should be left aside. These negative comments always affect a relationship in a detrimental manner because they negate others as valuable individuals. According to Murray (1964), "defendance" is the need of people to defend themselves from negative comments from other people. These comments tend to be perceived as threats by the receiver, which prompts this person to respond to them defensively. This response is related to the so-called fight-freeze-flight mode analysed in Chapter 3.

According to De Board (1978), when individuals adopt a defensive attitude, their mental energy is mostly used to protect themselves from the threatening factors, which prevents this energy from being used in more productive activities (for instance, analysis, creation, comprehension, etc.). To put it more simply, in a defensive mode, a person's analytical and reflective skills tend to shut down or be severely impaired. Therefore, when people feel attacked by comments from others, the performance levels of the former tend to naturally dwindle.

According to Webb (2016), the mental state opposite to the defensive mode is called discovery mode. A person who adopts a discovery mode does not feel endangered and is open to engaging in their interactions with others. In this mode, this person also becomes naturally curious and thoroughly analytical. The discovery mode makes people become more resourceful, which allows them to approach challenging situations more creatively. The aforementioned author also observed that in this mode, people tend to feel naturally competent, smart, and autonomous. When people are respectful towards others, the former prompt the latter to adopt this discovery mode.

A person who treats others respectfully provides them with full presence, active listening, and authentic and affirmative exchanges (Dutton, 2003). When a person listens to others attentively and thoughtfully, they are encouraged to express their ideas fully. By having the spotlight cast on them, these individuals feel acknowledged and appreciated.

A person who adopts a respectful attitude towards others welcomes each person's uniqueness and distinctiveness. This type of individual is interested in discovering and exploring people's different perspectives, values, opinions, and preferences. Respectful people always welcome comments from others, even when the comments of the latter differ from the views of the former. An individual with a respectful attitude towards others encourages them to express their uniqueness with phrases such as "Please tell me more about your viewpoint."

When a respectful person has views on a topic which are different from the ones of other people, they say phrases like "I understand your view and I respect it, and I have a different perspective on this topic." This type of individual kindly welcomes and acknowledges different points of view, which does not mean agreeing with them. When a company frequently uses this inclusive approach with its main stakeholders (employees, suppliers, etc.), the relationships with them become stronger over time.

The need for respect is related to a well-known "golden rule," which states: "Treat others as you want to be treated." This widespread rule is sensible and very practical and it has been promoted by the most important religions in the world. The business leader Richard Branson, who is behind Virgin Group, wisely quipped, "There's no magic formula for creating a great company culture. The key is to just treat your staff how you would like to be treated" (Jaf, 2022). At Southwest Airlines, employees are encouraged to adopt a servant attitude towards others, by putting others first and applying the golden rule (Syamasaki, 2008).

A person who applies the golden rule is inclined to adopt an attitude of benevolence (doing good) towards others, and avoid any attitude of malevolence (causing harm). For example, if employees do not feel that they are fully cared for, respected, and understood by the company they work for, they tend to behave in a reciprocal manner. In this case, the company is acting in an unloving manner towards its personnel; therefore, these employees will also tend to adopt an unloving attitude towards this company, which implies, for example, behaving in an uncooperative manner, and "doing just their job."

In this example, the company's lack of love to its employees has a very tangible effect, which is the decrease in employees' co-operation at work. Their uncooperative attitude, in turn, is likely to affect the company's productivity and quality levels, which can eventually drive profits down. It is important to highlight that the golden rule can be applied not only to a company's employees, but also to other relevant stakeholders (such as suppliers, retailers, customers, and community).

Some companies foster respectfulness through the implementation of a Code of Conduct, which includes rules regarding acceptable and unacceptable behaviour whenever people interact with others. A company like 3M, the global company which offers various products (cleaning products, adhesives, dental products, electronic material, components, etc.), includes the principle "Be Respectful" in its Code of Conduct. Through the application of this code, this company creates a work environment where all its staff members are appreciated. These employees are treated with respect, dignity, and professionalism, and their differences are acknowledged and valued. In addition, this company is strongly against any form of discrimination, reprisal, bullying, and harassment in the workplace (3M, 2022).

There is another topic to pinpoint. According to Alessandra and O'Connor (1998), the "platinum rule" states that you should always treat others in the way *they* want to be treated. From this perspective, a company should discover the most important and unique needs of each stakeholder in order to cater to these very needs. Companies that use a marketing approach, which implies being customer-oriented, try to thoroughly research their customers' needs in order to meet them in an effective manner, which includes treating them in the way they want to be treated.

Respectful people naturally treat others in a kind and loving manner. Hamilton (2010) observed that people are genetically wired for kindness, which means that kindness is in their genes. This author observed that when people are kind to others, not only will this better their relationships with them, but it will also improve their health condition and mood, slowing down their ageing process.

Not only do people feel respected when they are treated in a kind way, but also when they participate in agreements with others which are fair and reasonable, commonly known as win-win. In these agreements, the needs of both parties are duly acknowledged and considered. People are also more likely to feel respected when they perceive that others are not acting arbitrarily with them, but in a well-justified manner.

In the work and business environments, the concept of respect is closely connected to the term "face." In this context, "face" means a person's self-image in public (or public image). Goffman (1967) observed that face is a person's image of themselves, which is "delineated in terms of approved social attributes." According to this author, people are prone to react emotionally, positively or negatively, regarding their face whenever they interact with other individuals.

A person tends to experience positive emotions in those situations perceived as enhancing the face of this individual. Nonetheless, in circumstances that are perceived to put this individual's face at risk, this person is more prone to experience negative emotional states. The aforementioned author wisely concluded that "as sacred objects, men are subject to slight and profanation" from others (Goffman, 1967).

According to Brown and Levinson (1987), there are two main aspects of a public face: a positive aspect (the desire to be positively perceived, liked, approved, and accepted by others) and a negative aspect (the desire that one's actions are not prevented by others). When any of these two aspects are not duly considered by other people, a person's face is at risk, and the individual might feel disrespected.

These authors also observed that some actions of others can negatively affect the positive aspects of people's public face: ignoring these individuals, overtly disapproving or not valuing their comments, embarrassing them and harshly criticising them, and not allowing them to express their ideas, among others. According to these authors, there are some actions performed by others which can detrimentally affect the negative aspects of people's public face, for example, giving them manipulative commands, threatening them, giving them ultimatums, and refusing to provide them with help when requested. A person who adopts a loving attitude towards others naturally avoids actions which can potentially threaten the positive or negative aspects of the public face of others.

According to these authors, some valid strategies to protect the negative aspects of the face of others are, for example: delivering requests in a tactful manner ("Could you please move the chair?") instead of formulating direct requests ("Move the chair now!") and using apologetic words when making requests to others ("Sorry, could you please move a bit ahead?"), among others. These specialists also pinpoint actions to preserve people's positive aspects of the face of others, such as considering the person' interests and needs adequately, avoiding disagreements with the individual whenever possible, and allowing the person to partake in important decisions, among others. In relation to this, Goffman (1969) calls the techniques used by people to protect the impression conveyed by others "protective actions" or "tact."

Other examples of actions which can potentially enhance the positive aspects of the image of others are delivering compliments to them and being publicly appreciative of their contribution. Lastly, a person with a loving attitude towards others naturally respects them and tends to regularly use the aforementioned strategies to save their face.

The global retailer, The Home Depot, which sells various products (construction items, tools, appliances, etc.), is a clear example of a company that adopts a respectful attitude towards its stakeholders. This company has an Open Door Policy in force, which fosters sincere and respectful two-way communication among staff members. The application of this policy contributes to the development of a work environment which fosters open communication, where employees can overtly express their worries, highlight problematic issues, pose questions, and also give suggestions regarding work challenges (The Home Depot, 2018).

There is another topic to pinpoint. Porath (2016) observed that civility implies gestures of kindness, respect, and courtesy which prompt people to experience positive emotions. This author conducted a research study which concluded that, when employees are treated in an uncivil manner (publicly belittling them, taking their credit, etc.), a great percentage of these staff members reduced their effort and time at work. It also decreased their commitment and performance levels. Conversely, civil workplaces bring about more vitality, more motivation to learning, higher performance, increased mutual support; moreover, customers that see people in a company treating each other in a civil manner are more prone to use the company's products in a future time (Porath, 2012).

Wallace (2014) discussed an experiment conducted at Yale University's Infant Cognition Center. This study's main objective was to discover if people, when they are very young, can truly differentiate good from bad. In this valuable experiment, babies were shown a puppet which made an effort to open a box, while a second puppet kindly provided some help. Later, these babies were shown a puppet trying to open a box, but on this occasion, another puppet shut the box in an unkind manner and stopped the first puppet from opening the box. When given the opportunity to choose, most babies in this experiment chose the kind puppet (the one helping the other open the box) over the unkind puppet (the puppet that has unkindly shut the box). Researchers also concluded that people can innately distinguish kind from unkind behaviour; this capability seems to be inborn, not learned from others.

6.4.3.9 Love Is Having Positive Assumptions about Others

Assumptions are the termites of relationships.

Henry Winkler

We all have opinions of people … We have a screen of ideas between ourselves and another person so we never really meet that person.

Krishnamurti

Every time a person working for a company meets others for the first time (for instance, new employees, new suppliers, new customers, etc.), this individual should have positive assumptions about them. Whenever a person has positive assumptions regarding others (for instance, this individual assumes that they are benevolent, honest, credible, etc.), these assumptions affect the way this person perceives others.

It is interesting to note that people never relate directly to others, but through their own mental representations of these very people. These representations about other people are very subjective, but never precise nor complete. Steiner (1986) stated that our knowledge about others begins with, but cannot go beyond, our representation of them. These mental representations can have different names, for instance, assumptions or mental images, among others.

These assumptions (positive or negative ones) towards other people are mental projections, which act like glasses colouring the way others are perceived. For instance, when a person has positive assumptions about others, their words and actions are filtered through these assumptions and tinted positively in the eyes of this individual. A person who holds positive assumptions about others is also more inclined to treat them kindly, which contributes to the development of deeper and more meaningful relationships with them.

In other words, when a person intentionally has positive assumptions about others, this individual's overall attitude towards them becomes more constructive. This person is more inclined to have positive thoughts, emotions, words, and actions towards these people, which, in turn, prompts them to behave accordingly, that is, in the same positive way they are treated. According to the psychological principle of consistency, a person tends to naturally behave in accordance with how they are treated by others.

For instance, a person who assumes that others are co-operative treats these people as if they were really co-operative. In this example, these people will tend to behave collaboratively with this individual. Likewise, research demonstrates that when a person has high expectations of another individual, the latter is prone to show improved levels of performance. Psychologically speaking, this is also called the "Pygmalion effect."

There is a very simple technique people can use to have more positive assumptions about another person. Before interacting with this individual, people should say to themselves "My positive assumptions about this person are …." This sentence should be completed with some positive attributes and qualities regarding the other person.

When people use this technique, their perception regarding others is affected positively, as a result of the constructive assumptions of the former about the latter. Even though this technique is very simple to use, its powerful effects should never be dismissed. As a consequence, a company's people should give this tool a try in order to improve their relationships with the organisation's main stakeholders.

This technique of purposely adopting positive assumptions about others can be applied to people one meets for the first time. An individual can also apply this tool to known people, especially those whom were involved in past feuds or disagreements with this person. When a person has positive assumptions about others, this person's perception of them is shifted almost instantaneously, making the communication with them more constructive and pleasurable. The famous humanistic psychologist Abraham Maslow stated a series of paramount assumptions to be applied in business activities, such as "Assume that everyone is to be trusted," and "Assume that everyone can enjoy teamwork, friendship, (and) good group spirit," among others (Maslow, 1965).

To sum up, having positive assumptions about others always helps a person see them in the best light and prompts these people to adopt a congruent attitude, which, in turn, makes interactions more flowing and graceful. The opposite is also true; when a person has negative assumptions about others, they tend to behave according to these very unproductive assumptions, which makes communication less spontaneous and more defensive.

Kendra Scott is a prestigious fashion designer (necklaces, earrings, rings, bracelets, etc.) whose core values are Family, Fashion, and Philanthropy. In relation to the value "Philanthropy," this is a good example of a company which has positive assumptions about its employees. In that sense, this organisation assumes that its employees are keen to adopt a philanthropic attitude and contribute to relevant social causes. Consequently, this company provides its employees with paid time off for them to volunteer (Kendra Scott, 2022; The Muse, 2022).

Another example of a company where positive assumptions are prevalent is Netflix, the global movie streaming company and movie producer. This company provides its employees with a lot of freedom. At this renowned organisation, there are no unnecessary rules or procedures, which prompts its employees to act in the best way possible. This company assumes that employees will behave as adults; they are not children to take care of. For example, the company doesn't monitor the hours or days that employees work; this organisation doesn't even have a policy regarding vacation or travel, or rules for expense approval. In this organisation, there is an important positive assumption: staff members will behave in a responsible manner (Hastings and Meyer, 2020; Meyer, 2021).

6.4.3.10 Love Is Showing Compassion for Others

> Communication technologies are necessary, but not sufficient, for us humans to get along with each other. This is why we still have many disputes and conflicts in the world. Technology tools help us to gather and disseminate information, but we also need qualities like tolerance and compassion to achieve greater understanding between peoples and nations.
>
> **Sir Arthur C. Clarke**

Compassion implies listening to others in a non-judgemental manner, and oftentimes offering them care and support. When a person is compassionate with others, interactions with them become more flowing and relationships with them become stronger. Compassion always begets a stronger connection with others. People who face challenging circumstances are in need of a helping hand from others. From an evolutionary standpoint, compassion is prone to have developed in human beings as a way of taking care of their own offspring and developing co-operative ties with others (Goetz et al., 2010). The main characteristics of compassionate people are:

- **Non-judgemental:** According to Rosenberg (2005), a compassionate person does not make moralistic judgements or condemnatory comments about others. Compassionate people try to understand the challenges experienced by others in a non-judgemental way, taking into consideration the unique perspective of the latter.
- **Understanding:** A compassionate person is not self-centred, but instead is focused on others. This person is authentically concerned for others and identifies with their experiences as if they were their own. This person tries to be in the shoes of others to understand them in the best way possible, from the emotional, rational, and behavioural perspectives. The compassionate person tends to offer solutions which are suitable for the other person, when appropriate. A compassionate person is open to understanding the human side of the person affected by challenging life experiences. This individual shows authentic and friendly concern for others' challenges, which prompts the development of stronger relationships with them (Alexander, 2020). Kukk (2017) observed that compassion always implies a broad understanding of the suffering of others, accompanied by a clear commitment to take action to mitigate their suffering. This specialist observed that according to research, when people are compassionate, they use the neural circuits related to love (as compared with empathy, which uses the brain areas linked to pain) which nurtures their brain and makes them more prone to achievement. This prestigious scholar observed that while empathetic people relate to the phrase "I feel your pain," compassionate individuals are more likely to relate to the sentence "I understand your pain and will do something about this."
- **Oriented to others:** A compassionate individual tends to understand what really affects others, without grasping their issues in a superficial manner. Rosenberg (2005) stated that when a person is compassionate with others, these people tend to feel more empowered to dwell on deeper aspects of themselves. This exploration prompts people to experience a sense of relief regarding the issues affecting them.
- **Sensitive:** A compassionate person who interacts with people facing difficult times and experiencing pain or grief tends to authentically understand their feelings. Moreover, a compassionate individual validates the feelings and experiences of others and listens to these individuals in a loving and active manner. A compassionate person is fully present before others and willing to offer them full support, when appropriate.

Gray (2015) observed that compassion implies a person's skills to recognise pain in others, identify with their suffering, and connect with them because of this individual's own painful experiences. From this perspective, the compassionate person tends to use sentences such as "I can truly recognise your pain because of my own painful experiences." Compassionate individuals realise that painful experiences are commonalities affecting all human beings, which helps them authentically connect to others when they suffer. These circumstances are valuable opportunities to adopt a more nurturing, collaborative, and connecting attitude towards others.

Compassionate people are often good at identifying negative emotions (fear, anger, etc.) in others, and validating these emotional states to lower their intensity (Voss and Raz, 2017). A compassionate individual can observe those affected by challenges from an outside perspective, and provide them with much more useful suggestions than the ones these people could obtain by themselves (Grossmann and Kross, 2014).

Whenever requested, a compassionate person can offer support others. Sometimes, this support implies providing them with tangible things (funds, etc.). Other times, this assistance entails intangible things (active listening, technical advice, emotional support, etc.). Research has concluded that a person who kindly supports others feels competent, confident, and more connected to them (Regan et al., 2022).

People who are treated in a compassionate manner tend to feel understood, appreciated, and also calmer. So, these individuals are less likely to respond in a reactive manner. In addition, people who have been supported in a compassionate way are more inclined to adopt a compassionate attitude towards others (Goetz et al., 2010).

Renowned scholars Trzeciak and Mazzarelli (2019) observed that in the healthcare sector, compassionate treatment of patients has concrete positive psychological effects (decreasing their anxiety and distress, alleviating their depression, etc.), a physiological impact (reducing their perception of pain, lowering inflammation, decreasing their blood pressure, helping their wounds heal faster, and strengthening their immune system), but also improving the quality of medical care (providing patients with more detailed, personalised, and safer treatment, lowering malpractice), and prompting patients to follow medical directions and cope with illnesses more effectively. These authors also mentioned the case of an anaesthesiologist who treats patients compassionately – as part of therapy – before they undergo an operation, which lowers their anxiety, and as a result they need fewer sedatives.

The following example also aims to clarify how compassion looks like in practice. For instance, a person working for a company can adopt a compassionate attitude towards one of the organisation's suppliers. Let us imagine a supplier that was not able to deliver an order placed by the organisation on time because of unforeseen circumstances. In this case, the compassionate employee will kindly ask this supplier about the reasons for the delay of the delivery.

In this example, not only will this employee acknowledge the justifications given by the supplier, but this employee will give, when possible, additional time for that delivery without penalising this supplier. This compassionate employee is also likely to give valuable suggestions so that this supplier could avoid similar delays in the future. The compassionate attitude adopted by the employee towards this supplier is bound to have a positive impact on their relationship, increasing the trust levels between them.

It is important that a company's employees adopt this kind and assisting attitude towards a company's stakeholders, especially if they showed goodwill and commitment towards the company in the past. Compassionate employees understand the difficulties experienced by others in a caring and non-judgemental manner, providing them with assistance when possible.

Oftentimes, a compassionate person helps others abreact, which means prompting them to release their emotional tension in a cathartic manner, through their meaningful articulation of thoughts and emotions. Troubled people tend to feel more relieved when they can vent their feelings and ideas with a person who is not judgemental, but relaxed, supportive, and caring. In a similar vein, Gilbert (2009) observed that when a person is compassionate with others, they tend to feel more safe, nurtured, soothed and cared for, and less stressed, which can help them navigate their challenges in a more confident manner. When people suffer, their core skills (critical analysis, creativity, learning, etc.) are impacted negatively; when these staff members are supported in a compassionate manner, these skills are restored (Worline and Dutton, 2017).

There are some other aspects of compassion in the workplace to highlight. Employees can be affected by various stressful factors (accidents, death of a relative, serious health conditions, divorce, loss of belongings, etc.), which often impacts on their performance at work in a detrimental manner. In some cases, staff members can also be affected by conflictive situations with their colleagues (e.g., arguments) and other stressful factors in the workplace. In all these cases, employees should be treated in a compassionate manner.

According to Lilius et al. (2008), when an employee is treated in a compassionate manner by her colleagues, this individual tends to bring about positive inferences about themselves (e.g., "I'm valuable"), her colleagues ("I work with supportive staff members"), and the organisation ("This is a caring company"). These authors also pinpointed that, when an employee is treated in a compassionate manner at work, this individual is more prone to be committed to the organisation.

Armstrong (2015) observed that, in compassionate workplaces, staff members tend to be more content, and interact with others in a more collaborative manner, while also bringing about higher customer satisfaction, which can have a positive impact on the bottom line. Research has also concluded that compassion can also reduce healthcare costs, as a consequence of lower employee absenteeism, and lower employee burnout, among other factors (Trzeciack and Mazzarelli, 2019).

Kukk (2017) observed that the evolutionary process in humankind is more based on the "survival of the kindest" instead of "the survival or the fittest." According to this specialist, research has shown that people are hardwired for compassion and that compassionate behaviour towards others is a fundamental human instinct; when people adopt a compassionate attitude towards others, the hormone oxytocin is released in their brains, which makes them experience positive emotions. This prestigious scholar also observed that people who adopt a compassionate attitude tend to become more resilient and develop a higher self-esteem.

Some organisations can set up specific roles where employees act in a more compassionate way; for instance, a customer service officer will be empowered to adopt a compassionate attitude towards the suffering of customers (e.g., their complaints) (Lilius et al., 2012). A company can also have a counsellor onsite to discuss challenging situations affecting employees. Some companies can also have some policies in place which contribute to the development of a more compassionate workplace, for instance, compassionate leave (employees can take some time off to handle emergency issues related to their dependants). Companies can also offer employees training courses on the importance of compassion in business.

Some researchers have pinpointed the so-called empathic distress fatigue, erroneously named compassion fatigue. According to Brown (2021), this represents the emotional depletion stemming from continually supporting others in their challenging situations. This scholar stated that various caregivers like doctors, nurses, psychologists, and social workers are more prone to experience empathetic distress fatigue. Besides, employees in direct contact with customers (customer service officers, tutors, etc.) also tend to experience it. When people experience this exhaustion, they are less prone to treat others in a personalised manner.

Some research has shown that an effective way to combat this type of exhaustion is to treat others in a more impersonal manner (Zaki, 2019). In that sense, by being more disconnected or detached from others, people are less prone to experience this type of burnout. However, this attitude (treating others in an impersonal manner) is completely discouraged by this book.

In work and business environments, many people do not adopt a compassionate attitude towards others for different reasons, such as goal-orientation, busyness, lack of personal communication, over-reliance on formal procedures, self-centredness, and negative aspects of organisational politics (one-upmanship, gatekeeping, turf wars, etc.), among others. For example, a research study showed that people are less likely to behave in a compassionate way when they are under time pressure (Darley and Batson, 1973). However, research has observed that treating others in a compassionate manner often takes less than a minute, while it brings about an enormous positive impact on them (Dempsey, 2017). Lastly, research concludes that people with a powerful position in an organisation are less likely to behave in a compassionate manner with others. Instead, when people have low power in a company, they are more inclined to treat others in a compassionate manner.

The following is a good example of compassion applied to business activities, which was mentioned by Mackey and Sisodia (2014) and Sisodia (2017). In the past, Whole Foods, the company which sells healthy food products, was supported by some of its stakeholders, who adopted a compassionate attitude towards this organisation. Some months after starting up, this company was severely affected by a massive flood.

On that occasion, this company did not have any stock, savings, or insurance. Some of the company's customers and neighbours helped this organisation reconstruct what was destroyed by the flood, so that this company could start from scratch. In addition, the company's staff members worked for free until the organisation fully recovered. With a supportive attitude, the company's suppliers provided products on credit to help this company recover.

Financial institutions extended additional credit, to assist this company, and those who invested in the company at its onset decided to make the additional investments this organisation needed. All these stakeholders adopted a compassionate attitude towards this company. As a consequence, this company was capable of re-opening a couple of weeks after this predicament.

6.4.3.11 Love Is Acting with Integrity with Others

Integrity is closely related to the concept of fairness. In business, people want to be treated fairly by others. From this perspective, people believe that their good actions must be duly acknowledged, appreciated, and, if possible, rewarded. When people feel that their accomplishments are not properly recognised, they are prone to feel resentment towards those who should have acknowledged them.

For instance, an employee who works overtime every day for a company that does not acknowledge this person's additional contribution is likely to consider this situation unfair. In this example, the employee devoted additional valuable time performing the company's tasks, without receiving any recognition from the company. As a consequence, this employee is prone to become more demotivated and this person's support to the company will dwindle over time.

In the previous example, the company could have acted more fairly and recognised this employee's additional effort in different ways, for example, a salary rise, bonus, or additional annual leave, among others. This company could also have openly expressed its gratitude to this employee (for instance, a personalised thank-you letter). If the company had acknowledged this employee's valuable contribution, this individual might have been more inclined to keep on co-operating with this company in the future.

People who perceive unfair situations, tend to respond to these perceived threats in a defensive manner (Tabibnia and Lieberman, 2007). In the workplace, employees who perceive a lack of fairness are prone to act in arguable ways, such as lowering their work quality, being less productive at work, and withdrawing co-operation, among others (Shapiro and Kirkman, 1999).

From a wider perspective, people can also feel that they are treated unfairly when they are negatively affected by a win-lose agreement. In this type of agreement, there is one party that obtains all the gains at the expense of the other party. This type of agreement is not mutually profitable because only one party has their needs met, while the other not. The party that does not have their needs met is prone to consider that they have been treated in an unfair manner. In the example previously mentioned (the employee who worked over time and was unacknowledged), the company obtained all the gains at the expense of this employee.

Integrity is also linked to the concept of honesty. Even though deceitful behaviour is socially condemned, deceptive actions tend to be widespread in the business environment. However, most people do not tolerate dishonest individuals and companies. In other words, there is an urgent need to deal with transparent and authentic people and organisations.

A company like The Home Depot, previously mentioned, is an example of company with an attitude of integrity. This company's main values are Doing the Right Thing, Building Strong Relationships, Respect for All People, and Taking Care of Our People, among others. In the company's Code of Conduct and Ethics, there are various important activities related to integrity: developing a safe environment for workers and customers, fostering fair hiring practices, discouraging discrimination, promoting recycling and conservation of energy and natural resources, issuing truthful financial reports, and bolstering confidentiality and information protection, among others (The Home Depot, 2018). All these practices reflect an attitude of integrity.

In the business environment, many organisations act in a deceptive manner; they lack integrity. These businesses regularly implement a wide range of manipulative stratagems which affect their internal and external stakeholders in a negative fashion. Some examples of these deceptive behaviours are threatening others, making others feel guilty, lying to them, providing others with unfelt praise, using double discourse, and hiding relevant information, among others.

Organisations that use the aforementioned ruses intend to control others in order to take advantage of them. When these ploys are discovered, the individuals and companies affected tend to adopt a distrusting and uncooperative attitude towards these organisations, which affects the relationships with them in a negative manner.

Most individuals and organisations have the need to avoid being controlled by others. Murray (1964) calls "autonomy" the social need "to resist coercion and restriction" and "avoid or quit activities prescribed by domineering authorities." People who are controlled by others are prone to feel that their natural freedom of choice is reduced, which makes them experience negative emotional states. Conversely, people whose need for autonomy is satisfied tend to show heightened performance levels and an increased state of well-being (Deci and Ryan, 2000).

In Section 4.3.8, the main aspects of saving people's face or maintaining their public image were thoroughly explained. One of these aspects is people's desire to avoid their actions being prevented by others. When people's autonomy is reduced by other people, the former are likely to perceive that their public image or face is threatened, which makes them feel disrespected by the other people.

Research concluded that some common causes of stress in the work and business environments are situations in which individuals perceive that they have no control. When a person feels that the unfolding or outcome of a specific circumstance is in the hands of other people, this individual tends to feel fretful and restless.

There is another point to highlight regarding the topic of control and autonomy. When people feel that they are being controlled by others, the former tend to adopt a defensive attitude towards the latter. This protective response is related to the fight-freeze-flight mode which was previously explained in this book. As a consequence, when people develop relationships with those attempting to control them, these bonds are prone to be impacted in a negative manner.

Exerting control over other people can be overt and blatant, or oftentimes, subtle. For example, in most companies, employees are overtly controlled, when their superior gives them specific orders or commands regarding how these subordinates must act. Most companies also have an intricate myriad of procedures and policies in order to control employees' behaviour. These rules are set with the purpose of bringing more order and predictability to the work environment, but they often become utterly constraining and even stifling regarding employees' natural need for autonomy.

In other cases, employees are covertly controlled, especially when their roles offer little or no discretion to act spontaneously. In other words, these employees' freedom of action in the workplace is very limited, as they need their superiors' permission to make most relevant decisions. Employees' freedom of action can also be restricted when they are not encouraged to express their voice regarding company activities.

It is important to pinpoint that exerting control over others is never good, especially when it is excessive. Control generally creates friction in relationships, and it brings about different degrees of resistance from the person being controlled. In the business and work environments, the best way to relate to others is allowing them to have an important degree of autonomy. For example, instead of the superior commanding a subordinate on the actions to take, the former can invite the latter to make joint decisions on the steps to be taken. In other cases, the manager can give general guidelines on a project undertaken by the subordinate, so that the latter works out the details on how to proceed considering those guidelines.

These recommendations should not be applied only to a company's employees. The perspective of increased autonomy should also be applied, when possible, to other company's stakeholders, such as suppliers, customers, and intermediaries. Consequently, a company's people should frequently ask themselves questions like "How can I give this stakeholder more autonomy?" and "How does this stakeholder's increased freedom of action contribute to more efficiency regarding our business activities?"

A good example of an organisation which forsakes control is the innovative company Adobe, which offers computer software. In this company, managers prevent themselves from micromanaging their subordinates. Instead, these managers encourage employees to rely on their unique capabilities and develop creative ideas (Kashyap, 2022). As seen previously, in Netflix, the successful video streaming and movie producing company, unnecessary rules are scrapped (e.g., vacation, travel, and expenses approval policies), as employees are expected to behave in a responsible way.

6.4.3.12 Love Is Generating Trust-Based Bonds

> Trust is like the air we breathe—when it's present, nobody really notices; when it's absent, everybody notices.
>
> **Warren Buffett**

There is a generalised lack of trust in society. This attitude of distrust extends to some politicians, media organisations, but also to some businesses. Some unethical activities, like false advertising, employee exploitation, and environmental pollution, tinge many business activities with great suspicion.

The Edelman Trust Barometer Global Report which summarises research including more than 30,000 respondents in 28 countries brought about some interesting conclusions: business is perceived as the only institution to be trusted, more than 40% of respondents want businesses to be more engaged in relevant issues (climate change, inequality, etc.), more than 70% of people expect the CEOs to publicly address these issues and support their solution, and more than 40% of people expect business and government jointly to address these challenges (Edelman, 2023).

According to Rousseau et al. (1998), trust is a state where people accept being in a vulnerable situation, relying on their positive expectations regarding the actions of others. According to these specialists, trusting others always entails some risk, the risk they will behave contrary to what is expected. According to Feltman (2021), when a person trusts others, this individual renders something of value (money, property, etc.) vulnerable to the actions of others.

As a consequence, when others behave in the expected way, one's trust of them rises; when they do not act as expected, trust is lowered. Trust is increased or decreased throughout the interactions of people (employees, customers, etc.) who rely on one another.

When people trust others, they can share relevant information with others. These trusting individuals feel more at ease and calm when interacting with them, as their perceived uncertainty regarding others' behaviours is reduced significantly. These trusting people adopt an open and non-defensive communication with others. They feel empowered to overtly express their own ideas, including those related to sensitive issues, with no fear. These people also feel safe to disclose their emotional states to others, without fear of judgement. People who trust others are more willing to delegate tasks to them.

In an environment of trust, activities are performed in a more agile and unhindered manner. In this type of environment, some costs (like the ones linked to developing meticulously crafted contracts, implementation costs of these agreements, etc.) are substantially reduced. In addition, in trust-based environments, conflicts between people are substantially decreased, and any conflictive situation which arises is resolved in a prompt and friendly manner. Simons (cited by Feltman, 2021) observed that companies where managers are trustworthy tend to become significantly more profitable than those organisations whose managers are not trusted. In business, when people trust each other, they are more prone to develop co-operative endeavours.

In a trusting environment, people tend to behave in a supportive, kind, and compassionate manner, which brightens their relationships with others. In this type of environment, people are more willing to consider the advice given by others. In unclear or challenging situations, people who are trusting give others the benefit of the doubt (Edmondson, 2004). Trusting work environments bring about more job satisfaction, higher productivity, more collaboration, and less stress, which impacts positively on profits; in this type of environment, all projects – including challenging ones – are undertaken with more ease (Zak, 2017, 2019). Trusting workplaces are *not* fear-based, but instead full of kindness and supportiveness. In this type of environment, people proactively adopt a trusting attitude towards others, which brings about more enhanced trust-based bonds with them; trusting brings about a positive cycle of trust.

In a trusting environment, there tends to be fewer rules (organisational policies, etc.) to shape and monitor people's behaviour. In this type of environment, mistakes made by others are perceived as unintentional, and people are more prone to forgive them. In a trust-based environment, people can willingly contribute to others more than is expected (e.g., an employee working overtime to meet an important deadline) as they feel that others will not take advantage of them (Voehl and Harrington, 2016). In business, there are some activities which often generate trust:

■ People who avoid forcing others to do things, but instead respect their autonomy, generate trust. In that sense, Wagner (2020) observed that pushy sales techniques used to pressurise customers to buy specific products generate distrust. Other manipulative techniques (e.g., feigning scarcity of a product to make it more desirable in the eyes of customers) can also generate distrust.

■ People who are transparent with their own intentions – when interacting with others – generate trust. On the contrary, untrustworthy people often have vested interests, opportunistic or egotistical ones, which are not fully disclosed, to intentionally mislead others.

■ People who offer complete and truthful information to others generate trust. Instead, untrustworthy people purposefully distort information (e.g., untruthful adverts) or hide important information (e.g., fine print in a contract) which is relevant for others to make effective decisions.

■ People who keep relevant information regarding others (personal details, etc.) confidential generate trust. On the contrary, untrustworthy people share personal information with others (gossiping, selling this information to other organisations, etc.). In many countries, the confidentiality of personal data is legally protected by data protection regulations in force.

■ People who have deep knowledge and extensive experience – traits which characterise competence – generate trust regarding activities related to that area of expertise. On the contrary, inexperienced and unknowledgeable people regarding a topic generate distrust in activities related to it.

■ People who have shared values with others tend to generate more trust (Morgan and Hunt, 1994). These people are more prone to join collaborative projects with others. Instead, people who have opposing values to others tend to be distrusted by these individuals.

■ People who keep their promise, by delivering what they have committed to – or delivering something even better than promised – generate trust. To put it simply, people who match their words and actions act with integrity. Instead, untrustworthy people don't fully walk the talk and often deliver less (lower quality, smaller amount, etc.) than promised. In a company, its mission and values are actually considered promises, so when the organisation acts against them, it is perceived as untrustworthy.

■ People who avoid engaging in detrimental behaviour related to the dark side of politics (one-upmanship, favouritism, gossiping, slandering, turf wars, etc.) generate trust. On the contrary, untrustworthy people purposely engage in that behaviour to obtain personal gain.

■ People who always aim to solve conflictive situations with others in an amicable way generate trust. These individuals look for agreements which consider the needs of all parties involved. Instead, untrustworthy people are prone to personalise conflicts with others, by adopting an adversarial attitude (e.g., threats, lawsuits) to resolve these issues.

■ People who encourage others to give their views on a topic tend to generate more trust. Instead, people who only centre on their own views and ignore the perspective of others generate distrust.

■ People who acknowledge others' emotions – especially negative ones – with sentences like "You look upset" generate trust-based bonds with them (Yu et al., 2021). People who acknowledge emotions of others also show emotional intelligence. Instead, untrustworthy people ignore other people's emotional states.

■ People who offer honest and heartfelt words of support, thanks, or compliments, and demonstrate positive body language (e.g., sincere smiling) to others generate trust. Instead, untrustworthy people often offer positive words to others but in an insincere manner (and they also display inauthentic body signals, like forced smiling), with the only purpose to ingratiate themselves to others.

■ People who adopt a compassionate attitude towards other individuals generate more trust (McAllister, 1995). Instead, uncompassionate people, who are unwilling to soothe others' pain, tend to be distrusted by others.

■ People who avoid regularly and obsessively monitoring others' performance are more prone to bring about trust-based bonds with them (Dutton, 2003). On the contrary, when people do not refrain themselves from frequently scrutinising others' outcomes, they tend to generate lower levels of trust.

▪ People who look for win-win agreements with others – where all participants are benefitted – generate trust. Instead, untrustworthy people only seek win-lose agreements which benefit them at the expense of others.

People who are trusted by others tend to elicit trust in people completely unrelated to them. This is related to the so-called social proof concept. For example, a company which has very positive online customer reviews tends to be more trusted by new customers, as compared with an organisation with a lot of negative reviews. These reviews, also called word of mouth, represent valid evidence of the company's trustworthiness.

In addition, people who treat others in a kind, supportive, and respectful manner generate trust-based bonds with them. Trustworthy people are oriented to others and try to add high value to them; they want the best for them. These individuals adopt a compassionate attitude towards others. Instead, untrustworthy people act in a self-centred manner and they truly do not care for others' needs. For example, when a doctor treats patients in a compassion manner, these patients are more prone to trust this professional and follow medical directions (Trzeciack and Mazzarelli, 2019). In addition, when people trust each other, they use inclusive words (we, our, ours, etc.) to pinpoint the interdependence with each other (Dutton, 2003).

When a company is online, it looks more trustworthy when it discloses full, updated, and transparent information. This type of company also includes customer reviews and testimonials from people who interacted with the company. The terms and conditions of a purchase as well frequently asked questions are clearly stated on the website. This company also includes enough online visual material (pictures, videos, maps, etc.) regarding its products. In addition, this organisation shows some awards (Best employer, Most trusted company, etc.) on its platform.

This company allows stakeholders to use non-virtual sources to contact the company (phone number, etc.). Lastly, the main members of the team (with their pictures and brief bio and functions) are included on the online platform. This company may have some certifications (B Corp, ISO 9000 quality certification, Fair Trade certification, etc.) which are shown on its website. Lastly, this company includes relevant information of its socially and environmentally oriented projects.

Companies which care about making a positive social and environmental impact tend to be perceived as more trustworthy. According to Fombrun (1996), these companies have good reputations and are more enticing for staff members, customers, and investors, which has a positive effect on these organisations' economic results.

On the contrary, a company which brings about a negative social or environmental impact (pollution, customer deception, employee exploitation, etc.) is perceived as untrustworthy, and often repels these stakeholders. Not only do these questionable activities damage the company's reputation, but they also negatively affect the company's results. There is an interesting research study which concluded that companies with more unclear and obscure definition of its statement of values tend be perceived as less trustworthy, and its people are more prone to behave in an unethical manner (Markowitz et al., 2021).

Companies should look for examples of other companies which develop trust-based bonds with their stakeholders and emulate these organisations. Companies should also look at those that are untrustworthy and the specific ways they behave, in order to act in an opposite manner. A very important question to ask is "How can we generate more trust with our stakeholders?"

A good example of a trustworthy company is The Body Shop which brings about activities with a positive social and environmental impact benefitting various stakeholders (suppliers, employees, customers, etc.). This company is a B Corp organisation which means that it achieves high standards regarding social and environmental performance, accountability, and transparency (B Corporation, 2022). This company also has a fair trade certification. This organisation promises to fight against animal cruelty, and it delivers this promise: all its products are cruelty-free.

A company like Walt Disney which has developed a participative, inclusive, and diverse workplace is another example of a trustworthy company. This company is on Fortune's List of "World's Most Admired Companies" (The Walt Disney Company, 2021). These two companies disclose their socially oriented projects on their websites. Lastly, in a previous chapter, FAVI, a company that produces car parts was analysed. As seen, this company eliminated the time-clocking system, and unlocked all storage place (rooms, cupboards, and cabinets), as this organisation trusts its employees. In this company, staff members can also use the company's vehicles (without any approval) to visit customers or suppliers.

6.4.3.13 Love Is Expressing Creativity

All people have the relevant need to show others their uniqueness, which implies harnessing their distinct talents and capabilities, and standing out from others in a differentiated manner. To put it more simply, people have the need to express themselves, in various ways, openly and creatively.

When people connect to their creative essence, they become less bound to widespread rigid structures (social conditioning, well-ingrained assumptions, self-judgement, assessment from others, etc.). When these individuals aim to satisfy their creative needs, they feel empowered to develop things that did not exist previously (new projects, products, services, ideas, etc.). The need to be creative also includes going through novel experiences (visiting new places, learning new topics, etc.). People who dare to be creative can be more "themselves" because they harness their unique talents in a more complete manner.

Rogers (1961) observed that people who satisfy their natural creative needs tend to harness their potentialities more fully and actualise themselves. Fritz (1984) stated that the creative process is an act of love itself. The topic of creativity will be explored in Chapters 14 and 15 in a more thorough manner. Several recommendations on how people working for companies can become more creative will also be examined in detail.

An interesting example of a company that fosters creativity is Google, the company which developed the most famous search engine and other related products. In this company, employees can devote 20% of their work time to Google projects they are passionate about, or chosen or created by them. This approach encourages this organisation's employees to be more creative. Moreover, the ideas that contributed to the development of some of the company's most popular products (Gmail, AdSense, Google Maps, Google News, etc.) were originated during this allocated time for creativity (Adams, 2016).

6.5 Some Interesting Perspectives about Relationships with Stakeholders

6.5.1 Bank Account Approach

This perspective was suggested by the legendary management guru Covey (1992). This well-known perspective is called the "bank account approach." Metaphorically speaking, every relationship a company has can be likened to a bank account. In the same way as a bank account, the relationship has "deposits" and "withdrawals." The "deposits" are positive actions or gestures from one person to the other in the relationship. These "deposits" make the relationship stronger and increase the rapport and affinity between the relationship members. Some examples of these positive actions or gestures are:

- Being grateful, loving, and kind with the other person.
- Being generous to the other party, freely and unconditionally, offering them affection, time, advice, support, information, etc.
- Acknowledging the other person's opinions, interests, dreams, difficulties, and concerns.
- Respecting the word given to the other person and always acting with integrity.
- Recognising the other person's uniqueness, talents, and capabilities.
- Spending quality time with the person and listening to this individual actively.
- Recognising when the other person was hurt by one's actions.
- Admitting one's mistakes affecting the other person promptly and compensating this individual when possible.
- Being compassionate and forgiving for the other person's mistakes.
- Using positive vocabulary with the other person and avoiding delivering any snide remarks or abrasive criticism to this individual.

Negative actions and gestures or "withdrawals" are opposite to the aforementioned examples. An example of "withdrawals" is adopting an unloving attitude with others, which implies being ungrateful, self-centred, uncompassionate, etc. From this perspective, a relationship can only thrive when there are more "deposits" than "withdrawals" on both sides of the relationship.

When a member of the relationship has made continuous "deposits" over time and occasionally and unintentionally makes a mistake ("withdrawal") affecting the other, their relationship is unlikely to suffer in a relevant manner. The precedent of these "deposits" acts as a "cushion," which makes the relationship solid and strong enough for this type of contingencies. When, instead, at least one of the relationship members has "overdrawn" with the other, their relationship tends to wither. Consequently, some paramount questions people working for a company should ask themselves on a frequent basis are:

- How can I make more "deposits" in the "bank accounts" in each of my relationships?
- What "withdrawals" regarding these relationships must I avoid?
- What relationships are "overdrawn" and how can I reverse this?

As seen previously, companies like The Body Shop develop agreements where its suppliers are provided with a fair compensation for their inputs. In this example, this company acts in a generous and supportive way with its suppliers. In that sense, the company makes "deposits" in its "bank accounts" regarding its relationships with these suppliers.

In another company seen previously, The Home Depot, through its Open Door Policy, encourages its employees to express their worries, pinpoint their problems, as well as pose questions and provide suggestions. By acknowledging its employee's opinions and concerns, this company makes "deposits" in the "bank accounts" regarding its relationships with its employees.

6.5.2 Substance over Form

This approach was suggested by the insightful author Robert Fritz (2007). This perspective can be applied to any company stakeholders (employees, suppliers, intermediaries, etc.). From this standpoint, the different relationships with stakeholders must be regularly and thoroughly analysed to discover how they can become more vital, true, precious, and real. In order to do this, Fritz (2007) advises dwelling on the essence or substance of each person involved in these relationships.

Most companies tend to focus, not on the essence of people, but instead on their external aspects (role, function, position, etc.). When people only focus on the external aspects of others, their relationships tend to become cold or formal, and oftentimes lifeless. In a similar vein, Perelmuter (2021) observed that whenever people interact others using these labels (roles, etc.), instead of considering them as human beings with unbounded potential, they are treating them in a dehumanising manner. Therefore, each member of a relationship should aim to discover the "substance" of the other. Their essence is what makes them precious and unique as human beings, and it should be regularly analysed and acknowledged.

Not only is it important to examine the human side of the other person, but also the relationship as a whole. In this sense, Duncan (2002) stated that people tend not to focus properly on the essence of relationships, but instead on their formal aspects. When participants focus on the essence of their relationships, these relationships tend to become more meaningful and thrive. Some important questions people working for a company should frequently ask themselves are:

- What are the main human aspects of these relationships? Are these human aspects duly taken into account by our company?
- How can each person in these relationships uniquely contribute from the human perspective?
- How can I be more loving in these relationships?

The company previously analysed, 3M, fosters respectfulness as an important pillar of its Code of Conduct. In that sense, in this company, staff members are acknowledged, respected, and also appreciated. As previously seen, Walt Disney Company is also another example of a company with a loving attitude towards its employees, as it fosters an inclusive and diverse workplace.

6.5.3 Vulnerable Beings

This is an alternative perspective on relationships, suggested by certain psychological schools of thought, which can be used with any of the company's main stakeholders. People can use this approach especially when they engage in one-to-one interactions with others, in person, on the phone, or in any other way. The regular use of this perspective significantly increases the connection and rapport with others.

From this perspective, every time a person interacts with others, this individual should perceive them as vulnerable human beings. Most people see others and themselves as vulnerable only when they have had an accident, a serious illness, or a life-changing event. Nonetheless, all people are intrinsically vulnerable and sensitive; this is a common trait of all human beings. Consequently, all stakeholders should be perceived beyond their social masks, and treated with care, compassion, understanding, patience, and affection. All stakeholders are intrinsically valuable and special, with their skills and capabilities, and their contradictions and shortcomings.

In order to apply this perspective, it is advisable to see others as if they were newborns. Most people perceive babies as sources of utter innocence, purity, and brilliance. Babies only prompt most people to feel positive emotions, such as peacefulness or joy. When people interact with babies, they tend to adopt a tender, kind, and playful attitude. Therefore, by perceiving others as if they were vulnerable beings like babies, a person can connect to them in a more sensitive, smooth, and loving manner (De Botton, 2016b).

John Paul Mitchell Systems, the company which sells hair products, treats its employees in a caring manner. As seen previously, in this organisation, staff members are appreciated in a direct and overt way. This is a good example of a company which adopts a supportive attitude towards its employees.

6.5.4 Interdependence and Interconnectedness

> You are at once a beating heart and a single heartbeat in the body called humanity.

Wayne Dyer

> It really boils down to this: that all life is interconnected. We are all caught in an inescapable network of mutuality, tied into a single garment of destiny. Whatever affects one destiny, affects all indirectly.

Martin Luther King Jr.

All people are connected to others around, even if they are not aware of this. Covey (1992) observed that there is a constant state of interdependence which links all people. From the business perspective, no company can achieve its business objectives (increasing profits, decreasing costs, launching new products, etc.) without the participation of others (suppliers, employees, intermediaries, customers, community, etc.). From a wider perspective, Castells (1996) observed that our society is a complex grid composed of countless networks whose purpose is to develop activities related to production, consumption, power reproduction, and experience, through meaningful interactions.

The business environment is an intricate and dynamic network of relationships, in which each participant has its share of contribution to the whole. Cohen and Prusak (2001) observed that the participants of these networks are "brought together by common interests, experiences, goals or tasks" and "imply regular communication and bonds characterised by some degree of trust and altruism." These authors also observed that "networks form because people need one another to reach common material, psychic and social goals."

From a systemic perspective, each person is a relevant component of a system and interacts with others in various ways. Consequently, for this system to work flowingly and efficiently, the continuous contribution of all its components is needed. From this standpoint, there are systems, which belong to bigger ones. Each system also contains subsystems.

For instance, a company can be considered to be a system which is composed of subsystems (such as divisions, departments, and employees). In this example, the company also belongs to bigger systems (a group of companies serving similar customers, industrial sectors, etc.). From a wider perspective, a company also belongs to even bigger systems, such as communities, regions, countries, and the world itself, with all the implications this represents. Organisations which are oriented to social causes and those that are environmentally friendly consider this holistic perspective and contribute to the well-being of the community and the planet as a whole, respectively.

In other words, people and organisations that realise their interconnectedness with others relish belonging to the systems they form part of. They purposefully contribute with their best to these very systems. These individuals and organisations know that every positive action they take, even the smallest one, will make a significant beneficial impact on the whole. They are also aware of the subsystems they enclose.

People working for a company should frequently ask these questions: "How can I add more value to the systems I belong to and also to my subsystems?" and "What are the potential consequences of my actions on these systems and subsystems?" This systemic approach is analysed more thoroughly in Appendix D.

Companies discussed previously like The Body Shop, Disney, John Paul Mitchell Systems, and Ella's Kitchen, among others, clearly recognise their interdependence with their various stakeholders (employees, communities, etc.). In that sense, these organisations purposefully undertake meaningful initiatives to bring about a positive impact on these very stakeholders.

Questions for Self-Reflection

- How can I satisfy the unique needs of each our company's stakeholders more effectively?
- How can I acknowledge and respect our stakeholders in a clearer manner?
- How can I adopt a more compassionate attitude towards our company's stakeholders?
- How can I create a stronger connection with our stakeholders?

Chapter 7

Loving Ways to Relate to Stakeholders

7.1 Generosity

7.1.1 Generosity, Abundance, and Stakeholders

> Kindness in words creates confidence. Kindness in thinking creates profoundness. Kindness in giving creates love.
>
> **Lao Tzu**

Generosity is a very important way to improve relationships with a company's external and internal stakeholders. Some examples used in this chapter relate to specific stakeholders, but nonetheless, this powerful tool can be applicable to any stakeholder. The word "generosity" comes from the term "genere," which has its origins in an old Latin term that means "beget," "bring about," or "produce." Generosity is a valuable by-product of adopting a loving attitude towards others.

Most people only act generously only on specific occasions, such as birthdays, weddings, and graduations. It is important to pinpoint that this chapter suggests the adoption of a continuous generous attitude towards internal and external company stakeholders, not an occasional act of generosity.

People who are generous with others are focused on them, rather than on themselves. Fromm (1956) stated that "love is primarily giving, not receiving." This author also observed that the act of giving is an expression of real power and strength, but also a display of joy and aliveness. As in the case of respiration where inspiring is always linked to expiring, giving can never be separated from receiving.

When a person is generous with others, this makes them feel especially acknowledged and cared for, which, in turn, has a positive impact on this individual's relationship with them. In other words, the act of giving recognises others as valuable human beings, who always deserve to be supported. Schwartz (1979) observed that likeability is the natural consequence of generosity. In other words, a person who is generous with others is more prone to be liked by them. On a similar note, Hyde (2012) observed that a generous person erases the boundaries separating this individual from the receiver which makes their emotional connection stronger and closer.

DOI: 10.4324/9781003372684-9

In a company, a person who adopts a generous attitude towards other stakeholders gives with no strings attached. Authentic generosity means giving unconditionally, without expecting anything in return. A person who gives with the expectation of receiving back is not actually generous, but calculating. This type of manipulative attitude is easily detected by others and it often results in a negative impact on the relationship with them. An honest generous person is focused on others; this individual does not have any hidden agenda and gives selflessly. Authentic generous people only aim to add value to others through the act of giving.

Google, the global company which developed the most popular search engine and other significant products, through its philanthropic activities, aims to "help solve some of humanity's biggest challenges — combining funding, innovation and technical expertise to support underserved communities and provide opportunity for everyone" (Google, 2022a).

For example, Google has provided various resources (volunteers, technology, and funding) to assist communities – before the occurrence of natural disasters – to be readier for these events (e.g., through flood forecasting) and also support these communities during their recovery. In addition, the company also makes significant donations (funds and the company's products) and gives its own expert advice to various organisations (social enterprises and not-for-profits) which undertake climate action endeavours. These endeavours must be based on open data, as well as Artificial Intelligence and other types of digital technology (Google, 2022a). As it can be seen, this company adopts a generous attitude towards various communities and organisations.

Most companies tend to adopt the opposite attitude; they try to receive. Most forces in the business environment push organisations to "get," instead of being generous. Oftentimes, these organisations focus on "getting" in a very disguised way. For their projects, objectives, and actions, these companies use more subtle words such as "achieving," "developing," "attaining," "attracting," "obtaining," "cashing in," and similar terms. All these terms are synonymous with "getting" or "receiving." Some examples of organisations centred on receiving, instead of giving, are, for example:

- Companies that try to attract more new customers.
- Companies that try to retain current customers.
- Companies that try to obtain more profits and revenues.
- Companies that try to get more efficiency from employees.
- Companies that try to have a better brand image and reputation.
- Companies that try to obtain positive word of mouth in the marketplace.
- Companies that try to have lower costs regarding their business activities.
- Companies that try to achieve higher levels of quality and productivity.
- Companies that try to attain more overtime from their employees.
- Companies that try to obtain better deals from suppliers and intermediaries (wholesalers, retailers, etc.).
- Companies that try to achieve higher objectives over time.

It is important to pinpoint that there is nothing inherently wrong with the aforementioned activities. However, most organisations tend to be excessively focused on "getting" activities, while paying little or no attention to their "giving" ones. From the perspective explained in this book, companies should aim to keep their "getting" and "giving" activities more in balance.

The key to knowing if a company is giving or receiving can be deduced by a simple question: "Who is benefiting directly with this company's action?" If the company is the only party benefitting from its own action, then this organisation is not adopting a giving attitude, but a receiving attitude. If instead others (for instance, customers, employees, community, suppliers, etc.) are the primary beneficiaries of a company's actions, this company is adopting a generous attitude.

The adoption of a generous attitude is related to the abundance mindset, which was thoroughly explained in Chapters 3 and 4. People with a prosperity mindset give because they feel that they have enough abundance to share with others. These individuals give wholeheartedly, they do not experience any sense of loss, and their focus is on others, not on themselves; their giving is based on love, not fear.

By contrast, when a company's people focus on what they do not have and try to get it from others, they adopt a scarcity mindset. These people adopt a "receiving" mode, instead of a generous attitude. As seen in Chapter 3, this scarcity mentality is based on fear (of not having enough), which is never beneficial for the company's growth and development. These people do not dare to give because of their underlying fear of losing what they have. Oftentimes, a company's people who are primarily (or solely) focused on receiving from different stakeholders, instead of giving, tend to be perceived as manipulative, selfish, careless, forceful, and cajoling.

A good example of a generous company is Taylor Wimpey plc, one of the biggest responsible home-building companies in the UK. This company adopts a generous attitude towards its employees. The company provides its staff members with various benefits like bonuses depending on employees' specific roles, flexible work time, remote work, health care support, a generous pension scheme, and a massive discount when an employee buys a home built by this company (Taylor Wimpey, 2023a).

This company is generous with its customers by providing them with energy-efficient homes, which saves them hefty amounts of money on energy bills, while also bringing about a positive impact on the environment. Taylor Wimpey plc also assists some charitable organisations like Crash, which provides hospices and other organisations with advice regarding their building endeavours (Taylor Wimpey, 2023b, 2023c).

7.1.2 Generosity and Business Activities

> Put giving first and getting takes care of itself. The generous prosper. The selfish don't …
> Prosperity varies in relation to generosity.
>
> **David Schwartz**

Some will argue that if the company only gives, instead of focusing on receiving, this company will find it hard to perform any of its relevant business activities. But this is only a half-truth; all companies are actually giving, in many cases unwillingly, to perform their daily activities. For instance, when a company pays salaries, advisors' fees, taxes, supplies, or utility services, this organisation is giving.

An organisation is also giving when, for example, it allocates its resources (time, personnel, technology, etc.) to perform specific activities (showing its products to customers, arranging good deals with suppliers, recruiting and training employees, designing a customer-oriented strategy, developing new products, designing an attractive company website, setting up new branches, opening new markets, etc.). A company is also generous when it offers valuable incentives to its customers (free samples, trial period for its products, etc.). All these activities represent a company's expenses which are related to giving. In general, every item that appears as an expense (advertising, salaries, etc.) in the company's financial report known as an "income statement" is related to giving.

The generosity perspective explained in this chapter does not imply that companies should only be giving. As mentioned previously, it is important that a company achieves a balance between giving and receiving. A company should aim to progressively increase its "degree of giving," which implies being more generous over time. In relation to this, a company's people should frequently ask themselves this relevant question: "How can we be more generous with this stakeholder?" Most company's people ask the opposite question: "How can get more from this stakeholder?"

Companies with a generous attitude focus primarily on others. In other words, these organisations put others (customers, employees, community, suppliers, etc.) first, and by doing so, these organisations become naturally more prosperous and successful over time. For instance, a generous company will always try to offer customers the best quality possible, the most outstanding design regarding its products, and impeccable customer service, among other aspects of high value. This type of company acts in the same generous manner, not only with its customers but also with its other stakeholders (suppliers, employees, community, etc.)

Free People, a company that sells specialty women's clothes, is an example of great generosity. This company donates 1% of proceeds related to customer purchases, to support fitness and wellness training regarding its partner non-profit organisation (Girls Inc.). Girls Inc. inspires thousands of young girls to be confident, strong, and smart, through various pro-girl activities (mentoring, evidence-based programmes delivered by professionals, etc.). Free People has also donated thousands of apparel units to Girls Inc., and organised and hosted various community events for female teenage groups from this organisation (Free People, 2022; Girls Inc., 2022).

Not only do generous companies aim to offer the best value possible to every stakeholder they relate to, they also try to improve the value offered to them over time. As a consequence, customers tend to become more loyal and recommend the company's products and services to friends and acquaintances. Employees become more committed, suppliers become more obliging, and the community is more prone to offer its support to these organisations. Other stakeholders (intermediaries, etc.) also tend be more supportive with generous organisations.

As explained previously, when a company is generous with others, they are the main beneficiaries of the company's actions. Nonetheless, there are some specific benefits a company's people usually obtain from being authentically generous with others, as follows:

■ A generous person tends to develop stronger trust bonds with others. When a company's employee is genuinely generous with stakeholders, they tend to be more receptive and open to interacting with this individual. A generous person is more prone to bypass the default defensive attitude some stakeholders tend to adopt towards others, especially at the beginning of a relationship.

■ A company's people who adopt a generous attitude become a good example, or role model to be emulated by other stakeholders. These generous people are also less self-absorbed and more people-oriented. Employees who are generous with others also create a positive impact on the business environment, which makes their actions more meaningful. Research backs the fact that a generous attitude towards others has a triple positive effect: it makes the receiver feel appreciated, it generates good feelings for the giver, and it prompts people witnessing the giving act to experience positive emotions. Moreover, according to research, people who observe another individual behaving in a prosocial way (e.g., being generous and supportive to other people) are more prone to act in the same way. In simple words, generosity has an infectious effect on others. This applies when observers see this prosocial act in person or look at it in a more indirect fashion (e.g., through audio or visual material) (Jung et al., 2020; Suttie, 2020).

■ Some research studies have concluded that people who perform altruistic actions become less stressed, which improves their overall state of well-being. Wiseman (2009) observed that "people become much happier after providing others rather than themselves."

■ A generous person does not try to get anything from the receivers, but to benefit them instead, which brings about more rapport between them. A person with a generous attitude towards others prompts them to behave in a more attentive and co-operative manner.

■ A generous attitude is related to a principle known as reciprocity thoroughly analysed by Cialdini (2009). For example, when a company's employee adopts a generous attitude to other stakeholders, they naturally feel compelled to reciprocate and give back to this individual. In other words, receivers feel "indebted" to the giver, which prompts them to act in a reciprocal manner, which implies "paying their debt back."

■ According to Dr Hawkins (2012), a company's people who are in "getting mode" (which is opposite to a generous attitude) have a lower state of consciousness, commonly related to greed, fear, or any other negative emotion. Instead, in a company that adopts a generous attitude, the company's people have a higher state of consciousness, related to love and thankfulness. This specialist observed that an individual who has a high state of consciousness (e.g., a generous attitude towards others) positively affects thousands of individuals with lower consciousness states (such as fear, shame, and greed) (Hawkins, 2013).

■ According to Salzberg (1995), generous people tend to experience a state of freedom, glee, brightness, and expansion and become more welcome and popular in groups. This scholar also observed that giving is a powerful way to express equanimity, joy, and compassion for others, and also helps individuals let go of any state of withdrawal, aversion, and disconnection with others.

■ When a company's people act in a generous way towards other stakeholders, this company's image is improved exponentially. A generous company is likely to become more attractive in the eyes of talented employees, who work or might want to work for this organisation. Companies never want to be seen by stakeholders as exploitative, greedy, corrupted, or heartless. When a company is exclusively focused on getting (obtaining more profits, increasing market share, getting more customers, etc.), this company is prone to be seen in a negative light by its stakeholders. In addition, a company which is not generous is more prone to try to achieve its objectives by all means, even questionable ones (exploiting employees, polluting the environment, etc.).

Abrams (2017) observed that when a person is generous with others, his oxytocin levels are increased, which produces a flood of feel-good hormones (such as endorphins and the neurotransmitter called dopamine, which is highly addictive), prompting this individual to be generous again and again, to have this positive feedback loop repeatedly. This author interestingly stated that the aforementioned positive side effects are also experienced by a person who follows a meaningful purpose which contributes to the improvement of other people's lives.

Some research has concluded that being generous (e.g., giving to charity) activates areas of the brain in areas linked to the processing of rewards (Harbaugh et al., 2007). Some authors like Suttie and Marsh (2010) observed that people with a generous attitude enjoy other positive effects, like becoming more content, improving their health conditions, developing more robust bonds with others, and eliciting thankfulness. These authors also stated that being generous prompts others to become more generous as well.

An example of a generous company is Salesforce that has supported more various environmental projects worldwide, and supports the conservation, restoration, and growth of millions of trees, through the assistance of the global reforestation community. The development of healthy forests is a paramount factor to combat climate change, as well as to bolster biodiversity (1t, 2022; Salesforce, 2022a). This company has been analysed previously in this book.

There is a last point to highlight. Sometimes, a company provides another company (e.g., a retailer) with gifts or inducements (e.g., free merchandise) in order to be benefitted by this second company, preventing this company from acting in a proper or impartial fashion. For example, a seller gives a gift to the procurement staff of a global retail chain with the only intention of gaining a contract with this chain over other potential competing sellers.

Oftentimes, this type of gifts or inducement can be perceived as corrupted practices whose only aim is to obtain advantages by influencing the decision of another company in one's favour. In relation to this, some companies have specific procedures in their codes of conduct to avoid corruption and bribes regarding procurement activities.

For example, Hilton, the hotel chain, has clear rules in its code of conduct regarding when business courtesies (meals, travel and entertainment, gifts, etc.) are appropriate and their potential detrimental impact on this company's business decisions. In this company, employees – using their own judgement – might accept or offer these business courtesies providing they are legal, customarily accepted, aimed to foster successful relationships with the company's stakeholders, not very valuable, pertinent to the receiver's function, and unrelated to any contract decisions or any procurement and purchasing decisions, among other factors (Hilton, 2017).

7.1.3 Generosity and Corporate Social Responsibility

Generosity can increase wealth rather than decrease it.

Abraham H. Maslow

The whole concept of corporate social responsibility (CSR) is based on the concept of giving something back to the community. This CSR includes activities such as helping communities and specific groups, through charitable endeavours, donations, philanthropy, and other meaningful social causes. Oftentimes, companies have their CSR projects clearly separated from the rest of their other activities.

Many companies tend to misuse the CSR perspective because they support a community only with a purpose of "cleaning up" or improving their image. In these cases, the company is not adopting an authentically generous attitude because it only supports the community in order to get something back (for instance, an improvement of the company's image). This type of company does not behave generously in an unconditional manner and this tends to be perceived by stakeholders.

The generosity approach explained in this book is radically different. Firstly, companies that adopt this generous attitude give fully and wholeheartedly. Their attitude is unconditional and loving because they give with no expectation of receiving anything in return. These companies behave generously with only the aim of benefitting their stakeholders. Their generous attitude is not speculative, transactional, or manipulative. This type of company adopts a proactive and continuous generous attitude towards others. In other words, these companies act in a generous manner as a fundamental and natural way of doing business, which is fully integrated with all their activities.

A company which adopts this giving attitude acknowledges their interconnection with other stakeholders in the business environment. This company realises that all business activities are performed within a network of stakeholders, who are always interdependent. Therefore, for a company to thrive, its activities should always be flowing, which implies both giving to and receiving from stakeholders, instead of only receiving from them. When a generous company brings about benefits for its stakeholders, this very organisation also vicariously benefits, as a part of this intricate network.

An example of an organisation with a generous attitude is Ben and Jerry's, the well-known ice-cream company. This company donates part of their profits in support of philanthropic causes. In addition, they use Fair Trade ingredients ensuring that a fair price is paid to their suppliers for their inputs, such as cocoa, nuts, fruits, and sugar, among others. Through its Caring Dairy programme, this company also delivered a myriad of workshops to farmers to bolster sustainable dairy farming activities, as well as animal care (Ben and Jerry's, 2022a, 2022b). Other companies mentioned in this book, such as Ella's Kitchen and The Body Shop, among others, are also examples of generous companies.

7.1.4 Different Types of Gifts

Many companies argue that they cannot give because they lack resources. Nonetheless, any company can give two types of things: tangible and intangible ones, whose examples can be found below:

1. **Tangible things**: For example, the company can give free gifts to customers (samples, merchandising items like pens or calendars, etc.). Customers can also be given, for instance, bonuses and discounts. In relation to its employees, a company can pay them, for instance, a salary higher than the minimum legal wage, or additional holiday time. In the case of suppliers, the company can offer better conditions to them (for instance, a more lenient timeframe to deliver their supplies). In relation to retailers, the company can give them free goods with their orders. In the case of the community, a company can donate goods to social groups in need in that community. In the case of Chipotle's, the Mexican grill restaurant company, this organisation offers the reimbursement of 100% of tuition for its employee education (college preparation courses, high school diplomas, and degrees) allowing employees to become more qualified for free (Scholly, 2021). Wegmans Food Markets, the renowned supermarket chain, is known for adopting a very obliging attitude towards its stakeholders; this company donated huge amounts of food to local food banks as well as other organisations in need (Wilson, 2021).

2. **Intangible things**: A company can give, for example, thanks to its employees for their continuous commitment and contribution to the company's objectives. In relation to customers, for instance, an organisation can give them outstanding and comprehensive information regarding its products so they can make the best decisions according to their needs. A company can also provide customers with free services (free delivery, free training, etc.); services are intrinsically intangible, but with very tangible effects on customers. In relation to suppliers, a company can give them compliments for providing the goods ordered on time. In relation to retailers, for example, the company can give them ongoing support and advice on how to exhibit goods in their outlets and market these products more efficiently. In the case of a community, for instance, a company can give its own time to train its members free of charge. The company mentioned previously, Wegmans Food Markets, assists seniors by giving them free rides to its stores and medical appointments (Wegmans, 2020). Another

example of generous organisation is Ernst & Young (EY), the global consultancy company, which provides its employees with a set of free counselling sessions, as well as meditation sessions and mindfulness training, to support their emotional health (Ernst & Young, 2022).

People working for a company can also give other intangible valuable things to others. For example, a person can give a smile, a warm handshake, a supportive pat on the back, and valuable assistance. People can also give others their appreciation, encouragement, and a vision. Oftentimes, an individual can also give others valuable references, an expert opinion, relevant contacts, kind endorsements, constructive feedback, and the time to listen to them, among other things. In The Ritz-Carlton hotel, the renowned hotel chain, staff members are encouraged to smile at any person who is within 10 feet around them, which creates a friendlier atmosphere (Talavera, 2021).

There is one more point to highlight. The attitude of giving also implies giving up or letting go of one's own negative thinking and unproductive qualities. To that effect, people working for a company should give up deception, manipulation, untruthfulness, malevolence, and any other negative trait or detrimental behaviour. In other words, any unloving words and actions should be given up in order to adopt a loving attitude towards others.

7.1.5 Generosity and Employees

As seen previously, a company should be generous with all its stakeholders, for instance, customers, employees, suppliers, business partners, community, etc. In this section, some specific examples of the adoption of a generous attitude towards a company's employees will be explained.

Many employees feel that they participate in an unfair exchange with the company they work for. In this exchange, these employees feel that their work activities are not duly valued economically (e.g., a fair wage) and non-economically (e.g., respectful treatment of employees, acknowledgement of their achievements, gratitude for their contribution to company's projects) by this organisation. Oftentimes, these employees feel that the company takes all the gains at the expense of them; they feel short-changed or deceived by this organisation.

Many employees regularly complain, in an overt or silent manner, against the organisation they work for. Oftentimes, these employees say that they give the best of their time, energy, and skills to undertake projects in the workplace, but their efforts are not fairly recognised by the company they work for. These hard-working individuals perceive that the company does not adopt a generous attitude towards them.

Many companies pay the minimum salary established by the legislation in force. In those cases, companies do not take into account the unique contribution of each employee in order to compensate them accordingly. Consequently, these employees do not feel motivated to contribute with their valuable and distinctive skills and talents to forward the company's endeavours. Novak and Bourg (2016) wisely observed that "people won't care about you if you don't care about them."

These unmotivated employees are prone to act in an unproductive and uncooperative way in the workplace and do only the minimum work possible at their specific roles. These employees are unwilling to fully harness their analytical and creative skills; this uninterested attitude, in turn, tends to be negatively reflected in the company's economic indicators.

In these common situations, it is paramount that the company adopts a generous attitude towards employees, which, in turn, gracefully resolves issues with them. Generous companies always make sure that their employees are prodigally compensated. When a company is bountiful to employees, they will be grateful. A thankful employee is prone to work in a happier and more productive manner, and this, in turn, will have a positive impact on the company's economic development.

According to the principle of reciprocity analysed in this chapter, when a company acts generously with its employees (e.g., paying them higher salaries for their work), these individuals are more inclined to reciprocate (e.g., they willingly work harder and work overtime, when necessary). Besides, when a company adopts a generous attitude towards employees, its relationships with them are strengthened over time. Therefore, a company can be more generous with its employees in different ways, for example:

- A generous company offers higher salaries to their employees, as compared to the minimum set legally. The company pays employees bonuses and additional benefits not required by law. For example, Netflix, the movie producing and streaming company, pays the highest media employee salary, as compared to the wages paid by companies in the sector (Price and Rasay, 2021).
- A generous company allows employees to take longer breaks at work and allows more generous holidays. This extended non-working time will help employees resume their work tasks having been refreshed and revitalised. A company like Netflix has no specific limitation regarding holiday time for its salaried staff members. In that sense, this company encourages its employees to take as much time as they need to give their minds and bodies a break (Netflix, 2023).
- A generous company offers several benefits to employees (free coffee and tea or meals, discount vouchers, free transport passes, free relevant training, free use of technological equipment like laptops and mobile phones, free medical insurance, etc.). A good example of a generous company is the Delta Airlines. This company offers employees multiple benefits, such as profit-sharing, enticing retirement savings plan, professional development training, and comprehensive medical insurance which covers dental and optometry, among others. This company also offers its employees free and discounted flights, and gym membership, as part of its generous employee benefits (Perkupapp, 2022).

All companies, including the ones that adopt a generous attitude towards their employees, should frequently ask themselves this question: "How can we be more generous with our employees?" All companies can become more generous over time; there is no limit to generosity. These organisations should always remind themselves that satisfied employees tend to be more productive, co-operative, and creative in the workplace.

A company can also be generous with its employees via intangible things, such as congratulating employees on their contribution to the company's projects, for example, with a personalised letter signed by the company's management. As seen before, when a company is generous with its employees, these individuals tend to adopt a more generous attitude towards the company's customers. For example, a generous employee will be more willing to provide customers with the best advice according to their needs.

Motivated employees are also prone to adopt a generous attitude with other employees. For example, a generous employee is more prone to provide colleagues with advice, technical information, and warm support, and co-operate with other workmates, even when they are not formally required to do so. Moreover, generous employees also tend to adopt a generous attitude towards other relevant company stakeholders, such as the community and suppliers. In other words, when a company is generous with its employees, they act generously, which creates a virtuous cycle, spreading generosity gradually over the work environment and also towards external stakeholders.

A good example of a company which is generous with its employees is Google. Its employees are offered free high-quality savoury food at the workplace. This organisation also offers its employees various onsite services (doctors, dentists, physiotherapists, hairdressers, shoe-shine service, beauticians, etc.), most of them for free. They also have "sleep pods" or nap rooms, to be used by their employees to better their creativity, learning, and productivity (Rainey, 2017).

7.2 Gratefulness

Don't forget your thank-you notes! … Appreciation, applause, approval, respect – we all love it!

Tom Peters

7.2.1 Importance of Gratitude for Stakeholders

Feeling gratitude and not expressing it is like wrapping a present and not giving it

William Arthur Ward

The term *"appreciation"* has two main distinct meanings. The first meaning of this word is to recognise the value or quality of something (a person, a thing, a place, idea, or an experience). From this perspective, when people are appreciative, they tend to focus on the positive aspects of things around them; a person who is grateful cannot adopt a negative attitude.

Appreciation, also called gratitude or thankfulness, has a second meaning that is "increasing the value of things." For example, when a national currency has appreciated in relation to others, the former has a higher value than the latter. Likewise, when people appreciate things around them, these things become of higher value in their eyes; they are not taken for granted. According to Hyde (2012), gratitude implies a person's sense of indebtedness towards someone or something, which prompts this individual to value them.

Hellinger et al. (1998) observed that in all relationships, there is a natural need for members to keep equilibrium between what they give and receive. These authors stated that "expressing genuine gratitude is another way to balance giving and taking." For instance, employees who regularly work overtime to meet a company's deadlines might feel that the time and effort they devote is imbalanced compared to the salary they are paid by this organisation.

In this example, the organisation could show its thanks to the employees, and pay them a more attractive salary recognising their effort and dedication to company's endeavours. In this way, the organisation re-establishes the balance between what was given by these employees and what they receive. Oftentimes, the organisation can be more grateful to its employees in a simpler manner, for example, by giving them a personalised gratitude note.

Gratitude should never be occasional, but a continuous attitude. A company's people should make a habit of being thankful to other stakeholders, which will strengthen the relationships with them over time. All companies are interdependent with their internal and external stakeholders; no business is self-sufficient. Consequently, when an organisation is grateful, not only does it recognise these stakeholders' contribution to the company's activities, but it also values the interdependence with them.

Motley Fool is a prestigious company which provides financial and investing information. This company recognises its employees in a distinctive manner. At this company, all days need to be considered employee recognition days. Consequently, at this organisation, its employees regularly use a peer-to-peer recognition tool to appreciate each other (Koul, 2022).

In the following points, some positive effects of adopting a grateful attitude in the work and business environments will be analysed. It is important to pinpoint that this enumeration is only illustrative. To that effect, some positive effects of being thankful to stakeholders are:

- A person who is appreciative to others tends to behave in a more loving and thoughtful manner when interacting with them. A thankful person tends to see the positive in others, instead of their faults, which lifts their self-esteem and self-confidence. Schwartz (1986) observed that that all individuals want to feel needed and useful, and showing gratitude towards them is a good way to achieve this. In the business environment, adopting a grateful attitude creates a better connection with internal and external stakeholders.
- When people are thanked for their contribution, their mood tends to become more positive. Gratefulness gladdens the heart of the receiver and also the heart of the giver. Ashkanasy and Ashton-James (2007) observed that employees tend to experience positive moods in the workplace as a consequence of a series of cumulative small uplifts, such as being regularly appreciated for their work, which, in turn, motivates them to keep on contributing to the company's projects.
- When a company's people are appreciative with stakeholders, the level of conflict is diminished and oftentimes eliminated. Appreciative people tend to focus on the positive aspects of their relationships with others, instead of concentrating on their conflicting traits. In other words, when people are grateful to others, their relationships become more harmonious and peaceful. Research concluded that when people are frequently grateful to others, these positive effects build up.
- Thankful people tend to be more caring and compassionate to others. Gratitude also shows humility and kindness towards others. When a person is thankful to others, they tend to be more co-operative with this individual.
- Grateful people tend to be in a good mood. When people are grateful, their perception of circumstances is shifted towards the positive and their stream of thoughts tags along. A person who adopts a thankful attitude also tends to be more calm and peaceful. No person can be appreciative and experience negative emotional states (anger, sadness, fear, etc.) at the same time. When a thankful person interacts with others, their emotions are positively shifted because of this person's emotional state. People tend to experience the emotional states of others around them because of mirror neurons. The topic of mirror neurons was explained in Chapter 6 of this book.
- Grateful people are less prone to criticise, moan, or complain, as they become more aware of the positives surrounding them. In the business environment, grateful people naturally perceive the positive aspects of each situation they face, especially challenging circumstances. Moreover, thankful people are more prone to see business opportunities, even in situations which are seemingly dire. When people are grateful on a continuous basis, they build up positive habits and a virtuous cycle regarding gratitude which feeds itself over time.

McCullough et al. (2001) found that, by showing gratitude to people, a person reinforces the positive actions performed previously by these individuals, which makes them more prone to keep on acting in a benevolent way in the future. According to these authors, people who have been thanked are not only prompted to continue acting benevolently towards the person thanking them, but also to other people.

Childre et al. (2000) call gratefulness an "energy asset" or "heart feeling" because it contributes to the general state of well-being of an individual. As an "asset," thankfulness also helps people release any tension stemming from stress. Thankful people tend to feel more alive and happier, which has a positive impact on their overall performance.

Badger Maps, a company that offers route planning products for salespeople, shows its appreciation to its employees for their accomplishments on a weekly basis. Once a week, employees meet up and are encouraged to publicly appreciate their colleagues for their contribution. For example, an employee can appreciate the way another colleague recently dealt with a challenging buyer. This regular practice of appreciation brings about a sense of community among employees (Weiner, 2017).

At Whole Foods, the company that sells natural food products and other items, before employees finish a meeting, the following question is posed "Would anyone like to appreciate a fellow team member?" (Mackey et al., 2020). The purpose of posing this type of question is to foster appreciation within the workplace.

7.2.2 Practical Aspects of a Thankful Attitude towards Others

Reflect upon your present blessings of which every man has plenty; not on your past misfortunes of which all men have some.

Charles Dickens

Show the people in your life that you appreciate what they do, whether they are in your main cast or your background crew.

Jaime Thurston

Companies are urged to show their gratitude to their main external and internal stakeholders in an overt and authentic manner. As seen previously, a grateful attitude towards others can never be excessive; in other words, gratitude cannot be overdone. Rosenberg (2005) observed that a complete expression of gratitude should be specific and include the reasons why the person is grateful as well as the feelings related to that experience. Some examples of ways of expressing gratitude to stakeholders can be found below:

- I really appreciate your contribution regarding …. This is very important to me because … and I feel … because of this.
- Your co-operation regarding … is greatly appreciated because … and I feel … because of your kind assistance.
- You are very kind because …. Thank you very much for …. I feel … because of your support.

A thankful person can always add their personal touch to express their gratitude to others. For example, a person can give thanks to others by sending them a personalised, handwritten, and signed letter. Companies should not only recognise their stakeholders for their performance, but also for their distinctive contribution.

Figuratively speaking, every time a company's people express their gratitude to stakeholders, they act like gardeners tending to and watering their plants. Moreover, people who show their gratitude to others prompt them to act in a reciprocal manner, which contributes to the development of more fruitful relationships. A person can express gratitude regarding other people's significant achievements or contributions, but also be grateful for their small gestures.

In the case of a company's personnel, there are several reasons for being grateful to them. An example could be an employee offering creative insights to improve a company's systems and processes, or an employee treating customers in a warm and kind manner, among others. In some cases, a company can be appreciative to its employees in a more indirect manner, by involving them in relevant company decisions. In this case, the company can say, "We appreciate your commitment and hard work and we would like to hear your opinion on …." A very thorough research study concluded that one of most relevant factors that motivates employees is duly appreciating their efforts and contribution at work; this is an inexpensive and often underutilised motivator (Wiley, 1997).

An example of a company with a grateful attitude towards its employees is Groupon, which offers discount vouchers to customers. For each work anniversary, this company presents its employees with a track jacket, as a sign of the organisation's appreciation. This gift can also be personalised with their names (Koul, 2022).

A company can express gratitude to its customers for several reasons, for instance, these customers have trusted the organisation, the customers have recommended its products to others, etc. A company can also be thankful to its suppliers for a myriad of motives, for example, the suppliers have delivered their supplies on time, the goods provided are of the highest quality, and the packing used in their deliveries is safe, among others.

A company's employees can use gratitude in advance to make polite requests to others. For example, an employee can say to one of the company's suppliers, "I appreciate you sending the shipment by the end of the week" or "Your co-operation on this topic is greatly appreciated." In this case, the appreciation "in advance" also subtly prompts the supplier to deliver the goods on time.

This type of request is friendly and is prone to dissolve any type of resistance from the receiver. Besides, in this example, the grateful person has positive assumptions about the attitude of the other individual, which prompts the latter to behave congruently with these assumptions. This topic was explained more thoroughly in Chapter 6.

It is advisable not to use plain sentences like "Thank you" but to include the specific reasons for gratitude "Thank you for …" in order to make thankfulness more complete and meaningful for the receiver. When gratitude is accompanied by generosity, they are a powerful combination which enhances the relationships with others. For example, when a person is grateful to others, and also gives them a valuable present for their contribution, the positive effects of gratitude are significantly magnified.

An example of a company that appreciates customers is Zappos, which was already mentioned in this book. The following example will illustrate this point. A customer bought several pairs of shoes for her mother from this company. Her mother has sensitive feet, due to her medical condition. So, most of the shoes this customer bought did not fit well. When this customer wanted to return some of the shoes, an employee adopted a very empathetic attitude towards this customer. This staff member clearly understood the challenges faced by this customer's mother. Moreover, this employee warmly said that she had a relative with similar challenges regarding the fitting of shoes also due to illness. This employee engaged in a long heartfelt conversation with this customer and wished this customer's mother the best. Afterwards, the employee sent this customer some flowers by post, as a sign of support and appreciation (Wellington, 2021).

7.2.3 Ungratefulness and Its Negative Effects

A hundred of times every day I remind myself that my inner and outer life depends on the labour of other men, living and dead, and that I must exert myself in order to give in the same measure as I received and am still receiving.

Albert Einstein

Many people are not accustomed to being grateful. These individuals are more keen on criticising, moaning, or focusing on the negative. Oftentimes, these people take valuable things around them for granted, which prevents them from being appreciative. Some people behave ungratefully out of entitlement; they do not feel that they need to be appreciative for their belongings or experiences because they believe that they just deserve them.

Some individuals cannot be appreciative because their thoughts are focused on what is missing, instead of what can be cherished. Other people say that they do not have time to be appreciative because they have more urgent things to do, or because they do not believe that they have attained enough to be grateful for. Oftentimes, individuals negatively focus on their past (for instance, regrets) or on their future (for example, worries), instead of being centred on what there is to be grateful for at present.

In the business environment, many companies act in an ungrateful manner. This type of company demands a lot from their stakeholders but does not show its appreciation to them. An ungrateful company, for instance, demands its employees work long hours every day, but it does not recognise their additional contribution. In another example, a company receives goods from its supplier before the time agreed, but this organisation does not express its gratitude to this very supplier. A company can also be ungrateful to customers, for instance, when it does not send them an email to them thanking for their purchase.

In these previous examples, the company takes these stakeholders for granted; they are not acknowledged as valuable human beings. When stakeholders are not appreciated by a company, they are more likely to behave in a non-cooperative and unmotivated manner. Oftentimes, these stakeholders become resentful and might criticise the company because they feel that they are not being recognised and cared for. It is possible that the communication between the company and these stakeholders is negatively affected. An unappreciated employee, for example, might comply only with the minimum work requirements or might even sabotage the company's activities.

Goldsmith and Reiter (2008) observed that gratitude always represents a form of recognition of others; it is like the beautiful ribbon that wraps around the jewel boxes that other people are. These authors also stated that when a person is not grateful to others, they are deprecating them.

Lastly, a company that frequently celebrates its business achievements (increase in sales, growth in market share, launching of new products, etc.) tends to adopt a generous attitude towards its stakeholders. These accomplishments can be celebrated in several ways, for instance, providing gifts to employees and organising social events (dinners, balls, retreats, etc.). A company which celebrates its past successful outcomes does not take them for granted, but it also gives credit to people who contributed to these accomplishments. Some companies focus so much on achieving their goals and pursuing their purpose that they do not take the time to acknowledge and celebrate their past achievements. MonetizeMore is a renowned ad-tech organisation. In the past, when staff members reached a specific benchmark regarding revenues, this company fully paid for a retreat in the Philippines for all its employees to celebrate this achievement (Williams, 2022).

7.2.4 Appreciative Inquiry

The supreme happiness of life is the conviction that we are loved; loved for ourselves, or rather, loved in spite of ourselves.

Victor Hugo

Appreciative inquiry is another topic related to thankfulness. Appreciative inquiry is a tool that many organisations use on a regular basis. The concept of appreciative inquiry is indeed simple. Bushe (2013) stated that this tool "advocates collective inquiry into the best of what is, in order to imagine what could be" and it is "followed by collective design of a desired future state that is compelling." This author also observed that, when this tool is used, there is no need to incentivise people in order to introduce change in an organisation.

Companies are prone to use problem-solving techniques that tend to focus excessively on the negative aspects of issues affecting them. Organisations that use these tools tend to dwell on the causes of the problems in order to devise possible solutions to efficiently "fix" these issues. Oftentimes, this way of solving problems proves ineffective because its primary focus is on the negative aspects of a challenging situation which needs a solution.

People who use appreciative inquiry recognise and value the positive aspects of a troublesome situation, which means that they adopt a grateful attitude. These people also aim to envision possible ways in which this situation can work better for the company. When people focus on positive aspects of a challenging situation, and are appreciative of them, they are more capable of devising creative and compelling alternatives to deal with this very issue.

The main stages of appreciative inquiry are discovery (the company highlights what is working positively, such as strengths, processes, capabilities, and functions), dreaming (the company creatively visualises what is prone to work positively in the future), design (developing a suitable plan with an emphasis on what could work in a positive manner), and destiny (which implies the commitment to implementing specific actions to fulfil the goals previously set, as well as learning from this implementation). This tool can be applied to a specific issue affecting the organisation, or to the company as a whole (Bushe, 2013; McKenna, 2012a).

The approach of appreciative inquiry is closely related to the creative approach explained by Fritz (1999). This specialist observed that most companies use a "problem-solving approach," which implies analysing a problem to eliminate it. This author also suggested that a company should instead use a "creative approach," which implies acknowledging and recognising its current situation (and its problematic aspects) and generating the future desired state this organisation wants to create. This second approach is primarily focused on what a company wants to generate, as compared with the traditional problem-solving approach which is centred on what the company wants to eradicate.

The following example was discussed by Cooperrider (2022). Appreciative inquiry was used by Avon, the global cosmetics direct-sales company, for its activities in Mexico in order to foster gender equity. Here is a brief summary of the application of this tool by this company. At the beginning of the process, there were no female workers at the executive level. Through a myriad of interviews, the best practices and stories about men and women working together at this company were unveiled. It was also suggested that both men and women should be represented at various decision-making levels, including the executive committee.

In addition, the key learnings from the good examples already occurring at this organisation were synthesised. A vision for the possible future for gender equity was also developed, including the idea of women and men working together in project teams and co-chairing them. A specific action plan was developed to implement this. There were some significant positive outcomes of this process: the company developed policies that support women in the company. After a short time, a female worker became a member of the Executive Committee for the first time. As a consequence of these changes, the company's profits soared significantly.

7.3 Collaboration

7.3.1 Competition and Collaboration

> Competition is an acquired, not an inborn drive ... Competition is, however, not a basic need of any kind.

M. F. Ashley Montagu

As previously seen, society supports competition. In the business environment, for instance, many companies continually aim to outwit other organisations, known as rivals or competitors. In the work environment, employees compete for a promotion and candidates compete for a job. Different suppliers compete with others to provide a specific company with their goods and services.

However, a company that adopts a competitive approach with its stakeholders can never develop mutually beneficial relationships with them. This competitive approach implies a scarcity mindset, which is based on fear and implies that there are scarce resources available to fight for. Consequently, a company that acts competitively with its stakeholders always tries to outpace or defeat them.

The competitive approach implies a zero-sum game in which a company attempts to get all the gains at the expense of others. This approach (also called win–lose) implies that there is a winner that takes all the gains at the expense of others. Sometimes, a company can even use this approach with its customers, when it tries to get as much as possible from them, without giving enough value in return.

When a company adopts a competitive attitude towards its stakeholders, no fruitful relationships with them can be developed. The use of a competitive perspective generates negative emotional states, such as fear of losing, resentment, and mistrust. An organisation adopting a competitive attitude tends to act in a defensive manner, instead of being proactive, because it aims to care and defend its access to available resources, which are perceived as scarce.

From this perspective, the competitive approach is the opposite to the co-operative perspective. While the former is based on fear because resources are perceived as scarce, the latter is based on love and trust towards others and the view that resources are abundant. On the one hand, in the competitive approach, a company believes that it can only access resources when battling for them with others. On the other hand, from the co-operative perspective, a company aims to develop synergetic alliances with stakeholders because it believes that resources can be shared and even generated collectively. Some examples of the use of the co-operative approach can be found below:

■ A company adopts a co-operative approach with customers when it provides them with good value for their money. In other words, the company does not try to take advantage of customers, by misleading, manipulating, or ripping them off. Instead, this company offers customers the best products and services in a fair exchange for these customers' money. This company also provides them with the most complete and truthful information about its products and services so that they can make the most appropriate decisions according to their unique needs. A company adopts a co-operative attitude with customers when it offers them relevant incentives, such as samples, bonuses, free services, and discounts. As seen previously, Wegmans Food Markets and Zappos are valuable examples of companies which adopt a co-operative attitude towards customers.

- A company adopts a co-operative attitude with its employees when it fairly recognises the effort and time they devote to the company. This company offers employees a fair compensation (economic and non-economic one) for their services and aims to enhance employees' capabilities through training, mentoring, coaching, or other relevant upskilling activities. A company that adopts a co-operative attitude towards its employees allows them to overtly express their opinions regarding the company's important decisions. As seen, companies, like Google and Delta Airlines, adopt a co-operative attitude towards their employees, providing them with a myriad of benefits to support these staff members.

- A company adopts a co-operative approach with other companies (such as suppliers, wholesalers, and retailers) when it only looks for fair agreements (win–win) with them. In these agreements, the needs of both parties are duly satisfied. A company that adopts a co-operative approach towards other companies is understanding, supportive, and patient with these organisations when they face challenges. As discussed previously, companies like The Body Shop and Honest Tea use Fair Trade ingredients, which allows them to pay a fair price to their suppliers for their inputs.

- A company is co-operative with other companies offering similar products and services (commonly called rivals) when it tries to develop partnerships with them. Some objectives of these partnerships could be sharing resources, such as technology, contacts, technical information, customers, human resources, facilities, and distribution channels, among others. These partnerships can have other goals, for example, researching, manufacturing, and promoting in a joint manner, spreading business risks more effectively, and reducing costs by sharing resources, among others. In the case of Virgin Atlantic, this airline has partnered up with other airlines (Air France, Delta Airlines, KLM, etc.) to offer its customers a more extended set of destinations for places where this company cannot fly in a direct way (Virgin Atlantic, 2022b).

- A company that adopts a co-operative attitude towards the community tries to support social causes, through donation, free training of community members, and other activities. The co-operative company performs these philanthropic activities without expecting anything in return. This company only aims to benefit its community without any hidden agenda or ulterior motives. As a consequence, the company's ties with the members of this very community tend to strengthen over time. As seen previously in this book, companies like Ella's Kitchen and John Paul Mitchel Systems have partnered up with various organisations for socially and environmentally oriented projects.

When companies adopt a co-operative attitude with one another, some transaction costs linking these organisations are lowered significantly. Transaction costs are the expenses of buying or selling products or services in relation to other independent organisations. Some examples of these costs are preparation of contracts to be signed by the parties, the enforcement of these contractual aspects, and the supervision of the obligations assumed by the parts, among others.

For example, when a company and its supplier adopt a co-operative attitude, the costs of enforcing and monitoring contractual aspects tend to be significantly lower. In this case, the parties trust one another and are committed to complying with the terms of the contract linking them, which helps them lower the aforementioned transaction costs.

The following example illustrates the benefits of a collaborative alliance between two renowned companies. Uber (a company that provides customers with transportation services) and Spotify (the global music streaming company) have developed a collaborative partnership. As a consequence of this alliance, customers that use vehicles linked to the Uber network can stream their

Spotify playlists, while they are being transported. These customers enjoy a unique experience, as compared to those using other similar companies in the sector (e.g., Lyft), as Uber can provide these passengers with this personalised service. In addition, Uber's customers are subtly prompted to subscribe to Spotify Premium for an upgraded service, which can bring additional revenues to the streaming company (Huhn, 2022a).

7.3.2 Other Aspects of Co-Operation

> Alone we can do so little; together we can do so much.
>
> **Helen Keller**

Ricard (2015) observed that co-operation is paramount for the evolution of humankind and its outstanding attainments, as most of these accomplishments could not have been developed on an individual level. This author mentioned the case of one of the greatest inventors in history, Thomas Edison, whom had 21 assistants helping him with the undertaking of his outstanding innovative endeavours.

Some experts observed that people are naturally inclined to co-operate with others. Schrage (1990) noted that when people adopt a co-operative attitude towards others, their relationships can become purposeful. These relationships can have different aims, such as working together to solve intricate problems or creating something new.

When people support one another and consider each other's needs, they tend to act in a more cohesive manner. Co-operative people avoid social loafing, which is not to be fully supportive and proactive when working in a collective project. A co-operative person tends to pose questions like "Is there anything I can be of assistance with?" and "How can I help you with this?" This type of person also frequently uses statements like "Let's do this together," or "Let me help you."

A person who adopts a co-operative attitude towards others tends to purposely use more positive words (such as "right" and "good") instead of negative criticism or complaints (such as "impossible" and "not feasible"). A co-operative individual is also inclined to use a more inclusive vocabulary (for example, words such as "and," "we," "our," "ours," and "us"), instead of words which imply an individualistic approach (such as "I," "my," and "mine"). These inclusive terms connote a sense of togetherness with others, implying that everyone is on the same side and trying to achieve shared objectives.

Co-operative people tend to be grateful for the contribution of others ("Thanks for your kind support regarding …"). In a co-operative environment, every person feels that their support is of great value, and their unique contribution can improve collective projects in a significant manner. The adoption of a co-operative attitude towards others is related to a systemic approach to business activities. In this approach, a company and its stakeholders are perceived as relevant parts of the same system; all components are interdependent and their harmonious interaction is crucial to bring about valuable collective results.

A co-operative attitude helped our primitive ancestors co-ordinate resources to perform relevant survival activities, such as defending themselves from dangerous predators or obtaining food for the group, among others. Montagu (1957) observed that "man is born with strong co-operative impulses, and all that they require is strong support and cultivation."

This author also stated that co-operation has a biological basis which "has its roots in the same sources as social behaviour, namely, in the process of reproduction" and that "social co-operative behaviour is the continuation and development of the maternal-offspring relationship."

This specialist concluded that "social behaviour which is not co-operative is diseased behaviour" because "the basis that informs that all behaviour … biologically healthy is love." From this author's perspective, love and co-operation are closely related.

Most people's early upbringing unfolds within a network of co-operative relationships, which includes close relatives and friends. From a wider perspective, Montagu (1957) observed that a society is a complex set of co-operative interactions between its members for a common life, where co-operation has a relevant value for each individual's survival.

Human beings have a gregarious nature, which means that they are prone to socialise and relate to others in a co-operative fashion. Many social psychologists recognise "affiliation" as a relevant human need, which implies people's desire to belong to groups. People want to form part of a group because they want to feel identified with its values and activities, and also be acknowledged and valued by other group members.

In the same view, Murray (1964) observed that co-operation is closely related to affiliation which means "to draw near and co-operate or reciprocate with an allied other." The concept of co-operation can also be related to what is known as "brotherly love." Fromm (1956) observed that this type of love implies loving others, regardless of their differences and distinct attributes. An individual who adopts this loving attitude towards others is willing to assist them, whenever needed.

In business, there is another interesting example of co-operation between companies. Starbucks, the well-known coffee-shop chain, partnered with Barnes & Noble, the renowned bookshop chain. As the result of this strategic alliance, Starbuck's coffee shops have been set up in many of the Barnes & Noble's bookshops. These coffee shops are co-branded "Starbucks B&N Cafes." As a result of this alliance, readers visiting these bookshops can enjoy some nice hot beverages. In addition, Starbucks can grow its customer base, by targeting readers who visit these bookshops (Huhn, 2022a).

7.3.3 Co-Operation within the Company

If you don't believe in co-operation, look what happens to a wagon that loses a wheel.

Napoleon Hill

Within an organisation, co-operation is a key factor to develop strong relationships between employees. Employees have specific roles and activities related to these roles, which makes the interdependence of employees a relevant factor in the workplace.

Besides, most companies meticulously divide their work projects into specific tasks, which are assigned to different employees. Therefore, an employee almost never undertakes an entire project, but only a part of it. Sometimes, employees interact and work together for each of the stages of projects. Nowadays, many employees are connected in a virtual way, for example, by emailing or by using some applications (Sharepoint, Slack, etc.) when working on the same projects. Consequently, employees need to support one another for the company to thrive in the marketplace. Collaborative employees realise that successful outcomes often stem from everyone working on the same side.

Laudon and Laudon (2018) observed that, in the current era, collaboration is more prone to happen in workplaces due to different factors, like the prevalence of work endeavours which require regular co-ordination and interaction of staff members, and the increasing importance of group work to attain a company's outcomes. These authors also mentioned another factor that drives collaborative projects, which is a growing number of international businesses whose staff members are spread over different countries and need to work collaboratively.

According to Cornelissen (2017), co-operation contributes to the development of "communities of practice" within a company. These communities are self-managed networks composed of employees from the same or different departments, who have common interests and are linked by shared tasks or projects. In these communities, people adopt an attitude of mutual support and understanding towards each other, which aligns their actions. Some employees only behave co-operatively for specific collective projects; other employees adopt a co-operative attitude on a continuous basis. In most cases, co-operation among colleagues represents an expansive experience for them. In a research study, it was concluded that when participants engage in mutual co-operation, the parts of their brains related to the processing of rewards are clearly activated, which is prone to positively reinforce a mutual supportive attitude among these very participants (Rilling et al., 2002).

According to Fritz (1991), in the work environment, there are two possible types of co-operation: consensual and hierarchical. The consensual way is used when there is no chain of command and employees work at the same level. Hierarchical co-operation is used instead when superiors and subordinates work in a joint manner. Some advantages of adopting a co-operative attitude with other employees are:

- When employees adopt a co-operative attitude, a more amicable and loving work environment is developed.
- Co-operative employees have a team spirit and sharing attitude; they aim to frequently support one another because they realise that nobody is self-sufficient.
- When employees co-operate with one another, the tasks related to a collective project can be allocated among them in a more efficient manner.
- When employees work on a joint project, each participant's skills complement one another; no employee has an overarching set of skills to solve every single problem.
- In collective projects, employees are compelled to relate to others, which helps them know each other better and learn from one another.
- Co-operative employees develop a stronger bond with their colleagues; trust and rapport among them are naturally increased.
- In co-operative projects, participants are more prone to support one another whenever difficulties or challenges arise.
- In a co-operative work environment, each employee is recognised for their unique skills and capabilities and their contribution to collective results, which makes these employees feel more comfortable and engaged.
- Co-operative employees do not adopt a defensive attitude towards others; they can be more at ease because they form part of a group which contains and supports them.
- In complex projects, co-operative employees can jointly develop a deeper analysis of the different alternatives and generate more creative courses of action, as a result of profuse interactions between all participants.
- In joint projects, co-operative employees are naturally open to contributions from others; they willingly welcome different opinions from others.
- In collaborative endeavours, delays in production and design are reduced, more innovative ideas are brought about, better solutions to customer problems are developed, and fewer mistakes are made, which leads to better Key Performance Indicators (growth, higher sales, etc.) (Laudon and Laudon, 2018).
- Co-operative projects create synergy because the collective results are not the simple sum of employees' individual achievements, but an enriched combination of all of them.

Besides, the existence of a widespread co-operative attitude in the workplace often discourages some common detrimental practices in relation to an organisation's politics, such as backbiting, favouritism, one-upmanship, and gatekeeping, among others. These unproductive behaviours are related to a competitive approach, which is based on fear.

In a co-operative work environment, employees are not on their own; they know that they will be assisted by others. By being supported by others, these staff members feel more confident and empowered to face and overcome work challenges. To put it more simply, co-operative employees develop mutually supportive relationships with others.

This co-operative attitude also implies providing others with insights into relevant topics, giving others useful advice, creating value jointly, and clarifying unclear topics. Co-operative people also tend to solve disagreements with others in a fair and amicable manner. In co-operative environments, collective decisions are encouraged whenever possible.

A company like Badger Maps, an organisation which develops an application for routing outside sales, is a good example of a collaborative work environment. In this organisation, there are some cross-training activities which allow employees to share their own experience and specialism with others. These collaborative endeavours widen the employees' skill sets; these activities also improve productivity levels and bring about higher customer satisfaction (Moga, 2017).

There is another important point to discuss. Co-operation is closely related to love; employees who interact with others adopt a loving attitude towards them. In the workplace, co-operative employees avoid outpacing one another, but work side-to-side with colleagues. Co-operation also generates an atmosphere of camaraderie, where people are more inclined to support one another. Besides this, co-operative environments are very suitable spaces to use a creative technique like brainstorming, which will be analysed in Chapter 14.

Pixar, the studio that develops computer-animated movies, is an example of a co-operative workplace. In this company's workplace, creative ideas are nurtured through collaboration. Staff members are empowered to provide feedback in order to better the ideas developed by other teams. The feedback provided is candid, respectful, and constructive. This feedback is not focused on people, but instead on the improvement of creative ideas developed by them. In a co-operative environment, half-baked ideas, through various iterations, become more fine-tuned ones (Razzetti, 2020).

However, social psychology research has concluded that co-operative projects are also likely to have some disadvantages, for example, groupthink (which means that the group members conform to a unique view, without challenging it), less individual effort made by each participant, problems of co-ordination, taking a longer time to make decisions and perform activities, and interference of members in each other's actions, among others. Oftentimes, co-operative projects can have other negative effects, such as ineffective communication between the participants, formation of conflictive subgroups, and lack of consensus. When participants adopt a loving attitude towards one another, this mitigates these negative effects. Lastly, in some organisations, collaboration among employees can be used for detrimental purposes (embezzlement, deceit, bullying others, etc.).

7.4 Forgiving Attitude

When you plant lettuce, if it does not grow well, you don't blame the lettuce. You look for reasons it is not doing well. It may need fertiliser, or more water, or less sun. You never blame the lettuce. Yet if we have problems with our friends or family, we blame the other person. But if we know how to take care of them, they will grow well, like the lettuce. Blaming has no positive effect at all, nor does trying to persuade using reason and argument. That is my experience. No blame, no reasoning, no argument, just understanding. If you understand, and you show that you understand, you can love, and the situation will change.

Thic Nhat Hanh

7.4.1 Effects of a Lack of Forgiveness

The quality of mercy is not strained; it droppeth as the gentle rain from heaven upon the place beneath. It is twice blessed – it blesses him that gives and him that takes.

William Shakespeare, *The Merchant of Venice*

Forgiveness is not only applicable to non-business relationships (such as relatives, friends, and lovers), but also to business relationships. In the business environment, some individuals discriminate against others, make aggressive comments to them, behave in an intolerant manner, or use manipulative stratagems to deceive other people, which might prompt the recipients of this behaviour to feel resentful with these negative individuals. When people are affected by harsh criticism, unfair treatment, and lack of recognition from others, they are also prone to hold grudges.

In all these situations, the individuals offended by others have not had their personal needs duly met by them. Moreover, these people tend to become resentful because they believe that their personal limits have been trespassed on by others. Consequently, these resentful people are more prone to become bitter, unmotivated, aggressive, uncooperative, less productive, and more critical, especially with the people who disrespected them. These resentful individuals tend to cling to continuous negative ruminations about people who have mistreated them. These negative thoughts cloud their perception and affect their actions in a detrimental manner. Sometimes, these unforgiving individuals act in a revengeful manner against their offenders.

Resentment implies a lack of forgiveness because it keeps negative past issues in an unproductive loop. When a person is feeling resentful towards another individual, their relationship is not likely to thrive. Resentful individuals always adopt an unforgiving attitude towards their offenders, which prompts the former to continually grieve over the past wrongdoing of the latter. A person who is continually resentful tends to be avoided by others.

Resentful people carry very heavy emotional baggage; their intense emotions related to past offences prevent them from experiencing current circumstances fully. Their discerning skills tend to be clouded by these powerful negative emotions, which also make them act in a defensive manner. Resentful people find it difficult to be kind to those who have mistreated them; they also cannot acknowledge and appreciate the distinct positive qualities of their offenders. In the business environment, when people cannot forgive others, simple disagreements become more relevant and intense, leading to conflicts escalating and becoming more personal. Resentful people are also less prone to co-operate with others who they feel offended by.

Oftentimes, people do not forgive themselves because of negative words they have said to others, unintentional negative actions affecting other people, or mistakes made. These individuals hold on tightly to their own past errors, which keeps them stuck in a negative unforgiving attitude towards themselves.

Research has also shown that being forgiving to others brings about some personal benefits, such as lower stress levels, decreased anger, enhanced self-confidence, and improved relationships with others (Luskin, 2010). Fred Kiel is one the leaders of KRW International, a prestigious global consulting firm aimed at bettering the performance of organisations and leaders. This business leader observed that, according to his research, companies whose leaders rate high in some noble principles (forgiveness, alongside integrity, compassion, and responsibility) show a noticeably higher return on these organisations' assets, as compared with organisations whose leaders rate low in these very principles (Askew, 2017).

7.4.2 Meaning of Forgiveness

People who adopt a forgiving attitude are more capable of releasing grief and pain related to past issues that could have affected them negatively; these individuals are also more open to experiencing positive emotional states. When people forgive others, the attitude of the former has an impactful and restorative effect on their relationships with others. These people release any negative judgement or condemnation of those who offended them, as they realise that blaming others is useless because it does not make them feel better, nor does it improve their interactions with others. However, forgiving does not mean forgetting about hurtful actions from others, condoning or excusing them, or even minimising one's hurt, but instead being at peace at present with these past grieving experiences (Luskin, 2010).

Therefore, when people decide to give up any negative emotional wounds caused by other people, they allow themselves to relate to others in a more meaningful manner. Forgiving individuals realise that all suffering and frustration stemming from offences caused by other people prevent the former from harnessing their own innermost potential.

Forgiveness transmutes negative emotions towards others; it also transforms separation from others into connection with them. A person with a forgiving attitude towards others tends to treat them in a more compassionate manner. Dr Hawkins (2013) observed that many people wrongly believe that forgiving others is debilitating, when in fact it is very empowering. Toussaint et al. (2018) observed that, in the workplace, forgiveness is related to lower stress levels and it is also linked to enhanced well-being and higher productivity.

Some people have an unforgiving attitude towards themselves; these individuals should learn the lessons stemming from their own past mistakes in order to release them for good. People who cannot forgive themselves tend to feel guilty and fretful, which clouds their discerning skills and unique resources. In order to forgive themselves, people should realise that in the past, they have always done the best they could, according to the available knowledge and experience at that moment.

When people think that they (or others) could have done better in relation to certain issues, they analyse this in hindsight. These people examine the past mistakes from the present vantage point, considering the learning obtained and counting on a different set of circumstances and personal resources.

The Project Forgive, which is a global non-religious organisation, trains companies in the application of forgiveness in business activities. Some of its main clients are renowned companies like Bosch, General Motors, and Walt Disney International, among others. The founder of this project observed that, through training in forgiveness, companies can develop enhanced diversity, inclusion, and belonging, as well as joy and creativity. Moreover, this thought leader observed that forgiveness can also be considered a leadership tool (Project Forgive, 2022).

7.4.3 Resolving Misunderstandings Promptly

Life forgives you when you cut your finger … Newer cells build bridges to cover the cut.

Joseph Murphy

Lazare (2004) enumerates a series of situations where people might feel offended by others, such as if they were overtly rejected or avoided, taken for granted, mistreated verbally or physically, betrayed, reduced in their status, accused unfoundedly, threatened, embarrassed in public, and disrespected in their beliefs and values, among others. People might also feel offended when their contributions to others (e.g., employees working overtime for a company) are not duly appreciated.

As seen previously, when a person offends or disrespects others without apologising for this, these people tend to resent this individual. As a consequence, when a person realises that others are resentful towards them because of actions performed or words said by this individual, this person should tackle this issue in a prompt, friendly, and straightforward manner, leaving formalities aside, if possible.

The best way to handle this type of issue is to humbly apologise to the person who feels offended. People who offer authentic and overt apologies to others should take full responsibility for their own mistakes, without minimising, denying, or hiding them. When apologising, people should honestly, unequivocally, and thoroughly acknowledge their mistakes and their negative impact on the offended (without diminishing this effect), and also display regret or remorse for having hurt others. For their apologies, people should preferably use the first person ("I apologise for ..." or "I am very sorry for ..."), and avoid conditional sentences ("If I hurt you, I apologise ...") as in the latter case they seem as if they are not taking responsibility.

Whenever possible, apologies should be made in person in a private meeting; therefore, emails or letters should be avoided. Shapiro and Shapiro (1994) observed that asking for forgiveness puts people in a position of vulnerability in which they recognise the pain caused to others, as well as their participation in it; besides, asking for forgiveness also shows care and respect for those offended.

People willing to apologise for their past mistakes understand that relationships are the most precious resource in the work and business environments. They understand that their wrongdoing might have affected their relationships with others in a negative way; consequently, they are willing to offer their apologies to those affected in order to care for their relationships with them. When people apologise for their mistakes, they are also more prone to learn from these errors in order to avoid them in the future.

People should never be ashamed or hesitant to ask for forgiveness, but instead offer their apologies in a humble manner. People who truly recognise their mistakes adopt an attitude of humility and integrity towards others. Oftentimes, these individuals are prone to ask others to forgive them, even when they are not completely sure that they have offended them. Lazare (2004) mentioned several reasons why some people are reluctant to ask for forgiveness, such as fear of feeling inferior (weak, ashamed, humiliated, etc.), fear of their image being affected negatively, fear of being punished or unforgiven, and fear of the relationship ending; people can also avoid apologising out of insensitivity or self-centredness.

People who offer their apologies to others can also promise to avoid similar mistakes in the future. Sometimes, apologies are not sufficient and a compensatory action must be offered to people offended; this compensation aims to assuage the pain or trouble caused. These actions are beneficial to preserve and strengthen the relationships between the offender and those offended. Dr Maltz (2015) wisely observed that people who have been hurt by others should always be willing to forgive them, even when there is no sensible reason to do so because through forgiveness, their emotional wounds can be healed.

According to Lazare (2010), offering apologies to others can contribute to healing the relationship with them in different ways. From this author's perspective, the person apologising makes the person who was offended experience a sense of dignity; besides, the apologiser and the aggrieved person also agree on a mistake which should not have happened and that will not be repeated; and lastly, over these exchanges, both the person apologising and the one offended can open up about their feelings.

As seen previously, a person who forgives others forsakes judgement, grudges, or blame towards them, and negative emotions related to the incident. The forgiving person understands that all human beings make mistakes, which deserve to be forgiven. Some psychological schools of thought observe that people always try their best, according to their specific circumstances and personal resources. People with a forgiving attitude are aware of this and adopt a more compassionate attitude towards others.

Some years ago, Volkswagen, the vehicle manufacturing company, was involved in a scandal related to setting up illegal software in millions of cars in order to hide high emissions during the testing process. In a public speech, which was widely broadcast, the company's CEO at that moment said, "We all know that we have let down customers, authorities, regulators, and the general public …." This business leader continued to say, "I am truly sorry for that, and I would like to apologise for what went wrong with Volkswagen …" and "We are fully committed to making things right" (Associated Press, 2016).

7.5 Fun, Playfulness, and Humour

Play is the highest form of research.

Albert Einstein

7.5.1 What Is Not Playfulness

Seriousness is the only refuge of the shallow.

Oscar Wilde

We are most nearly ourselves when we achieve the seriousness of a child at play.

Heraclitus

Playfulness is not a topic traditionally related to business activities. On the contrary, most people tend to relate business activities with terms which are the complete opposite of playfulness, such as sacrifice, hard work, huge effort, Spartan discipline, and other similar words. Many people believe that business activities should be performed in a serious, hard, and monotonous manner.

Dodgson and Gann (2018) observed that most organisations set a myriad of rules, policies, and procedures, which oftentimes prevent people from being playful. Besides, many companies share a widespread but detrimental assumption that their employees must be on duty 24/7 (and more, if this were possible) to progress in a challenging and complex business environment. Most business people associate business success with abnegation. The term "abnegation" implies an attitude of self-denial, responsibility, dutifulness, and sacrificing one's desire to favour others' desires.

Consequently, abnegation does not seem to be related to the concepts of "fun" and "playfulness." In a company, abnegated staff are prone to renounce their own interests to achieve the company's goals. The business approach based on abnegation is borne out in different ways:

- Working hard, fatiguingly, and drudgingly in a continuous manner.
- Setting business activities as a priority over everything else.

- Taking massive action in the shortest time possible.
- Being worried about any problem, even small ones.
- Overanalysing situations in order to solve them.
- Forcing things to happen in a specific way.
- Performing activities on automatic pilot.
- Being over-committed to the goals previously set.
- Following successful formulas that worked for others.
- Doing things in the same way as usual.
- Focusing exclusively on "serious" and traditional activities.
- Being exclusively focused on economic aims.

The behaviours shown in these examples tend to generate negative feelings, unproductive thoughts, and tension in most people. When people act in any of these ways, they are prone to feel stressed and fretful. These people are also inclined to adopt a defensive attitude (fight-freeze-flight mode) which prevents them from harnessing their high mental capabilities (such as creativity, synthesis, and analysis). Likewise, Marden (1917) observed that "over-seriousness depresses the mental faculties and tends to lower efficiency."

In other words, being too "serious" or abnegated regarding work and business activities can bring about negative effects. For example, people who continually work hard are more likely to burn out. When people take massive action in a short time, in order to be efficient, they are more prone to make innumerable mistakes. Besides, people who perform activities on automatic pilot lack the minimum discernment regarding their performance. Individuals who consider work and business activities as their only priority tend to become imbalanced in other relevant areas of life (such as health and family) which end up affecting their productivity negatively.

People who are continually worried about business problems tend to be more stressed and less creative in tackling these issues. These people are prone to overanalyse possible solutions to their problems, which prompts them to feel tired and unfocused. When people push hard for things to happen, they are prone to affect their relationships with others in a negative manner.

People who are over-committed to their goals do not take enough time to reflect and change these objectives when necessary. These people tend to adopt a rigid attitude towards these aims, which is unproductive when relevant changes in the business environment make these goals meaningless.

When people follow the "successful formula" used by others, they are unwilling to tread their unique path, considering their own distinctive resources (skills, capabilities, information, etc.) and set of circumstances. In the same way, when people do things the way they have always done before, their conservative attitude prevents them from going beyond their comfort zone and exploring alternative approaches.

Lastly, when people exclusively focus on the economic rewards of their business activities (obtaining more profits, increasing revenues, etc.), they tend to dismiss other relevant aspects, for example, building fruitful relationships with stakeholders, offering a better service to customers, or creating a better work environment, among others. These other positive aspects of business activities tend to be as important as a company's economic returns.

Organisations like SAS, one of the leading software companies, is considered to be one of the best workplaces. This company purposely fosters playfulness in its workforce. In that sense, this company has an on-site health care centre, which is totally free to employees and also dependants. This company also has a centre for recreation and fitness with a swimming pool. They also offer fitness sessions, basketball courts, and massage therapy, among other activities (SAS Blog, 2019).

7.5.2 *Importance of Playfulness*

> Every now and then go away, have a little relaxation, for when you come back to your work, your judgement will be surer; since to remain constantly at work will cause you to lose power of judgement.
>
> **Leonardo da Vinci**

As previously seen, most people link business activities with struggle and hardship. These people cannot relate business endeavours with being spontaneous, playful, and adventurous. Playfulness can be defined as the attitude of letting go of the seriousness, rigidity, and formality related to work and business activities. Play allows people to embody their freedom and explore new possibilities in an imaginative, energetic, and passionate fashion, in the middle of (and despite) hindering routine activities and processes so common in work and business environments (Kane, 2011).

Playful people tend to adopt a more light-hearted attitude towards business activities and avoid being overeager or pushy. Maslow (1968) defines playfulness as a good-humoured and amusing trait, which naturally goes beyond any state of hostility. These playful individuals tend to be continually engaged with the present moment, even when they pursue their main goals. These people let go of any regret from the past or concern about the future because they know the only moment of power is now. These individuals are utterly delighted and joyful when absorbed in playing. This attitude makes their actions more vital and daring.

In other words, playful individuals are willing to fully harness the present moment with no fear. These people know that "now" is the most valuable stepping stone to what is about to come. Playful people are more open-minded and curious, but also more flexible and experimental. Even though goals are relevant for a playful attitude, these goals are not pursued in an anxious way, but in a more relaxed and detached manner. Some authors observed that play is *not* driven by the quest for efficient and reliable ways to satisfy goals (Glynn, 1994; Mainemelis and Ronson, 2006). Murray (1964) observed that all people have the social need for play, which implies:

- ▪ To act in a fun, purposeless manner.
- ▪ To make jokes, laugh, and smile.
- ▪ To perform activities which release stress.
- ▪ To partake in games, parties, dancing, etc.

Brown and Vaughan (2010) stated that play is a specific type of mindset, rather than a series of activities. When people adopt a playful attitude, they can interpret situations affecting them in a less dramatic and more resilient manner. People who stand for playfulness do not really believe in working hard, but instead they aim to work smart. These people tend to behave in a spontaneous and thoughtful manner, instead of acting mechanically and automatically. In the business environment, people with a playful attitude positively contribute to all stakeholders while enjoying what they do fully.

When people adopt a playful attitude, they become more receptive and open to new ideas. These people tend to avoid paths well-trodden by others and develop their own ones. Playful people tend to let loose, which prompts them to harness their creative skills and devise new ways to do things.

There is a well-known psychological school of thought called "transactional analysis" (Berne, 1964; Harris, 1969). From this perspective, a person's ego is composed of three parts, which are the parent, the adult, and the child. In different interactions with others, people use these different parts (parent, adult, child) and communicate and behave in specific ways which are related to the very parts used. From this perspective, when playful people relate to others, they tend to use their child part. This part is related to relevant traits such as adventurousness, openness, and expansiveness.

Their childlike and light-hearted perspective helps playful people release their imagination freely, which prompts them to envision scenarios beyond current limitations. Nobel (2012) observed that playful people tend to learn more effectively because they use their whole brains. Playful people are also more prone to experience a state of flow; they can be laser-focused on the task at hand and improve their performance without strenuous effort, but with grace. People who adopt a playful attitude enjoy engaging in challenges and let things unfold smoothly and without pressure.

People with a playful attitude do not follow the rules in force in the work and business environments (such as policies and procedures), which often makes them look anarchic. In other words, these individuals are experimental and improvisational, which might also make them look aimless. They enjoy the process of exploring non-traditional ways of doing things, and avoid getting upset whenever they face setbacks or predicaments. Moreover, these people tend to garner important lessons from their failures and put themselves back in the game.

Innocent is a company that provides healthy beverage products. This is a good example of a company that fosters playfulness at the workplace. In the company's premises in London, there are ping pong tables and picnic benches, which are set up to prompt employees to have a bit of fun at work (Burn, 2020).

7.5.3 *Playfulness and Stakeholders*

> If you have fun at what you do, you'll never work in your life. Make work like play and play like hell.
>
> **Norman Brinker**

> The world of work we are entering in demands that we are more creative, playful and available to have fun. If your work isn't fun, then consider changing something – either the way you work or the work itself.
>
> **Steve Nobel**

Brown and Vaughan (2010) observed that play activities are performed voluntarily (not driven by a "serious" purpose) and people feel the desire to continue playing because they experience good feelings. These authors also stated these activities prompt people to improvise and experiment creatively, which makes these individuals less focused on themselves and more concentrated on the activities. These specialists concluded that playful activities help people develop new connections in their brains which are valuable for dealing effectively with challenging circumstances; these authors wisely observed that play acts like a fertiliser for brain growth.

When people relate to stakeholders in a more playful manner, they avoid being overly formal with them, when not needed. Playful people tend to connect to others in a more personal and genuine manner, beyond any social masks or work roles. Besides, playful people aim to develop more constructive and co-operative relationships with other stakeholders, where each part can contribute with their unique talents and skills. These playful individuals are more willing to engage in exploratory and unstructured conversations with others in order to debate relevant topics from fresher and more creative perspectives.

Nobel (2012) observed that when people relate to others in a playful manner, work and business activities tend to become more productive and creative. Dodgson and Gann (2018) observed that the adoption of an explorative attitude tends to be relevant for business activities, especially when a company faces uncertain or complex circumstances. These authors also stated that "play at work brings progress, enhances our humanity and adds to the distinctiveness of what we can contribute as humans compared to machines."

Bolton and Houlihan (2009) stated that playful activities can increase a person's morale and prompt this individual to act in a more joyous and energetic way. People who adopt a playful attitude to others are less prone to respond in a defensive way. It is important to remember that when in a defensive mode called the fight-freeze-flight response, people cannot fully harness their innermost discerning and creative skills.

In IDEO, which is a consultancy and design company, people are open to performing playful activities. For instance, at its New York office, on Thursdays at lunch time, employees gather together for some fun activities, like writing haiku poems in groups, aromatic finger painting, and blind contour drawing. These activities prompt employees to adopt a playful attitude, and let their hair down (Fosslien and Duffy, 2019).

As a consequence of the aforementioned benefits, it is important that companies aim to develop more playful interactions with their main stakeholders. Some examples of questions a company's employees should frequently ask themselves to relate to other stakeholders more playfully are:

- How can we perform this specific activity in a more fun manner?
- How can we engage with this stakeholder in a more playful manner?
- What type of non-business activities can be performed with this stakeholder?
- What are different ways to add value to others while being playful?
- What business accomplishments can be celebrated in a fun manner?

Some examples of playful activities can be informal conversations and non-business meals, among others. Sometimes, companies organise relaxing retreats for employees, as an example of a fun activity. These organisations seriously consider these playful activities because they know that they prompt people to replenish their vital energy and help them become more efficient in their business activities. Oftentimes, these playful activities also foster a spirit of connection, belonging, and togetherness, especially when they involve the participation of others.

Playfulness can help a company's people adopt a more detached view of business activities. A story shared by Brown and Vaughan (2010) will illustrate this point clearly. According to this story, a CEO met employees at an all-staff meeting to talk about the company's negative outcomes. At the beginning, the CEO blamed himself for this negative performance; afterwards, this man asked attendees to look for foam darts placed under their seats.

Then this individual asked the attendees to shoot those darts at him. As soon as employees started shooting darts, the energy of the room lifted from gloom to glee. After this, the CEO proceeded to explain how future outcomes could be improved, and employees were more open to taking these recommendations on board. In this example, the playful interaction enabled attendees to perceive negative outcomes less dramatically.

There is another interesting example to pinpoint. Udacity, a company that offers online training courses, organises events (Fancy Fridays or after-hours recess) for its employees so that these staff members can have fun, as well as strengthen their bonds with others. At these events, employees can develop camaraderie and brighten their relationships with their colleagues (Anjos, 2022).

There are a few things which people working for a company can do to adopt a more playful attitude. As seen, people working for a company can organise playful events (contests, social dinners, etc.) on a regular basis. As mentioned, organisations can also set up the workplace in ways which allow fun activities to naturally unfold, for example, with board games or darts. In addition, a company can look for examples of other organisations with playful activities in order to emulate them. These companies can belong to the sector, or different industries. Lastly, a company can also set specific policies that foster playfulness (e.g., scheduling regular time for playful activities at work).

7.5.4 Playfulness and Laughing

> Those who approach life like a child playing a game, moving and pushing pieces, possess the power of kings.
>
> **Heraclitus**

Martin (2006) has observed that humour is a type of mental play, where unrelated thoughts and ideas are mixed up in non-traditional ways. The use of light-hearted and non-offensive humour is a good way to lighten interactions with others. Witty humour makes people feel more comfortable and at ease, especially during stressful circumstances. Good jokes have some incoherence in their scripts, oftentimes crowned by an unexpected punchline, which creates a powerful binding effect among people.

De Bono (1977) observed that humour is a valuable tool which is life-enhancing and accessible to anyone. This author also observed that humour is against any form of solemnity and arrogance, which are so common in business and work environments. Besides, the use of humour contributes to an overall state of well-being and helps develop smoother interactions with others. Ehrenreich (2006) concluded that some people feel naturally compelled to share their joy with others, which strengthens their relationships among them. However, oftentimes, people avoid using humour at work as they fear that their jokes will not be pertinent or they will not be perceived as professional or business-like.

Psychologically speaking, humour can be considered a mental defence mechanism, which people use to convey unpleasant ideas or emotions to others in an ingenious and pleasurable manner. These defence mechanisms are mental subconscious responses usually activated when a person has unpleasant thoughts or feelings (for instance, unacceptable, threatening, or antisocial) that the individual refuses to acknowledge in a proper manner.

Zander and Zander (2002) observed that "humour and laughter can bring us together around our inescapable foibles, confusions and miscommunications, and especially over the ways in which we find ourselves acting entitled and demanding, or putting other people down, or flying at each other's throats." Humour can also be considered an astute way to cope with the tediousness and routine sometimes related to work and business activities; it can also help people put challenging situations into perspective.

On a similar note, Ramanchadran and Blakeslee (1999) observed that jokes have the function of trivialising troublesome situations, by pretending that they do not have any real impact. These authors also concluded that humour helps distract people from anxious states, prompting them to turn off their defensive responses. According to Brown and Vaughan (2010), jokes "are the minimally invasive surgery of a relationship" and they added that jokes "penetrate to a deep entry level without leaving an entry wound." The reader can find below some of the positive effects of laughter on individuals:

■ Some studies have concluded that laughter not only creates the opportunity to share glee with others, but also to strengthen bonds with them. Laughter can also help people de-dramatise challenging situations and make them less frightening; complex circumstances seem more approachable and solvable.

- Laughter warms people's hearts because of its noticeable relaxing effect; people become less stressed and more revitalised. The appeasing effect of laughter helps people become more at ease with others and develop a deeper rapport with them.
- Gamon and Bragdon (2002) observed that laughter brings about benefits to the immune system and lowers stress levels. Goleman (1996) observed that laughter prompts people to fully harness their reflective, creative, and critical skills.
- Claflin (1998) observed that laughter increases the heart rate and blood pressure, dissipates any tension, and improves the working of the immune system. This author stated that when people laugh, they get a "mini-workout" for their body and brain.
- When people are engaged in laughter and are in a good mood, they are more likely to widen their views and consider a broader range of alternatives to approach current situations.
- Laughter has a therapeutic and cathartic effect on human interactions, which is very relevant during times of conflict. In other words, laughing is prone to brush away nervousness in people, making them less prone to adopt an adversarial attitude towards one another.

The use of humour makes the business environment less formal and more humane. People working for a company should use humour with their main stakeholders in a respectful way, which means avoiding deprecating jokes. Koestler (1964) observed that good humour is generally based on the unexpected, the original, the exaggerated, or the implicit. In a similar vein, De Bono (2004) stated that "humour permits exaggeration and absurdity to make a serious point."

A good example of a company with a good sense of humour is Taco Bell, the American chain of fast-food restaurants. Oftentimes, this company uses light-hearted humour in its messages, especially on social media platforms. For example, in the past, this company engaged in a humorous Twitter exchange with Old Spice, the company which sells perfume products. In that virtual conversation, Old Spice – referring to Taco Bell – posted a witty tweet which said "What is that 'fire sauce' isn't made with any real fire? Seems like false advertising." In response to this message, Taco Bell posted a jocular tweet saying "@OldSpice Is your deodorant made with really old spices?" (Garber, 2012). Twitter has been rebranded to X.

Plester (2009) observed that the use of humour in the workplace can contribute to the development of affinity, cohesiveness, and camaraderie among work colleagues. Price and Price (2013) observed that people who experience positive emotions – for example, the ones stemming from laughter – tend to become more productive and resilient, especially when they face setbacks. According to Martin (2006), "research has also confirmed that humour in the workplace is correlated to better working relationships, greater job satisfaction and increased productivity." A research study conducted by Mesmer-Magnus et al. (2012) concluded that humour in the work environment is linked to reduced burnout, lower stress levels, and decreased work withdrawal.

Positive emotional states – for example, the ones stemming from laughter – tend to be contagious. Goleman (2006) observed that people have mirror neurons that replicate the emotional states of others; this phenomenon is called "emotional contagion." When a person experiences a positive emotion, other people around them are more likely to be "infected" by that emotional state. Hatfield et al. (2011) observed that the contagion originates in the mimicry of the others' body language (facial expression, gestures, etc.) which prompts their emotions to converge. Research has concluded that humour patterns at work, where the humour brings about more humour, generate more positive interactions among employees and enhanced performance, especially in workplaces where there is low job insecurity (Lehmann-Willenbrock and Allen, 2014).

The appropriate use of humour can warm the work and business environments. The use of occasional jocular anecdotes and light-hearted comments are very effective tools to disrupt any atmosphere of tension in these commonly formal environments. Moreover, Harrold (2007) observed that humour is a good tool to develop rapport with people. Oftentimes, small humorous comments can be used to "break the ice" between stakeholders who have not met previously.

Innocent, a company that was already mentioned, infuses humour in its workplace. In this company, the best employee is chosen each month. On these occasions, the chosen staff members will be gifted with a top hat or tiara for their "services to fruit." In addition, these employees will be given a special treat of their choice (Burn, 2022).

There is another important point to highlight. O'Quins and Derks (1999) stated that humour prompts people to be more relaxed and positive, less rigid in their thinking, and more open to assessing various alternatives for specific problems because of the incongruity of humour; in addition, humour brings about a more playful environment which fosters creativity. These authors also observed that when people are exposed to humour (e.g., jokes), they are more prone to approach problematic issues in more creative ways (developing unusual mental associations, etc.).

The following is another good example of the use of humour in business mentioned by Aaker and Bagdonas (2020). When Spanx (a company which sells shapeware products) started up, its founder and former CEO faced some challenges in persuading the main retailers to buy these items of clothing, which at that moment were unknown. This entrepreneur rang these retailers, but none of them called her back. She then tried to grab the attention of these retailers in a non-traditional and jocular manner.

She put a new brand high heel shoe in a shoebox and posted this "gift" to each of these retailers. In each box, there was also a handwritten note which said, "Just trying to get my foot in the door. Can I have a few minutes of your time?" alongside her phone number. One of the retailers was grabbed by her humorous note and contacted her. A deal was closed with this retailer, which made her act with more aplomb with the rest of the retailers. One year later, the most relevant retailers were stocking Spanx's products.

In the airline sector, delivering safety announcements is considered a very monotonous but paramount task to be performed by flight attendants. Southwest Airlines' crew members introduce some humour into their safety announcements. For example, in one of the company's flights, a crew member said: "Pull the tab and the vest will self-inflate. For you overachievers you can blow on the tube and inflate it manually." The jokes used by crew members do not need prior approval by the company, as there is trust in these employees. However, when the airline industry faces challenging moments (e.g., plane crash), this company will remind staff members to be very sensitive (Sampson, 2019).

7.5.5 Smiling

Let us always meet each other with a smile, for the smile is the beginning of love.

Mother Teresa

In the business environment, smiling is a universal and inexpensive way of communicating with others. Every time a person smiles at another, a stronger sense of connection between them is developed. When people smile to others, they naturally tend to smile back. McLellan (1996) observed that a "smile is the lighting system of the face and the heating system of the heart." As in the case of laughter, smiling is contagious.

From the emotional perspective, smiling is an unmistakeable display of one's good mood. Smiling and laughing have a very powerful alchemic effect on interactions with others. When people smile (or laugh) with others, any negative emotional state is temporarily cast aside. In other words, people cannot experience a negative emotion (anger, fear, etc.) and smile (or laugh) at the same time. Some psychological schools of thought assert that when people put a smile on their faces willingly, this gesture releases hormones that prompt their mood to improve.

From the sociological perspective, smiling is a sign of friendliness or non-aggression. When a person genuinely smiles at strangers, their natural defensive responses tend to be turned off. From the communicational standpoint, smiling is a fundamental key to open up a more natural and meaningful conversation. When people smile during a conversation, the rapport between them is improved. Consequently, in the business environment, people should smile more frequently and authentically to develop a livelier connection with others.

Experts in body language agree that honest smiles always involve all the face muscles, while an artificial smile only includes the lower part of the face. In the case of inauthentic smiles, the lips tend to be stretched sideways, as compared with honest smiles where lips are naturally pulled upwards. An inauthentic smile seems calculating and dishonest and makes people look less trustworthy. Most people recognise a fake type of smile when being approached by those who intend to try to force them to buy a product or service.

Research has shown that when employees smile at customers alongside making direct eye contact with them, this body language tends to bring a more positive emotional response from these customers than if this employee smiles with indirect eye contact, or if this employee makes direct eye contact without smiling at all (Li et al., 2018). These findings highlight the importance of smiling at people and making direct eye contact with them.

In another research study, servers at a cocktail lounge who displayed a broad smile (mouth corners up showing front teeth) obtained significantly larger tips from customers, as compared with the tips received by waitresses who showed minimal smiles (mouth corners up without showing teeth). In this study, customers whose servers showed broader smiles also displayed more frequent departure smiles, as compared with those whose servers displayed minimal smiles (Tidd and Lockard, 1978).

The Ritz-Carlton, the hotel chain, was mentioned previously. At this company, employees apply the 10/5 rule. This means that if an employee walks within 10 feet of another person, for example, in any area to the hotel's premises, this staff member will make eye contact and smile. If the employee walks within 5 feet of another person, this employee will greet them with a "hello." In some hospitals, staff (medics, nurses and other employees) have been trained to voluntarily use the 10/5 rule. As a consequence of this training, people had more positive work experiences in those places. Moreover, some patients reciprocated and smiled in return. In general, people in those hospitals became more satisfied just because of the application of the 10/5 rule (Achor, 2013; Talavera, 2021).

Questions for Self-Reflection

- How can I adopt a more generous and grateful attitude towards our company's stakeholders?
- How can I collaborate with our stakeholders on a regular basis?
- How can forgiveness improve the work and business environments?
- How can I introduce more humour and playfulness at the workplace?

Chapter 8

Natural Conversations with Stakeholders

8.1 The Need for More Natural Conversations

> The first principle in good communication is to treat the other person as a neighbour. Look them in the eye ... and make real contact with them as sharing our human situation.

Godfrey Howard

> We don't need more "professionalism" in our workplaces. Instead, we need more of ourselves, and more human connection – especially as in-person meetings are replaced by video chats and more relationships are sustained entirely by email. Often, all it takes is a hint of levity to shift a moment, or a relationship, from transactional and robotic to relational and authentic.

Jennifer Aaker and Naomi Bagdonas

Clear, complete, truthful, and meaningful communication represents a very important resource in the business and work environments. This type of communication has a positive impact on companies' economic results. The opposite is true; communication problems can affect companies' performance negatively. Communication capabilities are part of what is known as soft skills and help people relate to one another in a more effective manner.

There is an increasing use of technology for communication, for example, emailing, social media, text messaging, and video conferencing, among others. In most cases, technology makes contact with other people easier, which lures most companies to these technological advancements. Honoré (2004) also observed that "technology made it possible to do everything more quickly" and, as a consequence, people are "expected to think faster, work faster, talk faster, read faster, write faster, eat faster, move faster," which is counterproductive for meaningful and authentic communication.

The use of technology often makes the communication process colder and more depersonalised, as compared, for example, with face-to-face interactions. According to Hallowell (1999a),

                                   DOI: 10.4324/9781003372684-10

when people use technological devices, they tend to feel more disconnected from one another because there is no "human moment" of real contact between them. Hallowell (1999b) also observed that in these human moments, people are fully present, pay close attention, and display sincere and heartfelt interest in one another; without these moments, people are prone to be more preoccupied about their tasks.

Hogg and Vaughan (2002) observed that the use of some technological devices for communication purposes presents other disadvantages, such as lack of body language and suppression of the amount of information exchanged by the participants. This is especially evident in the use of emails, and text messages. In a similar vein, Locke (1998) observed that computer-mediated communications flatten participants' self-expression. Oftentimes, this communication technology is purposefully used by companies to make the interaction more formal and less impersonal. However, with the widespread use of video-conferencing (Zoom, etc.), people can communicate with each other, while displaying some aspects of their body language (facial expression, etc.).

Schrage (1990) stated that the use of technological devices for communication purposes focuses more on the transmission of the message than on facilitating the understanding between the sender and the receiver. This can be observed in the use of emails or text messages, which can sometimes bring about misunderstandings. This author also observed that the use of technological instruments for communication purposes does not encourage collaboration between people because they passively share an experience, instead of actively creating one. However, over the last years, there is a widespread use of virtual meetings (Zoom, etc.) and applications like Sharepoint, Slack, and others, which allow people to collaborate in various work projects.

According to Ong (1982), many companies prevalently use the pipeline model for their internal and external communication. This is a one-way communication model in which one participant (e.g., a manager) sends chunks of information (directives, orders, deadlines, etc.) to another participant (e.g., employees). Oftentimes, these messages are insufficiently contextualised to be understood in an accurate way. This widespread and practical model leaves aside valuable real interactions between the participants. The use of some technological devices (e.g., email, text messages, etc.) is very suitable for the application of the pipeline model.

Keegan (2015) observed that "when communication is important, delicate and potentially ambiguous, you cannot beat face-to-face communication." Personal interactions are superior to other forms of communication because they allow people to obtain instantaneous feedback from others and express their emotions overtly. Lobel (2014) observed that face-to-face conversations make people feel close, not only physically, but also emotionally, creating a more empathetic connection between them. The CEO of Allianz Global Corporate & Specialty (AGCS) Canada, a corporate insurer, actively endorses and bolsters face-to-face conversations. This business leader observed that engaging in face-to-face exchanges with colleagues is often the most effective way to resolve conflictive issues (Schawbel, 2018). As mentioned previously, over the last years, companies are increasingly using virtual meetings (Zoom, etc.) for some of their business exchanges.

Personal communication is more expressive because it includes verbal language (words) and also body language (tone of voice, gestures, posture, etc.), which makes it less prone to misunderstandings. Some technology, like emails and text messages, does not reproduce this level of expressiveness. Therefore, a company's people should always attempt to establish contact with its stakeholders in the most direct manner, whenever possible. For instance, personal meetings and conversations on the phone should be preferred over emails or letters. For many companies, the use of video conferencing (Zoom, etc.) is an interesting option as well.

Virgin Media takes its internal communication, which entails exchanges between staff members, as one of its main priority business factors. This organisation stated that regular connection among employees is a paramount factor for the company's success. As a consequence, this company aims to enhance its internal communication, by switching from more traditional ways of communication among employees (emailing, long-form content, etc.) towards open conversations, alongside videos and live content (Newson, 2021).

8.2 Business Formalities and Natural Conversations

Life is a conversation with the world around us and within us.

Simon Parke

Humans have already changed the world several times by changing the way they had conversations.

Theodore Zeldin

Ong (1982) observed that natural conversations allow people to have more close-knit communion, as compared with written communication, which is more distancing and disengaged. It is important to pinpoint that in the business environment, a great part of the communication is written. According to the aforementioned author, written communication is sequential, with closure but no clear context, where the recipient is often absent and fictionalised.

This specialist concluded that, in contrast, natural conversations are "empathetic and participatory rather than objectively distanced," and that there is "real speech and thought" that "exist essentially in a context of give-and-take between real persons." Carlson (1999) observed that in natural conversations, people tend to become more positive, generous, trusting, nurturing, and honest. People who engage in natural conversations are more open and spontaneous because they feel comfortable with being themselves, as they truly are.

In Honda, the prestigious car manufacturing company, they believe that some tools like email and social media are relevant for communication purposes, but these tools can also be difficult to respond to, as well as cumbersome. In this company, face-to-face conversations are considered the easiest and most vital communication tools, as they allow people to understand each other more easily (Honda, 2022).

There is another relevant point to highlight. According to Zeldin (2000), conversations are joint enterprises and humbling experiences where minds meet, and facts are exchanged and reshaped, bringing about new trains of thoughts. Angell and Rizkallah (2004) observed that these interactions aim to co-ordinate and maintain relationships with others. These authors also stated that business conversations create structure because of the way a company manages its own resources, which includes "dividing up work tasks, creating business goals, and establishing levels of authority." All these tasks are co-ordinated through human interactions.

In the business environment, there is a myriad of formalities which oftentimes hinder the communication process, making conversations structured, distant, and cold. These business conversations do not play out flowingly; they are rigid and unnatural. Consequently, these interactions only help people connect on a superficial level.

For example, in traditional conversations between a company and its suppliers, the most significant topics tend to be the commercial conditions (price, quality, specifications, etc.) of the transactions between both companies. Any personal aspects related to the individuals engaged in these conversations (their personal preferences, values, etc.) are purposefully left aside. These non-business topics are considered "irrelevant" for companies' transactions.

Another example can illustrate the previous point more clearly. In the workplace, employees mostly talk to others about topics related to their organisation, such as work tasks to undertake, relevant deadlines to meet, main goals to achieve, projects in progress, and others. Informal topics unrelated to the company's activities are not discussed because employees are only acknowledged from the perspective of their work roles. Other relevant topics related to employees beyond their work positions (other roles of employees, for instance, as friends, parents, siblings, etc.) are left aside in most companies' conversations.

In traditional conversations, blue-collar employees are prone to be acknowledged regarding their manual skills. White-collar personnel are more prone to be acknowledged for their rational aspects. None of these business conversations recognise employees as whole human beings with several dimensions, such as emotional, spiritual, physical, and mental aspects.

Work and business roles are predetermined, fixed, and encapsulated categories, which never fully represent the wholeness of the valuable human beings behind them. In the same vein, Rogers (1961) stated that people are always more than their roles because these very people are intrinsically fluid and living. This prestigious author observed that a person is a "changing constellation of potentialities, not a fixed quantity of traits." In a similar way, Maslow (1965) observed that workers prefer to be whole, utilising all their capacities, not just an instrument or a "hand" in the workplace.

In work and business environments, people continually enact their roles, which makes them feel separate from others. According to Goffman (1969), people play their work roles in a coherent and homogeneous manner, showing the unequivocal signs of these roles, which are intended to be believed by others. These roles have specific ways of expressing and behaving, which are intrinsically limiting. Consequently, this author observed that, when people play their roles, they are prone to suppress heartfelt feelings and impulses to avoid showing their "all-too-human selves," so they can be accepted by other people. Argyle (1994) observed that people comply with their roles because these roles are interlocked with those performed by the other individuals who they interact with. Mirivel (2014) observed that these roles are enacted in moments of communication exchanges, as these roles are dependent on the ways people talk to each other.

However, natural conversations empower people to go beyond these social masks in order to show themselves as they truly are. Johnstone (1987) observed that "masks are surrounded by rituals that reinforce their power." In other words, every time people "wear" these social masks, they act and speak in an unnatural manner and their conversations become ritualised and structured. This is a very common trait of most traditional business conversations.

These masks often result in people communicating with others in a manufactured, rigid, and unfeeling manner. People's true expressiveness lies concealed behind these social façades. However, when people hold natural conversations, they drop these masks and become more aware of their shared humanness, which prompts them to interrelate in a more expansive and meaningful manner. In simple words, natural conversations bring people much closer.

A person can never be entirely defined by their business role (employee, buyer, supplier, etc.). Natural conversations prompt people to show themselves beyond their roles and functions. Carlson (1999) stated that natural conversations always put the human side of people first, and the role second, which makes people feel that they are treated like human beings. Natural conversations leave aside unnecessary formalities to make interactions more real and meaningful. This type of interaction has a more horizontal approach, which means that participants are perceived at the same level, rather than within a hierarchical (vertical) structure.

From the linguistic perspective, the specific traits of the relationship between people engaged in a conversation are implied in the specific words and body language (gestures, tone of voice, etc.) used by them during that interaction. For example, when a boss and an employee hold conversations, the former is more prone to use a more directive tone of voice and more commanding words over the latter than the other way around. In natural conversations, participants tend to use non-directive words and body language, which implies the connection between two human beings in equal conditions, beyond roles, functions, or aspects of status.

In Honda, the renowned car manufacturer, employees hold frequent informal and unstructured meetings, called Waigaya – which means hubbub or noisy meetings. In these meetings, hierarchy is not taken into consideration. In these agenda-free conversations, all employees are considered equals, as they engage in conversations about topics and ideas in a free-flowing manner. In this type of unplanned conversations, all ideas are welcome and disagreements among participants are perceived as fruitful. All participants can express their ideas openly. There are no silly questions or topics in these conversations. Some meetings can extend for a significant period of time (Honda, 2022; Rothfeder, 2014).

There is another important point to highlight. As previously seen, traditional business conversations fail to embrace the participants' human side and their complex and unique experiences because these interactions only cover narrow business topics related to their roles. Natural conversations instead include both business and informal topics. Sometimes, natural conversations can be solely based on personal topics, such as interests, preferences, hobbies, pastimes, family topics, and others, without including any business topic.

Natural conversations acknowledge the fact that each individual has a unique set of values, dreams, preferences, emotions, and expectations. In other words, natural conversations do not have a one-dimensional perspective, as in the case of most traditional business conversations, because participants are considered in a more complete and integral manner, beyond their specific functional role (employee, supplier, customer, etc.).

People who engage in natural conversations can overtly express their needs, values, and dreams. People can be authentic and show their human side, without any fear of being judged by others. These individuals do not feel obligated to "edit" their messages, as commonly happens in most traditional business conversations.

People working for a company should have frequent natural conversations with internal stakeholders (other employees) and external ones (suppliers, customers, etc.). These conversations should include, when possible, both business topics and non-business ones. Natural conversations create a deeper connection between all the people involved and also strengthen their relationships. These conversations also tend to have a positive impact on a company's performance indicators, such as productivity, quality levels, and customer satisfaction.

8.3 Assumptions in Business Conversations

When you're authentic, you create aliveness and excitement. People instantly tune into you and find you interesting. Sanitised and predictable speaking on the other hand, whether unconscious or deliberate, cuts off connection and creates boredom, disappointment and even mistrust.

Judy Apps

All relationships, including business ones, are the result of a series of conversations. Therefore, the destiny of these relationships is mostly affected by the quality of these interactions. In natural conversations, people put aside their own assumptions about others. Assumptions about other people include an overarching set of aspects, such as status, level of intelligence, and character. Oftentimes, assumptions about other people mislead the communication process with them.

These assumptions are like screens which cloud people's perception regarding others; therefore, these assumptions have a powerful impact on the communication process. Oftentimes, these assumptions are fragmentary, and also false or unfounded. When people can purposely leave their own assumptions aside, their connection with others becomes more humane and genuine.

Some great philosophers like Descartes observed that people should cast aside preconceptions to gather a true knowledge of reality (Buckingham et al., 2011). Outstanding psychologists like Rogers (1961) stated that flexibility and openness to the communicational experience and unconditional acceptance of one another allow participants to enjoy their interactions more fully. In other words, people are more open and flexible when they drop their assumptions about others.

When engaging in conversations, people can discover their own assumptions regarding others by asking themselves a simple question like "What am I assuming about this person?" This type of question creates more awareness regarding assumptions about others. At the same time, this question facilitates the process of leaving these assumptions aside.

Another relevant question people can ask themselves is: "How can I perceive this person from an innocent and childlike perspective?" The insights via this question can help a person forsake his own assumptions about others in order to perceive them in a more unpolluted manner. This question also helps people connect with the essence of others, their human side.

When a person can perceive others free from these rigid mental labels, the communication process becomes more natural and spontaneous. In those cases, the person can discuss with others relevant topics in a flowing and engaging manner. People who drop their assumptions develop a deeper level of rapport with others because they can go beyond what is apparent.

As mentioned previously, in these informal meetings held at Honda, called Waigaya, there is an important assumption: hierarchy is unheeded. Consequently, at these unplanned conversations, all staff members are considered equals, regardless of their role in the company. In these conversations, all participants are encouraged to express their views in an open and unrestrained manner. The views of all participant are valuable; none of these views is better than others (Honda, 2022; Rothfeder, 2014). In this example, this valuable assumption helps improve the communication process. The impact of assumptions on relationships was thoroughly explained in Chapter 6.

8.4 Connecting to Employees in a Natural Way

Words are windows, or they're walls.

Ruth Bebermeyer

In the work environment, typical conversations have covert aspects of power (for instance, company's hierarchical levels) embedded in them. These aspects make conversations in the workplace intrinsically hierarchical and imbalanced (for example, superior–subordinate). In the workplace, people tend to enact their specific work roles in a full and automatic manner.

As seen previously, employees' continuous role-playing hinders the development of a deeper connection between them. In many conversations, roles stand up as borders between people, which hampers their real connection. For example, when a manager talks to a subordinate, the distance and respect for each other's role make the conversation excessively formal, cold, and impersonal. In most cases, if an employee dares to engage with a manager in a more casual and unstructured way, these attempts are often deemed to indicate a lack of respect towards the hierarchical organisational structure.

As a consequence, most conversations in the workplace are far from being natural. Countless formalities (policies, procedures, etc.) pervading these conversations override any chance of people being spontaneous and connecting with each other in an authentic fashion. In the workplace, but also in business environments, conversations are affected by these hindrances. In extreme cases, conversations become mechanical and dehumanised, resembling interactions between blind automatons.

As seen previously, typical work conversations tend to avoid acknowledging participants' human side. Employees focus on important work tasks during their work time, but they also have other relevant aspects affecting their lives (family, relationships, health, etc.) which are never considered to be relevant topics in work conversations. Nonetheless, these personal aspects always play out silently but relentlessly in the background of employees' minds. Moreover, these personal affairs usually affect employees' performance, in most cases, unknowingly.

"Does this mean that employees should only talk about non-business topics?" Not necessarily. There should be a fair balance between organisational topics (deadlines, company objectives, projects, etc.) and non-business ones (emotions, values, preferences, beliefs, habits, etc.).

HubSpot is a renowned developer of software for sales, inbound marketing, and customer service. This is an example of a company where employees can engage in conversations about non-business topics. Staff members are prone to adopt an exploring attitude during live chats with its customers, which often include varying non-commercial topics. For example, in one of these live chats, a sales team member engaged in a conversation with a customer, which included non-business topics, like Star Wars movies, the Jedi (the main characters in those movies), and Spider-man (Bergstrom, 2021).

There is another relevant point to highlight. A simple way to hold more natural conversations in the workplace is to ask others their opinion about any non-business topics, such as sports, well-being, and others. When these non-business topics are included in chats, employees tend to become more engaged and connected to others. Most employees are very opinionated regarding these topics; these themes make these employees reflect on aspects of their humanity.

Therefore, these topics should never be restricted in the work or business environments. These topics are common in all natural conversations; they facilitate valuable interactions between real human beings who connect with one another in a borderless fashion.

8.5 Emotions in Business Conversations

> Organizations fear if people were to bring all of themselves to work – their moods, quirks, and weekend clothes – things will quickly dissolve into a mess.
>
> **Frederic Laloux**

From a psychological perspective, emotional states which are not expressed keep on running on a subconscious level, colouring people's perceptions, thoughts, and actions. Several experts advise people to express their emotional states, not to repress or suppress them. It is also recommended to observe one's emotional states without judging them as negative (sadness, anger) or positive (happiness, etc.). People who openly communicate their emotions to others are prone to experience a cathartic relief.

A natural conversation represents a safe context where people can share their authentic emotions, as a valuable part of their humanness. When people share their emotional states with others, a deeper rapport is developed between them; the latter will also feel compelled to open themselves up emotionally as well. This reciprocal opening of the participants contributes to the development of more meaningful and honest communicational experiences.

Most traditional business conversations are excessively rational and analytical, without including any emotional aspects. Some might argue that in most business conversations, individuals often ask others questions like "How are you?", which implies an indirect reference to the emotional aspects experienced by others.

Nonetheless, this type of question is often posed in a merely formal, ritualistic, and mechanical manner, not in an honest way. In other words, the person asking this question does not really intend to connect to another in deep and wholehearted manner. This question's objective is generally to look more sociable in the eyes of others, and not to connect to their human aspects.

Instead, a person who engages in natural conversations with others asks them how they feel, and really means it. In a natural conversation, emotions and other relevant human aspects are an essential part of the chat. When emotional aspects are integrated to conversations, these interactions become more personal and enriched.

In natural conversations, each participant is encouraged to openly express their thoughts, but also the emotions underpinning them. Instead, in most traditional business conversations, people are prone to repress or suppress most of their own emotional states. People use these self-censoring mechanisms to avoid looking vulnerable before other people, and also as a way to avoid being taken advantage of by them.

On an organisational level, research shows that there is a positive correlation between companies which are emotionally intelligent with stakeholders and high growth rates. These emotionally intelligent companies also add more value to stakeholders and outperform other organisations (Dentsu, 2022).

In natural conversations, participants' emotions provide the interaction with more substantial texture, meaning, and depth. In these conversations, people show themselves as real emotional beings, which makes them appear more human. These informal encounters gather two human beings in presence who are authentically interested in knowing more about each other's internal worlds.

Zak (2013) observed that when people share their vulnerable side with others, more trust between them is generated. In a similar vein, Hallowell (1999a) stated that, as a result of the emotions conveyed by the participants, these natural encounters have more lasting positive effects on them, such as increased trust, respect, and rapport.

Qantas is an example of a company where employees hold empathetic conversations with its customers. A woman was on holiday when she was told that her father had died in an accident. This grieving woman talked to employees working for Qantas airline, who understood her challenging situation and kindly and quickly got her on a flight back home. On that flight, a couple with a baby asked the lady to move to another seat, which made her feel enraged with these passengers. Despite this, the crew members made her flight very comfortable (Thackray, 2022).

These staff members listened to this woman attentively throughout the flight, as she tearily commented about her hard day. Besides, the crew members also treated her with red wine and gave her toddler food and snacks to make their flight more comfortable. Crew members also helped her disembark first on the arrival. This staff even arranged for her baggage to be taken out of the plane first, and her bags were already on the carousel as she and her child arrived. She was very appreciative for these crew members' kind gestures and their empathetic attitude (Thackray, 2022). In this example, staff members prompted this customer to express her emotions openly and listened to her attentively, which helped her deal with her issues more effectively.

8.6 Goal-Setting and Natural Conversations

> Human life has its own laws, one of which is: we must use things and love people.
>
> **John Powell**

In the business environment, most conversations are unnatural; they tend to be utterly goal-oriented. When talking to others, people have clear and rigid agendas on their minds to follow. These agendas can include, for instance, tasks to perform, projects to implement, deadlines to meet, and other business-related topics.

Agendas set for conversations are generally topic-oriented, not person-focused. Consequently, when a business conversation is based on specific agendas, this interaction tends to unfold in a colder and more formal manner. Traditional business conversations tend to be rigid and controlling, and the topics discussed by the participants do not come up spontaneously.

Oftentimes, an agenda makes people objectify others, which means considering them as specific means to achieve specific goals related to their own agenda. Instead, natural conversations flow because the topics analysed are not scripted; people do not aim to tick off predetermined topics from their personal lists.

Sometimes, people participating in a traditional business conversation show their agendas by proposing the topics of interest for the conversation. Other times, people have ulterior hidden motives, which make them subtly sway the conversation towards their own topics of interest.

Besides, many typical business conversations are held in a very limited time. This time limitation prompts people to focus exclusively on the topics related to their own agendas, which makes small-talk irrelevant. Some business conversations do not look like real dialogues, but complex entanglements of each participant's agendas.

As an example, the representatives of two different companies A and B are holding a business conversation. In a typical interaction, the representative of company A will consider the representative of the company B as a "means" to fulfil company A's objectives, and vice versa. The parties do not aim to know each other on a personal level, but to achieve their own goals. Instead, in natural conversations, the other person is never perceived as a means to an end, but as an end itself. Natural conversations aim to explore the human side of others and strengthen relationships with them.

Traditional business conversations have a utilitarian approach; people interact to see what they can get from one another. Instead, in natural conversations, people are not determined to obtain anything from others, but to know others better. In these conversations, the topics to discuss often roll off in a spontaneous and unrehearsed manner, as the result of dynamic interactions between the participants. People are fully immersed in meaningful dialogues, where personal ideas and stories are articulated and amalgamated in an unstructured manner. These conversations are likened to jam sessions performed by the musicians of a jazz band, who "talk" to each other with their instruments in an unrehearsed manner.

In natural conversations, each person is genuinely curious about one another. When people hold these types of chats, people discuss topics in an experimental and open-minded manner, and not in a definite, directive, or absolute way. Grice (1989) observed that in these interactions, people can make relevant contributions to one another, when required, according to the orientation of the conversation.

As previously seen, in Honda, there are some unplanned, open, and formless meetings called Waigaya, where all employees are entitled to give their views, voice their opinions, and disagree with others in an informal and unstructured manner. These agenda-free meetings can be held in different forms; they can last 30 minutes or sometimes they can go on for several weeks. Even though these shapeless meetings might seem an ineffective use of resources, these gatherings often bring about enhanced productivity, as well as improved process and systems, and higher performance. Some of these meetings end up bringing insightful ideas for the development of valuable products (Honda, 2022; Rothfeder, 2014).

8.7 Natural Conversations and Mutual Exploration

We share the same biology regardless of ideology.

Sting

Natural conversations are dynamic and generative; the main purpose of these encounters is to explore each other's views in a non-adversarial manner. This type of interaction is always open-ended, which means that there is uncertainty about how it will unfold. During these conversations, a person can propose a topic considered of great value and interest and the other person can engage with it or not, or even change it.

Natural conversations are co-constructed by participants, with no one controlling the interaction. Senge (1990) observed that, in these conversations, people are willing to drop their own assumptions to observe their own thoughts and others', and also grasp a deeper understanding of the topics discussed. Participants drop assumptions about one another and also assumptions about how the conversation should develop. People also avoid drawing preliminary conclusions regarding topics in progress, which makes the conversation more insightful and meaningful and less constraining.

In natural conversations, people are more prone to find some common aspects (preferences, values, hobbies, places visited, things learned, etc.) with each other. Research has observed that when people engage in conversations and find commonalities between them, these interactions tend to have a higher engagement and a deeper rapport. In other words, when people find common factors between them, they feel more connected to one another.

Johnson (1997) observed that, in authentic conversations, each participant willingly comments about their ideas, emotional states, and experiences, which is called reciprocal self-disclosure. In other words, natural conversations are made up of personal and revealing comments, including negative experiences, which create an enhanced sense of intimacy and trust between the participants.

Locke (1998) observed that self-disclosure is more prone to happen upwardly in a hierarchical structure. This author explained that "in a corporate life an employee is far more likely to divulge personal facts about himself to an immediate superior than the superior is to reveal intimacies to his subordinates." Nonetheless, in natural conversations, all participants feel spontaneously encouraged to use self-disclosure with others, regardless of business or work roles.

From the psychological perspective, when people disclose their personal experiences to others, the latter tend to like the former more. Lieberman (2001) observed that people who share their feelings about their negative experiences to others prompt the latter to act in a reciprocal manner, which creates a more trusting bond between them.

Schafer (2015) has observed that self-disclosure generates more attraction in others if the comments have an emotional base, rather than factual, and are specific rather than general. However, this author stated that if a person makes comments which are too intimate, especially when they are early in a relationship, this individual is perceived as less likeable in the eyes of others. An author like Mirivel (2014) observed that self-disclosing, when it is authentic and personal, "has a range of positive functions for the person who is disclosing, including improving well-being, mood, and physical and mental health"; besides, "disclosure fosters connection, intimacy and cohesiveness."

As seen previously, the employee working for HubSpot was not adopting a rigid attitude towards the customer. In other words, this employee did not engage in a traditional conversation with this customer to sell the company's products. Instead, their conversation was more focused on the customer's personal likes and preferences, like Spider-man, Star Wars movies, and the Jedis.

8.8 Natural Conversations and Comfort

Most work and business environments have an accelerated pace and tend to be time-is-money orientated. In these environments, there are some common practices, such as overworking, continuous busyness, multiple deadlines, multitasking, and time-management practices, which make people behave in a hurried and unreflective manner and pursue tasks as something to be ticked off from a list.

Consequently, most traditional business conversations are rushed, especially when organisations have plenty of things on their plates. In most companies, time is considered a precious resource, which should never be wasted on non-priority topics or trivial issues. Most companies are continually constrained by various tight deadlines, which, in turn, limits interactions with others in the work and business environments. In these cases, personal conversations are only held when absolutely necessary.

This time limitation also constrains the length of personal encounters, which prevents people from expressing their ideas fully. These rushed conversations make people feel pressurised and uncomfortable; their need for expression is severely curtailed. In hectic environments, casual or informal conversations are considered a waste of time, and sometimes, plain diversions from the process of achieving a company's objectives. Consequently, these "idle" conversations are strongly discouraged, sometimes in a very subtle manner.

Most dictionaries define the term "slow" with negative connotations such as "sluggish," "dull," "laggard," and others. Honoré (2004) stated that "fast is busy, controlling, aggressive, hurried, analytical, superficial, impatient, active, quantity-over-quality." This author also observed that natural conversations have a slower pace; slow is "calm, careful, receptive, still, intuitive, unhurried, patient, reflective, quality-over-quantity." From this author's perspective, a slower pace allows people to make "real and meaningful connections." In these conversations, people place no restraints on their interactions because they are willing to experience these conversations fully, without rushing them.

Natural conversations can be mindfully savoured and reflected on because people are not pushed by any time pressure. Arnold and Plas (1993) observed that "when people take the time to share a joke or a cup of coffee, to pause, think, share and truly listen, trust starts to build." These authors wisely concluded that any time people invest in being more human with others is always well invested.

In natural conversations, the participants can have different opinions on a topic. In those cases, they are inclined to use sentences like "It is interesting to know your specific view on this topic … I feel that this can also be perceived in this way … (exposing the speaker's own view)" or "I understand your perspective on this and I have an alternative viewpoint on this topic, which is …." These sentences are delivered in a calm and friendly tone of voice.

In these conversations, the participants never express their own positions on a topic in an aggressive manner, but treat each other with kindness. These individuals adopt a loving attitude with one another because they each want the other to feel comfortably acknowledged. Therefore, any comments are warmly welcomed, never judged.

Some adversarial sentences like "Your view is wrong because …" or "I know what you said is not right …" tend to disconnect people and prompt them to adopt a defensive mode (fight-freeze-flight). In natural conversations, this type of sentence is avoided, because subtle or overt confrontation creates friction and disrupts the flow of the interaction.

In natural conversations, people do not seek approval or acceptance from others – they feel comfortable showing themselves as they truly are. In these conversations, people also feel comfortable with the analysis of an overarching range of topics, which go from external aspects (facts, news, trends, etc.) to internal ones (their own experiences, challenges, desires, etc.).

Consequently, in natural conversations, people tend to adopt a more open-minded attitude, which make them more likely to find commonalities with others as human beings (moments of tribulation, hard challenges, hopes and dreams, etc.), instead of things separating them. These conversations are more alive because people can express themselves fully. Participants are empowered to break free from any rigid structures which hamper traditional conversations.

In this chapter, there are some examples of natural conversations held in companies like Honda and HubSpot. In these organisations, people regularly engage in conversations with its stakeholders in a free and spontaneous manner. In these exchanges, topics can be explored in an unrestrained and unstructured manner.

8.9 Natural Conversations and Active Listening

> Seek first to understand; then to be understood.
>
> **Stephen Covey**

The majority of people tends to be self-centred most of the time; their main focus is on themselves, not others. Instead, in natural conversations, each person is also focused on the other; when a participant talks, the other listens mindfully. People who listen to each other actively tend to fully enjoy the encounter.

Warren (2002) observed that giving undivided attention to others is always an act of love. This author also stated that active listeners concentrate so intently on the speaker that they totally forget themselves. In other words, active listening makes people less self-conscious and more connected to others.

An active listener shows natural interest in what others say, to understand their states of mind and feelings. This individual considers others' ideas enriching because valuable things can be learned from them. When this person shows interest in others, this individual connects to them on a deeper level. These listeners adopt a generous attitude towards others; they do not try to get anything from others, but give them their attention. Research has stated that when participants listen to each other attentively, more trust is generated (Ramsey and Sohi, 1997).

An active listener acts like a sounding board which helps speakers articulate and elaborate their message with more clarity and depth. Some authors like Ray and Myers (1989) observed that a person should always listen to others as if this individual was a therapist, willing to discover what is relevant to them, without judging them. Besides, speakers who are given undivided attention tend to feel as if they were the most relevant voice to be heard, which positively contributes to their self-esteem and confidence. Metaphorically speaking, this listener acts like a movie maker who purposely directs the filming lights and cameras on the other person. From this perspective, the speaker is considered the main "protagonist" on the communication stage set.

An active listener is fully present, which means that this person is centred on the now, avoiding any distracting thoughts about the past or future. The listener is not trying to guess what the speaker is about to say next. Instead, the listener is totally absorbed and engrossed in the speaker's message, which is the most important thing at that moment. This also means that the listener avoids multitasking (reading, taking calls, etc.) during the interaction. Some authors like Tuckle (2015) have observed that, even when a mobile phone is nearby, people tend to engage in a more superficial conversation and their attention becomes less engaged.

In most traditional business conversations, active listening is not possible because people are continually pressurised by multiple deadlines, policies, procedures, and processes. These people have an impending sense of urgency to achieve organisational goals, which prevents them from listening to others in a mindful manner.

Instead, in natural conversations, even though people have priorities to focus on and objectives to achieve, they allow themselves to be more patient and listen to others actively in order to connect to them more deeply. Moreover, these individuals enthusiastically encourage others to express their ideas fully and openly.

Besides, an active listener is never anxious about providing the speaker with responses, advice, or suggestions. This type of listener is patient, relaxed, and calm when others are speaking and avoids interrupting their train of thought. The active listener is never interested in blaming, criticising, or arguing with the speaker. This listener acknowledges the message conveyed, in a kind, warm, and respectful manner.

Rackspace is a company specialising in cloud infrastructure. In this company, employees listen to customers actively. For instance, at this company, an employee was advising a customer on the phone on how to solve several issues. This conversation was going on for an extensive period of time. During this chat, this staff member overheard this customer saying to someone nearby that she was hungry. As a consequence, this employee put this chat on hold and bought a pizza for this customer. This pizza was received by the customer, while she was still chatting on the phone with this employee. The customer was happily surprised by this employee's thoughtful gesture. This staff member thought that it was a good idea that this customer could have an energy boost until the issues were sorted out (Wellington, 2020).

8.10 Other Aspects of Active Listening

It is the province of knowledge to speak, and it is the privilege of wisdom to listen.

Oliver Wendell Holmes Sr.

Most people have overanalytical minds, crowded with agendas, expectations, and concerns, which prevent them from listening to others more actively. Carlson and Bailey (1998) observed that during a conversation, a person should slow down in order to fully experience others without being distracted by restless thoughts. Listeners who slow down become more attentive to what is being said by others and increase their understanding of it. To put it simply, active listeners tend to quieten their mental dialogue to focus only on the ideas expressed by others. Some techniques like deep breathing can help people calm down.

An active listener is always willing to know more about others and understand distinct views on different topics. This type of listener fully absorbs the messages conveyed by others and reflects on their ideas. This listener acts like a curious child who silently observes the world around and pays close attention to each of its details. Not only is an active listener attentive to the words expressed by others, but also their body language (tone of voice, gesture, movements, etc.).

An active listener tends to make frequent nods to non-verbally encourage speakers to deliver their ideas in a complete manner. These listeners also use regular eye contact and certain words ("aha," "hmm," etc.) to show their engrossment in the speaker's message. With these signals, the listener aims to satisfy the speaker's need to be fully heard.

When a person listens actively to another, the latter is more likely to listen to the former because of the principle of reciprocity. Cuddy (2016) observed that when a person listens actively to another, they can develop a more trusting bond. This author also concluded that an active listener is more inclined to provide others with useful suggestions based on what they previously said. Based on ideas previously delivered by others, this person can also ask them insightful questions about their interests, desires, and needs.

Richard Branson, the dynamic and charismatic leader behind Virgin Group, observed that, in business, people should listen more than they talk, as they cannot learn anything new from hearing themselves talk (Blaschka, 2019). This business leader always adopts an inquisitive attitude when he interacts with various stakeholders. As seen previously in this book, when this entrepreneur talks to any customer or employee, he listens to them attentively, and takes note on their insights on his notebook. Then, he reviews these notes and takes specific actions on them, when possible (Krapivin, 2018).

8.11 Active Listening, Paraphrasing, Analogies, and Recaps

An authentic active listener also lets others finish their ideas and uses paraphrasing on a regular basis. People who paraphrase repeat the message conveyed by an individual in their own words, to verify that the message was understood accurately. In natural conversations, a person can paraphrase what the speaker said (textual paraphrasing) and also how this person felt (emotional paraphrasing).

Paraphrasing is a valuable skill used to learn more about the other person. The use of this tool can be improved with continuous practice. Rosenberg (2005) observed that paraphrasing should be used when it contributes to a better understanding of others and to adopt a more compassionate attitude towards them, especially when their messages are emotionally charged. A person who paraphrases another uses sentences like "Let me see if understood well what you said … You told me that …," and similar phrases. With this type of sentence, people show that they paid close attention to the messages conveyed by others, which also implies that their opinions are relevant.

An active listener can also use analogies to clarify what was previously said by another. An analogy is a sentence which relates two things which look similar in some way (for instance, "This lake is like a clean mirror"). To that effect, this individual can use sentences, such as "What you said is like …? Isn't it?" Lastly, an active listener can also recap what the other person said, by observing "I would like to summarise what you told me …." The use of the aforementioned tools prevents people from misinterpreting the message conveyed by the others.

8.12 Natural Conversations and Co-Operation

Love is at the same time the foundation of dialogue and dialogue itself.

Paulo Freire

Plowman (1998) observed that there are several types of interactions involving communication, such as contending, collaborative, compromising, avoiding, accommodating, and reconciling. Natural conversations are always collaborative and constructive; participants always aim to co-operate and support each other during these interactions.

According to Rogers (1961), in natural conversations, people are genuine and show others warm regard, considering them as individuals with unconditional self-worth, regardless of their personal conditions. In these conversations, people contribute to developing a loving environment for others to express their ideas and emotions in a transparent and unrestrained manner. People also show others that they are not being taken for granted, but valued greatly. Moreover, in these conversations, participants relish the togetherness created by these interactions.

Lowndes (2003) said that, in order to have more natural conversations with others, people can imagine that they are talking to old friends. These individuals can ask themselves: "How can I connect with this person if he/she was a close friend?" This simple mental "trick" generally makes conversations more flowing, warm, and amicable.

When a person treats others in a friendly and kind manner, they feel compelled to adopt a reciprocal attitude. Besides, a person who considers others as companions avoids detrimental behaviour towards them, such as

- Keeping people waiting before a meeting.
- Not returning their phone calls.
- Not answering their emails.
- Ignoring their comments.
- Talking only about business topics.
- Centring the conversation on themselves.
- Being disrespectful or rude with others.
- Not showing appreciation to them.

A person who treats others as friends is more inclined to help them explore their ideas and emotional states openly and confidently. According to Rogers (1961), when a person treats others in a conversation like close companions, this individual avoids trampling on their valuable worlds of meaning and feelings, but instead accepts these worlds with no reservation.

The Ritz-Carlton, the prestigious hotel chain, is a valuable example of a company where employees adopt a warm and friendly attitude towards customers. These staff members engage in meaningful conversations with others. A family, who was staying at one of the company's hotels in Bali, brought special eggs and milk because of various allergies of one of these family members. As they arrived at the hotel, they realised that these food products were in a bad condition. Through some exchanges with these guests, staff members working for this hotel became aware of this issue. These employees looked for these food products in town, with no avail. One of the hotel's staff members knew that these products were sold by a shop in Singapore. This employee contacted a relative in that country and asked this person to buy these products. This relative ended up swiftly flying to Bali to deliver these products. As a consequence, the hotel's employees were able to provide the family with these items which were so needed, with no additional cost for this family (Wellington, 2020).

8.13 Natural Conversations and Learning

Sometimes the greatest adventure is simply a conversation.

Amadeus Wolfe

In natural conversations, people share valuable parts of their personal universes with one another. In these encounters, people truly want to learn more from others about their specific views and perspectives on various topics. Each person is willing to submerge themselves in the strangeness of the other. In these natural conversations, participants never adopt an omniscient attitude towards one another; omniscience implies behaving as a know-it-all person. In a similar vein, Freire (2005) observed that "dialogue cannot exist without humility" and "cannot be an act of arrogance."

These conversations can also help people learn more about themselves. For example, people who talk to others about their own emotions relating to a specific situation can gain more clarity about these emotional states. However, some people tend to naturally adopt a defensive attitude towards others and, therefore, are less likely to fully convey their emotional states to them.

In these conversations, any topic can be discussed from a wide range of perspectives. In other words, people are always open to discovering valuable insights from others, regardless of their specific knowledge, background, or business role. Figuratively speaking, in this type of conversation, participants act like inquisitive explorers navigating uncharted territories teeming with hidden treasures to be unearthed. People who engage in a natural conversation always assume that others have valuable things to share with them. Consequently, participants are empowered to talk about any topic, including personal ones.

Luft and Ingham (1955) developed a very useful model which includes four types of topics to be potentially included in a natural conversation. The first type is called the "façade" because it is a topic about one of the participants which is known by this person, but unknown by the other. The second type is called the "blind spot," which is a topic related to one of the participants, unknown by this individual, but known by the other. There is a third type of topic called "arena," which is related to one of the participants and known by both of them, and the last type is named "the unknown" which is a topic about one participant, but none of them know about this topic (Scoular, 2011). Natural conversations can include any of these four types of topics.

Natural conversations are replete with interesting stories about participants' past experiences, challenges, motivations, dreams, and aspirations. It was previously explained that in natural conversations, people are focused on the present moment regarding the topics that unfold during the interaction. Nonetheless, participants can comment on their past experiences and future expectations, but perceived and analysed from the present perspective, which means rooted in the now.

Lastly, in natural conversations, each participant adopts a receptive and validating attitude towards each other's comments. In this type of interaction, a person can even show their appreciation to others by saying "Thanks for sharing this; I appreciate your comments." This appreciative attitude represents a powerful way to validate others as unique and valuable human beings.

8.14 Natural Conversations and Meaning

When minds meet, they don't just exchange facts; they transform them, reshape them. draw different implications from them, engage in new trains of thought. Conversation does not simply reshuffle the cards. It creates new cards.

Theodore Zeldin

In traditional conversations, the level of communication is commonly kept on a surface level These conversations are business-related and formal, which does not connect people in a deep manner. Instead, natural conversations are intrinsically deep and meaningful because participants connect with one another beyond their business objectives, roles, formal hierarchies, or power games.

In general, people tend to consider that a conversation is meaningful when they feel acknowledged, cared for, and respected during the interaction. In meaningful conversations, participants adopt a curious attitude towards each other, which makes their bond stronger. In these meaningful interactions, people ask others interesting questions, for example:

- Could you please tell me more about this?
- How did you deal with that situation?
- What are your hopes and expectations about this topic?
- What are your unique strengths and capabilities regarding this?
- What are the challenges you faced regarding this?
- Why is this situation relevant to you?
- What did you learn about this situation?
- How do you feel about this issue?

These questions are generally posed in a friendly tone of voice and they are related to an inquisitive attitude towards others. The purpose of these questions is to know more about others, without making them feel pressurised. These questions empower others to contribute to the dialogue with their particular views. When a person asks these questions to another, the latter tends to feel acknowledged, understood, and respected.

Natural conversations are meaningful because they truly transform participants in a positive manner for two main reasons. Firstly, these individuals are transformed because they end up knowing more about one another (their preferences, challenges, values, fears, insecurities, etc.). Secondly, participants also feel transformed because they are able to express themselves in an overt and authentic manner.

In a previous example in this chapter, employees working for The Ritz-Carlton in Bali clearly knew that it was relevant to get special milk and eggs for that family because of one of its members' allergies. These employees also understood that these products were needed in an urgent manner, and acted accordingly. In the example of HubSpot, previously seen in this chapter, the staff member knew that it was important to engage in a conversation about Spider-man, Star Wars, and the Jedis, as these were the customer's preferences.

8.15 Natural Conversations, Inclusiveness, and Empathy

> Love is our shared identity. The differences we experience in our gender, nationality, politics and religion do not exist in love.

Robert Holden

Natural conversations are more casual and personal than traditional business conversations. In the former, people avoid using impersonal phrases, such as "It is said …," "It's been completed …," etc. Instead, participants tend to use personal sentences, which involve others more directly. Some examples of these sentences are: "You said …" or "I said …," and similar ones.

In this type of conversation, people frequently use inclusive words (such as "we" and "our,"), which denote a strong affective connection between the participants. Natural conversations are also inclusive because, as mentioned previously, participants perceive one another as equals, so they experience a deep sense of togetherness.

Kotler (2021) observed that these chats are additive: participants make valuable comments about what was said by the other. For instance, participants are more likely to use words like "Yes, and …," instead of using sentences like "Yes, but …." The former brings about dynamism and momentum; the latter generates friction and opposition. Positive sentences like "Yes, and …" can be used even when participants have different views on a topic ("Yes, your idea is interesting, and I want to mention an alternative view of this topic which is…").

In natural conversations, participants are empowered to show all their aliveness to the other. In the work and business environments, and oftentimes outside it, most people are afraid to show themselves in an overt manner because they fear being misinterpreted, rejected, or harshly criticised.

According to Mipham (2017), in these natural exchanges, participants adopt a generous attitude towards each other, as they spontaneously give their attention and support. During these conversations, people tend to adopt an empathetic attitude towards one another. Participants put themselves in the positions of one another in order to perceive things from the viewpoint of the other. A compassionate person feels a natural identification with the predicaments and tribulations of others, acknowledges their emotional states, and provides them with loving support. According to Hanh (2014) in natural conversations, people can use phrases like "Please help me understand" and "I am here for you" to show an empathetic attitude towards others.

An example of an empathetic company is Glossier. This company offers women skincare products; most of them are vegan and cruelty-free. This company empowers its customers to express themselves in an open manner. In that sense, this company has a full team which continually gathers customers' opinions (likes, dislikes, etc.) which are duly considered. For instance, the company took into account these customers' various calls and launched a new customer-oriented product (e.g., a non-sticky and non-smelly sunscreen), which customers have greatly appreciated. Moreover, some customers sent messages on social media to the company, thanking this organisation for having listened to them and launching this new product. At this company, customers' opinions are regularly gleaned in different ways (emails, social media, blogs, calls, etc.) by the customer service team. In addition, the team also sends personalised messages, which include answers to customers' comments and clarifications (Bernazzani, 2021).

There is another significant point to highlight. A compassionate person has the ability to "read" others' emotional states, through changes in their body language (posture, tone of voice, etc.). The ability to be sensitive to emotions experienced by other people is part of what Goleman (1996) calls "emotional intelligence skills." When a person adopts a compassionate attitude towards others, this individual tends to use phrases such as:

- I understand your viewpoint …
- What you said is very important …
- If I were you, I would feel the same.
- In your position, I …
- I really got what you meant …
- I know that this is challenging for you …
- I comprehend how you truly feel …
- Thank you for sharing this.

In natural conversations, people also engage with others in a more compassionate manner, when they use some sentences in an active voice, for example: "I understand you." Sentences in a passive voice (for instance, "You are understood by me") should be avoided, not only because they sound unnatural, but also because they do not create a real connection with others.

Besides, compassionate people are willing to help others who deal with challenging issues, whenever possible. In that sense, a compassionate person uses sentences like "Have you thought of …?" or "What about … to deal with this situation?", among others. As mentioned previously, compassionate people can provide others with support in different ways (advice, technical information, etc.).

People who adopt a compassionate attitude towards others bring more love into their relationships with them. When an individual is treated in a compassionate manner by others, this person tends to act in a similar way towards them. Consequently, adopting a compassionate attitude is valuable in any type of relationship, including business ones.

It is more difficult for people to adopt a compassionate attitude towards others when they use written communication (emails, letters, etc.) because some aspects of humanity (such as gestures and tone of voice) are lost in the interaction. Therefore, when the emotions of the participants are involved, it is preferable that people use one-to-one conversations over alternative forms of communication.

A good example of people at work offering emotional support to others was presented by Fosslien and Duffy (2019). These authors mentioned the case of Laszlo Bock who founded Humu, a company specialising in machine learning. In the past, this leader received an important call and travelled to see and stay with his family. When he came back, he told the staff members that his brother had died. People working for that company regularly asked him how he was feeling, and displayed other types of supportive behaviour towards him. This business leader felt supported and understood by the company's staff members during that challenging time.

8.16 Natural Conversations and Free Expression

In natural conversations, people can express their opinions in a free and overt manner. In this type of conversation, nobody imposes their views on others. Participants share their ideas eloquently and without editing them. In these interactions, participants do not pretend to show a perfect image of themselves to be accepted by others, but honestly share what is inside themselves. According to Apps (2014), natural conversations also include heart talk, which encompasses comments about feelings, values, meanings, and topics of great value to the speaker.

In natural conversations, people say what they mean, but also mean what they say. These dialogues are so honest and revealing that people feel safe, even when they talk about their own negative experiences, mistakes, flaws, and problems. In these conversations, participants fully own their comments using personal sentences, like "I think …," "I feel …," "I know …," and similar ones. In natural conversations, participants avoid misleading or manipulating one another, and speak their words with integrity and transparency.

In these conversations, people welcome the discussion of any topic. However, the discussion of potentially contentious topics (such as politics and religion) is always friendly and respectful. Each participant is curious to know each other's opinions; they are sensitive to the views of others. Participants express their ideas using words that are right for them.

In natural conversations, people tend to avoid convoluted or complex vocabulary to impress others. They also avoid the use of euphemisms and intricate jargon. Instead, participants tend to choose casual and simple words. The use of clear, spontaneous, and straightforward conversational style helps people create a deeper connection with others.

The well-known quote "condemnation is the root of all evil" is commonly applied to natural conversations. In these interactions, people are prone to adopt a non-judgemental attitude towards others, which means avoiding criticising them, mentally or aloud. When a person avoids condemning others, this individual is addressing their need to be respected and treated with care. Rogers (1961) called this attitude "unconditional positive regard."

In natural conversations, people never behave in an aggressive or defensive manner with others; nor do they attempt to exert their power over them. If participants have divergent views on a topic during the conversation, these perspectives are always expressed in a gentle and caring way. In natural conversations, participants are also inclined to adopt an attitude of curiosity towards others. The use of sentences like "This sounds quite relevant/interesting/attractive/important …" and "Can you please tell me more about this?" is suitable for this type of conversation.

Natural conversations are warm and friendly, which makes people feel safe, at ease, and physically relaxed. From the scientific perspective, there is a continuous connection between a person's physical and mental aspects. Consequently, when people do not feel tense, they are inclined to express their ideas in a more open, spontaneous, and flowing manner. Comfortable people tend to adopt an exploring and inquisitive attitude towards opinions expressed by others. Tense or uncomfortable individuals are prone to adopt a more cautious attitude (connected to the fight-freeze-flight mode). As seen in a previous chapter, in Netflix, the streaming and movie producer company, staff members are empowered to engage in conversations to give feedback to one another in a candid, honest, but also constructive manner.

8.17 Clarity in Natural Conversations

From the perspective of neuro-linguistic programming (NLP), whenever people engage in conversations, they tend to omit, generalise, and distort their messages. People are also prone to simplify their messages for practical conversational purposes, leaving relevant aspects out of the conversation. Their messages also include various assumptions, which oftentimes are not necessarily connected with reality.

NLP provides a series of questions to help people clarify messages received from others. These questions form part of a tool called the Meta Model of Language. People who apply this tool to their conversations obtain more details about unclear and unspecific messages conveyed by others.

For example, some people use very general sentences like "I am stressed." In this case, these individuals can be asked a question like "Stressed specifically about what?" in order to know more about the causes of their stress. People who use generalisations like "I am always stressed" can be asked questions such as "Always?" or "Are there any exceptions to this?" Similar questions can be asked to clarify statements, including terms like "everyone" and "everywhere," and similar ones.

Most people use nominalisations or terms linked to intangible or abstract things, which cannot be perceived by the senses. Examples of nominalisations are "fairness," "satisfaction," "rest," etc. If a person says, "I need motivation," the word "motivation" represents various things to different people (specific training, recognition, more economic rewards, etc.). In this example, the other person could ask a question like "What do you specifically mean by motivation?" to understand the thinking of the other individual.

Sometimes, people use sentences which imply apparent limitations, for example: "I cannot attain a balanced life." In this case, the other person can ask: "What are the obstacles preventing you from having balance?" to probe the apparent limitations. Sometimes, people use statements which entail mind-reading skills, for instance: "I know that this person will not like my work." A person listening to this statement can challenge this idea by asking: "How do you know that this person will not like your work?"

In some conversations, people use statements which include a cause and its related effect. For example, a person says "I feel demotivated because I have a lot of work." The listener can ask: "How is it that having a lot of work makes you feel demotivated?" to understand details regarding the link between the cause (having a lot of work) and the effect (feeling demotivated).

Oftentimes, people use sentences which include vague expressions, for example: "I rest too much." In this example, this person can be asked the following question: "In which way are you resting too much?" to garner more details about this. People often use other unclear words like "it," "that," or "this," and similar ones. For example, a person who says "It's stressful" can be asked questions like "What is stressful?" to obtain more detailed information.

In the previous examples, people express their ideas unclearly, and the listener adopts an inquisitive and loving attitude and asks them for more details about the ideas expressed. The frequent use of the aforementioned questions helps the listener clarify messages expressed by others, but also shows them that this individual has authentic interest in their ideas, which contributes to the development of more clear and meaningful conversations. As mentioned in the previous example, Glossier has a full team devoted to interacting with different customers in a personalised manner, for instance, clarifying their specific doubts or responding to their requests.

8.18 Body Language and Natural Conversations

Body language (gestures, movements, eye contact, etc.) is the natural complement of verbal aspects (words) in any conversation. Research shows that body language contributes to the communication process more significantly than verbal language. Mehrabian (mentioned in Pease and Pease, 2004) observed that communication is composed of 55% gestures, movements, and other non-verbal aspects, 38% vocal aspects (which includes the inflection and tone of voice), and only 7% verbal (words). Body language is used to stress certain points of the message or illustrate them more eloquently. These non-verbal cues also help people express their emotions more overtly. Some authors like Goman (2012) observed that, in the previous research study, the 93% previously mentioned (which includes 55% gestures, movement, and other non-verbal aspects, and 38% vocal aspects) is only related to communication of emotional aspects of a message, not the full content of the message.

In natural conversations, people use warmer and more relaxed body language, as compared with traditional business interactions. People who engage in natural conversations use their body language for positive purposes, for example, to show respect to others, pay attention to them, or express appreciation. Some examples of positive uses of body language are mentioned below.

- When a person listens to others, this individual should face them either from an angle or communicate side-by-side, to make them feel more at ease. This person should never point at others directly because this type of body language can be perceived as confrontational or intimidating by others.
- A listener should use regular eye contact with others, without staring at them in a fixed manner. This person should remain relaxed and lean towards others while they express their ideas. This non-defensive body language conveys comfort and engagement with whatever others comment on.
- During a chat, nodding is frequently perceived as a valuable non-verbal signal to acknowledge messages being conveyed by others. People who nod to speakers are encouraging these individuals to continue expressing their ideas. Borg (2011) observed that nodding can also be used to acknowledge others or show understanding or agreement.
- A positive body language cue commonly used in natural conversations is smiling frankly and openly at the other person, which increases the rapport between them. Lastly, tilting the head to one side when the other person is speaking demonstrates interest in what is being said.

Some scholars like Pease (2014) observed that, in typical business conversations, people tend to look at the point between the other's eyebrows. This point is commonly used for formal interactions. Instead, in more casual and natural conversations, people are prone to focus on the whole face of their participants. This second point of attention (the whole person's face) is used for the so-called "social eye contact."

Another important body language cue which most experts highlight is showing the palms up when conversing with other; this signal conveys transparency and honesty. All these microgestures make other people feel comfortable and valued. In natural conversations, negative body language (e.g., visual avoidance, crossing arms tightly, darting eyes, and staring continually) should be avoided because it does not contribute to the development of a loving connection between the participants.

A very relevant part of body language is the tone of voice. In traditional business meetings, people tend to use a monotonous and formal tone of voice, to appear more serious and professional in the eyes of others. Oftentimes, people can also use this type of tone of voice to hide their own negative emotional states, like fear, and appear confident and calm.

Instead, in natural conversations, people use a warmer and more friendly tone of voice to express their ideas. In these interactions, people naturally use their tone of voice to express various nuances of their feelings in a more expressive manner. The use of a natural tone of voice helps people express ideas to others in a more transparent and trustworthy manner.

8.19 Body Language, Emotions, and Synchronicity

Heart is sea,

language is shore.

Whatever sea includes,

will hit the shore.

Rumi

In natural conversations, people avoid repressing their body language, but let it unfold in a spontaneous and lively manner. Instead, in typical business conversations, people tend to display body language which is rigid and ungraceful, for instance, arms crossed, clenched fists, tight and raised shoulders, etc.

This stiff non-verbal language conveys tension, lack of confidence, and a state of defensiveness. These non-verbal signals do not inspire trust, but create distance from others. Goffman (1969) observed that people tend to hide traits (verbal and non-verbal ones) incompatible with their roles in order to be accepted by others.

In most traditional business conversations, people display solemn and stiff body language, which creates distance from others. According to Giddens (2009), these people are concerned about how they are seen by others, and consequently use different ways of impression management, for example, controlling their body language consciously or unwittingly. Oftentimes, these signals look inauthentic and make others feel uncomfortable.

In business, most people expect others to communicate in a non-emotional manner. In that sense, rational aspects are the default foundations of most traditional exchanges. Moreover, in those environments, people's expression of their own emotions is often perceived as a potential threat or obstacle to the achievement of relevant business objectives.

In traditional business interactions, many people try to hide their undesirable emotional states (sadness, fear, anger, etc.) by controlling their body language, which makes them look untrustworthy. According to Goffman (1969), these defensive practices are used by people to preserve a positive impression when they interact with others.

Tense people tend to show a body language which is incongruent with their verbal language, and this can be detected by others very easily. Their non-verbal "armours" prevent these individuals from expressing their ideas more openly and creatively. Besides, fretful people have more difficulties conveying messages that come from their hearts.

According to Apps (2012), individuals are more prone to hold authentic conversations when they reconnect the energy of their thoughts and emotions with their voice. This author observed that honest conversationalists are emotionally truthful; their tone of voice, gestures, and corporal movements naturally tell others a congruent story, which makes them credible.

Consequently, people who hold conversations with stakeholders should be aware of not controlling their own body language. If their non-verbal expression is restrained, they should slightly tense their muscles and then relax them. A second way to become more relaxed is to breathe deeply a few times and relax, causing gestures and posture to become more at ease physically. When people show more relaxed body language, their conversations tend to become natural and flowing.

From the perspective of NLP, natural conversations commonly show spontaneous synchronicity between the body language of participants. Participants seem to mirror one another with their movements, posture, gestures, tone of voice, and other non-verbal signals. Their body language seems to flow, like dancers in a graceful choreography, which increases their connection and rapport during a conversation. Pease and Pease (2004) observed that mirroring is generally perceived as a co-operative behaviour, which makes others feel more comfortable. This convergence is also related to liking, inclusion, and closeness (Mirivel, 2014). In a research study, it was concluded that, when people use self-disclosure in their exchanges with others, these individuals showed orchestrated movements of their bodies (known as behavioural synchrony), which led to more positive and vital interactions between these individuals (Vacharkulksemsuk and Fredrickson, 2012).

Some NLP specialists recommend that people should purposely aim to "match" other's body language to increase the rapport with them. However, other scholars observed that it is not advisable because this might look inauthentic and unnatural. In natural conversations, the alignment of participants' body language occurs unforcefully and spontaneously.

An example of the effect of contagion of body language can be observed in business meetings. For instance, at meetings held at Microsoft, the giant software company, it has been reported that Bill Gates, one of its co-founders, was doing certain gestures while expressing his ideas (adjusting his eyeglasses, rocking the chair, etc.), and the other people around him at the table were replicating his body language (The Mind Gym, 2007).

8.20 Natural Business Conversations

Entrepreneurs should remember the quotation which goes "thriving business activities are always based on thriving relationships." Natural conversations allow people to bring to the table their authentic human side which benefits the business aspects of their relationships. These conversations also help people connect more deeply in their interactions with others. Natural conversations should never be considered one-off interactions; these conversations should be held on a regular basis.

When people talk to stakeholders, they can use natural conversations in three distinct ways. The first way is to convert the entire interaction into a natural conversation and combine business topics and personal topics in a balanced manner. These interactions consider both the business roles of the participants (manager, subordinate, supplier, customers, etc.) and their valuable human side. These conversations are more relaxed and insightful because people are recognised as worthy human beings, not as cogs in the business machinery.

The second way is to use this sequence: natural conversation – formal conversation – natural conversation. These encounters start as a natural conversation (where personal aspects are expressed), then continue with a more traditional conversation (where business topics – deadlines, projects, requirements, etc. – are discussed), and end up with another natural conversation (where personal aspects wrap up the encounter). Even though this second way looks less spontaneous than the previous option, it can create good engagement and support between participants.

The third way is to have a brief natural conversation only at the beginning of the interaction. This preliminary conversation, known as "small-talk," has the objective of "breaking the ice" before entering a formal discussion on business topics for the rest of the interaction. These natural preludes aim to put people in a more positive mood, which often lowers their default mental defences towards one another. This third way does not consider the human dimension of individuals extensively, so this conversation can still sometimes be perceived as an unnatural interaction.

In some cultural environments, known as "high context cultures," local companies consider the human side of interactions with others as important as their business side. In these cultural environments, companies' representatives want to personally know their counterparts in other companies, before doing any business together. In these cultures, companies understand that transactions are based on relationships, which must be developed and nourished over time.

Lastly, it is important that companies encourage the development of natural conversations among their employees. According to Cohen and Prusak (2001), an organisation can do this in several ways: developing comfortable spaces (communal rooms, lounges, etc.) where people can hold informal frequent conversations, allowing employees to take regular breaks to talk to one another in an informal manner, and privileging whenever possible personal interactions over other ways of communication (email, etc.).

At Buffer, a company which offers software products to manage social media accounts, employees are encouraged to have regular natural conversations. Once a week, employees are paired up with another colleague to have a Zoom video conversation. In these exchanges, employees are encouraged to chat about anything occurring in their own lives on a personal level, as well as what they want to attain at this company during that week (Seiter, 2014).

Questions for Self-Reflection

- What formalities can be eliminated to make communication with our stakeholders more natural?
- How can I listen to our company's stakeholders in a more active manner?
- How can I express myself to our stakeholders in a more spontaneous manner?
- How can I encourage our stakeholders to express their ideas and emotions more openly?

Chapter 9

The Use of Positive Language with Stakeholders

9.1 The Importance of Words for Communication Purposes

Words are the materialisation or overt expression of people's thoughts and emotions. Words are important in business conversations (and also in non-business ones) because they help people to analyse, describe, and justify circumstances in specific ways. Words are like building blocks which sustain and strengthen relationships with others. Besides, words act like maps helping people navigate the circumstances affecting them. Other important traits of words are:

- Words are powerful attention-grabbing resources; they can emphasise or direct the attention to different aspects of specific situations. Words can be used to ask questions, to create possible scenarios, and to draw definite or provisional conclusions.
- Some words can describe positive sides of a situation, and other words can describe its negative aspects. Words are powerful tools to frame, shape, and interpret reality in different ways.
- Words can be used to express one's values, preferences, desires, objectives, and feelings. Words can also help people describe their beliefs and behaviours, as well as justify them. Words are specific ways people enumerate their own qualities and the ones related to others.
- Words can be used to analyse situations and ideas. Words can be used to compare, synthesise, and create alternatives. Words can also be used to persuade others, instruct them, and remind them of relevant things.

The human brain uses words when it processes information; consequently, the use of words not only affects the thoughts a person has, but also the emotions and physical sensations related to them. In the business and work environments, words can be used in a loving manner: for instance, to acknowledge and praise stakeholders, empower them, support them, and express gratitude to them. Positive words can be used to provide people with feedback about their performance. People who use positive words with others tend to elicit positive emotions and thoughts in themselves and the other people.

The use of positive words shortens the distance between people. Most people have the need to hear positive words about them from others; praises or compliments are like a soothing balm to these individuals.

DOI: 10.4324/9781003372684-11

Google is a company which understands the power of using positive words. At Google, managers rate employees' performance, using positive sentences, like "needs improvement," "consistently meets expectations," "exceeds expectations," "strongly exceeds expectations," and "superb." As can be seen, this company's managers do not use any derogatory comments when they provide employees with feedback regarding their performance. All statements these managers use have a positive tone; even the statement "needs improvement." This company has been considered one of the best workplaces worldwide (Nguyen, 2022).

9.2 Detrimental Impact of Negative Words

In the business environment, people can use negative words with others to condemn them, threaten them, and complain about their unproductive behaviour. People can use negative words to express their anger, regret, or worry about others' behaviour or ideas. In the work environment, words can also be used to backstab others, discriminate against them, and bully them. Every time people use negative words with others, their relationships are affected in a detrimental manner.

It is important to remember that when people receive negative comments from others, they tend to shut down, adopting a fight-freeze-flight mode. This mode has been thoroughly explained in Chapter 3. These individuals often behave in a resentful or uncooperative manner. Sometimes, they feel angry, sad, or ashamed in relation to the people who offended them. Therefore, people working for a company should frequently ask themselves the following questions:

- Are we using positive words to convey our messages to others?
- Can we word our messages in a more positive manner?
- Are our words nourishing our relationships with others?
- How can we make our words more loving towards others?
- Are we using the same type of words we want to hear from others?
- How can our words be more grateful, supportive, or full of praise?
- Are we communicating at all with the company's stakeholders?

These questions will help people to reflect on the words they use on a regular basis. Frequent self-reflection on this topic will help these individuals use more positive vocabulary when interacting with others.

In Netflix, the global video streaming and movie producing company, employees give actionable feedback to others in order to assist them, never to deprecate them. In other words, these employees' feedback is always given in a constructive, kind, and sincere manner. Employees provide their colleagues with action-oriented feedback, with the only objective to bring about some improvement in their performance (Hastings and Meyer, 2020).

9.3 The Power of Using Positive Language

As perfume to the flower, so is kindness to speech.

J. Katherine Francke

Some social psychology experiments have concluded that people tend to react more productively to positive words, as compared to negative ones. Positive words have a powerful priming effect on people, prompting them to experience positive emotions and dwell on positive circumstances. In a company's environment, the frequent use of positive words could contribute to an improvement in that organisation's performance and productivity levels.

A very large number of words commonly used in the business environment have a negative connotation. Some examples of these words are "attack," "competition," "strategy," "tactics," "defence," and others. These words have a warmongering connotation, which prompts people to adopt an adversarial perspective towards others. Underneath these words, there is an impending sense of fear; people tend to use these terms to protect themselves from external threats. Some examples of these threatening factors are current competitors, potential entrants to the market, etc.

Cialdini (2016) suggested that people in a company should frequently use terms with positive connotations when performing their business activities. From this perspective, companies should use words related to accomplishment, such as "vision," "mission," "goals," "objectives," and similar ones. This specialist observed that, when people use positive words, their attention is engrossed in these very terms, instead of concentrating on competing words (negative terms). Some ways to use more positive words in the business environment are:

- People should regularly use words related to thankfulness. For example, the use of sentences with stakeholders like "Thank you very much for your comments" has a very positive effect on people receiving this message. Individuals should also offer honest compliments to internal and external stakeholders. For example, managers can say to their subordinates "I like the way you contributed to this project because …," which will impact on these employees in a positive manner. Positive words can affect the receiver's self-image positively.
- People who tell others that they share some positive traits, interests, or preferences with them create a more positive connection, affinity, and sense of togetherness with these individuals. For instance, a person can say to another "I enjoy working on this project, knowing that you are committed in the same way I am."
- People can also comment about their own ideas or experiences, stressing only their positive aspects. For example, these individuals can say to others "The best part of this …" or "The most positive aspect of …," and contribute to a more constructive dialogue with others. This tool can also be used when a person listens to others. In this case, this person can ask others, "What are the most positive aspects of what you said?" to redirect their focus towards the positive.
- In a conversation, a listener can also select the most positive comments the speaker has made and ask questions such as "Could you tell me more about …?" to obtain more detailed information about the positive aspects of the message conveyed. In this way, people are also prompted to concentrate on their own previous positive comments.
- An individual who receives a negative comment from another can reword this message in a positive manner. For example, if a person says "Our levels of sales are very low," the other individual can reframe this comment by saying, "I can see that you aim for higher levels of sales; which are the levels you look forward to obtaining?" In this example, the reframing of the message prompts people to feel more positive because it does not focus on what people do not want, but on their goals and desires.

Robbins (2001) advised to use words which magnify the intensity of positive emotions. For example, people should say "I feel exhilarated," instead of saying "I am having fun," to bring about more positive feelings and thoughts. This author also observed that people should use softening words in relation to negative emotional states. For instance, the person can use words like "I feel slightly concerned," instead of saying "I feel desperate."

A person can also use this tool to comment to others about their emotional states, for example, by saying to them "You look very exhilarated," instead of "You seem to be in a good mood." A person can also say "You look slightly concerned," instead of "You look desperate." In short, these "intensifiers" and "softeners" relabel people's emotional states and improve interactions with others.

According to Howard (1989), some examples of positive words which can affect the business communication in a beneficial manner are "agree," "care," "fair," "good," "heart," "hope," "love," "sincere," "special," and "new," among others. This author also provides examples of negative words to avoid in business conversations: "afraid," "but," "cannot," "disappoint," "disagree," "dislike," "doubt," "risk," and "unfortunately," among others. For example, instead of saying "Unfortunately, we cannot send the merchandise until you make the payment," a person can say "We would love to send the merchandise once you make the payment."

The use of positive language in the business environment is not limited to spoken words. Some researchers analysed the impact of placing banners with inspirational messages on the walls of the workplace. According to the research findings, the use of these positive notes (for example, "You can achieve your goals") affected employees' performance positively. Therefore, it is advisable that companies use this type of positive visual cues in the workplace to boost employees' productivity (Cialdini, 2016).

Mary Cullen, the founder of Instructional Solutions, an international business communication trainer and executive coach, has observed that organisations should be careful with the words they utilise. This entrepreneur recommends that, in business, people should frequently use positive words, such as "You're welcome," "It was my pleasure," "We're here to help you," and "We appreciate your business," among others (Cullen, 2020).

9.4 Positive Vocabulary and Criticism

As seen previously, a company's employees should frequently use positive language with other stakeholders and avoid delivering negative criticism to them. The well-known saying which goes "Condemnation is the root of all evil regarding relationships" is very applicable to the business and work environments.

When harsh criticism is used in organisations, people affected by these remarks are prone to respond in a reactive mode (fight-freeze-flight). A person can express negative criticism to others in several ways. For instance, threats, ultimatums, sarcasm, humiliating comments, guilt-tripping, and personal accusations are negative forms of criticism.

In the business environment, a person who delivers derisory criticism to others generally does so because of mistakes they made – for instance, missed deadlines, important documentation lost, low-quality supplies, delays in the delivery, wrong products offered, etc. For example, managers who say to their subordinates "You cannot do this job well!" do more harm than good to their relationships with these employees.

In this example, managers communicate with employees in an aggressive manner, personalising the conflict, instead of focusing on the problem itself. Managers' snide remarks prompt subordinates to adopt a defensive attitude, which, in turn, prevents them from improving their work performance. These employees do not feel acknowledged as valuable human beings and might even feel rejected and unappreciated.

These employees are prone to feel attacked by their managers' negative remarks, which makes these subordinates feel more vulnerable and unsafe. Their natural fear-based response is related to the fight-freeze-flight mode, which prevents them from harnessing their unique analytical and creative skills. In this example, these employees might even become less receptive due to the comments received.

9.5 A Positive Way to Deliver Criticism

Any criticism expressed to a company's stakeholders should be delivered in a non-harmful manner. A person who delivers critiques to others should adopt a compassionate, understanding, and caring attitude towards them. It is important to pinpoint a generally neglected fact: all human beings, with no exceptions, make mistakes.

When mistakes made by others are highlighted in a non-judgemental manner, people are more prone to learn from these mistakes and to act more effectively next time. When stakeholders are given critiques in a respectful way, they are more likely to treat others in a reciprocal manner. Some important characteristics of constructive criticism delivered to a company's stakeholders are discussed in the remainder of this chapter.

9.5.1 Positive Wording

Criticism provided to others must always be formulated in a constructive manner. When possible, the critique should not refer to things that are wrong or mistaken ("This task was done in the wrong way because …"), but instead focus on things that can be improved ("Next time, this task should be improved in this way …"). Consequently, a person who delivers criticism to others should avoid guilt-tripping others ("This is your fault") because it makes them feel as if they acted wrongly on purpose.

Critical comments should never be delivered in a pushy manner ("You must do it this way next time!") because people are likely to feel controlled and pressurised. As seen previously, accusations should also be avoided when delivering criticism to others. Whenever a person adopts an authoritative or accusatory attitude towards others, they are prone to adopt a defensive attitude (fight-freeze-flight) towards this individual.

A person who delivers critical feedback to others should start with some positive comments on what they have done correctly in the past (for example, "I want to highlight your performance last year because …"). After this, the person can continue with the specific critique, "Your performance during the last few months can be improved significantly because …." When criticism is accompanied by an initial positive comment, receivers tend to feel cared for, which makes them feel more at ease and receptive.

Criticism should always be delivered in a respectful manner; harsh words and tone of voice must be avoided. The use of a conversational and warm tone of voice is preferred over a "formal" or "solemn" one. People delivering a critique to others should demonstrate that they want the best for them.

Criticism is also prone to be well-received by others, when it includes previous empathic comments about them, for instance, "I know that you have been dealing with a massive workload during the last few weeks." This introductory comment makes people receiving the criticism feel acknowledged as valuable human beings, which makes them more open to the remarks received.

After people deliver their critiques to others, they can also offer their assistance for the implementation of the suggestions proposed. For example, these individuals can say "I know that the change I am proposing may be challenging for you, but I want you to know I am willing to support you during the process in this way ....." These people adopt a loving attitude to the receivers, which makes the latter feel cared for by the former. As a consequence, this critique is more likely to be taken on board. Whenever possible, the person offering support to another should act as if the latter was a close friend.

When people deliver critical remarks to others, the latter are more likely to act on these comments when they feel appreciated. For example, the person who delivered a critique can say to the other "Thanks in advance for considering these comments" or "Your co-operation on this topic is greatly valued." This type of sentences assumes that the other person will take the comments on board, which makes this individual more prone to act congruently with this positive assumption.

In the case of Netflix, the video streaming and movie producing company, employees are encouraged to give feedback to others (including to superiors) whenever they consider it necessary, even in the middle of a work presentation. For example, subordinates can provide their bosses with feedback, whenever needed. However, as mentioned previously, this feedback should always be delivered by using candid, honest, and constructive words (Hastings and Meyer, 2020; Meyer, 2021).

9.5.2 Behaviour-Oriented

Criticism must always be expressed with the core objective of preserving the relationships with others. In a similar vein, Fisher et al. (1999) observed that people should always be soft with others, but hard with problems involving them. Unproductive criticism is generally centred on the characteristics of the person criticised (personality, mental capabilities, manual abilities, etc.). When a person delivers criticism to others based on their qualities ("You are not good for anything"), they are prone to feel negatively labelled and adopt a defensive response.

Instead, constructive critiques delivered to others are focused on their behaviour (writing a report, delivering information, etc.), which can be improved in the future. This type of criticism makes people less defensive towards the critiques. Rosenberg (2005) observed that critiques about others' behaviour should always include observations about this behaviour, but not evaluation.

Criticism based on observations describes the current state of reality related to the receiver, in the most objective way possible. An example of this type of criticism is "You have arrived one hour late for the last three weeks" (observation). By contrast, an example of unproductive critique can be "You are incapable of arriving on time." This second example includes the personal evaluative word "incapable," which makes this feedback detrimental.

A person who delivers the critique to a stakeholder should be as clear and specific as possible. General or vague remarks are never of value. For example, instead of saying "I feel that performance can be improved," people should be informed of the specific actionable steps to take in practice to improve their performance. A better way to word this remark is: "Next time, it is important for things to be done this way ...."

Lastly, unclear generalisations like "always," "never," "all," "none," and others should be avoided. Critiques given to others should always be centred on specific issues. In the business and work environments, situations are unlikely to be "black or white." As a consequence, it is not advisable to use rigid generalisations because they do not allow any nuances or exceptions to them. Criticism must refer to a particular situation, for instance: "On this occasion ..." or "In this circumstance ...."

In the case of Pixar, the renowned animation company, whenever working on the development of a movie, animators assess the draft of the movie in progress on a daily basis. In this assessment, staff members purposefully make suggestions on improvements to the movie. For instance, animators can suggest changes regarding the characteristics of the characters (shape, colour, etc.), and their pace, among other aspects. In other words, in this assessment, the feedback is about the movie and how to improve its different parts. This feedback never includes personal criticism of the animators who have participated in the development of the movie (Fosslien and Duffy, 2019).

9.5.3 Change-Oriented

Sometimes, the receivers of criticism can be offered an incentive for them to change their behaviour in the future. For example, if an employee has a very low performance, the manager can say to this person, "If your performance for the next term is improved by 20%, you will be paid a bonus …." Oftentimes, the offer of a stimulus makes the critique more actionable. Nonetheless, some scholars are of the opinion that offering this type of incentive to others can paradoxically discourage individuals to take action.

As seen previously, when a person delivers constructive feedback on a specific unsolved problem, the receiver should also be given the proposed solution to be implemented, when possible. An example of this could be, "I noticed that your performance can be increased by 20% as compared with the previous year. There are some actions such as … for you to consider that could help you improve your performance."

Sometimes, the person delivering the criticism and its receiver can work out potential solutions to a problem together. An example of this critique could be, "I noticed that your performance can be increased by 20% as compared with the previous year. Let's talk about possible ways that will help you improve your performance. Please let me know your opinion about this and I will tell you mine." This approach tends to be more effective because the individual who should make changes is involved in the design of the action to be taken. From this perspective, criticism also represents an opportunity to enhance the receiver's creative capabilities.

As explained previously, criticism should include specific advice on how the receiver should act, which is considered practical support. Besides, the person delivering criticism to others should provide emotional assistance, for example, encouraging them to act or thanking them for their previous contribution to the company. In this way, the person delivering the critique adopts a compassionate and understanding attitude towards the receiver of the remarks.

When people want to prompt others to make some changes in their behaviour, they should accompany their criticism with the potential positive impact that this change will generate. An example of this is "There are some actions such as … for you to consider that could help you improve your performance for next year. If you could perform these actions next time, this will benefit our department in this way …." From the psychological perspective, when the person who delivers the critique explains to the other the specific benefits of introducing some changes in the future, the latter is more likely to become emotionally invested in the change process.

The founder of the communication training company Instructional Solutions, previously mentioned, observed that the words used in business conversations, especially when a person provides another with feedback, should be change-oriented. From this perspective, people should use sentences like "To complete your report, you will need…," instead of using sentences such as "You neglected to include… in your report." The former is focused on specific changes to be made; the latter is focused on harsh criticism and blame (Cullen, 2020).

Sometimes, the critique that a person provides to another can be linked to a goal shared by them. For example, a shared objective can be highlighted in sentences like "If next time you could …, our relationship will be greatly benefitted in this way …." The enunciation of a shared goal ("improvement of the relationship") makes the criticism more actionable to the receiver.

As mentioned previously, unproductive criticism makes people feel that they are being commanded or told what to do, which makes them less prone to generate any positive change. For example, critiques like "You have to do … this way …" generally creates a lot of resistance in the recipient of this order. Instead, when a person uses more indirect phrases, for instance, recommendations, advice, or suggestions to give feedback to others, they are more inclined to accept the remarks.

Sentences like "You could get better results if …" and "It would be advisable that …" are more likely to be taken on board. The use of phrases such as "You could …" or "You can …" also helps deliver more constructive critiques to others because they introduce an element of choice or possibility. Zhou (1998) has concluded that when a person receives positive feedback and has autonomy to act in the best way possible, this individual's creative skills are enhanced. According to this researcher, this feedback should always be constructive, supportive, and also not-controlling; in that sense, this feedback should suggest what the person *might* do, but not what this individual *must* do.

Whenever possible, criticism should be accompanied by the reasons why it is relevant for the recipient to take action on it ("It is a good idea that you could … because of …"). Research has shown that people are more likely to comply with a suggestion when it is accompanied by the reason supporting this advice, even in cases when the reason is obvious.

Criticism can also be delivered as a question, for example, "What about changing …?" Once people have delivered their critique to others, they can also say to them, "Thanks for considering this suggestion" or "Thanks for your co-operation regarding this." This type of sentences makes the recipient more likely to take on board the remarks received.

There is an interesting example of a company whose employees' feedback has led to a specific change. Centerfield is a company which offers digital marketing solutions. In an anonymous survey conducted by this company, a group of staff members requested that the system for employee bonuses and commissions should be made clearer. This company took this employee's feedback on board, and made sure that each of its staff members had a thorough understanding of the calculation and payment of bonuses and commissions (Famakinwa, 2018).

9.5.4 Other Aspects Related to Feedback

People who provide others with criticism should clearly explain to them the objective reasons for their comments. For example, a person can provide another with the following, "There is a better procedure to use such as …, which is more adequate because …" In this case, the person delivering the critique will explain the most appropriate procedures that the receiver should have used, according to regulations, conditions, or any other valid criteria. Critiques supported by objective evidence regarding why things must be done in a certain way are perceived as fairer by the receiver because they are less prone to subjective interpretation.

When a person delivers criticism to others that might make them feel ashamed, these remarks must be delivered in private. In those cases, the delivery of a private critique is a sign of caring for others' public image. When a person is not sure if the remarks could be perceived as shameful, this individual should deliver these critiques privately.

There is an interesting example regarding this topic. John Paul DeJoria, the cofounder of John Paul Mitchell Systems, the prestigious hair products company, observed that when an employee makes a mistake, this individual should never be told off publicly, but instead in a private manner. According to this business leader, this type of criticism should always be delivered in a private way, so that this staff member does not adopt an aggressive attitude (Bilyeu, 2017).

From the perspective of social psychology, there is a phenomenon known as "fundamental attribution error" which means that oftentimes a person tends to link other people's behaviour to their personal traits (character, personality, intention, etc.) instead of relating that behaviour to external circumstances. For instance, if a person arrives late to a meeting, another person is prone to explain this late arrival by mostly emphasising the characteristics of the former (for example, "This individual arrived late because he is irresponsible and lazy"), instead of considering possible external reasons affecting that individual (for example, "This person arrived late because of a public transport strike").

Therefore, the person who delivers the criticism should always probe for any external reason which might have affected the other person's behaviour to avoid assuming that this behaviour is related to this individual's characteristics. For example, the person who delivers the critique can ask the other questions like "Were you affected by any external factor which prevented you from arriving on time?" In this way, the person delivering the feedback can be more compassionate with the other.

When criticism is of great relevance, the person delivering the remarks should hold a personal meeting with the receiver, whenever possible. In the delivery of critiques face-to-face, the person delivering the critical remarks shows the receiver respect and care which strengthens the relationship between them. People who deliver their criticism in person also take personal ownership of the critique delivered. Some people might use video conferencing (e.g., Zoom) for that purpose.

Sometimes, a person can double-check the main aspects of an issue with the people involved in it, before delivering any critique to them. Sentences like "I would like you to confirm if ..." can be used to avoid mistakes or misunderstandings when delivering remarks to others. The use of these phrases helps confirm that the issue the critique is being delivered on is based on correct information.

Sometimes, critiques can be formulated in a personal way, for instance: "From my perspective ..." or "I think that ...." In other cases, criticism can be expressed in a more impersonal manner, for example: "It will be interesting ..." or "It is necessary ...." From the perspective of this book, oftentimes the personal approach is more authentic and natural than the impersonal one, making the person receiving the critique feel more at ease and receptive.

On some occasions, criticism can be delivered to others in a less forward manner. These remarks are delivered in a less straightforward way, which makes them more likely to be accepted by others. Some softeners, such as "I am a bit curious about one thing ...," can be used to deliver more indirect criticism. There is another important point to highlight. Rosenberg (2005) stated that, when people make a request to others, they should ask them if their message was correctly understood, for example, with some questions like "Is this clear?" This type of question allows the receiver to avoid mistakes regarding the request made.

PepsiCo, the global company which sells beverage, food, and snack products, prompts its employees to fearlessly provide this organisation with feedback in various ways. For instance, this organisation gathers feedback through different channels such as regular surveys which measure employee commitment and engagement (PepsiCo, 2022).

General Electric is the global conglomerate specialising in different sectors (aerospace, power, renewable energy, etc.). This renowned company developed a smartphone application which aims to generate more regular and significant exchanges among managers and their subordinates. Through this app, exchanges among staff members could be developed in different ways (voice, text, attached documentation, and written letters). With the use of this application, staff members can provide continual feedback all year long. In addition, employees can receive valuable suggestions from any person in their network, including those in the upper management team, as well as those working in other teams (Perform Yard, 2021).

Questions for Self-Reflection

- Why is the use of positive words important for business activities?
- What are the main traits of constructive feedback?
- How can I make other stakeholders feel comfortable when I give them feedback?
- What is the best way to deliver feedback which can potentially affect others negatively?

LOVE AND SPECIFIC STAKEHOLDERS

Chapter 10

Adopting a Loving Attitude towards Employees

10.1 Main Aspects of a Company's Work Environment

> Man becomes a "nine to fiver," he is part of the labour force, or the bureaucratic force of clerks and managers … They all performed tasks as prescribed by the whole structure of the organisation, at a prescribed speed, in a prescribed manner. Even the feelings are prescribed: cheerfulness, tolerance, reliability, ambition, and an ability to get along with everyone without friction.
>
> **Erich Fromm**

Some organisations treat employees as interchangeable parts of the organisational machinery. Oftentimes, these employees are treated in a dehumanised way, like cogs that can be easily replaced when they do not contribute to a company's objectives. These employees resemble automatons, whose only objective is to be productive. This is more prone to occur in achievement-oriented companies which adopt a mechanistic view of business and use words such as "efficacy," "efficiency," "moving the needle," "bottlenecks," and "reengineering," among others (Laloux, 2014). Cohen and Prusak (2001) wisely expressed that the word "employee" has an implicit negative connotation, which means to be utilised or employed. The word "employee" has its origins in the era of the industrial revolution.

Some companies use the term "human resources" instead of "employees." However, the word "resources" can also have a negative connotation because resources are something to be used and oftentimes abused by organisations. Lastly, from a financial perspective, most companies treat employees as "costs," which also has a negative meaning. This type of organisation tends to reduce these costs in different ways (for instance, through work overload, downsizing, etc.) in order to increase its profits, or reduce its losses.

An organisation generally hires people so that they can contribute to achieving the company's business objectives effectively. From this perspective, employees are considered a means to achieve an end or goal (the company's goals). Companies usually set various goals, such as a bigger market

204   DOI: 10.4324/9781003372684-13

share, more productivity, higher levels of profitability, more efficiency, and higher levels of quality, among others.

Many organisations set their goals without considering the potential impact of the achievement of these objectives on employees and other relevant stakeholders. For example, a company can set an objective of increasing its market share, which might imply that employees have to work overtime for many hours every day. This overtime might create an imbalance between their work time and their personal activities (family, leisure, etc.), which, in turn, might bring about employees' dissatisfaction.

Oftentimes, employees are pushed to achieve the company's goals by any means necessary. In those cases, these objectives tend to have a higher priority than employees' well-being. In these situations, the work environment becomes utterly stressful, which prompts employees to adopt a negative attitude towards others. These employees are prone to shut down and act in a passive-aggressive manner; they often become burnt out or overworked. Consequently, the pressure exerted on staff generally does not help them achieve a company's objectives.

Work has a very important impact on the majority of people's lives. Many employees devote a great part of their energy and time to their work activities. Oftentimes, it is difficult for employees to perceive their work as a fulfilling project. Nonetheless, work can be perceived as a gratifying and meaningful activity, especially when it helps employees develop their unique capabilities and harness their full potential.

Work can also be perceived as a valuable endeavour when it makes employees feel acknowledged and accepted as unique human beings. In short, work can significantly contribute to employees' overall well-being and can represent one of the worthiest sources of employees' personal development, growth, and inspiration.

From the perspective of human resources, employees can be considered the most important "asset" of a company, the visible face of an organisation, and the main connection with its customers and other external stakeholders. Employees are also the main creative forces of any organisation and a *meta-resource*, which means a resource with the ability to generate other resources (such as information, products, services, technology, contacts, and funds).

Each employee should be considered a unique human being with distinct valuable characteristics. As seen previously, none of an employee's traits (such as role, background, and qualifications) defines this individual in a complete manner; employees are intrinsically complex and multidimensional because of their physical, emotional, rational, and spiritual facets.

Consequently, when managers relate to their subordinates only considering their roles in the company, other relevant aspects of these employees are unfairly left aside. Most employees cannot be as authentic as they would like to in their workplace, if they are not considered from a holistic perspective.

10.2 Limiting Factors in the Work Environment

The basic philosophy is that if management wants its employees to do a great job with customers, then it must be prepared to do a great job with its employees. Unhappy employees will make for unhappy customers, so unless employees can be successfully taken care of, the success of the organisation on its ultimate, external markets will jeopardised.

Helen Peck, Adrian Payne, Martin Christopher, and Moira Clark

In the following points, several aspects that prevent employees from being treated in a more integrative manner will be thoroughly analysed. These aspects also prevent employees from showing their authentic selves fully.

10.2.1 Organisational Structure

An organisational structure presents different levels of complexity which vary from company to company. This internal structure includes different layers, such as departments, divisions, and roles. For instance, a company like General Electric – also known as GE, the global manufacturer – has its business activities divided into additive, aerospace, capital, digital, and power, among others (General Electric, 2022).

Some theories of social psychology state that when a person is assigned a specific role (for example, a role within an organisation), this individual is inclined to act congruently with functions and responsibilities related to this role. In an organisation, these roles have specific levels of authority and responsibility, and are located on different levels in a hierarchy within a chain of command.

In the work environment, each role has thorough specifications which the respective employee is expected to fulfil. The specific characteristics and functions of each employee's role tend to be continually reinforced by the interaction with other employees. In the workplace, most employees reinforce their own roles by their natural tendency to comply with the role's specifications and meet related expectations.

Whenever employees enact their roles in a company, their other human aspects (spiritual side, emotional states, values, preferences, etc.) cannot be shown overtly because these aspects are overridden by their work roles. In the workplace, employees' roles are considered more significant and valuable than their other human aspects. Therefore, the latter aspects are put aside, preventing employees from fully showing their unique essence.

10.2.2 A Company's Planning Processes

Every company, regardless of its size, develops strategies or plans, which include objectives, tactics, and deadlines. Every plan includes goals, which are the future desired states which a company intends to achieve in a very specific and realistic manner. Some examples of goals are reducing costs, improving profit margins, increasing productivity levels, entering new markets, developing new products, and raising quality standards, among others. These objectives (and the majority of other work topics) tend to be quantitative (based on figures), which makes them easy to measure.

Patel (2005) stated that most companies tend to adopt an attitude which is over-reliant on numbers. Companies are very keen on quantifiable parameters because their achievement is verifiable and easy to document. The use of quantitative indicators can also be used to compare a company's performance levels in different periods. Besides, sometimes employees receive part of their compensation based on these quantitative parameters (for instance, commission based on sales levels) (Klein, 2003).

Cameron (1963) observed that "not everything that can be counted counts, and not everything that counts can be counted." This quote is often wrongly attributed to Einstein. By over-emphasising quantitative aspects, many companies dismiss qualitative aspects (kindness, rapport, fulfilment, supportiveness, empathy, etc.) which are equally important, but cannot be easily measured. These qualitative parameters are fundamental to foster strong, long-lasting, and mutually beneficial relationships with the company's stakeholders.

Chip Conley was the former Airbnb's Head of global Hospitality and Strategy. This entrepreneur is the founder and CEO of the Modern Elder Academy, an organisation which provides people in their midlife with high-value learning (Modern Life Academy, 2023). This business leader posed an insightful question, "What counts that we are not counting?" This business leader said that companies often measure their profits, as well as their cash flow and other aspects. However, this entrepreneur also observed that there are other relevant aspects that are difficult to measure (employee commitment, company's reputation, etc.) and they should be duly considered (Buchanan, 2014).

There is another relevant point to highlight, which is related to a company's objectives. A company sets these quantitative goals, as part of their plans, to improve its performance in the marketplace. However, these goals tend to be set in an impersonal manner, which means without considering the specific and unique characteristics and capabilities of people in charge of achieving them.

Companies' plans also include specific actions to be taken to attain these objectives, as well as clear ways to measure their achievement. As a consequence, whenever employees participate in the implementation of these plans, the possibility of being totally spontaneous is limited by the actions predetermined by the plan.

Companies' plans are like structures which determine what to achieve, how to act, and specific resources to be used for that purpose. All these aspects limit employees' discretion, as they are oftentimes required to abide by them. Therefore, the full use of employees' creative skills is generally constrained by the structural aspects of these plans. In some companies, plans are more flexible, which provides employees with more leeway to act spontaneously and innovatively.

Some companies are relentlessly goal-orientated; their employees are continually pushed to achieve a company's objectives, which generally brings about potential negative effects for employees, such as burnout, employees' alienation and irritability, lack of balance between employees' work and personal activities, and other work-related issues.

Some media (e.g., Travel Weekly) frequently publish the economic results of companies. For example, the news which says "Marriott saw global leisure room nights increase more than 10%" is clearly related to quantitative objectives (Jelski, 2022). However, Marriot is very well-known for considering both quantitative objectives (profits, etc.) and qualitative goals (supportiveness, empathy, etc.). In relation to the latter, this company fosters a diverse and inclusive workplace. Moreover, this organisation supports the recruitment, retention, as well as development of its staff members. As an example, this company has partnered up with an organisation (Vital Voices) to bring about opportunities for women in Mexico, as well as on a global level through mentoring projects. This organisation also undertakes a programme to provide training to disabled youngsters and hire them (Marriott, 2022).

10.2.3 A Company's Rules and Procedures

> Rules tend to show up when people are not clear or trusted. When you know that people have bought into standards, you can give them freedom for decisions and behaviours. If this alignment does not exist, you must micromanage with regulation, expending much more energy in the long run.
>
> **David Allen**

Many workplaces have excessive formal and rigid procedures which regulate employees' activities. These internal regulations can cover a wide variety of topics: procedures regarding data protection, work dress code, ways of addressing a company's communication, format of documents and meetings, etc. This intricate tapestry of rules aims to standardise employees' behaviour and make it predictable and easier to monitor. Oftentimes, some rules in force in an organisation are completely non-sensical, but they are not challenged, as people are fearful of dissenting.

In many cases, organisations assume that workers tend to behave unproductively, make wrong choices regarding their work tasks, or even remain inactive, if internal rules are not in force. Companies set these regulations for their employees to act with efficiency and professionalism. These rules also aim for certainty, regularity, consistency, and clarity, which also contributes to increased efficiency and productivity.

Rules always shape people's expectations because they clearly prescribe what is expected from people and purposefully restrict the ways these people should act (Sheth and Mittal, 1996). On the one hand, some rules are very detailed, thoroughly indicating how employees should act in business. On the other hand, other rules are like general benchmarks which give staff members some leeway for discretion. The latter are often better than the former, as employees are always more keen on some level of autonomy. When employees have higher autonomy, they tend to experience higher well-being.

There are some rules, known as substantive rules, which stipulate how people should perform different business activities (e.g., how to prepare a financial report). Other rules are relational: they regulate how people should interact with one another, for instance, the specific ways a meeting should be held. Some companies set up relational rules which do not foster strong long-lasting relationships with various stakeholders, but instead prompt these interactions to become mechanical, cold, or excessively formal. Some of these rules might even generate more distrust and less co-operation regarding these stakeholders.

All rules in force in an organisation are related to the concept of organisational culture, which means how things are commonly done in an organisation. Most rules are explicit (written), but some are implicit, for example, topics that can be conversed about during work time. Even though all these rules aim to provide certainty and order within the organisation, sometimes they become constraining or even stifling for employees.

In an organisation, rules are intrinsically controlling and directing because they tell employees what to do and how to perform their work activities. Some regulations can also affect the way employees show themselves to others at the workplace. Oftentimes, these formalities do not allow people to express themselves in a genuine and authentic manner, but only in accordance with the company's rules. When these formal constraints are too limiting, they can also become demotivating.

Ekval (1999) observed that, in organisations where rules are too constraining, staff members are more prone to become slow and less alert, which does not contribute to the generation of new initiatives. People who are overburdened by regulations are also more prone to become stressed at work; they also tend to become more thoughtless, as they are not fully harnessing their discerning skills.

As a consequence of these rules, in most work environments, the overt expression of employees' feelings is discouraged. The expression of this rich fabric of human aspects is often considered inappropriate because it is not congruent with the company's rules. Therefore, employees are prompted to show a sterilised and bland version of themselves, leaving aside valuable aspects of their human side.

In many workplaces, employees' aspirations, dreams, and other personal affairs do not count as relevant to the company's aims either. Some work environments have an aseptic attitude towards employees' personal aspects, which are considered to be "domestic issues" that could potentially disrupt the natural dynamics of work activities.

Oftentimes, employees are also discouraged from developing new ideas and innovative alternative ways to do things, especially when these ideas contradict or confront well-ingrained rules in the organisation. Therefore, the rules that provide the organisation with stability and protect the status quo also prevent the organisation from treading non-traditional paths. However, these rules can prove to be inefficient when the organisation navigates turbulent environments, where a more flexible and adaptive approach is required.

Some companies enforce harsh monitoring and disciplinary rules in the workplace which are not aimed at enhancing employees' performance, but punishing them because of their mistakes. Oftentimes, these rules are applied in a mechanical manner, without considering specific circumstances affecting each employee.

The relentless application of these regulations makes many employees feel scared and they tend to adopt a defensive attitude (fight-freeze-flight mode), which affects their performance negatively. These employees feel threatened by these rules; consequently, their need for safety and security is not duly satisfied. Employees who adopt this fearful attitude cannot harness their utmost capabilities fully.

Oftentimes, an organisation is more worried about enforcing varying rules and monitoring their compliance in order to control employees' behaviour, than widely clarifying its most relevant values. As seen previously, a company's values imply what the company stands for and what is relevant to the organisation, for example, honesty, care for the environment, and integrity. As compared with rules, values tend to be willingly adhered to, not compulsorily complied with, as in the case of rules.

With the development of technological advancements (such as electronic employees' cards to open gates and doors, websites with restricted access, emailing, intranet, and CCTV cameras at the workplace), employees' performance can be monitored to an unimaginable extent. Employees' work "footsteps" become easily "trackable" by the company. However, employees who are controlled on a strict and continual basis by the company feel that they are not trusted; these employees often feel constrained, restless, and unappreciated.

A company like Netflix, the video streaming company and movie producer, is an example of an organisation which does not set countless rules for its business activities. Instead, this organisation is keen on hiring high-performance staff. In addition, this company trusts their employees' self-discipline, creativity, and their ability to deal with relevant issues effectively, and rewards these staff members accordingly. As mentioned previously, this company does not have any policies regarding travel and expenses. This company has the assumption that responsible employees, those this organisation aims to hire, deserve to act freely in an environment which is unhampered by rules. The company assumes that, in this type of workplace, staff members are more prone to succeed (Hastings and Meyer, 2020).

10.2.4 The Organisation's Politics

All companies are affected by their own political aspects. In general, a company's politics includes behaviour of employees at work, which is intentional and sometimes covert, aimed at attaining their personal goals. From the political perspective, employees try to persuade others to increase the influence of the former in an organisation, so that these employees' individual goals are attained. Therefore, politics always implies the practical application of different aspects of power by people working in an organisation. Morgan (1986) observed that people's power within a company can be based, for instance, on the control of scarce resources, formal authority, and information management, among other factors.

When people use politics in a positive manner, they try to relate to others in a constructive manner, for example, looking for mutually beneficial agreements with others, being generous and kind with them, and use of objective criteria for decision-making which affect others. These people also tend to recognise others' valuable contributions and unique capabilities, by praising their efforts and commitment. These positive factors imply the existence of a co-operative and supportive work environment.

However, most people tend to assign a negative connotation to the words "organisational politics"; this type of behaviour tends to be perceived as self-serving. From this perspective, a company's politics can include various aspects, such as gatekeeping, gossiping, one-upmanship, turf wars, favouritism, an unfair system of rewards and promotions, backbiting, taking others' praise, and lobbying at top management, among others.

Negative aspects of politics tend to be based on zero-sum game, where some employees win at the expense of others. These factors imply the existence of a competitive work environment where there are scarce resources to fight for. Besides, these negative aspects of politics prevent employees from harnessing their full potential at the workplace; when affected by these factors, employees cannot act in a totally spontaneous and honest manner. Most of these unconstructive practices are based on fear and keep employees from having honest and meaningful communication with others. These practices generate distrust among employees, which is detrimental to the undertaking of co-operative work projects.

These negative aspects of organisational politics prompt employees to act in a defensive manner, taking care of what they do and say to others. In order to navigate all these negative factors, employees tend to develop façades to interact with others in a politically correct, but inauthentic manner. These protective social masks allow employees to perform their work tasks in a less conflictive manner.

Cohen and Prusak (2001) observed that behaviour, either good or bad, spreads by example. These authors stated that workers regularly look for cues in the work environment about how to behave, and what behaviour is banned and which is rewarded. Therefore, negative political behaviour from a group represents a detrimental cue, which prompts other people to act in the same way. In a similar vein, Cialdini (2009) observed that when people have uncertainty regarding how to act, they look at others' actions, which is called "social proof."

Some organisations develop kind and supportive workplaces, which prevents the upsurge of the negative side of politics. As mentioned previously, in companies like Netflix and Pixar, employees are encouraged to continually provide others with constructive feedback, which prompts the other staff members to give this type of feedback as well. It was also mentioned that, in some hospitals, staff were trained to apply the 10/5 rule (making eye contact and smiling at others within 10 feet, and saying "hello" to people within 5 feet); this behaviour creates a more harmonious work environment. Some patients, who have not been trained in this rule, also displayed a smile in return.

10.2.5 Division of Labour

In many organisations, work projects are broken down into tasks. Each task is generally undertaken by specialised employees, who perform it in a routine manner. In those cases, employees are prompted to act in an interdependent and co-operative manner with others who perform other complementary tasks for the same projects. The objective of this division of labour between members of staff is that each employee gets very knowledgeable and efficient in the performance of one or few tasks, which contributes to increasing the company's productivity.

Consequently, most employees do not have access to the overall work project, but only part of it. In these environments, employees are prone to perform the same type of specialised tasks in a continuous manner, which prompts these employees to feel bored and de-skilled. These employees are also demotivated because they cannot harness their innermost skills fully, but only in a limited manner, in relation to their specialised routine tasks.

In some companies, the division of labour is more accentuated, through the development of departments (finance, marketing, administrative, etc.) with very specialised functions. In some organisations, these internal areas tend to act like "silos" which hold significant shares of power. Oftentimes, these silos act in an uncoordinated way with others, and even create feuds between them over perceived scarce resources (e.g., funds).

As a consequence, these employees only enhance skills related to the functions of their positions, leaving aside their other valuable capabilities. Nonetheless, some companies allow employees to work in other posts or departments, or to be trained at skills unrelated to the ones necessary for their position or department.

At Google, there is a clear division of labour. This company is internally structured in teams, such as Engineering & Technology (which is in charge of developing products for users), Marketing & Communications (whose function is to bring users and the company's products together), Business Strategy (which provides with insightful information for company's innovation), and Legal (which is in charge of Internet policy and legislation), among others (Google, 2022b). At most organisations, there is a clear division of labour.

There is one more point to highlight. According to De Pree (2004), in any company, relationships are always more important than structures. The structure of an organisation (e.g., how it is divided into departments) has the main benefits of providing stability, order, and certainty, allowing people working in that organisation to be more efficient. Nonetheless, when a company is too centred on its structural aspects, this organisation is more prone to neglect the development of strong bonds with its stakeholders.

10.2.6 Fast-Paced Environment

The continual upsurge of changing factors (e.g., new technological gadgets, changing legislation, and the entry of new competitors in the marketplace) prompts companies to catch up with these changes. Most organisations are teeming with various impending deadlines, multiple schedules, and a multiplicity of business challenges. All these factors tirelessly pressurise organisations, prompting them to develop hectic agendas and rushed projects. Oftentimes, employees are so pressurised by time limitations that they cannot even hold casual conversations with colleagues to strengthen their bonds with them.

In these organisations, employees are trapped in busy schedules, with their time compartmentalised in carefully designed slots filled with countless pending activities to tick off. These employees do not have much leeway to develop meaningful connections with others. These employees tend to have a limited vision, mostly oriented to short-term issues.

In the marketplace, there are several types of software that help employees manage their busy schedules. Some examples are Todoist (complete software for time management), Toggl Track (an app for tracking time related to activities), TimeTree (software that allows users to share calendars with others), and Trello (software that allows users to see what others are doing, and manage tasks and projects effectively). For example, companies like eBay, the popular e-commerce platform, and Fender, the prestigious producer of musical instruments and amplifiers, are currently using the Trello software pack (Lauretta, 2021).

There is another point to highlight. Fast-paced organisations tend to prioritise the urgent over the significant. For example, a company might give priority to paying suppliers' invoices over the development of mutually beneficial relationships with its main stakeholders. Most companies have difficulties setting a balance between urgent affairs and paramount ones.

Oftentimes, driven by this continuous change, many companies rush to implement new structures, systems, and processes which are not "staff-friendly." These changes create additional friction and busyness in the workplace.

10.3 Other Aspects Preventing Employees' Full Expression

10.3.1 Widespread Collective Activities

In most organisations, various work activities exist which require team-playing among different employees. Working in teams can be very productive because employees can fully express their unique views to others in an open manner. Oftentimes, groupthink is prevalent in teamwork. In those cases, teams have a set of ingrained tenets and ways of performing work activities which cannot be fully challenged by employees. Groupthink has negative effects on employees because they cannot confront the dominant team's viewpoint in order to offer alternative ideas.

As briefly mentioned in this book, in the past, the company Volkswagen, the car manufacturer, installed a software in millions of their cars which purposefully made these vehicles look as if they were safe for the environment. When these cars were tested, this software triggered emission controls that made the cars look like they duly met the emissions standards. Nevertheless, when not being tested, the car emissions were actually significantly higher than the emissions standards. This dishonest stratagem was discovered, and this company was penalised economically and it also had to recall the vehicles which had this software. The main driver of this disloyal ploy was groupthink which was widespread in that organisation at that moment. In that company, the most important decisions were made by a few major top leaders, and employees were frightened to dissent from the leaders' prevailing views (Edmonson, 2019; Schawbel, 2018).

10.3.2 Prevalence of Company's Values

A company's values include the different aspects of importance for an organisation. Values are widespread beliefs about what is considered relevant in an organisational environment. These values affect how employees think, feel, act, and interact with others. A company's values are like a lens through which employees perceive reality within the work environment. According to Barrett (1998), values bring about trust, cohesion, and sense of community within an organisation.

When a company recruits new employees, not only does it verify that candidates have the required skills for the job specifications, but it also checks that these individuals have values which are aligned with the company's prevalent values. Besides, when performing work tasks, employees tend to abide by the company's values, to avoid conflicts with other members of staff.

Nonetheless, some of the company's prevailing values are often at odds with those of employees. In those cases, employees tend to show others that they are aligned with all the company's values. This pretence prevents employees from acting in an honest and authentic way, which is according to their own personal values.

A company like Salesforce, the global software developer, has very significant values, like Trust, Customer Success, Innovation, Equality, and Sustainability. As a consequence, employees working for the company are encouraged to align with these core values when they perform tasks at work (Salesforce, 2022b).

Zappos, the giant shoes retailer, offers to new employees immersive and extensive training where they become knowledgeable of the company's main values (Deliver WOW Through Service, Embrace and Drive Change, Create Fun and A Little Weirdness, etc.) and other aspects of this company's culture. After a short time working for the company, these new employees are offered an interesting amount of money to leave the company, if they feel that they are not a good fit regarding the company's values. This company does not want any employee who is not fully aligned with the organisation's values to work there (Razzetti, 2019b; Zappos Insights, 2023).

10.3.3 Resistance to Change

Many companies are very conservative and tend to avoid significant changes in the way they do business. These organisations prompt employees to perform their activities in a traditional manner. In these organisations, non-traditional business perspectives proposed by employees are not truly welcome. Therefore, employees' creative expression is constrained by the traditional ways of doing things. Sometimes, innovative proposals made by employees are considered, but only after going through a lengthy and thorough scrutiny process. Change tends to be resisted by people, especially when they perceive that its costs exceed its benefits. There are different factors which can prompt people to resist change, as follows:

- Change to be introduced is incongruent with the company's main values.
- Lack of clear information about the change to be implemented.
- Change is seen as meaningless.
- Lack of adequate resources (technology, etc.) to introduce change.
- Perceived lack of support from management during the change process.
- Change is decided unilaterally without consulting those affected by it.
- Lack of competence to undergo change.
- Change is perceived as threatening, overwhelming, unjustified, or unfair.
- Attitude of conformity or complacency, which prevents any opportunity for change.

Other relevant factors of resistance are perceived complexity of change, previous negative experiences regarding change, and untimeliness of change, among others. The aforementioned list of factors is indicative. These factors often vary from company to company.

The following is a good example of resistance to change. The company Godrej and Boyce shut down several years ago. This organisation was the last manufacturer of typewriters in the world. In the past, typewriters were in huge demand by customers for many decades. The manufacturers of this product could not catch up with the fast technological change (microprocessors, Internet, etc.). Consequently, numerous substitute products (computers, electronic pads, etc.) pushed these companies out of the market (Jackson, 2011).

10.3.4 Perceived Limited Resources

Most companies perceive that their own resources (technology, funds, personnel, etc.) are scarce. This perceived limited availability of resources within an organisation tends to be a source of intra-organisational conflict. Employees working in different areas and departments (e.g., marketing, administration, finance) are prone to fight over these resources. This perceived scarcity of resources prompts employees to act in a competitive manner with other members of staff. In this type of scenario, every employee aims to get the best share of the limited resources, at the expense of the rest of the employees.

This perceived limitation of resources, so common in most companies, also reduces the chances of employees expressing themselves in an authentic manner. As seen in Chapter 3, the assumption that company resources are limited is related to a scarcity mindset. This perceived scarcity of resources often prevents employees from different areas (finance, human resources, etc.) from working in a co-operative manner.

10.3.5 *Over-Reliance on External Factors*

Most companies are overly dependent on factors related to their external environment when they perform their activities. These external factors include, for example, competitors' activities, changes in legislation, shifts in fashion trends, upswings and downswings of economic factors, and changes in customer behaviour, among others.

Even though these external factors are relevant to the company, they are generally beyond its control. Many companies perform activities solely driven by these external factors, not focusing on the development of internal factors. Some examples of internal factors are a company's quality levels, productivity, development of new products and services, etc. Among these factors, the development of strong relationships between the members of staff can also be included.

These internal factors are within the company's control, but they are often dismissed for being focused exclusively on external factors. In other words, when a company is mostly focused on factors relating to its external environment, employees are prevented from improving the company's internal factors (e.g., developing new products).

10.3.6 *Over-Emphasis on Rational Aspects*

Most companies' activities are rationally based. The application of this rational approach can be observed in some examples, such as efficient use of resources, meeting deadlines, efficacious cost-cutting, and thorough analysis of problems, among other aspects. These rational aspects are also shown in the development of meticulous procedures, processes, and systems aimed at making a company more effective and competitive in the marketplace.

This over-emphasis on rational aspects limits the enhancement of other relevant aspects of employees, for example, their spontaneity and creative expressiveness. Overly rational work environments leave no leeway for employees to express emotional or spiritual aspects either because these aspects are not relevant to the organisational activities. In extreme cases, employees are perceived as mechanical parts contributing to the organisation's machinery.

However, there is a myriad of companies that adopt an approach of emotional intelligence (EQ). In that sense, a research study has confirmed that the most emotionally intelligent brands have a higher performance in the stock exchange market than other organisations, but they also perform better than some indexes (FTSE100, S&P500). Some examples of these emotionally intelligent brands are Google, Samsung, Microsoft, Netflix, and Disney, among others. To assess the EQ of these brands, five key Brand EQ drivers (Motivation, Empathy,

Self-Awareness, Self-Regulation, and Social Skills) were taken into consideration (Dentsu, 2022).

10.3.7 Other Aspects

The aforementioned factors characterise the majority of work environments. It is possible to add to those factors others, such as the progressive use of telecommuting (also called remote working), the growing use of outsourcing, the increased use of digital resources and automation, the ongoing need for employees' continuous training, the widespread use of flexible work contracts, and the upsurge of new economic sectors which bring about fresh job opportunities, among others.

This book does not suggest the elimination of these factors, which are intrinsic parts of many companies' internal environments. Instead, companies should take into account these factors, but also set conditions which empower employees to harness their unique skills in a more complete manner and express themselves more authentically.

10.4 Nurturing Relationships with Employees

> Overworking happens when people make the mistake of taking care of business instead of taking care of relationships.

Robert Holden

The following points will provide practical advice on how to adopt a more loving attitude towards a company's employees. When these recommendations are applied, the work environment becomes kinder and friendlier, which, in turn, prompts employees to fully harness their unique skills and talents. Four relevant factors which make a workplace more loving are:

- Warm work environment.
- Diversity and inclusion at the workplace.
- Social events.
- Time off.

10.4.1 Warm Work Environment

> Companies and management teams vibrating at a low level can be arrogant, forceful, self-serving, non-caring, and even deceitful. On the other hand, organisations with a higher vibration are much more likely to be socially and environmentally responsible, and committed to higher standards of business ethics and customer service.

Jason Chan and Jane Rogers

10.4.1.1 Main Characteristics of a Negative Work Environment

A company's work environment can either facilitate or hinder employees' performance. The work environment is composed of the physical aspects of the workplace and also the verbal and non-verbal interactions between employees. Knight (1999) observed that a work environment sends a "metamessage" to others, a story of what is going on inside it. When people visit a workplace for the first time, they can infer some of the main traits regarding that company. In a workplace, individuals can pick up specific clues about the company, such as:

- The attitudes adopted by people when interacting with others.
- Main characteristics of employees' conversations (body language and verbal language).
- Emotional ambience of the workplace (enthusiasm, pessimism, anxiety, etc.).
- Specific uses of technology by the members of the staff.
- Proneness to individualistic activities or collective ones.
- Levels of formality and respect for authority.
- Levels of comfort and stress experienced by employees.
- Employees' pace when performing work tasks.
- Level of tidiness and orderliness.
- Existence of formal or informal dress code.
- Aspects related to planning and strategies (use of charts, graphs, etc.).
- Use of signage and livery at the workplace.
- Architectural aspects of the place (spaciousness, luminosity, etc.).
- Specific location and use of furniture.
- Use of shared spaces for socialisation purposes.

Ekval (1999) noted that all observable attitudes, feelings, and behaviours in a work environment are called work climate, and distinctively define the dynamics of employees' interactions in a company. This author also observed that these actions, feelings, and attitudes are responses to various factors (policies, practices, plans, the physical environment in an organisation, etc.) and have an unarguable impact on how staff members learn, sort out problems, communicate with one another, co-ordinate resources, and become motivated and committed, among other aspects. From this author's perspective, this work climate always has concrete effects on the various aspects, like productivity, job satisfaction, profitability, and innovation, among others.

Without the intention to make any generalisations, the reader can find below a list of factors which contribute to the development of an unloving work environment. This list is not exhaustive.

- These environments are overly formal and oftentimes extremely goal-oriented and competitive. Staff are only committed to the tasks at hand and avoid talking about non-business topics. Employees' personal topics (dreams, aspirations, emotional issues, health problems, hobbies, etc.) are discouraged.
- Employees adopt an unloving attitude towards others and oftentimes act without integrity. Their actions are based on detrimental values, such as selfishness, impoliteness, untruthfulness, dishonesty, and carelessness, among others. Some examples of this behaviour are lying, censoring, condemning, threatening, bluffing, ultimatums, and gossiping, among others.
- In these environments, there are several negative aspects of political behaviour (such as favouritism and backbiting) which stem from the adoption of an unloving attitude towards others. Employees are treated in an unloving manner and tend to reciprocate, which makes the whole workplace more hostile and demotivating. In this type of environment, the well-known saying which goes "negativity begets more negativity" is applicable.
- Employees are prompted to be over-committed to achieving goals set by the company. For example, they are pushed to overwork and they are given unreasonable deadlines. These employees are prevented from having work-life equilibrium. Oftentimes, these employees become workaholics and isolated individuals, with a proneness to stress and burnout.

■ Employees manipulate others to achieve the objectives of the former. These employees consider others as a simple means to achieve their own ends, instead of treating them as valuable human beings. In these work environments, employees have a short-sighted perspective on relationships; they aim to attain swift gains from others, instead of cultivating mutually beneficial relationships with them.

All these practices create an ambience of distrust between employees. Oftentimes, these staff members also have low morale, which prompts them to adopt an uncommitted and detached attitude towards work activities. These employees frequently experience negative emotional states (frustration, worry, anger, etc.), which affects their performance in a detrimental manner. In a similar vein, Frost (2007) observed that the emotional toxicity prevalent in a workplace depletes employees' energy, decreases their hope, undermines their confidence and self-esteem, diminishes their productivity, and increases their stress levels. In these negative workplaces, there are corrosive connections (e.g., people treating others in a disrespectful manner) which prompt employees to feel frustrated, distract them when doing their work, and lower their motivation (Dutton, 2003).

Oftentimes, these employees' negative emotions are based on fear, which impacts negatively on their work relationships. According to Keegan (2015), in unloving environments, employees are more prone to experience different types of fear (losing jobs, bullying, harsh criticism, intimidation, arbitrary decisions made by others, losing discretion, not fitting in, etc.), which becomes widespread and normalised. This author also observed that in this type of environment, the best employees tend to leave their jobs because they cannot express their views openly. In these companies, people feel that they are *apart* from these organisations, instead of being *a part* of them (Lewin and Regine, 2001).

Unloving work environments prompt employees to continually adopt a defensive attitude to others, which is related to the fight-freeze-flight mode. This protective mode is closely linked to the reptilian brain, which is the most primitive part of the human brain. In this mode, people tend to protect themselves against perceived threatening factors (for instance, unloving practices from others).

As seen previously, when in this mode, people tend to act in a hyper-vigilant manner and their focus is narrowed down to the threats affecting them, which prompts them to dismiss other aspects. Consequently, their innermost analytical and creative capabilities are temporarily impaired, which creates a negative impact on their productivity and performance.

10.4.1.2 Main Characteristics of a Positive Work Environment

Companies should aim to develop heart-warming work environments. Figuratively speaking, their work environments should be like vessels through which kindness, co-operation, and supportiveness can be continually channelled and spread between staff members. Loving workplaces are intrinsically inspiring and motivating. Every member of staff feels valuable and valued. This type of environment is not arid, stagnant, or inert, but welcoming, dynamic, and warming. These environments celebrate the interdependence of employees, and welcome and appreciate their unique contribution.

In a loving work environment, high-quality connections are more prone to develop. These energising connections foster learning and growth and are characterised by a sense of aliveness, feelings of being taken care of and supported, and a sense of mutual engagement and participation (Dutton and Heapy, 2003). In these connections, people are prone to talk about their own suffering and receive a compassionate treatment from others. In these connections, people display enhanced cognitive skills, better learning capabilities, higher resiliency, more engagement, and commitment at work (Dutton, 2014).

In a loving work environment, every person is willing to assist others and care for them. This attitude of collaboration and solidarity generates a positive impact on the employees, but also on other stakeholders interacting with these employees directly or indirectly. Employees are the human interface between the company and its external stakeholders; therefore, anything that affects staff members (either positive or negative) also impacts other stakeholders in the same way. Other relevant characteristics of a warm work environment are:

- Staff members can perform their work activities at a reasonable pace, without feeling pressurised or stressed. Work activities allow employees to have a good work-life balance, including non-work activities (friends, family, recreation, etc.). It was seen in this book that in the case of companies like Netflix, the video streaming and movie producing company, employees can take as much holidays as they actually need. Companies like Juniper, specialising in IT networks, cloud services, and software, have set up on-site dining and gyms in order to bolster employee physical fitness (Juniper, 2022).

- Members of staff feel acknowledged, appreciated, and valued. If employees have work challenges or personal issues (health, family, etc.), they know that they will be supported. For example, a company like GitHub, an Internet hosting services company, offers its staff members four months family leave for either parent. This company also offers unlimited sick time (Srivastava, 2022).

- Employees are encouraged to act in a creative manner. Their insightful ideas and innovative behaviour are considered valuable for the company's productivity and competitiveness. In companies like 3M, the global conglomerate that offers various products, employees can spend 15% of their time on developing creative insights (3M, 2022b).

- Personnel have all necessary available resources (stationery, technology, etc.) for them to perform tasks effectively. These employees are provided continuous support and training to enhance their skills and talents. It has been seen in this book that, in companies like Dell, the computer giant, its employees are trained on various topics (critical thinking, growth mindset, creativity, etc.).

- The emotional atmosphere of the workplace is positive. People are enthusiastic, kind, and supportive. People show a spontaneous vitality, grit, and willingness to make social connections. In this type of environment, creative ideas tend to flourish on a regular basis. Research has concluded that when staff members share positive emotions in the workplace, there is more co-operation, enhanced co-ordination, heightened creativity, more robust bonds, and better service rendered to customers (Rhee and Yoon, 2012). As previously seen in this book, a company like Walt Disney, the prestigious entertainment organisation, fosters a warm, inclusive, and diverse work environment which supports underrepresented voices.

- Employees adopt a continuous attitude of care, trust, and understanding, which improves connection and rapport with others. Employees can co-ordinate the resources to be used in complex endeavours in a more flowing manner. This type of environment is suitable for the development of collective projects where employees are interrelated in a synergetic manner. As seen in this book, a company like Pixar, the animation giant, fosters a collaborative work environment, where creative ideas can be nourished more effectively. Moreover, people are encouraged to give feedback regarding ideas developed by other teams.

- Staff members are encouraged to regularly hold formal conversations, as well as informal ones. The topics of these conversations are not limited to work matters, but include personal issues. These meaningful dialogues strengthen the relationships between employees. The importance of natural conversations was discussed in Chapter 8. The case of Honda, the car manufacturing company, was discussed in that chapter. This company fosters regular face-to-face conversations, where all employees are considered equals and can express their ideas in a natural and unstructured manner. As seen previously, at Buffer, a company which offers software products to manage social media accounts, once a week, employees are paired up with another colleague to have a Zoom video conversation. In these exchanges, employees chat about anything related their own lives on a personal level. These employees also discuss what they want to attain at this company during that week

- Employees attend non-work activities (dinners, informal meetings, etc.) with colleagues, which helps them revitalise their energy and develop stronger bonds. As seen in this book, a company like Udacity, an online training organisation, organises regular non-business events (Fancy Fridays, after-hours recess, etc.) as a way to foster camaraderie and goodwill among its staff members.

- Staff members feel fulfilled with the performance of their work tasks because they know that they are contributing to the company's purpose, which is meaningful and impactful for the marketplace and the community. In Chapter 1, some examples of companies with a meaningful mission, like Numotion, The Body Shop, Honest Tea, and others, were discussed.

In warm environments, employees are more prone to experience positive emotional states (joy, peace, etc.) on a continuous basis. These positive emotional states tend to affect a company's economic parameters (sales, profits, quality, etc.) in a positive manner.

In this type of environment, employees are more prone to act with integrity when they relate to others. Their actions tend to be aligned with positive values, such as care, respectfulness, selflessness, transparency, honesty, trustworthiness, fairness, and others. These individuals are more inclined to adopt a loving attitude towards others, which is generally expressed through praise, encouragement, thankfulness, and recognition of others. IKEA is a good example of a company with positive values. Its main values are togetherness, caring for people and planet, cost-consciousness, simplicity, renew and improve, (be) different with a meaning, give and take responsibility, and lead by example.

In a warm work environment, positive social capital is more likely to develop. This valuable social capital represents the net of relationships at work which stems from mutual respect, engagement, support, co-operation, and affinity. When this capital is developed in the workplace, people experience a sense of community which implies familiarity, belongingness, membership, and trust. This valuable social tapestry facilitates the learning process in an organisation and helps people stick together during dire circumstances. People perceive their interdependence with others in a positive way which allows them to develop close-knit work relationships.

Cohen and Prusak (2001) observed that this capital prompts the development of a deep understanding, sharing, and rapport between people, bridging the distance between them; this capital builds up and accrues over time. This capital is what makes people more loyal and committed to the company and less prone to leave it in search for other opportunities.

In many companies, when dire challenges arise, most employees tend to respond negatively (feeling overwhelmed, becoming anxious, etc.), which prevents them from surmounting issues effectively. These stressful situations make people feel tense and irritable, and oftentimes prompts them to treat others unlovingly.

However, in warm work environments, employees feel supported on a continuous basis, even if the company faces hardship and struggle. In these circumstances, staff members are less inclined to feel stressed, but more empowered to tackle challenges constructively and encourage others to do so. A warm work environment holds people together, especially during rough times. To put it more simply, in difficult times, employees adopt a co-operative and supportive attitude towards others.

ThermoFisher Scientific, a company which offers laboratory supplies, equipment, and instruments, among other products, is very supportive with its employees, especially when they face difficult times. This company offers its staff members the following benefits: national medical plan, dental plan, and vision plans, and wellness programmes, fertility and pregnancy assistance, as well as accident insurance and critical illness plan. This company also provides its employees with a paid second expert opinion on their health issues delivered by renowned doctors (ThermoFisher, 2022).

In warm work environments, people's loving attitude towards others is contagious. As previously seen, the human brain has mirror neurons which tend to replicate the emotional states of others around. When people act in a loving manner towards others, the latter tends to experience similar emotional states. This phenomenon is called emotional contagion (Goleman, 2006).

Likewise, Cialdini (2009) observed that when a person treats others lovingly, they feel compelled to reciprocate to the former. Hawkins (2012, 2013) stated that a person who adopts a loving attitude towards others positively transform their attitude in a positive manner. As explained in Chapters 2, 3, 6, and 7, this scientist stated that love is a high consciousness state which transmutes the lower consciousness states (guilt, fear, shame, etc.) of people around it. In short, when people treat others lovingly, the whole work environment tends to become more loving.

In a warm workplace, employees experience psychological safety. When employees feel psychologically safe, they are able to show themselves, and also employ themselves, without being fearful of any detrimental consequences to their status, career, or self-image (Kahn, 1990). In this type of workplace, employees can express themselves spontaneously and also show themselves as they truly are, without the fear of being punished or harshly criticised. In these work environments, staff members feel relaxed and comfortable; these employees are less prone to adopt a defensive attitude (e.g., freeze-fight-flight mode).

According to Edmondson (2004), in a psychologically safe workplace, employees are more prone to seek assistance from others, look for feedback, talk about one's own mistakes and difficulties, and act in an innovative manner. This specialist also stated that this type of workplace fosters better communication among staff members so they can co-ordinate resources and goals more effectively.

In a similar vein, Newman et al. (2017) observed that psychologically safe workplaces enhance interpersonal communication; for instance, people are more inclined to solve their disagreements in a friendlier manner, and they tend to provide each other with more constructive feedback. These authors also pinpointed that a psychologically safe workplace brings about better learning work experiences, improves performance, increases employee engagement and commitment, and also fosters innovation. In a psychologically safe workplace, there are reduced stress levels and turnover, increased collaboration and productivity, enhanced life satisfaction, and higher skills preparedness that stem from a faster learning process at work (Monet, 2021).

Barry-Wehmiller, which is a global company that offers manufacturing technologies and services, is an example of an organisation with psychologically safe workplace. This company is of great assistance and care with its staff members. At this organisation, staff members are offered listening sessions to express their views and opinions in a free fashion (Edmonson, 2019).

In Spotify, the audio streaming company, staff members accept mistakes as relevant factors in the learning process. In this company, engineers are allowed to spend 10% of their work time to work on anything they want to; in addition, this company also has a hack week, where employees can explore new ideas (innovative products, betterment of processes, etc.) that they are keen on, or that they lack time to reflect on. They can work with others on these ideas in a collaborative manner (Sundén, 2013).

Spotify makes it safe for people to take risks and fail, while encouraging them to learn from one another to do things better. In this organisation, teams share their mistakes thorough Fail Walls and internal blog posts for staff to learn from these errors, which bring about a psychologically safe workplace (Minaar, 2020; Razzetti, 2019a).

There is a last point to highlight. Barrett (2017) observed that, over a period of 10 years, an investment of $25,000 in each of the 40 best American companies to work for has shown, on average, an annualised return of 16.39%, as compared to the return of 4.12% related the S&P500 Index. This specialist also stated that, in these top workplaces, employees are truly engaged; they care about the company and are willing to make a meaningful contribution at work, and provide insightful advice on how to better the company's performance.

10.4.1.3 Positive Layout of the Workplace

The work environment also includes its physical aspects: its architectural design. Warm workplaces are designed in a worker-friendly manner; they allow employees to perform their activities in a focused manner and harness skills effectively. These workplaces are spacious and people can walk around them in an unencumbered manner. These places are well-lit and ventilated and they abide by hygiene and safety legislation.

These spaces have comfortable areas for people to socialise, where employees can take some time off and have informal chats with other colleagues. These places are equipped with dispensers for employees to have beverages and some snacks. These leisure spaces should include comfortable furniture for employees to relax and replenish their energy. Some companies include magazines, books, arcade games, or board games for employees to be entertained and to clear their minds.

Wiseman (2013) stated that positive bodily sensations bring about positive emotions. This specialist observed that, when a workplace is set in a way that prompts people to experience *physical sensations* of comfort and warmth, these individuals tend to *feel* (from the *emotional* standpoint) that this place is friendly and warm. Some examples of "warm" conditions that companies can consider for their workplaces are placing hot water dispensers for beverages (such as tea or coffee), using comfortable chairs with soft cushions, keeping the place well-heated in winter, etc.

The Hollister Group is a staffing agency; its main four core values are open communication, integrity, passion, and community (The Hollister Group, 2022). At the organisation's office, there are workstations which have automatic desks where employees can either sit or stand. These premises also have various soft and high-top seats to make employees feel as if they were at home. This place has natural lighting and brightly coloured furniture. All this unique decor brings about a warmer work environment (Berns, 2022).

Warm workplaces are also orderly and clean. Lobel (2014) observed that spotless places are associated with morality and ethical behaviour, which means that people working there look more trustworthy. This author stated that people tend to link a sensory experience (for example, seeing a clean workplace) with a related state of mind called "embodied cognition" (e.g., thinking that people working there have "pure" intentions).

The workplace is also perceived as warmer when it is kept decluttered. In order to avoid clutter, old documents and paperwork (not necessary to be kept by law) should be regularly binned. The same applies to useless and broken items. Sometimes, certain documents and other items used occasionally can be stored in a room separate from the main work area.

Wiseman (2009) observed that the use of green in the workplace has a positive effect on employees because this colour is linked with relaxation and positivity. This author advised locating some plants and greenery in the workplace because they symbolise creativity and generativity. Hale and Evans (2007) observed that "green symbolises growth, fertility and harmony; it is restful and refreshing." In Google, plants are seen in different areas of the workplace. In the company's premises, there is also natural lighting (Edays, 2022).

Lobel (2014) observed that red is associated with danger, which prompts people to feel anxious. Therefore, red should be avoided in the workplace, when possible. Some recommend that workplaces should be scented to make the place more pleasant and uplifting for employees. Lobel (2014) observed that the smell of cinnamon and peppermint can enhance employees' cognitive skills.

Positive visual cues can enhance employees' performance when they are included in the workplace. Research concluded that the existence of banners with positive images in the workplace prompted employees to be more productive. These positive messages continually imprint on the minds of employees prompting them to adopt a more optimistic attitude.

An example of positive imagery can be seen in an organisation called Bernstein Litowitz Berger & Grossmann LLP, which is a law company that prosecutes securities fraud. In its new offices, in the reception, this company placed a big arty painting of Batman. One of the company's founders observed that, as Batman aims to guard Gotham city, this law firm aims to protect victims from security fraud stratagems. In that sense, this person actually knew that the reception was the right place for that painting (Keswin, 2019).

The workplace should include natural light, when possible. Fluorescent lighting should be avoided. In relation to this topic, Brown (1997) observed that this type of lighting "emits a different colour of light and also gives off more radiation" which tends to lead to poor concentration or mental tiredness.

SnackNation is a company which delivers healthy snack products for offices. One of the most relevant features at this company' headquarters is a 20-feet tranquility waterfall. At the company's premises, there is a spot in front of a window, where water flows, and plentiful natural light comes in throughout the day. On a regular basis, employees use this luminous spot to contemplate, become more creative, and solve relevant issues (Murphy, 2022).

Workplaces should convey when possible principles of equality. This means that all employees should have the same allocation of space, including superiors. Managers should avoid having carefully guarded and luxury offices in order not to create a sense of separation from the rest of the staff. Workplaces with open spaces, for example, without cubicles, tend to encourage employees to act in a more trusting and supportive manner with one another.

IKEA, the company that offers furniture and houseware, has developed its headquarters offices, including an open office plan. The company's premises have three large rotating light wells. These premises also have a big staircase connecting all storeys. At every storey where the offices are located, there are views between the storeys. Because of the unique shape of this building, staff members are naturally prompted to have authentic and regular interactions (Aleksandrova, 2021).

Open spaces foster collaboration and interaction between employees. However, Bernstein and Turban (2018) observed in a research study that open spaces actually decrease face-to-face interaction and co-operation between employees, who are more likely to use different ways to communicate with colleagues, such as email. This can be due to overstimulation or a lack of privacy which characterises open spaces.

10.4.2 Diverse, Inclusive, and Participative Workplace

Work is love made visible.

Kahlil Gibran

10.4.2.1 The Importance of a Diverse and Inclusive Environment

Most people tend to categorise others in clear-cut groups, for instance, leaders and followers, proactive and reactive, etc. Oftentimes, people who use these classifications tend to stereotype others, for instance, with sentences like: "All these people are ...." Stereotyping is about categorising the members of a group in a stringent and simplistic manner, assigning them homogeneous traits without taking into account their distinctive individual qualities. Some examples of stereotyping are "All Italian people are..." or "All women are..."

Social psychologists have observed that people naturally tend to stereotype because of their subconscious biases. However, human beings are far more complex than simple categories. Each person is unique and can never be pigeonholed in rigid compartments. Moreover, all people need to be recognised by their distinct and unique qualities. Toyota, the prestigious car manufacturer, introduces its new employees to the topic of unconscious bias from the first day of the onboarding sessions (Vlad and Bankson, 2022).

As mentioned in Chapter 6, people generally get on better with others with similar characteristics. However, a person with a loving attitude towards others intends to relate to them, beyond their apparent differences or dissimilarities. A loving person recognises that other people are valuable human beings. Not only should these valuable beings be respected, but their distinctive views and values should also be duly acknowledged.

A company which adopts a favourable attitude towards diversity does not focus on any limiting social categories, but on the individual as a human being. This type of company aims to develop a pluralistic work environment that supports the harmonious coexistence and interrelation of people with different qualities. A company recently mentioned, The Hollister Group, fosters a diverse and inclusive workforce. This company makes employees staff members comfortable to be themselves at work. In addition, this company appreciates and celebrates various views from employees. This organisation is fully committed to avoiding any type of discrimination based on nationality, gender, race, disabilities, or any other personal qualities. As a consequence, this company has been given various awards and accolades (best company for women, best company regarding work-life balance, best company regarding happiness, etc.) (The Hollister Group, 2022).

In inclusive work environments, the unique attributes of each employee (experience, training, qualification, age, cultural background, etc.) are continually acknowledged, celebrated, and enhanced, when possible. A company's employees feel comfortable showing their unique qualities and they are also open to learning from other members of staff. In relation to this, research has observed that when a person feels excluded by others, the same areas of this individual's brain are activated as if this person was experiencing physical pain (Lieberman and Eisenberger, 2009). Discrimination and exclusion tend to become a very important stress factor.

There is another important point to highlight. Kandola and Fullerton (1994) stated that a diverse work environment has several benefits, such as easier recruitment of talented people, reduction in costs of training and turnover, increased employee commitment and satisfaction, improved customer service, higher quality and productivity levels, and a more enhanced company's image, among others. In addition, diverse workplaces foster more innovation (Lorenzo et al., 2017). In diverse workplaces, people with different viewpoints, distinct expertise, and unique experiences can interact and discuss relevant issues with one another, which can bring about richer creative insights. This provides companies with more flexibility which is very suitable for fast-changing business environments.

Richard (2000) has observed that diverse workplaces are positively correlated with a higher performance level, as compared with less diverse ones. Some characteristics of diversity-centred companies are:

■ According to Maslow (1968), this type of work environment is growth-fostering because it is promoting the satisfaction of all the relevant needs of employees. The different types of needs have already been analysed in Chapter 6. Some examples of companies satisfying these needs were also mentioned in that chapter.

■ In diverse workplaces, every employee is given fair chances to access different work opportunities regardless of their personal qualities and unique background. In this type of work environment, there are widespread and transparent procedures regarding employees' promotion; new employees are recruited from a perspective of equal opportunity. Employees' appraisal and promotion are based on specific set objectives and merit, instead of being centred on employees' personal qualities. Yahoo!, the popular online portal, is an example of a company which has a workplace with equal opportunities. In any recruitment campaign regarding this organisation, all qualified candidates are taken into account for employment, without any type of discrimination (gender, race, nationality, religion, etc.) (Yahoo, 2022).

■ In diverse work environments, activities related to favouritism are strictly avoided. Favouritism means unfairly preferring some employees over others. This is a common negative practice part of organisational politics. Skift, a travel industry news online platform, is an example of a company that discourages favouritism. Once a year, all the company's employees are invited to attend a retreat in a touristy destination. These retreats aim to strengthen the sense of community among all staff members (Lanier, 2022).

■ In diverse workplaces, all employees are genuinely encouraged to express their distinct views on relevant topics. As a consequence, the analysis of relevant issues becomes wider and enriched. Any discrimination based on specific ages, genders, physical abilities, races, religions, or type of personality (extroverts, introverts, etc.) is unwelcome and penalised. The previously mentioned The Hollister Group is a company that welcomes all employees' diverse views; this organisation is committed to combating any type of employee discrimination. Another company which encourages employees to express their views without restraints is Cisco. This is a company specialising in digital communications technology. On a regular basis, this organisation conducts an employee confidential online survey to assess staff members' level of engagement and satisfaction, with the aim to better its workplace. This survey covers various topics, like empowerment, teamwork and co-operation, and career development, among others. In addition, the company uses focus groups, composed of various employees, in order to debate specific issues. This company has received various awards as one of the best places to work (Cisco, 2008, 2023).

■ A diversity-centred company is committed to the continuous development of a diverse work environment. For instance, employees can be encouraged to informally express their objections and suggestions regarding the work environment. More formal ways of gathering information can also be used, for instance, surveys where staff members are asked about their satisfaction regarding the work environment. For instance, Intel, a company that produces semiconductor chips, conducted an employee inclusion survey. This survey wanted to measure the employees' perception of inclusion in the workplace. According to this survey, the majority of employees stated that the company provides them with an inclusive and safe place to work (Intel, 2022).

- Sometimes changes in the physical aspects of the workplace are introduced in order to develop a more diverse environment. An example is fitting special lifts for people with mobility difficulties (people using crutches/walkers, individuals in wheelchairs, etc.). For example, Cisco, a company previously analysed, has undertaken the initiative called Project Lifechanger which developed technology that provides staff members with disabilities with the possibility to work in a remote manner. This valuable technology also ended up being used by other organisations to support their own employees (Roberts, 2022).

- In diversity-centred organisations, employees are trained through workshops and seminars to make them aware of the importance of a diverse environment. Sometimes, the training can also include the development of specific capabilities necessary to support a diverse work environment. Intuit, a company that sells financial software, offers its staff members multiple courses and training sessions regarding diversity and inclusion (Postelnyak, 2022). Another well-known company, Delta Airlines, delivers a course titled "Promoting inclusion" for its employees in order to raise employees' awareness on this topic and bolster an inclusive work environment at every level of this organisation. Thousands of staff members working for this airline have already done this training (News Delta, 2020).

Some companies take the initiative and spontaneously foster diverse work environment because they want all employees to be treated in a fair and respectful manner; these companies realise that having a diverse workplace is the best thing to do. However, other companies often become more diverse as a result of the pressure of legal rules (for instance, equal opportunities legislation) or pressure from different groups (such as employees, unions, and community).

Many countries have specific legislation which encourages and protects diversity in the workplace. Some regulations aim to prevent discrimination and prejudice against employees in the work environment. For many organisations, respect for diversity represents an important value; these companies have their own organisational policies to guarantee and care for a diverse work environment.

10.4.2.2 Employees' Participation and Acknowledgement

Fromm (1956) observed that all human beings need to overcome their state of separateness from others. In other words, people are intrinsically gregarious, which means social beings who feel compelled to relate to others and be accepted by them. In a work environment, employees need to be regularly validated as relevant parts of the company. Whenever possible, employee recognition should be merit-focused, positive, fair, personalised, specific, timely, and frequent; this recognition can come from both superiors and colleagues (Mosley and Irvine, 2020). According to research, honest and personalised recognition of employees reinforces their positive behaviour, and prompts them to perform better (Luthans and Stajkovic, 2009).

On the one hand, companies that regularly recognise the contribution of their employees tend to have higher employee engagement and lower turnover (Schawbel, 2018). On the other hand, when employees do not feel recognised at work, this has a negative impact on their morale and productivity levels, which, in turn, affects the company's profits in a detrimental manner (Novak, 2016).

Consequently, a company should make its employees feel they are a special part of the organisation. A company can clearly highlight the reasons why employees are valuable and acknowledge them in different ways:

- Employees can be regularly informed of the company's most relevant achievements. The organisation can pinpoint how employees contributed to these successful outcomes. When employees' contributions are recognised, their engagement tends to increase significantly. Sometimes, employees can be given unexpected gifts for their contribution, for example, sending them thank you letters, inviting them to non-business events, and others. Black n Bianco is a company that sells children formal items of clothing online. In this company, there was a big purchase order regarding an international buyer; it took more than half a year to close the deal. As a consequence, this organisation gave each employee a performance bonus and a hand-written note to appreciate their contribution to this successful deal (Williams, 2022).
- Employees can also be told about the new endeavours the company will undertake. In these cases, the organisation can highlight the specific contribution expected from employees. Employees can also be invited to give their views on projects in progress, or even past endeavours. In these cases, the employees' voice is acknowledged and considered. For instance, AT&T is a huge provider of pay TV which reaches millions of customers with movies, sporting events, and shows. This company has a suggestion box called The Innovation Pipeline and employees all over this organisation are empowered to propose any innovative idea (Boogaard, 2022).

Oftentimes, companies use storytelling techniques to make their employees feel more acknowledged and proud of their contribution. These tales show how employees impacted on the company's endeavours in a positive manner. These stories include employees' feelings, opinions, and actions regarding the company's projects. Impactful stories show the human side of the company: the flesh-and-blood human beings who contribute to its projects. These stories also include the business aspects of the company's achievements (such as profits, revenues, and costs).

Some companies tend to wrongly include in their stories more faceless facts and quantitative parameters than aspects related to their most precious resources, their employees. This makes their stories cold and impersonal, which prompts employees to feel not fully acknowledged by them.

Poignant human stories create a stronger sense of belonging and identification between employees and the company. People easily identify with stories because they convey relevant ideas, values, and experiences in a memorable manner. These stories make employees feel that they are a relevant part of a community that contributes to the company's objectives. These stories can be told in different ways, for example, via the company's workshops, emailing, newsletters, internal magazines, press releases, newsboards, blogs, and websites. For instance, a company can use a story related to its new business branch. This story could include several elements, such as the challenges faced by employees before opening the branch and activities performed by employees to overcome these challenges, among others.

In the case of Marriott International, every year, this company gives the Marriott Awards of Excellence to recognise its best staff members who represent relevant values like achievement, character, dedication, effort, as well as perseverance. On its website, this company publishes the names of the winners of this award accompanied by rich details of their personal stories, as well as videos where these employees comment on their own lives (Marriott, 2023b).

The Chief Marketing Officer of Numotion, a company that offers wheelchairs and equipment for people with mobility problems, observed that, in business, it is important to make it personal, especially when using storytelling within the company (e.g., management, employees) or towards external stakeholders (customers, suppliers, etc.). In the past, one of the company's employees had lost all her belongings in a tragic house fire. The company's staff members all over the country, guided by the CEO, acted jointly to replace some of this employee's belongings. After these significant contributions, this employee's story was shared in a video conference, which was broadcast all over the company, and where every employee could participate in the "big reveal." This event increased employee morale throughout the whole company (Barczak, 2022).

10.4.3 Social Activities

10.4.3.1 Importance of Social Activities

> Far from standing in opposition to each other, play and work are mutually supportive. They are not poles at opposite ends of our world. Work and play are like timbers that keep our house from collapsing down on top of us … Work does not work without play.
>
> **Stuart Brown and Christopher Vaughan**

Most people have a need for novelty and fun; they want to explore new experiences and diverse sensations. Nonetheless, most work environments make people feel bored and burdened, and oftentimes trapped and overwhelmed. Most work activities are structured, goal-oriented, and logic-based, which renders these workplaces dull and barren.

Consequently, most employees crave social activities, which are intrinsically more interesting and engaging than work. In these events, people can be fully present and let their hair down, away from work pressures. However, most companies perceive these light-hearted activities to be of low value for business purposes. These recreational activities are usually considered irrelevant; therefore, most companies discourage them.

From this book's perspective, these social activities are not frivolous, slacking, or superficial, but of high value. These activities represent the perfect complement to work activities. These activities encourage improvisation and team-playing, and spice up social interactions, which creates more affinity and rapport between people. During these social activities, most people tend to have fun and experience positive emotions, which, in turn, is very positive for their work tasks. Copious research concludes that people in a positive mood are prone to act more productively and creatively at work. In a similar vein, Achor (2011) observed that positive emotional states are very important indicators of high success in the work environment.

Asana is a company which offers work management software. This organisation offers its employees social activities that foster employee well-being. For instance, this company's staff members are offered daily yoga programmes, as well as free gym memberships (Edays, 2022).

10.4.3.2 Importance of Social Activities and Events

> The brightest and most lucrative futures are going to belong to organisations whose people have the courage to risk being human in the workplace.
>
> **William Arnold and Jeanne Plas**

Some of the world's biggest industries are related to entertainment and leisure, for example, tourism, movies, and music. These activities are ludic, which means related to play. These playful activities connect people to their early childhood, when their only concerns were to be fed and to play with toys.

A company that regularly organises social events and activities for their employees adopts a loving attitude towards them. Most people working for a company, even boring individuals, want to have fun, once in a while. The majority of employees, including those in the highest positions, feel attracted to social activities and events. Some examples of these activities are cocktails, celebrations, award ceremonies, etc. In MVF, an organisation which offers digital marketing services, employees can partake in various clubs (bingo, board game, book, movie, etc.). These social activities help foster connectedness among its employees. This company also provides its employees with yoga sessions twice a week (Parris, 2022).

Social activities have a common trait: most formalities and bureaucratic procedures can be temporarily left aside. In these activities, work roles lose their importance. In this type of event, people can interact with others more spontaneously. People working in different areas (finance, marketing, etc.) are brought together which increases the affinity between them.

Dr Zak (2013) observed that these social activities foster the natural release of a powerful hormone called oxytocin, which makes people experience an enhanced sense of well-being. As seen previously in Chapters 5, 6, and 7, oxytocin is produced by the human brain and prompts people to feel good and fosters prosocial behaviour like bonding, co-operating, and trusting others.

In social events, there are no work objectives to achieve or pressing deadlines. People can relax and recharge their batteries to resume their work activities more energised. In addition, at these events, most people let their guard down and have no hidden agenda, which makes their communication more spontaneous and rooted in the moment. Therefore, conversations include non-business topics (personal preferences, past experiences, etc.) which make these interactions more real and meaningful. These events constitute a valuable parenthesis over a tedious work schedule.

At these events, the negative aspects of an organisation's politics (one-upmanship, gatekeeping, favouritism, etc.) are of little value. These social events prompt participants to feel more at ease and calm. At these events, people are less prone to adopt a defensive mode towards others, as compared with the working hours when people tend to act in a more reactive manner.

Some companies organise social activities in a very limited manner, for instance: Christmas dinner, year-end celebration, etc. When social events are infrequent, employees are left with a glimpse of them. Some organisations argue that these social activities are not a priority due to their busy schedules. Other companies believe that these activities are a waste of time because they do not generate any profits. Nonetheless, when these events are frequent, employees' performance is affected positively. At the renowned media agency The7stars, people love to celebrate; there is always a good excuse for a party (birthdays, Christmas, monthly payday, etc.). This company even has an office bar with a prosecco tap, which is used for some of these events (The7stars, 2022).

10.4.3.3 A Different Standpoint on Social Events

All companies should organise social events on a regular basis to bring their employees closer to one another. As seen previously, these events should be fostered in every company because they strengthen relationships between staff members. Some examples of social activities a company can organise are:

- Regular meetings for socialisation purposes.
- Retreats to practise yoga, qi gong, and meditation.

- Sports and board games tournaments.
- Picnics and other outdoor gatherings.
- Cultural visits to museums, galleries, etc.

When a company informs its employees of upcoming social activities, these staff members should be told of the positive effects of these events for them (for instance, better connection, improved rapport, etc.). Sometimes, these events can be linked to specific employees' accomplishments. In these cases, these social activities represent a great way of celebrating these attainments and appreciating employees' contribution.

For instance, Procter & Gamble, the company that offers beauty items and care products, provides its staff members with meditation sessions as well as tranquil places in order to bolster their well-being. HBO, the television company that offers movies and episodes, also provides its employees with meditation lessons in its workplace, as well as free yoga sessions (Duffy, 2020).

There are companies that consider these social activities irrelevant. Companies which are reluctant to organise social events can gradually add them in an experimental manner to test their outcomes. Here are some of the additional positive effects of these social activities:

Positive energy: All these activities have a celebratory energy, which prompts people to feel positive, which tends to be contagious. As explained previously, people attending these feel-good events tend to adopt a non-defensive mode; at these events, people also tend to be more spontaneous than usual, showing themselves as they truly are.

Improvement in productivity: At these events, people tend to feel less constrained by work obligations, but more energised. As previously seen, these activities are valuable time off which disrupts the monotony and dullness of work time. These fun activities always have a positive impact on employee productivity due to their revitalising effect.

High-quality communication: At these events, people can interact with others in a more personal, open, and lively manner. Participants tend to access human aspects of others beyond their social masks (job or business roles). This type of events is suitable for natural conversations, explained in Chapter 8. These social activities enrich people's interactions and have a positive impact on their relationships.

Enhancing of mental capabilities: Research states that playful social activities contribute to the development of neural pathways in the brains of the attendees, which, in turn, enhances their creative skills. Researchers also observed that, at these events, people enhance their improvisation skills, which can be applied to other real-life social situations, especially challenging ones.

Relaxing effect: Many employees regularly suffer from different degrees of stress during working time. When intertwined with work time, social activities have a refreshing effect on these employees. This type of activity helps stressed employees "unplug" from the fight-freeze-flight mode adopted at work. When employees release stress, their utmost mental capabilities are naturally enhanced.

There is a very popular organisation called The Events Company which offers different events for companies. This organisation offers companies various themed events (Arabian Nights, Alice in Wonderland, Casino Royale, etc.). In addition, the organisation offers various indoor team-building events (cheese making workshops, cocktail making experience, etc.) and outdoor ones (circus skills workshop, company sports day, GPS treasure hunt, etc.). Some renowned companies like AT&T, Johnson & Johnson, Astra Zaneca, and American Airlines are among this organisation's corporate clients (The Events Company, 2022).

10.4.4 Time Off

In many organisations, an employee's working time as well as rest time are meticulously regulated and monitored. Oftentimes, organisations believe that time off impacts negatively on their employees' productivity and efficiency levels. Consequently, employees' working time is used in the most fruitful way possible to contribute to the company's objectives.

Some employees are prompted to work on a non-stop mode or for long hours. Some companies wrongly believe that employees become more effective when they overwork or perform without being interrupted. However, research has shown that extended and uninterrupted work decreases employees' productivity because these individuals become mentally and physically tired.

Employees who overwork also create an imbalance between work activities and non-work ones (family, entertainment, etc.), which makes them feel demotivated. As a consequence, these employees become less engaged with the company, which impacts negatively on its main economic indicators (productivity, quality, etc.).

Full contact is a company that offers cloud-based software for companies and developers. This technology company is committed to paying a hefty amount of money to its staff members if they disconnect from work activities when they are on a holiday. In order to access this benefit, employees need to prove that on their vacation, they were not looking at their work emails or any other type of work-related messages (Zavvy, 2022).

Research also shows that employees who have regular breaks during work time and work only a reasonable number of hours are more motivated and productive. In other words, employees need this downtime to replenish their energy levels. Consequently, companies should realise that employees are not machines but human beings, which implies the need to recharge their energy regularly.

Schwartz et al. (2010) observed that employees should break every 90 or 120 minutes of working time to avoid becoming restless, irritable, and unfocused. This downtime should never be considered slackening time, but revitalising one. These authors concluded that people become more productive at work when they move between periods of concentrated focus and intermittent rest time. During these breaks, employees can replete their energy levels, for example, taking a short walk, stretching their muscles, or breathing deeply.

Companies should discourage employees from overworking. Employees' overtime can be simply avoided through reasonable allocation of tasks and by avoiding tight deadlines. With these simple practices, employees are prone to achieve a better balance between their work activities and personal ones.

Employees who do not overwork have more spare time for other activities. In their spare time, people have more choice and control, as compared to the commonly regulated and predetermined activities at work. Russell (1994) observed that workers should have more spare time, not to recover from work toil, but to express themselves through their non-working skills (artistic, sporty, etc.).

Some employees use their spare time to offset needs unmet in the work environment. This spare time also helps employees take their lives less seriously and more light-heartedly, which, in turn, has a positive impact on their work productivity. Research showed that leisure contributes to people's well-being and gives their lives more meaning, especially when people perform high-quality activities, such as mingling with others, reading, practising sports, hobbies, artistic endeavours, being in contact with nature, volunteering for social causes, etc.

Netflix, the international video streaming and movie producing company, has no vacation policy. In practice, this company's employees have been able to take unlimited holiday since this organisation started up. In this company, employees are entitled to take the time off they need. In that sense, the number of days off these employees take is in no way limited or monitored. This organisation focuses on specific accomplishments of its employees, rather than the specific time they work (Hastings and Meyer, 2020). There seems to be a link between unlimited vacations and reduced time off because of sickness; unlimited holidays also seem to be correlated with decreased staff turnover (Benton, 2022).

There is another point to highlight. Employees should be encouraged to have a minimum of daily sleep. Medina (2014) observed that insufficient sleep time drains the brain and hurts attention, memorisation, and reasoning skills. In other words, when employees do not sleep enough, they are less sharp, more unfocused, and less engaged, which diminishes their productivity levels and the quality of their work. Lack of adequate sleep makes people more irritable, less communicative, and more prone to become stressed. A research study has concluded that employees troubled sleeping is linked to higher absenteeism, lower work performance, and higher healthcare costs (Hui and Grandner, 2015).

Blackburn and Epel (2017) observed that a minimum of a regular seven hours of quality sleep has several restorative benefits, such as appetite control, consolidation and healing of memories, refreshment of mood, contribution to learning process, and reduction of stress-proneness. These authors suggested some tips for better quality sleep, like going to bed at a regular time, doing relaxation exercises, and drinking warm herbal infusions just before going to bed. Lastly, scientists have stated that all body functions have their own built-in daily rhythmical patterns, called *circadian rhythms*, which can be negatively affected by scarce sleeping time.

There are some companies that set up nap pods in their workplaces for employees to take short naps during work time. Some examples are Google (the developer of the most popular search engine and other information products), Zappos (the online retailer that sells shoes and clothes), and The Huffington Post (the prestigious newspaper) (Shoen and Singh, 2022).

Research has shown that a great a part of staff experiences fatigue at work which negatively affects productivity levels (Ricci et al., 2007). In an interesting research study, it was observed that short naps, especially those taken just after lunch, seem to bring about heightened employees' alertness at work (Takahashi et al., 2004).

Questions for Self-Reflection

- What are the limiting factors in a work environment?
- How can I make the work environment warmer?
- How can I encourage employees' inclusion and participation?
- What fun and social activities can be introduced in our company?

Chapter 11

Additional Aspects of a Loving Attitude to Employees

11.1 Relationships between Superiors and Subordinates

Work brings far more than just money. A satisfying job can also bring structure and meaning to one's life, mental and emotional stimulation, personal relationships, regular opportunity to develop to use and develop skills, social status, self-esteem and a sense of identity.

Paul Martin

Most organisations have an internal structure, which generally consists of different areas (departments, divisions, etc.). This hierarchical structure commonly has people at higher levels (known as management or superiors) who provide people in lower levels (also called subordinates) with commands and directions. The former are also in charge of monitoring the performance of the latter, according to specific policies and procedures. Besides this, managers are often in charge of the planning process, and the co-ordination and allocation of resources to be used by subordinates. In small companies, this structure tends to be simpler than in bigger organisations.

Some people might argue that the terms "superiors," "subordinates," and others have an unloving connotation. However, in this chapter and the rest of this book, terms such as "superiors" and "subordinates," "managers," "employees," and others will be used for practical purposes and simplicity.

Oftentimes, employees feel that their managers are rudely commanding them. In other words, managers adopt an unloving attitude towards employees. In these cases, not only do superiors' unkind directions make subordinates feel unsupported, but these commands also prompt these employees to adopt a defensive mode (fight-freeze-flight).

As seen previously, when employees have a defensive attitude, their mental capabilities are temporarily impaired, rendering them more ineffective at performing their work tasks. Superiors' rude orders can make employees feel unacknowledged as valuable human beings. These careless directions prevent employees from giving their best at work.

Employees are linked to the company through work contracts, which meticulously stipulate their rights and obligations at work. However, from the psychological perspective, the employer

DOI: 10.4324/9781003372684-14

and employees are also linked by the so-called "psychological contracts," which include the expectations that each party (employer and employee) has about one another. Some common expectations that employees have when they work for a company are:

- To be treated with respect.
- To be appreciated for their contribution.
- To have stability regarding their post.
- To use their skills and talents at the workplace.
- To work with supportive and friendly people.
- To have the necessary resources to work (e.g., computers, etc.).
- To have time for a work-life balance.
- To have a reasonable workload.
- To have access to rest time and leisure time.
- To express ideas and opinions freely.
- To receive fair compensation for their work.
- To contribute to a meaningful business purpose.
- To have a comfortable and safe space to work.
- To access opportunities for promotion.
- To be taken into account in relevant decisions.
- To acquire new valuable skills.
- To be supported when personal issues arise.

On the other side, employers have expectations as well. Some common examples of employers' expectations about employees are:

- To contribute to the company's objectives on a continuous basis.
- To go the "extra mile" when possible.
- To respect hierarchy and authority.
- To abide by the company's regulations.
- To perform tasks efficiently and diligently.
- To use their creative and analytical skills to solve the company's problems.
- To keep the company's information confidential.
- To use the company's assets (computers, etc.) in a caring and responsible manner.
- To contribute to a positive work environment.
- To be supportive and co-operative with colleagues.
- To relate to external stakeholders in a friendly manner.

It is important to pinpoint that these psychological contracts are never carved in stone, but evolve over time. These psychological contracts are unwritten, but their effects are very noticeable.

This unwritten contract is affected by the subjective perceptions of people involved in this agreement, which often differ in a significant manner. An example will clarify this point. A staff member is convinced that working overtime will make this employee be promoted by the manager. These are this employee's expectations. However, this manager has different expectations regarding this staff member's work. This manager believes that, if this employee works overtime, this staff member deserves to be given a hand-signed thank you letter.

In this example, the expectations of the employee and the manager are very different, so one of them is likely not to meet the other's expectations. If this happens, the participant with unmet expectations is prone to feel disappointed. As a consequence, this person is likely to adopt an uncooperative attitude towards the other. In this example, if this staff member employee is given a thank you letter as a reward for overtime work, this employee might feel angry and start working by the book. In this example, the relationship between this employee and the manager is affected negatively.

Some companies tend to focus too much on the work contracts (explicit agreements) and dismiss the psychological contracts (implicit agreements). In the workplace, relationships with employees are more prone to thrive when their expectations, embedded in these psychological contracts, are met. Therefore, a good question to ask to employees on a regular basis is "What are your expectations at this company?" and "Are your expectations being met?" This type of question can provide the company with valuable insights in order to strengthen its relationships with employees.

11.2 Guidelines for More Balanced Relationships with Employees

Business must view people not as a resource but as sources. A resource is a lump of coal; you use it and it's gone. A source is like the sun—virtually inexhaustible and continually generating energy, light, and warmth. There is no more powerful source of energy in the world than a turned-on, empowered human being.

Raj Sisodia

Bauman (2017) observed that employees have two opposite desires: the desire for stability, certainty, and safety on the one hand, and the desire for freedom and self-expression on the other hand. The first need is satisfied through a stable job, steady pay cheque, and clear rules to abide by. The second need is satisfied when employees can freely express their voice and show themselves as they truly are, with their distinct attributes, views, and talents. These personal qualities should be duly acknowledged and welcomed by the company. In the work environment, these two opposite needs should be satisfied in a balanced manner.

According to this standpoint, if employees only satisfy their need for stability without any freedom, they are prone to feel coerced and censored by the company. Instead, if employees are given absolute freedom (for instance, no rules to abide by) without taking into consideration employees' need for stability, the workplace can become haphazard and chaotic.

Most companies tend to be biased towards satisfying employees' need for stability, but dismiss employees' need for freedom and expressiveness. Some guidelines regarding a more effective satisfaction of both employees' need for stability and their need for freedom and self-expression are explained in the following points.

11.2.1 Treating Employees Kindly

Relationships between superiors and subordinates must be nourished on a continuous basis. Superiors must always instruct employees in a warm manner in order to strengthen their relationships. Moreover, employees must feel recognised and valued on a regular basis. Superiors should aim to lovingly engage with subordinates and guide and empower them on a continuous basis. However, it is also important that superiors deliver instructions to employees, so that the company objectives can be achieved in an effective manner. The reader can find below some guidelines to delivering directions in a more loving manner. These guidelines apply to relationships between superiors and employees, and also between colleagues.

- **Soft requests:** Sometimes, superiors believe that if they are warm with subordinates, they will lose authority over them. Nonetheless, superiors can be authoritative and also loving with employees under their control. In the discipline of negotiation, there is a well-known saying which goes "You have to be hard with problems, but kind with people," which implies focusing on solving relevant problems, but also being considerate and caring with relationships (Fisher et al., 1999). An example of a soft request is "I would really appreciate it if you could please ..."
- **Non-intrusive requests**: Sometimes, superiors can make their requests to employees in non-intrusive ways. For instance, a boss asks employees for some relevant personal information of theirs for work purposes; in this example, the superior should kindly request employees for their permission, so they do not feel that their privacy is being invaded. This loving attitude towards employees makes them feel more respected, which prompts them to act more collaboratively. An example of a non-intrusive request "I was wondering if you could please provide me with your ...."
- **Requests as suggestions:** When possible, superiors should frame requests as kind and caring suggestions. For example, instead of saying "You must do this ...!", the superior could use sentences like "It is advisable for you to ...." Sometimes, the superior can adopt an empathic attitude towards an employee using sentences like "If I were you, I would think about ...," and similar ones.
- **Caring requests:** The comments mentioned in the previous point can be accompanied by caring sentences such as "I sympathise with you ...." Sometimes, requests can be made in an impersonal manner, such as "It is important that ..." or "It is necessary that ...." In most cases, the use of personal sentences should always be preferred above impersonal ones.
- **Indirect requests:** A superior can give directions to subordinates framed as questions, for instance, "What do you think of doing ...?" These requests tend to be perceived as friendlier and warmer than direct statements (e.g., "You must do ..."). Some requests can be accompanied by some introductory sentences, such as "I know it might be a tall order, but I would like to know if ...," and similar ones. These "softeners" make the conversation smoother and more flowing.
- **Plural requests:** Some directions can be formulated using plural sentences, like "We should do ..." and "What do you think of us changing ...?", among others. The superior can use the plural ("us," "we") even when messages are entirely related to the subordinate. These messages are more comforting because the employees feel as if they were accompanied by their superiors. This approach can also be used to highlight improvements to be made by the employee, for instance, "We should be more careful with ... next time."
- **Justified requests:** A superior should make requests accompanied by the specific reasons underpinning them. Research indicates that when people explain the reasoning underlying their requests, recipients are more inclined to act on these requests. Superiors can justify their requests, by using words like "because," or "due to," and others.
- **Very indirect requests:** This type of request is suggested by Feltman (2021). Sometimes, a very indirect request is not perceived by others as a real request. For instance, a superior can make requests, by using general comments like "There is a lot of customers to call on the phone today." In this example, the superior is subtly suggesting that the employee can help with the phone calls.

Most work conversations tend to be structured and formal. However, conversations between employees should not only be about requests and related business information. Employees should also be encouraged to have frequent casual chats, even with people higher in the hierarchical structure. In these conversations, employees can discover each other's qualities (preferences, values, etc.) and needs (self-expression, security, etc.).

When possible, managers should take the time to talk to subordinates about these topics in personal meetings in order to cultivate these relationships. Cohen and Prusak (2001) observed that many managers wrongly believe that taking time for meetings outside business activities is generally perceived as a luxury, when in fact it is a necessity.

These conversations allow people to develop a deeper heart-to-heart connection with others and show that they truly care for them, on a human level. When superiors hold this type of conversation with subordinates, they can know the staff that work for them better and will be more capable of assigning these employees tasks more aligned with their innermost needs. The topic of natural conversations was analysed in Chapter 8. In that chapter, there are also various examples of companies which foster natural conversations.

There is one more point to highlight. Research has shown that small-talk conversations, which are those exchanges not necessary for the completion of tasks, enhanced staff members' positive emotional states in the workplace, but these talks can also be distracting (Methot et al., 2021).

11.2.2 Providing Employees with Care

Many companies must contend with red tape and regulations which are more likely to hamper employees' tasks, rather than making them easier. When managers adopt a caring attitude towards their subordinates, they wholeheartedly aim to strengthen their relationships. These managers genuinely want to help their employees, instead of hindering their performance. Consequently, when employees feel supported, their work performance tends to improve. As seen previously, when a person adopts a loving attitude towards others, their intellectual skills are also enhanced significantly.

Managers should always adopt an encouraging and enabling attitude towards their subordinates. Besides, this type of attitude will strengthen the relationships of the former with the latter. In relation to this, Lieberman (2001) stated that people tend to like those they help. In other words, when a person helps another, a stronger connection and rapport between them is developed.

Conversely, Schwartz et al. (2010) observed that "leaders who operate from anger and negativity literally have the power to make their employees sick." These authors also stated that managers should act like "Chief Energy Officers" who are in charge of inspiring, refuelling, and mobilising employees' energy. Moreover, managers should contribute to the development of an empowering work environment, where employees can enhance their unique skills and capabilities.

Everyone deserves to be supported in the workplace, regardless of their current or past level of achievement in the company. As seen previously in this book, research has concluded that employees who are continually supported identify more with the organisation they work for and develop a deeper sense of closeness and belonging to this company.

In some workplaces, people are less prone to support others. In these places, staff members are not used to being grateful to others for their achievements and are less inclined to engage in co-operative projects. In this type of environment, there are no supportive activities, such as mentoring, coaching, and others. Consequently, managers should regularly scan the work environment to detect non-supportive practices and gradually introduce activities which foster support towards employees. For instance, Caterpillar, the company specialising in construction machinery and equipment, is known as one of the best places to work. This company offers its employees extensive mentorship programmes; younger staff members are supported by senior members for two or three years to develop the specific capabilities (including leadership skills) needed for their success in the workplace (Reeves, 2022).

Arnold and Plas (1993) observed that management should always support employees' personal and family lives. From this perspective, a company should adopt an understanding and flexible attitude with its employees, especially when they undergo challenging personal issues, such as new parenthood, death of relatives, illnesses, and divorce. Managers should be available for employees to talk to about the main issues affecting them and give their staff members kind and warm assistance.

A company should adopt a caring approach towards employees affected by these challenges, which can include flexible work time, the possibility of working from home, and leave time, among others. In these situations, a company has a golden opportunity to show that it cares for its employees as human beings, beyond their specific work positions.

For example, several years ago, Cisco, the global conglomerate specialising in digital communications technology, introduced an on-site nursery for its employees' children which is located a short distance away from this company's premises in the UK. Employees can visit their children at the nursery during their work day. This nursery brought about some positive effects, like more employee engagement (Nimalan, 2021). People working there see these workers in their parenting roles, which makes them appear more human.

Airbnb, the accommodation networking organisation, offers various benefits to support its employees working in America. For instance, these employees are offered paid parental leave (a maximum of 10 weeks to bond with their newborn, adopted, or foster child) and medical paid leave (a maximum of 12 weeks because of pregnancy, childbirth, or medical issues linked to it). This company also offers parents a gradual return to work. This means that, for 12 weeks on return after their parental leave, employees can work 80% of the time while being paid 100% of their salary. Lastly, this company offers caregivers paid leave, with a maximum of 12 paid weeks off to assist a family member with grave health issues (Airbnb, 2021).

Vodafone is a renowned telecommunications company. This company has the Ready Parents & Carers network, a group which was originally set up by employees working for this organisation who faced challenges regarding parenting and work. Now composed of hundreds of employees, this group provides employees with actionable parenting suggestions, webinars on parenthood, and one-to-one support. As managers have a relevant impact on employee well-being, this group also provides managers at Vodafone with training on parental support at work to foster a compassionate workplace (Nimalan, 2021).

Another example of an organisation which is caring with its employees is Netflix, the movie producing and streaming company. In relation to parental leave, this company understands that birth or adoption is a paramount event in people's lives, so the only company's policy regarding this is "take care of your baby and yourself." On its website, this organisation stated that a new parent generally takes four to eight months of parental leave (Netflix, 2023).

11.2.3 Supporting Employees during Challenging Times

In relation to change affecting a company, most employees are comfortable with the status quo, and therefore they have a natural resistance to change. In the business environment, most of the time, changes are inevitable. These changes can affect different aspects of the organisation, for example, the way it is organised internally, its policies and procedures, the products the company sells, the type of customers it serves, and the employees' functions, among others.

When a company supports its employees on a continuous basis, they tend to feel more at ease when they perform their work tasks. Nonetheless, most employees tend to feel anxious when their company goes through challenging times (downsizing, potential bankruptcy, mergers, etc.). Employees might also feel restless when the company is affected by relevant changes in the business environment, for example, new competitors, new technology, or changes in legislation.

In some of these situations, employees tend to feel threatened, which prompts them to respond to these factors in a defensive manner. Schein (2009) observed that employees' fear can have different origins, for example, fear of losing their share of power, and fear of being incompetent in the new scenario. In these situations, employees are likely to become overwhelmed, which prevents them from tapping into their skills and talents.

Oftentimes, these anxious employees become incapable of tackling challenging circumstances effectively. Goleman (1996) stated that anxious individuals' cognitive functions become severely impaired, which affects their capacity to generate creative solutions to troublesome issues. Sometimes, employees feel powerless and left to their own devices, as if they had to face these challenging situations on their own. Some tips for managers to take into account during challenging circumstances are:

- Some employees are very fearful of the negative effects of specific changes affecting the company they work for. These employees must be thoroughly informed of the main aspects of these changes and the reasons that justify these very changes. In this way, employees' uncertainty and apprehension regarding changing circumstances can be lowered.
- Angell and Rizkallah (2004) observed that during periods of change, managers should always avoid any communication vacuum, where employees do not know or understand what is going on in the organisation. Managers should provide subordinates with loving support and reassurance during turbulent times. In addition, managers should show employees the potential implications of the changing circumstances, especially highlighting benefits that these changes will bring about for these staff members. Managers should be a sounding board for subordinates to navigate these changes confidently.
- Hardingham (1992) suggests that managers should help employees to perceive challenging situations in a less threatening manner. This author observed that management should be more encouraging and patient with employees than usual, so that they can feel safe and assisted.
- Sometimes, employees can be thoroughly trained regarding the actions to be compliant with the upcoming changes. Employees can also be directly involved in the discussion of potential actions to implement in relation to these changes.
- When changes affect the organisation, managers can set a transition period for employees to adapt to the new circumstances. In this period, these changes can be introduced gradually and smoothly to allow employees to become comfortable and familiar with the new situation.

A valuable example of an organisation that supported employees during challenging times is Yodel, which is a company that provides parcel delivery services. Some years ago, this company was affected by financial challenges, and had to close down some of its premises, and lay off some employees. In order to assist the employees being dismissed, this company introduced an initiative which provided the laid off staff members with CV development capabilities and suggestions regarding their preparation for job interviews. This company also contacted other organisations for alternative work positions for these employees (Bradley, 2019).

There is another point to highlight. Sometimes, employees can be valid participants of changes to be introduced. In those cases, employees are consulted and their opinion is duly taken on board before any change is implemented. In these cases, employees are also thanked for their contribution of ideas. When a company uses this participative attitude towards change, employees tend to feel more valued, which prompts them to be engaged with the implementation of the change.

Oftentimes, changes affecting an organisation imply a learning process, which includes unlearning old ways of doing things to learn new ones. In some companies, there are people assigned to explain to employees the specific aspects of change affecting them. In this way, employees can feel more supported and can engage with the overall process of change in a more committed manner.

Sometimes, management can even offer valuable incentives to employees who have adopted change, or to encourage people to adopt it. These incentives can be very valuable, especially when some employees feel that their situation worsens after the implementation of change.

In a warm work environment, there is a continuous atmosphere of togetherness, which allows employees to handle changing situations in a more effective way. In those cases, employees do not feel on their own, but are accompanied by their colleagues to face the effects of change. This supportive environment acts as a safety net for employees; in this type of environment, the most important values are empathy and solidarity.

11.2.4 Allowing Employees to Express Their Views

Oftentimes, companies have topics which are banned from an open discussion with some staff members. Employees should be continually encouraged to give their opinions regarding any topic relevant to the company. Employees' distinct voices must be acknowledged, heard, and respected. When employees' opinions are duly heard, the company's relationship with them is strengthened.

A company should personally thank its employees for their unique valuable suggestions, whenever possible. When employees' contributions are not properly appreciated, these staff members are less likely to express their perspectives in the future.

Employees should be encouraged to fearlessly express their objections, frustrations, and complaints, and management should make these staff members feel that their opinions actually count. As seen previously, employees should also be empowered to express their opinions about changes to be implemented by the company (new policies and processes, innovative systems and structures, non-traditional activities, etc.) because their views can provide valuable insights into the potential impact of these changes.

At work, employees should be able to express their needs and views assertively, which means being upfront but polite about their own requests and opinions. Assertive employees tend to express their ideas in a firm but non-aggressive manner. These employees do not want to beat others with their arguments, but instead consider the needs of all parties involved.

Assertive employees do not want their own needs and wants to be dismissed. Instead, they want to feel empowered to make requests or express their opinions with confidence and respect. Therefore, these employees avoid being hesitant, tentative, pushy, or abrasive, and tend to use sentences which start with "I know …," "I feel …," "I would like …," and similar ones.

Many employees are very opinionated regarding different topics and feel the need to express their views when working for a company. These employees are willing to make proposals to improve the workplace and specific tasks related to it. Nonetheless, in many cases, these employees do not express their opinions in the workplace because they do not want to "rock the boat" or intrude into company affairs. In other cases, employees do not express their views because they are fearful of being penalised for giving their opinions.

Asking employees for their opinions is always very valuable, especially in relation to topics which affect them directly at work. Most employees are generally open to suggesting alternatives which could improve the company's future performance. Some of their views might challenge well-ingrained assumptions prevailing in the company. In order to elicit opinions from employees, managers can ask them questions like "What is your opinion on changing …?" or "Is there anything regarding … that you think could be improved?" This type of question always makes employees feel acknowledged and valued; they realise that their opinions really count.

3M, a global company previously analysed in this book, is very keen on employee feedback through an open-door policy, which encourages staff members to express their views directly to their managers, members of the employees' networks, as well as the HR team, in order to introduce positive change. This company conducts regular surveys to find out employees' opinions on different topics. This organisation also analyses employees' views about the company posted on external platforms such as Glassdoor, which is an independent platform where employees freely express their views about the companies they work for. This company examines this employee feedback (both gathered from internal sources and external platforms) and assesses the actions to be taken regarding issues highlighted in that feedback (3M, 2022b).

Some companies are open to hearing employees' views through formal channels, for example, surveys to find out different aspects of employees' satisfaction regarding different topics (training, characteristics of the work environment, economic compensation, etc.). This type of survey empowers employees to make contributions to improve work conditions. In those cases, employees' opinions are analysed and oftentimes specific actions are taken to address employees' objections. If these actions are taken, employees should be duly informed of them. According to Blundel (2004), the company can also garner feedback from employees through gatherings known as consultative meetings, where employees can voice their opinions openly.

Target is a very successful general merchandise retailer, which has stores in different states of America; this company has more than 400,000 employees (Target, 2022). On a regular basis, this company conducts surveys which allow team members to give their sincere views on various topics, as well as provide valuable insights on products or services. All this employee feedback is carefully analysed by the Head of the Human Resources Department (Anjos, 2022).

Cornelissen (2017) observed that some managers are not open to receiving any feedback or suggestions from subordinates for several reasons: fear of receiving negative feedback from employees, the assumption that managers possess better knowledge than subordinates, and intolerance to any dissent stemming from employees, among others. When employees are not actively encouraged to provide suggestions, they are more likely to feel dismissed and unappreciated by the company. In these cases, employees are less prone to be engaged with the company's activities. As a consequence, superiors should always be open to receiving unsolicited suggestions from employees, which must be seriously valued and taken into consideration. When managers are open and easy-to-reach, and request feedback and insights from their subordinates, these employees are more prone to feel their opinions count, which contributes to the development of a more psychologically safe workplace (Edmondson, 2004).

Employees who do not express their views spontaneously should be regularly asked for advice on potential improvements that could be introduced by the company (new products, services, markets, etc.). Sometimes, employees can be encouraged to use creative techniques (brainstorming, mind-mapping, etc.) with other staff members to generate innovative proposals for the company. These creative techniques will be analysed in Chapters 14 and 15.

In most companies, big decisions are made by the members of the staff working at higher hierarchical levels. However, employees on the lower levels can always provide the company with valuable ideas. Employees can give their unique perspectives on topics relevant to the company. Once suggestions are made by employees, these members of the staff must be updated on the progress of their ideas. As mentioned previously, when ideas suggested by employees are taken on board by the organisation, these employees should also be informed when the respective changes will be implemented.

There is another important point to highlight. Collins (2001) observed that companies should encourage employees to regularly provide brutal facts affecting the company in a negative manner. Some examples of these facts can be a drop in the company's sales, shrinking of its market share, massive increase in costs, etc. In some work environments, employees are fearful of conveying bad news to others, so these staff members tend to be silent about these negative facts. Toyota, the renowned car manufacturer, is also keen on knowing the truth on the ground; when negative information arises, this is communicated to executive management – instead of hiding this – which prompts this organisation to take timely action (Sisodia et al., 2015).

Employees should continually be empowered to discuss these facts with management in an open and authentic manner, instead of eschewing them, so that remedial actions can promptly be taken. Collins (2001) also observed that, paradoxically, successful companies are those that are willing to know and face hard facts, but maintain faith in themselves to overcome these challenging issues and eventually thrive.

The company 1-800-GOT-JUNK? is an organisation that offers junk removal services. In the past, the Vice President of Finance cautioned on the company's rapid growth and the importance of not spending in certain ways. These brutal facts were not duly heeded by the company's top executives. As a consequence of ignoring the brutal facts, this company went through a swift expansion, ending up with no cash, which made this organisation encounter significant financial challenges at that moment. The company survived and also learned to accept the truth (Holtzer, 2021; Stibitz, 2015).

11.2.5 Delegation of Tasks

In the work environment, all types of control over employees imply that the company does not trust them fully. When a company does not trust its employees, it is adopting an unloving attitude towards them. Most control procedures in a company are based on fear, for example:

- Fear of employees not knowing how to act in certain situations.
- Fear of employees not working effectively.
- Fear of employees doing things differently.
- Fear of employees not achieving company objectives.
- Fear of employees wasting company resources.
- Fear of employees acting in a deceptive manner (embezzlement, etc.).

In many companies, employees feel that they cannot act freely to pursue the organisation's goals in the most effective manner. In these cases, companies do not have full confidence in employees' discernment regarding how to act in the best way. Consequently, these organisations are prone to put in force a myriad of control procedures to guide, discipline, and monitor their staff members. Consequently, employees' actions are not spontaneous, but thoroughly prescribed. Sometimes, employees are not even able to make the most minimal decisions at work without asking their superiors for authorisation. This type of work environment is disempowering for employees because they cannot feel in control of their work activities.

Delegation of relevant tasks to employees is a key factor for a company's success. Delegation allows employees to make relevant decisions without others' approval. The existence of delegation practices within a company is a signal of trust towards employees. From this perspective, employees are not considered to be naughty children requiring control, but instead adult people who can take full responsibility. When employees feel in control of their tasks, they tend to adopt a more collaborative attitude. Instead, when a company adopts a parental (controlling) approach towards employees, they tend to feel resentful and behave in a non-cooperative manner.

Delegation, especially in the case of complex tasks, might need to be implemented in a gradual way, in stages. Oftentimes, when a task is delegated, some achievement benchmarks, principles, and standards are set in advance so that the employee takes them into consideration when performing that task. Sometimes, the delegation of a task needs additional training to perform it more effectively. Oftentimes, when tasks are delegated to employees, the outcomes stemming from the performance of these tasks can be supervised by the employees' managers.

When employees are given relevant discretion at work, they are more motivated and engaged. Not only do these employees feel autonomous, but they also feel more creative, skilful, and capable. In these cases, employees can take ownership of the delegated tasks and enhance their performance in a genuine and unhindered manner. Emerson (1981) wisely said, "Trust people and they will be true to you; treat them greatly and they will show themselves great."

Some superiors adopt a cautious attitude, which implies not delegating anything to their subordinates, until the latter fully gain their trust. Nonetheless, a different perspective is needed; managers should assume employees' capability beforehand in order to delegate tasks to them. When superiors trust subordinates, the latter are more likely to act in a trustworthy manner. These staff members also tend to trust these managers more (Deci et al., 1989). In those cases, relationships between managers and their employees become more robust over time.

As seen previously in this book, delegation of tasks satisfies employees' relevant need for autonomy. D'Souza and Renner (2014) observed that "feelings of mastery, agency, autonomy and control are important and are connected with our sense of wellbeing." When employees are granted freedom to act more spontaneously at work, they feel less pressurised and coerced, which prompts them to contribute to business endeavours in a more willing and meaningful manner. Amabile and Kramer (2011, 2012) observed that autonomy must be accompanied by the supply of enough resources and time to execute the tasks, continuous support from management, and setting of clear goals in order to foster and stimulate employees' work life.

An example of employee's autonomy is seen in Spotify, the music streaming company. This company allows its employees to decide where they want to work. This organisation understands that some staff will be more productive working in the office, and others will do better working from home. This company has a programme called Work From Anywhere Program that allows staff members to choose the work location, and also the work mode (Spotify office, a co-working space, or the employee's home) (Spotify, 2022).

As mentioned previously, a person who delegates tasks to others lovingly trusts their capabilities. Moreover, by delegating specific tasks to others, this person implicitly trusts that others will do their best to complete these tasks, using their capacities in the most competent manner. A company that trusts employees makes them feel more competent and resourceful; they realise that their contribution is valuable and meaningful. When people are encouraged to act in an autonomous manner, their self-efficacy skills can be enhanced. Research has shown that autonomous employees are more likely to continue working for their company, and even invest in it.

Delegation implies switching from micromanaging subordinates to allowing them to be self-managed. With delegation, employees are encouraged to take the initiative, without being thoroughly told how to act in each situation. Superiors who delegate implicitly convey to others this idea: "You are a responsible individual and know how to care for yourself and handle things effectively." As seen previously, when delegating tasks, managers should be available to offer their assistance when requested by employees.

As mentioned previously, employees should be given access to relevant resources (technology, information, etc.) to perform their task autonomously and effectively. Pink (2011) suggests that, when possible, workers should be given autonomy over what to do (choosing the task), when to do it (time for performing the task chosen), the team (who to work with to perform a task), and the technique (how to perform a task). As previously explained, employees who are given more autonomy are prone to feel more empowered, capable, and committed.

Spotify, the company previously mentioned, fosters autonomy among its employees. In this organisation, there are cross-functional teams named "Squads" These teams have absolute discretion over what functionalities they want to develop and the ways this should be done. These teams also have control over the ways the team members should work together (Razzetti, 2019b).

Morning Star is a renowned company which processes tomato, offering some overly popular products like paste and diced tomato, which was discussed by Hamel (2011) and Laloux (2014). This company's workers are self-managed. At this company, staff members set their own individual mission statement (known as Personal Commercial Mission), which includes the objectives they want to achieve at work and that they will be committed to. In that sense, employees are responsible for attaining their personal mission and for obtaining any resources and co-operation from others needed.

These workers also develop action plans (called Colleague Letters of Understanding – CLOUs) which define their specific roles to take in order to attain their personal mission. These CLOUs are negotiated – one to one – with staff members affected by their work. At this company, employees can also make the decision to buy equipment or hire staff, if needed, but they look for advice from other staff members affected or those knowledgeable. At this company, there are no management roles, purchasing division, or HR area.

There is another important topic related to autonomy. Some authors like Wrzesniewski and Dutton (2001) propose the idea of job crafting. From their perspective, employees who act as job crafters purposefully and creatively modify the number, scope, as well as the type of tasks performed (e.g., using their own practices instead of standard ones); they can also change who they interact with at work and the way they interact with others (e.g., avoiding frequent interactions with certain people, and relating more to others, such as people from other departments); and they cognitively shift the way they perceive their own work (e.g., instead of seeing themselves as sellers, these employees see themselves as "customers' emotional supporters"). Research has concluded that job crafting positively affects the meaning related to a job and its identity and brings about higher employee satisfaction and commitment, enhanced performance, and role mobility (Wrzesniewski, 2014).

There is another point to highlight. Delegation can also be related to collective projects. In such cases, the projects can be self-managed by a team, or led by a member of management. In the former case, employees tend to feel more empowered and willing to contribute with their unique skills and talents, as compared with the latter.

Lastly, Hackman and Oldham (1976) observed that, besides autonomy, there are other relevant motivators for employees at work, such as variety of work tasks to perform, meaningful work activities which enhance their skills, the possibility to create valuable outcomes and take ownership of them, and access to feedback about their performance from others. All these factors contribute to employees' satisfaction in a significant manner.

Some companies like WL Gore & Associates, Inc., a manufacturer that offers products stemming from fluoropolymers, foster self-management at work. In this organisation, staff members manage themselves; they are not micromanaged. In this company, employees are encouraged to achieve their own objectives in the ways they consider most appropriate. Staff members are free to look for the necessary resources to attain these goals, and they are accountable for their commitments (Hlupic, 2018).

11.2.6 Harnessing Employees' Skills

> Every organisation is as healthy as its workforce.
>
> **Bill and Cher Nolton**

Rogers (1961) observed that all individuals have an "actualising tendency," which means a relevant need to grow and achieve their full potential. Sometimes, companies prompt employees to perform activities totally unrelated to their distinct capabilities, and employees find these activities demotivating. When performing these tasks, employees do not feel empowered to give their best; instead, they are more likely to feel deskilled.

In those cases, employees are also prone to feel unappreciated regarding their distinct qualities. On the contrary, employees tend to love what they do when they can harness their skills and capabilities. These employees are more engaged at work because they perceive that they are distinctively contributing to the company's projects.

Therefore, one of the most relevant company goals should be to harness the unique capabilities of each employee. There are many tests in the market which help companies discover the core strengths of each employee. Managers who adopt a loving attitude trust employees' resourcefulness and encourage them to harness their full potential. These managers avoid allocating tasks to employees which might constrain the unique skills of the latter. These managers instead encourage employees to participate in projects and activities where the employees can contribute with their distinct capabilities.

UPS, the international courier company, is an organisation which aims at enhancing its employees' capabilities. This company has a programme named Earn and Learn tuition assistance programme. Through this programme, this company provides its employees with hefty sums of money to assist them with the payment of the expenses regarding the college course of their choice. Since the onset of this programme, thousands of employees benefited from this financial assistance, contributing to their career development in a significant manner (UPS, 2022b).

There is another important point to highlight. When employees are given the opportunity to perform some tasks in sync with their unique capacities, they feel more involved and committed to the company. According to Fritz (1991), involvement means that people are genuinely interested and connected to a project because they feel that they can contribute to it with value.

Employees who perform tasks not fully aligned with their talents should be encouraged to use their distinct skills to handle these tasks in the most effective manner. Employees need to feel that they are using their unique talents, even in tasks that are not completely suitable for them. Employees must also be given tasks where they can unleash their creativity. Most employees feel more fulfilled when they perform tasks where they can be playful and creative.

Superiors should enrol subordinates into projects that help them connect with their innermost capabilities. Zander and Zander (2002) stated that "enrolling is not about forcing, cajoling, tricking, bargaining, pressuring, or guilt-tripping someone into doing something your way." These authors observed that "enrolment is the art and practice of generating a spark of possibility for others to share." In other words, managers should always adopt an affirmative and encouraging attitude towards their employees, so that they can share their talents and apply them to the company's activities.

Besides, by highlighting employees' unnoticed talents, managers can also help employees to learn from their own mistakes, so they can improve their actions in the future. Moreover, managers can help these employees go beyond their self-imposed limitations. When managers adopt this employee-centred attitude, employees are more prone to hone their unique skills so that they can handle work challenges more effectively. Some research stated that companies which harness employees' upmost capabilities, like in the case of Toyota – the global car manufacturer – tend to become very profitable (Ton, 2014).

Marriott International, the prestigious accommodation chain, is a good example of a company that enhances employees' capabilities. This organisation offers two employee development plans: The Global Voyage Leadership Development programme (aimed at supporting new university graduates), and The Marriott Development Academy (which assists aspiring managers to develop the necessary skills for leadership positions). These two programmes allowed the company to fill a great part of their leadership positions with internal applicants (D'Sa-Wilson, 2022).

11.2.7 Developing New Skills

> In a very positive way, top businesspeople look upon their staff as if they were their children, constantly seeking ways to encourage them and help them develop their full potential both as employees and individuals.
>
> **Brian Tracy**

Most employees abhor routine and mechanised activities. However, in many companies, employees have to perform the same tasks at work, day in, day out; these monotonous activities leave no leeway for employees' creative expression. Employees have the need to express themselves in a creative manner, and repetitive work activities prevent them from satisfying this relevant need.

Sadly, many companies deskill employees by forcing them to perform hyper-specialised activities over and over. This type of routine also makes employees feel demoralised because they cannot utilise their creative skills. Some companies have job rotation which allows employees to vary the tasks they perform or work in different areas or departments, which oftentimes make employees more motivated and engaged. Research has shown that increasing variety of tasks in the workplace can bring about higher satisfaction and performance (Dutton, 2003).

Some companies adopt a perspective of corporate social responsibility (CSR) which implies contributing to social causes (caring for the environment, donating money to charity, etc.). In these companies, employees should regularly be allocated specific tasks which are aligned with their skills and talents, but also have a positive social impact. The performance of these meaningful social activities tends to make employees feel more fulfilled and self-actualised in the work environment. Juniper, a company whose main offerings are IT networks, cloud services, and software, allows its full-time staff members to take one paid week per year, so that they can participate in charitable projects they want to support (Juniper, 2022).

Not only should managers harness employees' unique skills, but they should also support employees regarding the development of new skills. Superiors should never adopt a complacent attitude towards employees' natural talents, but instead encourage staff members to go beyond their current capacities. This is beneficial for employees' professional development, but also for the company's performance levels.

The work environment should be a place where the employees' learning is fostered on a continuous basis. As employees are regularly trained and their skills heightened, their awareness is progressively raised and their perspective of reality is widened as well. Employees who incorporate new skills also have more tools to analyse and interpret work circumstances; these individuals tend to deal with these situations more effectively. When employees are given the chance to enhance their skills, they can stand out in the work environment.

There are several well-proven ways to help employees learn new skills. These tools give employees the chance to "fail" in a safe environment. Some examples of these instruments are on-the-job training, online and offline workshops, coaching, shadowing others, mentoring, and participation in pilot projects, among others. These tools help employees safely develop capabilities beyond their comfort zone.

Juniper, the company previously mentioned, is a valuable example of an organisation which supports its employees on a regular basis. This company offers its staff members mentorship support, conferences, as well as training courses to enhance their capabilities (Juniper, 2022). Another good example is Atlassian, which is a renowned software company. This company provides its staff members with access to a business book platform and thousands of online courses (Parris, 2022).

Managers should adopt a positive attitude towards the development of subordinates' new skills. When companies have positive assumptions about their employees' ability to develop new skills, these employees are treated accordingly, as if they were truly capable of developing these very skills. When managers adopt this attitude, employees feel empowered to widen their set of skills in order to go beyond their current performance levels. The importance of assumptions was discussed in Chapter 6.

A manager can motivate employees to develop new skills with sentences like "You are the class of employee capable of ...." This positive assumption frequently prompts employees to behave consistently with the capability stated. Employees can also be rewarded for the acquisition of new skills. This reward can be symbolic, for example, providing employees with a training certificate as evidence of the new skills gained. In other cases, employees can receive more tangible rewards, for example, an economic compensation paid to employees for having developed new skills.

Buffer, a company that offers software applications to manage social media accounts, provides its employees with a specific amount of money to be used for learning and development activities (classes, courses, etc.). Besides, these staff members can have unrestrained access to Audible and Kindle books, to foster their self-development (Burn, 2020).

11.2.8 Friendly Assessment Process

Many companies have a penchant for assessing employees in a continuous and rigid manner. In these cases, sophisticated systems and processes are set in place to assess personnel's performance. Oftentimes, the intention behind the control instruments is positive, for example, encouraging employees to improve their performance. However, when the assessment is too strict, most employees tend to feel that they are not being trusted regarding their work activities.

Some employees feel fearful of this assessment process, especially when it is undertaken on a continuous basis. These employees are prone to feel judged or negatively criticised regarding their effectiveness at work, which prompts them to adopt a defensive attitude (fight-freeze-flight) towards the assessment. As seen previously, this reactive response keeps employees from fully harnessing their most relevant mental capabilities, which lowers their overall productivity levels.

Employees who adopt a defensive mode narrowly focus on the perceived threat (the assessment process), which hinders their learning process at work.

Many employees might even perceive the assessment process as inadequate and intrusive; sometimes, employees see themselves as objects whose qualities need to be assessed by the company. These employees feel hindered and continually subject to the company's control, which makes them perform work tasks in a fearful manner. Besides, these employees are also prone to be resentful because oftentimes superiors are not assessed by anyone. This perceived "unfairness" of the assessment process could also prompt employees to act in a less co-operative manner.

As seen previously, strict and continuous control over employees tends to stifle employees' natural freedom at work. In those cases, employees are prevented from acting in a more spontaneous and creative manner because of their fear of being detrimentally assessed. This does not mean that employees should never receive any feedback from superiors. On the contrary, assessment can positively contribute to an employee's learning process at work.

According to Egan (2011), for employees' assessments to be constructive, feedback should always be delivered with a caring spirit, which means in an affectionate and genuine manner. This author observes that good feedback is usually confirmatory and corrective. Confirmatory feedback includes actions that the employee performed well, and corrective feedback includes employees' activities that can be improved. Hounsell (2007) states that constructive feedback represents valuable feed-forward because it helps employees improve their tasks in the future.

Feedback is more constructive when it is delivered within a two-way communicative interaction between the manager and the subordinate. In these cases, employees actively participate in the assessment process. For example, the superior and a subordinate can review performance together. In this case, the manager provides the employee with feedback, and the former is open to receiving comments and requests for clarification from the latter.

This type of assessment puts the employees in a less defensive mode and generates more engagement. In some cases, employees' performance can also be appraised in a more complete manner, for example, by receiving feedback from different stakeholders, such as other employees, customers, and suppliers. This is known as 360-degree feedback.

In the case of Google, managers ask their subordinates to undertake self-assessment to appraise different aspects of their work (their alignment to the company's values, the quality of the execution of their tasks, their thought leadership, their problem-solving skills, etc.). This self-assessment is contrasted with a 360-degree feedback, which is provided by reviewing peers proposed by these very employees. The 360-degree feedback allows managers to discover any inconsistencies in the self-assessment undertaken by employees (Nguyen, 2022).

There is another relevant point to highlight. Managers should avoid providing employees with vague or general feedback from the assessment process. The information provided by managers should be specific and actionable. In that sense, constructive feedback should include:

■ Aspects that employees perform well. Research concluded that managers who centre on the employees' strengths bring about higher levels of engagement (Brim and Asplund, 2009). This can be accompanied by simply sending employees a message of gratefulness for their positive contribution at work.
■ Different aspects that employees can improve at work (with a focus on employees' behaviour, not on their personal qualities) and practical ways for employees to improve, including desired clear actionable strategies.
■ Specific reasons why things should be done differently (according to specific criteria such as regulations and company's strategy) and their potential positive impact on company activities.

■ Clear examples of how employees can harness their talents more effectively. The person providing feedback can also express confidence in the employees fully using their capabilities in the future. This can be accompanied by encouraging words, which can have a positive effect on the recipient's self-worth, aplomb, and development.

In relation to this, Yeager et al. (2014) observed that feedback could include sentences like "I'm giving you these comments because I have very high expectations about you, and I know that you can achieve them." According to these researchers, this type of sentences makes the recipient more prone to take the feedback on board, and act accordingly.

A caring manager not only provides subordinates with useful feedback, but also follows up with praise when they implement these suggestions. This manager also directly assists them, when necessary. Some authors suggest that positive feedback (what employees do well) should be delivered in a separate way, in relation to any negative feedback (what employees do not do well), as the real meaning of the latter can be diluted or obscured by the former (Von Bergen et al., 2014).

In psychology, there is the concept of negativity bias, which means that people tend to react more intensely and continually to negative situations than to positive ones. Consequently, when the main focus of feedback given to employees is negative, they tend to become more negatively self-aware of their performance, which prompts their performance levels to plummet. For this reason, superiors should provide feedback which mostly focuses on specific ways for employees to improve their performance in the future, instead of concentrating on their mistakes. From this perspective, the feedback is reassuring, as a relevant part of the employee's process of learning and development.

Constructive feedback always has an empowering and reinforcing effect, which makes employees feel valuable and recognised. This type of feedback represents a valuable source of information which employees can use to improve their performance at work. In other words, this feedback contributes to enhancing employees' self-efficacy skills. This means that employees are prompted to understand, reflect on, and develop strategies to accomplish work objectives more successfully. The enhancement of these self-efficacy skills also entails employees developing positive beliefs about their capability to perform at work in a more productive manner. As previously seen in this book, in Netflix, employees are encouraged to give others actionable, kind, and constructive feedback to contribute to their development (Hastings and Meyer, 2020).

When feedback is delivered in a constructive manner, employees are likely to feel more in control, which helps them improve their work tasks in a progressive manner. This type of feedback can represent a very significant tool for employees' encouragement, motivation, and empowerment. Additional aspects on how to deliver constructive feedback were explained in Chapter 9.

11.2.9 Supportive Feedback

Love is the basis, the foundation of everything, for it is a virtue that is blind to human mistakes, and is never offended. Even in the worst mistakes, it only sees something positive.

Peter Deunov

There are other aspects regarding feedback which must be highlighted. As seen previously, superiors should start focusing firstly on what employees are doing well, and secondly, discuss aspects to be improved. In these cases, employees are less likely to adopt a defensive mode. Besides, feedback should always be provided in a kind and gentle manner, with a focus on preserving and strengthening relationships with employees.

When providing feedback, superiors should show an authentic interest in employees' professional development. In addition, feedback stemming from assessment should always be delivered in a personalised manner, considering employees' unique strengths and capabilities. Therefore, feedback should avoid comparing an employee with others.

When employees have made mistakes at work, superiors must be compassionate with them. Superiors who adopt a compassionate attitude towards employees are fully aware of challenges affecting them, and they are willing to understand and support these employees in the best way possible. Compassion implies positive qualities (e.g., tenderness, care, thoughtfulness, and loving kindness) regarding others, which strengthens the connection with them.

Superiors must be patient and loving with their employees. From this perspective, employees' setbacks represent stepping stones for them to learn new capabilities and do things better in the future. Most employees obtain valuable insights into their mistakes. Superiors must always believe in their subordinates and their natural capability to overcome challenges successfully. In relation to this, Fritz (1991) observed that "if something is worth doing, it's worth doing poorly until you can do it well."

However, many managers act in a punitive way regarding subordinates' mistakes. This ruthless approach does not help employees overcome work challenges, but instead damages the relationship with them. As a consequence, superiors should always adopt a supportive attitude towards employees, especially when they make mistakes; managers should consider that every employee is a human being, in the process of improving and developing, not a finished work. This positive attitude contributes to strengthening employees' capabilities at work.

Some business coaches observe that the learning process at work always includes making some mistakes; this is inevitable. When subordinates make mistakes at work, managers should ask themselves some interesting questions:

■ How would I like to be treated by others if I am the one making this mistake?
■ How can I adopt a more supportive attitude this employee?
■ What is the most loving way to provide this employee with feedback?
■ What actionable tips can make this employee feel more confident and capable?
■ How can I help this employee while I care for my relationship with this individual?

These questions provide managers with interesting insights. When a superior adopts a compassionate attitude towards employees, these staff members are more likely to co-operate and improve their future performance. Conversely, when a superior is harshly judgemental of employees, they are more prone to adopt a defensive mode, which lowers their productivity levels. Besides, a compassionate attitude always creates a warmer work environment, a place where all employees are comfortable working.

If an employee makes a mistake, a compassionate manager tends to show this employee some examples of how things could be done in the future. The manager's explanation is generally delivered in a warm and kind manner. Due to the superior acting in a non-judgemental manner, the employee is prone to feel more confident and self-assured, and act more assertively.

It was previously seen that in Pixar, the animation company, staff members are encouraged to provide one another with feedback in a non-judgemental manner. For example, in the process of movie development, employees can provide others with feedback on aspects of the movie (colours, characters, etc.) that can be improved in the movie. This assessment never encloses personal criticism regarding the staff members who participated in the movie.

11.2.10 Appreciation of Employees' Contribution

The topic of gratitude has been explained in Chapter 7. Many companies tend to take employees' work for granted, and avoid being thankful to staff members for their contribution. Some companies adopt an ungrateful attitude towards their employees, dismissing their human side, and ignoring the fact that employees always need to be valued and recognised.

Managers that acknowledge employees' contribution do not look weak, but more humane. When a manager is grateful with subordinates, they tend to behave more co-operatively, which affects their productivity in a positive manner. When employees are overtly appreciated for their positive contribution to the company, they feel encouraged to keep on contributing. A manager who is grateful with employees can also explain to them how their work specifically contributes to the company's overall progress.

Sometimes, companies use personal letters to thank employees for their contribution to company objectives. It is possible to highlight employees' contributions by posting thank you messages or articles in different publications (the company's magazine, official website, newsletters, blogs, etc.). A company that wants to be grateful with employees publicly should primarily pinpoint the aspects of real people (their dedication, their commitment and grit, etc.) who contributed to the company's positive outcomes, instead of exclusively focusing on impersonal raw data (figures, statistics, percentages, etc.).

When a company adopts a grateful attitude towards employees, they tend to feel proud of their contribution to the organisation. Sometimes, recognising employees is symbolic, for instance, by acknowledging the most productive employee of the year. For example, every single year, Unilever, a company that offers various consumer goods, recognises those employees who have performed in an outstanding manner, by giving them Unilever's Heroes Award. Those employees who receive the awards are invited to an exclusive event, Change Leaders Conference, where hundreds of senior managers meet up on an annual basis (Recognize, 2021; Unilever, 2022).

Some companies with a grateful attitude promise a reward to employees who contribute more to the company's objectives. Wiseman (2013) expressed that when a company offers an employee an economic incentive to perform a task, this activity tends be perceived as less valuable and, in turn, becomes less likely to be performed. On a similar note, Sutherland (2007) observed that "material rewards reduce the attractiveness of pleasurable activities and have little effect on less pleasurable activities once they have been withdrawn."

If a company wants to be grateful, it should instead give its employees sincere praise for their valuable contribution to company's purpose. In a similar vein, Pink (2011) suggested that companies should give employees relevant feedback regarding their performance, instead of giving them material rewards (e.g., bonuses), to boost employees' motivation. This author also observed that these material rewards often decrease motivation, lower performance levels, foster dishonest tackling of tasks, and reduce creativity. However, this author also observed that there is an exception to this: rewards like bonuses and similar ones can be effectively used to motivate people who only perform mechanical activities which require basic or rudimentary capabilities (Pink, 2010).

In a similar vein, Cerasoli et al. (2014) concluded that for simple, repetitive, and less enjoyable tasks entailing some type of performance quantity (e.g., putting together piece type A and piece type B on a manufacturing assembly line), these activities can be incentivised through extrinsic motivators (e.g., paying a specific bonus for every two pieces assembled). According to these researchers, these quantity-type tasks do not require a deep analysis and are based on structured behaviour to obtain successful outcomes.

These researchers also observed that, for complex tasks, which imply more absorption and individual investment, and lead to performance quality (e.g., making personalised offerings of products for different customers), the use of external rewards (e.g., bonus based on performance level) should be avoided, whenever possible. According to their research study, this type of quality-type tasks seems to be more linked to intrinsic motivation. In these cases, employees are more inclined to be motivated by some factors such as the meaningfulness and purposefulness of the tasks they perform.

There is an interesting example to discuss. MonetizeMore, a well-known ad-tech organisation which helps digital publishers, has employees in the different parts of the world. In the past, when this company reached a specific milestone regarding its sales, it offered its staff members a costly, fully paid retreat in the Philippines. Not only was this retreat a gesture of appreciation from this company to its employees, but this event also allowed staff members to meet in person and bond with one another (Williams, 2022).

Questions for Self-Reflection

- How can I adopt a kinder and more grateful attitude to our company's employees?
- How can I support our company's employees during dire circumstances?
- How can I give our employees more constructive feedback?
- How can our company's employees' skills be harnessed more effectively?

Chapter 12

Adopting a Loving Attitude towards Customers

There is only one boss. The customer. And he can fire everybody in the company from the chairman on down, simply by spending his money somewhere else.

Sam Walton, Founder of Wal-Mart Stores, Inc.

12.1 Love and Customers

Put service first, and money takes care of itself – always.

David Schwartz

Many decades ago, in a business meeting, a famous businessman, who preferred to remain anonymous, emphatically asserted, "Customers will wish you well as a company if you truly wish them well." This simple but insightful idea is not commonly applied by many companies, not even those with extensive experience in the business arena. This valuable idea can be applied to any business activity, with no exception whatsoever.

Companies have to care for their customers if they want to succeed in business; to love customers is to appreciate them in an unconditional manner. Many companies focus on the improvement of economic parameters (more sales, increased profits, bigger market share, etc.) without realising that all these indicators are directly related to the degree to which customers are satisfied with the company's products and services. In simple words, when customers are duly satisfied by a company's products and services, these parameters tend to improve accordingly.

There are many good books on marketing which address the topic of customer satisfaction from a strategic perspective. Most of these books do not take into account the human aspects of customers. Every time a company relates to customers, it should acknowledge them as valuable and unique individuals. Customers deserve to be respected and loved; their needs must be duly recognised by companies on a regular basis. Each customer has dreams and preferences which are legitimate, significant, and distinct, and which companies must take into consideration.

252

DOI: 10.4324/9781003372684-15

As mentioned in Chapters 5 and 6, all individuals long for love from different sources; love is one of their most important needs. It is possible to say that customers look for love each time they buy products and services from companies. This idea might seem strange to many people, but it happens to be true. Customers primarily buy goods and services because of the positive emotional states they seek to experience when using or consuming them.

These sought-after positive emotions can comprise happiness, peace, and other positive states. Some schools of thought have observed that all these positive emotional states are directly and indirectly related to love. From this standpoint, there are only two qualities of emotion: the ones related to love (glee, peace, etc.) and the ones related to fear (sadness, anger, shame, etc.). The emotions related to love are always positive (as compared with the ones related to fear), and these are the ones sought by customers every time they make a purchase.

Oftentimes, customers buy products and services to be accepted by others (peers, family members, friends, colleagues, etc.). In these cases, customers make these purchases because of their urge to fit in with others and be complimented by them. In this case, the customer's need for acceptance implies the need to be loved by other people.

In the business environment, many companies tend to take customers for granted; these organisations adopt an unloving attitude to customers. When a company adopts an authentic loving attitude towards customers, it tries to improve the way they are served on a continuous basis. Below, there are some questions companies should ask themselves on a regular basis in order to serve customers in a warmer and kinder manner:

- How can we discover more about our customers' distinct needs?
- How can we acknowledge these unique needs more effectively?
- How can we give customers valuable advice regarding their decisions on our products and services?
- How can we enhance their experience and make them feel more fulfilled?
- How can we solve their problems more effectively?
- How can we offer them more valuable products and services?
- How can we be more appreciative and generous to them?
- How can we be more available to sort out their doubts and objections?
- How can we connect to them in a more natural and spontaneous way?
- How can we acknowledge them as valuable human beings?
- How can we be warmer, kinder, and friendlier to them?
- How can we adopt an authentic and wholehearted attitude of service?

Companies can also ask themselves: "How can we be more loving to our customers in a practical and specific manner?" It is important to pinpoint that when customers buy products or services, they generally look for self-fulfilment. Therefore, companies can use these questions to brainstorm and discover more effective ways to make customers feel fulfilled. In the following points, several examples of companies which ask themselves the aforementioned questions will be discussed.

Dr Daniel Goleman, one of the leading scholars in emotional intelligence commented about his experience as a customer, as follows (Goleman, 2013). On one occasion, he went to a luxury restaurant with his wife. He had a cold. At this restaurant, his wife ordered a soup, and he asked the server if he could bring him an empty bowl to share her soup. This waiter looked at him in a very disparaging manner (implying that type of request was never made in a place like that restaurant) and then said to him, "Let's see what I can do." The server dashed out and then returned, flinging the bowl on the table. Goleman thought that this rude waiter did not deserve a tip; he also thought that it was not worth returning to that restaurant.

At the end of that meal, Dr Goleman's cold worsened; consequently, he decided to have some herbal tea. So, he called another server and asked him if they could offer him any herbal tea. This second waiter empathetically looked at him and said that Dr Goleman looked like he had a cold. Then, this waiter commented about all the types of tea his mother gave him, which types of tea the restaurant had, and which tea he would recommend. Goleman thought that this second server really deserved a tip, and that it was worth returning to that restaurant. As can be seen, the first waiter adopted an unkind attitude towards the customer, while the second waiter was very caring and supportive with the customer. The way that each waiter treated Dr Goleman affected his willingness to give a tip, as well as his desire to return to that restaurant.

12.2 Importance of Customers' Well-Being

> Friendliness is to human understanding what freedom is to men in society – the very atmosphere of growth and development.
>
> **Elmer Letterman**

Many companies use a vast arsenal of techniques to persuade customers to buy products and services; in most cases, these stratagems tend to be counterproductive. In relation to this, research in social psychology concludes that people are more likely to do something when the message they receive is *not* intently seeking to persuade them.

Instead of purposely trying to persuade customers, a company should treat them as valuable individuals. Therefore, a company's employees should always try to connect to customers more from the heart, instead of the head. For instance, Zappos, the global online retailer, trains its workers at its call centres to engage with customers in a deep manner, from their hearts. These employees are encouraged to connect with customers in a spontaneous and personal fashion to develop robust relationships with them (Mechlinski, 2021).

From this perspective, each customer is a unique human being, who deserves kindness, love, and respect from the company. It is interesting to note that many companies treat customers in the opposite manner; these organisations consider customers as faceless figures or statistics who contribute to the organisation's economic results.

Whenever a company interacts with its customers, it should contribute to their well-being on a continuous basis. Companies and customers are deeply interrelated; when customers are fully satisfied, their well-being also impacts on the company's economic results. In other words, customers who are served well by a company tend to come back to buy more products and services, which generates more revenue and profits for this organisation.

The following is an example of a company which adopts a loving attitude towards its customers, mentioned by Farber (2019). Marco's pizza is a franchising chain of pizza restaurants. While delivering a pizza, one employee saw that the light in the customer's porch was out, and this staff member fixed it. In winter, a delivery person noticed that the pathway to access the customer's house was covered by snow, so this employee shovelled it. On one occasion, an elderly woman had to be taken to the hospital because she had fallen down. People at the hospital asked her for a person to ring to take her back to her home. She did not have anyone to call, but she gave them the local Marco's pizza's phone number. Despite being puzzled, people at the hospital called this restaurant, which sent a staff member to take this lady home safely.

There is another important point to highlight. Besides, when a company adopts a loving attitude towards customers, this brings about additional benefits for the company, such as more loyal
customers and abundant positive reviews from customers on the company's products and services,
among others. A company treats customers in a loving manner when:

- The company makes customers aware of the best products for them.
- The company adopts a kind, patient, and friendly attitude towards them.
- The company educates customers to help them learn things that are useful for them.
- The company aims to develop a mutually beneficial relationship with them.
- The company satisfies their needs more effectively over time.
- The company acts with integrity on a continuous basis.
- The company provides them with truthful and meaningful information.
- The company assists them whenever they need help.
- The company suggests insightful ideas to meet their preferences.
- The company helps them discover their innermost needs.
- The company makes them feel good whenever they interact with the company.
- The company gives them some free goods and services.

Most customers truly value these aspects; companies should pay close attention to them every
time they deal with customers. These aspects truly strengthen the relationship between a company
and its customers, which makes them more inclined to become loyal to the organisation. Since its
onset, Zappos, the prestigious online retailer previously mentioned, has been using a great part
of its marketing budget on developing outstanding customer service, while spending a minimal
amount of money on advertising. A former company's executive has quipped that Zappos is actually a customer service organisation which sells shoes (Huhn, 2022b).

12.3 Main Qualities of a Loving Attitude towards Customers

A customer chooses a product based not only on objective appraisal of its use but also
on how he or she feels about it. The fact is that the subtle, working as it does on the
level of emotions, hunches and intuition, influences the gross; there is no way around
it. And business always has to be tuned in to this fact.

Amit Goswami

Dr Hawkins (2012) recommends that employees in direct contact with customers should adopt a
loving attitude towards them. This prestigious scientist also observed that employees with a loving attitude tend to become more creative, which helps them recommend to customers products
and services which are more suitable for them. Besides, this author concluded that an employee
with a loving attitude "often converts customers to friends, and customers tend to become loyal."
Consequently, when employees treat customers in a loving manner, they tend to develop mutually
beneficial relationships with the company.

Customers who feel that they are being treated in a loving manner by a company tend to treat
the organisation in a reciprocal manner. These customers tend to write positive reviews online on
company's products and services or recommend the organisation to other people (relatives, friends,
colleagues, etc.). These positive comments from customers are commonly called positive "word of
mouth."

These positive comments are spontaneous unbiased expressions of customers' love towards a company which has previously served them lovingly. According to Cialdini (2009), these recommendations provided by satisfied customers also represent prized "social proofs" which validate products and services offered by the company. These comments also help to reduce other customers' uncertainty regarding the reliability of the products and services recommended. When customers spread positive word of mouth regarding certain products and services, they act like unpaid ambassadors who wholeheartedly endorse these goods and services, and want other people to try them. Consequently, oftentimes, companies have to spend less on some marketing activities like advertising campaigns, and others, as their customers become the paramount promoters of the products offered by these organisations. For example, Starbucks, the popular coffee shop chain, became renowned with virtually no advertising activities (Sisodia et al., 2015).

Casper is a company that sells mattresses and other bed products on its online platform. This company has been greatly relying on the power of word of mouth. This company has a referral marketing programme, through which they provide customers with gift cards if they refer someone who buys the company's products. This company also gives discounts on the purchases made by customers who were referred. This organisation also uses social media platforms to display various customers' positive testimonials regarding its products (Casper, 2022a, 2022b; Rice, 2021).

Another example of passionate customers who wholeheartedly endorse the company's products are many of the users of Harley Davidson's products. Harley Davidson is a company which sells high-quality expensive motorcycles. Not only are these customers proud to show up with these motorbikes wherever they ride them, many of these users also join the Harley Owner Group, which is a community that offers various benefits (participation in the community's events, merchandise, community inside emails, free access to Harley Davidson's museum, access to Harley Davidson authorised tours, etc.) (Harley Davidson, 2023).

This type of group is known as a brand community where its members – who have shared interests – are enthusiastically committed to a brand, and praise, celebrate, admire, and proudly endorse this very brand. In the case of Harley Davidson Group members, their shared interests are their passion for these motorcycles and their keenness to ride them in a flowing and unhindered manner. In this group, members participate in this community because this group serves them, by meeting their needs for connectedness, developing relationships with others, and fostering riders' brotherhood (Fournier and Lee, 2009).

There is another important point to highlight. Customers who are treated in a loving manner by a company's employees are also prone to defend this organisation and its products when other people attack them. These customers tend to be more understanding with the blunders made by an organisation, and also provide this company with kind insights on how to improve their products and services.

In the following points, no specific selling techniques will be explained. Instead, some relevant principles which can help a company adopt a more loving attitude with its customers will be analysed.

12.3.1 Over-Performing

In marketing, the main objective is to satisfy customers' needs appropriately. In other words, companies should offer products and services which meet customers' expectations. However, a company which loves its customers tries to exceed their needs, which implies *over-performing*. This means that a company offers customers more than what is expected by them. Chaston (2004) called it "positive disconfirmation" when the performance of an organisation exceeds customers' expectations. It is interesting to pinpoint that most customers can distinguish between a company with purely economic objectives (more sales, higher profits, etc.) and one whose main priority is to meet and even exceed their expectations.

Sometimes, a company serves customers by unexpectedly going beyond their expectations, and its customers experience deeply positive emotions (joy, etc.); this is known as customer delight (Oliver et al., 1997). As seen, delight includes an element of positive surprise. According to neuroscience, when customers are surprised in a positive manner with specific products or services provided by a company – which means that they exceeded these customers' expectations – their dopamine levels have a sharp increase, making these customers more prone to buy these very products or services in the future (Bogacz, 2020). Dopamine is also known as the feel-good hormone, which tends to be released in bursts before unexpected rewards.

A company can delight its customers in various ways. In relation to this, Barnes et al. (2011) observed that a company can potentially delight its customers in several ways, such as:

- Significant amount of effort made by employees to satisfy customer needs.
- Outstanding technical skills and expertise displayed by employees when serving customers (knowledge of policies, provision of technical suggestions, etc.).
- Superb quality of the products or services provided to customers.
- Capabilities of effectively solving customer problems (product return, delays in the delivery, etc.).
- Friendly, caring, and courteous treatment of customers to enhance their connection with the company.
- Undivided attention to customers and authentic interest in their needs.
- Flexible application of the company's rules (e.g., return policy) in ways which can benefit customers.
- Provision of high-value incentives (e.g., free stuff) to customers.

Crotts and Magnini (2011) observed that, when customers experience delight with a product, they are more prone to recommend it to others (e.g., positive word of mouth). According to these researchers, delighted customers are also more likely to purchase the product again in the future, and even become loyal.

An example of an over-performing company is Magic Castle Hotel in Los Angeles, United States. This company aims to bring outstanding and memorable experiences for its guests; it is very well-rated on social media. This company has a red phone called the Popsicle Hotline, which is very close to the heated pool. When guests use this phone, a waiter wearing a suit and white gloves brings popsicles to them on a tray. Besides, guests can also have unlimited savoury snacks, ice cream, and drinks. This hotel also has free breakfast for its guests; thrice a week, a magician performs tricks at the tables during breakfast time (Heath and Harbinger, 2018; Mott, 2020). This is a clear example of a company that delights its customers.

According to Wattles (2013), a company should always give customers more than it takes from them. To put it simply, a company should add more value to customers than the value it receives from them. By creating a deliberate imbalance in the value exchanged with customers, not only does the company serve them better, but these customers are also more likely to develop strong relationships with this organisation.

Moreover, a company which is generous with customers, which means providing them with higher value, makes these customers feel "indebted" with this organisation. As a consequence, because of the principle of reciprocity, these customers tend to act in a generous manner with this company. For example, these customers might come back to the organisation to buy new products and services, or they might recommend this company to other customers. This principle can be applied not only to customers, but also to other stakeholders of the company, such as employees, suppliers, and intermediaries.

Besides, when a company delights its customers, which is giving more than they expect, this organisation creates a long-lasting impression on them. This type of organisation aims to develop a long-term relationship with customers, instead of focusing only on a one-off transaction.

The Ritz-Carlton Hotel is an example of a company that aims to exceed customer expectations. In the past, one of its guests checked out, and unknowingly left his laptop charger in the room. The customer planned to call this hotel after he went back home by plane. Before he could do this, he received a swift air package delivery from the company. This next-day pack included not only his charger but also an additional one, alongside a personalised note signed by a company's employee (Bernazzani, 2021).

Another example of a company that exceeded customer expectations is the Dutch airline KLM. In the past, this company had a campaign called "Cover Greetings" which allowed people seeing off their relatives or friends at the airport to leave them a farewell message on a cloth that the airline crew members then stuck on the headrests of the respective passengers before the plane took off. Passengers felt very touched by this unexpected poignant gesture (KLM, 2014).

An alternative perspective states that customers have problems which should be solved by companies in the most effective manner. For example, when customers are looking for a package holiday, they have a problem (they experience boredom, stress, etc.) and want specific companies (e.g., tourism agencies) to solve it in the best way (for instance, package holidays). The companies more prone to become wealthy are the ones which solve customers' problems most effectively, which also implies adopting a loving attitude towards customers.

A company with a loving attitude towards customers also provides them with valuable presents. Customers are likely to feel more connected to the company because of having received these gifts. These presents must always be given by the company with no strings attached, which means unconditionally. To put it more simply, if a company only provides customers with gifts if they meet specific conditions (for instance, they get free gifts only if they buy other products offered by this company), these customers are prone to feel bribed. Some examples of items a company can give customers free of charge are:

- Product samples.
- Free e-books, reports, newsletters.
- Free services (delivery, repair, training, installing, etc.).
- Free advice and consultation.
- Vouchers.
- Free trial period.

This generous approach implies a demonstration of love from the company to its customers. However, the majority of companies adopt the opposite approach; they are primarily focused on *getting* something from customers, which implies obtaining more sales, increasing the level of profits, gaining more loyalty from customers, etc.

Instead, when a company gives its best to customers first, revenue and profits will later ensue in a spontaneous and effortless manner. If a company adopts a generous perspective, the company will not have to pursue and retain customers because they will be naturally attracted and pledge allegiance to it.

HubSpot sells software products for sales, inbound marketing, and customer service. This is an example of a generous company. This organisation offers a myriad of free online courses on its platform, with no strings attached. These free courses cover several topics, such as email marketing, digital advertising, and business writing skills, among others (HubSpot, 2022).

12.3.2 Trustworthiness

When a company is offering products and services with a superior performance, it is generating trust with customers. Trust is a very important factor when a customer and a company depend on each other. Morrison and Firmstone (2015) list some factors which create trust, such as reputation, accountability, and familiarity, among others. From the psychological perspective, familiarity between customers and a company not only increases trust, but also brings about liking between them. According to Pearce (mentioned in Baumeister and Leary, 1995), familiarity between people also brings about mutual assistance, as it also does in the case of dependency between them.

When trust between a company and its customers is increased, their relationship is strengthened, and potential disagreements and misunderstandings are prone to be reduced. High levels of trust also increase rapport, connection, and commitment in the interactions between a company and its customers. When people trust each other, over time, this bond of trust tends to get stronger, but trust can also disappear in the blink of an eye.

According to Mitchell et al. (1998), some factors which allow companies to develop bonds of trust with their customers are reliability, benevolence, probity, and satisfaction. Other relevant aspects are fairness in the deals and fulfilment of what was agreed by the company and the customer. It is interesting to pinpoint that these bonds of trust tend to develop over time, as a result of a positive assessment of each other's actions.

Rosseau et al. (1998) observed that trust implies the acceptance of a situation of vulnerability, where a person has positive expectations regarding the intentions and actions of another. As seen previously, trust is generally built over time and assessed in a continuous manner. When a person trusts another, the former believes that the latter will not take advantage of the former. In other words, when customers trust a company, they believe that it will behave in a predictably benevolent manner towards them. Consequently, these customers are less prone to adopt defensive or aggressive behaviour towards this organisation. To put it simply, when customers trust a company, they are less prone to adopt a fight-freeze-flight mode towards this organisation.

Trust represents a compass that guides customers through their relationships with a company. When trust towards an organisation is broken, customers realise this in a retrospective manner, by analysing the company's past actions. Even when countless rules and conditions can be set to protect customers, these regulations are generally a poor substitute for authentic trust. Moreover, sometimes a bond of trust makes these rules unnecessary.

Many companies resort to a wide range of cajoling stratagems in order to "force" customers into buying products and services. From this book's perspective, customers' needs must always be satisfied in a loving manner, which implies avoiding manipulative techniques and gimmicks. These cajoling techniques tend to create distrust between customers and the company using these tools.

Sisodia et al. (2015) observed that some companies tend to adopt a perspective of hucksterism – which implies the use of aggressive selling techniques that have no regard for customer needs. These authors stated that this type of selling behaviour is more noticeable in companies whose employees' main compensation is tied to sales quotas.

Some other examples of these manipulative ploys are to exaggerate products' benefits to mislead customers into buying them, to increase the customers' "pain" in order to offer a way to assuage it, to deride products and services offered by other organisations in order to differentiate a company's own offerings, to hide the fine print in contracts so that customers make uninformed decisions, etc. Some additional aspects regarding manipulative marketing techniques will be discussed in Appendix C.

Uber, the developer of the app that connects drivers and passengers, has acted in the opposite way by avoiding the use of any manipulative techniques. To that effect, this company has thoroughly assessed all the problems that passengers usually encounter when looking for taxi services (uncertain waiting time, unknown final cost of the ride, etc.) and eliminated each of these issues. In that way, customers who book a ride with Uber clearly know the estimated waiting time as well as the final cost of the transport service. In that way, Uber is able to provide customers with better transport services (Radu, 2022).

Besides, this company aims to improve these transport services through real-time feedback. When the ride is finished, customers can leave feedback about the driver through a survey by using the company's app. On the one hand, positive customer feedback provides evidence of the high value added to customers during the journey. On the other hand, negative customer feedback often prompts Uber to take corrective actions to improve the service. Moreover, extremely detrimental feedback regarding a driver might even prompt the company to disconnect this driver from the network (Qualaroo, 2022).

12.3.3 Attitude of Service

Render more service than that for which you are paid and you will soon be paid for more than you render.

Napoleon Hill

Most companies focus on selling their products and services to customers; however, the traditional sales approach tends to create different levels of friction between the company and its customers. Instead, companies that adopt a loving attitude towards customers focus on serving them, not on selling them products and services. This type of company realises that their business activities are more about serving customers (which means being customer-oriented) than focusing on the company itself.

Some employees tend to feel inferior when serving customers. It is important to clarify that serving never means servitude; instead, serving always implies adding value to customers and improving their lives to a small or large extent. An authentic attitude of service towards customers also entails treating them in a loving manner. Employees who serve customers lovingly feel that it is an honour to assist them. A company previously mentioned, The Ritz-Carlton, aims to deliver outstanding services to its customers on a regular basis. At this company, each staff member, regardless of their position (receptionists, cleaners, waiters, etc.), is allowed to spend up to 2,000 dollars a day in order to better guest experience (Bernazzani, 2021).

From a perspective of providing the best service, companies encourage customers to make the best decisions regarding their purchases of goods and services. These companies understand that customers' needs are relevant, and for this reason they try to satisfy them effectively. This type of company is determined to support customers before, during, and after the selling process. From this standpoint, a company wants its customers to make the best decisions for them, even when this implies not buying anything at all, or buying products and services from other organisations.

When a company changes its intent by adopting an attitude of service, customers can feel this in a subtle but powerful manner. As seen previously, when a company serves customers, they do not feel coerced into a commercial transaction, but instead truly acknowledged, supported, and respected. Customers do not want to feel bullied into purchasing a product or a service.

When an employee has a serving attitude, this person relates to customers in a more open manner, wholeheartedly wanting the best for them. As seen previously, when adopting a loving attitude, the employee will aim to inform customers of their best options, indicating the most suitable one for them.

Besides, when a company serves customers, it wants them to only buy products or services which they have full confidence in. In other words, the company wants customers to make fully informed purchase decisions, without any hesitation. When customers make their purchasing decisions based on the best information to hand, they are less prone to feel regretful afterwards. This type of company does not want customers to feel that they have bought a product which does not actually meet their most important needs.

If the company instead "pushes" customers to buy its products and services, they are more likely to become resentful with this organisation, and their relationship will be harmed. As seen previously, many companies regularly use stratagems to cajole customers and prompt them to buy products and services they do not really need. These ploys generally work once; when customers discover that they have been deceived, they tend to cease their relationships with that company. These commercial ruses never contribute to the development of long-term relationships between the company and customers.

With a loving attitude, a company's employees act as supportive coaches with customers. As mentioned previously, this type of employee provides customers with the most valuable information and advice for them to make the most well-informed decision. In other words, the attitude of service implies guiding customers to make their best choice, which entails total respect for their sovereignty when they make purchasing decisions.

Customers always want to know what is in it for them regarding a product or a service. A company with a serving attitude towards customers always considers their well-being and avoids keeping these customers by any means. For example, some years ago, the pharmacy chain CVS took all cigarettes from their shelves in all its stores. This decision was the result of the company's rebranding strategy, which repositioned this organisation as a provider of health services, CVS Health. As a consequence, this company decided to stop selling cigarettes because selling this unhealthy product was totally incongruent with this company's new brand image and mission. On the one hand, this decision had a very important impact on the company's sales, which dropped in several millions of dollars. On the other hand, this decision not to sell cigarettes to customers any longer prompted some of the company's customers to quit smoking. Consequently, this company's health-oriented decision has generated a positive impact on these customers' well-being (Cohen, 2017; Glazer, 2020).

There is another point to highlight. When a customer is effectively served by a company instead of being manipulated, a bond of trust is created and strengthened between them. In order to serve customers in the best way, employees should always ask customers questions like:

- What is the most relevant attribute of this type of product/service?
- What benefits do you want to obtain from this type of product/service?
- What are your real motivations when buying this type of product/service?
- What type of experience do you want to have regarding this type of product/service?
- How can this product/service make your life better?
- What are the ideal characteristics of this type of product/service?

When customers provide the company with specific answers to these questions, the organisation can know customers better in order to offer them products and services matching their criteria and preferences. Sometimes, customers might not have accurate or definite answers to the aforementioned questions. In those cases, it is the function of sellers, based on their expertise and experience, to educate and provide specific information about the alternatives that are potentially suitable for these customers.

It is important to highlight a very obvious point, which is generally dismissed by many companies. Some products and services which could be beneficial for certain customers could be totally detrimental for others. Therefore, company employees should treat each customer as a distinct human being with specific needs and preferences. This point will be thoroughly discussed later in this chapter.

For example, there is a company called Stitchfix, which sells items of clothing online. This company takes into account customer's unique characteristics and preferences in order to provide them with personalised offerings. In that sense, each customer is treated in a distinctive way. Customers take a stylist quiz on the company website, where they enter their personal traits (sex, height, weight, size, body shape, etc.) and distinct tastes (shirts' fit, trousers' fit, preferences regarding outfit, etc.). Based on this information, this company makes personalised suggestions on the most suitable items of clothing for them. This company has a myriad of personal stylists who evaluate each user profile to give them expert personalised advice (Brooks, 2022; Stitchfix, 2022).

Wolhorn (1977) observed that a company's employees should treat customers in the same way these employees would like to be treated if they were customers. In relation to this, Greenleaf (1991, 1996) observed that leading companies are the ones that make customers happier and fulfilled while being served.

Many salespeople become too eager to obtain a purchase from customers, and customers frequently feel the salespersons' anxiousness. When salespeople act in an anxious manner, customers are likely to be put off. In those cases, customers feel that the salesperson does not want the best purchase for them, but for the company.

Many employees want to close the sale at all costs and forget to thoroughly explore the customer's distinctive needs. In those cases, it is advisable that salespeople change their focus from "selling mode" to "serving mode," which implies knowing more about the customer's unique preferences. In relation to this, customers have different criteria when buying a product or service, such as trustworthiness, quality, branding, packaging, delivery services, and financing.

Sometimes, a company can also help its customers discover their latent or unobvious needs; in other words, customers might not be clear about their preferences. In these cases, company employees can kindly interact with customers to discover and explore their hidden preferences and needs, as well as potential products and services which can be suitable to them.

The company's employees should position themselves as experts about the product and services being offered to the customers. By standing out as knowledgeable about a company's products and services, salespeople can provide the best advice to customers. The main purpose of the salesforce is to guide customers throughout the buying process in a friendly manner.

However, the expert knowledge possessed by salespeople should always be balanced with the knowledge that customers have about themselves, which includes their own needs, desires, and values. The harmonious combination of these two types of knowledge places the seller in a better position to offer customers loving support so that they can make good purchasing decisions.

As explained previously, a company which adopts a loving attitude towards its customers is aimed at offering them the best value possible regarding its products and services. When a company focuses on offering outstanding value to customers, their needs are more likely to be met. Moreover, when customers have good experiences stemming from a company's products and services, they tend to feel cared for and loved by this company. These positive emotions experienced by customers make them more likely to be loyal to that company, and their relationships with the organisation tend to become stronger over time.

In marketing, the concept of value is defined as the relationship between the perceived benefits related to a product and the perceived costs associated with it, from the perspective of customers. If the customer perceives that a product offers more benefits than costs, this customer is more prone to buy this product. Instead, when a customer perceives that a product offers fewer benefits than its costs, customers will feel discouraged to buy it. The costs associated with a product include the price to be paid for this product, but also the cost of time (e.g., time spent to buy the product) and the level of risk assumed by a customer (e.g., more expensive products often represent a higher risk for customers). Oftentimes, customers compare the value regarding a specific product with the value offered by alternative products, in order to choose the item that offers the highest value.

An example of a company that aims to provide customers with the best value possible is Trader Joe's, the well-known grocery chain. This company offers a range of high-quality and low-price products, in a cheerful and friendly environment; a great part of these products is own-brand items. In stores, employees are engaged with customers on a regular basis, to assist them in whatever they need. This company's sales level per square feet is one of the highest in the sector (McKinnon, 2022). As seen, the company offers a lot of benefits (wide choice of high-quality goods, friendly environment, etc.) as compared with the costs (very affordable products).

Some online merchants like Amazon provide customers with value by reducing the cost of time. In this case, the customer does not have to travel to the shop to buy the product; instead, purchases can be made from home 24/7. Some companies which offer free samples also add high value to customers as they allow them to test these products with no strings attached (without the need to buy the product) eliminating the risk related to the product (which is linked to its cost).

Some companies use processes and systems that help customers analyse, select, and buy products without any assistance from a seller. This is part of the self-service trend, where customers can become self-reliant. Some examples of this are websites where customers can buy or book online, and supermarkets where customers select and buy products on their own and pay for them through an electronic cashier. Oftentimes, companies justify the use of this technology by saying that it put customers in full control of the process, and making it simpler, faster, and more convenient, while also reducing the company's costs.

In all these cases, there is no interaction between customers and a company's employees, which can make the company's service to customers look impersonal. In these cases, the company should provide customers with assistance from its employees in different ways (on the phone, in person, virtual chat, etc.) in order to make their customers' experience warmer and less impersonal.

In the case of Trader Joe's, which belongs to a sector where self-service is so widespread (self-checkout, etc.), this company is increasing the number of staff members to help customers in the best way possible regarding their in-store experiences. Many of the organisations in this sector prompt customers to do everything on their own (self-service, self-checkout, etc.). Instead, in this company, employees are devoted to helping customers as much as possible. For example, these enthusiastic staff members regularly assist customers regarding the best products for them, offer product samples to try, present new items, and even provide tips on serving food products (McKinnon, 2022; Trader Joe's, 2019).

12.3.4 A Sharing Attitude

Research states that when a person shares anything personal with another, the latter tends to be more open with the former. Moreover, Cialdini (2009) observed that every time a person gives something to another, this person feels naturally compelled to naturally reciprocate, which means acting in a similar manner. This principle is known as reciprocity and affects all social interactions.

A company's employees can apply this principle to all interactions with customers. When talking to a customer, sellers can make a casual comment about their own needs. For example, when showing a specific product to a customer, a seller can say, "In relation to this type of product, I generally like …." When sellers are open to confessing their own personal needs and preferences to customers, the latter are more inclined to talk about their own needs.

At Trader Joe's, employees often help customers with serving advice for food products, as mentioned previously. These employees are prone to engage in conversations with customers and provide them with valuable suggestions about the products offered by this company. Moreover, these staff members themselves are keen on the products the company sells in its stores (Trader Joe's, 2019).

There is another point to highlight. In order to improve their communication with customers, salespeople can make comments not only about their own personal preferences, but also about their own values, hobbies, interests, and any other personal aspects. By doing so, salespeople present themselves as more authentic individuals, which prompts customers to open up reciprocally. When customers hear these comments from a salesperson, they tend to lower their defensive barriers during the sales process.

Bryant (2009) observed that when people show themselves vulnerable before others, which implies being transparent, honest, open, and accepting of their own shortcomings and mistakes, this attitude helps create a stronger connection with them. Consequently, when sellers show themselves to be vulnerable and human, they are more prone to build deeper rapport with customers. In other words, when salespeople trust customers with aspects of their own personal stories, customers are more likely to trust these sellers with their own.

Besides, when salespeople share their own personal information with customers and they reciprocate, some common aspects between the speakers are likely to be found, for example, similar tastes and identical preferences. As seen previously, research has demonstrated that when a person finds commonalities with another, more affinity is created between them. In relation to this, Wiseman (2009) has observed that, according to research, people tend to like each other more when they agree on things they dislike, rather than on things they like.

The principle of reciprocity and sharing can be applied in other ways. As mentioned previously, companies, for example, can give away different things to customers: free samples, truthful and relevant information, useful advice, technical support, etc. According to the principle of reciprocity, customers that received these gifts from a company are prone to give something back to this organisation. For example, customers can give positive recommendations about the company to their friends, and customers can also give their loyalty to the company.

The principle of reciprocity can be illustrated with an example. As seen previously, Trader Joe's is a grocery chain that regularly supports its customers in an outstanding manner. As a consequence, customers act in a reciprocal manner: they spontaneously support this company on social media platforms. This company has countless followers on various social media platforms (YouTube, Pinterest, and Instagram) where it shares visually enticing posts.

Supportive customers write reviews on this company's customer service on social media, bringing about a positive impact on the company's brand image. There are also some Trader Joe's-related social media accounts with thousands of followers, which are led by customers. These popular social media accounts review this company's new products and also post food recipes, contributing to the promotion of these items (Esbenshade, 2019; Smith, 2020).

12.3.5 Spontaneous Approach

Many employees engage in conversations with customers in a scripted and unnatural manner. Some companies make salespeople memorise scripts to use with customers. When talking to customers, these sellers appear artificial, like robots, and no authentic rapport is developed between these salespeople and customers. This structured way of communicating is ineffective in developing relationships with potential or current customers. Customers are very intelligent and easily perceive when a company uses canned stories to meet its own interests.

A company can adopt an alternative perspective by leaving its own hidden agenda aside and approaching customers in a natural and spontaneous manner. Natural communication is a key factor for companies to engage with customers from a long-term perspective. From this standpoint, the company's priority is to serve its customers in the best manner, not to entice them with verbal gimmicks. When customers are really deemed important, employees let the conversation unfold spontaneously and effortlessly. In this communicational approach, salespeople do not try to veer the conversation in any specific predetermined direction.

Not only does this conversational approach improve the connection with customers, but it will also make them feel more comfortable, which contributes to building mutually beneficial relationships. The topic of natural conversations has been thoroughly explained in Chapter 8.

Zappos, the prestigious online retailer, makes workers at the call centres feel more engaged in the workplace. These employees are trained for several weeks to feel more empowered at work. In this training, employees are encouraged to connect to customers on a deep and personal level. These employees are encouraged to avoid using scripted talk when engaging in conversations with customers. These staff members are keen on communicating with customers in a natural and hearty manner in order to brighten their relationships with them (Mechlinski, 2021).

This is aligned with one of the company's main values "Build open and honest relationships through communication." Through this value, Zappos' employees are encouraged to build robust and emotionally based relationships with customers and other stakeholders. These relationships are based on relevant principles like openness, friendliness, compassion, and integrity (Zappos Insights, 2023).

12.3.6 Full Connection

Most companies get in contact with their customers on several occasions: before, during, and after the purchasing process. According to McGrath and MacMillan (2005), the consumption chain is the sequence of interactions between a company and its customers. Some examples of these interactions are: customers' requests for information about products or services, arrangement of the main purchasing conditions, delivery of products, sorting out complaints, etc. It is important to highlight that a company's employees should always add value to customers in each of these interactions.

The aforementioned authors advise companies to identify the main employees that get in contact with customers in each of these interactions and encourage these staff members to fully acknowledge customers' needs in a responsive, diligent, and friendly manner. In other words, in each interaction, employees should make things easier, faster, and simpler for customers. However, some companies tend to relate to customers in a halfway fashion. In relation to this, there are several obstacles which affect the quality of the connection between a company and its customers. Some examples of these hindrances are:

- **Lack of full information:** Sometimes, companies withhold information that is relevant to customers. These companies act in a very calculated or dishonest manner, which prevents the chance of a real and deep connection with customers. Customers should always be provided with the most significant information for them to make the best purchasing decision. A company like Southwest Airlines, a low-cost airline, is transparent with its customers by informing them of the price of its tickets in a sincere and direct manner, without any additional fees, such as change fees and unexpected bag fees. This company stated that its low fares remain low, by avoiding any pesky fees (Southwest Airlines, 2022).

- **Lack of personalised approach:** According to Brandenburger and Nalebuff (1996), when a company does not take the time to develop its relationships with customers, it is as if this company was selling standardised and undifferentiated products and services, similar to the ones offered by any other organisation. The development of strong relationships with customers adds value to customers, in the same way products and services offered by a company do. Therefore, it is important to care for the relationships with customers and nurture them on a regular basis, avoiding treating customers as "numbers" or "undifferentiated" individuals. As previously analysed, Stitchfix, a company that sells items of clothing, offers personalised suggestions for each of its customers according to their unique preferences (preferred fit, etc.) and features (size, etc.). Zingerman's is a community of various businesses – which includes delicatessen products, bakehouse catering and events, creamery, etc. –. One of the owners observed that this enterprise is focused on serving one customer at a time, through small gestures (recalling customers' names, thanking them for their purchases, devoting time to show new customers around, etc.) to deliver outstanding service (Weinzweig, 2023).

- **Lack of undivided attention:** Some companies do not develop a deep connection with customers because they do not provide them with full attention. Company employees must have a laser-focus on customers when engaging with them. All distractions (picking up a phone call, etc.) must be avoided in order to acknowledge customers in a respectful manner. A company's employees can use active listening skills when the customer is talking. These employees can also paraphrase what customers say and clarify relevant points to avoid misunderstandings. As seen in the case of Zappos, the prestigious online retailer, employees at the call centres are encouraged to connect to customers in a spontaneous, deep, and hearty way. These employees aim to develop robust relationships with customers, so they do not try to keep the talk for a short period of time, as it is common in other companies' call centres. For instance, the lengthiest phone call between an employee at the company's call centre and a customer was 10 hours and 43 minutes (Mechlinski, 2021).

- **Lack of presence:** Some employees are not fully present when interacting with customers. Presence implies being focused on the now. Many employees tend to be distracted by thoughts about the past (e.g., memories) or the future (e.g., worries, expectations). For example, when talking to customers, some employees think about the best way to close the deal with them; other employees are concerned about potential customer objections. The previous examples are focused on the future, which prevents employees from being fully engaged with the customers in the now. When employees focus on the present moment, their main priority is to understand customer's needs in order to meet them effectively. Starbucks, the coffee shop chain, has a continuous focus on customers, engaging with them on social media where it has millions of followers. For instance, when customers make comments on social media platforms about this company or its products, Starbucks posts swift and personalised replies to these comments. This company is continually monitoring social media to engage in virtual conversations with its customers. For example, if a customer comments online about her tastes and preferences regarding the company's products, Starbucks responds to this customer in a personalised and warm manner. The company often provides friendly suggestions on specific products suitable for customers on social media. This company also uses these platforms to publish attractive content (news, product launch, etc.), which brings about a deeper connection with its customers (Aktas, 2022).

- **Lack of kindness and warmth:** A full connection with customers also implies treating them in a polite and amicable manner. For instance, a company can kindly request customers' permission to ask about their personal information in order to recommend the company's products. Employees can also show their kindness towards customers in other ways. For example, some power gestures of warmth are grinning or smiling to customers in a friendly manner. Some other positive body language signals are nodding and making regular eye contact when the customers are speaking. All these actions improve the rapport between a company and its customers. A good example of a company which treats its customers with warmth and kindness is Trader Joe's. This company's employees always adopt a joyful and friendly attitude towards customers. For instance, on one occasion, a child began with his tantrums at the checkout in store. An employee started to sing a song and dance rhythmically with other colleagues in order to distract and calm down that child, who was fascinated by that impromptu performance (Lakritz, 2019).

- **Lack of continuous support:** Some companies are limited to offering assistance to customers during the buying process. In order to develop more affinity with customers, a company should also offer them kind support after they have bought the product. This includes, for example, listening to customer complaints and providing customers with clarification about the use of a product. A company can also offer customers valuable support before the buying process, for instance, by providing them with the most complete online information regarding the organisation's products and services, so that these customers can check it before interacting with this company. An example of a company that offers continuous support is GoDaddy, which sells Internet domains, website development products, and hosting services. This company has an award-winning team which offers customer support round the clock (24/7). To that effect, customers can contact the company's team on the phone at any time seven days a week, for various reasons, such as technical assistance and pricing (GoDaddy, 2022).

- **Lack of comfort:** Some employees do not make customers feel at ease. When an employee engages with customers, this person should prompt them to feel comfortable. When customers are treated in a friendly manner, they are more prone to experience positive emotions and link these emotional states to the company. Most purchasing decisions have an emotional component. Therefore, when customers feel good during their interactions with a company, they are more likely to develop a deeper connection with this organisation. Qantas is an example of a company where employees bring emotional support to its customers. As seen previously, on a flight, the company's employees (air hostesses) listened attentively to a mourning passenger whose father had died recently and treated her with red wine and her toddler with snacks to make them more comfortable on their journey (Thackray, 2022).

- **Lack of high value:** Some companies provide customers with little or no value. In order to develop long-lasting relationships with customers, companies must offer high value, but also add more value to them on a continuous basis. For example, a company should improve their products and services on a regular basis because customers are very demanding and their expectations tend to become gradually higher over time. If a company does not innovate on a regular basis, other companies in the market will. An example of a company that offers high value to customers is IBM, which was previously analysed in this book. This company has an award-winning publication which offers free online high-value insights about the sector conveyed by various renowned specialists. This publication has priceless articles covering various significant topics (Quantum computing, Artificial Intelligence, Cybersecurity, etc.), which are of great value for customers (IBM, 2023; Radu, 2022).

As seen previously, no customer wants to feel pulled or rushed into purchasing a company's products and services as a result of frightening, manipulating, or misleading strategies. These ploys create no connection with customers, but push them away. Not only do customers want to feel in total control of their actions when buying a product or a service; they also want to be acknowledged as valuable and unique human beings who deserve to have their need for full connection duly satisfied.

12.3.7 Soft-Touch Approach

The majority of sales workshops teach selling techniques (different alternatives to close deals, ways to answer customers' objections, scripts to identify customers' needs, etc.) which are unnatural, and sometimes blatantly manipulative. As seen previously, the right approach of a company's employee when relating to customers is not to try to sell something to them, but instead to show genuine interest in their needs. When a salesperson is truly interested in a customer, the latter is more prone to show interest in the former.

Salespeople commonly use traditional selling techniques which includes elements of control and manipulation. When sellers use these techniques, customers often feel "forced" to make decisions in a certain way, as a result of the pressure exerted on them. Most customers perceive these sellers as untrustworthy and unreliable. Salespeople who are pushy typically take actions like:

- Trying to focus on their company, instead of centring on customers.
- Treating customers in an inauthentically kind manner.
- Hiding or distorting information which is relevant to customers.
- Talking only about commercial topics and avoiding talking about personal ones.
- Talking negatively about competitors.
- Enunciating needs which customers do not actually have.
- Trying to offer products and services convenient for the company, but not for customers.

Customers can usually "smell" when a seller is pushy, sleazy, and inauthentic; they can easily perceive when the selling process does not feel "correct" or "real." Customers can also perceive the feeling of desperation from a forceful seller, which pushes them away. When customers perceive a lack of integrity in the salesperson, they automatically adopt a defensive attitude (fight-freeze-flight). In those cases, customers are prone to shut down their interactions with the seller.

No company can gain customers by pushing them into buying its products and services. Instead, when a company's employee acts in an unworried manner, which means not being continually centred on getting sales, customers tend to feel more comfortable. Moreover, when a company focuses on serving customers, they naturally respond in a more positive manner to its products and services.

As seen previously, hard-selling and pushiness are never related to a loving attitude towards customers. To that effect, when a salesperson adopts a loving attitude towards customers, this seller avoids trying to persuade them by using cajoling or misleading ploys. Social psychologists have observed that when a person is purposely trying to persuade others, they are less likely to be effectively persuaded because the former tends to be distrusted by the latter.

Yeti, a company that sells cool boxes and other products, avoids using a hard-selling approach in its promotion videos. One of its videos shows a renowned chef in a stunning natural landscape, who is fishing, picking plants, and cooking. Despite the company's products (cool boxes) being subtly shown in that video, they are not promoted in an explicit, direct, or pushy manner. Instead, throughout that video, the company wants to show the details of these experiences (fishing, cooking, etc.) in that magnificent natural place. In this example, viewers are more prone to develop an emotional bond between the company's brand and these experiences in nature (Wagner, 2020; Yeti, 2022).

There is another point to highlight. It is interesting to pinpoint that customers can feel when they are being treated in a fair and supportive manner. Customers can easily distinguish a company that wants to thrust its products onto them from a business which wants to serve them in the best way. This second type of company is primarily aimed at providing customers with the best advice, so that they can make the best decision to satisfy their needs. Consequently, when approaching customers, sellers should ask themselves, "Am I being pushy with customers or am I trying to help them in the most honest manner?"

There is another relevant point to highlight. Companies that sell products or services with several technical characteristics (sizes, materials, functions, etc.) often have to educate customers. These technical aspects should always be explained to customers in the clearest and most simple way, avoiding any technical jargon when possible. A seller who provides customers with information about these technical aspects should avoid bragging about this knowledge, so that customers do not feel ashamed of not having this knowledge (Allen and Wotten, 1998).

In those cases, a seller can say to a customer, "You might have realised that there are different models of … I would like to explain this further …" or "It is relevant for you to know a bit more about …," so that customers can feel acknowledged and respected. In order to clarify these technical traits, sellers can use visual props (such as photos, samples, and drawings) to make their explanations clearer (Allen and Wotten, 1998).

Oscar is a prestigious American health insurance organisation. This type of service (health insurance) is often intricate because it includes a myriad of technical terms which can potentially mislead customers in their choices. To that effect, this company has an online platform which avoids using any complex language or jargon (words like deductibles and premiums). The use of plain and simple language on that webpage helps customers select the best plan for them (Fiorella, 2021; Ireland, 2014). One of the founders observed that they have started up that company so it could behave as it were a doctor in the family (Oscar, 2022).

12.3.8 Transparency

Lack of transparency is related to the previous points regarding a seller's manipulative attitude. When sellers are transparent, they avoid providing customers with misleading or untruthful information. Instead, sellers' lack of transparency tends to generate distrust, which, in turn, harms the relationship with customers. Some examples of stratagems purposed to misguide customers are:

- Provision of incomplete information.
- Disclosure of false information.
- Incremental requirements to buy the product.
- Unreal scarcity of products and services.

In relation to the last example, a company pretends that the supply of their products (or services) is limited, when this is not true. In those cases, most customers tend to covet these items more intensely because they are perceived as scarce.

None of the aforementioned stratagems create a bond of trust with customers. In all these cases, customers perceive that the company is lying to them. In other words, a company promises something to customers, which is not the real deal. The use of this type of ploy backfires, making a company appear untrustworthy in the eyes of customers.

Consequently, a company should always aim to supply its customers with truthful and complete information so that they can make well-informed buying decisions. A company with integrity always provides customers with honest information and lovingly guides them before, during, and after the buying process. These companies actually want the best for their customers; their helpful attitude makes customers feel more supported, as well as comfortable. Figuratively speaking, these companies behave as a loving parent who continually gives their best advice to their children, but also encourages them to make the best decision.

Transparent companies always communicate the full range of aspects regarding their products and services. These companies are always willing to educate customers in a caring manner, so that they can make their most well-informed buying decisions. When a company acts with integrity, it is more likely to capture customers' minds (making them aware of the company's products and services), but also their hearts (which implies building a long-lasting bond of trust with them). As seen previously, companies like Southwest Airlines inform the price of its tickets in a transparent, straightforward, and clear manner, avoiding any additional fees. Another example of a transparent company is Lush. This is an ethical company that sells cosmetic products. On its webpage, Lush thoroughly lists the ingredients of every product. This detailed description of each product is accompanied by information about the places the product's ingredients come from, as well as how the product benefits customers (Lush, 2022).

12.3.9 Openness

Many companies try to sell their products and services to customers without knowing their distinct needs in detail. Customers are wise and insightful; they can thoroughly inform any company of their unique needs. Therefore, companies should always be open to being introduced to the customers' unique world, which includes their needs, values, and expectations.

Amazon sells millions of products on its online platform. This company becomes aware of each customer's unique needs and preferences through their past purchases, or through the searches they made in the past. Based on this information and using complex algorithms, this company makes personalised suggestions to each of its customers. For example, if a customer has bought a book about a specific discipline (Marketing, etc.) on Amazon, this company will post messages with specific recommendations of other books similar to the book bought previously (Khandelwal, 2022).

There is another point to highlight. It is important that companies be empathetic, which means seeing reality through customers' eyes. A very effective way to know what customers want is to listen to them actively on a continuous basis. The main aspects of active listening have been explained in Chapter 8, which is about natural conversations.

Another powerful way is to ask customers various open questions, such as "What …?", "Why …?", "Who …?", "When …?", and similar ones. These questions prompt customers to share more insightful information about themselves. The regular use of open-ended questions brings about richer and more expansive interactions, enhances trust and rapport, and fosters self-disclosure, which can help a company know more about its customers (Mirivel, 2014). When interacting with customers, companies should avoid asking them closed questions, which generally have short answers, for instance, "yes" or "no." This type of question does not provide as much relevant information about customers' preferences.

12.3.10 Specific Approach

Many companies say that they want to serve customers in the best way. Nonetheless, it is important to highlight that the word "customers" is just a general and abstract concept which never defines clearly the specific, particular, and concrete human beings who look for products and services according to their distinct preferences. In simple words, not all customers are alike, even when they share some characteristics with others, such as age and income.

When the company focuses excessively on the concept "customers," it runs the risk of missing the unique human aspects of the individuals to be served. According to De Mello (1990), concepts like "customers" are not fixed and unchanged; instead, each customer is a living being and therefore dynamic. He added, "words are pointers, they're not descriptions." Oftentimes, words hinder the real connection with reality. In relation to this, Watts (1955) observed that "in practice we are all bewitched by words," and "we confuse them with the real world, as if it were a world of words …," and "we are dismayed and dumbfounded when they do not fit."

Companies must realise that each customer has unique tastes and preferences. Consequently, companies should discover and acknowledge these distinct needs in order to offer customers products and services that are actually suitable for them. A company which adopts a loving attitude towards its customers tends to do its best to meet their distinct expectations.

Some questions a company's employees should ask themselves are: "What are the specific needs and motivations of this customer?" or "What unmet needs do I perceive in this customer?" These questions create more awareness and understanding of what specific customers are looking for, which, in turn, helps a company serve them in a more loving manner.

Care/of is a company that sells vitamins and health supplements. On its website, this company prompts customers to take a quiz in order to offer them personalised backed-by-science products which are suitable for their unique and distinctive needs. In this quiz, each customer is asked about their age, sex, current level of knowledge about vitamins and supplements (informed, curious, and sceptical), past use of vitamins, personal goals (immunity, sleep, energy, digestion, etc.), and stress levels, among other relevant aspects (Brooks, 2022; Care/of, 2022).

There is another relevant point to highlight. According to Wellemin (1998), customers have needs related to the tangible aspects of the products or services (such as quality, design, and reliability) and other needs which are more related to intangible aspects of the purchasing process. This second group of needs (intangible) are as important as the first group (tangible). Some examples of needs of customers related to intangible aspects of the purchasing process are:

- To be acknowledged regarding their unique needs and preferences.
- To be treated with care and respect throughout the purchasing process and also after it.
- To be actively listened to regarding comments and objections about products and services.

- To be provided with accurate information about the product or service in order to make their best decision.
- To feel comfortable (physically, emotionally, and mentally) during the buying process.
- To be offered a relevant set of alternatives in order to choose the most appropriate one.
- To receive continuous support from the company in case of clarifications or claims.
- To be delivered what was promised by the company.
- To be offered the possibility of changing, replacing, or returning products or services.
- To have the terms and conditions of the purchase respected by the company.

It is important to understand that customers do not only buy specific products and services from a company. At the same time, customers are "buying" how the company behaves with them and how this organisation treats them over time, and this counts as much as the products and services themselves.

Lastly, whenever customers buy products and services, these customers always seek the benefits these very products and services will provide them with. For example, when a family buys a holiday pack, this group also seeks the benefits which this pack will provide them (e.g., having a relaxing time together in a nice place). Let's relate this to a recent example. In the case of Care/of, customers who aim to buy vitamins and health supplements on the company's website want to obtain specific benefits from these products. These benefits can be, for example, better digestion, improved immune system, more energy, and better sleep. As also seen previously, these sought-after benefits will vary from customer to customer. For this reason, in the quiz which each customer has to fill out on this company's online platform, there is an important point: customer's personal goals regarding the use of vitamins and supplements. This point is related to the benefits sought by the customer.

12.3.11 Segmentation and Uniqueness

In marketing, there is a well-known concept called "segmentation" which means dividing the market (total group of customers) into segments (parts of market). Each segment is composed of customers with the same characteristics (age, occupation, gender, income, lifestyle, etc.). Even though customers are commonly gathered in homogeneous subgroups (called segments), each single customer must also be considered as a distinctive individual.

Each person – considered an individual customer – has distinctive beliefs, values, personality, interests and preferences, past experiences, income, occupation, family life cycle stage (single, married with children, etc.), cultural aspects, and groups of influence (family, friends, partner, colleagues, etc.), among other factors. These factors make each customer one of a kind. In some cases, companies sell their products to other companies, which is known as B2B or business to business. These corporate buyers – also called industrial customers – also vary from one another regarding different aspects: size of company, corporate culture, sector the company belongs to, geographical location, etc.

Above all, each buyer is a unique human being, who cannot be replicated. Consequently, each time a company interacts with a customer, the organisation should focus on discovering that customer's distinctive needs in a thorough manner. In the health sector, patients are the customers. In this industry, research has shown that 35% of medical doctors show some signs of depersonalisation, for example, by using sentences like "the chest pain in room six," instead of talking about the patient as a whole human being with unique health conditions, personal preferences, and fears (Trzeciack and Mazzarelli, 2019).

By treating each customer in a personalised manner, a company is more prone to satisfy their unique needs in a more effective way and add enhanced value to them. As a consequence, the company can brighten its relationship with each customer significantly. Chandra et al. (2022) observed that, when customers are treated in a personalised fashion, these customers tend to reduce the time they spend and the mental effort they make regarding their purchasing choices.

One of the owners of Zingerman's, an enterprise previously mentioned, insightfully observed that when a company becomes big and considers customers as statistical segments or as a contribution to its sales, the company is prone to lose customers as the organisation cannot serve one customer at a time to provide them superior service according to their unique needs. As mentioned previously, this company aims to serve one customer at a time (Weinzweig, 2023).

A company like Netflix, the movie producing and streaming company, is an excellent example of an organisation which uses an approach of personalisation with its customers. When subscribers log in on the company's website, they see posts of suggested movies to watch, which are personalised to them as viewers. In order to do this, this company uses its own machine learning algorithm, which takes into consideration the movies each user has clicked, watched, or searched for, and then makes personalised suggestions of specific movies to see, based on that information (Fiorella, 2021; Netflix, 2022).

There is another relevant point to highlight. Many companies tend to treat customers in a quantitative manner, which means that each customer is a number to the company. This approach towards customers is unloving because it aims to depersonalise them. Instead, when a company adopts a loving attitude towards customers, they feel that they are not a figure or a component of an impersonal group to that organisation; each customer is considered a valuable and distinct individual.

A loving company also prompts customers to express and articulate their own needs in a clear and overt manner. When interacting with customers, this type of organisation makes customers feel a deep sense of conviction that they are making the right choice regarding the products and services offered by this company. This organisation adopts a humanised approach towards customers, which contributes to the development of stronger relationships with them.

A loving organisation shows continuous genuine curiosity regarding customer preferences. This type of company adopts a learning attitude; it honestly wants to know more about customers in order to serve them better. In other words, when a company is fully aware of each customer's unique needs, the organisation is more capable of offering products and services which resonate with them. When a company is fully aware of the singular needs of each customer and understands them in a thorough fashion, customers are more inclined to feel connected to this organisation.

It is important to remember that all customers want to be cared for by a company. Consequently, whenever customers complain against a company, this organisation should always take their objections as signals of these customers' unsatisfied needs. This company should exhaustively analyse this valuable feedback to adopt a more loving attitude towards these customers and address these objections in a more effective manner. Moreover, negative feedback received from customers often helps to develop better products and services in order to satisfy customers' needs more effectively.

Starbucks, the global coffee shop chain, is an example of a company which adopts a caring attitude towards its customers. In this company, for instance, a barista perfectly knew her frequent customers' preferred breakfast and drinks. This barista engaged with these customers in a natural and unscripted manner, for example, asking them how they were on that day, as she served them. Her caring attitude brought about personalised and unique customer service for these customers (Keswin, 2019).

There is another interesting point to highlight regarding this company. At this organisation, staff members also add a tiny personal touch when they write the name of each customer on their respective cups. This is a standard practice for all Starbucks' stores which has two main objectives: bringing about a more personalised customer experience and preventing customers from picking up the wrong order (Angry Espresso, 2019).

12.3.12 *Emotional Enhancement*

The main purpose of the marketing discipline is to satisfy customers' needs. The concept of satisfaction implies that customers experience pleasant emotional states in relation to the products and services they buy. These positive emotional states could be of a different kind, for example, peacefulness, happiness, and excitement. In all these cases, products and services are connected to specific emotional experiences triggered by them.

From the psychological perspective, all human actions, including buying behaviours, are motivated by two main drivers: experiencing pleasure or avoiding pain. For example, a person goes to the cinema because he wants to have fun (pleasurable experience). A person, for example, who contracts insurance policy does so because he wants to be covered in case of an accident (avoidance of pain). In these cases, customers want to experience positive emotions or, at least, shun negative ones.

Nonetheless, if we look more closely into these examples, it is possible to say that customers always want to experience positive emotional states. When the person buys the insurance, for example, this individual does not only want to avoid the pain of not having insurance coverage (avoidance of pain), but he also wants peace of mind (pleasure-seeking).

The main responsibility of companies is to enable customers to have a positive emotional experience. Oftentimes, this experience can be composed of an array of various encounters or episodes, which should make a positive impression on customers. For example, customers can have a good emotional experience when consuming the products and services bought, but also during the buying process itself. Consequently, if a company adopts a loving attitude towards its customers every time it interacts with them, they are more likely to experience positive feelings. When a customer is prompted to experience positive emotional states, this individual becomes more co-operative with the company and open to receiving support from it.

Many companies only focus on offering the best products and services and managing specific aspects of the sales process. However, these companies forget to enhance the customers' overall experience. A company should always do its best to make customers feel positive emotions each time they interact with the organisation. These interactions do not include only the buying process, but are also related to activities after sales, such as delivery of products, returns, and repair or replacement of products, among others.

Ikea, the renowned company that sells furniture and houseware, aims to regularly enhance the interactions with its customers, by prompting them to experience positive emotions. In Ikea's premises, there are cafes and recreation zones, which are intended to purposefully make customers feel more comfortable and at ease when shopping. In addition, Ikea has a mobile app which includes augmented reality, which can be used by customers to check how specific furniture would fit and look in their own homes (Om, 2022).

Starbucks, the coffee shop chain, also aims to prompt its customers to experience positive emotions. This organisation sets up its venues with nice decoration, warm sofas, and comfortable nooks to relaxing. These coffee shops have a chill-out atmosphere, as well as signature drinks and an interesting range of savoury pastry to spoil customers. This company does not offer coffee products, but instead coffee experiences. These places are ideal for long conversations and having a relaxing time. The business leader Howard Schultz insightfully observed, "We are not in the coffee business serving people, but we are in the people business, serving coffee" (Schultz, 2012).

There is another point to highlight. A customer-oriented company should purposely enhance different points of contact with customers to prompt them to experience positive emotional states. For example, the company should have an attractive and interesting website, develop enticing packaging for its products, and have visually appealing layout for its stores, etc.

Sometimes, customers feel restless or uncomfortable during the buying process because of different reasons (confusing information, limitation of time, etc.). In most cases, the company can do something to make customers feel more at ease, so that they can experience positive emotional states during the buying process. For example, if customers experience negative emotions because they are confused about the information regarding a product, the company should provide comprehensive clarification so that they can experience a more positive emotional state.

It is important to pinpoint that when buying products or services, customers commonly face different types of risks, which vary depending on the type of product or service. Solomon et al. (2006) observed that customers face:

■ Monetary risk (customers want to spend money wisely and not waste it on products or services which do not satisfy their needs).
■ Functional risk (customers want the product and service to be effective, which means that it provides the benefits promised).
■ Physical risk (customers want the product or service to be safe, secure, or healthy, without affecting their health or physical integrity).
■ Social risk (customers want the product or service to be accepted by their close circle, for instance, relatives and friends).
■ Psychological risk (customers want the product or service to contribute positively to their self-esteem and status).

In relation to this, a loving seller when interacting with customers can make them feel more at ease and confident regarding these risks. In other words, when purchasing a product or a service, customers should feel that the aforementioned risks are eliminated. For example, in relation to monetary risk, the seller can explain why a product or service is good value for money; in relation to the functional risk, the sales individual can explain to the customers how a product or service satisfies their needs. In relation to the physical risks, the seller can explain, for example, how to use the product in a safe way.

At Trader Joe's, a company already mentioned, customers can have a sample of any product in the store, providing the item does not need to be cooked. This can help customers test these products with no risk, before making any purchasing decision (McKinnon, 2022). In that sense, the use of product samples to be tasted by customers represents the biggest marketing cost incurred by this company (Yohn, 2018).

There is another important point to highlight. In some cases, a customer can experience negative emotions after buying the product or service (for instance, regret, guilt, etc.). From the marketing perspective, this is called cognitive dissonance, which is the result of incongruence between a customer's beliefs and behaviours. Customers tend to experience negative emotional states because they believe that the product or service they purchased was not the right choice. When buyers experience this dissonance, they feel that the product or service purchased really does not satisfy their needs, or might not be fully convinced about it.

In this case, the company can interact with customers to clarify doubts they could have about the products bought. The company can also provide buyers with reassuring comments that they made the right buying choice. However, in the case that the customer really believes the product does not meet their needs, the company should be willing to provide customers with a refund. All these actions generally make customers feel better; these actions can transmute customers' post-purchase regrets into positive emotional states.

There is an interesting example of a company which tries to ensure that its customers always make the right purchasing choices. For instance, the supermarket chain Aldi offers a double guarantee policy. This allows those customers who are not fully satisfied with the quality of a product bought at this company to have both the product replaced and the money refunded. This policy applies to various products, except some specific items (alcoholic drinks, etc.) (Aldi, 2022).

BLQK Coffee is a company that offers ethically and sustainably sourced artisanal coffee. This enterprise is so confident in its products that they offer their customers a 30-day money-back guarantee. This organisation states that if a customer does not truly love its products, they can comment about their experience and offer feedback for improvement, and they will obtain a full refund for their purchase (BLQK Coffee, 2023).

There is another point to highlight. When customers regularly experience positive emotions in relation to a company and its products, they are more likely to be loyal to this organisation and develop a long-term relationship with it. In those cases, customers are also more prone to recommend the company's products or services to relatives, friends, and acquaintances.

As previously explained, this positive customer experience does not have to be limited to the sales process. The relationships between the company and its customers can be reinforced over time. A company can strengthen its relationships with its customers in different ways; for example, by sending customers emails with the latest news about product launches or valuable articles, or sending customers free gifts or coupons. Companies can also use this nurturing approach even with customers that got in contact with the company but did not buy any products from them.

From a wider perspective, all departments which make up an organisation (manufacturing, administrative, finance, etc.) should be customer-oriented. All these departments should contribute, directly or indirectly, to a more positive customer experience. For example, the manufacturing department should aim to produce goods which cater to the customer's needs, not the company's needs. Likewise, the administrative department should send documents (for instance, invoices, receipts, etc.) in a way that makes the customer's purchasing process easier.

All the company's employees should be reminded and even trained so that they adopt a customer focus on a regular basis. These employees should be devoted to the satisfaction of customer needs, which means making these customers feel positive emotions. All the company's departments (manufacturing, administrative, etc.) should work in a co-operative and integrative way in order to serve customers in the best fashion.

12.3.13 Warm Appreciation

> Your customers don't just want the product or service. They want what your heart has to give them.
>
> **Mark Silver**

Appreciation has several meanings; one of them is being thankful. A company can develop a strong link with its customers when it is grateful to them. For example, some companies show their appreciation to customers by sending them letters or emails and thanking them for their custom. When a customer buys a product from a company, this organisation should express its gratitude in a personalised manner, whenever possible. For example, the message of thankfulness sent to the customer should include a personal touch, including specific aspects of this particular custom. This personalised approach makes the expression of gratitude look warmer.

In other words, companies should avoid using the same standardised templates to express their gratitude to all customers, when possible. An example will clarify the aforementioned point. If a letter is sent to customers, their names and the specific characteristics of the products bought should be included. Some other particular aspects of that purchase should be highlighted, for example, why the customer made a good choice buying the products.

That gratitude note can also include the honest desire that the customer fully enjoys the products purchased. This letter can also comment on the continuing willingness of the company to provide this customer with additional information of value, whenever needed. Lastly, the desire to strengthen the relationship with this customer beyond this specific purchase can also be expressed in that letter.

There is another relevant point to highlight. From the psychological perspective, when an employee is grateful with customers, they are more prone to have positive thoughts and experience pleasant emotions, which contribute to these customers having a more positive attitude towards this organisation.

As recently explained, customers must always be thanked for their custom. Besides, customers must also be genuinely appreciated when they do not make any purchase from the organisation. In those cases, the company can be grateful to customers for having spent their time looking at its products, or for having shown interest in them.

Lastly, there is another meaning of appreciation, which is to realise the intrinsic value of something or someone. There is a saying which goes: "what you appreciate increases in value." From this perspective, a company which appreciates customers values them greatly and is truly interested in thoroughly knowing their preferences in order to meet their expectations more effectively.

HEX sells fashion bags, cases, and other products online. This company is a good example of an organisation with a grateful attitude towards its customers. In the past, this company sent 13,000 personalised thank you notes to its customers handwritten by its employees. Each letter included the customer's name, as well as the product this customer bought. The main purpose of these personalised notes was to bring about a positive impression and to develop strong relationships with these customers (Mann, 2021; Solomon, 2014).

12.3.14 Welcoming Feedback

Many companies really hate when customers complain about their products and services. However, when a company adopts a loving attitude towards its customers, their complaints and objections are instead kindly welcomed and appreciated. This type of company also informs customers that their feedback is valuable and therefore it will be thoroughly analysed.

When customers complain, the company should always be inquisitive and sympathetic to them. To that effect, customers should be asked about the specific motivations of their complaints in order to deal with them effectively. In other words, companies should always be open to amicably discuss with customers their complaints in order to address them accordingly.

At Trader Joe's, the well-known grocery store chain, employees regularly listen to customers. In the past, this company carefully listened to some customers' complaints about this organisation using excessive plastic packaging for its products. To that effect, Trader Joe's stated that it would begin to utilise more environmentally friendly packaging. As a consequence, they refrained itself from offering single-use plastic bags in all their stores. This company also changed its plastic produce bags, and now it offers compostable and biodegradable choices.

Besides, this company sells more of its produce in a loose way, instead of using plastic bags (Martichoux, 2019; Morgan, 2019).

There is another significant point to highlight. When customers have complaints about a specific product or service, a company's employees should always act as supportive advisors. Customers' comments must be acknowledged with no delay. In those cases, the company should show a spirit of service and willingness to introduce necessary changes to satisfy customers' needs in a proper manner. Sometimes, the company cannot offer a quick solution to customers' complaints. In those cases, the company should promise customers that their issues will be analysed more thoroughly in order to offer them specific answers as soon as possible.

Oftentimes, customers' complaints or objections are not clear enough. As a consequence, the company should ask for clarification, for example, by paraphrasing or recapping customers' critiques. Sometimes, a company can also use a pre-emptive approach in relation to customers' complaints. For example, after having shown a product, an employee can ask customers a question like "Are there any points regarding this product which you are not sure about?" In all the aforementioned cases, any feedback given by customers is worthy information which should be thoroughly analysed to offer a better service to customers. Oftentimes, customer feedback represents valuable information for a company to develop more innovative products and services.

Hyatt, the global accommodation giant, takes into consideration customer feedback to improve their services. For instance, this company encourages customers to make suggestions on the improvement of its services on a specific website. On this platform, customers can leave feedback regarding their recent stay at this company. This organisation also tracks customers on social media platforms, like Twitter (now X) and Instagram, to assess the shortcomings of their experiences with this organisation. In this way, the company can look for ways to improve its services (Qualaroo, 2022).

The concept of welcoming customer feedback is closely related to the so-called "innovation flywheel." According to Gildehaus et al. (2021), the innovation flywheel includes various stages in an innovation cycle. The cycle starts when a company gathers knowledge from customers (feedback, reviews, etc.); then, this organisation reflects on these insights to unearth potential innovation opportunities. According to these authors, after this stage, the company tests some innovative ideas in the marketplace (e.g., through experiments) to select those of highest value, and finally introduce higher value innovative products or services, which, in turn, brings about more customer engagement. After this stage, the cycle starts over and over in order to offer even higher value to customers over time.

These authors applied the concept of innovation flywheel to Google. In its origins, this company only offered its customers a search engine. Nowadays, customers are connected to Google through an increasing set of products (Google Maps, Gmail, Photos, Google Docs, etc.). This company has progressively increased its interactions with customers, through regularly launching new products. As a result of this increasing engagement of customers with the company (and the vaster information gathered from these customers), for instance, this search engine can anticipate the preferences of each customer and make personalised offerings (e.g., videos to watch).

12.3.15 Story-Telling

> A man is always a teller of tales, he lives surrounded by his stories and the stories of others, he sees everything that happens to him through them, and he tries to live his own life as if he were telling a story.

Jean-Paul Sartre

The use of story-telling helps people comment (from their own perspective) about the different aspects of reality, including intangible and non-measurable aspects such as experiences, preferences, and others, in a lively and verisimilar way (Lewin and Regine, 2001). Stories allow people to experience the similarities between themselves and others; these tales flowingly connect the past, with the present and also the future (Stanton, 2012).

Some customers love to be engaged in simple stories about the company and its products and services, as well as its experiences and viewpoints. When a company uses the story-telling technique, the stories must be presented in an engaging, simple, and clear way so that customers can identify and connect to these tales. A good story can create a state of intimate connection between the company and the customer.

When story-telling is used, the stories must be delivered in a natural, articulate, and spontaneous manner. In other words, customers must never perceive the stories as canned or scripted. Besides, the stories used must always be relevant to the situation at hand, for instance, the demonstration of a product. If possible, the story should also include real people who customers can identify with. For example, if a seller is explaining the potential benefits of a specific product to a customer, some examples of other customers who have benefitted from this product in the past are significant. The story can include different elements, such as:

- Reasons which make the story relevant and suitable for the situation at hand.
- Descriptive analysis of the context of the story (where and when this story unfolds).
- Relevant facts or highlights regarding the story.
- Thoughts and emotions experienced by the participants of the story.
- Sensory comments (related to the five senses, sight, hearing, touch, taste, and smell).
- Specific evidence underpinning different aspects of the story (for instance, objective facts).
- Metaphors, examples, comparisons, rhetorical questions, and analogies.
- Situations of conflict or predicaments faced by participants, and how these challenges were overcome over time.
- Brief recap or summary of the story and recommendations stemming from the tale.

The story-telling should implicitly include clues about values, principles, and the purpose of the organisation the salesperson (story-teller) is working for. As mentioned previously, when a company uses story-telling with customers, it should link facts to real people. For example, if a seller comments about the company's recent outstanding selling performance, the data of sales can be related to specific salespeople working for this organisation, including their real names when possible. When story-telling is used in a genuine manner, tales told to customers can easily touch their hearts and prompt them to take action (e.g., buying a specific product).

Cohen and Prusak (2001) stated that stories which start like "This happened to me ..." or "I witnessed ..." are more engaging and authentic than second-hand tales. Guber (2011) observed that people are prewired to engage with good stories that are attention-grabbing, which means providing listeners with an emotional experience in order to spur them into action.

A company can also use stories to make its customers imagine the experience of enjoying a certain product or service if they bought it. In those cases, story-telling techniques prompt customers to have an approximate vision of their future experience with the product or service offered by the company. To that effect, Yeung (2011) suggests that companies use sentences such as "Imagine that you ..." as part of their story-telling process. The use of story-telling becomes more relevant in the case of services offered by a company (training, transport, etc.) which are intangible by nature.

Krochet Kids is a social enterprise that is keen on story-telling when selling its products. This organisation widely shares its own story (its origin, its dream, its growing community, etc.) on its website. This socially oriented organisation offers crafted headware and other products, supporting communities from less developed countries. The product makers from these communities receive a fair compensation for these products, which supports their families. Each product offered by this organisation is signed by the person who produced it, and customers are encouraged to find out about the personal stories of these product makers (who they are, their dreams, their hobbies and tastes, etc.) on the organisation's website. This organisation also shares these stories on social media (Krochet Kids, 2022).

There is another point to highlight. Companies should empower customers to share their stories with others. In those cases, these customers become unpaid promoters of the company's offerings, which, in turn, can attract new customers. As seen previously, a company, like Trader Joe's, has a myriad of customers who share their own experiences with the products offered by this organisation on social media. For instance, some customers share some recipes to prepare these products on Instagram.

The following example about the relevance of story-telling was presented by Phillips (2017). Some years ago, a journalist aimed to test the power of story-telling. He purchased 200 items on eBay, the online platform. Each item cost him about 1 dollar. Then, he convoked 200 authors and asked them if they wanted to write a story regarding each of these items, and they agreed to do so. This journalist then posted these 200 items on eBay accompanied by these stories. As a consequence, the gross amount these products sold for was 8,000 dollars collectively when accompanied by their respective stories, when originally their collective cost was 129 dollars.

Questions for Self-Reflection

- How can I make customers feel more comfortable?
- How can I create more trust in relation to customers?
- How can I adopt a more obliging attitude towards customers?
- How can I use story-telling when I interact with customers?

Chapter 13

Adopting a Loving Attitude towards Other Stakeholders

13.1 Suppliers and Intermediaries

Most companies are fully reliant on suppliers of products and services for their business activities. Sometimes, a company does not sell its products and services directly to customers, but through intermediaries such as wholesalers, retailers, and agents. Both suppliers and intermediaries add significant value to the products and services offered by the company in a direct or indirect manner.

Some of the principles regarding other stakeholders (employees and customers) previously explained in this book can also be applied to suppliers and intermediaries, taking into consideration the specific characteristics of these stakeholders (suppliers and intermediaries). A company should adopt a continuous loving attitude towards its suppliers and intermediaries, by taking specific actions, for instance:

13.1.1 Continuous Communication

Companies should always be open to interacting with their intermediaries and suppliers on a continuous basis. When a company has frequent communication with these organisations, the number of misunderstandings and conflicts is significantly reduced. Sometimes, a company can contact its suppliers and intermediaries for no specific business reason. In those cases, the company approaches these organisations just to have some small-talk with them to nurture the relationships with them. A company can also organise non-business activities to improve its relational aspects regarding these stakeholders. Some examples of these activities are:

- Informal lunches or dinners with suppliers and intermediaries.
- Casual visits to their venues.
- Sending them presents or letters on special occasions.
- Phoning them to talk about trivial topics (politics, sports, etc.).

Besides, a company can congratulate its suppliers and intermediaries on their recent achievements (opening up a new branch, obtaining a quality certification, etc.), or greet them on their

DOI: 10.4324/9781003372684-16

anniversary. All these activities create an atmosphere of comfort and trust between the organisation and these stakeholders. Throughout these activities, the company can develop more humanised contact with its stakeholders.

However, some companies act the opposite way; their interactions with these stakeholders only have specific business objectives (placing orders, renegotiating terms and conditions of agreements, etc.). Other companies contact suppliers and intermediaries in such an infrequent manner that their relationships with them are never strengthened significantly.

In some cases, the lack of communication with these companies is related to an attitude of impoliteness, for example, when a company receives a phone call or email from one of its suppliers and it does not to return this call or answer that email promptly. This careless behaviour affects the relationships between the company and these external stakeholders negatively.

Some companies argue that they are "overly" busy (multiple business projects, several tight deadlines, etc.) to cultivate their relationships with external stakeholders, such as suppliers and intermediaries. However, the core factor of any successful business activities is the development of strong relationships with stakeholders. For instance, any relevant business aspects (launching new products, generating more revenue, increasing the market share, increasing profits, etc.) are built on healthy relationships with a company's stakeholders.

As mentioned previously in this book, a very effective way for a company to strengthen its relationships with suppliers and intermediaries is to be authentic and trustworthy. In other words, a company should always provide reliable and accurate information to these stakeholders. Truthfulness always generates trust between the company and its suppliers and intermediaries. A company which acts in a dependable manner prompts its stakeholders (e.g., suppliers and intermediaries) to act in the same manner. When a company provides credible and complete information to its suppliers and intermediaries, its relationships with them are strengthened in a significant manner.

Sometimes, when a company and its intermediaries and suppliers trust one another very well, there may be no need to develop a formal contract; the word given suffices. In those cases, not only do companies save the cost of drafting, enforcing, and monitoring a contract, but their commitment also grows much stronger over time. However, not using contracts will not be a suitable way of working for many companies.

But bonds of trust can also be broken up, despite relevant economic interests between the parties. An example is The Body Shop, a socially oriented company which sells cosmetic products. In the past, this company cancelled its contract with its major palm-oil supplier because this supplier had tried to evict hundreds of local people to set up its new plantation. This issue was thoroughly and extensively investigated by The Body Shop before this company decided to part ways with this supplier. Before breaking up with this supplier, this company supplied The Body Shop with the majority of palm oil for its beauty products (Syal and Brodzinsky, 2010).

On this occasion, The Body Shop prioritised the protection of these people and their communities over the company's own economic aspects (the supply of palm oil by the aforementioned supplier). In simple words, this supplier's behaviour was unacceptable in the eyes of The Body Shop. The way this supplier acted was incongruent with The Body Shop's core values, such as growing partnerships and supporting communities, and championing sustainability, among others (The Body Shop, 2022b).

There is another important point to highlight. A company should always be confidential with its stakeholders. Confidentiality means keeping critical or strategic information about them in a safe manner. A confidential company shows a caring attitude by continually protecting this information and avoiding any data leakage. When a company adopts this attitude towards its stakeholders, they are more prone to disclose sensitive information. The principle of confidentiality applies not only to suppliers and intermediaries, but also to other stakeholders (for instance, employees, customers, etc.).

Besides, when a company is trustworthy with its suppliers and intermediaries, it is willing to admit its own mistakes as quickly as possible. This honest attitude commonly generates even more trust between the company and its stakeholders. However, many companies are reluctant to admit their mistakes, which makes them less credible before other organisations.

13.1.2 Unselfishness

Every time a company negotiates agreements with its suppliers or intermediaries, it should avoid adopting a bargaining attitude towards them. A bargaining company tends to ask itself, "What can I get from this organisation?" This unloving attitude is only centred on the company's needs and dismisses completely the needs of the other party. When a company adopts this selfish approach on a continuous basis, its relationships with its stakeholders are prone to become weaker over time. Instead, when a company adopts a loving attitude, it is more prone to negotiate with stakeholders in a friendly way and ask itself the following questions:

■ How can we be more considerate with this organisation's specific needs?
■ What can we give to this organisation to satisfy their needs properly?
■ How can we strengthen the valuable relationship with this organisation?
■ What agreement can be proposed that fairly satisfies the needs of both parties?

A company should always aim to develop tailor-made agreements with its suppliers and intermediaries and avoid the use of standardised contracts. The company should use customised contracts which can fairly take the specific needs of both parties into account. Besides, a company should only look for business agreements with stakeholders which are mutually beneficial, which means that the unique needs of each party are properly met.

These win-win agreements endure the passage of time, as compared with lopsided agreements which tend to be short-lived. A win-win agreement is possible when the organisation thoroughly knows the distinctive needs of the other party. When a company does not thoroughly know the main needs of the other organisation, it should ask it about its main interests.

Some useful questions a company can ask its stakeholders for this purpose can be: "What are the main aspects you are looking for in a potential agreement between us?" and "Why do you want …?" A company can also ask itself the following question: "How can we satisfy their needs in a more effective manner?"

Whenever a company does business with its suppliers and intermediaries, all contractual terms and conditions between them should be the result of a fair exchange of proposals from both sides. In other words, both companies should participate in the construction of agreements, which means that none of them should impose any terms on the other. Agreements with stakeholders should always be based on consensus and aim to have a long-term perspective, when possible.

In mutually beneficial agreements, the interests of each party are cared for; no participant obtains unfair benefits at the expense of the other. These business contracts always bring about the highest good for all parties involved. In other words, this type of agreement is always transparent, fair, and amicable.

During the process of arriving at these agreements, the parties should avoid performing manipulative actions, such as exaggerated requests, offering false alternatives, bluffing, ultimatums, and unnecessary delays, among others. Some companies tend to use this type of detrimental behaviour in order to obtain more benefits from the agreement than the other party. From the perspective of this book, the relationship of a company with these organisations (suppliers and intermediaries) should always be consensual; no parties must be forced to be with one another.

Toyota, the renowned car manufacturing company, is a great example of an organisation which continually adopts a supportive attitude towards its suppliers. This company always allows its suppliers to obtain adequate returns regarding the contracts they have with this company. In addition, Toyota respects the price agreed with its suppliers and regularly assists them in the betterment of their operational aspects. In the past, Toyota's Thai suppliers were affected by the economic crisis in that country, and Toyota helped them financially by making big upfront payments to them, instead of making payments over time. This helped to significantly relieve the financial pressure on these suppliers. This type of actions has allowed Toyota to develop long-term bonds with its suppliers (Kalkofen et al., 2007).

13.1.3 Respecting Commitments

> The truth of the good old maxim, that 'Honesty is the best policy,' is upheld by the daily experience of life; uprightness and integrity being found as successful in business as in everything else.
>
> **Samuel Smiles**

An organisation that trusts another expects that the latter will abide by contractual obligations agreed by both parties. A trustworthy organisation is expected to act in a benevolent manner with others; this type of company tends not to perform any opportunistic or deceptive action to take advantage of others. It is interesting to highlight that when a company expects another organisation to behave honestly, this often becomes a self-fulfilling prophecy. Oftentimes, companies tend to act in congruence with others' expectations of them.

When a company and its external stakeholders (for instance, suppliers and intermediaries) trust each other, they know that they will naturally keep their commitment to one another over time. However, some companies promise things to their suppliers and intermediaries in the heat of the moment, which later cannot be delivered. These organisations do not keep their word with these stakeholders. A company which fails to respect its commitments with other organisations is prone to be distrusted in future transactions.

Consequently, a company should only assume commitments with these organisations if it can fulfil them in a proper manner. This type of organisation acts with integrity. According to Hendricks and Ludeman (1996), integrity is the foundation of any business relationship; the lack of integrity creates "entanglement" between companies, not real relationships. These authors observed that integrity is about being honest with oneself and others.

Before assuming any commitment, a company should always ask itself "Will we be really capable of delivering what we are about to promise?" and "Will this agreement positively contribute to the business objectives of both companies?" A company which answers these questions honestly is more likely to act with integrity with other organisations.

Lastly, a company which could not deliver its promises should sincerely apologise to the organisation affected. A company in fault should always take full ownership of this situation, making no excuses or untruthful comments. Besides, this company should clearly and swiftly explain the reasons for not keeping its word and offer compensation, when possible, for the inconveniences created. When a company adopts this attitude, its relationships with its external stakeholders are strengthened.

The Body Shop is a company which acts with integrity while positively contributing to both its own objectives and its suppliers' goals. For many decades, this company has been sourcing the ingredients for its products from a myriad of suppliers worldwide, through a community fair trade programme. This programme has various objectives: developing long-lasting and robust relationships with its suppliers, contributing to their financial independence, supporting projects in their local communities, and accessing high-quality ingredients for the company's products (The Body Shop, 2022c).

Through this programme, the company's suppliers are offered beneficial contractual conditions; they are always paid fair prices for their inputs. Some suppliers also receive additional economic support from The Body Shop to develop community initiatives regarding significant issues (education, healthcare, etc.). For example, The Body Shop obtains boxes and handcrafted paper from a supplier based in Nepal. This supplier employs artisans; the majority of them are women. These artisans utilise some recycled and waste materials (cotton cut-offs, etc.) to develop this paper. Besides, this supplier pays all these artisans equal and fair wages for their work. This supplier also supports children from families with low resources to access education at school. In addition, this supplier creates awareness in the local communities regarding relevant issues like human trafficking (The Body Shop, 2022c).

13.1.4 Soft Conflict-Solving

A company should always treat its suppliers and intermediaries in a warm and kind manner, even during arguments or disagreements with them. If external stakeholders behave rudely with the company, this organisation should remain calm and loving all the same. A company should never reciprocate when it is treated disparagingly, condescendingly, or abrasively by others; if it does, the conflictive situation tends to escalate and becomes personal. Companies should also use calming and constructive statements which help each other release any state of tension and overwhelm, and be at ease. Consequently, a company which adopts a loving attitude to its suppliers and intermediaries is more inclined to solve problems with them in an amicable manner.

Nonetheless, many companies use antagonistic methods, such as lawsuits, to resolve controversies with their stakeholders. These "hard" methods should never be a priority for a company; they should be left as the last resource to be used. Oftentimes, not only do these hard methods not mitigate the conflicts, but they exacerbate them.

A company which has conflicts with its stakeholders should be flexible and open to exploring different alternatives with these organisations in a creative manner. Conflictive situations must be resolved in a way that brings about the best outcomes for all parties involved. These agreements should be based on valuable principles, like fairness, mutual care, respect, and co-operation, among others. In addition, when there are conflicts with its stakeholders, a company should use friendly ways to solve these disagreements, like negotiation, mediation, and arbitration, among others.

The potential solutions to a conflictive situation between two organisations should be the result of the active participation of all parties involved. Therefore, companies should avoid taking unilateral actions (e.g., a lawsuit) to solve problems with their external stakeholders because this is detrimental to their relationships with them. Butler and Hope (2008) observed that a relationship is like a system, where each party is a component of the system; therefore, when one party tries to introduce changes that could negatively affect the other, these changes tend to be resisted and this affects the whole relationship.

In order to solve an issue sensibly, companies should adopt a co-operative attitude with one another. This attitude implies the use of empowering sentences like "I propose that we work on this together …," and similar ones. A company which faces conflicts with its suppliers and intermediaries can also create more affinity with them by regularly using inclusive vocabulary. A company can use inclusive terms like "we," "our," and "ours" when it interacts with stakeholders. For example, a company can use sentences such as "We can develop a mutually beneficial relationship over time."

A company should always approach any conflictive situation with its suppliers and intermediaries in an upfront but kind manner. Therefore, companies should avoid unproductive behaviour, like threats, accusations, blaming, offending, and similar ones. In relation to this, Dooley (2010) recommends to "fight fire with kindness." In other words, a conflict between companies can never escalate if these organisations avoid personalising this issue. The main objectives regarding a conflictive issue are not only to try to solve it in the best way possible, but also to preserve the relationship between the organisations involved.

An effective way to handle conflicts with stakeholders is using kind and assertive communication. Davis et al. (2008) observed that being assertive implies recognising any differences of perspective regarding others, but also being willing to express these differences in a calm, clear, and firm manner. Assertive people are not aggressive with others; these people do not feel uncomfortable expressing their distinct views on an issue in a kind manner. Moreover, assertive people are empathetic because they are always open to considering the perspectives of others.

All business transactions include commercial aspects (such as price, volume, and quality) but also relational aspects (such as trust, confidence, comfort, and respect). These two aspects, commercial and relational ones, are inextricably interrelated. As a consequence, a company should never focus exclusively on the commercial aspects of an agreement and dismiss the relational ones. Both aspects are equally important for the development of a long-term relationship with suppliers and intermediaries.

UPS, the renowned courier company, is a company which fosters relational aspects (empathy, understanding, respect, inclusion, etc.) regarding the bonds with its suppliers. For instance, this company has a suppliers' diversity programme which welcomes, appreciates, and celebrates differences among thousands of suppliers. This company strongly believes in its diverse suppliers' unique beliefs and distinctive capabilities, which can bring about innovative ideas and also adds high value to the diversity of communities that UPS provides its services (UPS, 2022c; UPS, 2020).

According to Bateman et al. (2020), diverse suppliers can be defined as those which are at least 51% owned and run by an individual or group related to underrepresented groups (minority-owned businesses, women-owned businesses, businesses owned by LGBQT groups, businesses operated by people with disabilities, etc.). According to these specialists, UPS fosters supplier diversity and has developed strong bonds with various organisations (Women's Business Enterprise National Council, the U.S. Hispanic Chamber of Commerce, etc.) to offer mentoring and training to support the growth of diverse suppliers.

13.1.5 Co-Operative Attitude

A company with a collaborative attitude towards its suppliers and intermediaries tries to support them in the best way possible. This type of company continually collaborates with its stakeholders, especially in circumstances beyond what was contractually agreed with them. This collaborative company usually asks: "How can we be more helpful to these stakeholders?"

For instance, a company signs a contract with a retailer to sell their products. In this contract, there is no condition which obligates the company to provide free samples to this retailer. Nonetheless, a company which adopts a co-operative attitude towards this retailer will tend to provide this intermediary with free samples, even if this has not been stipulated in the contract. In this case, the company gives the retailer the samples because the company knows they are of value to this intermediary. When a company adopts a co-operative attitude towards its external stakeholders, its relationships with them become stronger and more stable over time.

Besides, a company should express its gratitude to its suppliers and intermediaries for adding value to the products bought by customers. For example, a company buys high-quality raw materials from its suppliers; these materials add value to the product manufactured by this organisation. Customers are also prone to appreciate the quality of the materials used in the product they buy from that company. In this case, suppliers indirectly add value to the final customers. In this example, the company should be grateful to its supplier for the quality of the material provided by the latter.

Another example will also clarify this point. For instance, a company sells its products to retailers and these intermediaries show these products in very well-located and finely decorated places, which grab customers' attention. In this case, the retailer also adds value to the products to be purchased by final customers. In this example, the company should be grateful to these retailers for showing its products in their premises in a very effective manner. Consequently, a company should frequently express its gratitude to its suppliers and intermediaries for the value they add to final products to be bought by customers.

A company should also co-ordinate with these stakeholders (intermediaries and suppliers) on any remedial action to be taken, based on the feedback provided by customers that already bought the company's products. Let's imagine that a customer left an online review saying that the packaging (e.g., a carton box) containing a product broke down easily. The company that sold this product to the customer should contact its supplier of carton boxes in order to discuss effective ways to reinforce these boxes, or look for alternative materials to use in the development of this packaging. If this supplier takes these suggestions on board, and improves the quality of packaging, the company will be able to offer higher value to its customers.

There is another point to highlight. A company which co-operates with its suppliers and intermediaries provides them with valuable information (customers' feedback, latest market trends, etc.) on a regular basis. This valuable information can help these stakeholders enhance their performance and add higher value to their products and services. This company should also be open to receiving valuable advice from these organisations according to their own expertise and experience. The main purposes of these exchanges are (a) the company and its suppliers and intermediaries are more prone to act in a more congruent manner, and (b) they can jointly add more value to final customers, for example, by reducing delays, increasing quality levels, and making the products more accessible.

Toyota, the prestigious car manufacturer, develops collaborative bonds with its suppliers. The contracts signed with these suppliers include precisely set targets and parameters to monitor performance, which prompts these suppliers to act in an accountable manner. These agreements also prompt these suppliers to look for better quality levels, costs, and delivery on a regular basis. Toyota uses a steering committee for its relationships with suppliers; this committee includes senior staff members from this car manufacturer and its suppliers. The committee is in charge of specifying the goals and other aspects of this collaboration, monitoring progress, and resolving problematic issues (Gutierrez et al., 2020).

There is another point to highlight. Companies should always aim to engage with business partners (suppliers, retailers, etc.) that bring about a positive social and environmental impact. According to Seuring and Müller (2008), there are various factors which can prompt a company to request its suppliers and intermediaries to have a social and environmental orientation: requests from customers and other stakeholders (pressure groups, etc.), enhancement of the company's reputation, compliance with the current regulations, etc. However, these authors mentioned other factors (insufficient communication and deficient co-ordination between a company and its suppliers and intermediaries, higher costs involved, etc.) which can make this process more difficult.

Lush, an ethical company which offers cosmetic products, selects its suppliers by considering those providers which offer high-quality and safe inputs, and are fully aware of their environmental and social impact. For instance, this company looks for suppliers which respect employees' rights, care for the environment, and protect animals, among other criteria (Lush, 2023).

Natural mica is a shiny ingredient which provides cosmetic products with sparkle. The mining activities related to natural mica are often associated with child labour. In the past, Lush used to buy materials which included natural mica from a supplier which clearly guaranteed that there was no child labour involved in the production process, and provided Lush with a clear proof of this (audit reports). The pigment division of this supplier was acquired by another company, which could no provide Lush with convincing proof – through independent verification – that there was no child labour involved in the production process of natural mica. As a consequence, Lush decided to drop the use of natural mica in its products, and instead switched to the use of synthetic mica, which is a man-made and environmentally friendly material which does not include unethical sourcing (Shepherd, 2023).

For this company, it is very important *how* things are produced (Moon, 2017). If things are produced in a way which brings about a negative social (or environmental) impact, like in the case of natural mica, it is a good decision that the company looks for alternative sources of supply or materials for its products. This approach also applies to the company itself not only to its suppliers.

There is another good example of ethical sourcing. In IKEA, the home products giant, more than 98% of the wood this company used for its products is recycled or comes from responsibly managed forests – FSC-certified (IKEA, 2023). FSC certification means that trees are harvested responsibly with no net loss of forest over time, workers are trained, kept safe, and paid fair wages, and plants, animals, and communities are protected (FSC, 2023).

13.2 Competitors

13.2.1 Love and Competitors

Companies invest millions to find out inside knowledge about their competition, their products and customers, and even their plans. Most business books include numerous strategic approaches to outpace competitors. Moreover, the concept of "competitors" is well-used not only in the business environment, but also in other areas, like sports.

Competition implies that there is a "race" that companies have to "run," in which there can only be one "winner" and many "losers." As seen previously in this book, the whole concept of "competition" is based on fear. The concept of "competitors" is related to a scarcity mindset, previously seen in Chapters 3 and 4. Some misleading but common assumptions stemming from this concept are:

■ There is not enough space for all companies in the market.
■ Customers are scarce, so each company has to compete to secure them.
■ Competitors are always considered impending external threats to a company.
■ The marketplace is a battlefield where companies only thrive by outpacing one another.

- An important part of a company's resources needs to be allocated in order to outsmart competitors.
- Competitors' activities must be monitored on a continuous basis.
- If a company does not beat its competitors, it will be beaten by them.
- All companies must continually offer better products to not be defeated by competitors.
- Almost all types of strategies are justified to outpace competitors.

From this book's perspective, companies should stop using the words "competition" and "competitors." The use of these concepts implies that other organisations are perceived as threats a company should fear, or forces that it should defend itself from. Moreover, a company which uses terms like "competitors" or "rivals" to identify other organisations in the business environment tends to respond to them reactively.

From the psychological perspective, this defensive response is related to the fight-freeze-flight mode. As previously explained, in this survival mode, people's analytical and creative capabilities are temporarily impaired. Besides, a company which considers other organisations as "competitors" is prone to be excessively aware of their activities, which prevents this company from adopting a more proactive attitude. Sometimes, this type of company can be tempted to outpace its competitors by all means, even immoral or illegal ones, for example:

- Stealing or copying intellectual property (e.g., patents) owned by other companies.
- Slandering other organisations.
- Hacking into other organisations' websites.
- Entering into price wars with other companies.
- Performing activities related to industrial espionage.
- Using comparative advertising to debase other companies.
- Limiting the access of competitors to markets.
- Poaching talent from other companies.
- Use of predatory prices to push other companies out of the market.
- Intentional distortion of the information in the financial statements (balance sheet, income statement, etc.).

Some countries penalise some of these activities with stringent legislation. In other cases, some of these activities are not regulated legally, but nonetheless, they are considered immoral or at least questionable. Oftentimes, a company which performs any of these activities does not act with integrity regarding other organisations in the marketplace.

An example of company that behaved in a very questionable manner is Enron, a trading organisation. This company went bankrupt several years ago. In a trial, people working for its company were accused of intentionally misusing the accounting rules, as well as concealing the company's huge losses and liabilities, among other unethical practices. Several leaders working for this company went to jail for their various unethical practices (Segal and Stapleton, 2022). De Waal (2019) observed that this company's lengthy code of ethics resembled the safety manual regarding the infamous ship the Titanic.

13.2.2 A More Positive Approach Regarding Other Companies

This book offers an alternative view on organisations traditionally considered "competitors." These businesses can be perceived as positive forces, instead of threatening factors. To that effect, "competitors" can be a valuable source of feedback for an organisation. From this perspective, a company should avoid adopting an aggressive or defensive attitude towards these so-called "competitors," but instead have an open and curious perspective regarding them.

Oftentimes, a company can be inspired by "rival" organisations in valuable ways that help it improve its business activities. A company can also take these "competing" organisations as powerful motivators, preventing it from dwelling in stagnation and complacency. Besides, a company can consider organisations selling similar products and services as teachers to learn from. Moreover, a company can obtain relevant information about successful approaches used by other organisations regarding:

- Their distinctive customer service.
- Their outstanding quality standards.
- The unique value delivered to customers.
- Their relationships with stakeholders.
- Their innovative products and services.
- Their non-traditional recruitment processes.
- Their creative business models.
- Their ingenious ways to price products.
- Their partnerships with other companies.
- Their environmental consciousness.
- Their alternative distribution.
- The sophistication of their product design.
- Their non-traditional use of technology.
- Their unique promotional strategies.

In other words, these companies can be considered models to emulate. A business can consider these companies as worthwhile references to orientate its own activities. In the business literature, when a company "borrows" some outstanding aspects or processes from other companies, it is called external benchmarking. When a company benchmarks, it adopts certain aspects of excellence used by other organisations, but generally adapts them to its specific and unique needs.

For example, Lego, the toy bricks company, is a good example of an organisation to be emulated. This company has partnered up with the World Wide Fund for Nature (WWF), previously named the World Wildlife Fund, to bring about climate solutions. Lego has been committed to reducing carbon dioxide emissions, and decreasing its own energy consumption and waste in the production process. This company has invested in renewable energy projects both onsite and offsite. As a consequence, their locations are fully balanced by renewable energy. This means that the energy brought about from renewable sources owned by the company – onsite or offsite – is equal to or higher than the energy that this organisation utilises at its premises. All these practices bring about a positive impact on the environment (Lego, 2022a, 2022b). Lego is a good example of a company to be emulated by others regarding the care for the environment.

There is another point to highlight. Sometimes, other companies represent the living evidence of wrong business behaviour. This is the other side of the topic discussed recently. When other organisations act in unethical and unloving ways, a company can use them as reminders of the business practices *not* to be adopted. Some examples of negative practices are companies which mislead buyers to obtain their business, organisations which are reluctant to take customers' complaints seriously, etc. A company can take these negative models in order to act in the opposite manner, for instance, by treating customers with honesty and integrity. As seen previously, Enron, a company which has hidden relevant accounting information leading to fraud, is an example of an organisation *not* to be emulated.

Competitors can also be considered potential business partners. In other words, companies who offer products or services of a similar type or category can develop strategic alliances, in which all participants benefit. These alliances represent synergetic platforms where business partners are more prone to share various resources (technology, information, sources of supply, contacts, distribution channels, customers, funds, etc.) with one another. Oftentimes, these partnerships help members share business risks and reduce costs.

These partnerships imply a certain degree of affinity between the participants, and a sense of camaraderie and companionship between them. However, a company which only perceives other organisations as competitors to be beaten will not be able see them as potential partners for business activities.

From the traditional perspective, different airlines in the world compete with one another. However, there is a partnership among 26 diverse airlines (Aegean, Air Canada, Air China, Air India, Air New Zealand, etc.) to improve the passengers' experiences. This partnership is known as Star Alliance. This alliance has created a network of smooth connections to most of destinations in the globe. Some of the main projects undertaken by Star Alliance are co-location of these airlines at various hub airports, seamless flight connections regarding passengers' transfers, and recognition of premium passengers throughout their trips by all the members of this alliance, among others (Star Alliance, 2022).

There is another relevant point to highlight. Some business coaches observe that a company should never compete with other companies, but with itself. From this perspective, a company should take itself as the main reference to outpace. Over time a company should gradually raise its bar, and commit to improving their products, services, processes, and systems in a proactive and sustained manner. A company should continually better itself, not for the fear of "competitors," but because it wants to serve customers and other stakeholders in a superior way.

13.3 Communities

> I am I plus my surroundings and if I do not preserve the latter, I do not preserve myself.
>
> **José Ortega y Gasset**

13.3.1 Relevance of Communities

McIntosh et al. (1998) observed that companies have different types of responsibilities: economic (related to economic viability of the organisation in the marketplace), legal (related to the company's strict abidance with legislation), and social and environmental (considering a society and the environment as relevant factors when performing business activities). Some businesses only aim to respond to economic and legal aspects, dismissing the environmental and social ones. In any case, all business activities have an impact on each of the aforementioned aspects, which companies should be fully aware of.

Businesses are social organisations. Consequently, a community is always a relevant factor for any company's business activities, because without a community, there is no business. In other words, companies are never run in a vacuum; there cannot be companies offering their products and services without people buying them. Without a community, there cannot be people who work for companies either. As mentioned, community members purchase some of these companies' products and services. Besides, without a community, there cannot be intermediaries and suppliers. Companies also benefit from other resources from a community, such as infrastructure (roads, bridges, etc.).

Therefore, all companies should be supportive and committed to their communities. To put it more simply, organisations must always be caring and generous with their communities. Moreover, businesses must act as catalysts for positive social change and add significant value to their communities by improving the lives of their members.

A company which has a loving attitude towards its community abides by some relevant principles, such as responsibility, solidarity, benevolence, respectfulness, honesty, and fairness, among others. This type of company will support its community without compromising any of these values, even if doing so could achieve economic benefits for the organisation. Community-oriented organisations have a higher level of awareness than other companies.

Cascade Engineering is a company with various business units offering a myriad of products (automotive, office furniture, material handling, waste and recycling, etc.) This organisation has a programme named Welfare to Career which has allowed people to move away from welfare support to employment with this company in order to develop a meaningful career. This company has in house a social worker (related to government, namely Michigan Department of Human Services) who has been supporting people in surmounting any challenges of going from being on welfare support to being employed by this company. Hundreds of staff members who were previously on benefits have been employed by the company through this programme, providing them with a livelihood with dignity and confidence. Since this programme was instituted, the company's employee turnover dropped dramatically reducing costs in millions of dollars (Cascade Engineering, 2023; Davis and White, 2015). This is a very good example of a company that supports the members of its community.

There is another point to highlight. A company which adopts a loving attitude towards its community goes beyond the well-known perspective of corporate social responsibility (CSR). In the case of CSR, the company supports certain causes (donations, social events, foundations, etc.) which can contribute to the community in a positive and specific manner. From the CSR perspective, a company aims to solve some significant problems affecting communities and positively contribute to their development. These CSR projects tend to be more successful when they are fully supported and endorsed by top management level.

Instead, when a company has a loving attitude towards its community, this represents the general perspective the company uses to perform *all* its business activities, not specific ones. In other words, this is an ongoing perspective, which is not limited to specific activities or projects. A company which adopts a loving attitude towards its community aims to support it in a proactive manner. This community-oriented perspective is imbued in everything that the company does. From this standpoint, all business decisions (strategic, tactical, and operational ones) are analysed and implemented considering their social impact on the community.

Divine Chocolate is a good example of a socially oriented endeavour which supports communities. This organisation is a social enterprise that sells certified fair trade organic chocolate bars. This organisation states that every chocolate bar a customer buys will better farmers' lives. Kuapa Kokoo Farmers' Union, a co-operative composed of more than 100,000 cocoa farmers from a myriad of Ghanian communities who provide high-quality cocoa, co-owns Divine Chocolate. This co-operative receives distributed profits from the company's chocolate sales. Two representatives of this co-operative are Divine Chocolate's directors, which means that farmers also participate in the business decisions (Divine Chocolate, 2022).

These farmers are fairly compensated as suppliers to sustain their own families and farms. In that sense, farmers receive a guaranteed fair price for their ingredients (e.g., cocoa beans) which covers production costs and also provides their families with a relevant income. This Fairtrade price is a minimum price, so when the ingredient's price in the world marketplace is low, the farmers will receive the Fairtrade price. Instead, when the ingredient's world price is higher, farmers will receive that higher price. This system guards the farmers from any international price volatility. There is also a Fairtrade price premium which is paid in addition to the price farmers receive for their inputs. The co-operative (Kuapa Kokoo Farmers' Union) has been using these price premiums to support various community projects, like building schools in some villages, constructing wells to access clean water, etc. (Divine Chocolate, 2021).

There is another important point to highlight. In economics, the impacts of a company's production of goods and services on the social environment are called "externalities." These externalities can be positive, for example, the beneficial impact on the environment stemming from the use of renewable energy, such as wind power and solar energy. These externalities can also be negative, for instance, a detrimental impact on the environment because of throwing industrial waste into a river. From this perspective, a company with a loving attitude towards its community consistently avoids any business actions which might cause harm to the community; in other words, this organisation will aim to eliminate any negative externalities.

At the same time, this type of company is also committed to continually increasing the number of activities which have tangible positive effects on the social environment, benefitting it directly or indirectly. In other words, this organisation wants to purposefully bring about positive externalities.

Many companies perform activities related to CSR because they want to improve its image and reputation. In this case, the support to the community is a mere exchange; the organisation offers more assistance to the community in exchange for a better image. Instead, a company with a loving attitude towards its community does not look for anything in return for this organisation's good actions. A company who truly cares for its community spontaneously connects with and impacts on it in a meaningful manner. As seen previously, all of the company's activities and practices are driven by their direct or indirect contribution to the community.

As seen previously in this book, Sackcloth & Ashes is a company which sells blankets, bringing about a positive impact on the community. Every time a customer buys a blanket, this company donates another blanket to a homeless shelter (Sackcloth and Ashes, 2022b). This company also has a positive impact on the environment. This company's blankets are made of various materials (scraps from factories and donated clothes) which are converted into fibres using a process which does not use any water or chemical products. Then, the material is spun into yarn with a process which is free from any touching dye. Afterwards, the material is weaved, brushed, and twisted on its ends (Sackcloth and Ashes, 2022c).

13.3.2 Community-Oriented Activities

A company with a loving attitude understands that the community is one of the most important resources to count on. This company understands that it is closely and continually linked to its community; all the benefits the company obtains from its business activities (revenues, profits, company image, reputation, etc.) come directly or indirectly from its community. Therefore, these companies understand that these communities should be continually assisted and cared for.

A company cannot fully thrive if its community does not meet its basic needs. Therefore, a company and its community are inextricably bound; they have a shared destiny. They are interdependent because they need each other to prosper. Companies with a loving attitude to communities can positively contribute to them in different ways, such as:

- Not polluting the environment and having green policies (use of renewable sources of energy, recycling, use of ecological manufacturing technology and processes, efficient management of waste material, green quality certifications, etc.). Terracycle is a company which gathers seemingly unrecyclable waste from various companies and other organisations. This company has the technological advancements and processes to recycle all this material, while reducing waste and obtaining profits (Terracycle, 2023a). The recycling process includes several stages, like research on various types of waste, analysis of regulations regarding waste, receipt of waste, sortation and aggregation, cleaning, and processing. After recycling the waste and converting it into raw material, Terracycle sells this material to companies which manufacture specific end products, like containers, furniture, etc. (Terracycle, 2023b). This company also offers products made from waste material for sale. Some examples of these products are small tables made from toothbrushes and toothpaste tubes, a coffee table made from cigarette waste, and playground equipment made from various types of waste (air and home care products, etc.), among others (Terracycle, 2022).
- Performing business activities in a warm and friendly manner. As seen previously, Walt Disney company, the entertainment organisation, has a warm, inclusive and diverse work environment which supports underrepresented voices.
- Respecting the cultural traditions, values, and customs of its community. For example, in the case of food products, a company can cater for the specific tastes and preferences of local customers. Dunkin' Donuts is a company that offers doughnuts in restaurants in different parts of the world. For instance, this company offers the most popular donuts (Jelly Filled, Glazed, etc.) internationally, but it also offers specific types of doughnuts to local customers from different regions or countries to address their unique tastes. In that sense, Stroopwafel Donut can be found in the Netherlands. The development of this type of doughnut was inspired by the typical pastry in this country. The Pork Floss Donut, which includes vanilla frosting, covered by shredded pork, is offered in China considering the local preferences of customers in that country (Dunkin' Donuts, 2019). This company uses the so-called a *glocal* approach, which includes global aspects (standardised brand and business model used all over the world) and local or adapted aspects (local doughnut flavours are offered in different countries).
- Leading social projects, such as charities, donations, organisation of community events, free training, internships, and sponsoring events, among others. BLQK is a social enterprise that offers ethically and sustainably sourced artisanal coffee. This organisation gives 25% of its profits to organisations which bolster social justice (BLQK Coffee, 2023).
- Treating other companies fairly, considering the possibility of them becoming business partners. For example, Lego – the Danish toy company – has developed partnerships with companies like IKEA and others. As a result of the partnership between IKEA and Lego, the former offers a specific range of co-branded household products (storage solutions, brick sets, etc.) which are more fun and functional and foster play activities between children and parents (Lego, 2023).
- Developing joint projects with non-governmental organisations, governments, and local communities. BLQK Coffee supports organisations that foster endeavours related to educational, economic, and food justice. For instance, this social enterprise has developed alliances with Brotherhood Crusade (whose aim is to improve the lives of the low-income, disenfranchised, underrepresented, and underserved people) and Thrive Scholars (whose

mission is to assist ambitious, low-income, and underrepresented students in accessing high-quality college courses to unleash their full potential). BLQK Coffee assists its partners through donations, with funds but also in kind. BLQK Coffee also devotes time to assist these partners in projects that support the communities that are the focus of these organisations (BLQK Coffee, 2023; Daily Nomad, 2021).

- Developing fair deals with all company's suppliers and intermediaries, continually supporting them, especially during difficult times. As seen previously, companies like The Body Shop and Divine Chocolate develop fair trade agreements with their suppliers, which implies paying a fair compensation to these suppliers for their inputs. Another good example is Toyota, a company which kindly supported its suppliers when they needed financial assistance.

- Hiring people with low resources from the local community. Khaya Cookies is an enterprise which offers natural bakery products (shortbread, etc.). It employs previously unemployed women, primarily from the township of Khayelitsha (in South Africa), in order to improve the quality of their lives. In this area, there are around one million people living in poverty conditions. These people live in one-room abodes made from timber or corrugated iron. In these communities, there are high malnutrition and unemployment rates. Khaya Cookies' employees have received training from this enterprise which converted them into very capable bakers. This training covers a wide range of areas of this business (baking, customer service, etc.) (Khaya Cookies, 2023).

- Abiding by relevant legislation (work regulation, quality norms, etc.) regarding business activities and avoiding any illegal activities (smuggling, bribing, forfeiting, hacking, tax evasion, etc.) Hilton is one of the renowned leaders in the accommodation sector. They have an extensive Code of Conduct to foster a culture of integrity, which enhances this company's reputation. This comprehensive code includes valuable guidance on how to address paramount topics, like diversity, harassment-free workplace, non-discrimination, safety and health at work, confidentiality, and avoidance of bribery and corruption, among others. The company's employees, officers, and directors should abide by these guidelines (Hilton, 2017).

- Treating employees with respect and dignity, paying them fair salaries, and allowing them to enhance their natural skills and develop new ones; not violating employees' rights in the workplace. As seen, in the case with Khaya Cookies, these jobs provide women from communities in need with dignity, as their skills are enhanced and their potential is unleashed. These jobs also provide a noble way for these staff members to sustain their families.

- Development of partnerships with different representatives of communities such as councils, associations, chambers of commerce, etc. The socially oriented company Warby Parker, which sells eyeglasses, was analysed previously in this book. This company has created the so-called Pupils Project. Through this initiative – which includes various organisations and local government agencies (e.g., Department of Education in New York City, and the Department of Health in Baltimore) – children at school are provided with free vision tests and eyeglasses (Warby Parker, 2022).

- Encouraging its suppliers and intermediaries to behave in a supportive and kind way with all stakeholders, including the community. In relation to this last point, Dell, the computer giant, has set up very high expectations for its suppliers. In that sense, Dell prompts its various suppliers to adhere to the supplier's principles of responsible and ethical business set up by this company. These principles include protection of human rights, responsible sourcing, as well as avoidance of child labour, modern slavery, or human trafficking practices, among others. If suppliers want to do business with this company, they must strictly abide by these principles (Dell, 2022).

Companies can positively contribute to communities in other ways. Among these activities, the investment in companies which have a positive impact on the community can be included. For example, a conscious company, when investing, prefers to buy shares in organisations that have a positive social impact. Some examples of this type of company are educational institutions, recycling companies, communication companies, health organisations, etc.

On the contrary, companies that have a negative social and environmental impact are, for instance, mining corporations, gambling organisations, weaponry manufacturers, tobacco manufacturers, etc. A conscious company tends to avoid investing in this second type of companies, which means, for example, not buying shares of these companies.

Besides, conscious companies also aim to provide products and services which contribute positively to the community. Oftentimes, when a company acts in a conscious manner, its activities are also related to the concept of sustainability. A sustainable approach implies that the company's activities have a positive impact not only on the current social environment, but also on future generations. An example of this sustainable activity is the implementation of green policies, whose main purpose is to care for the environment, which impacts positively not only on current communities, but also on future ones.

A company who has a positive impact on present and future generations is TOMs, which is a company that sells shoe products. In the past, this company donated a pair of shoes to children in need for every pair bought by a customer. Millions of shoes have been donated by this organisation. These shoes were donated to children of communities in need, so that these children could go to school and were protected from uneven terrain and soil-transmitted diseases (Murphy et al., 2017. Lately, this company's approach is different, but with the same social orientation. At present, this company donates one-third of its profits to nonprofit organisations, which address relevant social causes, like boosting mental health, ending gun violence, and increasing access to opportunities (TOMs, 2022).

Mackey and Sisodia (2014) stated that a company should behave as a citizen of the community. Companies should always assist their community, especially when it faces relevant challenges. For instance, there are many examples of companies who helped communities who were affected by natural disasters, like floods and tornados. As mentioned in this book, Google has provided various resources (volunteers, technology, and funding) to support communities - before the occurrence of natural disasters - to be more prepared for these challenging events (e.g., through flood forecasting) and also support these communities during their recovery.

Some conscious organisations thoroughly analyse the main problems affecting their community and develop specific action plans to offer the community support regarding these issues. Moreover, some conscious companies monitor the impact of their community-oriented activities and summarise these positive impacts in a report; this report can be presented to the community and other relevant stakeholders.

When a company publishes this type of report, the information of the organisation's social and environmental impact can be of high value for different stakeholders (community members, customers, government, investors, etc.). A company that issues this report looks more transparent and trustworthy in the eyes of its main stakeholders, which brings about a positive impact on the company's reputation. This type of report can also help a company reflect on ways to improve its future social and environmental impact. This type of report tends to complement the company's traditional financial reports (balance sheet, profit and loss statement, etc.) which only include financial aspects of business activities.

For example, The Body Shop issues a report of their non-financial outcomes, which is called Sustainability Report. In this report, the company analyses its involvement in projects which have a positive social and environmental impact. Some of these projects have noble objectives like protecting the Amazon by decreasing CO2 emissions, and defending human rights by supporting staff members, suppliers, and communities, among others (The Body Shop, 2021). In a similar vein, the prestigious company General Electric issues a sustainability report, where it thoroughly analyses its socially and environmentally impactful activities (utilisation of decarbonising gas turbines, donation of medical equipment to communities in need, etc.) (General Electric, 2021).

There is another relevant point to highlight. When a conscious company is about to implement a business project with a potentially relevant impact on a community, this organisation tends to consult some representatives of the community before taking any action regarding this project. The purpose of this consultation is to hear these representatives' views and consider their suggestions regarding the business project. As seen, in the case of Divine Chocolate, in the board of directors of that organisation, there are two representatives of the co-operative of suppliers from local communities. These representatives have a voice in all Divine Chocolate's business decisions.

Some companies state that governments and non-governmental organisations are those truly responsible for bringing about social impact, not businesses. In relation to this, Porter (2013) stated that businesses obtain profits by satisfying customer needs, which makes them very adequate for tackling relevant social needs. This prestigious scholar insightfully observed that companies can aim to obtain profits as a consequence of addressing social needs, while creating shared value, a combination of economic value and social value. From his standpoint, businesses can also work in partnership with governments and NGOs to jointly sort out relevant social issues.

This specialist gave the example of Jain Irrigation Systems Ltd., which provides various farmers with an overarching range of irrigation systems. This company's mission is to "leave this world better than you found it." In that sense, this company brought about a positive impact on more than ten million farmers, by providing them with the highest quality technology regarding micro-irrigation and green energy, which helped them save resources (water, electricity, and fertilisers) and also improve their produce significantly (Jains, 2023).

13.3.3 Other Aspects Related to Communities

When a company adopts a loving attitude towards its community, its activities are based on integrity. This type of company becomes a model to emulate for other organisations because of its positive impact on society. The products and services offered by a community-conscious company have a social plus, which makes them preferred by many customers over offerings from non-conscious organisations. These thoughtful customers do not focus only on the satisfaction of their individual needs (hunger, thirst, socialisation, safety needs, etc.) but through their purchases, they also support products and services from companies which bring about a positive social impact.

When a company develops strong relationships with its community, multiple benefits are brought about for both parties. The most obvious benefits are the tangible positive effects of the company's activities on its community. Besides this, the company also obtains relevant benefits, such as an improvement in its image and reputation, higher employee motivation and engagement, and wider company visibility, among others. Community-oriented companies also act like a magnet for talented human resources; many highly skilful people are very keen to work for this type of organisation.

There are a number of certifications that companies can obtain which prove that they are bringing about a positive social impact. For example, B-Corp Certification validates that a company achieves high standards regarding social and environmental performance, accountability, and transparency (B Corporation, 2022). For example, TOMs, which was previously analysed, is a B-Corp-certified company (TOMs, 2022). There are more specific certifications that businesses can obtain, for instance, SA 8000. In that sense, SA 8000 certifies that a company treats its employees in a fair and decent manner, by abiding by the highest social standards (SAI, 2022). A company analysed previously in this book, Jaipur Rugs, which sells high-quality rugs with an outstanding design, has the SA 8000 certification (Jaipur Rugs, 2022).

Therefore, it is important that organisations adopt a community-oriented attitude. In order to adopt a more loving attitude towards its community, a company can ask itself these questions on a regular basis:

■ What is the actual impact of our activities on the community?
■ Are our activities creating a positive impact on our community?
■ How can the lives of community members be enhanced by our activities?
■ How can we make a more significant positive impact on our community?

Lastly, it is important to pinpoint that there are other stakeholders which will not be analysed in this book, such as financial organisations, government, business partners, potential and current investors, the media sector, unions, pressure groups, regulatory bodies, non-governmental organisations, academia, and trade associations, among others. Nonetheless, most principles explained in this text can be applied to these stakeholders.

Questions for Self-Reflection

■ How can our relationships with suppliers and intermediaries be improved?
■ How can we adopt a more constructive attitude towards competitors?
■ How can our relationships with the community be improved?
■ What activities can we perform that will have a positive impact on the community?

MAIN ASPECTS OF
LOVE AND CREATIVITY

Chapter 14

Love and Creativity

14.1 Meaning of Creativity

> Life itself is a creation, a work in progress, unfolding and revealing itself even as it is being created.

Robert Fritz

Every good product, service, or organisation started with an idea in the mind of someone. Consequently, creative skills are a meta-resource, which means a valuable resource that helps individuals and organisations generate other resources. People are masterful artisans of each thing they do in their life; each of their actions, thoughts, emotions, and words has the distinctive signature of their creative craftsmanship. When people create, a part of them is splintered into their creations. As seen previously, creativity is a very important human need, which is closely related to the need for self-expression. Even though it is not easy to define creativity, some suggested meanings of this term are:

Creativity is the development of new valuable alternatives beyond traditional ones.
Creativity is going beyond the status quo, the current state of things.
Creativity is stretching one's mind towards uncharted territories.
Creativity is being as endlessly inquisitive as a child.
Creativity is bringing thoughts into being.
Creativity is becoming aware of new aspects of reality.
Creativity is going beyond ingrained assumptions.
Creativity is a generous act which gives new ideas away.
Creativity is unfolding one's mental landscape from the inside out.
Creativity is imagining situations beyond current limitations.
Creativity is playing with several hypotheses on a topic.
Creativity is widening one's perception beyond the known.
Creativity is using one's imaginative skills to produce something original.
Creativity is dwelling on potential future scenarios.
Creativity is welcoming fresh perspectives on long-standing issues.

DOI: 10.4324/9781003372684-18

Creativity is the restructuring of current categories or developing others.
Creativity is gracefully going beyond any resistance to change.
Creativity is the eradication of self-censorship.
Creativity is going beyond hackneyed ways of doing things.
Creativity is generating potential perspectives on a topic.
Creativity is devising innovative ways of perceiving reality.
Creativity is being playful and freely engaged with ideas.
Creativity is being curious and spontaneous, like an explorer.
Creativity is mentally experimenting with the untested.
Creativity is developing new ways to solve current problems.
Creativity is giving birth to uncharted worlds.
Creativity is adding incremental value to others.
Creativity is a relevant asset in fast-changing scenarios.

McKenna (2012b) states that "creativity is a neurophysiological state … where we have seemingly unlimited access to our greatest potential." All human beings are natural creators; they are continually developing new activities, thoughts, and perspectives – they cannot avoid it. People's creative potential is embedded in their DNA; creativity is an innate capability of all human beings. People are more creative and resourceful than they believe they actually are.

Fritz (1984) observed that creating is always an act of love. This author stated that "in the creative process, love is generative rather than simply responsive" (Fritz, 1991). This prestigious scholar concluded that people who create bring about something out of nothing and they love their creation to exist (Fritz, 1984, 1991). In other words, every creation has its creator's love embedded in it. In a similar vein, Montagu (1957) observed that "love enables the person to treat life as an art which the person as an artist is continually seeking to improve on in all its aspects."

14.2 How Creativity Works

To see things in the seed, that is genius.

Lao Tzu

The creative process works through different mental operations, for example, the innovative combination of existing elements of a topic, modification of its current elements, simplification or sophistication of them, and partition of a topic into different subcomponents. The human mind has the capacity to store information (facts, objects, people, circumstances, etc.) into limiting and rigid mental models (De Bono, 1970). However, the use of creative techniques helps restructure the information enclosed in these models in a different manner.

In that sense, creativity implies combining, linking, or modifying the information contained in these mental structures, but it also implies developing metaphors, analogies, imagery, and various types of categorisation (Ward et al., 1999). The application of creative techniques brings about non-traditional insights which are worthy. In the next chapter, different ways to assess the worthiness of these novel ideas will be discussed.

A good example of creative mental associations can be found in the Wright brothers, who had their own bicycles. Throughout extensive experimental and playful time periods, these two brothers linked their deep understanding of bicycles with their own observation of birds. As a result, they were capable of developing the first flying aeroplane in the world (Jacab, 1999).

The renowned inventor Johannes Gutenberg put together two ideas seemingly disconnected. This luminary combined the coin punch (used to set up an image on tiny surfaces like coins) with the wine press (used to exert a force on a large surface to obtain the juice from grapes). He set up several coin punches to be pressed by the force of the wine press in order to print an image on paper. This brought about one the greatest inventions in mankind, the printing press with mobile type (Von Oech, 2011).

There is another relevant point to highlight. People who create are willing to explore uncharted territories. Consequently, these people avoid being traditional, or complacent, but instead are inquisitive and open to new perspectives. Klein (2003) observed that creative insights help people change the way they understand, perceive, feel, and desire.

Osborn (1948) observed that our mind is composed of two parts: a judicial part which assesses, analyses, and makes comparisons and choices, and a creative part, which develops ideas and visualioos. Theoo two parto are complementary; the creative mind can provide the judicial part with new insights, and the judicial mind can set some limits on the creative part.

For example, when a car manufacturer like Toyota develops a new car model, this company's employees will use the creative part of their minds, by depicting the external design of the car, and sketching the layout of the car's interior, among other aspects. These staff members will also use the judicial part of their minds, by choosing adequate materials for the car that comply with security and safety regulations, and assessing the productions costs.

There is another topic to pinpoint. From the psychological perspective, the mind can be divided into the conscious mind and the subconscious mind. The conscious mind is related to one's waking state: reasoning, perception, and interpretation of the environment. This part of the mind is continually related to the subconscious part, which acts below the level of people's awareness. The subconscious mind is related to one's beliefs, values, intuition, emotions, creativity, past conditioning, and management of bodily functions. This part of the mind manages a massive amount of information, as compared with the data dealt with by the conscious mind.

Scientists have observed that the human brain is composed of the two hemispheres, which have different functions. The left hemisphere is more lineal, logical, verbal, numerical, and analytical. The right hemisphere is more related to creative thoughts, imagery, symbolism, spontaneity, playfulness, intuition, and emotional aspects.

When a person is creative, the two hemispheres interact collaboratively. Some specialists have observed that creative people are more prone to use their right hemisphere, which helps them have a more holistic view of things. Nonetheless, other specialists like Sawyer (2006) concluded that there is no clear evidence of the relationship between creativity and the right brain. From this perspective, creative skills involve the whole brain. Greene (2012) observed that creative activities do not involve only the mental processes, but the whole self, which includes the emotions, character, energy, and also the mind.

Gardner (2006) states that there are seven types of intelligence: body intelligence (related to physical skills), verbal (related to expression), spatial (related to the use of space), logical (related to solving problems), emotional (related to understanding one's own feelings and the feelings of others), spiritual (related to spiritual aspects, like one's role in the world), and creative. From this perspective, creative intelligence implies the capability to create new realities. Even though people are related to all these types of intelligence, each individual will be naturally prone to harness some types of intelligence more than others. Creative intelligence can be enhanced by using the techniques suggested later in this book.

Wallas (1926) observed that the creative process has four stages: preparation (when people garner and organise sufficient information about a topic), incubation (when the topic is left aside, people focus on unrelated or trivial tasks and leave their subconscious minds to work on the issue), illumination (when insights about the topic spontaneously arise, oftentimes in an unfinished manner), and verification (the final idea is tested and conveyed to others). The aforementioned four stages tend to overlap in practice.

From this perspective, creativity implies the use of both the subconscious mind (for the incubation and development of ideas) and the conscious mind (to gather initial information, and to assess and select the most appropriate ideas). Creative skills are generally used in combination with logical skills: people can use a creative approach to generate multiple options to tackle issues, and then use their logical capabilities to select the most suitable one. As explained previously, creativity often implies breaking down an issue into its sub-elements, to use them as they are, or to modify them or even recombine them with others.

The following example will shed some light on the use of the conscious mind and the subconscious mind. Some decades ago, the famous entrepreneur Richard Branson was stuck on a grounded flight which was meant to go from Puerto Rico to British Virgin Islands (BVI). This was an unsettling situation, as he had not seen his partner for several weeks, and was unable to arrive at his destination. While his flight was grounded, and on the plane, this entrepreneur calculated the costs to charter an aeroplane to the destination, and the cost per passenger if the total expense was covered. Then, he walked around offering passengers on the grounded plane some charter plane tickets with a note which said, "$39 one way to BVI." After this entrepreneur chartered that simple flight towards the BVI, he rang the aeroplane manufacturer Boeing to request if he could buy a 747 aeroplane (second-hand). He thought he could start up his own airline aiming to deliver outstanding customer service. He also assessed the potential downside of this project. This story is about the origin of Virgin Atlantic (Kachroo-Levine, 2019).

In this example, when he assessed the situations of being stuck on a grounded aeroplane, he used his conscious mind. However, when he had the insight of renting a charter aeroplane, this valuable idea popped up from his subconscious mind. When this business leader started to research the charter plane and calculated the costs of chartering this plane, he was using his conscious mind. When he tested the interest of other passengers in finishing their journey on a charter plane, this business leader was also using his conscious mind. However, when he had an insight into starting up his own airline with superior customer service, this idea spontaneously popped up from his subconscious mind. Then, he used his conscious mind again, when he rang an aeroplane manufacturer to check the costs of purchasing a second-hand plane for his new business endeavour. Lastly, he also used this conscious mind to assess the downside of this promising business project and start up this project. As can be seen in this example, in this process, this entrepreneur used both the conscious and subconscious parts of his mind.

14.3 Characteristics of People Who Create

New ideas start with some recognition of an incomplete pattern. This is about noticing that there is something missing or that something could be improved.

Max McKeown

People are always creating either purposefully or unintentionally. It does not really matter if their creations are small (preparing an attractive dinner for friends, engaging in an interesting conversation with a relative, etc.) or big (e.g., discovering a new medicine, developing new technology). Oftentimes, people are not even aware that they are thinking and acting in a creative manner. Some characteristics of people who use their creative skills are:

Endlessly curious: Creative people are inquisitive and non-complacent regarding current facts and circumstances. These people are very flexible and believe that products, services, processes, and individuals can always improve. Ray and Myers (1989) call the process of discovering new symbols and forms regarding a topic "creative courage." Rogers (1961) stated that creative people are prone to "toy with elements and concepts" in an exploratory manner. These ruthlessly curious individuals tend to ask countless questions, such as "What are other ways to ...?" and similar ones. They are playful; they approach issues in a childlike and lighthearted manner, continually looking for new approaches and perspectives. These individuals explore things playfully, which makes them more resilient and enduring when their attempts fail. Sawyer (2006) observed that creative people are internally motivated; they find the exploration of new alternatives so enjoyable that they often find themselves losing the notion of time. Creative individuals have a knack of exploring new ideas, while they enjoy the process. These unremitting people have a high tolerance to uncertainty and ambiguity. An example of a curious entrepreneur is James Dyson, the founder of the Dyson Company. He observed that the traditional vacuum cleaner used bags which were full of dust and needed frequent replacement, which also generated a lot of waste. He tirelessly and inquisitively tested more than 5,000 prototypes to end up developing a fully functional bagless vacuum cleaner. This vacuum cleaner was the first of its kind in the world: it could separate dust from air by using centrifugal forces. This appliance did not need to use any bag, and it was ready to be produced. This thoughtful business leader wisely quipped, "Failure is interesting ... it's part of making progress" (Dyson, 2022; Goodman, 2012).

Open-minded: As seen previously, the human brain stores information in very rigid structures or mental models, which makes it difficult to devise new alternatives and options. To that effect, creative people go beyond their mental structures, and temporarily put them aside, or completely dismiss them. Oftentimes, creative people are capable of observing a well-known situation from different fresh perspectives. These people are prone to delay their judgement on a specific topic for a while in order to explore a myriad of different approaches related to that topic. These individuals are also prone to develop new ideas, considering elements from completely unrelated fields. For example, fast-food chains have taken the concept of the assembly line, which comes from an unrelated sector like the automobile industry, in order to serve customers more quickly. The renowned businessman, Henry Ford, developed the assembly line concept, which significantly reduced the production time of a car (from above 12 hours to only 1 hour and 33 minutes). Taking into account Henry Ford's valuable idea, McDonald brothers were the first to apply the concept of an assembly line to kitchen tasks. In that sense, these businessmen hired several unqualified workers; each of these employees was told to only do one little specific task over the process of preparing food. This made the place truly look like a factory, and the food-preparation process became more productive (Plant, 2016).

Visionary: Creative people are prone to stretch themselves beyond the ideas commonly held by average people. Creative individuals' revolutionary spirit does not conform to what is currently done, used, or established for a long time. They can shape the future by developing innovative products, services, and ways of solving problems, which most people do not even dare to imagine. Creators are willing to take risks in order to explore untraditional perspectives, risks which are considered unacceptable by other people. Creative people have forward vision which helps them to develop potential scenarios to deal with challenging circumstances more effectively. Oftentimes, creative individuals are perceived by other people as daydreamers or naïve thinkers. Creative people hold on to their innovative vision tightly and aim to put it into action. Marden (1917) observed that "men succeed in proportion to the fixity of their vision and invincibility of their purpose." An example of a truly visionary individual is Thomas Edison. He is considered one of the wisest entrepreneurs of his time. This entrepreneur has developed countless inventions. At the beginning of the twentieth century, this entrepreneur worked on the electric vehicle storage batteries, as he had a strong vision for transportation in cities which could use clean energy. In that sense, this luminary has anticipated the current significance of electric vehicles. In the 1920s, this businessman also foresaw the relevance of non-traditional types of energy (wind and solar energy), as he predicted scarcity problems regarding fossil fuel, as well as pollution issues (Edison Innovation Foundation, 2022).

Prolific: Creative people generate multiple ways to approach challenging topics. Firstly, creative people are prone to develop a myriad of options to approach an issue. In other words, creative individuals firstly focus on the quantity of alternatives over their quality; all possible approaches are welcomed without being judged prematurely. In a second stage, these people concentrate on quality over quantity. In other words, from the pool of ideas generated previously, creative individuals select the most feasible to be later analysed more thoroughly. An example of a prolific individual is Thomas Edison, previously mentioned. This business leader developed several inventions, such as the electric light bulb, motion pictures, and the phonograph, among others. This luminary has been awarded 1,093 patents in the United States (Edison Innovation Foundation, 2022).

Questioning: Creative people are tenaciously committed to treading unknown and untested paths, and go beyond prejudices, assumptions, and widespread beliefs. They never believe that things should be a certain way. Stengberg (mentioned in Garnham and Oakhill, 1994) observed that these people are mentally self-governed; they prefer to set their own rules rather than follow or assess the rules of others. By being self-governed, they are more prone to generate original and valuable ideas. James Dyson is an entrepreneur who questioned what was established in the vacuum cleaner sector. In the past, vacuum cleaners used to utilise non-reusable bags, which represented a multi-million dollar market worldwide. This business leader daringly questioned the practicality of these vacuum cleaners and developed the first bagless vacuum cleaner, which provided customers with higher value (Dyson, 2022; Goodman, 2012).

Receptive: Creative individuals are more open to receiving new insights in a non-judgemental manner. Creative people know that illumination, or the generation of new ideas, cannot be forced; it happens spontaneously. Oftentimes, creative insights come unexpectedly, as a result of a combination of specific activities (thinking about an issue, researching on a topic, etc.) and taking a rest (not doing anything). Moments of silent contemplation are ideal to receive creative insights because one's mental chattering is temporarily paused. Besides, a creative person knows that insights can be whispered to them in different ways (words, images, symbols, emotional states, physical sensations, conversations with people, books, etc.). In the case of Edison, many of his insights were depicted in various sketches he painstakingly developed in countless notebooks (Edison Innovation Foundation, 2022).

Determined: Creative people are proactive; they continually aim to reach out for new ideas. Creative people are also patient because they know that good ideas often take time to incubate and develop. Sometimes, new ideas come up half-boiled and need more time to develop.

Hall (1995) says that ideas are like babies who should be cared for and nourished during their growth. Creative individuals try out new ideas on a continuous basis, knowing that sometimes their ideas will work well in practice, and some will not. These individuals consider these "failures" as learning experiences, which can be used to do things differently in the future. Creative people never give up, especially when their ideas don't take off. As seen previously, James Dyson has developed more than 5,000 prototypes before he could come up with a fully functional bagless model of vacuum cleaner. This determined business leader did not consider these prototypes as failures, but as valuable sources of feedback which helped him improve the product over time. Another valuable example of determination is Edison, the great inventor. When the entrepreneur was developing the electric bulb, he ended up testing thousands of types of materials for the filament of this bulb until he found the most appropriate one (FI, 2023).

Creative people tend to experience positive emotions on a regular basis. Profuse research observes that people who experience positive emotions are more prone to engage in creative thinking because they tend to analyse varying data in a broad manner (instead of narrowly focusing on specific information) and develop various high-level mental connections with that information. In other words, when people experience positive emotional states, they are more inclined to explore information in non-traditional ways.

In a similar vein, Fredrickson and Branigan (2005) observed that positive emotional states widen people's range of thoughts and actions, prompting these individuals to go beyond their typical ones. According to these specialists, this wider range of thoughts and actions helps people develop physical resources (health, etc.), intellectual resources (knowledge, etc.), social resources (e.g., relationships with others), and psychological resources (e.g., optimism, creativity). These resources are long-lasting, which means that they last more than the positive emotional states that contributed to their development.

There is a last point to highlight. Creative individuals relish a myriad of valuable discoveries developed by many people who painstakingly devote their time to innovation. Moreover, creative people also feel compelled to move in that direction, providing mankind with their own valuable contribution in order to make the world a better place. As seen previously, Gutenberg took into account two previous inventions, the wine press and coin punch, in order to develop his renowned brainchild: the printing press.

14.4 Business Objectives and Creativity

If we listened to our intellect … we'd never go into business because we'd be cynical … You've got to jump off cliffs all the time and build your own wings on the way down.

Ray Bradbury

Many of the ideas you have, if not immediately and obviously valuable in the moment, contain the germ of something that may be useful.

David Allen

Many people strongly believe that creative techniques are more related to artistic disciplines (such as painting and sculpture), not to business activities. Nonetheless, creativity is suitable for business activities, but also fundamental to any company's success. Oftentimes, business activities are performed in scenarios characterised by ambiguity, constant change, uncertainty, and unpredictability. Consequently, creativity represents a paramount tool that can help companies to thrive in these challenging scenarios.

From the business perspective, the fundamental role of creativity is to add more value for customers and other stakeholders (employees, intermediaries, community, suppliers, etc.). Consequently, creativity can be applied to any business situation and activity. Moreover, some companies adopt the creative approach as part of their business philosophy. The use of creative tools has different objectives. The list below includes some examples of potential uses of creative tools; this list is only indicative, not exhaustive.

- To develop new products and services.
- To improve the characteristics of current products and services (performance, speed, etc.).
- To define new uses for current products and services.
- To create intellectual property assets (trademarks, patents, etc.).
- To increase customers' satisfaction and loyalty.
- To generate alternative business models.
- To analyse business problems in several ways.
- To harness a company's main capabilities differently.
- To simplify products, services, procedures, and processes.
- To develop a better work environment.
- To manage data more efficiently.
- To add new services (delivery, prepayment, etc.) to current products.
- To strengthen relationships with the company's stakeholders.
- To improve the company's productivity and competitiveness.
- To obtain information in non-traditional ways.
- To prepare different assortments of products and services.
- To re-position products and services in customers' minds.
- To develop and implement new management methods.
- To design new packing and packaging for current products.
- To improve the company's image and reputation.
- To develop new ways of buying products and services.
- To develop innovative solutions to conflicts with stakeholders.
- To improve the company's internal communication.
- To manage business information in a more innovative manner.
- To generate word of mouth in a non-traditional manner.
- To re-locate company activities in an innovative manner.
- To train and motivate employees in different ways.
- To dispose of waste in an alternative manner.
- To reduce company costs (R+D, manufacturing, marketing, etc.).
- To outsource activities to external organisations.
- To develop new categories of customers.
- To use different materials or manufacturing processes.
- To implement non-traditional ways of transporting and storing goods.
- To develop different ways to contribute to the community.
- To use innovative distribution channels.
- To recruit personnel and professionals in a non-traditional way.

- To implement different environmentally friendly actions.
- To design more attractive promotional activities and events.
- To develop new ways to price the offerings.
- To offer innovative financial conditions for buyers.
- To make products and services available to customers in non-traditional ways.
- To enter unexplored markets.
- To develop beneficial partnerships with other companies.
- To create attractive offers in a negotiation process.
- To develop other ways to increase an online presence.
- To develop new ways to improve quality levels.
- To develop new company strategies.
- To develop more socially responsible activities.
- To reformulate the company's mission and vision.
- To restructure the organisational chart (departments, areas, etc.).
- To develop different ways of managing time.
- To design new customer service activities.
- To develop the layout (decoration, furniture, etc.) of a place (sales outlet, office, etc.).
- To implement non-traditional ways of using technology.

For example, Levi's, the denim clothes producer, is committed to supporting the environment. The production of denim products often utilises great amounts of water. Several years ago, this company introduced a myriad of creative techniques in its garment production process which saved (and also recycled) billions of litres of water since this change was implemented. The implantation of these processes reduced the environmental impact of the production process of these denim products. For instance, instead of washing the jeans with softener to bring about the worn-in feel, this company may tumble these items of clothing with golf balls and bottle caps in order to eliminate the water in the process. This company also provides its customers with creative tips to save water regarding their jeans, for example, washing them less frequently. Another tip is washing the jeans with cold water to decrease energy consumption (Levi's, 2020).

There is another relevant point to highlight. The current global era makes creativity even more necessary than before. The globalisation process includes several factors, such as continuous launches of new products and services, countless technological breakthroughs, interconnectedness of the countries' economies, and development of new disciplines (robotics, nanotechnology, etc.), relevance of global brands, among others.

In the global arena, many companies realise that the enhancement of their staff's creative skills can help them thrive, especially in fast-changing and tumultuous scenarios. Kao (1996) observed that in the past, organisations pursued technology, capital, and raw material as their differential advantage in the marketplace, but nowadays companies are looking for the creative advantage, which includes "imagination, inspiration, ingenuity, and initiative."

It is important to pinpoint that organisations themselves are creations as well; their projects constantly unfold and readjust with the aim to fulfil their business purpose. Kim and Mauborgne (2015) observed that some creative companies develop new marketplaces (named blue oceans), instead of focusing on the well-known marketplaces (called red oceans). These authors stated that companies which implement blue oceans strategies create differentiated value but at a low cost, by bringing about new demand, and developing (as well as capturing) an unchallenged market space. Moreover, the company which develops a blue ocean strategy adopts an innovative approach regarding its business activities, in relation to what is conventionally done in a specific industry.

An example of a company which implemented a blue ocean strategy is Airbnb, the global accommodation network. This company has disrupted the accommodation sector by not owning hotels or any other accommodation facilities. Instead, this organisation connects owners of properties (flats, houses, etc.) with individuals that look for a short stay at these properties (potential guests). These two parties (property owners and potential guests) seamlessly connect with one another through the outstanding online platform developed by Airbnb. As a consequence, this company's elegant and revolutionary business model has allowed this company to swiftly expand on a global level (Uta, 2020).

14.5 Main Hindrances to Creativity

Every new idea is a mashup or remix of one or more previous ideas.

Austin Kleon

Just as weeds choke out flowers in a garden, too much judgement tends to choke out the imaginative talent with which we were born.

Alex Osborn

Even though creativity seems to serve uncountable objectives in the business environment, many companies do not take the chance to develop creative activities. For example, when things are going well, most companies are not compelled to innovate. Good ideas often come out of dissatisfaction, when things are not working in the way they expected. For instance, when a company is pleased with its customer service processes, this organisation will be less incentivised to innovate these processes. In contrast, a company which is frustrated regarding its business activities tends not to act in a complacent manner, and instead looks for alternative ways to improve these very areas.

A valuable example of how creative ideas can often stem from a state of dissatisfaction was mentioned previously. Richard Branson was upsettingly stranded on a plane, without the possibility to arrive at his ultimate destination. As seen previously, this leader researched a charter plane and calculated its costs, and offered this alternative means of transport to the other passengers on the grounded aeroplane. In this state of dissatisfaction, an insight came to his mind: he could start up his own airline and offer superior customer service. This prompted him to ring an aeroplane manufacturer to check the costs of buying a second-hand plane for his new business endeavour: Virgin Atlantic. As seen previously, a dissatisfactory situation (being on a grounded plane) prompted this entrepreneur to launch its own airline.

Another incentive to developing non-traditional ideas is when customers provide the company with negative reviews and complaints. This negative criticism can represent a valuable trigger for a company to find new ways to improve their products, services, and processes. Some traditional companies are threatened when change needs to be implemented. These organisations resist change, and fear the unknown. They prefer to do things "as usual." Oftentimes, these organisations become quickly outdated and their products and services become obsolete. In those cases, these organisations keep on using the same old methods, even when they do not work any longer. These companies have a functional fixation on how they perceive circumstances. Narang and Devaiah (2014) call this resistance to change "gravity mindset."

Some common expressions of these companies are: "We have tried similar ideas previously," "There is no need to change what works ...," "It is not possible to change this ...," or "This will take a lot of time or effort ...," among others. Hamel and Prahalad (1996) observed that "what prevents companies from creating the future is an installed system of thinking," which includes unchallenged assumptions and narrow views of threats and opportunities.

Complacent companies tend to act in a non-creative manner. These short-sighted organisations consider that their products, services, and processes, and even their business models cannot be improved. Morgan (1997) observed that "many products and services become 'prisoners' of their underlying concept," and even though they stem from good ideas, these ideas become unchallenged and prevent companies from innovating. For example, Blockbuster, the once successful movie hiring company, could not foresee the massive potential of the movie streaming sector, and this was one of the main reasons for this company's decline.

There is another relevant point to highlight. Creative processes imply different degrees of change that companies should be willing to take. Some other hindrances preventing companies from adopting a creative attitude are:

Short-term orientation: Many companies have hectic schedules, which include countless meetings, tight deadlines, overworking, etc. Oftentimes, these companies tend to focus mostly on the short term, for example, activities like paying the bills, and serving current customers, among others. In these organisations, creative activities are not prioritised because employees have to deal with urgent tasks. In contrast, creative companies are strategic; they tend to adopt a long-term perspective. These organisations understand that some innovative insights take time to develop; therefore, these organisations avoid rushing creative ideas. These organisations also realise that some creative ideas need to go through a process of experimentation, adjustment, and testing to see if they are feasible or not. People working for creative companies acknowledge their errors, look into them in an unemotional manner, gaining valuable insights into these mistakes. Pixar Animation Studio became well-known for its various blockbusters (Toy Story, Monsters Inc., Finding Nemo, etc.), which have been collectively developed by its team of talented employees. These movies are made up of a myriad of creative ideas and include the participation of a big number of staff members. Each of these movies takes a long time to develop, from story development to production, which makes this company a good example of an organisation not oriented to the short term (Catmull, 2008; Trott, 2012). As seen previously, in the case of the development of the definite version of his bagless vacuum cleaner, James Dyson went through a painstakingly long process of trial and error with thousands of failed prototypes (Goodman, 2012).

Rigid mental categorisation: As seen previously, the human mind has a natural tendency to categorise and store information in rigid mental classifications. Consequently, any new information is kept in one of the pre-existing categories. Oftentimes, these mental categories do not have any practical application, especially when people face new circumstances. Most people tend to stick to their limiting mental categories without challenging them. Creative people are instead prone to question their mental categories, modifying or recombining them, or even creating new classifications. In the case of Uber, this company successfully challenged the rigid conventions in the transport sector, where competing companies own their vehicles. In that sense, Uber has become a relevant player in the sector while not owning any vehicles. Instead, this organisation connects the vehicles' owners and passengers through an easy-to-use app.

Copying others: Some companies adopt the same perspectives and methods used by other organisations, regardless of their suitability for the specific dynamics of the former. Many companies are prone to thoughtlessly emulate what is in fashion or currently trending in the marketplace. Companies which adopt this passive attitude are unwilling to undertake creative projects that would harness their unique resources. Nonetheless, some companies analyse what works for other organisations, but also creatively adapt these aspects to apply them to their own specific reality. This approach is called benchmarking and is considered a creative tool, which will be analysed later. As seen previously, James Dyson has avoided copying other companies in the industry. As mentioned before, when other companies offered vacuum cleaners which non-reusable bags, this business leader has purposely opted for developing a bagless vacuum cleaner. There is another interesting example of an original entrepreneur. In the past, Walt Disney was looking for a new character; he originally thought about a cat. He discussed this idea with his close circle and he opted for a mouse who is known as Mickey Mouse. The reason he did not choose a cat is to avoid copying others; at that moment, there was a famous feline character named Krazy Kat. Walt Disney opted to be unconventional and this mouse became known worldwide (Runco, 1999).

Fear of uncertainty: Most business people have a fear of uncertainty. These people perceive unpredictable situations as threatening, which makes them feel anxious and powerless. Therefore, these individuals tend to develop patterns, routines, and regularities to avoid uncertainty. As seen in Chapter 4, companies aim to counteract uncertain scenarios in different ways: researching, planning, budgeting, agreeing on contractual terms, etc. Moreover, when companies face threatening factors (economic recession, etc.), they are even less inclined to experimentation as they tend to protect their own resources (funds, technology, time, etc.) (Mainemelis and Ronson, 2006). Executives who aim to control business results give priority to incremental or gradual innovations, which are seen as less risky; these leaders are less inclined to experiment in a more ambitious way (Furstenthal et al., 2022). People who fear uncertainty are less prone to develop creative ideas, which always implies taking risks. Creativity is naturally related to possible courses of actions, which involve ambiguity and uncertainty. In the creative process, no positive results can be guaranteed; at first, people who develop new ideas cannot know if their ideas will work on a practical level. In Pixar, its employees fully accept the uncertainty of the creative process, and take the risk of being original. This company continually looks for non-traditional themes for their movies, while rising its quality parameters over time (Catmull, 2008; Trott, 2012).

Strict planning: In most companies, work tasks need to be purposeful; these organisations aim to achieve specific objectives, such as increasing productivity and improving customer service. These companies develop plans which include realistic goals to help them prioritise their tasks, use their resources effectively, and reduce uncertainty about future scenarios. As seen previously, goals are future desired states or educated guesses, which are based on the analysis of relevant internal factors (company's talents, capabilities, etc.) and external ones (customers, suppliers, etc.). Unfortunately, these goals are often set in an inflexible manner, which renders them useless when the situation motivating them has changed significantly. Companies with rigid goals act in predictable ways to achieve them, which makes these organisations incapable of taking non-traditional actions. These companies are keen on "predicting" their future outcomes. In relation to this, Klein (2003) observed that creative insights are never predictable, but disruptive: "they come without warning, take forms that are unexpected, and open up to unimagined opportunities." Most people have heard of YouTube, the most popular video online platform. Its origin highlights the importance of being flexible when planning in business. A few decades ago, this enterprise started as a dating website where users uploaded videos of themselves. This business idea shortly tanked, but the founders realised that people were uploading any type of videos (their pets, holidays, etc.) on that platform. This idea was welcomed as the founders re-developed the online platform, by making the uploading process of any video more facile and accessible to anyone. Later on, this company was acquired by Google, and nowadays this platform has billions of videos watched every day (Koebler, 2015; Ludwig, 2020).

Lack of confidence: Some people do not consider themselves creative because they have self-limiting beliefs regarding creativity. As seen in Chapter 3, beliefs always dictate how a person thinks, feels, and acts. Therefore, people who have detrimental beliefs about creativity will not make any attempt to use creative techniques. Some examples of these negative self-dialogues are: "Artists are the only creative people," "I was not born creative," "I am not a genius," "I do not have a creative mindset," and "I cannot see creative ways to do this." These people are unwilling to explore new perspectives because they believe that they are not capable. In other words, they do not trust their innermost creative skills. All creative people mentioned previously like Thomas Edison and James Dyson have full confidence in their creative skills, which was shown through their outstanding creative endeavours.

Stress: In stressful situations, people tend to adopt a defensive attitude, which is related to fight-freeze-flight mode. In this mode, their analytical and creative capabilities are temporarily diminished. Their minds are focused on the threatening factors affecting them. In stressful circumstances, there is no need for the exploration of new ideas, which is the basis of the creative process. Stressed people tend to be tense, fretful, and agitated. Creative insights are more likely to emerge when people are calm and relaxed. Tomasino (2007) observed that when people experience negative emotions, their discerning skills and intuitive assessments are impaired, leading them to have more inflexible thoughts and actions. In a similar vein, Wiseman (2009) observed that stressed people are less creative and more risk-averse; they tend to use routine methods to analyse circumstances and have more rigid behaviour. As seen previously in this book, a company like Google has set up nap pods in its workplace for its staff members to take short naps during work time. When staff members use these pods, their stress levels are reduced, while their alertness at work is heightened (Shoen and Singh, 2022; Takahashi et al., 2004). In addition, naps enhance people's creative and problem-solving capabilities, and improve their productivity levels (Williams Cosentino, 2021). To that effect, Google is a clear example of an innovative company with dazzling products like Google Scholar, Google Maps, and Google Translate, among others.

Mental biases: As explained previously in Chapter 4, people have mental biases, also called cognitive distortions. These subconscious patterns of thought prevent people from apprehending circumstances clearly and directly. Oftentimes, these mental biases stop people from accessing their inner wisdom and prevent them from tackling life circumstances effectively. Some examples of these mental distortive patterns are exaggerating or minimising things, neglecting relevant factors in a situation, relating uncorrelated matters, "predicting" future scenarios, jumping to conclusions swiftly, among others. Not only do these biases prevent people from harnessing their discerning capabilities, but also their creative ones. For instance, companies, like Airbnb, avoided jumping to swift conclusions, a very common mental bias. When starting up, this enterprise avoided concluding that, in order to be competitive in the accommodation sector, this organisation would need to own properties. As seen previously, this company connects owners of properties (flats, houses, etc.) with individuals who look for a short stay at these properties (potential guests) through a simple online platform developed by this company.

Thoughtless abidance by the rules: Many companies are beset by countless rules (formal procedures, policies, etc.) which are not critically questioned over time. In general, these purposeful restraints are mechanisms for control and order within a company; they are generally based on fear of uncertainty and chaos. However, creativity always implies freedom, improvisation, and experimentation. Companies which are burdened by rules tend to act in a mechanistic manner; this is opposite to a creative approach, which implies flexibility and open-mindedness. Most employees abide by these norms thoughtlessly and automatically. Kahn (1990) observed that people who respect the prevalent rules in a company tend to feel more psychologically safe, as compared with those who strayed beyond these regulations, who are considered rebels or mavericks that risk losing their jobs. In these work environments, people are criticised and even punished when they use experimental approaches and do not do things "by the book." When criticised, these staff members tend to adopt a fight-freeze-flight mode, which prevents them from harnessing their creative capabilities. People who abide by the company's regulations are prone to behave in a serious and structured manner. Instead, creative people tend to adopt a playful and even rebellious attitude, which defies rigid formalities. Creativity implies going beyond the rules, and oftentimes breaking them and making new ones. As analysed previously in this book, Netflix, the movie producing and streaming company, does not set countless rules for its business activities. This company hires high-performance staff and trusts their creative skills and self-discipline to solve problems effectively. In this company, it is firmly believed that employees are prone to thrive when they are allowed to act freely, in a workplace unencumbered by rules (Hastings and Meyer, 2020).

Groupthink: Many organisations show a phenomenon called groupthink. In these companies, people want consensus and avoid considering other alternatives besides the ones already accepted by the majority. Dissent is overtly or subtly dismissed by group pressure. Consequently, people tend to provide the same opinions as the rest in order to avoid being disapproved by them. McKenna (2012a) observed that groupthink "amounts to an intentional erosion of one's critical faculties as a result of adopting group norms." Research shows that the internal dynamics of these organisations is based on unanimity and homogeneity of views. The open discussion of topics is discouraged and nobody wants to stand out. According to Wiseman (2009), decisions made in these organisations can be riskier and more daring, or more conservative than the ones made individually by each member because their opinions tend to reinforce one another. As seen previously in this book, in Netflix, groupthink is regularly avoided by the regular exchange of valuable feedback among its employees. In that sense, employees are continually empowered to provide others (even their superiors) with kind and honest feedback to others, whenever necessary (Hastings and Meyer, 2020; Meyer, 2021).

Lack of awareness: Profuse research has observed that many of the actions that people take daily are on autopilot. Oftentimes, people are unaware of their routine ways of doing things. Scientists have observed that repeated actions strengthen specific neural pathways in the brain, and make them more active, which reinforces the routine behaviour. These habits become more ingrained over time, which prevents people from developing alternative behaviours. Sometimes, habitual behaviour is useful to save time and be more effective, but this behaviour becomes unsuitable in novel or ever-changing situations, which generally require a more proactive and creative approach. The Ugly Company, previously discussed in this book, is a good example of an organisation with enhanced awareness. When starting up, this company was fully aware that above a third part of all food that is produced ends up as waste, which brings a valuable opportunity for upcycled food products (made from ingredients which normally would not have been utilised for human consumption). The development of this type of products has a positive environmental impact, as the greenhouse gases stemming from food waste are decreased (Sritharan, 2022). In that sense, The Ugly Company offers sustainable natural snack products made from ugly fruit. This fruit is visually imperfect, which often prompts companies to dispose of it, despite being completely appropriate to be eaten (The Ugly Company, 2022).

Silo structure: Most companies have a compartmentalised internal structure where each department (finance, human resources, etc.) acts as a "silo," which often has scarce interaction with others. This silo structure is based on an effective division of labour; each internal area is specialised in specific tasks. The incomplete data possessed by each silo prevents it from developing an integrative and holistic analysis of a company's issues. This rigid organisational structure hinders the development of innovative and synergetic solutions because inputs from different silos or departments cannot be duly considered and integrated. This bureaucratic structure kills the possibility of collective creativity. Pixar is a company which challenges the silo structure. Each of its movies is made up of countless creative ideas regarding characters, plotline, lighting, pace, and other aspects. Consequently, this company encourages its employees from different artistic and technical areas to work in a collaborative fashion and welcome feedback from one another regarding any work in progress (Catmull, 2008; Trott, 2012).

Perfectionism: As mentioned previously, most people working for organisations are goal-oriented; they want to do things in the right way to attain these goals. However, when people generate creative ideas, a few of them might be successful, but most will not be. Besides, creative ideas are developed gradually, and are often tested and modified several times. The "errors" found during the creative process represent necessary stepping stones to develop future fruitful ideas. Successful creators are not ashamed of making mistakes because they know those errors provide them with insightful clues on their path to outstanding creations. Errors show people what does not work and prompts them to act in alternative ways. As mentioned previously, James Dyson tested thousands of prototypes over several years before coming up with the final version of his bagless vacuum cleaner. Each of these prototypes provided this determined entrepreneur with valuable information about what did not work, which prompted him to act in alternative ways.

There are a few other relevant topics to analyse. Most companies tend to use black-and-white patterns of thinking. In these organisations, employees tend to classify facts and situations in a binary manner, such as profit – loss, co-operation – competition, traditional – modern, winner – loser, growth – decline, etc. From this limited perspective, a company is less likely to develop alternative views, which generally includes nuances, new combinations, reformulation of traditional classifications, use of analogies, and development of innovative categories.

It is important to acknowledge that creativity is related to imagination and the development of new ideas. Because of this intangible element, many companies consider that creative activities do not contribute to the company's economic results in a tangible and substantial manner. Therefore, the actual usefulness of a creative approach is harshly criticised by many organisations. These companies tend to use a quantitative approach which gives priority to what is precisely measurable (sales, profits, number of customers, etc.) and dismiss what is not quantifiable (e.g., intuitive insights). Levi's, a company previously analysed, stated that "Saving water is more important than profits." Consequently, this company developed and implemented numerous creative techniques to save water during the production process of its jeans (Levi's, 2020).

It is important to analyse the relationship between knowledge and creativity. In general, knowledge constitutes a relevant springboard on which creative techniques can be applied. People must be educated to interpret circumstances affecting them in a more complete manner. Moreover, most psychologists agree that creativity is centred on a specific domain or discipline, and previous preparation (which implies training and collecting related information) on that discipline is needed to develop creative ideas.

This knowledge represents the "raw" input that the creative person will work on to develop non-traditional insights. It is a myth that people create *ex nihilo* (out of nothing); they always create based on combining and transforming their current knowledge. However, when people have solemn respect for the knowledge they possess, without challenging it, these individuals are less prone to develop new ideas.

Many knowledgeable people think in a structured and rigid way, which prevents them from developing non-traditional approaches. Moreover, Sawyer (2006) observed, that beyond a certain point, education becomes a *hindrance* for the enhancement of creative skills. Some experts also state that specialised knowledge can prevent a person from developing fresh ideas to deal with complex and dynamic circumstances. Creative people continuously challenge established and well-accepted knowledge and are open to and flexible about exploring innovative ideas.

For example, at Pixar, new employees are encouraged to take training directly related to their posts, so they can develop deeper specialised knowledge in topics related to their positions, and consequently become more capable of contributing effectively with creative insights and dealing with complex issues. However, once these staff members become specialised, they are prompted to take training in other topics different from their specialisms. For instance, animators are encouraged to take training in topics like production. This company also offers these employees various training courses in diverse topics, like belly dancing, yoga, and sculpting. This cross-training which goes beyond employees' specialisms aims to avoid cognitive rigidity, which often stems from specialising in a specific topic. Oftentimes, this cognitive rigidity hinders the development of creative insights (Catmull, 2008; Mannucci, 2016; Pixar, 2022).

14.6 Traditional Creative Tools

> The thoughts that come often unsought, and, as it were, drop into the mind, are commonly the most valuable of any we have, and therefore should be secured, because they seldom return again.
>
> **John Locke**

> Genius is no more than childhood recaptured at will.
>
> **Charles Baudelaire**

A very simple creative tool anyone can use is note-taking. Business people should form the positive habit of taking note of any relevant topics related to business activities; valuable ideas come up and disappear fleetingly. Rando (2014) observed that "language is the oxygen of thinking; it allows thoughts to breathe and live, to become full-blooded."

People who put their ideas on paper do not have to depend on their memory skills. Besides, taking notes gives people a clearer and more articulate description of a topic. When taking notes, people can retrieve information, assess it later, modify it, and even combine it with other data. For instance, people can write down 20 potential solutions to a problem per day. By making the list, people can "unload" or "map" the ideas they have in their minds. Whenever people enumerate these ideas, they should not restrain or censor themselves; any idea should be included, even those considered to be "unreasonable" or "far-fetched." Some ideas on that list can be modifications of previous ideas. At the end of the week, this list should be rationally analysed to select the most promising ideas.

Another way to do this exercise is to write any idea about a topic down in a non-stop way and without editing. Later, these notes can be thoroughly analysed to find relevant patterns and insights into them. Afterwards, these notes can be refined and edited if necessary. Geniuses like Leonardo da Vinci kept countless notebooks with handwritten and graphical ideas.

Written ideas are longer lasting as compared with spoken ones; therefore, these notes can be reviewed more thoroughly later. Afterwards, these notes can also be elaborated, illustrated, edited, or reformulated. In other words, written notes represent a valuable source of additional ideas to be utilised in the future. The successful entrepreneur Richard Branson, from Virgin Group, is accustomed to taking notes, especially when he listens to anyone. In that sense, he carefully jots down any significant point, to later review them and take action on them. For example, this business leader often uses his notes to harness interesting business opportunities, deal with philanthropic issues, or develop posts for social media platforms (Branson, 2019).

However, some authors like Buzan and Buzan (2003) observed that note-taking tends to obscure significant words among all the notes taken and represent time wasted because it tends to include unnecessary notes. These authors are of the opinion that note-taking does not necessarily stimulate creativity. In conclusion, there are different views on the effectiveness of this tool. Therefore, everyone should try note-taking and see if it works for them because each individual is different. A great inventor like Thomas Edison, who was mentioned previously, was very keen on note-taking. He has thoroughly recorded his work in more than 4,000 notebooks (Edison Innovation Foundation, 2022).

Below, there are some examples of other valuable creative techniques. This list of tools is indicative, not complete. Companies can use these tools to achieve any of the objectives mentioned in Section 14.4. The use of creative techniques should be a positive habit that everybody takes up. The use of these tools helps people unearth their unique creative skills.

14.6.1 Mind-Mapping

This well-known technique was popularised by Buzan (2002). In order to use this tool, people must consider a relevant idea (e.g., a problem to be solved) and put it in a circled box in the middle of a blank page. This main topic should be broken down into subcomponents which branch out and are shown as little boxes around the main topic, connected to it with lines.

This technique helps people see relevant topics visually. These topics can be analysed in a holistic manner, including their main components. Buzan (2002) observed that this tool stimulates "whole-brain" thinking (the use of both left and right hemispheres) and gathers a large amount of information in one place, which helps people make more creative choices.

Some organisations use these mind-maps to develop their strategies, to deliver business presentations, to organise meetings, and to manage product innovation projects, among others. These maps can be prepared individually or collectively and they can be reformulated several times. In an insightful interview, Tony Buzan, the famous developer of this tool, enumerated several well-known companies which use mind-maps, such as HP, Walt Disney, and Microsoft, among others (Frey, 2007).

14.6.2 Drawing

The use of words limits the possible mental associations between valuable ideas. Instead, drawings allow people to develop more links between ideas, without being hampered by the intrinsic limitations of words. Edwards (1993) observed that "drawing is a global (whole) skill" which represents "a particular way of seeing" that allows people to tap into their "inventive, imaginative, intuitive powers."

Koestler (1964) stated that visual images are powerful "vehicles of thought" and non-verbal or pictorial representations, which are beneficial for creative purposes. This author observed that oftentimes "language can become a screen which stands between the thinker and reality." The use of images is related to the right brain hemisphere which is linked to a non-linear, intuitive, and holistic perspective. Instead, the left brain is more related to rational, critical, and structured thinking. As seen, creative people use both their left and right brain hemispheres.

For instance, people working for an organisation can draw a business problem affecting them. This visual representation of the issue can prompt these people to draw potential approaches to solve it. These potential solutions can be drawn in a clear, vivid, and detailed manner. The use of drawings help people hone their creative skills because these drawings are not constrained by the specific meaning of words or the structure of sentences.

The ideas originally drawn can be modified and fine-tuned as more ideas come up. Ferrucci (1982) suggests that people should use different colours in their drawings, and thoroughly assess the main aspects of these graphical representations (their style, the relationships among their parts, etc.) in order to gather some insights into them. A great visionary like Edison developed a myriad of sketches to meticulously depict the intricate details of his inventions, for instance, his drawings regarding telegraph circuits and relays (Edison Innovation Foundation, 2022).

At Honda, the renowned car manufacturing company, its designers develop their ideas in drawings (e.g., using notebooks). At this company, design development includes drawings which do not only display simple shapes, but also represent various aspects of the product, such as its essence or "aura," people who would use this product, how these people would feel about the product, the way this product would work, and how comfortable this product would be, among other aspects (Honda, 2022).

14.6.3 New Viewpoints

This is a well-used creative tool which involves the analysis of a topic from different viewpoints. An organisation regularly analyses its problems from its own perspective. Nonetheless, these problems can be analysed from the perspective of different stakeholders, for instance, employees, customers, suppliers, competitors, community, media, etc. Each of these stakeholders has a unique way of perceiving and interpreting circumstances.

For example, when a problem affects one department (e.g., the marketing department), the problem can be analysed from the perspective of other departments (administrative, finance, etc.). The problem can also be analysed, imagining it from the perspective of other companies in the sector or different industries.

In the past, PepsiCo, the food producer, aimed to decrease the amount of salt in its snacks without affecting their flavour. This company was not able to find a viable solution to this issue in its own sector. This company looked for solutions in other industries (pharma, engineering, etc.). This company found some interesting insights from the Orthopaedics division of a laboratory. This division was researching the development of nano-particles regarding osteoporosis. This research provided PepsiCo with a fresh perspective on its problem, which helped this company develop a more innovative solution to the issue of sodium in its snacks (Zynga, 2013).

A topic can also be analysed, imagining how it would be approached by different professionals or experts (doctors, lawyers, musicians, etc.). A topic can also be analysed from the perspective of several personalities (Richard Branson, Chris Rock, etc.). Some useful questions for imagining these alternative perspectives "How would … analyse this situation?", "What specific solutions would … provide?", and "What would … do?"

Some other ways to use this tool are to imagine how other unrelated people would analyse a topic. For example, a person can ask questions like "How would a person from Mars analyse this topic?", "How would a beggar analyse this topic?", or "How would a toddler perceive this subject?", among others.

This tool helps analyse issues with fresh eyes and in a multidimensional way, including a wide range of distinct viewpoints. People who use this technique can generate new perspectives on a topic, without being "polluted" by their previous knowledge about it. These individuals can temporarily leave aside any of their rigid categories, assumptions, values, or beliefs.

A company that used different perspectives is Tata Motors. Several years ago, its business leader had the insight to produce a small, safe, and affordable car, after having seen full families perilously travelling in two wheelers on Indian roads. When developing this car, this company took into account different perspectives (Blythe, 2012; Tata Motors, 2022):

- The company's own perspective: in relation to this car's production aspects, this small vehicle should be cost-effective regarding its manufacturing process.
- The customers' perspective: the car should be affordable and accessible for the average Indian customer who has low income.
- The government's perspective: this small vehicle should abide with all the requirements regarding passengers' safety and security, as well as environmental aspects.

After having thoroughly assessed all these perspectives, Tata Motors successfully launched a small, affordable, and no-frills car named Tata Nano. This car met all the requirements of these multiple perspectives.

14.6.4 What If Method

This creative method is simple and straightforward. When people use this tool, they should imagine possible scenarios, in which there are no limitations of resources (funds, technology, time, etc.). A person who uses this technique is thinking in a hypothetical manner.

When a person does not set any limitation to the analysis of an issue, this individual is more capable of generating potentially fruitful alternatives to tackle it. The use of this method is speculative and based on potential options regarding an issue, which do not include any hindrance. The use of this tool also helps people shift from a negative mood (based on the problem) to a positive emotional state (based on possible solutions).

In order to use this technique, a person can ask questions like "What if …?", "What will happen if …?", or "How would things be if …?", and similar ones. When these probable scenarios are imagined, it is easier for a company to work out specific ways to achieve them from a backward perspective.

A company like Uber, which developed the most popular ride-sharing app, surged from a very insightful question. Several years ago, on one cold night, two entrepreneurs during an event could not find a taxi. This situation triggered a very worthy insight: "What if people were able to ask for a ride from their phones?" This insight drove the development of Uber's business model (Blystone et al., 2022).

The What if tool can also be used by setting some specific limitations (specific deadline, limited funds, etc.); these limitations often prompt people to bring about more creative insights. For instance, skyscrapers have been brought about as a consequence of the constraints of limited and costly pieces of land, and the need for big space for offices (Von Oech, 2011).

Acar et al. (2019) observed that constraints can be classified in three types: input constraints (which are limitations of resources to be used during the creative process, such as time, technology, people, funds), process constraints (rules or procedures set up for the creative process, for example, use of brainstorming sessions), and output constraints (which are limitations set up affecting the final outcome, for example, the final product must have a specific size, or be made of specific material). Constraints often sharpen people's focus, allowing them to assess a more limited set of alternatives in a more in-depth way. These constraints should be set in a reasonable number, avoiding too many of them or very few. Research has concluded that the so-called focusing constraints (e.g., use this type of material for the product) tend to bring about more creativity as compared to exclusionary constraints (e.g., don't use this type of material) (Tromp and Baer, 2022).

14.6.5 Benchmarking and Analogies

Benchmarking is a technique commonly used by companies and it involves taking into account traits, processes, or procedures used by other companies and applying them to their own organisations, with the adaptations needed. Oftentimes, a company can consider outstanding aspects of other organisations as starting points and improve these aspects in order to apply them internally. A company can take as a reference those organisations with practices of excellence from the same industrial sector or different industries. As seen previously, the McDonald brothers took the concept of the assembly line (originally developed by Henry Ford) to apply it to kitchen tasks in the fast-food sector, to increase productivity levels in the food-preparation process.

These benchmarks can also be internal, for instance, when a company sees excellent aspects in one of its own departments (marketing, finance, etc.). In these cases, the organisation aims to apply these outstanding aspects to other departments whose performance needs to be improved. The application of these aspects tends to require adaptation to the distinct characteristics of the receiving department.

This technique is related to the use of analogies. An analogy implies the use of certain similarities between the topic being analysed and aspects taken from unrelated topics (components of nature, functions of the body, dynamics of societies, etc.). When ideas are taken from different fields, the creative tool is also called cross-fertilisation. A company like Pax Scientific uses biomimicry, which means considering the distinctive principles in nature to develop processes and products. For example, this organisation developed fans and water mixers, inspired by the dynamics of nature's vortices and spirals (hurricanes) (Hoffman and Haigh, 2012).

There is another point to highlight. Some people confuse analogies with metaphors. To put it simply, a metaphor is an implicit comparison (e.g., "Our company is a rocket"). Instead, analogies are explicit comparisons (e.g., "Our company is like a rocket"). The connection between the two elements (in this example, "our company" and "a rocket") in metaphors and analogies can be direct or indirect. According to Bragg and Bragg (2005), the use of these tools often helps transfer the underlying principles of a situation (in the example, how a rocket works, why it works, etc.) to another situation ("our company").

Kim and Mauborgne (2015) used metaphors to distinguish two types of markets: red oceans and blue oceans. Metaphorically speaking, a red ocean is a well-known space, where a myriad of sharks devour fish simultaneously and frantically, reddening the seawater with the blood of the fish being eaten. In practice, this is a saturated marketplace where countless competing companies with marginally differentiated or commoditised products and services eagerly fight for market share. Instead, metaphorically speaking, a blue ocean is a space with clear, radiant, uncharted waters. In practice, this represents the market space that is unknown, unexplored, and consequently, teemed with countless opportunities (Uta, 2020).

There is another interesting example of metaphors. In the past, people used to use the insightful metaphors "horseless carriages" and "iron horses" to name the first automobiles and the first locomotives respectively (Von Oech, 2011)

14.6.6 Brainstorming

This is a meeting where participants take turns to express their views on a common topic. These opinions are expressed freely, without any fear of being censored. In other words, all ideas are welcome and nobody criticises others' ideas. The use of this tool entails the temporary abandonment of criticism in order to allow non-traditional ideas to pop out.

The ideas expressed by each participant can be noted on a blackboard or flipchart for everyone to see. In these meetings, there could be a person who is responsible for taking note of all the ideas exposed during the encounter. All types of ideas are taken on board, even the seemingly outlandish. Sometimes, these meetings are attended by employees working for different departments (marketing, manufacturing, etc.), which makes the interaction richer and more diverse. Brainstorming events foster divergent thinking, which implies the development of numerous free-flowing insights related to a specific topic.

The use of this tool helps a company generate a large number of non-traditional ideas about a specific topic. The ideas expressed in the meeting are later analysed by attendees from a rational perspective. Companies can also break a problem into parts with each part being analysed by specific brainstorming groups. However, brainstorming can end up being ineffective when participants are centred on very few types of ideas, or when participants feel inhibited to communicate their insights (Sawyer, 2017).

On the one hand, Wiseman (2009) observed that, according to research, the use of brainstorming proved to be less effective than the individual development of creative ideas. This is due to a phenomenon called "social loafing" or "diffusion of responsibility," which implies that in a group each member is less inclined to make their best effort, because they become over-reliant on other people's contribution. On the other hand, Johnson (2010) observed that brainstorming always represents a valuable tool to develop serendipitous connections. Companies like Dell, the computer giant, regularly organises brainstorming sessions, within the context of the company's culture of innovation (Dell, 2022).

There is another version of this tool called *brainwriting*. When participants use this technique, they individually write their ideas on small pieces of paper, and then they are shown on a board. Another version of brainwriting is when there is only one piece of paper which is passed around, and everyone takes turns to add their own ideas to it.

14.6.7 Disney Strategy

This strategy was explained by Robert Dilts (1994) and it is said to have been used by Walt Disney. This strategy includes three sequential stages: the dreamer, the realist, and the critic. In the first stage (the dreamer), people envision what can be done creatively regarding a specific topic. In the second stage (the realist), people aim to analyse how creative ideas stemming from the previous stage (the dreamer) can be implemented in practice, considering their feasibility.

In the last stage (the critic), people focus on any criticism of these ideas: for example, why these ideas can fail in practice. In this last stage, people will also consider information from their previous unsuccessful experiences, as well as projected potential setbacks related to the ideas.

14.6.8 Scamper

This technique was originally developed by Osborn (1948). This acronym is S for substituting elements, C for combining with other factors, A for adapting, M for magnifying or modifying, P for putting or using for other purposes, E for eliminating or reducing, and R for reordering (or inverting). This technique can be used to solve problems related to products, services, processes, and business models.

For instance, a food company analyses one of its products (cereal). In this case, the company can modify part of that product (for example, its packaging) or combine this product with others in an assortment (for example, launching a package which includes boxes of cereal with different flavours). This organisation can also adapt the product for specific users (for example, cereal for children) or magnify the product by offering a family pack instead of an individual one.

This company can also promote the product for other uses, for example, if the cereal is promoted as nourishing, it can be promoted as energy-boosting. This organisation can also eliminate some aspects of the product, for instance, taking out some ingredients (sugar, preservatives, etc.), or reordering the product, for instance, offering individual cups with cereal for daily use.

A product can be broken down into its main parts (packaging, label, ingredients, etc.) and different aspects of SCAMPER can be applied to each of them. Bragg and Bragg (2005) suggest a very interesting question when using this model which is: "What factors can be reduced/eliminated/created regarding this product or service in relation to the prevailing standards in the sector?" In the case of James Dyson previously analysed, this entrepreneur has eliminated the bags from the vacuum cleaner to develop a bagless model.

In the case of Walt Disney, this entrepreneur combined ideas from different sources to develop Disneyland, the renowned theme park. In that sense, this entrepreneur's vision of this emotionally engaging park included ideas from different sources (The Henry Ford, 2020):

■ On one occasion, his two daughters were riding the carousel at a park. This image prompted him to develop the idea of an amicable, fun, and safe place for parents and their children.
■ His vision for the park also stemmed from his keenness on steam railroads. Once, he went to the Chicago Railroad Fair. He also dropped by the Greenfield Village and was delighted by the environment in that tiny town.
■ This entrepreneur was also inspired by various sites around Los Angeles. He looked into Knott's Berry Farm, as well as the shops located on Olivera Street which had a Spanish colonial-style. He went to the Farmer's Market which triggered some insights into the park.

- This businessman carefully assessed traffic flow, entrances, and exits at various places (fairs, circuses, museums, etc.) as he was worried about people becoming tired in those sites. Based on these insights, he planned to develop a single entrance for his park.
- This entrepreneur was helped by artists regarding the development of this theme park.

This is only a short list of sources which prompted this entrepreneur's insights. As seen previously, this entrepreneur combined several elements from different sites he visited and analysed in order to develop his park.

14.6.9 Use of External Words

These are trigger words, which are randomly related to the topic subject to analysis. Any words can work as a trigger and these words can be taken from a dictionary, any other book, TV programmes, etc.

For example, if the company is looking for a new "customer service approach," this topic can be related to any random word, such as "tree," "cup," "running," and any other words. The use of random words prompts the creation of new mental connections which can contribute to the development of new ideas.

14.6.10 Framing

A topic can be reformulated in many ways by changing its focus. Framing is a very useful tool to generate fresh ideas stemming from different perspectives. In a similar vein, Isen (1999) observed that creativity entails adopting various standpoints and changing from one to another. Some examples of framing can be found below:

- A topic can be defined in a more general manner, or in a more detailed way. In the case of Edison, this inventor defined his ideas in a general manner (e.g., a telegraph) but also meticulously sketched the details of his inventions through his drawings.
- A topic can be examined from a long, medium, or short-term perspective. As seen in this book, a company like Honesty Tea offers organic beverage products, which do not include any pollutants, preservatives, or chemical ingredients. These drinks are aimed to bring about a positive impact on both customers' health and the environment, which implies a long-term perspective.
- A topic can be analysed considering its impact on a department, the whole organisation, or the business environment. As seen previously, in Pixar, the development of each movie takes into consideration the contribution of the specialists of each department (animators, technical staff, etc.).
- A topic can also be analysed taking into account its rational aspects or emotional aspects. In the case of Walt Disney Company, when developing its entertainment parks, this organisation took into account rational aspects (costs of development, location, etc.) but also emotional aspects related to these parks (e.g., type of experiences customers would have when visiting the park).
- A topic can also be evaluated from the viewpoint of its positive aspects, or from the perspective of its negative aspects. As seen previously in this book, Uber, has meticulously analysed all the negative issues passengers usually face when looking for taxi services (e.g., unknown waiting time, uncertain cost of the ride) in order to provide superior transport services through its innovative app (Radu, 2022).

■ A topic can be considered from the perspective of its past aspects, or considering its future implications. Airbnb has wittingly considered a perspective of the past when it analysed the accommodation sector, where the main companies (hotels, hostels, etc.) own properties. Based on this analysis, Airbnb developed a creative business model to enter the accommodation sector without owning any properties.

■ A topic can be analysed taking into account all its aspects or structure (holistic view), or its components (partial view). For example, Pixar often analyse the movies they will develop both from the holistic perspective (e.g., the whole movie) and from the perspective of its components (characters, music, etc.).

■ A topic can be examined considering its main aspects, or taking into account secondary traits. In the case of the Tata Nano car, Tata Motors carefully assessed the main aspects of this small car (affordability, safety, compliance with legal aspects, etc.) and avoided including any secondary traits (e.g., frills).

■ A topic can be analysed from the perspective of possibility, or from the viewpoint of certainty. James Dyson when he was developing the bagless vacuum cleaner used a perspective of possibility, because before introducing his bagless model into the marketplace, all vacuum cleaners offered by other companies utilised non-reusable bags.

The aforementioned examples are not exhaustive. Organisations can use framing considering other perspectives besides the ones mentioned previously. The use of different alternatives allows people to overcome functional fixedness. Plucker and Runco (1999) defined functional fixedness as the "inability to consider other alternatives when facing problems," for example, different unusual uses of an object beyond its traditional purpose. According to research, young children (five-year-old children) do not seem to be affected negatively by functional fixedness (German and Defeyter, 2001).

When people are affected by functional fixedness, they tend to think in a rigid manner, while avoiding any non-traditional ways to approach relevant issues. Their cognitive rigidity can be underpinned by their previous experiences, expertise, or specialism in a specific area. Other tools seen in this chapter, for instance, new viewpoints, can also be of value for surmounting functional fixedness.

As seen previously, a company like Terracycle has overcome functional fixedness, as this organisation gives garbage various non-traditional uses. As mentioned, this company sells coffee tables made from cigarette waste, and playground equipment made from various types of waste (air and home care products, etc.), among other products.

14.7 Additional Comments on Creativity

The aforementioned set of techniques should be used even in cases where things are working well. Everything is perfectible, which means things can always be improved; it is important not to rest on one's laurels and to avoid being complacent. People are naturally resistant to change, so the use of creative tools stretches their views beyond their comfort zone and beyond their natural ways of perceiving things. Companies can use a combination of these creative techniques in different orders: for example, first using brainstorming, and then mind-mapping.

Lastly, some people are resistant to change and prefer the status quo, which is related to the "endowment effect." This means that these people are comfortable with what they already have, even when it is negative. These people are less likely to use creative tools. Other people are affected by the *Einstellung effect*. This means that when people find a specific solution to a given problem, they are less likely to come up with new ideas. These people are also less prone to use creative techniques. As seen previously, Blockbuster was affected by the Einstellung effect, as it was comfortable with its business model of offering movies for hire, despite the increasing development of the movie streaming trend.

Questions for Self-Reflection

- What does creativity mean to me?
- What are the attributes of creative people?
- What are the main obstacles in our company regarding creativity?
- Which techniques can be used to perform more creative business activities?

Chapter 15

Additional Aspects of Love and Creativity

15.1 Creating Is Asking New Questions

Look and you will find it – what is unsought will go undetected.

Sophocles

15.1.1 Importance of Questions

We hear only those questions for which we are in a position to find answers.

Friedrich Nietzsche

Solving the problem is the exciting part, not knowing the answer. Once the conjuring trick is explained, it loses its magic.

Paul Arden

Most people have a few default responses when they face a problem: for instance, they gather additional information, listen to experts, and analyse the issue thoroughly. Oftentimes, people avoid tackling the problem or decide to postpone its analysis. A good way to solve a problem is to ask several questions related to it. Toddlers learn through continually asking questions to explore the world around them; their relentless curiosity prompts them to ask countless questions in a repetitive and varying manner. Adults are also prone to ask questions about different topics (such as relationships, health, and career). However, sometimes, people refrain themselves from asking questions as they do not want to appear less intelligent (Adams, 2001). In history, various scientific discoveries have been driven by simple, but powerful and insightful questions.

Companies also tend to pose questions, such as "Will this product work?", "Which is the best way to obtain new customers?", or "Where are the most interesting markets to sell our products", among others. Many companies enrol their staff on seminars, workshops, and other training events with the purpose of answering those relevant questions.

DOI: 10.4324/9781003372684-19

Consequently, a very straightforward creative technique is to ask varying questions, especially non-traditional ones. These questions could be asked in relation to any aspect of a company's activities, for instance: business challenges, issues relating to a product or service, relationships with specific stakeholders, strategy aspects, etc. Every time a question is posed, new alternatives regarding a target topic are more likely to come up. To that effect, questions represent wonderful creative tools to solve seemingly unsolvable problems.

Questions are empowering and expansive starting points; they develop a field of valuable possibilities. People who ask frequent questions tend to loosen their mental processes and leave any ingrained assumptions aside. Besides, questions help people challenge statements which include the words "must" and "should" like "We must act this way" or "We should enter that market." The most creative questions are not comforting, but instead challenging and daring.

An airline like WestJet is keen to test the power of insightful questions. In the past, this organisation asked questions like: "What are our brand values?", and "How can we display this in our marketing?" One of this company's values is "Care from the heart." By posing these questions, the company developed more authentic adverts showing its caring focus on customers. For example, in a Christmas advert, this company's passengers were at the airport and Father Christmas asked these passengers, both adults and children, about the gifts they wanted for that festivity. Then, the company's staff members swiftly dashed into various shops to buy the gifts for these passengers. On their arrival at their destination, these passengers received their wrapped Christmas gifts which unexpectedly popped up on the luggage conveyor belt. This advert also showed the glee experienced by passengers when unwrapping these gifts. This simple but heart-warming advert was seen by millions of people (Mulholland, 2018; Westjet, 2013).

According to Robbins (2001), questions shape people's thoughts and their responses to experiences, and create a more fulfilling life. Moreover, questions act like lenses which allow people to see reality in different ways. When people are stuck in a rut, they can use questions to find and develop new paths. Sometimes, people do not find the answers to questions straightforwardly; in those cases, these answers are incubated subconsciously before they pop up in a clear manner.

Some people refrain from asking questions because they are shy or because they do not want to look silly or ignorant. However, asking questions is always a wise approach which implies inquisitiveness and exploration. Questions are expansive, because they help clarify topics in order to explore uncharted avenues related to them. Different questions focus on distinct aspects of a topic, which helps analyse it in a multifaceted way.

From the creative perspective, there is no such thing as a silly question; therefore, any question is welcome. Some other functions of asking questions as a creative tool are:

- Questions can help people reflect on relevant topics.
- Questions can challenge perceived limitations.
- Questions can help individuals formulate problems more clearly.
- Questions can open new lines of research on a topic.
- Questions can identify priorities regarding a topic.
- Questions can prevent people from swiftly jumping to conclusions.
- Questions can help define a problem in a wider or narrower manner.
- Questions can help connect different problems.
- Questions can help analyse different aspects of an issue.
- Questions can disrupt automatic patterns of thinking and ingrained perceptions.
- Questions can be the starting point for asking additional questions.

- Questions can help restructure information in a non-traditional manner.
- Questions can help find meaning regarding unclear situations.
- Question can identify the key elements of a topic.
- Questions can probe hypothetical scenarios.
- Questions can develop new alternatives and widen choice.
- Questions can help summarise or recap relevant ideas.

From the creative perspective, the objective of asking questions is to generate the largest number of answers possible, even those that are seemingly unfeasible or far-fetched. At a later stage, these answers will be screened out from a perspective of feasibility and practicality.

Questions always imply an attitude of curiosity. According to Brown (2021), curious people realise the gap in their knowledge regarding something of their interest, and become engaged on an emotional and cognitive level in bridging this very gap. This author also observed that being curious also entails being vulnerable, as one admits being uncertain regarding a specific topic. In business, this passionate "appetite for knowledge" can be driven by specific and clear objectives, such as satisfying customers more effectively, developing new products, and designing new business models (Loewenstein, 1994).

15.1.2 Examples of Useful Questions

A prudent question is one-half of wisdom.

Francis Bacon

We live in worlds our questions create.

David Cooperrider

Questions stimulate creative thinking, which helps companies navigate the business journey in a more meaningful and insightful manner. Sometimes, it is necessary to ask different questions to probe a specific topic. Some examples of questions to be asked are:

- What are other less known characteristics/uses/objectives/dimensions/perspectives of …?
- What are the unwanted consequences of …?
- What can be added to/taken from …?
- What is possible in relation to …?
- What other factors are related to …?
- What are the underlying assumptions regarding …?
- What is the opposite of …?
- How would … be approached if we started afresh?
- What are the proactive/reactive aspects of …?
- How can … be examined more thoroughly?
- Why is … relevant to our company?
- What are the main obstacles preventing …?
- What are the main principles underpinning …?
- What was learned from …?
- How can … be simplified?
- What is the exception to …?

- How can I satisfy customers' needs more effectively with …?
- How might … be worsened/solved?
- What are other ways to reduce costs/increase performance/improve the design …?
- What are the traditional and non-traditional activities related to …?
- Who are the main people affected by …?
- How can … be seen differently?
- How can this be improved regarding …?
- Does … feel right?
- How can I differentiate … from …?
- Where can information about … be obtained?
- What are the main time aspects related to …?
- How can I surmount the obstacles related to …?
- What do I already know about …?
- What resources can be leveraged to improve …?
- How can … be more useful in other contexts?
- How can … be reframed?
- What is the best/worst scenario regarding …?
- What are the unique or distinct aspects of …?
- What are the reasons for …?
- What are the different ways that … can fail/succeed?
- What are the missing aspects/repetitive aspects of …?
- What are the ambiguous/uncertain/uncontrollable aspects of …?
- What are the rational/emotional aspects related to …?
- Which are the internal/external factors affecting …?
- How do other companies deal with …?
- Why is … urgent for our company?
- What should have happened when … was solved?
- What are the precedents for …?
- What are the priorities regarding …?
- What is the most radical idea regarding …?
- How can I add more value to…?
- What are the advantages/disadvantages/strengths/weaknesses of …?
- How can I convert the weaknesses regarding … into strengths?
- If we had unbounded resources, what could be done with …?
- What aspects of … can be emulated?
- Who will benefit from …?
- How will they benefit from …?
- What are the other meanings of …?
- What actions should be taken regarding …?
- How would an outsider perceive …?
- How would an expert deal with …?
- How can conflicting goals regarding … be resolved?
- What are the main and secondary factors related to …?
- What other aspects of value are related to …?
- What is the best choice regarding …?
- What are other ways that … can work?
- What are the ideal circumstances for … to succeed?

- What are the limits of ...?
- How can I articulate the idea of ... more clearly?
- How can ... provide customers/employees/community with great value?
- What were the previous solutions to ...?
- What are the main drivers fostering ...?
- What are the main trends affecting ...?
- What are the causes/consequences of ...?
- What are the main parts/structure related to ...?
- What are the commonalities/differences ...?
- What metaphors/analogies can be applied to ...?
- What is the main pattern in relation to ...?
- Which are the temporary/permanent aspects of ...?
- How can the parts of ... be organised in a different manner?
- How can I effectively deal with a challenging situation like ...?
- How is the top organisation in the market dealing with ...?
- What partnerships can be developed to deal with ...?
- What are the simple traits/complex traits of ...?
- Which disciplines/fields can I learn more about ...?
- What are the qualitative/quantitative traits of ...?
- What are the compulsory/voluntary features of ...?
- What are the strategic/tactical aspects of ...?
- What would an improved version of ... be?
- What are other examples of ...?
- What are central/peripheral characteristics of ...?
- What are the general/particular aspects of ...?
- How can ... be modified/reduced/augmented/combined with other factors?
- How is ... aligned with the company's values and mission?
- How can ... bring about a positive social and environmental impact?

Matthew May, a renowned innovation specialist and writer, posed an interesting question "What one word do we want to own in the minds of our customers, employees, and partners?" This expert observed that this simple question aims to provide companies with more clarity. This pundit observed that, in the case of Toyota, this car manufacturer can be linked to one important word "quality." Instead, Google can be related to the word "search" (Buchanan, 2014).

In some cases, it is important to ask questions whose answers seem obvious. These questions tend to prompt new insights into what is already known, which often challenge well-ingrained assumptions. Creative people also ask seemingly silly or non-sensical questions to stretch their minds towards non-traditional ways of thinking.

It is also useful to ask questions from the opposite perspective of a topic to generate new ideas. For example, if the topic is "good customer service," a creative question regarding this topic is "What is bad customer service?" In this example, the question can provide insights into how *not* to act in relation to customers. O'Connor (2001) observed that people can also ask questions about questions, for example, "What is the most valuable question we need to ask about ...?"

When posing the aforementioned questions, people should adopt an attitude of curiosity, flexibility, and open-mindedness. Not all questions enumerated previously will be applicable to every topic. Companies should choose the most suitable questions for each situation under analysis, leaving irrelevant questions aside.

There is another important point to highlight, which is the topic of concepts. Concepts are general ideas. Atkinson et al. (1981) observed that "concepts foster cognitive economy by dividing the world into manageable units" because "the world is full of so many different objects that if we treated each one as distinct, we would soon become overwhelmed."

In relation to this topic, De Bono (1998, 2013) suggests a very interesting question, which is "What is the main underlying concept of this?" This specialist observed that concepts are general and abstract "junctions in the mind" which help people develop different alternatives to put these concepts into action. Consequently, concepts cannot be implemented directly, but through specific ideas. This author also mentioned that in the case of fast food restaurants, the main underlying concepts for their business activities can be "good location," "savoury food," "fast customer service," and others. A company can ask relevant questions regarding each of these concepts. By analysing and clarifying these concepts, a company can devise different creative alternatives to put these very concepts into practice. For example, in relation to the concept of "savoury food," a company can consider different alternatives, such as pasta, barbecue, stew, and soup.

15.2 Non-Traditional Tools for Creativity

> Unless man can make new and original adaptations to his environment as rapidly as his science can change the environment, our culture will perish. Not only individual maladjustment and group tensions, but international annihilation will be the price we pay for a lack of creativity.
>
> **Carl Rogers**

15.2.1 Meditation

Even though some consider meditation a non-business practice, it has been used by several companies to develop creative ideas and concepts. For instance, Google provides its employees with meditation sessions; in its premises, this company has areas to do meditation. This company fosters the practice of meditation, as it positively contributes to its staff members' overall well-being. Yahoo! also offers areas specifically allocated for meditation, as well as free meditation classes at work, for its staff members to become calmer (Duffy, 2020).

Some studies have demonstrated that regular meditation enhances mental capabilities and reduces levels of stress, rendering the body more relaxed. People's inner wisdom is generally clouded by their continual mental ruminations. However, when people meditate, their minds become more tranquil, which allows these individuals access to their valuable inner knowledge. Research has also stated that a frequent brief meditation (around 13 minutes each session every day) in inexperienced meditators enhanced their memory, focus, mood, and their ability to control their emotional states when faced with stressful events (Basso et al., 2019).

There are other benefits of meditation, such as revitalisation of the body and decluttering of the mind. Meditation also helps people cast a fresh and light gaze into their inner world. People who meditate are more prone to achieve a state of balance, peacefulness, and overall well-being. All these benefits contribute to the generation of more creative ideas.

There are different ways to practise meditation. One well-known way to meditate is to sit in or lie down in a comfortable and quiet place. Then close the eyes, relax the body, and focus on the breathing, feeling the air on the upper lip when inhaling and exhaling. People can mentally scan their bodies to detect any tension and imagine that it flies away, like a passing cloud. The meditative process can be performed by repeating a mantra such as "Om," "love," or any other, but meditation can also be done silently.

As mentioned, when people meditate, they should continually focus on their breathing, by following each inhalation and exhalation. Whenever the meditator's mind goes astray or is distracted, this individual should gently bring it back to the original point of concentration (the mantra or the breathing, whichever is used). If thoughts or emotions come up during this process, people should observe them in a non-judgemental way and let them go. Some practical uses of meditation for business activities are:

■ During meditation, a person can pose questions like "What are alternative ways to improve our customer service activities?" to look for creative insights. Answers to these questions might come during the meditation process or afterwards. During meditation, a person is more prone to incubate innovative alternatives to solve an issue.

■ Meditation brings serenity which allows the analysis of challenging situations in a more focused manner; people who regularly meditate are less prone to worry and complain. Consequently, meditation is useful for business people who are continually challenged by troublesome issues.

■ A meditative state is optimal for the generation of creative thoughts, because it naturally squashes any defensive state (fight-freeze-flight) which people tend to adopt in a great part of work environments. As seen in this book, this reactive state is detrimental to the generation of creative insights.

Don Arney is a renowned inventor who developed Bambi Bucket, a collapsible light tool which has been used to fight fires in a myriad of countries. This inventor said that the regular practice of meditation (every day, twice a day) helped him become a better inventor. In that sense, this person observed that meditation has been helping him clear his mind and gather valuable insights which have been used for his inventions (Swift, 2023).

15.2.2 Development of Intuition

Neither a lofty degree of intelligence nor imagination nor both together go to the making of genius. Love, love, love, that is the soul of genius.

Wolfgang Amadeus Mozart

Intuition is information obtained from the subconscious mind. This information is received as insights, not stemming from the use of rational capabilities. These insights are obtained in the form of thoughts, images, sounds, or sensations. This information summarises complex ideas simply, and it can often be obtained through specific experiences, for example, meeting a person, engaging in a conversation, or reading a certain book.

People should avoid reacting negatively to these insights, but welcome them instead. Intuitive insights are creative and beyond people's habitual way of thinking. Many people tend to distrust these sudden and often unexpected insights, because they often cannot be rationally explained or justified. Sometimes these insights do not make sense immediately, which prompts people to discard them without giving them a second thought.

In business activities, intuitive insights can be very valuable, especially when there is limited time to make decisions. When people follow their intuition, their actions tend to be more graceful and effortless. In uncertain business scenarios, intuition can also provide valuable clues on how to proceed. Many entrepreneurs built their business empires based on their hunches.

The charismatic business leader, Richard Branson, observed that he has been relying on his intuitive insights on several occasions to make relevant business choices, to confide in certain people, and to calculate risks related to business endeavours. He wisely quipped "There are some things that can't be summed up in a statistic, and this is when you need to use a bit of intuition." In addition, he stated that, as people become more driven by data, they are not so much in contact with their intuition, and end up behaving conservatively. In his view, data analysis is relevant to take educated risks and become more efficient, but intuition is significant as well. When his airline Virgin Atlantic started up, he encountered various risks (e.g., the dominant position of another airline in the sector, selling his company Virgin Records). On that occasion, if he had considered only the main risks, he might not have gone ahead with this business endeavour. However, in the depth of his heart, he knew the sector could be disrupted by an airline like Virgin Atlantic, which would provide superior service to customers (Branson, 2019b).

There is another relevant point to highlight. There are different ways to be more receptive to intuitive insights, which will be thoroughly explained. The list below is only enunciative.

15.2.2.1 Contact with Nature

According to Li (2018), people have a relevant need to engage with natural places, known as biophilia. This need is the consequence of human beings originally evolving in natural environments. People who are in regular contact with nature are more prone to receive creative insights. The passive observation of natural landscapes has a soothing effect, which contributes to the generation of intuitive insights. When people are in contact with graceful, lush, and harmonious natural places, their mental chattering is lessened and their minds are more receptive to insightful ideas.

In natural places, people are not besieged by a myriad of jarring stimuli (car passing by, adverts in the street, etc.) so these individuals tend to be calmer and more at ease, which makes them more prone to receive intuitive insights. Research has shown that, when people are immersed in natural places while being temporarily disengaged from technology (mobile phones, etc.), their creative skills seem to be enhanced (Atchley et al., 2012).

Pukka Herbs is a company which offers organic herbal tea products and supplements. This company has developed a partnership with The Eden Project, an English ecologically oriented education charity. Pukka's mission is to connect people to the might and allurement of nature, through the company's herbal creations. The Eden Project's mission is to link people with nature, so that they comprehend their relationship with it, and contribute to actively shaping the future. This charity offers learning programmes at its site, and has the world's biggest rainforests in an enclosed space. As a consequence of this partnership, Pukka's employees are able to participate in groups in a series of activities, like walks in nature, as well as private visits to the indoor rainforests situated at The Eden Project. Throughout these activities, these employees can become connected to their hearts, and also spend some time reflecting on Pukka's values – both at a company and individual level (Balch, 2022; Pukka Herbs, 2022; The Eden Project, 2022).

15.2.2.2 Asking Questions

> People with high levels of personal mastery cannot afford to choose between reason and intuition or head and heart, any more than they would choose to walk on one leg or see with one eye.
>
> **Peter Senge**

People can ask themselves relevant questions to solve specific challenging situations. These questions can be asked before going to bed, when meditating, or when in a calm and relaxing state, for example, having a shower or taking a bath. Spontaneous intuitive insights into these questions tend to come up afterwards, in the moment least expected. As seen previously. the main idea of developing Uber, the famous ride-sharing app, stemmed from the question, "What if people were able to ask for a ride from their phones?" which was posed by two entrepreneurs when they were looking for a taxi on a cold night during an event they attended.

15.2.2.3 Delving into the Issue

For instance, a person wants an answer to a question regarding an issue: "What materials can I use for this new product?" Firstly, this person can obtain introductory information about this topic from different sources: books, magazines, websites, etc. This person can also enumerate possible solutions on a piece of paper. After dwelling on this topic for a while, it is best to give this issue a rest, which means not thinking about it. During that time, the answer to the question incubates "behind the scenes" and tends to arise effortlessly.

Entrepreneurs like Richard Branson, Thomas Edison, and James Dyson, who are discussed previously in this book, are good examples of entrepreneurs who are keen on delving into an issue thoroughly before developing creative insights. For instance, in the case of Richard Branson, before launching Virgin Atlantic, he analysed various issues thoroughly, such as the cost of chartering an aeroplane and the cost of purchasing a Boeing second-hand plane.

15.2.2.4 Being Calm

Intuitive insights are more likely to arise when a person is calm, emotionally and mentally, and physically relaxed. Activities like yoga, swimming, or walking in a quiet place are a few examples of activities which make people slow down and become more receptive to intuitive insights. For example, HBO, the series and movie company, offers free yoga classes to its employees (Duffy, 2020).

15.2.2.5 Being in the Present

Insights are more likely to pop out when people are fully focused on the now. When individuals are engrossed in the activity at hand, their minds are less prone to ponder the past (guilt, criticism, etc.) or the future (worry, fear, etc.). People who are centred on the now do not resist what is, but engage with it. These people can be fully aware of the current experience, which opens their minds to insightful information. Companies like Google, Aetna, and Intel offer mindfulness programmes to their employees, which makes staff members more thoughtful and focused on the tasks at hand, and also less stressed (Lau, 2020).

There is another topic to highlight. People are more prone to receive intuitive or inspirational insights when they adopt a humble and open-minded attitude. Intuitive insights can never be produced at will or forced; they come spontaneously. However, people can be more prone to receive these insights when they adopt a calm and receptive attitude. Other ways to generate intuitive insights are mentioned in Appendix G.

Klein (2003) observed that intuition is the way people translate their own experience into action; consequently, people become more intuitive regarding a field or discipline, as they gain more experience in it. This scholar stated that people with intuitive skills perceive relevant cues from a situation at hand, which leads them to see other cues. From this perspective, intuitive people can imagine future scenarios based on these patterns, which can help them decide how to act in specific circumstances.

In other words, intuitive people have the ability to make diligent and subtle distinctions, in a split second, without going through a lengthy analytical process. Klein (2003) observed that intuitive skills are useful for situations where there is time pressure, expert knowledge is needed, when there are unclear goals, and in dynamic (but not complex) conditions.

15.3 Selection of Creative Ideas

> Creativity in business is not different from all other expression of creativity: They begin with questions, not answers.
>
> **Amit Goswami**

The techniques explained in this chapter and the previous one can be used to generate a myriad of creative ideas regarding a topic. From the creative perspective, being prolific with ideas is always recommended. As seen previously, creative thinking and rational thinking complement each other; the former generates a wide range of options on a topic and the latter narrows down the options within those viable alternatives according to specific criteria.

The objective of this realistic screening of creative ideas is to minimise risks (financial, commercial, etc.) relating to their implementation. De Bono (2013) explains that companies that are sensitive to value can appreciate the value of an innovative idea. Consequently, ideas stemming from the use of creative techniques can be analysed from a rational perspective, considering different practical aspects, such as:

- Distinct benefits of the idea.
- Intelligibility and simplicity of the idea ("Is the idea easy to understand?").
- Main audiences benefiting from the innovative idea (customers, employees, etc.).
- Main audiences affected negatively by the implementation of the idea.
- Social and environmental impact of the implementation of the idea (e.g., benefits for the community and the environment).
- Time necessary to implement the idea.
- Potential co-operation needed from specific stakeholders (suppliers, intermediaries, etc.) to develop or implement the idea.
- Suitability of the idea for customers/employees/suppliers/intermediaries ("Will they welcome and embrace the idea?").
- Accessibility to technology (machinery, computers, etc.) to develop the idea.
- Availability of economic resources (funds, etc.) to implement the idea.
- Estimated risk/return related to the implementation of the idea.
- Compliance of the potential implementation of the idea with current legislation.
- Feasibility of technical aspects related to the idea (specifications, designs, etc.).
- Possibility of prototyping the idea.
- Possibility of enhancing or improving the idea.
- Alignment of the idea with well-known ideas or concepts.
- Potential replicability of the idea by others in the market.

- Possibility of legal protection of the idea (patents, etc.).
- Possibility of the application of the idea to various products, services, or processes.
- Alignment of the idea with the company's mission.
- Potential unforeseen consequences of implementing the idea (delays, staff training, etc.).

When analysing creative ideas, people can also ask if these ideas make others' lives easier, safer, more comfortable, and more pleasurable. Oftentimes, innovative ideas have a relevant positive impact on the world, to a small or big extent. Murray (n.d.) suggest that, when testing an idea, business people can ask questions like "How do we feel about this idea?" to obtain some intuitive insights on the topic.

From the sociological perspective, creative ideas are ultimately validated by the social context (also called the "field"). In the entrepreneurial world, this field is composed of customers, other companies, media, community, government, and experts, among others. Oftentimes, different departments of the company (finance, marketing, manufacturing, etc.) are consulted regarding ideas; in other cases, ideas are discussed with external specialists on the topic. Other stakeholders can be consulted by the company in order to test the viability of an idea: for instance, customers, business partners, suppliers, intermediaries, etc. The company can even consult the community, if the implementation of an idea has a significant social impact.

Hippo Roller is a social enterprise which discovered that, in many less developed countries (e.g., some African countries), women living in rural villages collect and transport water regularly for their basic needs (sanitation, irrigation, etc.). Oftentimes, this chore is carried out with buckets over very long distances, which brings about negative health conditions (e.g., spinal issues) and this work can take a lot of time, stopping these women and girls from going to work or school (Hippo Roller, 2022; MacMillan and Thompson, 2013).

This enterprise developed a barrel-shaped container – made of durable plastic – which holds 90 litres of water, and the roller has a handle on the axis of the barrel. The user is able to push or pull the barrel with great ease. This product saves significant time when used to collect and transport water. This is an example of a product which adds great value to customers (Hippo Roller, 2022; MacMillan and Thompson, 2013). In relation to this successful distinctive product, several aspects of its feasibility have duly been tested, among others (Hippo Roller, 2022):

- The product is simple to understand and use, and it provides tangible benefits (access to water in a more practical, quicker, and comfortable manner).
- The product has a positive social impact on relevant needs (hygiene, irrigation, etc.) of specific groups (rural communities of less develop areas).
- The product is maintenance-free, enduring, light-to-carry, and suitable for tough rural trails (gravel, stones, etc.). Various tests were carried out to improve its durability.
- The users can access this product in different ways. For instance, this company developed partnerships with the World Food Programme and other non-governmental organisations, which act as sponsors. This enterprise also undertakes fundraising campaigns and receives donations.

This innovative product has been successfully benefiting hundreds of thousands of users over 56 countries, providing them with a high-value way of accessing water. As an example, several Hippo Roller products were given to the St Augustine's Centre for Teenage Mothers, which is located in Lesotho. This event was economically supported by Rotary Club International (Hippo Roller, 2022).

15.4 Innovation and Creativity

Before you can think out of the box you have to start with a box.

Twyla Tharp

15.4.1 *Main Aspects of Innovation*

Innovation involves a natural tension between chaos and order. If too many new ideas are followed nothing ever gets finished. If too many old rules are followed nothing ever gets improved.

Max McKeown

Trott (2012) highlights that innovation is "the management of all activities involved in the process of idea generation, technology development, manufacturing and marketing of a new (or improved) product or manufacturing process or equipment." The idea of innovation can be extended to services, management activities, administrative processes, and also marketing activities.

Innovation means the practical application of fresh ideas by a company, including their commercial exploitation. Drucker (2007) observed that innovation is motivated by various factors, for example, changes in the industry and market, changes in demographic factors (employment levels, population growth, literacy levels, etc.), the upsurge of new knowledge, and changes in people's perception regarding a topic, among others. Below there are other interesting ideas about the innovation process:

- All products and services need improvement; if not, over time, they run the risk of becoming useless or obsolete. As seen in this book, the typewriter was a popular and in-demand product for many years; however, the last manufacturer of this product shut down several years ago.
- During the development of innovative products and services, the company should harness its unique talents and core capabilities. Every time that Google develops innovative products (Google Maps, Google Docs, etc.), this company harnesses the skills and capabilities of its talented team members, such as programming and information management.
- Innovation is not related to one specific department (marketing, R+D, etc.); it should always be part of a company's philosophy which pervades all its aims and activities. In relation to this, Ringel et al. (2021) observed that, on average, 31% of companies have weak collaboration bonds between their Research and Development departments and their marketing departments, which impacts negatively on the return of these companies' investment on their innovation projects. In order to prevent this from occurring, companies can develop cross-functional teams, which include representatives from different departments, who can work jointly on innovative projects. The main benefits of using cross-functional teams are: access to different types of specialised knowledge, better rapport, improved co-ordination of resources, higher productivity levels, and enhanced creativity (Buchanan and Huczynsky, 2019).
- The novel combination of knowledge possessed by an organisation and knowledge from external sources can prompt the generation of outstanding ideas. The generation of innovative ideas can come from different sources: contact with customers, employees' comments, other companies' activities, trends, publications, highlights in other sectors, etc. Any

information can be a valuable input for creative insights. Hilton, the renowned hotel chain, carefully assessed the changes in customer tastes (e.g., the increasing importance of companies like Airbnb). As a consequence, this company launched a new brand known as Tru by Hilton, which offers customers "get in and get out" accommodation services (rooms with bathroom of a more reduced size, free coffee instead of free breakfast, no front desk, no swimming pool). These rooms have more affordable prices as the result of lower operative expenses (Baeza et al., 2021).

■ Observing how customers relate to products and services can provide valuable insights for innovation purposes; the most relevant judge of the value of the outcomes of the innovation process is the market. Innovative companies tend to adopt an outstanding attitude of service towards customers; these organisations want to satisfy customers' needs in the most effective manner. Amazon developed various innovations (one-click-to-buy button, Amazon Prime, etc.) as a result of its continual engagement with its customers. In relation to the increasingly popular Prime service offered by Amazon (which includes quick delivery of specific products, access to online music and movies, etc.), the average Prime subscriber spends more than double the amount of money spent by the average non-Prime customer (Gildehaus et al., 2021).

■ The innovation process should harness a company's main strengths and capabilities and also consider the opportunities and threats in the business environment. The quest for new business opportunities and innovative ideas should never end or become stagnant; innovation routines and habits should be continually fostered all over the company. Any opportunity to solve a relevant problem in a better way is a starting point for innovation; problems are opportunities (in disguise) for innovation. Play-Doh, a well-known moulding product which most children know very well, is an interesting example of a company that harnessed new business opportunities. Its inventor originally presented this product as a non-toxic, non-staining cleaning product for wallpapers. A teacher tested this product with children who enthusiastically played with it and shaped it in various ways. After this realisation, the company started selling this product to schools as a modelling compound. In simple words, the product was re-positioned as an educational toy. Over time, this product was re-worked, for example, some changes in its packaging (cans, plastic tubes, etc.). Over the years, this product became increasingly popular, not only locally but also internationally (Kindy, 2019; Marsh, 2022).

■ Perceiving flaws in things that apparently work well can be a very important source of innovative ideas; therefore, companies should always monitor what seems to work in order to introduce further improvements. Dominant ways of doing things and ingrained conventions must always be challenged, questioned, and rebelled against during the innovation process. Assumptions about what is preferred by the market as innovation ("Customer will never like this type of product") should be avoided; market preferences must be carefully researched and fully tested. In the past, there was a prevalent assumption in the accommodation sector which stated that companies in that industry needed to own their premises. There was another assumption in the passenger transport sector which stated that companies in that industry needed to own their vehicles. Companies like Airbnb (the global accommodation online platform) and Uber (the passenger transport app) successfully challenged these ingrained assumptions in their sectors.

■ A company should never start with the innovation process when its products become commoditised or copied by others; the company should start this process much earlier. In the car manufacturing sector, companies are continually launching new models of their products (e.g., vehicles which have more streamlined design, enhanced performance, etc.).

- Forsaking old ideas gives place to the unfolding of new ideas; ideas which are not fruitful at present can later become productive, reformulated, or combined with other ideas. In the previous chapter, it was mentioned that Walt Disney used and combined ideas from different sources to develop his entertainment park.
- The first vision of a new product or service is not always crystal-clear; oftentimes, ideas develop gradually over time and consequently, patience and determination are key factors in innovation. As seen previously in this book, YouTube, the most popular video platform started as a dating website where users could upload videos of themselves. This original idea failed and the founders re-developed the platform, by making the uploading process of any video easy for anyone, which proved to be extremely successful.
- Any feedback from customers (requests for clarification, complaints, etc.) in any of their interactions with a company is a valuable input for further innovation regarding its products and services; thus, customers can actually be considered to be co-creators. Customers can be considered in any of the stages of the innovation process (development of a product according to their needs, launching a new product, etc.); customers can be a relevant factor to test the commercial feasibility of a new product as well. A company like Lego, the Danish toy company, develops new products taking into account creative insights from its customers. To that effect, customers can submit their proposals for innovative Lego models to a community online, which has millions of members. In that community, each project proposed by a customer is voted on by the other members. If the proposal receives the support from 10,000 members, this project is assessed by Lego's review board. If a project is chosen as a new Lego set, the person who proposed this new product is recognised as its legitimate creator and will receive royalty payments on the sales of the product. For instance, a journalist proposed "Women of NASA" Lego idea and this innovative project obtained the necessary votes from other supporters. As a consequence, Lego decided to manufacture this product, and it ended becoming a best-selling item (Blythe, 2012; Qian, 2020).
- Potential economic outcomes stemming from the innovation process are often difficult to quantify; this should not prevent a company from adopting a proactive innovative approach. Companies that are extremely risk-averse are prone to prevent themselves from innovating; innovation implies risk and uncertainty, and potential rewards are not easily measurable. Innovative companies tend to face two types of uncertainty: uncertainty about the final outcome of their innovation process ("Will this idea end up working out successfully?"), and uncertainty about specific ways to achieve a desired result ("How can we achieve this specific outcome successfully?"). There is always uncertainty and unpredictability regarding the results of the innovation process. Therefore, adaptiveness and open-mindedness are needed throughout the process. The following is an example of a company's innovation which did not work out successfully. Evian is a company with a few centuries of history in the mineral water sector. Some decades ago, this company attempted to enter another industry: the clothes sector. In order to do so, this company launched the Water Bra, which was a bra designed to cool down the breast area during hot weather. This innovative bra had pads with mineral water. In addition, this bra had a filter funnel which could be used to top off the water, according to the woman's preferences. This product even featured a pouch, to hold a small water bottle. However, this product did not succeed, and its production was terminated a short time after being introduced into the marketplace (Menges and Frater, 2021).
- A company's innovation process should be flexible due to its intrinsic uncertainty, so tight deadlines should be avoided. Companies should always allocate sufficient time and resources for innovation; the innovation process tends to take more time and resources than estimated;

delays or unforeseen issues (e.g., lack of adequate technology) often hinder the process. As seen previously, James Dyson developed countless prototypes over a very extensive period of time, until he eventually developed a successful bagless vacuum cleaner.

■ Many brilliant ideas are generated in response to employees' or customers' dissatisfaction; all products and services should be improved on a regular basis, even the ones that serve customers effectively. As seen previously, the idea of starting up Virgin Atlantic originated out of the dissatisfaction Richard Branson experienced as a customer, when the plane that was meant to take him to his destination was grounded. This dissatisfactory situation drove this renowned business leader to start up his own airline, Virgin Atlantic, in order to offer superior customer service.

■ Current industrial sectors are never still; they are always dynamic and coexist with emerging and declining sectors. A company should aim to go beyond the limitations of the sector it belongs to, by reshaping that sector, creatively combining elements from different sectors, or even creating a new sector. As seen previously, the accommodation sector and the passenger transport sector have been reshaped by the upsurge of companies like Airbnb and Uber, respectively.

■ The innovation process should not be handled in an extremely serious and formal manner; a playful and exploratory attitude should preferably be adopted. As seen previously, Wright brothers were adopting a playful attitude when experimenting with the development of the first aeroplane.

■ All innovative products and services impact on the organisation and its environment; the development of innovative products and services should always consider the potential ethical implications for the company's stakeholders ("Can this innovation potentially bring about a negative impact on specific stakeholders?"). Some innovative products and services can also benefit other stakeholders besides customers (e.g., communities); these innovations must always be preferred over the rest. The innovative product developed by Hippo Roller, which is a big barrel-shaped plastic container with a handle is a valuable example of an item which adds great value to members of rural communities where water is scarce. As discussed previously, a very important benefit brought about by this innovative product is that people in those areas can access water in a quicker and easier manner.

■ Innovation not only implies the development of non-traditional ideas, but also the testing of these ideas from a commercial, technical, and financial perspective. As previously seen the innovative product developed by Hippo Roller was tested from different perspectives (commercial, technical, etc.).

■ Some innovations are disruptive or radical (they create a new market); some instead are a modification or natural progression of what already exists (they serve current markets). An innovative product does not always have to be disruptive or ground-breaking; any change, whether slight or significant, that adds more value to customers can be considered innovative. For example, there are some disruptive technological products like the 3D printer. This technology is used by some companies to build houses in a very expeditious, safe, waste-saving, and economical manner. The walls and other structures of the buildings are printed, layer by layer, with a huge 3D printer which is loaded with a special construction material, and uses information from models. The German company Peri uses 3D printing technology for residential construction, as well as individual prefabricated parts (Peri, 2023; The B1M, 2020).

■ Some outcomes from the innovation process can be applied to more than one product and service; an innovative product or service can also stack up the characteristics of various current successful products and services. For example, 3D printing technology, which was previously discussed, can be used for various purposes, like developing tools, prototypes and components for the aerospace sector, tools and spare parts for the automotive sector, and dental appliances and implants for the dental and medical sector, among others. Companies like Ford Motor Company and Porsche are a few examples of organisations which are already using 3D printing technology (AMFG, 2023).

■ There is no limit to the improvement of any product or services; creative development is unbounded. However, excessive formalities or rigid control procedures within an organisation could limit innovation. As seen previously, companies like Netflix, the popular streaming and movie producer company, eliminated all unnecessary rules in its workplace to foster more creativity and innovation among its staff members.

■ No innovation is an island, but directly or indirectly related to a previous series of innovations developed by the organisation, or other companies and individuals. Failed attempts during the innovation process can become stepping stones to successful tries; companies can always learn from unsuccessful products, services, processes, and business models. As seen in the case of James Dyson, each of his thousands of failed attempts got this insightful entrepreneur much closer to the definite version of the bagless vacuum cleaner. As seen previously, Thomas Edison, in his process of developing the electric bulb, tested a myriad of types of material for the bulb filament until finding the most adequate material.

■ All innovative products or services should have some points of contact with the products they replace; customers must identify common traits between old products and new ones, even in the case of radically innovative products. An example is the computer which uses a keyboard which resembles the one used in a product which preceded it: the typewriter.

According to Lafley and Charan (2008), innovation is the process of converting new ideas into economic results (revenues and profits), which always entails being customer-focused. These authors stated that innovation is also a social process which implies getting on board with staff from different departments and areas, who should share their learning, challenges, and ideas. This perspective implies fostering open communication among the different areas and departments of a company. According to McKeown (2014), all innovative ideas should also take into consideration relevant habits and ingrained traditions, which can represent relevant hindrances to the acceptance of non-traditional ideas.

The following is a very interesting example of innovation. Unilever is a renowned company that sells various consumer products. In order to develop more environmentally friendly detergents, this company has partnered with one of its main suppliers, Novozyme, which supplies enzymes to this organisation. In a collaborative way, these two companies contributed with their own specific technical knowledge and developed two enzyme innovations, which made the product perform more effectively and become more energy-saving, as well as decrease carbon dioxide emissions (Gutierrez et al., 2020).

There is another important topic to discuss. Dr Coelho stated that creative destruction implies economic evolution by eliminating the old and welcoming the new. For example, at present, ice is a very popular product used in different ways (keeping food fresh, cooling down beverage, etc.) In the faraway past, this product was not very accessible. This scholar observed that, in the sixteenth century, prosperous people used to cut ice from lakes and kept it in ice houses for their personal use. In the nineteenth century, the commercial ice trade started; organisations were producing ice at a big scale, but it was only affordable by the wealthy (Coelho, 2014).

This scholar observed that, in 1940, there were about 2,500 ice producers in America with around 30,000 workers. In the 1950s, the automatic ice maker was invented. Nowadays, most of the ice is produced by ice makers privately owned by people. This specialist stated that, at present, there are approximately 500 commercial ice producers with about 7,000 workers. Thousands of jobs were destroyed with the development of the personal maker, but this creation also made the ice widely accessible (Coelho, 2014).

15.5 Tips for Companies to Enhance Their Creative Resources

Great minds discuss ideas; average minds discuss events; small minds discuss people.

Eleanor Roosevelt

In organisations, creativity and innovation can be fostered not only to resolve problems, but also to exploit untapped opportunities. Managers should continually remind employees that creative thinking and experimentation is not only legitimate, but greatly welcomed. Management should encourage and reinforce creative behaviour in their staff. In order for the company to thrive, all staff members should get involved in creative activities on a regular basis.

When possible, all company departments (marketing, administrative, manufacturing, etc.) should directly or indirectly contribute with their insights to the innovation process. As seen previously, all sources of information, internal or external, are potential drivers to prompt innovation activities. However, chance and serendipity can also become relevant factors in the innovation process.

Sometimes the innovation process can be developed in partnership with other organisations, which provide the valuable input for the innovation process. Acme Whistles is a company based in Birmingham, UK, which manufactures dozens of original models of whistles (for pets, police force, sports, etc.). For its innovation process, this company works with the University of Birmingham because of the expertise of this institution's staff members and its high-quality labs (Acme Whistles, 2022).

As explained previously, all non-traditional ideas should be tested regarding their usefulness and their operative and practical aspects. Companies can purposefully take specific actions to increase innovation in their organisations. Some actions to be considered by companies are shown below.

15.5.1 Declaration of Innovation

Sloane (2007) suggested that all companies should write their own declaration of innovation. According to this author, this declaration should include the reasons for innovation (why), the areas to innovate (what), and the request that employees commit to a continuous innovation process. Additionally, this author mentioned that this statement can include specific resources to be allocated for innovation, aspects related to management and monitoring of the innovation process, the commitment to looking for ideas from various sources, and the declaration of continuous involvement in this process. This statement should be made public to all the company's employees, who should be reminded of it on a continuous basis.

Procter & Gamble, the well-known company which offers various products (home care, baby care, beauty, etc.), includes a declaration of innovation on its website. This declaration of innovation includes the reason for innovation (being inspired by people's needs and desires, seeking solutions to problematic issues, etc.), main areas for innovation (fabric care, beauty care, grooming, etc.) and the main resources allocated to innovation (the company's own team of world-class experts, partnerships with inventors and other innovators, etc.). This declaration also mentions some external sources used for the company's innovations (inventors, entrepreneurs, speakers, etc.) and internal sources (the company's scientists and designers). This declaration of innovation also includes the company's management and monitoring aspects of innovations. In relation to this, this company ensures its innovations meet the sector's benchmarks, high safety standards, legal requirement, and sustainable aspects (PG, 2023).

15.5.2 *Creative Time and Spaces*

All employees should have specific time compulsorily blocked off to generate new ideas for the company, as part of their work time. This is important because many employees avoid trying to develop creative ideas because of their hectic and busy schedules. For example, at 3M, a company previously analysed in this book, there is the 15% rule: the company's employees are entitled to use 15% of their time at work to focus on explorative scribbling or projects which can potentially bring about innovative products (Black, 2016).

Organisations should also have designated rooms, known as "safe environments" for employees to perform creative activities. Thompson (1992) suggested the development of bright workplaces (with incandescent or natural lighting), whose walls show the company's vision and mission to foster innovation. This author also suggested playing calming baroque or classical songs as background music in the workplace because this type of music stimulates creativity.

The workplace can have furniture which encourages open interaction between employees, which can help generate collective ideas. Wiseman (2013) observed that the use of natural plants in the workplace also prompts people to be more creative. Whiteboards can be stuck on the walls and can be used if intuitive insights arise. A research study stated that rooms with high ceilings prompt people to develop abstract and creative thinking (Meyers-Levy and Zhu, 2007).

An organisation like Refinery 29, which is a thriving media organisation centred on female youngsters, holds brainstorming sessions on a regular basis. These meetings are held in a place with peach walls. In these sessions, participants are empowered to chat in an inclusive but unstructured way. In these meetings, attendees eat peach-flavoured candies and drink rose wine. The place is set up in this way, in order to trigger creative insights (Keswin, 2019).

There is another good example to pinpoint. SnackNation is a company which offers healthy snack for offices. This company has set up the so-called Crush Cubes at its premises. These are small soundproof pods, which allow staff members to perform tasks without being distracted. Oftentimes, employees use these pods for developing creative ideas, for example, through brainstorming (Murphy, 2022).

15.5.3 *Creative Meetings*

The company should organise frequent brainstorming sessions, within each department. These meetings should last around 15 minutes and each participant should be able to freely and openly express their ideas on a common topic. Participants of these meetings should avoid using phrases that reject new ideas, such as "It is not practical," "It seems too difficult," and other similar sentences. There should be a person designated to jot down all the ideas suggested by the participants. These meetings could include members from other departments. The ideas obtained in these meetings should be analysed later in order to test their feasibility (financial, technical, commercial, etc.).

There are two examples of companies which organise creative meetings. The first example is about a company previously mentioned, Acme Whistles. For the development of the company's new models of whistles, staff members who work for each of its departments are engaged (Acme Whistles, 2022). As seen in this book, Spotify, the renowned streaming company, has a hack week, which is a period of time when employees can reflect on new ideas (analysis of innovative products, discussion of potential betterment of processes, etc.) and engage with people from other departments to share, reflect, and discuss these ideas (Sundén, 2013).

15.5.4 Fun Activities

As seen previously, research has shown that activities which prompt people to experience positive emotional states help them harness their creative and intuitive capabilities more effectively. Positive emotional experiences (e.g., joy, relaxation) are prevalent in play. Research suggests that the engagement of employees in playful activities transitorily suspends obligations and conventions which are so prevalent in some workplaces. These playful activities bolster creativity, as participants can bring about uncommon mental associations and propose diverse ideas (Mainemelis and Ronson, 2006).

For instance, the workplace can be equipped with arcade and board games to be used during break time. Besides this, the company should organise social fun events (such as staff dinners, sports competitions, and retreats). In this type of events, staff members are more prone to "let their hair down" and forsake the fight-freeze-flight mode, which is common in most work environments. By being relaxed and at ease, employees' creative skills are naturally enhanced. As seen previously in Chapter 10, these events are revitalising and re-energising; they empower employees to later go back to work and adopt a fresher approach on challenging work issues, which also impacts positively on productivity levels.

Southwest Airlines is a company which encourages fun and celebration, both in good times and in challenging ones. In this organisation, employees are encouraged to participate in various events, such as Chili Cookoffs, Spirit Parties, as well as the so-called Southwest Rallies (Southwest Air, 2023).

15.5.5 Avoiding Groupthink

In some companies, groups are formed and their members are unwilling to stand out with their own opinions; these individuals tend to conform to the prevalent views within their own groups. Any suggestions which can potentially defy these shared views are discouraged. This is known as groupthink; sometimes, it can be detrimental to business activities. Consequently, in any group, dissent should be encouraged and alternative perspectives on topics welcomed. People outside the group should also be able to give their alternative views on specific issues; external consultants or advisors can also provide disruptive opinions on relevant topics. In order to avoid groupthink, McKenna (2012a) suggested dividing a group into different subgroups, which will each analyse different aspects of the same topic. Scoular (2011) suggests that some of the participants in a group can adopt a critical view on a topic, by playing "devil's advocate." These people can often challenge others' ingrained beliefs, and offer them some fresh perspectives on an issue.

An example of groupthink was seen in Swissair, the national Swiss airline. In the past, this airline was very profitable and financially sound. This company was once such a financially thriving airline, that it was known as the "flying bank." Nevertheless, a short time before this airline filed for bankruptcy, this company had decreased the number of its board members, which prompted this organisation to lose a great part of its managerial expertise and dissenting views. The members who remained in the board had similar views, assumptions, and backgrounds, which made it more difficult for them to detect detrimental choices. This company went bankrupt in 2002 (Sherman, 2021; Wooll, 2022).

15.5.6 Records of Brilliant Ideas

Companies should keep collective records of creative ideas, including those whose implementation is not immediate or temporarily not suitable. All employees should contribute to these records. These records can include ideas stemming from the use of creative techniques, including those ideas that did not pass the feasibility test (e.g., ideas which are not economically viable). These ideas can also come from other sources, such as suppliers, customers, intermediaries, competitors, organisations from other sectors, and the community. These attractive ideas can come from other non-traditional sources, such as movies, magazines, songs, books, and the cultural environment. These brilliant ideas can also come from different disciplines, such as physics, philosophy, and history. These records are useful because the company can recombine, adapt, simplify, or augment these ideas to apply them to the company's issues. These records could include different categories of topics, and creative ideas can appear in more than one category. The access to these records should be open to all employees. There is specific software in the marketplace to keep records of creative ideas and projects.

An example of the use of this tool is the Cisco Community online. Cisco is one of the most renowned companies specialising in digital communication. This company developed this online community. In order to become community members, people can register and engage with others, for example, by posting questions and answers. This community is a self-service, collaborative, and technical environment, where members can find answers to various relevant issues. In this online community, members can also find various connectivity tools, reviews on products, how to troubleshoot issues, and relevant events to consider, among other aspects. In this community, members can also find videos, blogs, and forums to access and share relevant technical knowledge. This community has a myriad of members and discussions on various topics (Community Cisco, 2023). This group provides the company's customers with the so-called crowd service, where community members help each other (Van Belleghem, 2015).

15.5.7 Idea Incubators and Crowdsourcing

These are projects or areas inside the company whose main objective is the development of new ideas. In these incubators, people can freely and openly work on new perspectives or different issues, and develop innovative ideas in a prolific and unhampered manner. These incubators represent a safe haven where unconventional or non-traditional ideas are developed and welcomed. These incubators can even thoroughly explore areas which seemingly work well for the organisation.

Another important tool is crowdsourcing. Starbucks, the renowned coffee shop chain, uses crowdsourcing – the collection of online insights from its audiences. Some years ago, the company introduced My Starbucks Idea, an online platform where customers made suggestions, voted, and discussed some insights. The company collected and analysed thousands of ideas, and some of them were implemented, for instance, mobile payment for Drive-Thru stores, cake pop treats, and new flavours (Hazelnut Macchiato, Mocha Coconut Frappuccino, etc.), among others. The platform was later shut down, but nowadays customers can still provide Starbucks with suggestions through social media, or through the company's webpage (Livescault, 2022; Skonord, 2021).

15.5.8 Rewarding Creativity

The company should set organisational policies that stimulate the generation of new ideas by its employees. To that effect, a company should provide employees with specific incentives for the development of creative perspectives. These incentives could be economic (additional compensation, bonus, etc.) or non-economic (free transport tickets, additional annual leave, etc.). There could also be regular contests where members of the work team can propose their innovative approaches and be awarded valuable prizes. The generation of creative ideas should not be limited to specific departments (e.g., marketing or research and development), but affect the whole organisation.

Every year, the Tata group, the renowned conglomerate that offers products from different sectors (car, drinks, etc.), gives the InnoVista awards to acknowledge and appreciate innovations within the various companies in the group. Through this award, the Tata group fosters a corporate culture of innovation and collaboration, encouraging teams to resolve relevant issues and problems creatively. Some examples of innovations that obtained this award are the multi-function autonomous mobile robot, and Zero Carbon Logistics, among others. This award has different categories, such as Implemented Innovations, Piloted Technologies, Design Honour, Sustainable Impact Innovations, and Dare to Try. The last category is to acknowledge and appreciate those innovations that did not attain the desired results through the innovation process (Tata InnoVista, 2023).

There is another point to highlight. Sometimes, when a company rewards creative ideas from others (e.g., employees), this can foster creative behaviour. In relation to this topic, there was research conducted on a utility company. In that study, this company set up a suggestion box, but the number of creative ideas proposed by staff members was very small. Then, this company set up a system of monetary rewards to be given to those ideas which were rated to be precise and have potential benefits. After implementing this reward system, the number of creative ideas suggested by employees increased exponentially, and some of these ideas were implemented by the company on a practical level (Epstein and Laptoski, 1999).

15.5.9 A More Loving Environment

Maturana and Bunnel (1998) observed that love enhances people's creative capabilities and also expands their intelligence. When the workplace is warm, and people treat each other in a more caring, kind, and respectful manner, and they feel safe and appreciated, these people are less prone to adopt the fight-freeze-flight mode which temporarily impairs all thinking skills, including creative ones. The main characteristics of a warm workplace have been explained previously in Chapter 10. In that chapter, several examples of organisations with warm, kind, supportive workplaces were analysed.

15.5.10 Creative Brief

This tool has been suggested by Udall and Turner (2008). This a one- or two-page report, which includes the following elements: a question prompting an insightful analysis regarding a specific topic, the motives as to why this question is strategically relevant, the aim and objectives of the activities to be performed in relation to this question, the desired results and what they should look like, the main deadlines and timelines for the process, and support and resources available. This brief can prompt the company's employees to generate innovative ideas.

15.5.11 Open Feedback

Companies can adopt an open attitude to criticism from staff. To that effect, companies should welcome any type of comments from its personnel, both positive and negative ones. For instance, the company can set a suggestion box in order to encourage employees to provide anonymous suggestions. Cornelissen (2017) observed that this tool opens up the company's internal communication channels. Some know-it-all managers are very reluctant to use this tool, because they are afraid of any criticism from employees. Companies should encourage feedback from both internal and external stakeholders.

This feedback provides the company with valuable insights that are stepping stones to develop non-traditional approaches: new processes, new products and services, new business models, new goals, etc. As seen previously in this book, Netflix, the movie producer and streaming company, and Pixar, the animation company, foster the exchange of open, continuous, and constructive feedback at work. As discussed, in the case of Uber, passengers can use the app to leave their feedback on their rides.

15.5.12 Embedding Creative Techniques during Work Time

It should be a policy to train employees in the use of different creative techniques, which have been described in this book. These training events could be workshops, seminars, or conferences. In these events, trainers should explain practical tools for employees to apply to real-life scenarios. When employees perform their work activities, they should be granted a minimum "leeway" for them to explore creative perspectives. Medium- or long-term projects should also include a percentage of the work time to be devoted to the generation and testing of new alternatives. As seen in this book, companies like Dell, the computer giant, provides its in-house manufacturing team members with creativity training to sharpen their personal capabilities.

15.5.13 Opportunities Audit

When a company discovers a valuable opportunity, this could be a relevant starting point to develop creative ideas to harness this opportunity. However, most organisations do not allocate any time to discover and explore opportunities because they are focused on urgent tasks (paying the bills, chasing suppliers, etc.). De Bono (1978) suggests that companies should formally implement a process to find new opportunities. This author observed that the opportunities detected can be listed in a report (which includes a description of the opportunities, benefits, potential actions to take, resources and assistance needed, sticking points, and timing).

This author also observed that there could be an Opportunity Manager who facilitates and co-ordinates the tasks of the Opportunity Team. This independent team is in charge of looking for opportunities, using inputs within the company and outside it. This team will be in contact with other areas of the organisation. From this perspective, there could also be an opportunity Task Force, which will deal practically with the opportunities discovered by the Opportunity Team, using specific resources allocated for that purpose.

15.5.14 Continuous Improvement Quality

Companies should monitor all their activities, products, and services on a continuous basis in order to assess their potential for improvement. All areas of the company should be evaluated, not only those which do not work well. When carrying out this assessment, all assumptions on how things "are" and "must be" should be left aside temporarily. The company should adopt an approach of possibility, exploration, and openness. This perspective is based on the principle that everything is perfectible and can be improved over time.

Toyota, the prestigious car manufacturer uses Kaizen as one of its core principles for its production system. The meaning of Kaizen is continuous improvement; this principle allows this company to reach the highest quality, eliminate waste, and increase efficiency regarding equipment and work procedures. In its production system, this company fosters a humanised work environment which empowers employees to look for areas to improve in order to make practical suggestions. From this perspective, this company reconsiders every single process, from the ground up, to increase its efficiency (McIvor, 2022; Toyota, 2013).

15.5.15 Encouraging Collective Creative Activities

As seen previously, some important collective activities are brainstorming meetings. However, research has concluded that virtual meetings (e.g., via Zoom) are prone to generate fewer creative insights – as compared with in-person meetings – because attendees are focused on a screen during those exchanges, which prompts their cognitive focus to become much narrower (Brucks and Levav, 2022) Nonetheless, in virtual gatherings, participants seem to be more capable of choosing the most promising idea, as compared with in-person meetings in real life (Stokel-Walker, 2022).

There is another important point to highlight. Collective creation can also be attained through the development of partnerships with varying institutions, such as universities, research centres, other companies, associations, and government organisations. This type of alliance with creative aims represents a fertile environment for the generation of insightful and fresh ideas.

For instance, Siemens, the giant technology company with focus on various sectors (digital industries, smart infrastructure, mobility, etc.), developed a partnership with Nvidia, which specialises in Artificial Intelligence (AI) and graphics. The main objective of this partnership is to jointly develop the Industrial Metaverse, which is a visually rich, immersive, virtual space that allows companies to employ physics-based and photorealistic digital twins, and interact and cooperate with one another, in order to sort out various challenges (developing industrial innovations, etc.) (Siemens, 2022).

15.5.16 Creativity Audit

Kao (1996) observed that companies can audit some indicators regarding their creativity on a regular basis. This author suggest that companies ask questions like "What are the main creative resources possessed by our organisation?", "How many creative projects have come into fruition?", "What were the circumstances that prompted our company to undertake creative projects?", "What are the current hindrances to our creativity?", "How can our company emulate outstanding creative organisations?", "Who are the most creative staff members in our organisation?", and "What systems are in place to generate, store, and apply creative ideas?", among others.

15.5.17 Innovation Goals

A company can set specific and realistic objectives regarding its innovation process. For example, an organisation can set a goal of developing three new products or services per year. By clearly setting specific and clear goals, staff members are naturally prompted to reflect on these very objectives, behave in a more creative manner, and adopt a more experimental attitude when analysing non-traditional alternatives (Ekval, 1999). The progress of attainment of these goals should be monitored on a continuous basis. The topic of goals is explained more thoroughly in Appendix G.

Acme Whistles sets the objective of developing a specific number of new products over a period of time. This company has had more than a century and a half of continually introducing innovative products. For instance, for over 150 years, an innovative whistle has been developed and patented by this company, at least once per decade. Its current range is about 80+ products, with various applications like sports, dog training, policing, locomotive, and others (Acme Whistles, 2022; Blythe, 2012).

15.5.18 Attributes Assessment

McGrath and MacMillan (2005) recommend a valuable tool to continually improve products and services. These authors suggest that a company should map the main attributes of its products and services using classifications like satisfiers, neutral attributes, and dissatisfiers. From this perspective, satisfiers are positive attributes which prompt customers to experience positive emotions, neutral attributes make customers behave nonchalantly, and dissatisfiers are negative attributes which prompt customers to experience negative emotions. Companies should hold regular meetings to brainstorm ways to increase the satisfiers for their products, and reduce or eliminate their neutral factors and dissatisfiers. In a similar vein, Kim and Mauborgne (2015) observed that a company can analyse a product or service offered by companies in the sector, and identify elements which can be eliminated, those which can be reduced, factors which can be increased, and elements which can be created.

There is an interesting example regarding this topic. As seen previously in this book, when James Dyson started developing a new model of vacuum cleaner, this entrepreneur considered that the non-reusable bags, which all vacuum cleaners used, were a dissatisfier. Therefore, this entrepreneur developed a bagless vacuum cleaner, which became very popular in the marketplace. There is another interesting example. As seen previously in this book, when Google developed its first search engine, this company considered that the multiple weblinks, which clogged the other search engines, were a dissatisfier. Consequently, this company opted for developing a slim, clutter-free search engine, which became the most popular engine worldwide.

15.5.19 Premortem Assessment

This tool was suggested by Klein (2003). This technique consists of imagining the worst result for a project, product, or activity. From this failure, the company should thoroughly visualise and analyse the sequence of factors and actions bringing about that negative outcome. The purpose of this analysis is to discover what would have been done wrongly if this negative result is obtained, and how actions could have been improved; a list can be made with the potential causes of the failure. This technique to anticipate negative scenarios was originally used by the ancient Stoics (who called it *premeditatio malorum*, or "pre-vision of evils"). Stoics used to mentally rehearse or predict things which could go wrong regarding specific situations by asking specific questions (such as "What if this goes wrong?") and then imagining the actions to take. Research has shown the use of this tool can help companies detect potential challenges affecting their endeavours in order to take effective action, in case they occur. This tool can also help companies take preventive action to avoid the potential causes of failure, when possible. Lastly, the use this tool also significantly decreases people's overconfidence when they assess business projects (Klein et al., 2010).

Companies like Paypal, the online payments company, uses the premortem assessment. For instance, in this company, an engineer develops a one-page report which includes the details of an unsolved problem, the reasons why this issue should be sorted out, the suggested solution to that problem, and any other relevant aspect. Then, colleagues in this engineer's team review this report and assess its potential shortcomings, while stating various ways this project could go wrong. This premortem assessment prompts the engineer to reshape the original report to address all the potential issues encountered by colleagues in the team (Thapar, 2021).

Questions for Self-Reflection

- Which questions can help me perform more creative business activities?
- Which non-traditional tools can help me become more creative?
- How does our company deal with innovation?
- How can a more creative work environment be developed?

APPENDICES

Appendix A: Stress and Business Activities

When we overwork, we under-enjoy

Susan Jeffers

Looker and Gregson (2010) state that stress is a "mismatch between perceived demands and perceived ability to cope," which implies that a person has too many demands or too few resources to deal with those demands. Sometimes, stress can also stem from few demands, even though this is less common. In other words, stress is a person's defensive response to a perceived threat from the environment.

Stressed people appraise that they will not be capable of dealing with the stress factors effectively. Csikszentmihalyi (2002, 2003) states that workers are more prone to become stressed when the level of work required from them is highly challenging as compared with their skills. From the psychological perspective, stressful events tend to be more impactful when they are uncontrollable or unpredictable.

Sometimes, people experience anticipatory stress, which means that they feel stressed before going through a potentially stressful event (Albretcht, 1979). For example, an employee has to deliver a training course to colleagues at work in two weeks' time. At present, this employee feels that she will not be confident or knowledgeable enough at this event, and starts feeling stressed in anticipation.

Stress usually brings about physical symptoms (tension, fast heartbeats, etc.), emotional states (anger, fear, etc.), thoughts (worries, ruminations, etc.), and behaviour (avoidance, inaction, self-medication, etc.). These aspects interact with each other in a negative cycle. Stress can also be contributory to the development of different health conditions, such as backache, lowered immunity, depression, headaches, and heart attacks.

Some say that a reasonable amount of stress improves achievement, but it is difficult to determine what is "reasonable." At first, when people feel stressed, they might feel more energised, but after a while, they become depleted, out-of-control, and fretful. The mind–body system is only built for arousal for a short time.

Perceived stressors trigger people's fight-freeze-flight response, which lowers their discerning and creative skills, bringing about temporary cognitive impairment. In this reactive mode, the person's focus is narrowed down to the threatening factor. If this alarm system is activated for a period of time long enough, the body is not allowed to recover properly.

Most business environments are intrinsically stressful because of multiple factors: multitasking, tight deadlines, scarcity of resources, absence of support, demanding requirements, unrealistic

DOI: 10.4324/9781003372684-21

objectives, etc. For example, at work, some common stressors are a lack of autonomy, countless bureaucratic procedures, technological fast-paced change, low pay, role ambiguity, shift work, unfair treatment, unfamiliar tasks, lack of feedback and support, insufficient skills, authoritarian commands, confusing goals, boredom, bullying, overworking, unhealthy work-life balance, lack of planning, low-quality communication, lack of recognition, etc. Some relevant changes (change of job, promotion and demotion, downsizing, mergers and acquisitions, etc.) can also represent stress factors. These stressful factors often bring about higher absenteeism and demotivation, lower productivity, as well as inefficiency.

In the business environment, stress also brings about other negative outcomes, such as avoidance of challenging tasks, harsh arguments, workaholic attitude, accidents, foggy thoughts, irrational decisions, low creativity, lack of co-operation, and slow judgement. Bevelin (2017) observed that stressed people tend to be more suggestible than unstressed ones. Stress also has a significant impact on other areas, such as family and health. In all cases, stress always indicates that some necessary changes must be made. If stress is no correctly managed or it extends in time, it can bring about burnout where people experience apathy, cynicism, despair, or disengagement at work and other areas of their lives (McIntosh et al., 2018).

There is another point to highlight. In a 20-year longitudinal study, it was concluded that younger adults (those who are less than 30 years old) have the highest exposure to stressful factors and also the highest reactivity to them. According to this study, their stress profile becomes better as they age, as their reactivity before stressful factors is reduced over time throughout the years, until they become 54 years old where their reactivity to stress remains stable (Almeida et al., 2023).

Below, there are some simple actionable tips to relieve the symptoms of stress in the business and work environments. Oftentimes, these suggestions are also prone to be applied in a preventive manner, which means before one becomes stressed.

A.1 Self-Awareness

A stressed person should purposely take some time off, when possible, to be more self-aware; these individuals should observe early signs of stress in their body (like muscular tension and accelerated breathing). The body of a stressed individual tends to become tense and its vital energy does not flow well. Bacci (2002) suggested that when practising self-awareness, individuals should focus on their breathing and internal states (e.g., emotions and physical sensations), instead of concentrating on what they want to achieve (e.g., aims and objectives). In other words, people should dwell on their internal states and observe them quietly. Besides, when individuals become aware of any tension in different areas of their bodies (shoulders, neck, etc.), they can intently tense their muscles and then relax. Individuals can also imagine that the tension is being released from their body like a flying cloud. People can also stretch their whole body like a slothful cat in order to relax their muscles.

Individuals can also use diaphragmatic or abdominal respiration to become more aware of their breathing and calm it down naturally. Research has shown that diaphragmatic breathing can help people decrease their anxiety levels (Chen et al., 2017). People can even be aware of their breathing while they go through their daily activities, especially when they face dire challenges. A person can also use introspective questions to prompt emotions and thoughts to pop up, such as "What is going on in me at this moment?" or "What am I feeling now?" The objective of these questions is to enhance people's internal awareness and help them articulate their own emotional states in words.

Research states that a good way to reduce stress levels and improve mood is the use of cyclic sighing. This form of respiration implies breathing in through the nose deeply filling up the lungs, followed by a second short inhale (which contributes to a deeper inhalation), and then exhaling through the mouth in a very slow and extended manner. This type of breathing should be performed for 5 minutes in order to benefit from its calming effect (Balban et al., 2023).

A.2 Exercise and Other Activities

Exercise is a powerful self-care tool, which helps release stress naturally. Exercise also revitalises muscles, bones, and tissues, improves blood circulation, and helps detox the body. Besides, exercise helps release endorphins, which contributes to an overall sense of well-being. Frequent exercise contributes positively to one's self-esteem. Research concludes that exercise reduces proneness to stress and increases life expectancy. One study concluded that regular aerobic exercise for a short time (six weeks) protects people against stress and depression (Herbert et al., 2020).

Some physical activities like jogging and gym exercises are excellent to release tension. Stretching exercises and aerobic exercises (such as dancing, cycling, and running) and exercise routines to tone muscles (e.g., lifting weights) are also advisable. Some disciplines are naturally de-stressing, for example, yoga, qi gong, tai chi, and meditation.

The regular practice of meditation helps people quieten their thoughts and relax their body. Frequent practice of meditation makes people feel more vital and energetic. As seen, meditation enhances concentration and problem-solving processes. As discussed previously, the meditative state is also suitable for receiving intuitive insights and creative ideas.

A.3 Healthy Habits

In order to avoid worsening stress symptoms, a person should have a healthy diet. According to a research study, higher perceived stress is linked to an unhealthy diet (López-Cepero et al., 2021). In order to have a healthy diet, a balanced ingestion of fats, carbs, and proteins should be considered. A good nutrition programme generally includes a multivitamin and mineral complex, taken on a daily basis. Some specialists like Abrams (2017) suggest the intake of magnesium, calcium, vitamin C, vitamin B5, and vitamin B6, as well as Biotin. Some supplements like ashwagandha, L-theanine, and rhodiola can help decrease stress levels (Kubala et al., 2022). Advice from a doctor or nutritionist should always be sought by individuals on what constitutes a balanced diet for them, as well as what supplements are the most appropriate for them.

Some food recommendations are well-known and common sense. For example, some products to avoid are junk food, products with preservatives, canned food, overly salty or sugary items, foods with high-fructose corn syrup, fried products, caffeine, and alcohol. People should eat more leafy green vegetables, fruit, beans, whole grains, seeds, legumes, and nuts. Natural, organic, fermented, and vegetable-based food should be chosen over highly processed items. Some specialists also recommend eating lean protein and cold-water fish in moderation. Sufficient water should be drunk to remain hydrated all over the day.

Some healthy fats, such as olive oil, oily fish, and avocado, should be preferred over fats in processed food. Food ingestion should be unhurried, and over-eating should be avoided; small and regular portions should be ingested and chewed slowly. When eating, the person should mindfully concentrate on their food, avoiding mental wandering over work-related problems. It is important not to skip meals during the day. Emotional eating should be avoided; for example, eating to combat boredom, tension, or anxiety is not beneficial.

A.4 Alternative Activities

Rosenberg (2005) observed that oftentimes stress is caused by unmet needs, which makes it important for people to ask themselves "What are my unmet needs in this situation?" People who use this question can obtain some insights into their main needs, which will help these individuals meet their needs in alternative ways. For instance, if people do not feel fulfilled at work, they can look for other activities outside work (hobbies, pastimes, etc.) for their self-realisation.

A person should devote frequent time to activities that this individual yearns to do, not obligations. These activities help people recover their energy levels and become more revitalised. A person should choose activities which prompt them to experience positive moods and laughter, when possible. These activities will vary from person to person, but all of them help people slow down and become more at ease.

For instance, some people like reading positive literature (motivational books, spirituality, etc.), which is very inspiring and oftentimes calming. Others like to be in contact with natural places (parks, lakes, etc.) to become more revitalised. Some people are keen on activities like dance, sports, and creative activities (music, writing, etc.) which help the person wind down.

Some people like to give themselves treats, for example, bubble baths, sauna, dinners out, or some other activities like cooking and travelling. Research has shown that these self-care activities help decrease stress levels and increase resiliency (Ayala et al., 2018). Other people like to have professional massages, which improve circulation, release tension, and calm pain. Research has also shown that performing activities which prompt people to experience positive emotional states, such as watching comical movies, is of great help in overcoming stress. A study has shown that the use of aromatherapy, especially inhaling lavender oil scent, significantly decreased work-related stress levels (Chen et al., 2015).

Some specialists also advise helping others, for example, volunteering or charitable activities. These altruistic activities switch the focus from oneself to others, which makes people feel at ease. People also feel good because they contribute to noble social causes.

A.5 Better Work Organisation

Stressed people should slow down their work pace, avoiding hectic schedules when possible. Complex business projects should be broken down into more actionable and easier steps. A person should avoid undertaking tasks uninterrupted for lengthy periods of time. Some useful questions stressed people can ask themselves are "Am I overloaded with activities?" and "How can I manage my activities in a more calm and enjoyable manner?"

Regular short breaks should be taken during work time to avoid exhaustion and overwhelm. These breaks can also be included in the personal diary, to be respected as if they were carved in stone. Multitasking should be avoided because it goes against undivided focus and effectiveness. When people perform many simultaneous activities, they are more prone to make mistakes because their focus is scattered. Employees should be engrossed in one task at a time, and temporarily disengage from other activities. In addition, people should avoid procrastinating tasks, as it relates to higher stress levels (Khalid et al., 2019; Sirois, 2016).

At night, a person can make a list of things to do during the following day. To-do lists can also help people declutter and clear up their minds; these lists also give people an instant emotional boost. Relevant activities should always be prioritised over trivial ones; the former should have specific blocked time to tackle them. Sometimes, different ways to approach each of the forthcoming tasks can also be included on the list. Besides, realistic goals should be set and reviewed on a regular basis, avoiding adopting a perfectionist attitude when pursuing them. When possible, some tasks should be delegated to others, or worked on in co-operation with other colleagues.

A.6 Improved Discernment

When stressed people dwell on irrational ideas or catastrophic thoughts, they can ask themselves specific questions like "Are these threatening factors real or imagined?", "What are the chances of these threats occurring?", "What is the evidence of this?", "What is a more realistic view of this?", and "What is the worst that can happen in relation to this?", among others. These types of questions help people change their perception of external circumstances, and prompt them to feel calmer and more in control.

Stressful circumstances should be promptly recognised and can also be written down and framed more positively in order to avoid reacting to them. A person should identify the actions to be taken in relation to these situations. The person should also use more positive vocabulary, for example, "challenge" instead of "problem," or "I choose to feel more energised," instead of "I feel exhausted."

Blackburn and Epel (2017) observed that people can deal with stressful circumstances by framing them as challenges, instead of threats. These authors stated that people can feel excited and confident before these circumstances, by using phrases such as "I am excited" and "I have what it takes," which, in turn, will create positive effects in their minds and bodies.

Lastly, a person can reflect on current challenging circumstances in order to look for creative solutions to them. In Chapters 14 and 15, several creative tools (such as analogies and brainstorming) were thoroughly explained.

A.7 Social Aspects

People could look for support from others (colleagues, relatives, friends, etc.) when feeling overwhelmed with stress factors. These individuals can talk to others about their own worrying issues to unload their minds and also receive useful tips. In this way, stressed people can feel cared for and assisted by others, which reduces their anxiety and tension. A stressed person should always look for uplifting people and avoid surly ones. Positive social interactions can represent a very restful refuge from hectic business and work schedules. Research has shown that receiving support from friends and partners is linked to lower stress levels (Lee et al., 2020).

People tend to feel less stressed when they are more generous, supportive, and grateful with others. When a person adopts a loving attitude towards others, stress is naturally pushed away; love and stress are incompatible. People with a kind attitude take the focus off themselves and place it on others. Research has shown that when people are more grateful, they have lower stress levels, and their negative emotional states (fear, anger, etc.) are replaced with positive ones (peace, contentment, etc.).

Lastly, a person should seek for a balance between work and other life areas (health, family, hobbies, etc.) as a priority. Overworking always brings about several trade-offs and imbalances in other life areas.

A.8 Other Aspects

When individuals are stressed, they can use self-suggestions to calm themselves down. Some statements like "Relax," "I am capable," "I am tranquil," or "I allow myself to be still" can be effective to become more relaxed. By mentally repeating these sentences, a person can focus on positive things, instead of concentrating on threatening factors.

People can also become more positive by asking themselves questions like "What good things happened today?", "What good things are likely to occur?", and "What am I grateful for?", and similar ones. The objective of these questions is to prompt positive thoughts in order to replace stressful ones.

As seen, visiting natural places, like parks, lakes, mountains, and other places of natural beauty, can also represent relevant stress busters. According to Blackburn and Epel (2017), these natural places allow people to disconnect from the myriad of stimuli bombarding them on a continuous basis, which, in turn, makes these individuals feel more tranquil and at ease. Research has concluded that, when people visit natural places, their stress – both on a psychological and on a physical level – is reduced (Ewert and Chang, 2018).

Lobel (2014) observed that having a shower after a hectic day not only makes people feel cleaner, but it also helps them eradicate any trace of stressful experiences they have had during the day. When having a shower, the person will feel cleaner, more revitalised, and less prone to be burdened down by stressful circumstances.

Brewer (2010) suggests keeping a stress diary. In this diary, people should frequently jot down the time of the day they felt stressed, the stress intensity, the stressful situation, the feelings, and negative responses related to that situation. In this diary, potential effective courses of actions to respond to the stress factors can also be included.

There is another point to highlight. Some companies purposefully aim to reduce the stress level of employees with some specific practices. Some examples of these practices are flexible hours, clear work specifications, offering the option of working remotely, organisation of regular social events, and training on stress management techniques, among others.

Talking Rain is a sustainable beverage company which offers a series of activities to its employees to bust their stress levels and to enhance their fitness. As part of its Health and Wellness Program, this organisation prompts its employees to undertake activities like yoga and Zumba at work with the company's personal trainers, or do some regular exercise outside work. Moreover, staff members can receive monetary rewards when they do some physical activities. For instance, an employee ran various marathons, and these expenses have been refunded by this company (Talking Rain, 2023).

Appendix B: Mindfulness and Business

Most of the time, a person's brain is prone to focus on the future (worries, expectations, etc.) or the past (regret, guilt, etc.). The human mind is also naturally inclined to judge everything (good, bad, big, small, etc.). People who practise mindfulness concentrate on themselves (their thoughts, emotions, and physical sensations) or focus on different aspects of the environment around them (people, things, places, etc.) with undivided attention and in a non-judgemental manner. Consequently, mindful people tend to be less reactive.

Individuals who intently practise mindfulness are centred on the present moment and use their five senses (touch, sight, smell, hearing, taste) fully. As seen previously, people tend to see reality through the lens of their mental biases (exaggerating, mind-reading, drawing quick conclusions, etc.). Salzberg (2014) observed that mindfulness helps people cut through their mental biases to get in direct contact with themselves and their surroundings. Tart (mentioned in Fontana, 1999) observed that mindfulness helps people see things as they are, instead of how they want them to be.

Research notes several benefits of mindful practice, such as less tiredness, better communication skills, higher self-esteem, improved memory skills, fewer distractions, heightened awareness, improved decision-making, more creativity, lower stress levels, enhanced performance, and less emotional reactivity, among others (Good et al., 2016). Collard (2014) observed that mindful individuals tend to be more vital, enthusiastic, grateful, and compassionate. The continuous use of mindful techniques also has a positive impact on relationships and the overall well-being of a person. General Mills, the global food company, has implemented mindfulness exercises, as well as yoga as part of their employees' development. As a result of these practices, employees reported that they were more focused, more creative, and more connected to others (Gelles, 2012; Olejniczak, 2021). Below, there are some potential uses of mindfulness in the business environment.

1. Mindfulness can be used as part of active listening to a company's stakeholders. When a person is actively listening to another, the former can become a silent observer of the latter's movements, gestures, tone of voice, and words. Mindful listening contributes to a better comprehension of the speaker's message and emotions related to it. Mindful listeners temporarily silence their inner dialogue to pay full attention to what is being said and how it is being said. This type of listener adopts a more empathetic attitude towards a speaker.
2. With mindfulness, a business person can fully concentrate on projects of great importance (contracts, strategies, product innovation processes, launching of new items, etc.). Mindful

DOI: 10.4324/9781003372684-22

practice can help people focus on the priority tasks at hand, without being distracted by trivial ones. Mindful observation can also be used to avoid multitasking, which lowers productivity according to research. In other words, mindfulness also allows people to manage relevant tasks in a more productive manner.

3. Mindful practice can be used by business people who suffer from stress. Stressed people who practise mindfulness can become more aware of their thoughts, emotions, sensations, and the overall environment. When they do so, they can assess threatening factors (excessive workload, tight deadlines, etc.) in a calmer and more insightful manner. A mindful person will tend to avoid responding to stress factors in a reactive manner. Verni (2015) observed that mindfulness helps people focus on the "raw data" at present, lessening their ruminations and facing the business challenges in a less stressed manner.

4. Mindfulness can help business people become better learners. As seen in Chapter 4, running a business implies continuous self-education and training. When people practise mindfulness on a regular basis, they can fully focus on the knowledge to be learned and affect the learning process positively. Besides, a mindful learner has a clear understanding of relevant knowledge and reasons underpinning it. Lastly, mindful people tend to apply the new knowledge learned to specific situations in a more meaningful manner.

5. With mindful practice, business individuals can become more aware of their negative emotions, such as anger, sadness, fear, and others. These emotions negatively colour thoughts and activities when unchecked. A person with a mindful attitude does not aim to control these disturbing emotional states. Instead, this person observes their emotions and allows them to be, without judging or criticising them. By doing so, any turbulent emotion tends to naturally subside. Verni (2015) stated that mindful people are more inclined to recognise their negative emotions and disengage from them, if necessary. When people have full emotional awareness, they are less prone to have unproductive behaviours which could bring about negative consequences. Being mindful of detrimental emotions could be of great value in a negotiation process with different stakeholders to prevent oneself from responding to them in a reactive manner.

6. With the regular practice of mindfulness, a business person can avoid automatic behaviours. Many business people perform a great part of their daily activities on autopilot. For routine activities, a person has no need to be fully aware of the task at hand. Nonetheless, many business people tend to be less effective when they respond automatically to new challenges (e.g., entering a new market). In those cases, a more thorough and creative analysis is relevant. Mindful business people are fully aware of the task at hand and can develop more innovative ways of approaching it. Besides, many business individuals have negative habits (answering emails late, etc.) which affect the company's performance in a detrimental manner. People who start to act mindfully are more prone to replace their negative habitual responses for more positive ones. This type of person also tends to act authentically and spontaneously, instead of heedlessly and automatically.

7. Webb (2016) suggests that when people start feeling the signs of stress (irritability, tension, fatigue, clouded thoughts, reactiveness, etc.), they should take a mindful break. During this break, these individuals should pause any current activity and breathe deeply, focusing on the area of their bellies; this is called abdominal respiration. These people can also sit in an open space or natural landscape, and breathe slowly and calmly, while they are mindfully aware of the surroundings. During that break, people can also scan their body and imagine any tension subsiding. During the day, people should take regular breaks of around 5–10 minutes to start feeling more revitalised.

8. Mindful people can be more aware of the interconnectedness of all that exists. For example, when people are working for a company, they can be aware of their interdependence with other members of staff. A mindful person considers the workplace to be a co-operative space where each person supports one another and contributes to the company's purpose. From this perspective, successful work projects are never the result of an individual, but of collective effort. Likewise, a company's success is never considered a result of the organisation itself, but instead the contribution of all its valuable stakeholders, such as suppliers, intermediaries, external advisors, etc.

9. Mindful business people can make better decisions. Mindful people are fully focused on the present moment, which prevents them from being dragged down by turbulent thoughts and emotions from the past or the future. Mindful individuals tend to be calmer, which allows them to make unhurried and wiser business decisions. These people are less prone to respond to challenges in a reactive or thoughtless manner. These individuals tend to be more flexible and in control when they solve business problems. A business person who adopts a mindful attitude is prone to make decisions more clearly and objectively, without being taken by distracting thoughts and emotions.

10. Mindful people tend to pay more attention to the details. People with a mindful attitude are more observant; they can perceive details in any situation that most individuals have taken for granted. A person fully engaged in the present moment can discover different aspects of the environment (people, things, places, experiences, etc.) and also of themselves (thoughts, emotions, physiological states). When people are aware of what is going on around and inside themselves, their analysis of situations is more thorough and meaningful. This increased awareness can also help people detect hidden opportunities in the business and work environments.

11. A mindful person can deal with difficult conversations in a more compassionate manner. Some business people face challenging conversations with stakeholders, for example, talks about the cancellation of a supply contract, or a meeting arranged to fire an employee, and downsizing the company structure, among others. A mindful person is capable of telling others about a conflicting issue in a calm and kind manner. A mindful individual is also more prone to use objective criteria (statistics, market price, etc.) to solve conflictive situations with others in a fair manner. A person with a mindful attitude truly cares for the relationships with various stakeholders and tends to address conflictive situations more lovingly.

As previously seen, the regular practice of mindfulness brings about multiple benefits which have a positive impact on work and business relationships, as well as on a company's economic results. Some other examples of companies that foster mindfulness in their workplaces are Google (the developer of the most well-known search engine and other products), Intel (the developer of computer processors), and Green Mountain Coffee Roasters (which offers coffee products) (Olejniczak, 2021).

Appendix C: Marketing and Manipulation

Tricks and treachery are the practice of fools that have not wit enough to be honest.

Benjamin Franklin

C.1 Consumption and Consumerism

The majority of customers in the marketplace look for new products, services, and experiences on a regular basis. Most customers are utterly attracted by novelty and innovation. Hyde (2012) observed that, as customers, "sometimes we go to the market to taste estrangement, if only to fantasise what our next attachment might be." Oftentimes, customers obtain a very short-lived sense of satisfaction from their purchases, which prompts them to engage in buying again. Not only do customers create a continuous demand for innovative offerings from companies, but customers are also one of the main drivers of any national economy. Moreover, customers represent the main, and oftentimes the only, source of income of most companies.

Honoré (2004) observed that consumerism has contributed to the development of the fast-paced society and "tempted and titillated at every turn, we seek to cram in as much consumption and as many experiences as possible." In relation to this, Martin (2006) observed that "our consumerist culture encourages people to strive after things that they believe, often wrongly, will bring them happiness in the future" and "they find it hard to enjoy the present because their thoughts are focused on a future state they have not yet attained and perhaps never will." In a similar vein, Perelmuter (2021), who previously worked in the advertising sector, insightfully observed that marketing activities often aim to bring about a higher demand, by prompting people to want products they would never have sought after otherwise.

Some years ago, Patagonia, the prestigious company which sells items of clothing, posted an advert which stated, "Don't Buy This Jacket," accompanied by a picture of one of the jackets this organisation offers. The objective of this advert was to tackle unnecessary consumption by encouraging customers to think thoroughly before they buy any product. In that sense, this advert's main objective was to prompt people to consume less. This lower and more thoughtful consumption can contribute to a smaller negative environmental impact, as the production of any item of clothing brings about carbon dioxide emissions and uses precious freshwater (Patagonia, 2022c). Many companies in the clothing sector tend to act in an opposite manner; they prompt customers to buy their products as frequently as possible.

There is another point to highlight. Customers have different motives for buying products and services, like social acceptance, safety, simplicity, status, comfort, novelty, autonomy and independence, time-saving, entertainment, curiosity, and low cost, among others. The different types of needs of a company's stakeholders, including customers, were thoroughly explained in Chapter 6. As seen in this book, a human-oriented company aims to satisfy these customers' needs effectively, while also achieving its own business objectives and bringing about a positive social and environmental impact.

C.2 Marketing Strategies and Manipulation

Most companies actively use different marketing stratagems (events, advertising, free samples, etc.) to persuade customers to buy their products and services. In relation to this, Baker and Martinson (2002) observed that authentic persuasion is based on relevant principles, such as truthfulness, authenticity, respect, fairness, and social responsibility. In a similar vein, Parson (2004) highlighted the importance of veracity, non-malevolence (not harming others), beneficence (doing good to others), confidentiality (respecting privacy of others), and fairness when interacting with customers.

Patagonia is an example of a company which is very transparent to its customers. On its website, this organisation shows customers various aspects of the production process of its products, and their environmental and social impact. For example, this company explains that, in the current season, 94% of its product line is made from recycled materials, which reduces 4,300 metric tons of carbon dioxide emissions. This company also explains that 87% of its product line is Fair Trade certified, benefitting more than 64,000 workers of factories which provide this organisation with items of clothing. This company pays a premium for all clothes (with the Fair Trade Certified label on them) sold by these factories. This premium goes to the workers at the factories who decide their use (providing economic support to community projects, giving cash bonus to employees, etc.) (Patagonia, 2023).

There is another relevant topic to discuss. It is very common to see customers disappointed because of having been enticed by deceptive or manipulative stratagems implemented by companies. These manipulative ploys aim to reduce customers' natural freedom of choice and force them into choosing specific pre-selected alternatives.

Some examples of companies' disrespectful behaviour towards their customers are the use of pushy sales techniques, continuous unsolicited telephone calls, and the delivery of junk mail and intrusive spamming, among others. Some companies through attractive advertising campaigns aim to promote needs which are superfluous and also showcase idealised role models (the successful entrepreneur, the vital young man, the perfect lady, etc.) which can often confuse customers regarding their innermost fundamental needs. Some companies offer products (cosmetic plastic surgery, quick methods of losing weight, etc.) which promote helping customers get closer to looking like these idealistic images.

Some companies purposefully take advantages of vulnerable customers, for instance, organisations which offer unhealthy food products to toddlers, whose cognitive skills are not fully developed. Other companies offer products or services whose excessive consumption is potentially dangerous (alcoholic drinks, gambling, etc.) without any explicit and clear suggestions on the importance of the responsible consumption of these offerings. Sometimes, a company adopts a profit-oriented and careless attitude and purposefully offers products which are potentially unsafe for customers (food products with ingredients harmful for health, hazardous electric products, etc.).

There is another point to highlight. Some companies use an approach of planned obsolescence. This implies wittingly offering products of inferior quality which – when they are used – last a shorter time than their expected lifespan. The main purpose of this stratagem is to increase the sales levels of this product. In 1924, various producers which were members of the so-called Phoebus Cartel agreed to manufacture lower quality light bulbs, making them last a shorter time. Before this agreement, the bulbs had previously lasted 2,500 hours (on average). A decade later after this agreement, the light bulbs only lasted around 1,200 hours (Mihm, 2022).

Some companies use an approach of perceived obsolescence when they launch a new model of a product. This new model has different features which are only marginally superior ones, as compared to the current version of the product. In this case, through the launch of this new model, the company purposefully aims to make customers perceive that the existing model of a product they already own is unattractive or less functional, despite this current model working well, which will prompt these customers to seek out the new model. To that effect, the main objective of perceived obsolescence is to increase the company's sales levels. Some companies in various sectors such as car manufacturing, mobile phones, and fashion clothes are more prone to use the approach of perceived obsolescence (Ping, 2020).

Organisations that use manipulative ruses have no interest in developing sustainable relationships with customers which exceed specific transactions. These companies tend to put the development of any potential mutually beneficial relationships with customers on the back burner, which makes this approach extremely short-term oriented.

Many companies are not interested in taking the time to create an emotional connection and rapport with customers in order to discover and acknowledge their unique needs. In many cases, companies completely ignore customers' specific and unique preferences. Some companies do not have the least interest in making customers feel that the product they buy is right for them.

Sometimes, customers are not treated as human beings, but as mere means (impersonal figures in a company's database) to potentially contribute to achieving a company's economic results (profits, sales, etc.). In all these situations, customers tend to feel blatantly utilised, which makes them suspect a company's real intentions when they interact with this organisation. These customers perceive that companies are not being authentic, which prompts these very customers to act in a similar way.

Consequently, companies should adopt a thoughtful and loving attitude when they interact with customers. Each encounter with customers should be considered an opportunity to develop and strengthen fruitful relationships with them. These golden occasions should empower companies to offer more value than expected by customers in order to delight them.

C.3 Other Aspects of Marketing Strategies

Every time customers get in contact with a company, this organisation should kindly and warmly accompany and guide them over the buying process, which means before, during, and after the purchase. When a company assists customers in an insufficient manner, they can think that this organisation does not care enough for them. A company's employees should continually check if they are adopting a kind and warm attitude towards customers. A good question to be posed is "Are we supporting this customer enough?" Throughout this book, there were some examples of companies like Zappos or Trader Joe's where employees adopt a friendly and supportive attitude towards customers.

Customers tend to feel very upset when a company does not fulfil its promises (delays in the delivery of products, delivering goods of inferior quality, etc.). Therefore, whenever a company makes a promise, this organisation should meticulously deliver what was agreed. Companies should avoid over-promising and under-delivering because customers will feel deceived.

There are a few other points companies should take into account when interacting with customers. Interactions with customers should consider human contact, more especially in the case of online purchases. When possible, personal interactions or conversations on the phone should always be preferred over the ones which are only technology-based, like email or online chat. As seen in this book, GoDaddy, a company which sells Internet domains, website development products, and hosting services offers customer support on the phone round the clock (24/7).

Lastly, companies should be committed to continually improving the performance and quality levels of their products and services. Organisations should invest enough resources on research and development of new offerings for customers. When a company offers innovative products to customers, they are inclined to be very grateful for this. As seen, a good example of an innovative company is Google, as this organisation continually develops valuable products (Google Docs, Google Translate, etc.).

Appendix D: System Thinking and Organisations

No mind is an island, entire of itself; every man is a piece of the continent, a part of the main...

John Donne

D.1 Importance of Companies as Systems

Science suggests the next step of human evolution will be marked by the awareness that we are all interdependent cells within the super-organism called humanity.

Bruce Lipton and Steve Bhaerman

Companies can be considered dynamic and complex living systems with the capability to adapt to changes in the business environment. A system is a synergetic set of interrelated components which link to one another in a direct or indirect manner. Synergy means that the system is more than the simple summation of its components. A company is more than the simple addition of its main components (e.g., departments). O'Connor and McDermott (1997) observed that "a system is an entity that maintains its existence and functions as a whole through the interaction of its parts." From this perspective, a company behaves as the organising or structuring principle of its components.

In a company, each of the departments, sections, divisions, or teams can be considered subsystems. Despite being continually managed and monitored, the behaviour of a company's subsystems is often difficult to predict. Moreover, changes in any of these components (e.g., departments, etc.) affect the system (the company) as a whole. At the same time, a company belongs to bigger systems, for example, its industrial sector (group of companies offering similar products and services).

The company is also part of a wider system, the business environment, which includes not only competitors, but also suppliers, intermediaries, media, customers, business partners, and the community, among others. Not only does a company continually interact with its external environment, but this organisation also has a shared view of this environment, sets a common purpose, and acts towards it as a common front. The business environment is also considered a system affected by a myriad of uncontrollable and often unpredictable factors (economic, legal, cultural, technological, etc.).

DOI: 10.4324/9781003372684-24

Some examples of companies that adopt a systemic approach are Patagonia and The Body Shop, which have been previously analysed in this book. As seen, these companies regularly bring about a positive social and environmental impact. Every business activity performed by these organisations perform thoughtfully consider its effects on the bigger systems these companies are inserted in, such as communities and the planet.

There is another point to highlight. From a global perspective, the world is becoming increasingly interconnected. National economies are increasingly interrelated, as a result of international business flows (import, export, foreign direct investment, etc.), technological advancements (Internet, satellite, etc.), and financial aspects (international loans, etc.), among others. Therefore, it is also possible to consider the world as a complex and dynamic system.

D.2 Main Characteristics of Companies as Systems

As with any system, there are boundaries which separate the company and its internal environment from the external environment. From this perspective, the most important activity in an organisation is to effectively manage the flows (products, services, information, etc.) which go through and within the company's boundaries.

A company's activities should always be analysed from a holistic perspective, considering the contribution of each of its components. In a similar vein, Goleman (2014) observed that, in order to analyse systems, people should use a panoramic span of attention. An analysis considering, for example, the contribution of just one of a company's departments is incomplete. Consequently, when a company develops its strategies, this organisation should allow the participation of all its departments (finance, marketing, administrative, etc.) in the process of planning, when possible. As seen in this book, Acme Whistles is a company which sells various types of whistlers. When developing new products, this company encourages the participation of employees from its different departments.

There is another point to highlight. It is important to break down the components of the company as a system, and analyse how these components interact with one another. As in any system, all parts of a company contribute to the whole to different extents. This analysis should also consider the impact of the company on its external environment, which is the bigger system the company is inserted in, and vice versa.

Continuous feedback is obtained as the company's components relate to one other, and also when this company as a whole relates to its external environment. This feedback can confirm that the company is going in the right direction (e.g., increased customer satisfaction), so this organisation will keep on acting in the same way. This feedback can also indicate that the company should correct its course of action (e.g., decreased customer satisfaction), and choose an alternative one. In this case, feedback prompts the company to make some adjustments (e.g., offering better customer service) to achieve a state of balance (also known as homeostasis).

As a system, a company has inputs (e.g., raw material delivered by its suppliers) and outputs (e.g., products to be sold). An organisation also has throughputs, which is the transformation of inputs into outputs by adding significant value to them. Successful companies add value to these exchanges, which means that the outputs will have a superior value to the inputs.

When a company is considered to be a system, none of its parts should be analysed in isolation, but in relation to the whole. Thus, when a company adds value to customers through its products and services, it should take into account the contribution of different internal departments (manufacturing, administrative, marketing, etc.). This organisation should also consider the value added by components of the bigger system that the company is inserted in (the company's suppliers and professional advisors, wholesalers and retailers the company sells its products to, etc.).

D.3 Systems, Objectives, Decision-Making, and Environments

The majority of companies are goal-oriented. These organisations set objectives and perform activities to achieve these goals. A company on its way to attain its goals is always subject to changes in its internal or external environment. Therefore, when a company sets its objectives, it should consider both its internal environment (its employees, its technology, etc.) and its external environment (customers, suppliers, other organisations, etc.). Sometimes, the objectives must be reformulated according to changes in those environments. Besides, objectives set by a company should consider potential impacts on components of the bigger system the company belongs to (suppliers, customers, community, etc.).

From a systemic perspective, when a company takes actions to achieve its objectives, these actions are always related to external factors (macroeconomic factors, changes in the legislation in force, etc.), which are beyond the organisation's control. Oftentimes, these external factors bring about unpredictable and uncontrollable consequences. Besides, any change in the company system not only modifies the organisation itself, but also impacts on its external environment. Great and small changes (both internal and external) affect the whole company system. This complex interrelation of internal and external factors makes the long-term consequences of these changes difficult to predict.

For example, as seen previously, Khaya Cookie Company gives employment to women from communities in need, providing them with a worthy livelihood, which is a positive effect of this business endeavour. However, in this example, there could also be other effects, which might be difficult to predict. For example, these women, by becoming wealthier because of working for that company, might potentially be targeted by thieves. These women might also become the main source of financial support regarding their friends and relatives, who might borrow money from them (MacMillan and Thompson, 2013).

It is possible to see another simple example of these interrelated factors. For instance, if a company's employees become more engaged and motivated, they are more prone to serve customers more kindly, which, in turn, could create stronger loyalty ties between these customers and the company. These customers can also recommend the company's products to potential customers. Consequently, all business decisions should be made considering not only small components within the company system, but also the bigger context the organisation is inserted in. Oftentimes, each of the decisions a company needs to make is affected by various factors from its subsystems or from the bigger system the organisation belongs to. Some of these factors are often undetected.

As with any human system, the company has homeostasis, which implies that it will adapt to changes in its internal environment (employees, etc.) and its external environment (competitors' activities, changes in customers' trends, etc.) in order to remain stable over time. Both the internal environment of the company and its external environment are impermanent and subject to continuous development.

Not all factors in a company's external environment affect the organisation as a system in the same manner. Some companies as systems are more inclined to collapse when they are affected by impactful factors; for example, a company with low levels of sales is more prone to shut down when the national economy is in an economic depression. Fiebleman and Friend (1945) observed that a company is more likely to survive an ever-changing business environment when it is tenacious, determined, and flexible.

D.4 Other Aspects of the Systemic Perspective

The analysis of company problems (e.g., lack of qualified staff) tends to be related to other problems (financial problems, etc.). Therefore, problems should never be considered in isolation, but in relation to other troublesome issues. From this perspective, it is important for companies to step back and reflect on the whole set of problems and their interrelated aspects, considering the whole picture. From the systemic perspective, no problem occurs independently, but in relation to others.

Individuals working for a company, and outside it, can also be considered systems. People are multidimensional: they are affected by emotional, spiritual, physical, and mental aspects. These individuals also have different roles, such as worker, parent, friend, and relative. These people also belong to bigger systems, such as groups of friends, relatives, and colleagues.

From the employee's perspective, systems like family, friends, and others are equally as important, if not more so, as the organisation the employee works for. The way these individuals perform their activities in some of these systems (e.g., the family circle) tends to impact others in the systems they belong to (e.g., group of work colleagues).

Many companies consider their employees in a fragmented way; for example, taking into account only their job or work role. These companies also tend to consider their external stakeholders purely in relation to their specific business roles (suppliers, buyers, etc.). Instead, the systemic approach fosters a multifaceted perspective, which goes beyond reductionist work positions and business roles. From this perspective, work activities allocated by a company to its employees should always consider other employees' dimensions besides their work roles, so that employees can achieve a balance between their work tasks and other areas of their lives (family, friends, etc.). A company which takes into account its employees' work-life balance is Netflix, the movie producing and video streaming company. As seen previously, this company offers its employees unlimited paid leaves. As mentioned in this book, in relation to parental leave, the only company's policy is "to take care of your baby and yourself;" a new parent usually takes four to eight months of parental leave.

There is another point to highlight. In a company, each department or internal division should be aware of their valuable contribution to the whole company system. All parts of the company system should add value in a consistent manner. These subsystems should also be aware of their interactions with one another, considering the possibility of assisting each other and working in a co-operative and co-ordinated manner. Moreover, a company should hold frequent cross-departmental meetings, which implies the participation of different areas of this organisation (marketing, finance, etc.). These meetings can bring a more integrative picture of the company's challenges and opportunities, and can be a viable environment to brainstorm creative courses of action to deal with them. A few decades ago, Cisco developed a cross-functional team, which included people from its different departments (marketing, software engineering, manufacturing, etc.). The objective of this team was to improve security regarding router lines. As a consequence of the insights stemming from this team, the company's business activities grew significantly (Tabrizi, 2015).

Consequently, in any company, the interplay between its different parts (e.g., departments) should always be taken into consideration. The level of conflict among these components can be reduced significantly when each subsystem adopts an integrative and non-fragmentary view of business activities.

Sometimes, business activities are analysed in a fragmented manner: for example, from the viewpoint of the company itself. However, this analysis can also be more overarching when it considers the unique perspectives of customers, suppliers, community, government, etc. Most companies are prone to assess business situations by considering only one or few of these possible viewpoints. In those cases, the general picture is not perceived; the valuable interplay between these distinct perspectives is generally dismissed. As seen previously in this book, Tata Motors developed the Tata Nano, a very affordable small car. In relation to the development of this product, this organisation has taken into consideration various perspectives: the company's perspective (e.g., the achievement of its business objectives), the customers' perspective (affordability of the product), and the government's perspective (compliance of the car with all the regulations in force regarding safety and security).

There is one more point to highlight. A company's strengths, capabilities, and talents are interrelated to one another. All these elements add value in an integrative manner. Nonetheless, these positive internal aspects are also interrelated to negative ones (a company's weaknesses). Consequently, these negative factors often counteract positive ones, creating final negative outcomes.

From a systemic perspective, a system tends to be slowed down by its weakest factors. This principle can be applied not only to the level of strengths and weaknesses, but also on the level of departments, divisions, and teams. The weakest department, division, and team tend to slow down the whole company's system. Therefore, some relevant questions a company can ask itself on a frequent basis are:

- What is the contribution of this department, section, or team to the bigger company system?
- How does a change in this department, section, or team affect the company as a whole?
- What is the contribution of this company to the business environment system as a whole?

Appendix E: Compassionate Negotiation

E.1 Conflicts and Organisations

All organisations tend to have several conflicts within them and with other companies. These conflicts have various origins, such as different values and beliefs, emotional unrest, perception of limited resources, and diverse goals, among others. Some conflicts are internal, which include the same area or different areas within a company (marketing, finance, etc.). Other conflicts are related to the company's external environment, for example, between an organisation and its external stakeholders (suppliers, intermediaries, etc.). Companies use different techniques (negotiation, lawsuits, mediation, etc.) to solve these conflicts.

Some conflicts escalate because of a participant's personal aspects (e.g., personality) and others because of substantive aspects (quality, price, etc.). Oftentimes, these conflicts damage relationships, which are the most relevant assets in an organisation. From a traditional perspective, every conflictive situation tends to be perceived as a fixed pie; a participant can only get a bigger slice at the expense of the other. This perspective is based on a scarcity mentality, which is fear-based. This fear can adopt different forms, such as fear of losing resources, fear of not being right, and fear of being controlled, among others. The scarcity mentality was discussed in Chapter 3.

It is possible to say that most conflicts are based on the lack of a loving attitude towards others. The existence of conflict implies, to a certain extent, the participants' perception of separation from each other. Each party gives preference to their "right to be right" over their "duty to care for others." However, if companies adopted an attitude of open-mindedness and showed a warmer heart, most conflicts could be amicably resolved, and oftentimes avoided.

E.2 Importance of a Loving Attitude towards Conflicts

Companies which act based on noble principles (compassion, care, forgiveness, gratitude, etc.) are less prone to engage in any conflictive situations with their stakeholders. These organisations also give priority to the human aspects of each participant in any negotiation process in order to preserve and strengthen their relationships with them. There are some recommendations organisations can use when they have disagreements with their stakeholders:

- Express one's needs by using clear and simple language. Use positive vocabulary when possible and focus on what you want, avoid centring on what is not wanted.

DOI: 10.4324/9781003372684-25

- Invite others to convey their needs overtly. Acknowledge others' opinions overtly ("I appreciate your comments; thanks for letting me know!").
- Avoid mind-reading or guessing the other's opinions and preferences. Use open-ended questions, paraphrasing, clarifications, and recaps in order to understand other's comments clearly.
- Encourage others to elaborate on their ideas with sentences like "Tell me more about ...." Listen to them in an active manner, by being totally focused and absorbed in their comments and without interrupting them. Keep an inquisitive attitude, even during rough times.
- Look for similarities with the other participants. When people converse about their similarities, they are naturally prone to feel affection for one another.
- Don't ignore or avoid conflictive situations, hoping that they will be resolved by themselves over time. Perceive any conflictive situation as an opportunity to learn from one another in order to strengthen the relationship with each other.
- Try to interpret comments made by the other participant from the most loving perspective, even seemingly negative ones. When a person makes a detrimental comment, paraphrase it from a positive standpoint. Assume that others have the best intention to reach an agreement.
- Use words which imply a connection between the participants, for example, "let's," "us," "we," and "our," among others. When possible, eliminate words like "I," "my," or "mine."
- Avoid using manipulative stratagems, such as ultimatums, bluffing, and false deadlines, among others. All these ploys prevent participants from achieving a mutually profitable agreement and damage their relationship.
- Acknowledge others' emotions; allow them to be expressed overtly. Rosenberg (2005) observed that when each person can express their vulnerabilities, conflicts can be solved more easily. Emotional states generally signal the person's most relevant interests.
- Be empathetic with others' emotional states, using sentences like "It looks like you feel ...." Suggest break time when emotions are becoming increasingly heightened to avoid potentially destructive escalation.
- Avoid adopting a defensive attitude towards others which is generally based on fear. Never respond to aggressive comments in a reciprocal manner. Identify one's emotions regularly and express them calmly using sentences like "I feel ..." without blaming others.
- Avoid personalising the conflictive situation (for instance, discussing negative personal traits of the other participant). Personal conflicts are more prone to escalate.
- Approach the conflict in a positive mood, whenever possible. When participants experience positive emotions, they tend to develop more creative solutions to it.
- Know that the adoption of an appreciative and a generous attitude towards others prompts them to feel more positive emotional states. The use of sentences like "Thanks for your contribution" and similar ones is beneficial for the negotiation process.
- Acknowledge the significance of achieving a higher-level goal (e.g., a mutually satisfactory agreement), which not only preserves, but also strengthens the relationship between the participants.
- Realise that partial agreements often create momentum for bigger ones. Sometimes, agreements can have a trial period to test their effectiveness in practice. There could be a transition period from the current situation to the implementation of an agreement.
- Ask others to suggest solutions to the conflict; make them feel like valuable participants in the development of the agreement. Ask questions like "What do you suggest we should do?"
- Consider the other participant as a partner, not as an adversary. It is important to recognise and encourage others to continually contribute to the development of an agreement.

- Allow others to express their opinions openly. Focus on actively listening to others firstly in order to be heard by them afterwards, especially when discussing challenging issues.
- Avoid exerting power over the other party. Avoid any imbalance of power as it creates resentment, distrust, and unwillingness. Show care for others to prompt them to open up.
- Try to imagine creative solutions to the conflict alongside the other participant. Look for fair solutions which consider both parties' interest. Pose interesting questions like "What would a solution look like if we meet our interests and yours?"
- Break down the conflictive topic into subparts: for example, a price can be broken down into: money to be paid, currency used, possibility of financing, etc. Look for creative variations to these variables.
- Understand that negotiation processes are generally based on more than one variable (quality, price, transportation, etc.); these variables (and their subvariables) can also be recombined in a creative manner to arrive at an agreement.
- Avoid attacking, judging, criticising, and ignoring others, as this behaviour implies the adoption of an unloving attitude towards others. Realise that these strategies don't make people feel acknowledged and recognised as legitimate participants.
- Be flexible in the design of any potential agreement, which must be based on equality, co-operation, inclusiveness, and fairness. Solve obstacles or deadlocks in a co-operative and creative manner, and always avoid making decisions unilaterally. Ask others for their opinions, instead of commanding them.
- Learn more about values of the other participant, which indicate what is important for them. Ask questions like "What is really important for you in this situation?" to discover the other person's values.

Some other points can be highlighted. Participants should find a common ground during the negotiation process. O'Connor (2001) suggested that every participant should frequently use tools like "chunk up" and "chunk down." For example, a company has a disagreement with a supplier about the commercial terms of a transaction between them. In this example, the parties can use "chunk up" to agree on higher-order objectives. For instance, these participants might agree that beyond this specific agreement, they want to preserve their business relationship (high-level objective). The parties can also use chunk down; in this case, participants can explore more specific parts of the agreement (price, quality, etc.), when appropriate.

E.3 Other Relevant Aspects to Be Considered

Each party should aim to discover the other's interests, which are the real needs behind their positions (or requests). Positions are just one of many strategic ways to satisfy one's interests. However, there are often several ways to address each other's interests. Participants who do not know each other's actual interests can ask the other questions like "Why do you want this?" Conversations during the negotiation process should unfold around both participants' interests to find ways to fairly meet them.

According to Kelley (1990), participants in a negotiation process should avoid using *ad hominen* arguments, which dismiss the argument of others by attacking them in a personal way. According to this author, an example of this type of erroneous argument is: "The agreement cannot be reached because you are not capable of understanding the complexity of this transaction."

Caspersen (2015) suggested that one's comments should always be focused on the interaction with the other person based on one's observation ("You left the room suddenly"), instead of making personal judgements on how they are ("Your behaviour is rude"). All observations should be made in a warm and loving manner.

The participants should also aim to always use assertive vocabulary, which implies communicating one's needs in a calm and firm manner, instead of doing so in an aggressive way. Caspersen (2015) suggests the use of sentences like "When (the triggering event) happened, I felt (my feeling) because (my need/interest) is really important to me. Would you be willing to (request a doable action)?" to express one's emotions, needs, and requests.

All agreements should be based on objective principles (statistics, expert opinion, market average price, etc.), not arbitrary ones. Each participant should ask one another about the objective evidence that justifies their own position. Kelley (1990) observed that participants should avoid providing subjective arguments ("This is the price that I want") or emotional ones ("In your heart, you know that this is the best price …").

Lastly, Leech (1983) suggested a conversational maxim to contribute to an agreement with others. According to this maxim, each party should reduce the number of statements which imply disagreement, and instead maximise those statements which imply agreement. An example of statements which imply agreement is: "I am sure that we will develop a co-operative agreement working together."

The renowned car manufacturer Toyota adopts a compassionate attitude when negotiating with its suppliers. This company has been continually focused on developing fair deals with its suppliers. As seen previously, this company supports its suppliers and fosters co-operative long-term relationships with them. For instance, Toyota provides its suppliers with high-level specifications. At the same time, this company is open to receiving valuable feedback from these suppliers regarding potential modifications of these specifications, based on these suppliers' expertise (Kalkofen et al., 2007).

As seen previously in this book, Morning Star is a company which processes tomato. The main principles prevalent in this company are staff members work without exerting any force on each other, and workers always aim to keep their commitments. Any conflict between workers (different opinions, not respecting commitments, etc.) is resolved through a process, which includes a first stage where staff members meet up privately and one makes a request and the other agrees, disagrees, or offers something different. If the conflictive situation is still not resolved, a third employee can intervene as a mediator. If this does not work out well either, a panel of employees (who are significant to the issue) is gathered to listen and assist the parties in the achievement of an agreement. If this still does not work, the president can be called into this panel to contribute with some moral weight (Hamel, 2011; Laloux, F., 2014). As seen, at this company, the conflicts tend to be resolved in a friendly way, avoiding adversarial methods.

Appendix F: Empathetic Use of Social Media

F.1 Main Characteristic of Social Media

Social media platforms are valuable environments, through which companies can engage with their different stakeholders. These platforms allow companies to develop two-way communication, tantamount to personal conversations. These virtual tools are participative because people can openly and overtly express their opinions, either positive or negative.

Some companies use different social media platforms to enhance their image; these virtual environments provide organisations with priceless visibility and an online presence. All information published on social media is shown in real time and in a direct manner.

Social media is an easy-to-use, integrative, and democratic environment because it allows individuals and organisations to develop networks, whose members can be accessed directly. On these social platforms, information can be disclosed with immediacy. Belonging to a virtual community contributes to a sense of bonding between the participants. Nonetheless, in this virtual environment, it is often difficult to verify the trustworthiness and credentials of the participants.

These platforms are relevant socialising spaces, where virtual relationships with others can progressively be developed; they are also equalisers because of their free access for everybody. Relationships online tend to be strengthened by sharing common interests and learning from one another on a regular basis. Therefore, the use of specific ways of communicating ideas (like story-telling) is very common and valuable.

Virtual relationships cannot be compared with the realness and authenticity of offline relationships. Online interactions are less complete and deep, and more intermittent and ephemeral than offline ones. Many people argue that on social media, there is no human connection with real people, but with abstract profiles which seem to look good to try to grab others' attention.

Nonetheless, these platforms allow participants to connect with people or organisations which would otherwise not have been possible, if it were not for social media. Lindgren (2017) observed that online platforms represent computer-mediated environments of affinity where participants can experience "virtual togetherness."

Tuten and Solomon (2017) observed that social media has four main purposes: developing communities (which involves online networking sharing, socialising, and chatting), social publishing (which includes editorial activities with content generated by the user), social commerce (which includes retailing and customer service activities), and social entertainment (music, games, art, etc.). These authors also stated that people engage in social media for different reasons: affinity, utility or personal gain, helping others, curiosity, and ego-validation, among others.

DOI: 10.4324/9781003372684-26

Safko and Brake (2009) observed that there are several categories of social media, such as social networking (LinkedIn), publishing (blogs, wikis, etc.), photo (Instagram), audio (Clubhouse), video (YouTube), microblogging (Twitter, now known as X), virtual worlds (Second Life), gaming (Twitch), aggregators (gathering and sharing information, for example, Reddit), mobile applications (WhatsApp), and interpersonal tools (Skype). This list is not exhaustive.

F.2 Companies and Social Media

Social media, as audience-oriented platforms, allow companies to post messages, upload pictures and videos, or publish articles with no cost. As seen previously, the specific ways companies can communicate with others online will vary from platform to platform. In all cases, the barriers to entry to social media platforms are very low; all companies can publish content online, regardless of their size.

Companies who utilise social media should always adopt a generous attitude; they should provide their audience with valuable free content on a regular basis. The content published should be changed frequently, avoiding rehashing previous information. New content should be distinct and attractive, and aim to cater to the audience's needs.

Companies should never use these platforms to hard-sell their products or services. Any reference to company products or services should be subtly included, preferably after having provided substantial free high-quality content. McKenna (2012a) expressed the view that social media platforms can be used for story-telling, for instance, by telling tales about successful customer experiences. Safko and Brake (2009) state that the main objectives of the content published on social media should always be communication, collaboration, education, and entertainment. This content could include both opinion and factual information.

Companies like Lego, the Danish toy company is very popular in various social media platforms (YouTube, Facebook, Instagram, etc.) with millions of followers. This company develops continuous engagement with its followers by posting pictures and videos regarding its new products. As seen previously, there is an online community where member can propose these company ideas for new toy products (Qian, 2020).

There is another important point to highlight. Messages posted by a company should be congruent across all social media platforms, which means that they should not have any contradictions. All these messages published by an organisation should support one another, as part of the company's overall digital communication strategy. These messages should also be coherent with the rest of the messages conveyed by the organisation in other ways, for example, events, mail, adverts, and the company's website.

Most companies need to become more active on social media and regularly publish attractive content. The content published defines the company and distinguishes it from other organisations. A company should choose content which piques the audiences' curiosity and prompts them to participate willingly. There is a positive correlation between high-quality content posted by an organisation and the endorsement it receives from audiences.

Authentic and worthy content generates the spontaneous engagement of community members. A company which posts high-quality information on a frequent basis tends to be perceived by visitors as a caring organisation. Oftentimes, companies replicate their content in several platforms, using different formats. In those cases, several platforms can also be linked to one another.

When possible, after new content is posted, the company should invite their audience to participate and also express their views and opinions on the information published. Companies can also pose open-ended questions to prompt the audiences to participate. Most community members are very opinionated; they have the urge to express their views overtly and freely. Every time members of an audience give their opinions, a company can obtain valuable insights. Oftentimes, these insights have a commercial value for the company (improvement of its products, development of new services, etc.). On social media platforms, individuals are empowered to comment about topics in an open and fluid manner, through digital, sociable, and non-face-to-face interactions. As seen previously, Starbucks gathered a myriad of insightful ideas from the online platform My Starbucks Idea and some of these ideas became successful products.

F.3 Other Aspects of Companies and Social Media

These content-oriented platforms are popular because they foster the equal participation of individuals and organisations. Consequently, companies should never censor any opinion, even negative ones. By allowing diverse opinions to be posted, a company can be positioned as transparent in the eyes of the audience. However, companies should never allow community members to be offensive or aggressive with their comments. Clear participation rules based on respect and inclusiveness are set by social media platforms.

These virtual spaces are useful to debate relevant topics, oftentimes in a heated manner, and are paramount sources of relevant feedback about a company's activities, products, and services. Oftentimes, companies consider audience members' comments as starting points for making adjustments in their offerings, for example, developing higher quality products based on customer online complaints.

A company should regularly express its views regarding different topics on these platforms. A company's representatives can directly connect to audience members in order to clarify doubts or offer them valuable advice. Companies can also use social media as an online research tool to scan trends, consumption patterns, and technological advancements. As seen in this book, companies can also use social media platforms to gather innovative ideas from the audiences (crowdsourcing), as well as to test the likeability of the company's ideas with these very audiences.

Customers always leave valuable "footprints" on social media platforms to be used by a company as data to improve its products and services. Companies can assemble a myriad of traces left by customers on social media platforms for research purposes. The use of this online research tool is low-cost because all the information is available online, free for the taking. Organisations can complement this data with information from other sources, such as interviews and focus groups.

Social media always empowers individuals to express their views openly, without being subject to any gatekeeping or editing forces. This trait makes social media more credible than traditional media because customers can share their reviews and recommendations of products and services unrestrainedly. However, as mentioned, there are specific rules regarding users' behaviour that are set by these platforms.

HubSpot is a renowned developer of marketing software. A customer was so delighted with the customer service delivered by HubSpot's team that he posted a message on Twitter (now X) inviting this customer service team to have mimosas and pancakes, as a sign of his appreciation. The company responded to this tweet and thanked this customer for this kind gesture (Needle, 2021).

There is another point to highlight. On social media platforms, customers' comments cannot be controlled by companies, which makes these comments more trustworthy. These reviews and recommendations are known as word of mouth. Oftentimes, specific pieces of content become viral, which means that they are cascaded swiftly and profusely over a virtual community.

There is a last topic to mention. Companies can assess their performance on various social media platforms in two distinct ways. In that sense, companies can assess the qualitative aspects of its virtual interactions with stakeholders (relevance of topics covered by the company on social media, quality of the content of the company's posts, etc.). The company can also consider the quantitative aspects of these virtual interactions (number of followers, likes, shares, comments, etc.). As mentioned in this book, Trader Joe's has a myriad of followers on some social media platforms like Instagram.

Appendix G: Additional Ways to Generate Intuitive Insights

When people regularly focus on their desired states (the goals they want to achieve), they are activating their reticular activating system (R.A.S.). As seen In Chapter 1, the R.A.S. is the part of the brain which screens out irrelevant information in the environment and helps a person detect relevant data. The working of this system is congruent with a well-known saying which goes "what you focus your attention on, increases."

In simple words, if a person focuses on a topic frequently, this person will tend to receive valuable insights (e.g., opportunities, people, places, situations, and information) related to this very topic and any information unrelated to this topic will be automatically discarded. The activation of the R.A.S. can be obtained in different ways, which are prone to bring about intuitive insights:

G.1 Setting Objectives

Research has shown that people who set clear objectives for different areas of their lives are more prone to succeed than those who don't. Purdie (2010) observed that the objectives must be set using the SMARTENUP acronym, which means specific, measurable, attainable, realistic, time-bound, enthusiastic, naturally defined, understood by the individual or the company's people and (well-) prepared.

A company's goals should also be congruent with the business mission. From the systemic perspective, a company's objectives should also consider the impact on different stakeholders (employees, customers, suppliers, community, etc.). Whenever possible, goals should also be accompanied by a clear set of specific actions conducive to their achievement.

Objectives should be measurable in order to know that they have been adequately achieved. However, as seen previously, some qualities, such as kindness, generosity, gratitude, and compassion, cannot be measured accurately because they are not quantifiable.

O'Connor (2001) observed that a person or organisation that sets objectives should include other elements, such as specific evidence that will prove that the objectives are effectively achieved, necessary resources (people, technology, information, etc.) to achieve these outcomes, and potential benefits of achieving these goals. This author also observed that objectives must be congruent with the identity of the objective setter and aligned with other objectives set by this individual or organisation. This specialist also recommends that companies and individuals should set goals that are worthy and ambitious, especially for the medium and long term. However, it is also important that these objectives are also attainable; therefore, excessively

DOI: 10.4324/9781003372684-27

demanding goals should be avoided because these objectives are prone to lead the goal setter to potential disappointment.

As seen previously, companies like Acme Whistles set the goal of developing a specific number of innovative products over a specific period of time. This company has been developing a myriad of innovative products for more than 15 decades. As mentioned, for over more than 150 years of history, an innovative whistle has been developed and patented by this company at least once per decade.

There is another relevant point to highlight. Objectives are cues people use to meet their needs; a person who sets objectives tends to be more motivated to find effective ways to achieve them. Goals should always be worded in a positive way, by focusing on the desired state, not on what should be avoided. When a person words goals, they should avoid words which imply lack (e.g., "I want ..." or "I wish ...") and instead use positive wording (such as "I choose ..." or "I deserve ...").

From a rational perspective, Covey (1992) observed that objectives should always include what the person or organisation wants to achieve, why the person wants to achieve these goals, and how these objectives will be attained. From an intuitive perspective, when people set their goals, they should not be focused so much on "how" these goals will be achieved. Instead, these individuals should be centred on their desired states frequently, and be receptive to any useful intuitive insights into ways to achieve these goals. Some other relevant aspects related to objectives are:

- Setting goals is a powerful strategic and motivating tool which helps people move forward in a more effective and planned manner. When people are focused on specific goals, they are more likely to gain momentum and less prone to be sidetracked. Nonetheless, if the goals are too rigid, people can have difficulties adapting to changing circumstances.
- The objectives to achieve (e.g., to find a solution to a specific problem) can be written on a piece of paper in a clear manner. When people read their objectives regularly, their R.A.S. is reactivated, and their brain will tend to laser-focus on information relevant to these objectives.
- Amabile and Kramer (2011, 2012) observed that setting clear and meaningful objectives is a valuable tool to generate creative insights, especially when a person has time to work on their attainment. These authors also concluded that minimal daily progress regarding these objectives can contribute to the development of creative and outstanding ideas.
- Whenever possible, goals should be as ambitious as possible. An example of an audacious goal can be seen in Ford Motor Company. At the beginning of the twentieth century, this organisation set up the objective to make the automobile a widely affordable product for the population.

Fritz (1984, 2003) observed that not only should people set their goals, but also recognise and accept their current state (status quo) and confront both (goals and the current state) to create "structural tension," which tends to be resolved as people take creative action to achieve these goals. This author also stated that the objectives should be set to create end results (e.g., going towards wanted situations) and not to solve problems (e.g., getting rid of unwanted circumstances).

The aforementioned perspective is related to a well-known model used in business coaching activities called GROW, which means G for setting Goals (and envisioning them), R for comparing them with the current Reality (present circumstances), O for assessing the most adequate Options to achieve these goals, and W for taking respective actions (Will).

G.2 Use of Envisioning

The human mind cannot differentiate real things from imagined ones. Visualisation is a transformative tool which implies forming mental images, by using the five senses internally. When people visualise a desired state frequently, these images are embedded in their subconscious minds, which with the help of the R.A.S. will help these individuals find effective ways to achieve these very states. Visualisation has been used by great luminaries such as Einstein, da Vinci, and Tesla, among others.

Mike Tranter, a renowned neuroscientist, observed that, when people regularly visualise themselves doing something (e.g., holding successful conversations with customers), the neural connections in their brains are flooded with messages, as if they were actually performing this very behaviour. The frequent use of envisioning brings about neuroplasticity, which means developing changes in neural connections stemming from a learning process (Cook, 2022).

There is another significant point to discuss. People should visualise their desired state in a vivid and detailed way. Images must be as compelling as possible. When people visualise, they can use colourful images and also include other senses (tactile sensations, sounds, etc.). People can also imagine the positive emotions they would experience when their objectives have already been achieved.

During the visualisation process, the images must be in the "first person"; people should imagine themselves as the protagonists, not as mere witnesses. It is not advisable for people to view themselves in a detached way (as a witness of themselves). When people practise visualisation regularly, the gap between their current state and their desired one tends to be bridged gradually. Allen (2003) observed that positive envisioning improves the quality of a person's perception, feelings, thoughts, and decisions; this specialist also observed that "a vision of a desired future allows you to focus on an improved condition."

Envisioning is used by many companies worldwide. In some cases, when the company's people mentally see the future desired state, they can also envision in a backward manner the steps that would be required to arrive at the achievement of this desired state. The use of visualisation also imprints the subconscious with vivid images, which will help the person incubate innovative approaches to the situation visualised.

Lastly, Wiseman (2009) developed the concept of doublethink. From this perspective, not only should the people visualise their desired goals, but they should also devote some time to imagining potential issues which might affect the achievement of these goals, and imagine how to surmount these difficulties. This specialist stated that the doublethink tool proved to be more effective than only visualising future desired states because the imagining is accompanied by the realistic assessment of potential difficulties.

The famous and wealthy communication leader, Oprah Winfrey, observed that her success in the media and entertainment sector is due to her use of vision boards. These boards are posters where people stick images related to their dreams on it. Then, people regularly visualise these desired outcomes while looking at the board, as if these results have already occurred. In relation to this, this entrepreneur observed that it is important to "create the highest, grandest vision possible for your life, because you become what you believe" (Williams, 2015).

G.3 Use of Positive Statements

The use of positive statements also called "affirmations" is also a powerful tool to obtain intuitive insights. These statements are worded in a positive way and can stem from goals previously set. When a person continuously repeats these affirmations, mentally or aloud, they become embedded in their subconscious minds; with the help of their R.A.S., the person will be guided to find effective ways to attain the outcomes related to these affirmations.

A person should repeat these positive statements in an assertive manner. If possible, they should also evoke emotions congruent to the ones they expect to experience when these outcomes are attained. These positive commands should be worded in a personal and meaningful manner. Present tense should be used to word these statements ("I choose …," "I allow …," "I see myself …," "I deserve …," "I feel well doing …," "I am empowered to …," or "I enjoy …"), avoiding words which imply lack (such as "wish," "desire," "want," and any similar ones). When employed on a regular basis, these statements programme the person's mind positively, and help this individual develop insightful alternatives.

According to Critcher and Dunning (2015), the use of affirmations can help people become less defensive when faced with threatening situations. Some research has concluded that neural pathways are developed with the use of affirmations (Cascio et al., 2016).

Appendix H: Human-Oriented Leadership

We suspect that the best kept secret of successful leaders is love: Being in love with leading, with the people who do the work, with what the organizations produce and with those who honor the organization by using its work. Leadership is an affair of the heart, not the head.

James Kouses and Barry Posner

There are various definitions of leadership, as well as countless leadership styles. Some people consider leaders as those individuals who are at the top of the organisational hierarchy, who have a relevant share of power over others. However, from the perspective of this book, anyone can act as a leader whenever they inspire, influence, or impact others, regardless of the position they hold in a company (CEO, customer service officer, etc.).

Human-oriented leaders are aware of the importance in business of developing robust long-lasting relationships with various stakeholders. These leaders also recognise that a company is always interdependent with its stakeholders. To that effect, these leaders understand that an organisation can only succeed with the assistance of its stakeholders. These human-centred leaders have other distinct traits, which will thoroughly be discussed below.

H.1 Empathetic Attitude

Research concluded that those with high power in an organisational structure are less inclined to adopt the perspective of other individuals (Galinsky et al., 2006). In addition, O'Reilly and Chatman (2020) stated that grandiose and narcissistic leaders tend to naturally adopt a non-compassionate attitude towards others. Moreover, these leaders often behave in a hostile and self-centred manner.

Instead, human-focused leaders embrace noble values, such as integrity, honesty, transparency, benevolence, respectfulness, connectedness, supportiveness, and kindness. These leaders know that they are being taken as a model to emulate by others, so they always aim to show the best version of themselves. These leaders also understand that people (employees, customer, etc.) are the main pillars of any business endeavour. These leaders are always interested in learning about people around them.

In any exchange with people, these leaders are keen to know how others think and how they feel, and adopt an equanimous but supportive attitude towards them. When people face

DOI: 10.4324/9781003372684-28

challenges, these leaders are willing to assist them in the best way possible. As a result of their supportive attitude, these leaders often develop loyalty-based ties with others (Ross, 2019). These leaders care for others and respect them. A research study concluded that respectful leaders prompt people to behave in a more creative manner (Carmeli et al., 2015).

Besides, these leaders contribute to the development of a warmer and more supportive work environment. In this type of workplace, people help one another to harness their unique skills and talents. When interacting with employees, human-focused leaders foster psychological safety. In other words, these leaders make other people feel safe and at ease. In the leaders' presence, people can be themselves, and their views are welcomed and appreciated. Research has concluded that leaders who behave in a civil manner (treating others respectfully, caring for them, being polite, etc.) are perceived as competent and warm by employees (Porath et al., 2015). In a similar vein, a research study concluded that leaders with the best image are those who adopt a co-operative and caring attitude towards others (Kouzes and Posner, 2011).

Empathetic leaders always adopt a kind attitude towards employees. Seppälä (2016) observed that, when leaders are kind to employees, these staff members tend to act in a less reactive manner; they also feel less threatened at work, and become more loyal to these leaders. Johri (2018) stated that, with kind leaders, employees tend to be happier, more motivated, committed, collaborative, trusting, and productive; staff members become less stressed, and customers are more satisfied.

This author also observed that companies led by kind leaders attract more talented staff, and these organisations are perceived as having great work environments. In simple words, kind leaders foster a psychologically safer workplace. The concept of psychologically safety was explained in this book in Chapter 10.

Herb Kelleher, who co-founded Southwest Airlines and was previously the CEO of this company, is a good example of a kind leader. When walking over the company's hub, this business leader always kindly smiled at people, and gave handshakes to customers in a friendly manner. In addition, this business man even hugged staff members and overtly appreciated their contribution to the company. All employees felt like family with this business leader (Goleman and Boyatzis, 2008).

There is another relevant point to highlight. Empathetic leaders foster the development of an inclusive, diverse, and participative work environment, where everyone is considered a high-value contributor. Besides, these leaders avoid stubbornly imposing their ideas onto others. Instead, they are willing to collectively debate their insights and reflect on the views of other people. Moreover, these leaders adopt an inquisitive attitude towards others; they regularly ask relevant questions to others to learn from them.

These leaders adopt an understanding attitude when people make mistakes. In that sense, these leaders avoid criticising others harshly for their shortcomings, errors, and setbacks. These leaders clearly understand that all people, including themselves, are fallible human beings, who are valuable works in progress with unique capabilities to be harnessed. Consequently, these leaders regularly focus on others' unique capabilities, instead of centring on their weaknesses.

When relevant change needs to be introduced, human-oriented leaders always try to frontally explain the real motives driving that change, instead of keeping a secretive agenda. When change has a significant impact on some of the company's stakeholders, these leaders adopt a supportive attitude towards them. These leaders support those affected by change throughout the implementation process of change. This assistance could include, for example, training courses, counselling sessions, mentoring programmes, and other support activities. As seen in this book, at Caterpillar, the company specialising in construction machinery and equipment, mentorship is offered to its employees to provide them with valuable guidance.

Human-focused leaders understand the importance of inclusive conversations with others. These leaders listen actively and curiously to the opinions and ideas of others, avoiding dominating the exchanges. Whenever these leaders express their views, they aim to be clear, and use plain and straightforward words. In that sense, these leaders avoid using complicated technical terms to convey their insights, if possible.

These leaders are always willing to hold content-rich conversations with the company's stakeholders. These exchanges include both business topics (goals, prices, etc.) and personal aspects (pastimes, family, etc.). These conversations include rational aspects (plans, goals, etc.), but also emotional aspects (how people feel, what upsets them, etc.).

These leaders can wisely express their emotions to others, without being overwhelmed by these emotional states. Even when being pressurised by intense detrimental emotions, they can remain centred on the company's vision and purpose, and inspire others to follow them through. These leaders clearly know that all emotional states, either positive or negative, have an infectious effect on others around (Barsade, 2002). Therefore, whenever possible, these leaders willingly try to generate a good emotional environment for all people around them.

In workplaces infused with positive emotions, employees are more inclined to show higher productivity levels, more innovation, better decision-making, and more frequent prosocial behaviour (helping others, etc.) (Cameron, 2012). Research studies have concluded that leaders with an empathetic attitude prompt people to work in a kinder and more effective manner (Fosslien and Duffy, 2019).

Lastly, these leaders encourage others to express how they feel. To that effect, these leaders avoid stifling the emotional states experienced by others. On the contrary, these leaders are genuinely interested in knowing more about how people feel, and offer them support, when possible.

H.2 Relationship-Building

> The key to a leader's impact is sincerity. Before they can inspire with emotion, they must be swayed by it themself. Before they can move the team's tears their own must flow. To convince them they must themself believe.
>
> **Winston Churchill**

Human-oriented leaders understand that, in business, economic aspects (profits, market share, etc.) are as important as relational aspects (supportiveness, care, etc.). Consequently, these leaders aim to develop long-term and mutually beneficial relationships with all the company's stakeholders. When relating to these stakeholders, this type of leader adopts a supportive and co-operative attitude.

These leaders support a meaningful business purpose which includes economic aspects (profits, etc.), social impact (caring for different stakeholders), and environmental impact (caring for the environment). This type of mission was thoroughly explained in Chapter 1. These leaders are characterised for always putting this high purpose as the first priority (Mackey et al., 2020). These leaders embed this broader business perspective (including economic, social, and environmental aspects) into the organisation culture (Stubbs and Cocklin, 2008).

According to Freeman (2009a), these leaders try to add value to all the company's relevant stakeholders, both internal (e.g., employees and management) and external ones (customers, suppliers, etc.), because all these stakeholders are paramount for the company's success. These leaders realise that each of these stakeholders (suppliers, customers, etc.) are "living breathing human beings... with names and faces," who need to be treated in a compassionate fashion, and whose needs must be addressed and satisfied (Freeman, 2009b).

When making business decisions, these leaders carefully analyse and ensure that the actions to be taken do not bring about any negative impact on the company's stakeholders. These thoughtful leaders avoid any business project which could potentially harm stakeholders. The long- and short-term consequences of any business decision are mindfully assessed to avoid any detrimental impact on the company's stakeholders. As seen previously, companies like The Body Shop, the cosmetics company, cut off its ties with its main palm oil supplier because this supplier had tried to evict hundreds of local people to set up its new plantation.

These leaders develop a "we" perspective, which implies continually seeking the common good for all involved, instead of adopting a "me" attitude which is based on self-interest (Barclay, 2015). As seen in this book, Anita Roddick is a good example of human-oriented leaders. This woman is the founder of The Body Shop, a company which brings about positive social and environmental impact. Since its origin, this company offers cruelty-free products which have natural ingredients and supports local communities (The Body Shop, 2022b).

Human-oriented leaders bolster win-win agreements with the company's stakeholders, which means that all parties have their unique needs met. In these agreements, no party wins at the expense of others. Besides, these leaders deal with any conflict with these stakeholders in a friendly manner, avoiding adopting any adversarial attitude towards them.

These leaders also adopt a generous attitude towards others. In that sense, these leaders are always willing to offer others something of value, such as advice, support, technical information, or training. These leaders are also empowered to give others constructive feedback which helps them unleash their full potential.

These leaders always adopt an appreciative attitude towards the company's stakeholders for their contribution and support. For example, this type of leader can be grateful to the company's employees for their hard work and commitment to the company's projects. Oftentimes, these leaders show their appreciation overtly, for example, through the organisation of special events to thank people publicly. As seen previously, the business leader John Paul DeJoria, who co-founded John Paul Mitchell Systems, observed that when people do something well, one should praise them overtly to prompt them to feel good.

There is another point to highlight. Human-centred leaders aim to develop collective endeavours. These leaders always foster work in groups as well as collaborative projects, and aim to integrate the unique skills of various people in a synergetic manner. These leaders are also keen to develop valuable partnerships with various stakeholders. For example, these leaders are keen to develop alliances with other companies, government agencies, or non-profit organisations. In this book, there are some examples of partnerships developed by companies like IKEA, which has a partnership with Lego. Another example is Lego which developed a partnership with the WWF (World Wide Fund for Nature).

These leaders are so passionate and determined that they naturally inspire others to follow them. Their enthusiasm is so infectious that they become natural magnets to others. This type of leader has a strong vision, which naturally brings about momentum and inspires others (De Pree, 2004). When leading business projects, these leaders avoid controlling every single aspect of these endeavours. Instead, they trust others' knowledge and discerning skills, and delegate tasks accordingly. In other words, these leaders willingly prevent themselves from micromanaging others and allow them to act in the best way possible, to apply their unique skills and experience.

These leaders sparingly use humour to lighten relationships with others, and make these bonds more humanised. According to research, when business leaders use non-deprecatory humour with staff members, these workers tend to see these leaders in a more positive light, and experience enhanced job satisfaction (Decker, 1987). As seen in this book, the founder and former CEO of Spanx (a company which sells shapeware products) used humour to grab the attention of retailers.

H.3 Open-Mindedness and Humility

There is a greater need to extinguish arrogance than a blazing fire.

Heraclitus

Human-oriented leaders adopt a humble attitude towards others. By being humble, these leaders are always willing to learn from others. These leaders perceive their own strengths and shortcomings in a balanced fashion (Brown, 2021). These leaders never abuse their power or impose their own ideas. Instead, these leaders consider others as valuable collaborators to the company's objectives. Moreover, before making any important decision, these leaders are willing to welcome suggestions from other people.

In simple words, these leaders do not adopt an omniscient attitude. Instead, they admit when they do not know something, and look for insights from various sources. These leaders have a growth mindset; they believe that learning is a lifelong journey. These leaders are willing to learn from others, from the janitor up to the top executive. In relation to this, the CEO of Microsoft, Satya Nadella wisely quipped, "Don't be a know-it-all. Be a learn-it-all"; this is a leader with a growth mindset (Lindergaard, 2022). Research has shown that leaders with a humble attitude towards their employees bring about decreased employee turnover and heightened employee engagement (Engelberg and Aaronson, 2019).

There is another point to discuss. Humble leaders are interested in all types of knowledge, not only that related to business (e.g., data regarding the industrial sector). They are also keen on knowledge related to seemingly unrelated fields (psychology, sociology, etc.). In addition, their non-arrogant attitude prompts these leaders to look for assistance from professionals (coaches, mentors, consultants, advisors, etc.), whenever needed.

These leaders regularly resort to formal sources (books, seminars, etc.) but also more informal ones (reviews on social media, etc.) to become more knowledgeable on a specific topic. As seen in this book, Warren Buffett, is committed to reading several hours every day. As mentioned, these leaders regularly learn from internal stakeholders (e.g., employees, management) and external ones (customers, etc.). For instance, if the company's products received negative customer reviews, these leaders will dissect this feedback to look for alternatives to improve these products.

These leaders are explorative and look for innovative ways of doing things. These leaders know that, when things work well, they can always be improved even more over time. Therefore, they look for suggestions from others to do things in a better way. These leaders appreciate and value the unique knowledge and distinctive perspectives of those around them.

These leaders are always willing to ask others various questions, even those seemingly obvious. When asking others for advice, these leaders listen to them in an inquisitive and attentive manner and are eager to learn from others, as much as possible. An entrepreneur like Richard Branson is a good example of an inquisitive business leader; this entrepreneur always carries a notepad with him, and is willing to ask questions and learn from others, to add more value to stakeholders.

Oftentimes, humble leaders encourage stakeholders to provide them with valuable feedback. This valuable feedback could include insights into the company's economic parameters (sales, profits, etc.) and non-economic aspects (climate of the company's workplace, etc.). Not only do these leaders welcome the views of others, but they also change their own views when mistaken. It was seen that in companies like Netflix, people are encouraged to give feedback to others, including superiors.

Sometimes, humble leaders learn from other organisations in the sector or from other industries. These business people are prone to gather valuable insights from these organisations (the way they serve their customers, the packaging they use for their products, etc.) and adapt these insights or improve them.

Besides, humble leaders are willing to learn from their own mistakes, but also from errors made by others. As seen in this book, James Dyson is a valuable example of a leader who learned from countless mistakes when he was developing the bagless vacuum cleaner. When humble leaders make any blunders, they do not hide these errors away, but instead they own these mistakes and take responsibility with no delay. In addition, these leaders are not ashamed of apologising in an overt and heartfelt manner when they hurt others.

These leaders also welcome brutal facts, for instance, factors which affect the company's performance in a negative manner (e.g., drop in the company's sales). They never avoid these facts, despite their negative traits. Moreover, these leaders are open to overtly discussing these challenging issues with others in order to debate potential strategies to surmount them.

These leaders display "epistemic humility," as they realise that their views on any issue are always limited (Ozawa-de Silva and Karlin, 2017). These leaders adopt an open-minded attitude. They continually challenge their own assumptions, limiting beliefs, and mental biases; they let go of the need to be right at all times. Their humility prompts these leaders to admit that they have some blind spots, which can prompt them to unintentionally leave important aspects aside.

Human-oriented leaders also admit that their discerning skills can be faulty, and they can make mistakes. Consequently, these leaders avoid having any rigid views on any topic, but instead they are open to re-evaluating their own perspective on a regular basis. When leaders adopt a humble attitude, employees tend to be more engaged, especially when working in teams (Owens et al., 2013). These leaders are always willing to discuss relevant issues with others. The views of all stakeholders are considered relevant.

When analysing new endeavours to undertake, these leaders consider their potential positive aspects, but also their possible downside. As seen previously, when Richard Branson started up his airline Virgin Atlantic, he thoroughly analysed the potential risks related to that endeavour.

These leaders try to assess any business projects from different perspectives, emotional, rational, long-term, short-term, technical aspects, commercial aspects, legal factors, etc. These leaders always welcome people with different specialisms in order to analyse these projects in a multidimensional manner. These leaders also analyse these issues critically, considering the perspectives from different stakeholders (customers, competitors, etc.). As seen previously, when Tata Motors launched the small car branded Tata Nano, this company assessed various aspects, such as government legal regulations, company's costs, and customer needs. The case regarding Hippo Roller was also discussed in this book. This company assessed its own product from different perspectives, such as its simplicity to use, its positive social impact, its maintenance, its durability, and its availability.

Lastly, when analysing relevant business issues, these leaders look for insights from different areas within the organisation, for example, marketing department and human resources team. Sometimes, these leaders hold cross-functional meetings, which include representatives from different departments. These meetings can foster some creative activities (e.g., brainstorming) to assess issues in a non-traditional manner. As seen, companies like Cisco or Acme Whistles are keen on using cross-departmental meetings.

Bibliography

1t. 2022. 1t.org: A Platform for the Trillion Trees Community. https://www.1t.org/ (Accessed: October 17, 2022).

3M. 2022. Code of Conduct. https://www.3m.com/3M/en_US/ethics-compliance/code/respectful/ (Accessed: October 17, 2022).

3M, 2022b. 3M's SVP of HR Gets Honest about What's Great and What Could be Better About Working at 3M. https://www.3m.com/3M/en_US/careers-us/full-story/?storyid=8298f76a-754b-4ae6-954d-50a9d215b4ea (Accessed: November 17, 2022).

Aaker, J. and Bagdonas, N. 2020. *Humour, Seriously: Why Humour Is a Superpower at Work and in Life*. London: Penguin.

Abrams, R. C. 2017. *Body Wise. Discovering Your Body's Intelligence for Lifelong Health and Healing*. London: Blue Bird.

Acar, O. A., Tarakci, M. and Van Knippenberg, D. 2019. Creativity and innovation under constraints: A cross-disciplinary integrative review. *Journal of Management*, 45(1), 96–121. https://doi.org/10.1177/0149206318805832

Achor, S. 2011. *The Happiness Advantage. How a Positive Brain Fuels Success in Work and Life*. London: Virgin Books.

Achor, S. 2013. *Before Happiness*. New York: Crown Business.

Acme Whistles, 2022. https://www.acmewhistles.co.uk/ (Accessed: December 31, 2022).

Adams, B. 2016. How Google's 20 Percent Rule Can Make You More Productive and Energetic. *Inc.* https://www.inc.com/bryan-adams/12-ways-to-encourage-more-free-thinking-and-innovation-into-any-business.html (Accessed: October 17, 2022).

Adams, J. L. 2001. *Conceptual Blockbusting. A Guide to Better Ideas*. Cambridge: Perseus Publishing.

Airbnb, 2021. In Support of Paid Leave for Employees in the US. July 22, 2021 https://news.airbnb.com/in-support-of-paid-leave-for-all-in-the-us/ (Accessed: December 2, 2022).

Airbnb, 2022. Airbnb. https://www.airbnb.co.uk/ (Accessed: October 2, 2022).

Aktas, I. 2022. Starbucks' Social Media Customer Service Performance. December 16, 2022. Juphy. https://juphy.com/blog/starbuckss-social-media-customer-service-performance (Accessed: December 26, 2022).

Albretcht, K. 1979. *Stress and the Manager. Make It Work for You*. New York: Touchstone.

Alderfer, C. P. 1972. *Existence, Relatedness and Growth: Human Needs in Organizational Settings*. New York, NY: Free Press.

Aldi, 2022. ALDI Twice as Nice Guarantee. https://www.aldi.us/en/about-aldi/return-policy/ (Accessed: December 19, 2022).

Aleksandrova, R. 2021. 4 Modern Workplace Design Examples Your Office. AskCody. May 18, 2022. https://www.askcody.com/blog/modern-workplace-design-examples (Accessed: December 9, 2022).

Alessandra, T. and O'Connor, M. 1998. *The Platinum Rule. Discover the Four Basic Business Personalities and How They Can Lead You to Success*. New York, NY: Warner Book.

Alexander, R. A. 2020. Study on the impact of learned optimism and emotional intelligence on sales performance and turnover intention. *Altius Shodh Journal of Management & Commerce*. Jul 2020

Allen, D. 2003. *Ready for Everything. 52 Productivity Principles for Getting Things Done*. New York, NY: Viking.

Allen, P. and Wotten, G. 1998. *Selling*. Harlow, UK: FT Prentice Hall.

Almeida, D. M., Rush, J., Mogle, J., Piazza, J. R., Cerino, E. and Charles, S. T. 2023.Longitudinal change in daily stress across 20 years of adulthood: Results from the national study of daily experiences. *Developmental Psychology*, 59(3), 515–523. https://doi.org/10.1037/dev0001469. Epub 2022 Sep 29. PMID: 36174182; PMCID: PMC9993073.

Amabile, T. and Kramer, S. 2011. The Power of Small Wins. *Harvard Business Review*. [Online] Available at https://hbr.org/2011/05/the-power-of-small-wins (Accessed: September 16, 2018).

Amabile, T. and Kramer, S. 2012. The Progress Principle: Optimising Inner Work Life to Create Value. *Rotman Magazine*. pp. 28–33.

Ambadar, Z., Cohn, J. F. and Reed, L. I. 2009. All smiles are not created equal: Morphology and timing of smiles perceived as amused, polite, and embarrassed/nervous. *Journal of Nonverbal Behavior*, 33(1), 17–34. https://doi.org/10.1007/s10919-008-0059-5. PMID: 19554208; PMCID: PMC2701206.

American Express. 2022a. Who We Are. https://about.americanexpress.com/our-company/who-we-are/who-we-are/ (Accessed: September 23, 2022).

American Express. 2022b. Life at American Express: Winning as a Team by Backing Each Other. https://www.americanexpress.com/en-us/careers/about-teamamex/ (Accessed: September 23, 2022).

AMFG, 2023. AMFG, Autonomous Manufacturing. Industrial Applications of 3D Printing: The Ultimate Guide. https://amfg.ai/industrial-applications-of-3d-printing-the-ultimate-guide/ (Accessed: January 23, 2023).

Angell, P. and Rizkallah, T. 2004. *Business Communication Design: Creativity Strategies and Solutions*. New York, NY: McGraw-Hill.

Angry Espresso, 2019. Why Starbucks Writes Your Name on the Cup. https://www.angryespresso.com/post/why-starbucks-writes-your-name-on-the-cup

Anjos, A. 2022. Are Teamwork and Collaboration the Same? 9 Examples from Great Companies. Nutcache. https://www.nutcache.com/blog/are-teamwork-and-collaboration-the-same-9-examples-from-great-companies/ (Accessed: October 23, 2022).

Apps, J. 2012. *Voice and Speaking Skills for Dummies*. Chichester, UK: Wiley.

Apps, J. 2014. *The Art of Conversation. Change Your Life with Confident Communication*. Chichester, UK: Capstone.

Argyle, M. 1994. *The Psychology of Interpersonal Behaviour*. London: Penguin Books.

Armstrong, A. 2015. Compassion at Work - What's Your Business Case? HR Zone. https://www.hrzone.com/engage/managers/compassion-at-work-whats-your-business-case (Accessed: October 2, 2022).

Arnold, W. W. and Plas, J. 1993. *The Human Touch. Today's Most Unusual Program for Productivity and Profit*. New York, NY: Wiley.

Ashkanasy, N. M. and Ashton-James, C. E. 2007. *Positive Emotion in Organizations: A Multi-Level Framework*. In Nelson, D. and C. L. Cooper (Eds.). *Positive Organizational Behaviour. Accentuating the Positive at Work*, 57–73. London: Sage.

Askew, T. 2017. Forgiveness: A Key Tool for Business Success. Don't Look for Revenge. Look for Success. *Inc.* https://www.inc.com/tim-askew/forgiveness-a-key-tool-for-business-success.html (Accessed: October 12, 2022).

Assagioli, R. 1974. *The Act of Will*. London: Wildwood House.

Associated Press, 2016. Volkswagen CEO Apologizes for Emissions Scandal. Associated Press. https://www.youtube.com/watch?v=t7ne3cwqI4A (Accessed: October 30, 2022).

Atchley, R. A., Strayer, D. L. and Atchley, P. (2012). Creativity in the wild: Improving creative reasoning through immersion in natural settings. *PloS One*, 7(12), e51474. https://doi.org/10.1371/journal.pone.0051474 (Accessed: October 2, 2022).

Atkinson, R., Smith, E. and Bem, E. et al. 1981. *Hilgard's Introduction to Psychology*. New York, NY: Harcourt Brace College Publishers.

Autry, J. A. and Mitchell, S. 1998. *Real Power. Business Lessons from the Tao Te Ching*. London: Nicholas Brealey.

Ayala, E. E., Winseman, J. S., Johnsen, R. D. and Mason, H. R. C. 2018. U.S. Medical students who engage in self-care report less stress and higher quality of life. *BMC Medical Education*, 18(1), 189. https://doi.org/10.1186/s12909-018-1296-x. PMID: 30081886; PMCID: PMC6080382.

B Corporation, 2022. About B Corp Certification. Measuring a company's entire social and environmental impact. https://www.bcorporation.net/en-us/certification (Accessed: December 12 2022).

Baby2baby. 2022. Baby2Baby. https://baby2baby.org/ (Accessed: October 12, 2022).

Bacci, I. 2002. *The Art of Effortless Living*. London: Bantam Books.

Baeza, R., Allred, D., Brigl, M., Deutschländer, S., Gildehaus, C., Lovich, D., Schmidt, M., Stutzman, C. and Taylor, L. 2021. *Chapter 2: The CEO Innovation Agenda*. in *Most Innovative Companies 2021. Overcoming the Innovation Gap*. BCG. April. https://web-assets.bcg.com/eb/93/cfbea005442482b0 adc64b9f499f/bcg-most-innovative-companies-2021-apr-2021-r.pdf (Accessed: December 26, 2022).

Bailes, F. 2004. *Basic Principles of the Science of Mind*. Marina del Rey, CA: De Vorss Publications.

Baker, S. and Martinson, D. L. 2002. Out of the red-light district. Five principles for ethically proactive public relations. *Public Relations Quarterly*, 47(3), 12–15.

Balban, M. Y., Neri, E., Kogon, M. M., Weed, L., Nouriani, B., Jo, B., Holl, G., Zeitzer, J. M., Spiegel, D. and Huberman, A. D. 2023. Brief structured respiration practices enhance mood and reduce physiological arousal. *Cell Reports Medicine*, 4(1), 100895. https://doi.org/10.1016/j.xcrm.2022.100895. Epub 2023 Jan 10. PMID: 36630953; PMCID: PMC9873947.

Balch, O. 2022. Why More Managers Are Going Back to Nature. *Financial Times*. August 22, 2022. https://www.ft.com/content/e03cc4bb-2415-45fa-9f50-1a413ea76a6e (Accessed: December 31, 2022).

Bangladesh Accord, 2023. Accord on Fire and Building Safety in Bangladesh. https://bangladeshaccord.org (Accessed: January 31, 2023).

Barclay, J. 2015. *Conscious Culture. How to Build a High Performing Workplace through Values, Ethics, and Leadership*. New York: Morgan James.

Barczak, B. 2022. Using Internal Business Storytelling to Motivate Employees and Build Culture. https://www.llrpartners.com/growth-bit/internal-business-storytelling-motivate-employees-build-culture/ (Accessed: December 12, 2022).

Barnes, D., Ponder, C. and Dugar, N. K. 2011. Investigating the key routes to customer delight, *Journal of Marketing Theory and Practice*, 19(4), 359–376. https://doi.org/10.2753/MTP1069-6679190401

Barrett, R. 1998. *Liberating the Corporate Soul. Building and Visionary Organization*. Woburn: Butterworth-Heinemann.

Barrett, R. 2017. *The Values-Driven Organization: Cultural Health and Employee Well-Being as a Pathway to Sustainable Performance*. NY: Routledge.

Barsade, S. G. 2002. The ripple effect: Emotional contagion and its influence on group behavior. *Administrative Science Quarterly*, 47(4), 644–675. https://doi.org/10.2307/3094912 (Accessed: December 21, 2022).

Barsade, S. G. and O'Neill, O. A. 2014. What's love got to do with it? A longitudinal study of the culture of companionate love and employee and client outcomes in a long-term care setting. *Administrative Science Quarterly*, 59(4), 551–598.

Barsade, S. G. and O'Neill, O. A. 2016. Manage Your Emotional Culture. *Harvard Business Review*. Jan–Feb 2016. https://hbr.org/2016/01/manage-your-emotional-culture (Accessed: November 21, 2022).

Basso, J. C., McHale, A., Ende, V., Oberlin, D. J. and Suzuki, W. A. 2019. Brief, daily meditation enhances attention, memory, mood, and emotional regulation in non-experienced meditators. *Behavioural Brain Research*, 356, 208–220. https://www.sciencedirect.com/science/article/abs/pii/S016643281830322X?via%3Dihub (Accessed: January 2, 2023).

Bateman, A., Barrington, B. and Date, K. 2020. Why You Need a Supplier-Diversity Program. *Harvard Business Review*. August 17, 2020. https://hbr.org/2020/08/why-you-need-a-supplier-diversity-program (Accessed: December 26, 2022).

Baumeister, R. F., Bratslavsky, E. and Finkenauer, C. et al. 2001. Bad is stronger than good. *Review of General Psychology*, 5(4), 323–370.

Baumeister, R. F. and Leary, M. R. 1995. The need to belong: Desire for interpersonal attachments as a fundamental human motivation. *Psychological Bulletin*, 117(3), 497–529.

Bauman, Z. 2017. Being Populist Is Not Always Bad (in Spanish). Ser Populista No Es Siempre Malo. Perfil Newspaper. January 9, 2017. [Online] Available at https://www.perfil.com/noticias/internacional/zygmunt-bauman-ser-populista-no-es-siempre-malo.phtml (Accessed: September 16, 2018).

Bayer, L. 2016. *The 30% Solution. How Civility at Work Increases Retention, Engagement, and Profitability*. Melbourne: Motivational Press.

Bebchuk, L. A. and Tallarita, R. 2022. The Illusory Promise of Stakeholder Governance. *Harvard Law School Forum on Corporate Governance* Working Paper 2020-1, 24 March 2022. https://corpgov.law. harvard.edu/2020/03/02/the-illusory-promise-of-stakeholder-governance/ (Accessed: September 24, 2022).

Belyh, A. 2019. 8 Most Creative Entrepreneurs in History. Cleverism. September 23, 2019. https://www. cleverism.com/8-creative-entrepreneurs-history/ (Accessed: January 2, 2023).

Ben & Jerry's. 2022a. Ben & Jerry's Corporate Social Responsibility https://bjsocialresponsibility.weebly. com/index.html (Accessed: September 28, 2022).

Ben & Jerry's. 2022b. Ben & Jerry's Our SEAR Reports https://www.benjerry.co.uk/about-us/sear-reports (Accessed: September 28, 2022).

Benton, L. 2022. Unlimited Holiday – Good idea or Gimmick? 25 February 2022. https://libertymind. co.uk/unlimited-holiday-good-idea-or-gimmick/ (Accessed: November 28, 2022).

Ben-Ze'ev, A. 2000. *The Subtlety of Emotions*. London: Bradford Books.

Bergstrom, M. 2021. The Best Conversation I've Ever Had While Running My Company's Live Chat. June 10, 2021. https://blog.hubspot.com/marketing/snapengage-live-chat-example (Accessed: September 28, 2022).

Bernazzani, S. 2021. 6 Examples of Good Customer Service (and What You Can Learn From Them) https:// blog.hubspot.com/service/good-customer-service (Accessed: September 28, 2022).

Berne, E. 1964. *Games People Play*. New York, NY: Grove Press.

Berns, Y. 2022. Companies with the Coolest Office Layouts. Comparably. May 5, 2022. https://www. comparably.com/news/companies-with-the-coolest-office-layouts/ (Accessed: December 12, 2022).

Bernstein, E. S. and Turban, S. 2018. The impact of the 'Open' workspace on human collaboration. *Philosophical Transaction of Royal Society B*, 373(1753). [Online] Available at https://doi.org/10.1098/ rstb.2017.0239 (Accessed: December 19, 2018).

Bevelin, P. 2017. *Seeking Wisdom*. Sweden: Post Scriptum.

Bevelin, P. A. 2019. *Few Lessons for Investors and Managers from Warren E. Buffett*. USA: Post Scriptum.

Bilyeu, T. 2017. Billionaire Reveals The Key Habits that Will Change Your Life! John Paul DeJoria. May 2, 2017. https://www.youtube.com/watch?v=aIVCyp_7Cqc&t=2637s (Accessed: September 28, 2022).

Bishop. 2019. Eight London Companies that Are Revolutionizing Work-Life Balance WeWork Ideas. August 15, 2019. https://www.wework.com/ideas/professional-development/management-leadership/ eight-london-companies-that-are-revolutionizing-work-life-balance (Accessed: October 31, 2022).

Black, S. 2016. How the 15% Rule Became a Stepping Stone for 3M's Innovation. Market Realist. June 22, 2016. https://marketrealist.com/2016/06/15-rule-became-stepping-stone-3ms-innovation/ (Accessed: September 28, 2022).

Blackburn, E. and Epel, E. 2017. *The Telomere Effect. A Revolutionary Approach to Living Younger, Healthier, Longer*. London: Orion Spring.

Blaschka, A. 2019.Three Ways To Nail What Sir Richard Branson Cites as His Top Leadership Soft Skill. *Forbes*. March 11, 2019. https://www.forbes.com/sites/amyblaschka/2019/03/11/three-ways-to-nail-what-sir-richard-branson-cites-as-his-top-leadership-soft-skill/?sh=4021d8a85496(Accessed:November12, 2022).

Bloomberg. 2021. Chipotle Builds Virtual Community for Its Remote Workplace. Bloomberg UK. February 16, 2021. https://www.bloomberg.com/press-releases/2021-02-16/chipotle-builds-virtual-community-for-its-remote-workplace (Accessed: December 1, 2022).

BLQK Coffee. 2023. About Us. Our Mission Is to Spread Joy & Inspire Service through Great Coffee and a Dedication to Giving Back. https://blqk.coffee/pages/about (Accessed: January 12, 2023).

Blundel, R. 2004. *Effective Organisational Communication. Perspectives, Principles and Practices*. Harlow, UK: FT Prentice Hall.

Blystone, D., James, M. and Jackson, A. 2022. The Story of Uber. Investopedia. https://www.investopedia. com/articles/personal-finance/111015/story-uber.asp#:~:text=Uber%27s%20story%20began%20 in%20Paris,co%2Dfounded%20for%20large%20sums (Accessed: December 28, 2022).

Blythe, J. 2012. *Essentials of Marketing*. Harlow: Pearson Education Ltd.

Blythe, J. and Martin, J. 2019. *Essentials of Marketing*. Harlow: Pearson Education Ltd.

Bodian, S. 2006. *Meditation for Dummies*. Indianapolis, IN: Wiley.

Bogacz, R. 2020. Dopamine role in learning and action inference. *eLife*, 9, e53262. https://doi.org/10.7554/eLife.53262

Bolton, S. C. and Houlihan, M. 2009. Are we having fun yet? A consideration of workplace fun and engagement. *Employee Relations*, 31(6), 556–568.

Bonusly. 2022. 15 Unique Examples of Employee Recognition in Action. https://bonus.ly/employee-recognition-guide/employee-recognition-examples (Accessed: October 19, 2022).

Boogaard, K. 2022. 21 Companies Who Value Big Ideas. The Muse. https://www.themuse.com/advice/21-companies-who-value-big-ideas (Accessed: December 19, 2022).

Borg, J. 2011. *Body Language. How to Know What's Really Been Said.* London: Pearson.

Bradley, A. 2019. *The Human Moment: The Positive Power of Compassion in the Workplace.* London: LID Publishing.

Bragg, A. and Bragg, M. 2005. *Developing New Business Ideas. A Step-by-Step Guide to Creating New Business Ideas Worth Backing.* Harlow, UK: FT Prentice Hall.

Brandenburger, A. M. and Nalebuff, B. 1996. *Co-Opetition.* New York, NY: Doubleday.

Branson, R. 2014. Richard Branson: We Make Virgin Companies Fun. https://www.youtube.com/watch?v=IMAPpPzhh1A (Accessed: October 2, 2022).

Branson, R. 2019. Why Everyone Should Take Notes. April 24, 2019. https://www.virgin.com/branson-family/richard-branson-blog/why-everyone-should-take-notes (Accessed: January 2, 2023).

Branson, R. 2019b. Instinct in a World of Analytics. November 27, 2019. https://www.virgin.com/branson-family/richard-branson-blog/instinct-world-analytics (Accessed: January 4, 2023).

Branson, R. 2016. Sir Richard Branson on "How to Create a Winning Culture. May 31, 2016. https://www.youtube.com/watch?v=n0K0_icUUOc (Accessed: October 2, 2022).

Bridges, C. 2017. *In Your Creative Element. The Formula for Creative Success in Business.* London: Kogan Page.

Brim, B. and Asplund, J. 2009. Driving Engagement by Focusing on Strengths. Gallup Business Journal. November 12, 2009 https://news.gallup.com/businessjournal/124214/driving-engagement-focusing-strengths.aspx (Accessed: December 1, 2022).

Brewer, S. 2010. *Cut Your Stress. An Easy-to-Follow Guide for Stress-Free Living.* London: Quercus.

Brooks, A. 2022. 30 Killer Examples of Personalised Customer Experiences. February 7, 2022. True North. https://www.ventureharbour.com/personalised-experiences-examples/ (Accessed: December 24, 2022).

Brooksbank, R. 2002. *Hot Marketing. Cool Profits. 200 Proven Sales and Marketing Ideas to Grow Your Business.* Sydney: McGraw-Hill.

Brown, B. 2021. *Atlas of the Heart. Mapping Meaningful Connection and the Language of Human Experience.* Vermillion: London.

Brown, S. 1997. *Practical Feng Shui. Arrange, Decorate and Accessorize Your Home to Promote Health, Wealth and Happiness.* London: Ward Lock.

Brown, P. and Levinson, S. 1987. *Politeness. Some Universals in Language Usage.* Cambridge: Cambridge University Press.

Brown, S. and Vaughan, C. 2010. *Play. How It Shapes the Brain, Opens the Imagination and Invigorates The Soul.* New York, NY: Penguin Group.

Brucks, M. S. and Levav, J. 2022. Virtual communication curbs creative idea generation. *Nature*, 605, 108–112. https://doi.org/10.1038/s41586-022-04643-y

Bryant, J. H. 2009. *Love Leadership. The New Way to Lead in a Fear-Based World.* San Francisco, CA: Jossey Bass.

Buchanan, 2014. 100 Great Questions Every Entrepreneur Should Ask. *Inc.* April. https://www.inc.com/magazine/201404/leigh-buchanan/100-questions-business-leaders-should-ask.html (Accessed: December 28, 2022).

Buchanan, D. A. and Huczynsky, A. 2019. *Organizational Behaviour.* Harlow: Pearson.

Buckingham, W., Brunham, D., Hill, C. et al. 2011. The Philosophy Book. London: DK.

Buffett, W. 2012. Buffett An Interview With Warren Buffett Part 2 of 9. GMIRatings. September 17, 2012. https://www.youtube.com/watch?v=KCUL00-8dCo (Accessed: December 2, 2022).

Bunting, M. 2016. *The Mindful Leader: 7 Practices for Transforming Your Leadership, Your Organisation and Your Life.* Milton Qld: Wiley.

Burg, B. and Mahn, J. D. 2010. *The Go-Giver. A Little Story about a Powerful Business Idea*. London: Penguin Books.

Burn, C. 2020. Working from Home Best Practice – Buffer. Shine. December 15, 2020. https://www.shineworkplacewellbeing.com/working-from-home-best-practice-shine-workplace-wellbeing/ (Accessed: December 1, 2022).

Burn, C. 2022. Employee Wellbeing Case Study – Innocent Drinks. Shine. November 10, 2020. https://www.shineworkplacewellbeing.com/employee-wellbeing-case-study/ (Accessed: December 19, 2022).

Bushe, G. R. 2013. *The Appreciative Inquiry Model*. In Kessler, H. (Ed.). *Encyclopedia of Management Theory*. Los Angeles, CA: Sage. [Online] Available at http://www.gervasebushe.ca/the_AI_model.pdf (Accessed: December 19, 2018).

Business Roundtable. 2019. Statement on the Purpose of a Corporation. https://perma.cc/CMR8-WMXE (Accessed: September 24, 2022).

Butler, G. and Hope. T. 2008. *Manage Your Mind*. Oxford: Oxford University Press.

Butterick, K. 2011. *Introducing Public Relations. Theory and Practice*. London: SAGE.

Buzan, T. 2000. *Head First. 10 Ways to Tap into Your Natural Genius*. London: Thorsons.

Buzan, T. 2002. *How to Mind Map. The Thinking Tool that Will Change Your Life*. London: Thorsons.

Buzan, T. and Buzan, B. 2003. *The Mindmap Book. Unlock Your Creativity, Boost Your Memory, Change Your Life*. London: BBS Books.

Cameron, K. 2012. *Positive Leadership. Strategies for Extraordinary Performance*. San Francisco: Berrett-Koehler Publishers.

Cameron, W. B. 1963. *Informal Sociology, a Casual Introduction to Sociological Thinking*. New York, NY: Random House.

Canfield, 2022. About Jack Canfield. https://jackcanfield.com/about-jack-canfield/ (Accessed: October 12, 2022).

Canfield, J. 2005. *The Success Principles: How to Get from Where You Are to Where You Want to Be*. New York: Harper Collins.

Care/of, 2022. Personalized Vitamins. Results You Can Really Feel. https://takecareof.com/ (Accessed: December 22, 2022).

Carlson, R. 1999. *Don't Sweat the Small Stuff at Work. Simple Ways to Minimize Stress and Conflict While Bringing Out the Best in Yourself and Others*. London: Hodder and Stoughton.

Carlson, R. and Bailey, J. 1998. *Slowing Down to the Speed of Life. How to Create a More Peaceful, Simpler Life from the Inside Out*. London: Hodder and Stoughton.

Carmeli, A., Dutton, J. E. and Hardin, A. E. 2015. Respect as an engine for new ideas: Linking respectful engagement, relational information processing and creativity among employees and teams. *Human Relations*, 68(6), 1021–1047. https://doi.org/10.1177/0018726714550256

Cascade Engineering. 2023. Welfare to Career. https://www.cascadeng.com/welfare-career#:~:text=Exactly%20like%20it%20sounds%2C%20our,and%20into%20meaningful%2C%20thriving%20careers (Accessed: March 26, 2023).

Cascio, C. N., O'Donnell, M. B., Tinney, F. J., Lieberman, M. D., Taylor, S. E., Strecher, V. J. and Falk, E. B. 2016. Self-affirmation activates brain systems associated with self-related processing and reward and is reinforced by future orientation. *Social Cognitive and Affective Neuroscience*, 11(4), 621–629.

Cash, A. 2013. *Psychology for Dummies*. Hoboken, NJ: Wiley.

Casper. 2022a. Casper. https://casper.com/ (Accessed: December 26, 2022).

Casper, 2022b. Refer a Friend. https://refer.casper.com/ (Accessed: December 26, 2022).

Caspersen, D. 2015. *Changing the Conversations. The 17 Principles of Conflict Resolution*. London: Profile Books.

Castells, M. 1996. *The Rise of the Network Society*. Malden, MA: Blackwell Publishers.

Catmull, E. 2008. How Pixar Fosters Collective Creativity. *Harvard Business Review*. September. https://hbr.org/2008/09/how-pixar-fosters-collective-creativity (Accessed: January 2, 2023).

Cerasoli, C. P., Nicklin, J. M. and Ford, M. T. 2014. Intrinsic motivation and extrinsic incentives jointly predict performance: A 40-year meta-analysis, *Psychological Bulletin*, 140(4), 980. Advance online publication. https://doi.org/10.1037/a0035661

Chandra, S., Verma, S., Lim, W. M., Kumar, S. and Donthu, N. 2022. Personalization in personalized marketing: Trends and ways forward. *Psychology & Marketing*, 39(8), 1529–1562.

Chan, J. and Rogers, J. 2015. *Infinite Abundance. Becoming a Spiritual Millionaire*. Manchester, UK: Light Foundation.

Chaston, I. 2004. *Knowledge-Based Marketing. The 21st Century Competitive Edge*. London: Sage.

Chen, M. C., Fang, S. H. and Fang, L. 2015. The effects of aromatherapy in relieving symptoms related to job stress among nurses. *International Journal of Nursing Practice*, 21(1), 87–93. https://doi.org/10.1111/ijn.12229. Epub 2013 Nov 15. PMID: 24238073.

Chen, Y. F., Huang, X. Y., Chien, C. H. and Cheng, J. F. 2017. The effectiveness of diaphragmatic breathing relaxation training for reducing anxiety. *Perspectives in Psychiatric Care*, 53(4), 329–336. https://doi.org/10.1111/ppc.12184. Epub 2016 Aug 23. PMID: 27553981.

Chersniske, S. A. 1998. *The DHEA Breakthrough*. New York: NY. Ballantine Books.

Chicken Soup. 2022. Chicken Soup for the Soul. Facts & Figures. https://www.chickensoup.com/about/facts-and-figures (Accessed: September 26, 2022).

Childre, D., Martin, H. and Beech, D. 2000. *The HeartMath Solution. The Institute of HeartMath's Revolutionary Program for Engaging the Power of the Heart's Intelligence*. New York, NY: Harper Collins.

Cialdini, R. 2009. *Influence. The Psychology of Persuasion*. Boston, MA: Pearson.

Cialdini, R. 2016. *Pre-Suasion. A Revolutionary Way to Influence and Persuade*. London: Random House Books.

Cignacco, B. 2020. Why is Play Important for a Company's Work Environment? *European Business Review*. September. https://www.europeanbusinessreview.com/why-is-play-important-for-a-companys-work-environment/ (Accessed: October 22, 2022).

Cisco. 2008. Engaging Our Employees. https://www.cisco.com/web/about/ac227/csr2008/our-employees/engaging-our-employees.html (Accessed: November 20, 2022).

Cisco. 2022. Supply Chain Sustainability. https://www.cisco.com/c/en/us/about/supply-chain-sustainability.html (Accessed: October 02, 2022).

Cisco. 2023. Awards. https://www.cisco.com/c/en/us/about/careers/we-are-cisco/awards.html (Accessed: January 2, 2023).

Claflin, E. 1998. *Age Protectors. Stop Aging Now!* Emmaus, PA: Rodale.

Clare, J. 2018. *Storytelling. The Presenter's Secret Weapon*. London: Lionsden Publishing.

Clear, J. 2018. *Atomic Habits. An Easy and Proven Way to Build Good Habits and Break Bad Ones*. New York: Avery.

Clifford, C. 2020. From Chatty Employees to $5 Wine: How Trader Joe's Turns Customers into Fanatics. Make. It. July 20, 2020. https://www.cnbc.com/2020/03/09/psychology-behind-how-trader-joes-became-a-favorite-grocery-store.html (Accessed: November 20, 2022).

Coelho, P. 2014. Creative Destruction. February 24, 2014. https://www.youtube.com/watch?v=IaIek5MQ6Hs (Accessed: November 10, 2022).

Cohen, R. 2017. When CVS Stopped Selling Cigarettes, Some Customers Quit Smoking. March 20, 2017. https://www.reuters.com/article/us-health-pharmacies-cigarettes/when-cvs-stopped-selling-cigarettes-some-customers-quit-smoking-idUSKBN16R2HY (Accessed: December 20, 2022).

Cohen, D. and Prusak, L. 2001. *In Good Company. How Social Capital Makes Organizations Work*. Boston, MA: Harvard Business School Press.

Collard, P. 2014. *The Little Book of Mindfulness*. London: Gaia.

Collin, C., Benson, N., Ginsburg, J. et al. 2012. *The Psychology Book*. London: DK.

Collins, J. 2001. *Good to Great*. London: Random House.

Collins, J. and Lazier, B. 2020. *Beyond Entrepreneurship 2.0. Turning Your Business in an Enduring Great Company*. London: Penguin Random House.

Collins, J. and Porras, J. 2005. *Build to Last. Successful Habits of Visionary Companies*. London: Random House.

Collison, C. and Parcell, G. 2004. *Learning to Fly. Practical Knowledge Management from Leading and Learning Organizations*. Chichester, UK: Capstone.

Community Cisco. 2023. Welcome to the Community! https://community.cisco.com/?profile.language=en (Accessed: January 2, 2023).

Conner, D. 2010. *Spiritual Wholeness. Operationalizing the Intangible*. In Shelton, C. and M. Lynn (Eds.). *Good Business. Putting Spiritual Principles into Practice at Work*, 28–51. Unity Village, MO: Unity House.

Cook, J. 2022. How Entrepreneurs Can Leverage Visualization: A Neuroscientist Explains. *Forbes*. January 12, 2022. https://www.forbes.com/sites/jodiecook/2022/01/12/how-entrepreneurs-can-leverage-visualization-a-neuroscientist-explains/?sh=7837d9d31847 (Accessed: December 2, 2022).

Cooperrider, D. 2022. David Cooperrider and Associates. Case Studies. AI in diversity work: Avon Mexico. Consultants: Marge Schiller, David Cooperrider, Jane Watkins, and Rusty Renick. https://www.davidcooperrider.com/case-studies/ (Accessed: November 20, 2022).

Cooper, R. and Sawaf, A. 1998. *Executive EQ. Emotional Intelligence in Business*. London: Orion Business Books.

Cornelissen, J. 2017. *Corporate Communication. A Guide to Theory and Practice*. London: Sage.

Cottrell, S. 2015. *Skills for Success. Personal Development and Employability*. London: Palgrave.

Covey, S. 1992. *The 7 Habits of Highly Effective People. Powerful Lessons in Personal Change*. London: Simon & Schuster.

Crane, A., Matten, D., Glozer, S. and Spence, L. 2019. *Business Ethics: Managing Corporate Citizenship and Sustainability in the Age of Globalization*. Oxford. Oxford University Press.

Cranwell-Ward, J., Bacon, A. and Mackie, R. 2002. *Inspiring Leadership. Staying Afloat in Turbulent Times*. London: Thomson.

Critcher, C. R. and Dunning, D. 2015. Self-affirmations provide a broader perspective on self-threat. *Personality and Social Psychology Bulletin*, 41(1), 3–18.

Crotts, J. C. and Magnini, V. M. 2011. The customer delight construct: Is surprise essential? *Annals of Tourism Research*, 38(2), 719–722.

Csikszentmihalyi, M. 2002. *Flow. The Classic Work on How to Achieve Happiness*. London: Rider.

Csikszentmihalyi, M. 2003. *Good Business. Leadership, Flow and the Making of Meaning*. London: Coronet Books.

Cuddy, A. 2016. *Presence. Bringing Your Boldest Self to Your Biggest Challenges*. London: Orion Publishing Group.

Cullen, M. 2020. Instructional Solutions. Business Writing Style Top Tip: Positive Language. October 19, 2020. https://www.instructionalsolutions.com/blog/bid/87150/business-writing-style-top-tip-positive-language (Accessed: November 16, 2022).

Culture Partners, 2022. 4 Companies Winning with Feedback in the Workplace https://culture.io/resources/companies-that-understand-importance-of-feedback-in-the-workplace/ (Accessed: November 16, 2022).

Cyrulnik, B. 2009. *Resilience. How Your Inner Strength Can Set You Free from the Past*. London: Penguin Books.

D'Sa-Wilson, M. 2022. 10 Companies with Exceptional Employee Development Programs Together. April 29, 2022. https://www.togetherplatform.com/blog/best-training-and-development-programs (Accessed: December 12, 2022).

D'Souza, S. and Renner, D. 2014. *Not Knowing. The Art of Turning Uncertainty into Opportunity*. London: LID.

Daily Nomad, 2021. Pouring with a Purpose—BLQK Coffee Announces Inaugural Line-up of Philanthropic Partner to Champion Educational, Economic and Food Justice Initiatives. *Daily Nomad*. April 20, 2021. https://daily-nomad.com/news/pouring-with-a-purpose-blqk-coffee-announces-inaugural-line-up-of-philanthropic-partners-to-champion-educational-economic-and-food-justice-initiatives/0297343 (Accessed: November 23, 2022).

Dalmasio, A. 2012. *Self Comes to Mind. Constructing the Conscious Brain*. London: Vintage Books.

Darley, J. M. and Batson, C. D. 1973. "From Jerusalem to Jericho": A study of situational and dispositional variables in helping behavior. *Journal of Personality and Social Psychology*, 27(1), 100–108. https://doi.org/10.1037/h0034449

Davis, M., Eshelman, E. and McKay, M. 2008. *The Relaxation and Stress Reduction Workbook*. Oakland, CA: New Harbinger Publications.

Davis, G. F. and White, C. J. 2015. *Changing Your Company from the Inside Out: A Guide for Social Intrapreneurs*. Boston, MA: Harvard Business Review Press.

Dawes, R. M. and Kagen, J. 1988. *Rational Choice in an Uncertain World*. Orlando: Harcourt Brace Jovanovich, Publishers.

De Board, R. 1978. *The Psychoanalysis of Organizations. Psychoanalytic Approach to Behaviour in Groups and Organizations*. London: Tavistock Publications.

De Bono, E. 1970. *Lateral Thinking*. London: Penguin Books.

De Bono, E. 1977. *The Happiness Purpose*. London: Penguin Books.

De Bono, E. 1978. *Opportunities. A Handbook of Business Opportunity Search*. London: Penguin Books.

De Bono, E. 1986. *Tactics. The Art and Science of Success*. Dorset: Fontana.

De Bono, E. 1998. *Simplicity*. London: Penguin House.

De Bono, E. 2004. *How to Have a Beautiful Mind*. London: Vermillion.

De Bono, E. 2013. *Thinking to Create Value*. Malta: Kite.

De Botton, A. 2016a. Economic Demand. School of Life. January 11, 2016. [Online] Available at www.youtube.com/watch?v=VvTzaNUDVms (Accessed: September 16, 2018).

De Botton, A. 2016b. How to Remain Calm with People. School of Life. July 4, 2016. [Online] Available at www.youtube.com/watch?v=du035tg-SwY (Accessed: October 5, 2018).

De Mello, A. 1990. *Awareness*. Grand Rapids, MI: Zondervan.

De Pree, M. 2004. *Leadership Is an Art*. New York: Doubleday.

De Waal, F. 2019. *The Age of Empathy: Nature's Lessons for a Kinder Society*. London: Souvenir Press.

Dean, J. 2013. *Making Habits, Breaking Habits. Why We Do Things, Why We Don't, and How to Make Any Change Stick*. Boston: Da Capo Life Long.

Decety, J. and Ickes, W. (Eds.). 2011. *The Social Neuroscience of Empathy*. Boston, MA: MIT Press.

Deci, E. L., Connell, J. P. and Ryan, R. M. 1989. Self-determination in a work organization. *Journal of Applied Psychology*, 74(4), 580–590.

Deci, E. L. and Ryan, R. M. 2000. The "What" and "Why" of goal pursuits: Human needs and the self-determination of behavior, *Psychological Inquiry*, 11(4), 227–268. https://doi.org/10.1207/S15327965PLI1104_01

Decker, W. 1987. Managerial humor and subordinate satisfaction. *Social Behavior and Personality: An International Journal*, 15(2), 225–232.

Dell. 2022. Our ESG Reports https://www.dell.com/en-us/dt/corporate/social-impact/esg-resources/reports.htm#tab0=0 (Accessed: October 2, 2022).

Dempsey, C. 2017. *The Antidote to Suffering: How Compassionate Connected Care Can Improve Safety, Quality, and Experience*. New York: McGraw Hill.

Dentsu, 2022. Brands with High EQ Outperform Stock Markets. June 16, 2022. https://www.dentsu.com/see/en/emotionally-intelligent-brands-by-carat-2022 (Accessed: October 2, 2022).

Dilts, R. 1994. *Strategies of Genius* (Vol. 1). Capitola, CA: Meta Publications.

Dilts, R., Hallbom, T. and Smith, S. 2012. *Beliefs. Pathways to Health and Well-Being*. Carmarthen, UK: Crown House.

Disney Musicals in Schools. 2022. About the Programme. https://disneymusicalsinschools.com/about (Accessed: October 2, 2022).

Divine Chocolate. 2021. Why Fairtrade? August 26, 2021. https://www.divinechocolate.com/divine-world/why-fairtrade/ (Accessed: December 26, 2022).

Divine Chocolate. 2022. The Divine Difference. Delicious Chocolate Fighting Exploitation. https://www.divinechocolate.com/divine-world/the-divine-difference/ (Accessed: December 26, 2022).

Dixon, N. 2000. *The Organization Learning Cycle. How We Can Learn Collectively*. Aldershot, UK: Gowen Publishing Limited.

Dobelli, R. 2014. *The Art of Thinking Clearly*. New York, NY: Harper.

Dodgson, M. and Gann, D. 2018. *The Playful Entrepreneur. How to Adapt and Thrive in Uncertain Times*. Padstow, UK: Yale University Press.

Dooley, M. 2010. *Infinite Possibilities. The Art of Living Your Dreams*. Hillsboro, OR: Beyond Words.

Dove. 2022. The 'Dove Real Beauty Pledge' Dove. https://www.dove.com/us/en/stories/about-dove/dove-real-beauty-pledge.html (Accessed: October 2, 2022).

Drucker, P. F. 1973. *Management: Tasks, Responsibilities and Practices*. New York, NY: Harper and Row.

Drucker, P. F. 1999. *Managing Challenges for the 21st Century*. New York, NY: HarperBusiness.

Drucker, P. F. 2007. *Innovation and Entrepreneurship. Practice and Principles.* Oxford: Elsevier.

Duckworth, A. 2017. *Grit. Why Passion and Resilience Are the Secrets to Success.* London: Vermilion.

Duffy, J. 2020. 10 Big Companies that Promote Employee Meditation. January 2, 2020. https://www.morethanaccountants.co.uk/10-big-companies-promote-employee-meditation/ (Accessed: October 2, 2022).

Duncan, T. 2002. *High Trust Selling. Make More Money in Less Time with Less Stress.* Nashville, TN: Thomas Nelson Publishing.

Dunkin' Donuts. 2019. Seven Donut Wonders from Dunkin's around the World. Dunkin' Newsroom. June 06, 2019. https://news.dunkindonuts.com/blog/seven-donut-wondders-from-dd-s-around-the-world (Accessed: December 22, 2022).

Dutton, J. E. 2014. *Build High Quality Connections.* In Dutton, J. E. and Spreitzer, G. M. (Eds.). *How to Be a Positive Leader. Small Actions, Big Impact.* San Francisco. Berrett-Koehler.

Dutton, J. E. 2003. *Energize Your Workplace: How to Build and Sustain High-Quality Connections at Work.* San Francisco, CA: Jossey-Bass.

Dutton, J. E. and Heapy, E. D. 2003. *The Power of High-Quality Connections.* In Cameron, K. S. Dutton, J. E. and Quinn, R. E. (Eds.). *Positive Organizational Scholarship. Foundations for a New Discipline.* San Francisco: Berrett-Koehler.

Dweck, C. 2012. *Mindset. How You Can Fulfil Your Potential.* London: Robinson.

Dyer, W. 1976. *Your Erroneous Zones.* New York, NY: Quill.

Dyson. 2022. Doing More with Less https://www.dyson.co.uk/newsroom/overview/features/july-2020/dyson-sustainability (Accessed: December 2, 2022).

Edays. 2022. Employee Wellbeing: 7 of the Best Wellness Programs. https://www.e-days.com/news/7-of-the-best-employee-wellbeing-programs (Accessed: November 26, 2022).

Edelman, 2023. Edelman Trust Barometer Global Report. Edelman Trust Institute. https://www.edelman.com/sites/g/files/aatuss191/files/2023-03/2023%20Edelman%20Trust%20Barometer%20Global%20Report%20FINAL.pdf (Accessed: March 26, 2023).

Edelman, M. W. 1993. *The Measure of Our Success: A Letter to My Children and Yours.* New York, NY: Harper Perennial.

Edison Innovation Foundation. 2022. Thomas A. Edison. Edison Innovation Foundation. https://www.thomasedison.org/ (Accessed: January 2, 2023).

Edmondson, A. 2004. *Psychological Safety, Trust and Learning: A Group-Level Lens.* In Kramer, R. and Cook, K. (Eds.). *Trust and Distrust in Organizations: Dilemmas and Approaches,* 239–272. New York: Russell Sage Foundation.

Edmonson, A. 2019. *The Fearless Organization: Creating Psychological Safety in the Workplace for Learning, Innovation, and Growth.* New Jersey: Wiley.

Edwards, B. 1993. *Drawing on the Right Side of the Brain. How to Unlock Your Hidden Artistic Talent.* London: Harper Collins.

Egan, G. 1994. *The Skilled Helper. A Problem-Management Approach to Learning.* Monterey, CA: Brooks Cole Publishing Company.

Egan, J. 2011. *Relationship Marketing. Explore Relational Strategies in Marketing.* London: FT Prentice Hall.

Ehrenreich, B. 2006. *Dancing in the Streets. A History of Collective Joy.* New York, NY: Metropolitan Books.

Ekval, G. 1999. *Creative Climate.* In: M. A. Runco & S. R. Pritzker (Eds.). *Encyclopedia of Creativity* (Vol. 1). San Diego, CA: Academic Press.

Elkington, J. 1999. *Cannibals with Forks: the Triple Bottom Line of 21st Century Business.* Oxford: Capstone.

Elkington, J. 2018. 25 Years Ago I Coined the Phrase "Triple Bottom Line." Here's Why It's Time to Rethink It. *Harvard Business Review.* https://hbr.org/2018/06/25-years-ago-i-coined-the-phrase-triple-bottom-line-heres-why-im-giving-up-on-it (Accessed: November 30, 2022).

Ella's Kitchen. 2022. About Us. https://www.ellaskitchen.co.uk/about-us (Accessed: September 26, 2022).

Ellis, A. and Harper, R. 1997. *A Guide to Rational Living.* Hollywood, CA: Melvin Power Wilshire Book Company.

Emerson, R. W. 1981. *Emerson's Essays.* New York, NY: Harper Perennial.

Encyclopedia of World Biography. 2022. *James Dyson Biography.* https://www.notablebiographies.com/newsmakers2/2005-A-Fi/Dyson-James.html (Accessed: September 26, 2022).

Engelberg, M. and Aaronson, S. 2019. *The Amare Wave: Uplift Your Business by Putting Love to Work*. USA: Angel Mountain Press.

England, L. 2015. The Most Innovative Companies in the World (Hint: Apple Isn't in the Top 10). *Inc.* June 12, 2015. https://www.inc.com/business-insider/the-most-innovative-companies-in-the-world.html (Accessed: October 7, 2022).

Enterprise World. 2022. The Journey from Homeless to Becoming a Millionaire. https://theenterpriseworld.com/john-paul-dejoria-journey/ (Accessed: October 26, 2022).

Entis, L. 2014 Entrepreneurs: Your Irrational Optimism Is Necessary. *Entrepreneur.* February 14, 2014. https://www.entrepreneur.com/article/231549 (Accessed: September 26, 2022).

Epstein, R. and Laptoski, G. 1999. *Behavioural Approaches to Creativity.* In M. A. Runco & S. R. Pritzker (Eds.). *Encyclopedia of Creativity* (Vol. 1). San Diego, CA: Academic Press.

Ernst & Young. 2022. EY. How Can We Help You to Thrive, So We All Thrive? https://leplb0790.upoint.alight.com/web/ey/preauth-active#/routing (Accessed: October 26, 2022).

Esbenshade, E. 2019. How Trader Joe's Transforms Loyal Customers into Brand Advocates on Social Media. Flackable. October 21, 2019. https://flackable.com/blog/how-trader-joes-transforms-loyal-customers-into-brand-advocates-on-social-media (Accessed: December 26, 2022).

Ethos Esg. 2020. Top 50 Companies for Worker Health and Safety. https://www.ethosesg.com/blog/top-50-worker-safety (Accessed: October 26, 2022).

Ettlie, J. E. 2006. *Managing Innovation. New Technology, New Product and New Services in a Global Economy.* Oxford: Elsevier/Butterworth Heinemann.

Ewert, A. and Chang, Y. 2018. Levels of nature and stress response. *Behavioral Sciences* (Basel), 8(5), 49. https://doi.org/10.3390/bs8050049. PMID: 29772763; PMCID: PMC5981243.

Famakinwa, J. 2018. From Idea to Action: 3 Companies Where Employee Feedback Drives Real Change Built in LA. August 22, 2018. https://www.builtinla.com/2018/08/22/la-companies-where-employee-feedback-drives-change (Accessed: October 30, 2022).

Farber, S. 2019. *Love Is Just Damn Good Business: Do What You Love in the Service of People Who Love What You Do.* New York: McGraw Hill.

Fayol, H. 1949. *General and Industrial Management.* London: Pitman.

Feltman, C. 2021. *The Thin Book of Trust. An Essential Primer for Building Trust at Work.* Bend: The Thin Book Publishing.

Ferriss, T. 2017. Why You Should Define Your Fears Instead of Your Goals. July 14, 2017. [Online] Available at www.youtube.com/watch?v=5J6jAC6XxAI (Accessed: September 16, 2018).

Ferrucci, P. 1982. *What We Might Be. Techniques for Psychological and Spiritual Growth through Psychosynthesis.* New York: Jeremy Tarcher/Putnam Books.

FI. 2023. Edison's Lightbulb. The Franklin Institute. https://www.fi.edu/en/history-resources/edisons-lightbulb#:~:text=In%20the%20period%20from%201878,develop%20an%20efficient%20incandescent%20lamp (Accessed: March 16, 2023).

Fiebleman, J. and Friend, F. W. 1945. The structure and function of an organisation. *Philosophical Review*, 54, 19–44.

Fiorella, S. 2021. 20 Unique Customer Experience Examples & Best Practices to Boost Your Brand. February. https://bondai.co/blog/10-unique-customer-experience-examples-best-practices-boost-brand/ (Accessed: October 30, 2022).

Fischer, A. H. and Manstead, A. S. R. 2008. *Social Functions of Emotion.* In Lewis M, Havilan-Jones J. M. and L. F. Barrett (Eds.). *Handbook of Emotions.* New York. The Guilford Press.

Fisher, R., Ury, W. and Patton, B. 1999. *Getting to Yes. Negotiating an Agreement without Giving In.* London: Random House.

Fombrun, C. J. 1996. *Reputation: Realizing Value from Corporate Image.* Boston, MA: Harvard Business School Press.

Fontana, D. 1999. *Learn to Meditate. The Art of Tranquillity, Self-Awareness and Insight.* London: Duncan Baird.

Forgas, J. P., Bower, G. H. and Krantz, S. 1984. The influence of mood on perceptions of social interactions. *Journal of Personality and Social Psychology*, 20, 497–513.

Fortune, 2023. World Most Admired Companies https://www.fortune.com/ranking/worlds-most-admired-companies/ (Accessed: February 18, 2023).

Fosslien, L. and Duffy, M. W. 2019. *No Hard Feelings. Emotions at Work (and How They Help Us Succeed)*. London: Penguin Random House.

Fournier, S. and Lee, L. 2009. Getting brand communities right. *Harvard Business Review*, 87(4), 105–111.

Fox, E. 2010. *The Mental Equivalent*. Princeton, NJ: Princeton Licensing Group.

Frankl, V. 2006. *Man's Search for Meaning*. Boston, MA: Beacon Press.

Fredrickson, B. 2011. Positive Emotions Open Our Mind. Greater Good Science Center. June, 21, 2011. https://www.youtube.com/watch?v=Z7dFDHzV36g (Accessed: October 30, 2022).

Fredrickson, B. 2013. *Love 2.0. How Our Supreme Emotions Affect Everything We Think, Do, Feel and Become*. New York, NY: Hudson Street Press.

Fredrickson, B. L. 2003. *Positive Emotions and Upward Spirals in Organizations*. In Cameron, K. S. Dutton, J. E. and Quinn, R. E. (Eds.). *Positive Organizational Scholarship. Foundations for a New Discipline*. San Francisco: Berrett-Koehler.

Fredrickson, B. L. and Branigan, C. 2005. Positive emotions broaden the scope of attention and thought-action repertoires. *Cognition and Emotion*, 19(3), 313–332. https://www.ncbi.nlm.nih.gov/pmc/articles/PMC3156609/ (Accessed: December 30, 2022).

Free People. 2022. Free People Movement. https://www.freepeople.com/free-people-girls-inc/ (Accessed: October 30, 2022).

Freeman, R. E. 2009a. Stakeholders Are People - R. Edward Freeman. October 1, 2009. *Corporate Ethics*. https://www.youtube.com/watch?v=keED9l3zVi8&list=PL15B809B055A2C795&index=3 (Accessed: December 3, 2022).

Freeman, R. E. 2009b. What Is Stakeholder Theory? - R. Edward Freeman. October 1, 2009. *Corporate Ethics*. https://www.youtube.com/watch?v=bIRUaLcvPe8&list=PL15B809B055A2C795&index=1 (Accessed: December 3, 2022).

Freeman, R. E. and McVea, J. A. 2001. Stakeholder Approach to Strategic Management 2001. Darden Graduate School of Business Administration University of Virginia. Working Paper No. 01-02. https://doi.org/10.2139/ssrn.263511 (Accessed: December 30, 2022).

Freire, P. 2005. *Pedagogy of the Oppressed*. New York, NY: Continuum.

Frey, C. 2007. Tony Buzan Reflects on the Growth, Evolution and Future of Mind Mapping. Innovation Management. 2007/01/03. https://innovationmanagement.se/2007/01/03/tony-buzan-reflects-on-the-growth-evolution-and-future-of-mind-mapping/ (Accessed: January 3, 2023).

Friedman, A. and Miles, S. 2006. *Stakeholders. Theory and Practice*. Oxford: Oxford University Press.

Fritz, R. 1984. *The Path of Least Resistance. Principles for Creating What You Want to Create*. New York, NY: Fawcett Books.

Fritz, R. 1991. *Creating*. New York, NY: Fawcett Columbine.

Fritz, R. 1999. *The Path of Least Resistance for Managers. Designing Organizations to Succeed*. San Francisco, CA: Berrett-Koehler Publishers.

Fritz, R. 2003. *Your Life as Art*. Newfane, VT: Newfane Press.

Fritz, R. 2007. *Elements. The Writing of Robert Fritz*. Newfane, VT: Newfane Press.

Fromm, E. 1956. *The Art of Loving*. New York, NY: Harper & Row.

Fromm, E. 1966. *Fear of Freedom*. London: Routledge & Keegan Paul Ltd.

Fromm, E. 1976. *To Have or to Be?* London: Abacus.

Frost, C. 2019, Jack Ma, the Richest Man in China, Stepped Down as Alibaba Chairman — Here Are 27 of His Most Brilliant Quotes. Market Insider. September 11, 2019. https://markets.businessinsider.com/news/stocks/jack-ma-quotes-alibaba-inspirational-2019-6-1028295089 (Accessed: October 2, 2022).

Frost, P. J. 2007. *Toxic Emotions at Work and What You Can Do about Them*. Boston: Harvard Business School Press.

FSC, 2023. What's in a Label? FSC. https://fsc.org/en/what-the-fsc-labels-mean (Accessed: March 2, 2023).

Furstenthal, L., Morris, M. and Roth, E. 2022. Fear Factor: Overcoming Human Barriers to Innovation. McKinsey & Co. June 3, 2022. https://www.mckinsey.com/capabilities/strategy-and-corporate-finance/our-insights/fear-factor-overcoming-human-barriers-to-innovation (Accessed: October 9, 2022).

Galinsky, A.D., Magee J.C., Inesi, M.E., and Gruenfeld, D.H. 2006. Power and perspectives not taken. *Psychol. Sci.* 17(12):1068–74

Gamon, A. and Bragdon, D. 2002. *Building Mental Muscle. Conditioning Exercises for the Six Intelligence Zones*. London: Pocket Books.

Gamon, A. and Bragdon, D. 2003. *Building Left-Brain Power: Conditioning Exercises and Tips for Left-Brain Skills*. New York, NY: Walker & Company.

Gamon, A. and Bragdon, D. 2008. *Learn Faster, Remember More*. New Lanark, UK: Geddes and Grosset.

Garber, 2012. Taco Bell vs. Old Spice: The Twitter War that Wasn't. The Atlantic. July 11, 2012. https://www.theatlantic.com/technology/archive/2012/07/taco-bell-vs-old-spice-the-twitter-war-that-wasnt/259712/ (Accessed: October 19, 2022).

Gardner, H. 2006. *Multiple Intelligences. New Horizons in Theory and Practice*. New York, NY: Basic Books.

Garner, S. 2012. Entrepreneurial Inspiration – Anita Roddick and The Body Shop. Go Forth Institute. July 23, 2011. https://canadianentrepreneurtraining.com/entrepreneurial-inspiration-anita-roddick-and-the-body-shop/ (Accessed: October 29, 2022).

Garnham, A. and Oakhill. J. 1994. *Thinking and Reasoning*. Oxford: Blackwell.

Gelles, D. 2012. The Mind Business. *Financial Times*. August 24, 2012. https://www.ft.com/content/d9cb7940-ebea-11e1-985a-00144feab49a (Accessed: December 24, 2022).

General Electric. 2021. 2021 Sustainability Report. Sustainability at Core https://www.ge.com/sites/default/files/ge2021_sustainability_report.pdf (Accessed: December 20, 2022).

General Electric. 2022. General Electric. Businesses. https://www.ge.com/ (Accessed: November 20, 2022).

German, T. and Defeyter, M. 2001. Immunity to functional fixedness in young children. *Psychonomic Bulletin & Review*. 7. 707–712. https://doi.org/10.3758/BF03213010.

Giddens, A. 2009. *Sociology*. Cambridge: Polity Press.

Gilbert, P. 2009. *The Compassionate Mind*. London: Constable.

Gildehaus, C., Allred, D., Naidoo, E. and Podduturi, A. 2021. Powering the Innovation Flywheel in the Digital Era. BCG. March 12, 2021. https://www.bcg.com/publications/2021/driving-business-impact-with-the-innovation-flywheel-approach (Accessed: December 31, 2022).

Girls Inc. 2022. Girls Inc. https://girlsinc.org/ (Accessed: October 30, 2022).

Glazer, R. 2020. CVS Lost $2 Billion with 1 Decision—Here's Why They Were Right. *Forbes*. April 21, 2020. https://www.forbes.com/sites/robertglazer/2020/04/21/cvs-lost-2-billion-with-1-decision-heres-why-they-were-right/?sh=1bea9dbc689c (Accessed: December 14, 2022).

Glynn, M. A. 1994. Effects of work task cues and play task cues on information processing, judgment, and motivation. *Journal of Applied Psychology*, 79, 34–45.

GoDaddy. 2022. We're Here to Help 24/7. https://uk.godaddy.com/help/contact-us (Accessed: December 26, 2022).

Goetz, J. L., Keltner, D. and Simon-Thomas, E. 2010. Compassion: An evolutionary analysis and empirical review. *Psychological Bulletin*, 136, 351–374.

Goffman, E. 1967. *On Face-Work: Interaction Ritual*. Harmondsworth: Penguin Books.

Goffman, E. 1969. *The Presentation of Self in Everyday Life*. New York, NY: Penguin Books.

Goldsmith, M. and Reiter, M. 2008. *What Got You Here Won't Get You There. How Successful People Become Even More Successful*. London: Profile.

Goleman, D. 1996. *Emotional Intelligence. Why It Can Matter More than IQ*. London: Bloomsbury.

Goleman, D. 1998. *Working with Emotional Intelligence*. London: Bloomsbury.

Goleman, D. 2006. *Social Intelligence. The New Science of Human Relationships*. New York, NY: Bantam.

Goleman, D. 2013. Daniel Goleman - Leadership and Compassion - Empathy and Compassion in Society 2013. December 22, 2013. https://www.youtube.com/watch?v=TnTuDDbrkCQ (Accessed: March 2, 2023).

Goleman, D. 2014. *Focus. The Hidden Driver of Excellence*. New York, NY: Bloomsbury.

Goleman, G. and Boyatzis, R. E. 2008. Social Intelligence and the Biology of Leadership. *Harvard Business Review*. September. https://hbr.org/2008/09/social-intelligence-and-the-biology-of-leadership. (Accessed: January 2, 2023).

Goleman, D., Kaufman, P. and Ray, M. 1995. *The Creative Spirit*. New York, NY: Plume.

Goman, C. K. 2012. Busting 5 Body Language Myths. *Forbes*. July 24, 2012. https://www.forbes.com/sites/carolkinseygoman/2012/07/24/busting-5-body-language-myths/?sh=664c42a53922 (Accessed: January 22, 2023).

Good, D., Lyddy, C. J. and Glomb, T. M. et al. 2016. Contemplating mindfulness at work. An integrative review. *Journal of Management.* 42(1), 114–142.

Goodman Nadia. 2012. James Dyson on Using Failure to Drive Success. *Entrepreneur.* November 5, 2012. https://www.entrepreneur.com/article/224855 (Accessed: September 26, 2022).

Google. 2022a. Google.org. https://www.google.org/ (Accessed: October 30, 2022).

Google. 2022b. Google Careers. Teams. https://careers.google.com/teams/ (Accessed: December 09, 2022).

Gottman, J. 1994. *Why Marriages Succeed or Fail.* New York, NY: Simon & Schuster.

Gray, A. E. 2015. Speak: Some thoughts on somatic psychotherapies in international contexts. *Somatic Psychotherapy Beyond Borders.* Somatic Psychotherapy Today, 5(4), 30–37.

Great Place to Work. 2022a. Great Place to Work. Certified. August 2022–August 2023. https://www.greatplacetowork.com/certified-company/1000311 (Accessed: September 23, 2022).

Great Place to Work. 2022b Great Place to Work. Certified. August 2022–August 2023. https://www.greatplacetowork.com/certified-company/1000184 (Accessed: October 1, 2022).

Greene, R. 2012. *Mastery.* London: Profile Books.

Greenleaf, R. 1991. *The Servant as Leader.* Indianapolis, IN: The Robert K. Greenleaf Center.

Greenleaf, R. 1996. *On Becoming a Servant-Leader.* San Francisco, CA: Josey-Bass Publishers.

Grice, H. P. 1989. *Studies in the Way of Words.* Boston, MA: Harvard University Press.

Griffith, J. 2016. *Freedom. The End of Human Condition.* Sydney: WTM Publishing and Communications PTY Ltd.

Grossmann, I. and Kross, E. 2014. Exploring Solomon's paradox: Self-distancing eliminates the Self-other asymmetry in wise reasoning about close relationships in younger and older adults. *Psychological Science,* 25(8), 1571–1580. https://doi.org/10.1177/0956797614535400. Epub 2014 Jun 10. PMID: 24916084.

Guber, P. 2011. *Tell to Win: Connect, Persuade and Triumph with the Hidden Power of Story.* London: Profile Books.

Gutierrez, A., Kothari, A., Mazuera, C. and Schoenherr, T. 2020 Taking Supplier Collaboration to the Next Level. McKinsey & Company. July 7, 2020. https://www.mckinsey.com/capabilities/operations/our-insights/taking-supplier-collaboration-to-the-next-level (Accessed: December 23, 2022).

Hackman, J. R. and Oldham, G. R. 1976. Motivation through the design of work: Test of a theory. *Organizational Behavior and Human Performance,* 16, 250–279.

Haidt, J. 2006. *The Happiness Hypothesis. Putting Ancient Wisdom to the Test of Modern Science.* London: Arrow Books.

Hale, G. and Evans, M. 2007. *The Feng Shui Bible. A Practical Guide for Harmony and Well-Being.* Wigston, UK: Lorenz Books.

Hall, D. 1995. *Jump Start Your Brain.* New York, NY: Warner Books.

Hall, E. T. 1981. *Beyond Culture.* New York, NY: Anchor Book.

Hallowell, E. 1999b. *Connect. 12 Vital Ties that Open Your Heart, Lengthen Your Life and Deepen Your Soul.* New York: Pantheon Books.

Hallowell, E. 1999a. The Human Moment at Work. *Harvard Business Review.* Jan–Feb 1999 Issue. [Online] Available at https://hbr.org/1999/01/the-human-moment-at-work (Accessed: September 16, 2018).

Hamel, G. 2011. First, Let's Fire All the Managers. *Harvard Business Review.* December. https://hbr.org/2011/12/first-lets-fire-all-the-managers (Accessed: October 29, 2022).

Hamel, G. and Prahalad, C. K. 1996. *Competing for the Future.* Boston, MA: Harvard Business School Press.

Hamilton, D. 2010. *Why Kindness Is Good for You.* London: Hay House.

Hanh, T. N. 2014. *The Art of Communicating.* San Francisco, California: Harper One.

Harbaugh, W., Mayr, U. and Burghart, D. 2007. Neural responses to taxation and voluntary giving reveal motives for charitable donations. *Science* (New York, N.Y.). 316, 1622–1625. https://doi.org/10.1126/science.1140738

Hardingham, A. 1992. *Making Change Work for You.* London: Sheldon Business Books.

Harley Davidson, 2023. Harley Owner Group. https://www.harley-davidson.com/gb/en/content/hog.html (Accessed: March 2, 2023).

Harris, T. A. 1969. *I'm OK – You're OK.* New York, NY: Harper & Row.

Harrold, G. 2007. *De-Stress Your Life in 7 Easy Steps*. London: Orion.

Hastings, R. and Meyer, E. 2020. *No Rules Rules: Netflix and the Culture of Reinvention*. New York: Wh Hallen.

Hatfield, E., Rapson, R. L. and Le, Y. L. 2011. *Primitive Emotional Contagion: Recent Research*. In Decety, J. and W. Ickes (Eds.). *The Social Neuroscience of Empathy*. Boston, MA: MIT Press. [Online] Available at http://www.neurohumanitiestudies.eu/archivio/Emotional_Contagion.pdf (Accessed: December 20, 2018).

Hawkins, D. R. 2012. *Letting Go. The Pathway of Surrender*. London, UK: Hay House.

Hawkins, D. R. 2013. *Power vs. Force. The Hidden Determinant of Human Behavior*. Carlsbad, CA: Hay House.

Headspace, 2023. About Headspace. https://www.headspace.com/about-us (Accessed: March 23, 2023).

Heath, D. and Harbinger, J. 2018. How a "Popsicle Hotline" Turned an Average Hotel into a Beloved Destination. Next Big Idea Club. October 3, 2018. https://nextbigideaclub.com/magazine/conversation-how-a-popsicle-hotline-turned-an-average-hotel-into-a-beloved-destination/19130/ (Accessed: December 16, 2022).

Heinz Awards. 2014. Salman Khan. https://www.heinzawards.org/pages/salman-khan

Hellinger, B., Weber, G. and Beaumont, H. 1998. *Love's Hidden Symmetry. What Makes Love Work in Relationships*. Phoenix, AZ: Zeig, Toucker & Co.

Hendricks, D.2004. 5 Successful Companies that Didn't Make a Dollar for 5 Years. *Inc.* July 7, 2004. https://www.inc.com/drew-hendricks/5-successful-companies-that-didn-8217-t-make-a-dollar-for-5-years.html

Hendricks, G. and Ludeman, K. 1996. *The Corporate Mystic. A Guidebook for Visionaries with Their Feet on the Ground*. New York, NY: Bantam Books.

Herbert, C., Meixner, F., Wiebking, C. and Gilg, V. 2020. Regular physical activity, short-term exercise, mental health, and well-being among university students: The results of an online and a laboratory study. *Frontiers in Psychology*, 11, 509. https://doi.org/10.3389/fpsyg.2020.00509. PMID: 32528333; PMCID: PMC7264390.

Herzberg, F. 1968. *The Work and the Nature of Man*. London: Staples Press.

Hill, N. 1928. *The Law of Success*. Meriden, CT: Ralston University Press.

Hill, N. 2016. *Think and Grow Rich*. Shippensburg, PA: Sound Wisdom.

Hillman, J. 2006. *The Soul's Code. In Search of Character and Calling*. New York, NY: Warner Books.

Hilton, 2017. Hilton Code of Conduct. https://ir.hilton.com/~/media/Files/H/Hilton-Worldwide-IR-V3/committee-composition/hlt-code-of-conduct-en-rev-05-10-17.pdf (Accessed: December 23, 2022).

Hippo Roller, 2022. Hippo Roller. https://hipporoller.org/n (Accessed: December 2, 2022).

Hlupic, V. 2018. *Humane Capital: How to Create a Management Shift to Transform Performance and Profit*. USA: Bloomsbury Business.

Hochschild, A. R. 1983. *The Managed Heart: Commercialization of Human Feeling*. Berkeley, CA: University of California Press.

Hoffman, A. J. and Haigh, N. 2012. *Positive Deviance for a Sustainable World. Linking Sustainability and Positive Organizational Scholarship*. In Cameron, K. S. and Spreitzer, G. M. (Eds.). *The Oxford Handbook of Positive Organizational Scholarship*. New York: Oxford University Press.

Hogg, M. A. and Vaughan, G. 2002. *Social Psychology*. Harlow, UK: Pearson.

Holden, R. 2008. *Success Intelligence. Essential Lessons and Practices from the World's Leading Coaching Programme on Authentic Success*. London: Hay House.

Holtzer, M. 2021, Don't Ignore the Brutal Facts! https://www.linkedin.com/pulse/dont-ignore-brutal-facts-mike-holtzer-1c/ (Accessed: December 15, 2022).

Honda. 2022. Behind the Scenes of Honda Design Waigaya: Boisterous Meetings https://global.honda/innovation/design/process/behind-the-scenes.html (Accessed: October 22, 2022).

Honest Tea. 2020. 2020 Honest Mission Report. https://www.honestorganic.com/content/dam/nagbrands/us/honesttea/en/mission/CCD20-231-HT-Mission-Brochure-R10.pdf (Accessed: September 22, 2022).

Honest Tea. 2022. Our Mission. https://www.honestorganic.com/our-mission (Accessed: September 22, 2022).

Honoré, C. 2004. *In Praise of Slow. How a Worldwide Movement Is Challenging the Cult of Speed*. London: Orion.

Hounsell, D. 2007. *Toward a More Sustainable Feedback to Students*. In Boud, D. and N. Falchikov (Eds.). *Rethinking Assessment in Higher Education*, 101–113. London: Routledge.

House, J., Landis, K. and Umberson, D. 1988. Social relationships and health. *Science* (New York, N.Y.). 241, 540–545. https://doi.org/10.1126/science.3399889

Howard, G. 1989. *Getting Through. How to Make Words Work for You*. London: David and Charles.

Howells, A., Eiroa Orosa, F. J. and Ivtzan, I. 2015. Putting the 'app' in happiness: A randomised controlled trial of a smartphone-based mindfulness intervention to enhance wellbeing. *Journal of Happiness Studies*. 17. https://doi.org/10.1007/s10902-014-9589-1

Huberman, A. 2022. Using Play to Rewire & Improve Your Brain Huberman Lab Podcast #58. February 7, 2022. https://www.youtube.com/watch?v=BwyZIWeBpRw (Accessed: September 28, 2022).

Huberman, A. 2023. Dr. Emily Balcetis: Tools for Setting & Achieving Goals | Huberman Lab Podcast #83. August 1, 2022. https://www.youtube.com/watch?v=7YGZZcXqKxE (Accessed: September 28, 2022).

HubSpot. 2022. Free Courses https://www.hubspot.com/resources/courses (Accessed: October 10, 2022).

Huhn, J. 2022a. 10 Strategic Alliance Examples [and What you Can Learn From Them] ReferralRock. September 8, 2022. https://referralrock.com/blog/strategic-alliance-examples/ (Accessed: October 10, 2022).

Huhn, J. 2022b. How 11 Major Brands Have Successfully Used Word of Mouth. ReferralRock. December 19, 2022. https://referralrock.com/blog/brands-successful-word-of-mouth-marketing/ (Accessed: October 22, 2022).

Hui, S. K. and Grandner, M. A. 2015. Trouble sleeping associated with lower work performance and greater health care costs: Longitudinal data from Kansas state employee wellness program. *Journal of Occupational and Environmental Medicine*, 57(10), 1031–1038. https://doi.org/10.1097/JOM.0000000000000534. PMID: 26461857; PMCID: PMC4610176.

Humana. 2022. Humana's 2021 Impact Report The Humana Foundation https://www.humana.com/about/impact/community/humana-foundation/ (Accessed: October 10, 2022).

Humana Careers. 2022. Humana Careers. Job Search Results. https://careers.humana.com/job-search-results/?employment_type=Full_time&location_type=Remote&pg=2&source=Humana_Website (Accessed: October 10, 2022).

Humana News. 2020. Humana Again Ranked among Top Companies for Flexible Work. https://news.humana.com/ (Accessed: October 10, 2022).

Hyde, L. 2012. *The Gift. How the Creative Spirit Transforms the World*. Edinburgh: Canongate Books.

IBM, 2023. IBM Research. https://research.ibm.com/ (Accessed: July 20, 2023)

IKEA. 2023. The IKEA Vision and Values. https://www.ikea.com/gb/en/this-is-ikea/about-us/the-ikea-vision-and-values-pub9aa779d0 (Accessed: February 20, 2023).

IKEA. 2023b. The IKEA Forest Positive Agenda. https://about.ikea.com/en/sustainability/wood-forestry/forestry-beyond-our-business/ikea-forest-positive-agenda#:~:text=All%20wood%20used%20in%20IKEA,sugarcane)%20are%20deforestation%2Dfree (Accessed: February 20, 2023).

Ingram, J., Hand, C. J. and Maciejewski, G. 2021. Social isolation during COVID-19 lockdown impairs cognitive function. Applied Cognitive Psychology. https://doi.org/10.1002/acp.3821

Intel, 2022. Employee Inclusion Survey Results. https://www.intel.com/content/www/us/en/diversity/employee-inclusion-survey-results.html (Accessed: December 10, 2022).

Ireland, L. 2014. 4 Inspiring Customer Experience Examples. Customer Think. October 15, 2014. https://customerthink.com/4-inspiring-customer-experience-examples/ (Accessed: December 22, 2022).

Isen, A. M. 1999. *On the Relationship between Affect and Creative Problem Solving*. In S. W. Russ (Ed.). *Affect, Creative Experience, and Psychological Adjustment*. Philadelphia, PA: Brunner/Mazel.

Isen, A. M. 2008. *Some Ways in Which Positive Affect Influences Decision Making and Problem Solving*. In Lewis M, Havilan-Jones J. M. and L. F. Barrett. (Eds.). *Handbook of Emotions*. New York: The Guilford Press.

Jacab, P. L. 1999. *Wilbur and Orville Wright*. In M. A. Runco & S. R. Pritzker (Eds.). *Encyclopedia of Creativity* (Vol. 2). San Diego, CA: Academic Press.

Jackson, N. 2011. Last Typewriter Factory in the World Shuts Its Doors. The Atlantic. April 25, 2011. https://www.theatlantic.com/technology/archive/2011/04/last-typewriter-factory-in-the-world-shuts-its-doors/237838/ (Accessed: November 21, 2022).

Jaf, T. 2022. 7 Meaningful Internal Communication Examples for 2022. Staffbase. https://staffbase.com/blog/internal-communication-examples/ (Accessed: October 16, 2022).

Jains, 2023. Jain Irrigation Systems Ltd. https://www.jains.com/ (Accessed: March 1, 2023).

Jaipur Rugs. 2022. Jaipur Rugs. Sustainability. https://www.jaipurrugs.com/uk/sustainability#our_foot (Accessed: October 16, 2022).

Jaipur Rugs. 2023. Our Vision. https://www.jaipurrugs.org/about-us/ (Accessed: January 1, 2023).

Jaipur Rugs Foundation. 2022. Jaipur Rugs Foundation. https://www.jaipurrugs.org/about-us/ (Accessed: October 16, 2022).

Jeffers, S. 1991. *Feel the Fear and Do It Anyway*. London: Arrow Books.

Jeffers, S. 2003. *Embracing Uncertainty. Achieving Peace of Mind as We Face the Unknown*. London: Hodder and Stoughton.

Jelski, C. 2022. Travel Weekly. Marriott's Q1: Luxury is a Standout, Vacation Rentals Is a Focus. May 04, 2022. https://www.travelweekly.com/Travel-News/Hotel-News/Marriot-Q1-2022-results (Accessed: December 7, 2022).

Jobs, S. 2008. *Steve Jobs' 2005 Stanford Commencement Address*. March 7, 2008. [Online] Available at www.youtube.com/watch?v=UF8uR6Z6KLc (Accessed: September 16, 2018).

Johnson, D. 1997. *Reaching Out. Interpersonal Effectiveness and Self-Actualization*. Boston, MA: Allyn and Bacon.

Johnson, S. 2010. *Where Good Ideas Come From. The Seven Patterns of Innovation*. London: Penguin.

Johnstone, K. 1987. *Impro: Improvisation and the Theatre*. London: Methuen Drama.

Johri, L. 2018. *Kindness in Leadership. A Global Perspective*. In Hasking G., Thomas, M., Johri, L. (Eds.). *Kindness in Leadership*. New York: Routledge.

Jung, H., Seo, E., Han, E., Henderson, M. D. and Patall, E. A. 2020. Prosocial modeling: A meta-analytic review and synthesis. *Psychological Bulletin*, 146(8), 635–663. https://doi.org/10.1037/bul0000235 (Accessed: December 20, 2022).

Juniper, 2022. Juniper Networks. Benefits with You in Mind. https://www.juniper.net/us/en/company/culture-careers/benefits.html (Accessed: November 22, 2022).

Kachroo-Levine, M. 2019. The Incredible Reason Why Richard Branson Started Virgin Atlantic. July 12, 2019. https://www.travelandleisure.com/travel-tips/celebrity-travel/how-richard-branson-started-virgin-atlantic (Accessed: October 2, 2022).

Kahn, W. A. 1990. Psychological conditions of personal engagement and disengagement at work. *Academy of Management Journal*, 33(4), 692–724.

Kahneman, D. 2013. *Thinking, Fast and Slow*. New York, NY: Farrar, Straus and Giroux.

Kahneman, D. and Tversky, A. 1984. Choices, values, and frames. *American Psychologist*, 39(4), 341–350.

Kalkofen, M., Momin, Z., Mosquet, X., Singh, J. and Sticher, G. 2007. Getting to Win-Win. How Toyota Creates and Sustains Best Practice Suppliers Relationships. The Boston Consulting Group. https://studylib.net/doc/8401010/getting-to-win-win—the-boston-consulting-group (Accessed: December 28, 2022).

Kammok. 2022. Kammok. About. https://kammok.com/pages/about (Accessed October 2, 2022).

Kandola, R. and Fullerton, J. 1994. *Managing the Mosaic. Diversity in Action*. London: Institute of Personnel and Development.

Kane, P. 2011. *The Play Ethic: A Manifesto for a Different Way of Living*. London: Pan Books.

Kao, J. 1996. *Jamming. The Art and Discipline of Business Creativity*. London: HarperCollin.

Kaplan, R. S. and Mikes, A. 2012. Managing Risks: A New Framework. *Harvard Business Review*. June 2012. https://hbr.org/2012/06/managing-risks-a-new-framework. (Accessed: September 20, 2022).

Kashyap, V. 2022. 8 Companies With Enviable Company Cultures. Proofhub. https://www.proofhub.com/articles/8-companies-with-enviable-company-cultures (Accessed: September 20, 2022).

Kassorly, I. 1985. *Go for It*. London: Warner Books.

Kay, J. 2011. *Obliquity. Why Our Goals Are Best Achieved Indirectly*. London: Profile Books.

Keegan, S. 2015. *The Psychology of Fear in Organizations. How to Transform Anxiety into Well-Being, Productivity and Innovation*. London: Kogan Page.

Kelley, D. 1990. *The Art of Reasoning with Symbolic Logic*. New York, NY: W.W. Norton & Company.

Kendra Scott. 2022. Kendra Scott. https://www.kendrascott.com/careers.html (Accessed: October 21, 2022).

Keswin, E. 2019. *Bring Your Human to Work: 10 Surefire Ways to Design a Workplace That Is Good for People, Great for Business, and Just Might Change the World*. New York: McGraw Hill Education.

Khalid, A., Zhang, Q., Wang, W., Ghaffari, A. S. and Pan, F. 2019. The relationship between procrastination, perceived stress, saliva alpha-amylase level and parenting styles in Chinese first year medical students. *Psychology Research and Behavior Management*, 12, 489–498. https://doi.org/10.2147/PRBM. S207430. PMID: 31308770; PMCID: PMC6619418.

Khan Academy. 2023. Khan Academy. https://www.khanacademy.org/ (Accessed: January 16, 2023).

Khandelwal, A. 2022 How Does Amazon & Netflix Personalization Work? VWO Blog. November 11, 2022. https://vwo.com/blog/deliver-personalized-recommendations-the-amazon-netflix-way/#:~:text= The%20company%20uses%20customer%20viewing,should%20be%20recommended%20to%20 them. (Accessed: December 20, 2022).

Khaya Cookies, 2023. Welcome to the Khaya Cookies Company! https://khayacookies.com/ (Accessed: January 12, 2023).

Kim, W. C. and Mauborgne, R. 2015. *Blue Ocean Strategy. How to Create Uncontested Market Space and Make the Competition Irrelevant*. Boston, MA: Harvard Business School Press.

Kindy, D. 2019. The Accidental Invention of Play-Doh. Smithsonian Magazine. November 12, 2019. https://www.smithsonianmag.com/innovation/accidental-invention-play-doh-180973527/ (Accessed: December 21, 2022).

Kinni, T. 2021. All the Feels: Why It Pays to Notice Emotions in the Workplace. Insights by Stanford Business. May 13, 2021. https://www.gsb.stanford.edu/insights/all-feels-why-it-pays-notice-emotions-workplace (Accessed: October 21, 2022).

Klein, G. 2003. *Intuition at Work. Why Developing Your Gut Instincts Will Make You Better at What You Do*. New York, NY: Currency.

Klein, G. A., Veinott, B. and Wiggins, S. 2010. "Evaluating the effectiveness of the premortem technique on plan confidence," Proceedings of the 7th International Information Systems for Crisis Response and Management Conference, May 2010.

KLM. 2014. Schiphol & KLM: Cover Greetings. KLM Royal Dutch Airlines 18 Nov 2014 https://www. youtube.com/watch?v=DH8D2OHn18c (Accessed: October 2, 2022).

Knight, S. 1999. *NLP Solutions. How to Model What Works in Business to Make It Work for You*. London: Nicholas Brealey Publishing.

Koebler, J. 2015. 10 Years Ago Today, YouTube Launched as a Dating Website. Vice. April 23, 2015. https://www.vice.com/en/article/78xqjx/10-years-ago-today-youtube-launched-as-a-dating-website (Accessed: October 21, 2022).

Koestler, A. 1964. *The Act of Creation*. London: Hutchinson & Co.

Kofman, F. 2013. *Conscious Business. How to Build Value through Values*. Boulder, CO: Sounds True.

Kolb, D. A. 1973. *Organizational Psychology. An Experiential Approach*. Englewood Cliffs, NJ: Prentice Hall.

Kotler, S. 2021. The Art of Impossible: A Peak Performance Primer. New York. HarperWave.

Kotler, P., Keller, K. L. and Brady, M. et al. 2009. *Marketing Management*. London: Pearson Education.

Koul, A. 2022. 12 Examples of Employee Recognition for 2022 Together. January 18, 2022. https://www. togetherplatform.com/blog/employee-recognition-examples (Accessed: December 20, 2022).

Kouzes, J. M. and Posner, B. Z. 2011. *Credibility: How Leaders Gain It or Lose It, Why People Demand It*. San Francisco: Jossey Bass.

Krapivin, P. 2018. Sir Richard Branson's Five Billion Reasons to Make Your Employees and Candidates Happy. *Forbes*. July 9, 2018. https://www.forbes.com/sites/pavelkrapivin/2018/07/09/sir-richard-bransons-5-billion-reasons-to-make-your-employees-candidates-happy/?sh=276c11126710 (Accessed: December 20, 2022).

Krochet Kids, 2022. We exist to…Empower People to Rise above Poverty https://krochetkids.com/pages/ about (Accessed: December 18, 2022).

Kruse, K. 2016. Netflix Has No Rules Because They Hire Great People. *Forbes*. September 5, 2016. https://www.forbes.com/sites/kevinkruse/2016/09/05/netflix-has-no-rules-because-they-hire-great-people/?utm_source=TWITTER#1d6395159bc6 (Accessed: December 20, 2022).

Kubala, J., Jennings, K. and Wade, D. 2022. 15 Simple Ways to Relieve Stress. Healthline. January 20, 2022. https://www.healthline.com/nutrition/16-ways-relieve-stress-anxiety (Accessed: December 29, 2022).

Kukk, C. 2017. *The Compassionate Achiever. How Helping Others Fuels Success.* New York, NY: HarperOne.

Kumar, A. and Epley, N. 2022. A little good goes an unexpectedly long way: Underestimating the positive impact of kindness on recipients. *Journal of Experimental Psychology: General. Advance Online Publication.* https://doi.org/10.1037/xge0001271 (Accessed: December 31, 2022).

Lafley, A. G. and Charan, R. 2008. *Game-Changer. How You Can Drive Revenue and Profit Growth With Innovation.* New York, NY: Crown Business.

Lakritz, T. 2019. Trader Joe's Cashiers Danced and Sang to Stop a Toddler's Tantrum, and the Heartwarming Video Is Going Viral. Insider. August 13, 2019. https://www.insider.com/trader-joes-crew-members-dancing-singing-video-2019-8 (Accessed: December 20, 2022).

Laloux, F. 2014. *Reinventing Organizations: A Guide to Creating Organizations Inspired by the Next Stage in Human Consciousness: A Guide to Creating Organizations Inspired by the Next Stage of Human Consciousness.* Brussels: Nelson Parker.

Lanier, S. 2022. Favoritism at Work and How to Combat It. August 01, 2022. https://blog.hubspot.com/the-hustle/favoritism-at-work (Accessed: December 10, 2022).

Lau, Y. 2020. Increasing Mindfulness in the Workplace. *Forbes.* October 5, 2020. https://www.forbes.com/sites/forbeshumanresourcescouncil/2020/10/05/increasing-mindfulness-in-the-workplace/?sh=98b0a006956a (Accessed: December 31, 2022).

Laudon, K. C. and Laudon, J. P. 2018. *Essentials of MIS.* Harlow: Pearson Education Limited.

Lauretta, A. 2021. Best Time Management Apps. Very Well Mind. August 08, 2021. https://www.verywellmind.com/best-time-management-apps-5116817 (Accessed: December 6, 2022).

Lazare, A. 2004. *On Apology.* New York: Oxford University Press.

Lazare, A. 2010. *Making Peace through Apology.* In Keltner, D., Marsh, J., and Smith, J. A. (Eds.). *The Compassionate Instinct: The Science of Human Goodness.* New York: W. W. Norton

Lee, 2016. (Accessed: January 16, 2023).

Lee, F., Caza, A., Edmonson, A. and Thomke, S. 2003. *New Knowledge Creation in Organizations.* In Cameron, K. S. Dutton, J. E. and Quinn, R. E. (Eds.). *Positive Organizational Scholarship. Foundations for a New Discipline.* San Francisco: Berrett-Koehler.

Leech, G. 1983. *Principles of Pragmatics.* London: Longman Group Ltd.

Lee, C. S., Goldstein, S. E., Dik, B. J. and Rodas, J. M. 2020. Sources of social support and gender in perceived stress and individual adjustment among Latina/o college-attending emerging adults. *Cultural Diversity & Ethnic Minority Psychology.* 26(1), 134–147. https://doi.org/10.1037/cdp0000279. Epub 2019 Mar 28. PMID: 30920247.

Lego. 2022a. In Partnership with WWF. https://www.lego.com/en-gb/sustainability/environment/wwf-partnership (Accessed: October 16, 2022).

Lego. 2022b. Sustainability. https://www.lego.com/en-gb/sustainability (Accessed: October 12, 2022).

Lego. 2023. LEGO® Collaborations. https://www.lego.com/en-gb/lego-collaborations (Accessed: January 6, 2023).

Lehmann-Willenbrock, N. and Allen, J. 2014. How fun are your meetings? Investigating the relationship between humor patterns in team interactions and team performance. *The Journal of Applied Psychology*, 99. https://doi.org/10.1037/a0038083.

Leon. 2022. Pear & Ginger Seasonal Porridge with Organic Dairy Milk. https://leon.co/menu/ (Accessed: October 6, 2022).

Leonard, G. 1992. *Mastery: The Key to Success and Long-Term Fulfilment.* New York, NY: Plume.

Letterman, E. 1962. *Personal Power through Creative Selling.* New York, NY: First Collier Books.

Levi's. 2020. Water&ltLess® Born in 2011. Still Saving Water. Sustainability/March 2020. https://www.levi.com/US/en_US/blog/article/born-in-2011-still-saving-water (Accessed: December 2, 2022).

Lewin, R. and Regine, B. 2001. *Weaving Complexity and Business. Engaging the Soul at Work.* New York: Texere.

Li, Q. 2018. *Forest Bathing. How Trees Can Help You Find Health and Happiness.* New York: Viking.

Li, J., Canziani, B. F. and Barbieri, C. 2018. Emotional labor in hospitality: Positive affective displays in service encounters. *Tourism and Hospitality Research*, 18(2), 242–253. https://doi.org/10.1177/1467358416637253

Lieberman, D. 1997. *Instant Analysis.* New York, NY: St Martin's Griffins.

Lieberman, D. 2001. *Get Anyone to Do Anything*. New York, NY: St Martin's Griffins.

Lieberman, M. and Eisenberger, N. 2009. Neuroscience: Pains and pleasures of social life. *Science: New York, N.Y*, 323, 890–891. https://doi.org/10.1126/science.1170008

Lilius, J. M., Kano, J., Dutton, J. E., Worline, M. C. and Maitlis, S. 2012. *Compassion Revealed. What We Know About Compassion at Work (Where We Need to Know More)*. In Cameron, K. S. and Spreitzer, G. M. (Eds.). *The Oxford Handbook of Positive Organizational Scholarship*. New York: Oxford University Press.

Lilius, J., Worline, M., Maitlis, S., Kanov, J., Dutton, J. and Frost, P. 2008. The contours and consequences of compassion at work. *Journal of Organizational Behavior*, 29. https://doi.org/10.1002/job.508.

Lindergaard, S. 2022. Don't Be a Know-It-All...Be a Learn-It-All! September 5, 2022. Pulse. Linkedin. https://www.linkedin.com/pulse/dont-know-it-allbe-learn-it-all-stefan-lindegaard (Accessed: December 2, 2022).

Lindgren, S. 2017. *Digital Media & Society*. London: Sage.

Liu, E. and Nope-Brandon, S. 2009. *Imagination First. Unlocking the Power of Possibility*. San Francisco, CA: Jossey Bass.

Livermula, J. 2022. My Starbucks Idea: An Open Innovation Case Study. Braineet. https://www.braineet. com/blog/my-starbucks-idea-case-study (Accessed: December 22, 2022).

Lobel, T. 2014. *Sensation. The New Science of Physical Intelligence*. London: Icon Books.

Locke, J. 1998. *The De-Voicing of Society. Why We Don't Talk to Each Other Anymore*. New York, NY: Simon and Schuster.

Loewenstein, G. 1994. The psychology of curiosity: A review and reinterpretation. *Psychological Bulletin*, 116, 75–98.

Looker, T. and Gregson, O. 2010. *Manage Your Stress for a Happier Life*. London: McGraw-Hill.

López-Cepero, A., O'Neill, J., Tamez, M., Falcón, L.M., Tucker, K.L., Rodríguez-Orengo, J.F., Mattei, J. 2021. Associations between perceived stress and dietary intake in adults in Puerto Rico. *Journal of the Academy of Nutrition and Dietetics*, 121(4), 762–769. https://doi.org/10.1016/j.jand.2020.09.035. Epub 2020 Oct 24. PMID: 33109502; PMCID: PMC7981238.

Lorenz, E. 1993. *The Essence of Chaos*. Seattle, WA: Washington Press.

Lorenzo, R., Voigt, N., Schetelig, K., Zawadzki, A., Welpe, I. and Brosi, P. 2017. The Mix that Matters: Innovation through Diversity. BCG. April 26, 2017. https://www.bcg.com/publications/2017/people-organization-leadership-talent-innovation-through-diversity-mix-that-matters (Accessed: December 2, 2022).

Lowell, B. and Joyce, C. 2007. *Mobilizing Minds. Creating Wealth from Talent in the 21st Century Organization*. New York, NY: McGraw-Hill.

Lowndes, L. 2003. *How to Talk to Anyone. 92 Little Tricks for Big Success in Relationships*. London: Element.

Ludwig, S. 2020. 10 Hugely Successful Companies that Reinvented Their Business. December 4, 2020. https://www.uschamber.com/co/good-company/growth-studio/successful-companies-that-reinvented-their-business (Accessed: December 29, 2022).

Luft, J. and Ingham, H. 1955. "The Johari Window, a Graphic Model of Interpersonal Awareness." Proceedings of the Western Training Laboratory in Group Development. Los Angeles, CA: University of California.

Lundvall, B. A. (Ed.). 1992. *National System of Innovation: Toward a Theory of Innovation and Interactive Learning*. London: Pinter Publishers.

Lundvall, B. A. and Johnson, B. 1994. National systems of innovation and institutional learning. (Sistemas nacionales de innovación y aprendizaje institucional). *Revista Comercio Exterior*, 44(8), 695–704.

Lush. 2022. Super Powered Ingredients. https://www.lush.com/uk/en (Accessed: December 12, 2022).

Lush. 2023. From Source to Skin and Beyond: Our Stance on Ethical Buying. https://weare.lush.com/lush-life/our-values/ethical-buying/ (Accessed: January 2, 2023).

Luskin, F. 2010. *Forgive for Good: A Proven Prescription for Health and Happiness*. New York: HarperOne.

Luthans, F. and Stajkovic, A. 2009. *Provide Recognition for Performance Improvement*. In Locke, E. A. (Ed.). *Handbook of Principles of Organizational Behavior: Indispensable Knowledge for Evidence-Based Management*, 2nd Edition. 239–253. Chichester: Wiley.

MacCallum, L., Brew, E. and Howson, N. 2019. *Inspired Inc. Become a Company the World Will Get Behind.* Crowd Press.

MacDonald, S. 2021. Two Blind Brothers Reimagines Buyers' Trust. Commerce in The World. Shopify. March 8, 2021. https://www.shopify.com/uk/enterprise/two-blind-brothers-reimagines-buyers-trust (Accessed: October 2, 2022).

Mackey, J., McIntosh, S. and Phipps, C. 2020. *Conscious Leadership. Elevating Humanity Through Business.* New York: Portfolio Penguin.

Mackey, J. and Sisodia, R. 2014. *Conscious Capitalism. Liberating the Heroic Spirit of Business.* Boston, MA: Harvard Business Review Press.

MacMillan, I. C. and Thompson, J. D. 2013. *The Social Entrepreneur's Playbook, Expanded Edition: Pressure Test, Plan, Launch and Scale Your Social Enterprise.* Wharton Digital Press.

Mainemelis, C. and Ronson, S. 2006. Ideas are born in fields of play: Towards a theory of play and creativity in organizational settings. *Research in Organizational Behavior*, 27, 81–131.

Maltz, M. 2015. *Psycho-Cybernetics.* New York, NY: Perigree.

Manby, J. 2012. *Love Works. Seven Timeless Principles for Effective Leaders.* Grand Rapids, MI: Zondervan.

Mann, I. 2021. How One Company Built A Business with Thank You Notes. Postalgia Ink. June 4, 2021. https://postalgia.ink/how-one-company-built-a-business-with-thank-you-notes/ (Accessed: December 26, 2022).

Mannucci, P. V. 2016. How Knowledge Can Stimulate but Also Impede Creativity. HEC Paris. May 03, 2016. https://www.hec.edu/en/knowledge/instants/how-knowledge-can-stimulate-also-impede-creativity

Marden, O. S. 1917. *How to Get What You Want.* New York, NY: Thomas & Crowell.

Marker, A. 2021. Enterprise Risk Management Case Studies: Heroes and Zeros. Smartsheet. April 7, 2021. https://www.smartsheet.com/content/enterprise-risk-management-examples (Accessed: December 2, 2022).

Markowitz, D. M., Kouchaki, M., Hancock, J. T. and Gino, F. 2021. The deception spiral: Corporate obfuscation leads to perceptions of immorality and cheating behavior. *Journal of Language and Social Psychology*, 40(2), 277–296.

Marriott. 2022. Marriott International. Diversity and Inclusion. https://www.marriott.com/diversity/diversity-and-inclusion.mi#:~:text=At%20Marriott%2C%20the%20foundation%20for%20diversity%20and%20inclusion,and%20inclusive%20workforce%2C%20owner%2C%20guest%20and%20supplier%20base. (Accessed: December 5, 2022).

Marriott. 2023a. Core Values & Heritage. https://www.marriott.com/culture-and-values/core-values.mi (Accessed: January 12, 2023).

Marriott. 2023b. Stories of Excellence. https://www.marriott.com/culture-and-values/awards-of-excellence.mi

Marsh, B. 2022. A Few Fun Facts about Play-Doh & Its History. The Fact Site. August 25, 2022. https://www.thefactsite.com/play-doh-facts/ (Accessed: December 25, 2022).

Martichoux, 2019. Trader Joe's Listens to Customer Feedback, Making Big Changes. Houston Chronicle. March 1, 2019. https://www.houstonchronicle.com/food/article/Trader-Joes-plastic-packaging-waste-compostable-13653491.php (Accessed: March 2, 2023).

Martin, P. 2006. *Making Happy People. The Nature of Happiness and Its Origins in Childhood.* London: Harper Perennial.

Mashore, K. 2022. You Have to Read If You Want to Succeed. *Entrepreneur.* August 3, 2022. https://www.entrepreneur.com/leadership/successful-entrepreneurs-like-bill-gates-and-oprah-winfrey/430911 (Accessed: December 2, 2022).

Maslow, A. H. 1954. *Motivation and Personality.* New York, NY: Harper & Row.

Maslow, A. H. 1968. *Toward a Psychology of Being.* New York, NY: D. Van Nostrand Company.

Maslow, A. H. 1943. A theory of human motivation. *Psychological Review*, 50, 370–396.

Maslow, A. H. 1965. *Eupsychian Management. A Journal.* Homewood, IL: Richard D, Irwin, Inc and The Dorsey Press.

Maturana Romesin, H. and Verden-Zoller. G. 1996. *The Biology of Love.* In Opp, G. and F. Peterander (Eds.). *Focus Heilpadagogik.* Munchen/Basel: Ernst Reinhardt. Available at https://reflexus.org/wp-content/uploads/biology-of-love.pdf (Accessed: December 20, 2018).

Maturana Romesin, H. and Verden-Zoller, G. 2008. *Origin of Humanness in the Biology of Love.* Charlottesville, VA: Imprint Academic.

Maturana, H. and Bunnel, P. 1998. *Biology of Business. Love Expands Intelligence.* Presentation at the Society of Organisational Learning Members' Meeting. Amherst, MA. [Online] Available at www.researchgate.net/publication/240275459_The_Biology_of_Business_Love_Expands_Intelligence (Accessed: September 24, 2018).

Meyer, E. 2021. Netflix Treats Its Employees Like Adults, that's What Gets Speed and Innovation Going. France 24. English. April 19, 2021. https://www.youtube.com/watch?v=qV6b1Dzoebc (Accessed: October 22, 2023).

McAllister, D. J. 1995. Affect- and cognition-based trust as foundations for interpersonal cooperation in organizations. *Academy of Management Journal*, 38, 24–59.

McBride-Walker, S. M. (n.d.). Toward a Working Definition of the Construct of Fear in the Management Sciences. Cleveland, OH: Department of Organizational Behavior. Weatherhead School of Management Case, Western Reserve University. [Online] Available at https://weatherhead.case.edu/departments/organizational-behavior/workingPapers/WP-16-01.pdf (Accessed: September 24, 2018).

McCullough, M., Kilpatrick, S., Emmons, R. and Larson, D. 2001. Is gratitude a moral affect?, *Psychological Bulletin*, 127, 249–266. https://doi.org/10.1037//0033-2909.127.2.249

McEvilly, G. 2012. TEDx Westlake - Greg McEvilly - "The motivation for everything" https://www.youtube.com/watch?v=wfCZYvqVFKM - July 12, 2012 (Accessed: October 12, 2022).

McGrath, R. G. and MacMillan, I. C. 2005. *Marketbusters. 40 Strategic Moves that Drive Exceptional Business Growth.* Boston, MA: Harvard Business School Press.

McIntosh, D., Horowitz, J. and Kaye, M. 2018. *Stress. The Psychology of Managing Pressure.* London: DK.

McIntosh, M., Leipziger, D. and Jones, K. et al. 1998. *Corporate Citizenship Successful Strategies for Responsible Companies.* London: Financial Times Management.

McIvor, M. 2022. The Continuous Improvement Process of Toyota Kaizen: Discard, Replace, or Continue. Globis Insights. August 12, 2022. https://globisinsights.com/purpose/values/toyota-kaizen-improvement-process/ (Accessed: December 31, 2022).

McKenna, E. 2012a. *Business Psychology and Organizational Behaviour.* Hove: Psychology Press.

McKenna, P. 2012b. *I Can Make You Smarter.* London: Bantam Press.

McKeown, M. 2014. *The Innovation Book.* London: Pearson.

McKinnon, T. 2022. Trader Joe's Strategy: 12 Keys to Its Success. Indigo Digital. April 11, 2022. https://www.indigo9digital.com/blog/traderjoesstrategy (Accessed: December 1, 2022).

McLellan, V. 1996. *Wise Words and Quotes.* Wheaton, IL: Tyndale House Publishers.

Meares, K. and Freeston, M. 2008. *Overcoming Worry. A Self-Help Guide Using Cognitive Behavioral Techniques.* London: Robinson.

Mechlinski, J. 2021. How Zappos Builds Engagement with Its Call Center. February 2, 2021. https://www.shiftthework.com/blog/how-zappos-builds-engagement-with-its-call-center (Accessed: December 1, 2022).

Medina, J. 2014. *Brain Rules. 12 Principles for Surviving and Thriving at Work, Home, and School.* Seattle, WA: Pear Press.

Medrut, F. 2022. 28 Inspiring Bill Gates Quotes on How to Succeed in Life https://www.goalcast.com/2017/12/07/27-bill-gates-quotes/ (Accessed: October 1, 2022).

Menges, S. and Frater, J. 2021. Top 10 Failed Products from Famous Companies. Listverse. April 19, 2021. https://listverse.com/2021/04/19/top-10-failed-products-from-famous-companies/ (Accessed: December 1, 2022).

Mesmer-Magnus, J., Glew, D. and Viswesvaran, C. 2012. A meta-analysis of positive humor in the workplace. *Journal of Managerial Psychology*, 27, 155–190. https://doi.org/10.1108/02683941211199554.

Methot, J. R., Rosado-Solomon, E. H., Downes, P. E. and Gabriel, A. S. 2021. Office chitchat as a social ritual: The uplifting yet distracting effects of daily small talk at work. *Academy of Management Journal*, 64(5). https://doi.org/10.5465/amj.2018.1474 (Accessed: December 11, 2022).

Meyer, E. 2021. Netflix treats its employees like adults, that's what gets speed and innovation going. France 24. English. 19 Apr 2021. https://www.youtube.com/watch?v=qV6b1Dzoebc (Accessed: October, 22, 2023).

Meyers-Levy, J. and Zhu, R. 2007. The influence of ceiling height: The effect of priming on the type of processing that people use. *Journal of Consumer Research*, 34 174–186.

Microsoft. 2022. Microsoft. Our Corporate Values. https://www.microsoft.com/en-us/about/corporate-values (Accessed: October 1, 2022).

Mihm, S. 2022. The Curious History of a Forgotten Lightbulb Cartel. Bloomberg UK. https://www.bloomberg.com/opinion/articles/2022-05-04/cheering-for-led-bulbs-read-this-cautionary-tale-about-the-phoebus-cartel?leadSource=uverify%20wall (Accessed: October 2, 2022).

Miller, L. 2009. *Mood Mapping. Plot Your Way to Emotional Health and Happiness*. London: Rodale.

Minaar, J. 2017. FAVI: How Zobrist Broke Down FAVI's Command-and-Control Structures. Corporate Rebels. January 4, 2017. https://corporate-rebels.com/zobrist/ (Accessed: October 2, 2022).

Minaar, J. 2020. Psychological Safety: How Pioneers Create Engaged Workforces. Corporate Rebels. February 5, 2020. https://corporate-rebels.com/psychological-safety-79185/ (Accessed: December 2, 2022).

Mipham, S. 2017. Lost Art of Good Conversation: A Mindful Way to Connect with Others and Enrich Everyday Life. New York: Harmony.

Mirivel, J. C. 2014. *The Art of Positive Communication. Theory and Practice*. New York: Peter Lang.

Mitchell, P., Reast, J. and Linch, J. 1998. Exploring the foundation of trust. *Journal of Marketing Management*, 14, 159–172.

Modern Life Academy, 2023. Modern Life Academy. A School Dedicated to Helping You Navigate Midlife and Beyond. https://www.modernelderacademy.com/ (Accessed: January 12, 2023).

Moga, B. 2017. Real Life Examples of Successful Teamwork (9 Cases). ActivCollab. https://activecollab.com/blog/collaboration/real-world-examples-of-successful-teamwork (Accessed: October 12, 2022).

Moll, J., Krueger, F., Zahn, R., Pardini, M., Oliveira-Souza, R. and Grafman, J. 2006. Human fronto–mesolimbic networks guide decisions about charitable donation. *Proceedings of the National Academy of Sciences*, 103(42), 15623–15628. https://doi.org/10.1073/pnas.0604475103

Monet, T. 2021. Why Psychological Safety at Work Matters to Business. Accenture. Business Function Blog. Workforce. October 28, 2021. https://www.accenture.com/us-en/blogs/business-functions-blog/work-psychological-safety (Accessed: December 12, 2022).

Montagu, A. M. F. 1957. *The Direction of Human Development*. London: Watts.

Moon, J. 2017. Sustainable Business: It's Not Just about the Why. TEDxScottBase. January 25, 2017. https://www.youtube.com/watch?v=azM4n0zf4jw (Accessed: January 1, 2023).

Morgan, B. 2019. The Five Lessons from Trader Joe's Unbeatable Customer Experience. *Forbes*. https://www.forbes.com/sites/blakemorgan/2019/10/24/the-5-lessons-from-trader-joes-unbeatable-customer-experience/?sh=2db911694776 (Accessed: September 26, 2022).

Morgan, G. 1986. *Images of Organization*. Newbury Park, CA: Sage.

Morgan, G. 1997. *Imaginization. New Mindsets for Seeing, Organizing, and Managing*. San Francisco, CA: Berrett-Koehler/Sage.

Morgan, R. M., and Hunt, S. D. 1994. The commitment-trust theory of relationship marketing. *Journal of marketing*, 58(3), 20–38.

Morrison, D. and Firmstone, J. 2015. The social function of trust and implications for e-commerce. *International Journal of Advertising*, 19(5), 599–623.

Mosley, E. and Irvine, D. 2020. *Making Work Human: How Human-Centered Companies Are Changing the Future of Work and the World*. New York: McGraw Hill.

Mott, T. 2020. The Magic Castle Hotel – The Power of Moments. Risq Consulting. February 5, 2020. https://risqconsulting.com/the-magic-castle-hotel-the-power-of-moments/ (Accessed: December 26, 2022).

Mulford, P. 2015. *Your Forces and How to Use Them*. Hollister, CA: Yoge Books.

Mulholland, B. 2018. The Power of Asking Simple Marketing Questions. March 9, 2018. https://www.process.st/marketing-questions/ (Accessed: December 29, 2022).

Murphy, J. 2022. 14 Easy Ways to Create a Zen Office Space on a Budget. https://snacknation.com/blog/zen-office/ (Accessed: December 21, 2022).

Murphy, P. E., Laczniak, G. R. and Harris, F. 2017. *Ethics in Marketing. International Cases and Perspectives*. NY: Routledge.

Murray, B. (n.d.). *A Career Can Turn on a Big Idea*. Momentum.

Murray, D. 2009. *Borrowing Brilliance. The Six Steps to Business Innovation by Building on the Ideas of Others*. New York, NY: Gotham Books.

Murray, E. J. 1964. *Motivation and Emotion*. Englewood Cliffs, NJ: Prentice-Hall.

My Saint My Hero. 2023. Be Kind Humankind. https://mysaintmyhero.com/collections/be-kind-humankind (Accessed: March 31, 2023).

Narang, R. and Devaiah. D. 2014. Orbit-Shifting Innovation. The Dynamics of Ideas That Create History. London: Kogan Page.

Nardi, B. 2005. Beyond bandwith. *Computer Supportive Co-Operative Work (CSCW)*, 14(2), 91–130.

Needle, F. 2021. 7 Companies with Great Social Listening Strategies. September 06, 2021. https://blog.hubspot.com/service/social-listening-examples (Accessed: December 31, 2022).

Neill, M. 2013. *The Inside-Out Revolution. The Only Thing You Need to Know to Change Your Life Forever*. London: Hay House.

Nelson, D. and Cooper, C. L. (Eds.). 2007. *Positive Organizational Behaviour*. London: Sage.

Netflix. 2022. Netflix. Unlimited Films, TV Programmes and More. https://www.netflix.com/gb/ (Accessed: December 14, 2022).

Netflix. 2023, Netflix Jobs. Work Life Philosophy. https://jobs.netflix.com/work-life-philosophy (Accessed: March 14, 2023).

Newman, A., Donohue, R. and Nathan, E. 2017. Psychological safety. A systematic review of the literature. *Human Resources Management Review*, 27(3), 521–535.

News Delta. 2020. Promoting Inclusion: New Training to Reach 75,000 Delta Employees. November 18, 2020. https://news.delta.com/promoting-inclusion-new-training-reach-75000-delta-employees (Accessed: March 12, 2023).

Newson, R. 2021. From a Trend to a Tool – How We've Revamped our Internal Communications. May 26, 2021. https://careers.virginmedia.com/feeling-social/stories/from-a-trend-to-a-tool-how-weve-revamped-our-internal-communications/ (Accessed: November 14, 2022).

Nguyen, T. V. 2022. How Google Conducts Performance Review. https://blog.grovehr.com/google-performance-review (Accessed: November 14, 2022).

Nimalan, G. 2021. Supporting Parents' Wellbeing at Work. Shine. December 15, 2021. https://www.shineworkplacewellbeing.com/businesses-supporting-parents-wellbeing/ (Accessed: November 26, 2022).

Nobel, S. 2012. *The Enlightenment of Work. Revealing the Path to Happiness, Contentment and Purpose in Your Job*. London: Watkins.

Novak, D. 2016. Recognizing Employees Is the Simplest Way to Improve Morale. *Harvard Business Review*. May 09, 2016. https://hbr.org/2016/05/recognizing-employees-is-the-simplest-way-to-improve-morale.html (Accessed: October 24, 2022).

Novak, D. 2016. Recognizing Employees Is the Simplest Way to Improve *Morale*. *Harvard Business Review*. May 09, 2016. https://hbr.org/2016/05/recognizing-employees-is-the-simplest-way-to-improve-morale.html (Accessed: December 1, 2022).

Novak, D. and Bourg, C. 2016. *O Great One: A Little Story about the Awesome Power of Recognition*. New York, NY: Penguin Random House.

Nvidia. 2022a. Nvidia. About Us. Diversity and Inclusion. https://www.nvidia.com/en-gb/about-nvidia/careers/diversity-and-inclusion/ (Accessed: October 14, 2022).

Nvidia. 2022b. Nvidia. Environmental, Health, Safety and Energy (EHS&E) Policy https://www.nvidia.com/content/dam/en-zz/Solutions/about-us/documents/NVIDIA-Environmental-Health-Safety-Energy-Policy.pdf

O'Connor, J. 2001. *NLP Workbook. A Practical Guide to Achieving the Results You Want*. London: Thorsons.

O'Connor, J. and McDermott, I. 1997. *The Art of Systems Thinking*. London: Thorsons.

O'Quins, K. and Derks, P. 1999. *Humor*. In M. A. Runco and S. R. Pritzker (Eds.). *Encyclopedia of Creativity* (Vol. 1). San Diego, CA: Academic Press.

O'Reilly, C. A. and Chatman, J. A. 2020. Transformational leader or narcissist? How grandiose narcissists can create of destroy organizations and Institutions. *California Management Review*. 62(3), 5–27.

Oakley, E. and Kroug, D. 1994. *Enlightened Leadership. Getting to the Heart of Change*. New York, NY: Fireside.

Olejniczak, L. 2021. Why Google, Target, and General Mills Are Investing in Mindfulness. January 8, 2021. https://www.sbam.org/why-google-target-and-general-mills-are-investing-in-mindfulness/ (Accessed: December 17, 2022).

Oliver, R., Rust, R. T. and Varki, S. 1997. Customer delight: Foundations, findings, and managerial insight. *Journal of Retailing*, 73(Fall), 311–333.

Om, V. 2022. 8 Best Customer Service Companies in 2022 (Tips included). Freshdesk Blog. August 19, 2022. https://freshdesk.com/general/best-customer-service-companies-blog/ (Accessed: December 7, 2022).

Ong, W. J. 1982. *Orality and Literacy*. London: Matheun.

Ornish, D. 1999. *Love and Survival. 8 Pathways to Intimacy and Health*. New York, NY: William Morrow & Company.

Osborn, A. 1948. *Your Creative Power*. New York, NY: Charles Scribners.

Oscar. 2022. Oscar. Health Insurance that Actually Works for You. https://www.hioscar.com/ (Accessed: December 7, 2022).

Owens, B. P., Johnson, M. D. and Mitchell, T. R. 2013. Expressed humility in organizations: Implications for performance, teams, and leadership. *Organization Science*, 24(5), 1517–1538.

Ozawa-de Silva B. and Karlin, M. 2017. Compassionate Integrity Training. Center for Compassion, Integrity and Secular Ethics (CCISE) at Life University.

Palmisano, S. 2023. A Business and Its Beliefs. Icons of Progress. https://www.ibm.com/ibm/history/ibm100/us/en/icons/bizbeliefs/ (Accessed: January 7, 2023).

Panera Bread. 2021. Boldly Embracing Change. 2021 Responsibility Report. Panera. https://www.panerabread.com/content/dam/panerabread/integrated-web-content/documents/press/2021/panera-bread-2021-responsibility-report.pdf (Accessed: March 7, 2023).

Panera Bread. 2023. Eat Well, Share More and Take Care of Each Other. https://www.panerabread.com/en-us/food-values/community.html (Accessed: March 7, 2023).

Parikh, J. 2021. Ratan Tata. The Financial Pandora. April 16, 2021. https://thefinancialpandora.com/ratan-tata/ (Accessed: October 7, 2022).

Parris, R. 2022. 20 Best Companies for Employee Benefits and Perks. April 25, 2022. https://tech.co/hr-software/best-companies-employee-benefits-perks (Accessed: December 23, 2022).

Parson, P. 2004. *Ethics in Public Relations. A Guide to Best Practice*. London: Kogan Page.

Pasha, R. 2017. 55 Anita Roddick Quotes for Entrepreneurs. Success Feed. January 24, 2017. https://succeedfeed.com/anita-roddick-quotes/ (Accessed: September 23, 2022).

Patagonia. 2022a. Core Values. https://eu.patagonia.com/gb/en/core-values/ (Accessed: September 23, 2022).

Patagonia. 2022b. Earth is Now Our Only Shareholder. https://eu.patagonia.com/gb/en/ownership/ (Accessed: September 23, 2022).

Patagonia. 2022c. Don't Buy This Jacket, Black Friday and The New York Times. https://www.patagonia.com/stories/dont-buy-this-jacket-black-friday-and-the-new-york-times/story-18615.html?utm_source=goodonyou.eco&utm_medium=affiliate&utm_campaign=Custom%20Link (Accessed: December 23, 2022).

Patagonia. 2023. Everything We Make Has an Impact on the Planet. https://www.patagonia.com/footprint.html (Accessed: February, 1, 2023).

Patel, K. 2005. *The Master Strategists. Power, Purpose and Principle in Action*. London: Hutchinson.

Paul Mitchell. 2022a. John Paul Mitchell Systems. Culture of Giving. https://www.paulmitchell.com/company/culture-of-giving/ (Accessed: October 1, 2022).

Paul Mitchell. 2022b. John Paul Mitchell Systems. Sustainability. https://www.paulmitchell.com/sustainability (Accessed: October 1, 2022).

Paul Mitchell. 2022c. John Paul Mitchell Systems. Our Story. https://www.paulmitchell.com/company (Accessed: October 1, 2022).

Pease, A. 2014. *Body Language*. Usha, Madhya Pradesh: Manjul Publishing House.

Pease, A. and Pease, B. 2004. *The Definite Book of Body Language. The Hidden Meaning Behind People's Gestures and Expressions*. London: Orion.

PepsiCo. 2022. Employee Engagement. https://www.pepsico.com/our-impact/esg-topics-a-z/employee-engagement (Accessed: November 12, 2022).

Perelmuter, T. 2021. Aloneness to Oneness - Life Changing Spiritual Documentary Film on Non-duality. September 16, 2021. https://www.youtube.com/watch?v=9M56t0UoW5M (Accessed: September 24, 2022).

Perform Yard. 2021. How Does GE Do Performance Management Today? Perform Yard. June 14, 2021. https://www.performyard.com/articles/how-does-ge-do-performance-management-today (Accessed: October 24, 2022).

Peri. 2023. 3D Construction Printing. Peri. https://www.peri.com/en/business-segments/3d-construction-printing.html (Accessed: January 2, 2023).

Perkupapp. 2022. Perk up. The Delta Airlines Perks & Benefits that Attract Employees. August 11, 2022. https://www.perkupapp.com/post/the-delta-airlines-perks-benefits-that-attract-employees (Accessed: September 24, 2022).

Perttula, K. H. and Cardon, M. S. 2012. *Passion*. In Cameron, K. S. and Spreitzer, G. M. (Eds.). *The Oxford Handbook of Positive Organizational Scholarship*. New York: Oxford University Press.

Peters, T. 1994. *The Pursuit of Wow. Every Person's Guide to Topsy-Turvy Times*. London: McMillan.

PG. 2023. Innovation. https://www.pg.co.uk/innovation/ (Accessed: January 14, 2023).

Pham, L. B. and Taylor, S. E. 1999. From thought to action: Effects of process-versus outcome-based mental simulations on performance. *Personality and Social Psychology Bulletin*, 25(2), 250–260.

Phillips, D. J. P. 2017. The Magical Science of Storytelling | David JP Phillips | TEDxStockholm. March 16, 2017. https://www.youtube.com/watch?v=Nj-hdQMa3uA (Accessed: March 24, 2023).

Ping, J. 2020. Planned vs. Perceived Obsolescence. My Money Blog. June 25, 2020. https://www.mymoneyblog.com/planned-vs-perceived-obsolescence.html (Accessed: December 24, 2022).

Pink, D. 2010. RSA ANIMATE: Drive: The Surprising Truth about What Motivates Us. RSA. April 1, 2010. https://www.youtube.com/watch?v=u6XAPnuFjJc (Accessed: December 24, 2022).

Pink, D. 2011. *Drive. The Surprising Truth About What Motivates Us*. New York, NY: Riverhead Books.

Pixar, 2022. Internships at Pixar. https://www.pixar.com/internships (Accessed: December 4, 2022).

Plant, P. 2016. What Does Henry Ford, McDonald's, and Your Content Have in Common? *Medium*. December 7, 2016. https://medium.com/everydaymarketers/what-does-heny-ford-mcdonalds-and-your-content-have-in-common-fda8a36b4eea (Accessed: January 2, 2023).

Plester, B. 2009. Healthy humour: Using humour to cope at work. *Kōtuitui: New Zealand Journal of Social Sciences Online*. 4(1), 89–102. [Online] Available at www.tandfonline.com/doi/abs/10.1080/1177083x.2009.9522446 (Accessed: September 24, 2018).

Plowman, K. D. 1998. Power in conflict for public relations. *Journal of Public Relations Research*, 19(4), 237–261.

Plucker, J. A. and Runco, M. A. 1999. *Enhancement of Creativity*. In M. A. Runco & S. R. Pritzker (Eds.). *Encyclopedia of Creativity* (Vol. 1). San Diego, CA: Academic Press.

Polanyi, M. 1967. *The Tacit Dimension*. London: Routledge and Keagan.

Porath, C. 2016. *Mastering Civility: A Manifesto for the Workplace*. New York: Grand Central Publishing.

Porath, C. L. 2012. *Civility*. In Cameron, K. S. and Spreitzer, G. M. (Eds.). *The Oxford Handbook of Positive Organizational Scholarship*. New York: Oxford University Press.

Porath, C. L., Gerbasi, A. and Schorch, S. L. 2015. The effects of civility on advice, leadership, and performance. *Journal of Applied Psychology*, 100(5), 1527–1541. https://doi.org/10.1037/apl0000016

Porter, M. 2013. Michael Porter: Why Business Can Be Good at Solving Social Problems. TEDx Talk. October 7, 2013. https://www.youtube.com/watch?v=0iIh5YYDR2o (Accessed: November 2, 2022).

Post It. 2022. History Timeline: Post-it® Notes. https://www.post-it.com/3M/en_US/post-it/contact-us/about-us/ (Accessed: November 26, 2022).

Postelnyak, M. 2022. Top 10 Employee Engagement Companies. Contact Monkey. https://www.contact-monkey.com/blog/top-companies-employee-engagement (Accessed: November 27, 2022).

Post, J. E., Preston, L. E. and Sachs, S. 2002. *Redefining the Corporation, Stakeholder Management and Organizational Wealth*. Stanford: Stanford University Press.

Price, A. and Price, D. 2013. *Introducing Leadership. A Practical Guide*. London: Icon Books.

Price, S. and Rasay, S. J. 2021. Netflix Pays Top Median Employee Salary; Cable CEO Pay Ratios Skyrocket. October 26, 2021. S&P Global Market Intelligence. https://www.spglobal.com/marketintelligence/en/news-insights/latest-news-headlines/netflix-pays-top-median-employee-salary-cable-ceo-pay-ratios-skyrocket-67206389 (Accessed: March 2, 2023).

Project Forgive. 2022. Project Forgive. https://projectforgive.com (Accessed: November 26, 2022).

Pugh, D. S. and Hickson, D. 2007. *Writers on Organizations*. London: Penguin Books.

Pukka Herbs. 2022. Our Mission. https://www.pukkaherbs.com/us/en/our-mission (Accessed: December 26, 2022).

Purdie, J. 2010. *Life Coaching for Dummies*. Chichester, UK: Wiley.

Qian, J. 2020. LEGO: The Marketing Strategy behind the Toy Industry Titan. Contact Pigeon. December 11, 2020. https://blog.contactpigeon.com/lego-marketing-strategy/ (Accessed: December 29, 2022).

Qualaroo. 2022. How Top 15 Brands Use Customer Feedback Effectively. September 5, 2022. https://qualaroo.com/blog/the-best-ways-big-companies-use-customer-feedback/ (Accessed: December 1, 2022).

Race, P. 1995. *Who Learns Wins*. London: Penguin Books.

Radu, V. 2022. 12 Companies with Great Customer Experience. Omniconvert. https://www.omniconvert.com/blog/companies-great-customer-experience/ (Accessed: December 24, 2022).

Rainey, S. 2017. Inside the World's Wackiest Workplace: Staff at Google Take Catnaps in £5,000 Sleep Pods, Hold Meetings in Caravans, Get Staff Passes for Their Dogs and the Canteen Serves Free Lobster (But You Don't Dare Get Fat!) *Daily Mail*. July 5, 2017. http://www.dailymail.co.uk/news/article-4665838/World-s-wackiest-workplace-look-inside-Google-offices.html (Accessed: October 1, 2022).

Ramanchadran, V. S. and Blakeslee, S. 1999. *Phantoms in the Brain. Human Nature and the Architecture of the Mind*. London: Four State.

Ramsey, R. P. and Sohi, R. S. 1997. Listening to your customers: The impact of perceived salesperson listening behavior on relationship outcomes. *Journal of the Academy of Marketing Science*, 25, 127. https://doi.org/10.1007/BF02894348

Rando, C. 2014. *You Can Think Differently. Change Your Thinking, Change Your Life*. London: Watkins.

Ray, M. and Myers, R. 1989. *Creativity in Business*. New York, NY: Broadway Books.

Razzetti, G. 2019b. How Zappos Designs Culture Using Core Values. Fearless Culture. December 9, 2019. https://www.fearlessculture.design/blog-posts/zappos-culture-design-canvas (Accessed: December 31, 2022).

Razzetti, G. 2020. 12 Examples of Companies with Powerful Cultures. Fearless Culture. December 7, 2020. https://www.fearlessculture.design/blog-posts/11-examples-of-companies-with-powerful-cultures (Accessed: October 31, 2022).

Razzetti, G. 2019a. Spotify Agile Model: The Power of a Strong Engineering Culture. Fearless Culture. https://www.fearlessculture.design/blog-posts/spotify-culture-design-canvas (Accessed: December 12, 2022).

Razzetti, G. 2021. Leadership Is All about Mindset – What Assumptions Do You Hold about Your Employees? Fearless Culture. July 21, 2021. https://www.fearlessculture.design/blog-posts/the-assumptions-you-make-about-people-harm-your-company-culture (Accessed: November 10, 2022).

Read, S. 2021. Sainsbury's Takes on Aldi in Supermarket Price War. February 10, 2021. https://www.bbc.co.uk/news/business-56012719 (Accessed: October 1, 2022).

Recognize. 2021. Companies with the Best Employee Recognition Programs. https://recognizeapp.com/cms/articles/companies-with-the-best-employee-recognition-programs (Accessed: October 1, 2022).

Reeves, M. 2022. 10+ Examples of Successful Mentoring Programs. Together. September 21, 2022. https://www.togetherplatform.com/blog/examples-of-successful-mentoring-programs (Accessed: December 1, 2022).

Reforest Action. 2022. Reforest Action. Our Mission. https://www.reforestaction.com/en (Accessed: October 1, 2022).

Regan, A., Margolis, S. and Ozer, D. J. et al. 2022.What is Unique about Kindness? Exploring the Proximal Experience of Prosocial Acts Relative to Other Positive Behaviors. *Affective Science*. https://doi.org/10.1007/s42761-022-00143-4

Reivich, K. and Shatté, A. 2002. *The Resilience Factor. 7 Keys to Finding Your Inner Strength and Overcoming Life's Hurdles*. New York, NY: Broadway Books.

Responsible Business Alliance. 2021. Responsible Business Alliance. Version 7.0 (2021) Responsible Business Alliance Code of Conduct. https://www.responsiblebusiness.org/media/docs/RBACodeofConduct7.0_English.pdf (Accessed: October 1, 2022).

Rhee, S. and Yoon, H. J. 2012. *Shared Positive Affect in Workgroups*. In Cameron, K. S. and Spreitzer, G. M. (Eds.). *The Oxford Handbook of Positive Organizational Scholarship*. New York: Oxford University Press.

Ricard, M. 2015. *Altruism. The Science and Psychology of Kindness*. London, Great Britain: Atlantic Books.

Ricci, J. A., Chee, E., Lorandeau, A. L. and Berger, J. 2007. Fatigue in the U.S. Workforce: Prevalence and implications for lost productive work time. *Journal of Occupational and Environmental Medicine*, 49(1). 1–10. https://doi.org/10.1097/01.jom.0000249782.60321.2a. PMID: 17215708.

Rice, M. 2021. Casper Used Content and Creative Policies Get People to Buy Mattresses Online. Jilt. March 19, 2021. https://jilt.com/blog/casper-content/ (Accessed: December 1, 2022).

Richard, O. C. 2000. Racial diversity, business strategy, and firm performance: A resource-based view. *Academy of Management Journal*, 43, 164–177.

Rigby, G. 2014. Top Four Traits of a Successful Entrepreneur. The Telegraph. June 6, 2014. https://www.telegraph.co.uk/sponsored/business/national-business-awards/10877468/successful-entrepreneur-traits.html (Accessed: September 26, 2022).

Rilling, J., Gutman, D., Zeh, T., Pagnoni, G., Berns, G. and Kilts, C. 2002. A neural basis for social cooperation. Neuron, 35(2), 395–405. https://doi.org/10.1016/s0896-6273(02)00755-9. PMID: 12160756.

Ringel, M., Apostolatos, K., Kruehler, M., Panandiker, R., Manly, J., Backler, W., Harnoss, J. and Norihiko, S. 2021. *Chapter 3: How Leaders Bring Product and Sales Teams Together*. in *Most Innovative Companies 2021. Overcoming the Innovation Gap*. BCG. April. https://web-assets.bcg.com/eb/93/cfbea005442482b0adc64b9f499f/bcg-most-innovative-companies-2021-apr-2021-r.pdf (Accessed: December 26, 2022).

Robbins, A. 2001. *Awaken the Giant within. How to Take Immediate Control of Your Mental, Emotional, Physical & Financial Destiny!* New York, NY: Fireside.

Robbins, A. 2014. Tony Robbins: 6 Basic Needs that Make Us Tick. *Entrepreneur*. December 4, 2014. [Online] Available at www.entrepreneur.com/article/240441 (Accessed: September 25, 2018).

Robbins, M. 2017. *The 5 Second Rule. Transform Your Life, Work and Confidence with Everyday Courage*. Savio Republic.

Roberts, K. 2004. *Lovemarks: The Future beyond Brands*. New York, NY: Powerhouse Books.

Roberts, S. 2022. Top 10 Companies Empowering Employees with Disabilities, Verbit. https://verbit.ai/top-10-companies-empowering-employees-with-disabilities/ (Accessed: December 29, 2022).

Robertson, T. 2020. What 'Integrity Built In' Means for Microsoft Devices' Sustainability. November 17, 2020. https://blogs.microsoft.com/on-the-issues/2020/11/17/integrity-built-in-microsoft-devices-sustainability-report/ (Accessed: September 29, 2022).

Robles, M. 2012. Executive perceptions of the top 10 soft skills needed in today's workplace. *Business Communication Quarterly*, 75(4), 453–465.

Rogers, C. 1961. *On Becoming a Person*. London: Houghton Mifflin Company.

Rogers, C. 1969. *Freedom to Learn*. Columbus, OH: Charles and Merrill Publishing Company.

Rogers, C. 1991. *Client Centred Therapy*. London: Constable.

Rosenberg, M. 2005. *Nonviolent Communication*. Encinitas, CA: Puddledancer Press.

Rosenberg, R. 1998. Yes, There Is a Better Search Engine. While the Portal Sites Fiddle, Google Catches Fire. Salon.com. December 21, 1998. https://www.salon.com/1998/12/21/straight_44/ (Accessed: November, October 29, 2022).

Ross, M. 2019. *The Empathy Edge: Harnessing the Value of Compassion as an Engine for Success*. Canada: Page Two.

Rothfeder, J. 2014. For Honda, Waigaya Is the Way. Strategy + Business. August 1, 2014. Autumn 2014. Issue 76. https://www.strategy-business.com/article/00269?gko=48bd9 (Accessed: October 3, 2022).

Rousseau, D. M. 1989. Psychological and implied contracts in organizations. *Employee Responsibilities and Rights Journal*, 2, 121–139. https://doi.org/10.1007/BF01384942

Rousseau, D. M., Sitkin, S. B., Burt, R. S. and Camerer, C. 1998. Not so different after all: A cross-discipline view of trust. *Academy of Management Review*, 23, 393–404.

Rubenstein, D. 2016. The David Rubenstein Show: Microsoft Co-Founder Bill Gates. December 8, 2016. https://www.youtube.com/watch?v=KlV0fyDC3Gc (Accessed: October 3, 2022).

Runco, M. A. 1999. *Contrarianism.* In M. A. Runco & S. R. Pritzker (Eds.). *Encyclopedia of Creativity* (Vol. 1). San Diego, CA: Academic Press

Russell, B. 1994. *In Praise of Idleness.* London: Routledge.

Sackcloth and Ashes. 2022a. Founding Story. Sackcloth & Ashes. https://sackclothandashes.com/pages/about-new (Accessed: December 24, 2022).

Sackcloth and Ashes. 2022b. Share the Love. https://sackclothandashes.com/ (Accessed: December 24, 2022).

Sackcloth and Ashes. 2022c. Sustainably Made. Sackcloth & Ashes. https://sackclothandashes.com/pages/sustainability (Accessed: December 24, 2022).

Safko, L. and Brake, D. 2009. *The Social Media Bible. Tactics, Tools, and Strategies for Business Success.* Canada: Wiley.

SAI. 2022. SA8000® Standard. Social Accountability International. https://sa-intl.org/programs/sa8000/ (Accessed: December 26, 2022).

Salesforce. 2022a. FY22 Stakeholder Impact Report. https://stakeholderimpactreport.salesforce.com/ (Accessed: October 19, 2022).

Salesforce. 2022b. Salesforce. Bringing People Together Changes Everything. https://www.salesforce.com/company/our-story/ (Accessed: November 19, 2022).

Salzberg, S. 1995. *Lovingkindness. Revolutionary Art of Happiness.* Boston, MA: Shambala Classics.

Salzberg, S. 2014. *Real Happiness at Work. Meditations for Accomplishment, Achievement and Peace.* New York, NY: Workman.

Sampson, H. 2019. Southwest's Plan to Conquer the Airline Industry, One Joke at a Time. *Washington Post.* October 16, 2019. https://www.washingtonpost.com/travel/2019/10/16/southwests-plan-conquer-airline-industry-one-joke-time/ (Accessed: November 30, 2022).

Sangeeth, V. 2010. The Butterfly Effect and Your Employees. *Forbes.* May 17, 2010. https://www.forbes.com/2010/05/17/butterfly-effect-employees-leadership-managing-workplace.html#7f4671d25126 (Accessed: October 2, 2022).

SAS Blog. 2019. Our SAS Culture Code: Perks + Benefits. November 18, 2019. https://blogs.sas.com/content/efs/2019/11/18/our-sas-culture-code-perks-benefits/ (Accessed: October 27, 2022).

Sawyer, K. 2017. *Group Genius. The Creative Power of Collaboration.* New York: Basic Books.

Sawyer, R. K. 2006. *Explaining Creativity. The Science of Human Innovation.* Oxford: Oxford University Press.

Schafer, J. 2015. Self-Disclosures Increase Attraction. *Psychology Today.* March. [Online] Available at www.psychologytoday.com/us/blog/let-their-words-do-the-talking/201503/self-disclosures-increase-attraction (Accessed: September 25, 2018).

Schawbel, D. 2018. *Back to Human. How Great Leaders Create Connection in the Age of Isolation.* London: Piatkus.

Scheffer, M. 1990. *Bach Flower Therapy. Theory and Practice.* London: Thorsons.

Schein, E. 2009. *Corporate Culture Survival Guide.* San Francisco, CA: Jossey Bass.

Scholly. 2021. Programs. April 22, 2021 https://myscholly.com/50-companies-with-amazing-tuition-reimbursement-programs/ (Accessed: October 22, 2022).

Schrage, M. 1990. *Shared Minds. The New Technologies of Collaboration.* New York, NY: Random House.

Schultz, H. 2012. Howard Schultz - I Dreamed Big Dreams. December 2, 2012. https://www.youtube.com/watch?v=c75SF1HJSKo (Accessed: October 2, 2022).

Schultz, H. 2012b. People Business Serving Coffee (Howard Schultz). The LeapTV. January 30, 2012. https://www.youtube.com/watch?v=KOH5LSg5YQA (Accessed: October 23, 2022).

Schultz, W. 1999. The reward signal of midbrain dopamine neurons. *News in Physiological Sciences*, 14(6), 249–255.

Schwab, K. 2019. Davos Manifesto 2020: The Universal Purpose of a Company in the Fourth Industrial Revolution. *World Economic Forum.* December 2, 2019. https://www.weforum.org/agenda/2019/12/davos-manifesto-2020-the-universal-purpose-of-a-company-in-the-fourth-industrial-revolution/ (Accessed: September 24, 2022).

Schwantes, M. 2017. Richard Branson Reveals 3 Important Lessons Most Leaders Learn Too Late in Life at Virgin Group, It's OK to Encourage and Even Celebrate Failure. *Inc.* September 23, 2017. https://www.inc.com/marcel-schwantes/richard-branson-reveals-3-of-his-own-brilliant-habits-for-successful-leadership.html (Accessed: September 26, 2022).

Schwartz, D. 1979. *The Magic of Thinking Big.* London: Pocket Books.

Schwartz, D. 1986. *Maximize Your Mental Power.* London: Thorsons.

Schwartz, T., Gomes, J. and McCarthy, C. 2010. *The Way We're Working Isn't Working. The Four Forgotten Needs That Energize Performance.* New York, NY: Free Press.

Scott, D. M. 2017. *The New Rules of Marketing and PR. How to Use Social Media, Online Video, Mobile Applications, Blogs, Newsjacking, and Viral Marketing to Reach Buyers Directly.* Hoboken, NJ: Wiley.

Scoular, A. 2011. *The Financial Times Guide to Business Coaching.* Harlow: Pearson.

SDGS UN. 2023. The 17 Goals. https://sdgs.un.org/goals (Accessed: January 2, 2022).

Segal, T. and Stapleton. 2022. 5 Most Publicized Ethics Violations by CEOs. *Investopedia.* July 07, 2022. https://www.investopedia.com/financial-edge/0113/5-most-publicized-ethics-violations-by-ceos.aspx (Accessed: December 24, 2022).

Seiter, C. 2014. How We Stay in Sync as a Distributed Team: The Buffer Pair Call. Buffer. https://buffer.com/resources/buffer-daily-pair-call/ (Accessed: December 2, 2022).

Seligman, M. 2006. *Learned Optimism. How to Change Your Mind and Your Life.* New York, NY: Vintage Book.

Senge, P. 1990. *The Fifth Discipline. The Art & Practice of the Learning Organization.* London: Century Business.

Seppälä, E. 2016. Why Nice Guys Really Do Finish First … as Long as They Keep People from Taking Advantage of Them. *Psychology Today.* February 2, 2016. https://www.psychologytoday.com/intl/blog/feeling-it/201602/why-nice-guys-really-do-finish-first (Accessed: January 29, 2023).

Seuring, S. and Müller, M. 2008. From a literature review to a conceptual framework for sustainable supply chain management. *Journal of Cleaner Production,* 16(15), 1699–1710.

Seventh Generation. 2023. Our Company. We Believe in a Seventh Generation. https://www.seventhgeneration.com/company (Accessed: January 2, 2023).

Shapiro, D. L. and Kirkman, B. L. 1999. Employees' reaction to the change to work teams: The influence of "anticipatory" injustice. *Journal of Organizational Change Management,* 12(1), 51–66.

Shapiro, E. and Shapiro, D. 1994. *A Time for Healing. The Journey to Wholeness.* London: Piatkus.

Shawky, S., Kubacki, K., Dietrich, T. and Weaven, S. 2019. Using social media to create engagement: A social marketing review. *Journal of Social Marketing,* 9(2), 204–224.

Shelton, C. and Lynn, M. (Eds.) 2010. *Good Business. Putting Spiritual Principles into Practice at Work.* Unity Village, MO: Unity House.

Shepherd, A. 2023. Why Natural Mica Is a No-No for Lush. https://www.lush.com/au/en/a/faq-lush-and-mica (Accessed: March 25, 2023).

Sherman, S. 2021. Groupthink Examples in Business. *Chron.* May 24, 2021. https://work.chron.com/groupthink-examples-business-21692.html (Accessed: December 24, 2022).

Sheth, J. N. and Mittal, B. 1996. A framework for managing customer expectations. *Journal of Market-Focused Management,* 1(2), 137–158.

Shoen, S. and Singh, A. 2022, Nap pods. Sleep Foundation. https://www.sleepfoundation.org/sleep-hygiene/nap-pods (Accessed: October 12, 2022).

Siebold, S. 2010. *How Rich People Think.* London: London House.

Siemens, 2022. Siemens and NVIDIA Partner to Build the Industrial Metaverse. https://new.siemens.com/global/en/company/insights/siemens-and-nvidia-partner-to-build-the-industrial-metaverse.html (Accessed: December 31, 2022).

Simon, C. 2016. *Impossible to Ignore. Creating Memorable Content to Influence Decisions.* New York, NY: McGraw-Hill.

Simon, H. A. 1971. *Designing Organizations for an Information-Rich World.* In M. Greenberger (Ed.). *Computers, Communication, and the Public Interest,* 37–72. Baltimore, MD: Johns Hopkins Press.

Sirgy, M. J. and Lee, D. J. 2018. *The Psychology of Life Balance.* In Diener, E., Oishi, S. and L. Tay (Eds.). *Handbook of Well-Being.* Salt Lake City, UT: DEF Publishers.

Sirois, F. M. 2016. *Chapter 4 - Procrastination, Stress, and Chronic Health Conditions: A Temporal Perspective.* In Fuschia M. Sirois and Timothy A. Pychyl (Eds.). *Procrastination, Health, and Well-Being,* 67–92. Academic Press. https://doi.org/10.1016/B978-0-12-802862-9.00004-9

Sisodia, R. 2017. *Prologue*. In Worline, M. C. and Dutton, J. E. (Eds.). *Awakening Compassion at Work. The Quiet Power that Elevates People and Organizations*. Oakland, CA: Berrett-Koehler.

Sisodia, R. and Gelb, M. J. 2019. *The Healing Organization: Awakening the Conscience of Business to Help Save the World*. New York: HarperCollins Leadership.

Sisodia, R., Wolfe, D. and Seth, J. 2015. *Firms of Endearment. How World-Class Companies Profit from Passion and Purpose*. Upper Saddle River, NJ: Pearson.

Sisodia, R., Wolfe, D. and Seth, J. 2023. Firms of Endearment. https://www.firmsofendearment.com/ (Accessed: April 20, 2023).

Skonord, C. 2021. My Starbucks Idea Creates Mobile Drive-Thru, Cake Pops, and More. Ideawake. January 19, 2021. https://ideawake.com/my-starbucks-idea-creates-mobile-drive-thru-cake-pops-and-more/ (Accessed: December 31, 2022).

Sloane, P. 2007. *The Innovative Leader. How to Inspire Your Team and Drive Creativity*. London: Kogan Page.

Sloman, J. 2008. *Economics and the Business Environment*. Harlow, UK: Prentice Hall.

Smiles, S. 1859. *Self-Help*. London: John Murray.

Smith, M. L. 2020. A Look at Trader Joe's Social Media & Networking. Mustang Sailor Management & Public Relations. August 7, 2020. https://michaellsmith14.wixsite.com/msmpr/post/a-look-at-trader-joe-s-social-media-networking (Accessed: December 2, 2022).

Solomon, M. 2014. How 13,000 Handwritten Thank-You Notes Built a Thriving Business. *Forbes*. May 11, 2014. https://www.forbes.com/sites/micahsolomon/2014/05/11/thanks/?sh=4b87b76a735d (Accessed: December 26, 2022).

Solomon, M., Bamossy, G. and Askegaard, S. et al. 2006. *Consumer Behaviour. A European Perspective*. Harlow, UK: FT Prentice Hall.

Sony. 2021. News Releases. Sony Honored as One of "2021 World's Most Ethical Companies". February 24, 2021. https://www.sony.com/en/SonyInfo/News/Press/202102/21-017E/ (Accessed: October 2, 2022).

Southwest Air. 2023. Our Culture. https://careers.southwestair.com/culture (Accessed: January 21, 2023).

Southwest Airlines. 2022. https://www.southwest.com/html/air/transfarency/ (Accessed: December 22, 2022).

Spotify. 2022. Work Isn't Somewhere You Go, It's Something You Do. https://www.lifeatspotify.com/being-here/work-from-anywhere (Accessed: December 12, 2022).

Sritharan, A. 2022. Should We Embrace Upcycled Food? The New Food. https://www.newfoodmagazine.com/article/161476/should-we-embrace-upcycled-food/#:~:text=Essentially%2C%20it's%20a%20way%20of,the%20benefits%20of%20upcycled%20food (Accessed: October 14, 2022).

Srivastava, P. 2022. From Netflix to LinkedIn, Here Are 7 Companies that Offer Unlimited Leaves to Their Employees. May 20, 2022. https://www.scoopwhoop.com/career/netflix-hotstar-linkedin-offer-unlimited-leaves-to-employees/ (Accessed: December 2, 2022).

Stanton, A. 2012. Andrew Stanton: The Clues to a Great Story. March 21, 2012. https://www.youtube.com/watch?v=KxDwieKpawg (Accessed: March 23, 2023).

Star Alliance. 2022. About Star Alliance. https://www.staralliance.com/en/about (Accessed: December 2, 2022).

Starbucks. 2022. Starbucks. about Us. https://www.starbucks.co.uk/about-us#:~:text=Today%2C%20with%20more%20than%2032%2C000,specialty%20coffee%20in%20the%20world. (Accessed: October 2, 2022).

Steiner, R. 1986. *The Philosophy of Spiritual Activity*. New York, NY: Anthroposophic Press.

Steiner, R. 2014. *Knowledge of the Higher Worlds. How Is It Achieved?* London: Rudolf Steiner Press.

Stibitz, S. 2015. How to Really Listen to Your Employees. *Harvard Business Review*. January 30, 2015. https://hbr.org/2015/01/how-to-really-listen-to-your-employees (Accessed: October 2, 2022).

Stitchfix. 2022. Personal Styling for Women & Men. https://www.stitchfix.co.uk/ (Accessed: December 2, 2022).

Stokel-Walker, C. 2022. Virtual Meetings Make Creative Problem-Solving Harder. *New Scientist*. April 27, 2022. https://www.newscientist.com/article/2317566-virtual-meetings-make-creative-problem-solving-harder/ (Accessed: December 31, 2022).

Stone, M. and Hartmans, A. 2021. Jack Ma Hasn't Been Seen in 2 Months after Clashing with Chinese Regulators. Here's a Look at How the Alibaba and Ant Group Founder Got Started as a Scrappy Underdog and Amassed a $50 Billion Fortune. *Business Insider*. January 5, 2021. https://www.businessinsider.com/inspiring-life-story-of-alibaba-founder-jack-ma-2017-2?r=US&IR=T (Accessed: September 29, 2022).

Stories Starbucks. 2022. Starbucks Stories & News. People. The Starbucks Foundation. https://stories.starbucks.com/stories/the-starbucks-foundation/ (Accessed: October 12, 2022).

Strauss, V. 2017. The Surprising Thing Google Learned about Its Employees — and What It Means for Today's Students. *The Washington Post*. December 20, 2017. https://www.washingtonpost.com/news/answer-sheet/wp/2017/12/20/the-surprising-thing-google-learned-about-its-employees-and-what-it-means-for-todays-students/ (Accessed: January 2, 2023).

StrawberryFrog. 2023.We Help Leaders Build Their Business with Purpose. StrawberryFrog. https://strawberryfrog.com/about (Accessed: January 29, 2023).

Stubbs, W. and Cocklin, C. 2008. Conceptualizing a "Sustainability business model." *Organization & Environment*, 21(2), 103–127. https://doi.org/10.1177/1086026608318042 (Accessed: January 2, 2023).

Sundén, J. 2013. Organizing a Hack Week. February 15, 2013. Spotify. https://engineering.atspotify.com/2013/02/organizing-a-hack-week/ (Accessed: March 1, 2023).

Sunderland, M. 2007. *What Every Parent Needs to Know. The Incredible Effects of Love, Nurture and Play on Your Child's Development*. London: DK.

Sutcliffe and Vogus. 2003. *Organizing for Resilience*. In Cameron, K. S. Dutton, J. E. and Quinn, R. E. (Eds.). *Positive Organizational Scholarship. Foundations for a New Discipline*. San Francisco: Berrett-Koehler.

Sutherland, S. 2007. *Irrationality*. London: Pinter & Martin.

Suttie, J. 2020. How Kindness Spreads in a Community. *Greater Good Magazine*. November 18, 2020. https://greatergood.berkeley.edu/article/item/how_kindness_spreads_in_a_community?utm_source =Greater+Good+Science+Center&utm_campaign=e437d05929-EMAIL_CAMPAIGN_Special_ Edition_JAN+2023&utm_medium=email&utm_term=0_5ae73e326e-e437d05929-75011080 (Accessed: November 2, 2022).

Suttie, J. 2021. If Humans Evolved to Cooperate, Why Is Cooperation So Hard? *Greater Good Magazine*. August 24, 2021. https://greatergood.berkeley.edu/article/item/if_humans_evolved_ to_cooperate_why_is_cooperation_so_hard?utm_source=Greater+Good+Science+Center& utm_campaign=e437d05929-EMAIL_CAMPAIGN_Special_Edition_JAN+2023&utm_ medium=email&utm_term=0_5ae73e326e-e437d05929-75011080 (Accessed: November 2, 2022).

Suttie, J. and Marsh, J. 2010. 5 Ways Giving Is Good for You. *Greater Good Magazine*. December 13, 2010. https://greatergood.berkeley.edu/article/item/5_ways_giving_is_good_for_you/ (Accessed: November 23, 2022).

Sweetgreen. 2022. Sweetgreen. Our Mission. https://www.sweetgreen.com/mission (Accessed: September 23, 2022).

Swift, M. 2023. Bambi Bucket Inventor Don Arney Uses Meditation as a Tool for Innovation. Meditation Lifestyle. 2023/01/06. https://meditationlifestyle.com/bambi-bucket-inventor-don-arney-on-tm-as-a-tool-for-innovation/ (Accessed: March 3, 2023).

Syal, R. and Brodzinsky, S. 2010. Body Shop Drops Supplier after Report of Peasant Evictions in Colombia. *The Guardian*. October 3, 2010. https://www.theguardian.com/business/2010/oct/03/body-shop-palm-oil-supplier (Accessed: December 27, 2022).

Syamasaki. 2008. "Warrior" Spirit. Southwest. 03-18-2008. https://community.southwest.com/t5/Blog/quot-Warrior-quot-Spirit/ba-p/43921 (Accessed: March 2, 2023).

Sylwester, K. and Gilbert, R. 2010. Cooperators benefit through reputation-based partner choice in economic games. *Biology Letters*, 6659–6662. http://doi.org/10.1098/rsbl.2010.0209 (Accessed: December 2, 2022).

Tabibnia, G. and Lieberman, M. D. 2007. Fairness and cooperation are rewarding: Evidence from social cognitive neuroscience. *Annals of the New York Academy of Sciences*, 1118, 90–101.

Tabrizi, B. 2015. 75% of Cross-Functional Teams Are Dysfunctional. June 23, 2015. *Harvard Business Review* https://hbr.org/2015/06/75-of-cross-functional-teams-are-dysfunctional. (Accessed: December 12, 2022).

Takahashi M, Nakata A, Haratani T, Ogawa Y, Arito H. 2004. Post-lunch nap as a worksite intervention to promote alertness on the job. *Ergonomics*, 47(9), 1003–1013. https://doi.org/10.1080/0014013041 0001686320. PMID: 15204275.

Talavera, J. 2021. Service from The Ritz-Carlton Hotel Helped Hospitals Improve Healthcare Delivery after Hurricane Katrina. Pulse. March 19, 2021. https://www.linkedin.com/pulse/how-lessons-customer-service-from-ritz-carlton-hotel-helped-talavera/?trk=public_profile_article_view (Accessed: January 14, 2023).

Talking Rain. 2023. Rain Maker Spotlight. Better-for-you Innovation https://www.talkingrain.com/blog/post/better-for-you-innovation/ (Accessed: January 3, 2023).

Tapscott, D. 1996. *The Digital Economy. Promise and Peril in the Age of Networked Intelligence*. New York, NY: McGraw-Hill.

Target. 2022. All about Target. https://corporate.target.com/about (Accessed: November 3, 2022).

Tata InnoVista. 2023. Tata InnoVista. About. https://tatainnovista.com/ (Accessed: January 1, 2023).

Tata Motors. 2022. https://www.tatamotors.com/?s=tata%20nano (Accessed: December 31, 2022).

Taylor Wimpey. 2023a. Benefits. https://www.taylorwimpey.co.uk/jobs/how-we-work/benefits (Accessed: February 21, 2023).

Taylor Wimpey. 2023b. We Build Greener, Healthier Homes. https://www.taylorwimpey.co.uk/why-choose-us/we-build-greener-healthier-homes (Accessed: February 21, 2023).

Taylor Wimpey. 2023c. Charity and Local Support. https://www.taylorwimpey.co.uk/why-choose-us/charity-and-local-support (Accessed: February 21, 2023).

Te, N. 2021. This Social Enterprise Donates 100% of Its Proceeds to Foundation Fighting Blindness. NoProfit Pro. February 17, 2021. https://www.nonprofitpro.com/article/this-social-enterprise-donates-100-of-its-proceeds-to-foundation-fighting-blindness/ (Accessed: January 15, 2023).

Terracycle. 2022. Recycled Products. https://www.terracycle.com/en-GB/pages/recycled-products (Accessed: November 20, 2022).

Terracycle. 2023a. Eliminating the Idea of Waste®. https://www.terracycle.com/en-US/about-terracycle (Accessed: January 10, 2023).

Terracycle. 2023b. Discover Our Recycling Process. https://www.terracycle.com/en-GB/about-terracycle/our_recycling_process (Accessed: January 10, 2023).

Thackray, L. 2022. Grieving Woman 'kicked out' of Plane Seat for Family with Baby. November 10, 2022. *Yahoo News*. https://uk.yahoo.com/news/grieving-woman-kicked-plane-seat-124052764.html (Accessed: November 10, 2022).

Thapar, S. 2021. Pre-Mortem: Working Backwards in Software Design. *Medium*. July 6, 2021. https://medium.com/paypal-tech/pre-mortem-technically-working-backwards-1724eafbba02 (Accessed: December 1, 2022).

The B1M. 2020. Why This 3D-Printed House Will Change the World. December 16, 2020. https://www.youtube.com/watch?v=XHSYEH133HA (Accessed: October 3, 2022).

The Body Shop. 2021. 2021 Sustainability Report. https://thebodyshop.a.bigcontent.io/v1/static/The_Body_Shop_Sustainability_Report_2021. (Accessed: October 3, 2022).

The Body Shop. 2022a. The Body Shop. About Us. https://www.thebodyshop.com/en-gb/about-us/our-story/a/a00002 (Accessed: September 26, 2022).

The Body Shop. 2022b. The Body Shop. Our Values. https://www.thebodyshop.com/en-gb/about-us/brand-values/a/a00006 (Accessed: October 3, 2022).

The Body Shop. 2022c. Community Fair Trade. Our Pioneering Programme Has Been Going Strong Since 1987. https://www.thebodyshop.com/en-gb/about-us/brand-values/community-fair-trade/a/a00009%20 (Accessed: December 28, 2022).

The Ecolaundry. 2023. The Ecolaundry. https://www.ecolaundry.co.uk/ (Accessed: March 3, 2023).

The Eden Project. 2022. Eden's Mission. https://www.edenproject.com/mission (Accessed: December 31, 2022).

The Events Company. 2022. https://www.theeventscompany.co.uk/ (Accessed: October 23, 2022).

The Henry Ford. 2020. Walt Disney and His Creation of Disneyland. https://www.thehenryford.org/explore/blog/walt-disney-and-his-creation-of-disneyland/#:~:text=Walt%20claimed%20the%20idea%20of,children%20could%20have%20fun%20together! (Accessed: October 3, 2022).

The Hollister Group. 2022. Two Divisions, One Purpose: People. https://hollistergroup.com/about-us/what-we-do/ (Accessed: December 4, 2022).

The Home Depot. 2018. Business Code of Conduct and Ethics https://ir.homedepot.com/~/media/Files/H/HomeDepot-IR/documents/governance-documents/Code%20of%20Conduct%202018.pdf (Accessed: October 3, 2022).

The Mind Gym. 2007. *The Mind Gym. Wake Your Mind Up*. London: Sphere.

The Mind Gym. 2023. Mind Gym. https://themindgym.com/ (Accessed March 12, 2023).

The Muse. 2022. The Muse. Kendra Scott. https://www.themuse.com/profiles/kendrascott (Accessed: October 3, 2022).

The Ugly Company. 2022. The Ugly Company. https://www.theuglyco.co (Accessed: October 14, 2022).

The Walt Disney Company. 2021. Disney Ranks High on Fortune's 2021 List of "World's Most Admired Companies. The Walt Disney Company. February 1, 2021. https://thewaltdisneycompany.com/disney-ranks-high-on-fortunes-2021-list-of-worlds-most-admired-companies/ (Accessed: October 1, 2022).

The7stars. 2022. Why Work with Us? The7stars. https://www.the7stars.co.uk/careers/ (Accessed: December 29, 2022).

ThermoFisher. 2022. ThermoFisher Scientific. Total Rewards: Physical Wellness, https://jobs.thermofisher.com/global/en/total-rewards-physical (Accessed: December 31, 2022).

Thompson, C. 1992. *What a Great Idea. Key Steps Creative People Take*. New York, NY: Harper Perennial.

Thompson, G. 1995. *Fear: The Friend of Exceptional People*. Chichester, UK: Summersdale.

Thorndike, E. L. 1898. Animal intelligence: An experimental study of the associative processes in Animals. *Psychological Monographs General and Applied*, 2, 1–109.

Thurston, J. 2017. *Kindness. The Little Thing that Matters Most*. London: Thorsons.

Tidd, K. L. and Lockard, J. S. 1978. Monetary significance of the affiliative smile: A case for reciprocal altruism. *Bulletin of the Psychonomic Society*, 11, 344–346.

Tohidian, I. and Rahimian, H. 2019. Bringing Morgan's metaphors in organization contexts: An essay review, *Cogent Business & Management*, 6(1), 1587808. https://doi.org/10.1080/23311975.2019.1587808

Tom's of Maine. 2023. Our Reason for Being. https://www.tomsofmaine.com/our-promise/our-mission/our-reason-for-being#:~:text=Tom's%20of%20Maine%20Mission,information%20about%20products%20and%20issues. (Accessed: March 28, 2023).

Tomasino, D. 2007. The psychophysiological basis of creativity and intuition: Accessing "the zone" of entrepreneurship. *International Journal of Entrepreneurship and Small Business*, 4, 528–542.

Toms. 2022. A Message from our Chief Strategy & Impact Officer. https://www.toms.com/uk/impact-emea/report-emea.html (Accessed: December 28, 2022).

Ton, Z. 2014. *The Good Jobs Strategy: How the Smartest Companies Invest in Employees to Lower Costs and Boost Profits*. Seattle: Lake Union Publishing.

Topham, G. 2014. Sir Richard Branson's Setbacks: From Virgin Cola to Virgin Brides. *The Guardian*. October 6, 2014. https://www.theguardian.com/business/2014/oct/06/sir-richard-branson-failures-vigin-cola-brides (Accessed: September 26, 2022).

Toussaint, L., Worthington, E. L. and Van Tongeren, D. R. et al. 2018. Forgiveness working: Forgiveness, health, and productivity in the workplace. *American Journal of Health Promotion*. 32(1), 59–67. https://doi.org/10.1177/0890117116662312

Toyota. 2013. What is Kaizen and How Does Toyota Use It? *Toyota UK Magazine*. May 31, 2013. https://mag.toyota.co.uk/kaizen-toyota-production-system/#:~:text=Kaizen%20is%20one%20of%20the,Always%20a%20Better%20Way'%20slogan. (Accessed: December 12, 2022).

Trader Joe's. 2019. Why Trader Joe's? | It's Not a Secret, It's People. April 23, 2019. https://www.youtube.com/watch?v=xOpOAicgtSI (Accessed: December 12, 2022).

Tromp, C. and Baer, J. 2022. Creativity from constraints: Theory and applications to education, *Thinking Skills and Creativity*, 46, 101184, ISSN 1871-1871, https://doi.org/10.1016/j.tsc.2022.101184

Trott, P. 2012. *Innovation Management and New Product Development*. Harlow: Prentice Hall.

Trzeciack, S. and Mazzarelli, A. 2019. *Compassionomics: The Revolutionary Scientific Evidence that Caring Makes a Difference*. Pensacola, FL: Studer Group.

Tuckle, S. 2015. *Reclaiming Conversation. The Power of Talk in Digital Age.* New York, NY: Penguin.

Tuten, T. L. and Solomon, M. R. 2017. *Social Media Marketing.* London: Sage.

Tversky, A. and Kahneman, D. 1974. Judgement under uncertainty: Heuristics and biases. *Science,* 185(4157), 1124–1131.

Twice as Warm. 2023. Twice as Warm. https://twiceaswarm.com/ (Accessed: February 21, 2023).

Two Blind Brothers. 2023. Two Blind Brothers. https://twoblindbrothers.com/ (Accessed: February 01, 2023).

Uber. 2022. Uber. About Us. https://www.uber.com/gb/en/about/ (Accessed: October 11, 2022).

Udall, N. and Turner, N. 2008. *The Way of Nowhere. Eight Questions to Release Our Creative Potential.* London: Harper Collins.

Unilever. 2022. "I was born to cook!" Chef Gun Gun's Expertise at the Service of Customers and Community. January 6, 2022. https://www.unilever.com/news/news-search/2022/i-was-born-to-cook/ (Accessed: December 17, 2022).

UPS. 2020. The Power of Difference: UPS Supplier Diversity. UPS. May 14, 2020. https://www.youtube.com/watch?v=DFiFJDaYNAc (Accessed: December 15, 2022).

UPS. 2022a. UPS. Social Impact Reporting. https://about.ups.com/us/en/social-impact/the-ups-foundation.html (Accessed: October 17, 2022).

UPS. 2022b. Earn & Learn. UPS. https://www.jobs-ups.com/earn-and-learn (Accessed: December 15, 2022).

UPS. 2022c Supplier Diversity. UPS. https://about.ups.com/sg/en/our-company/suppliers/supplier-diversity.html (Accessed: December 31, 2022).

Uta, I. 2020. Blue Ocean Strategy: How to Differentiate from the Competition. *Brand Minds Blog.* May 13, 2020. https://brandminds.com/blue-ocean-strategy-how-to-differentiate-from-the-competition/ (Accessed: January 1, 2023).

Vacharkulksemsuk, T. and Fredrickson, B. L. 2012. Strangers in sync: Achieving embodied rapport through shared movements. *Journal of Experimental Social Psychology,* 48(1), 399–402. https://doi.org/10.1016/j.jesp.2011.07.015. PMID: 22389521; PMCID: PMC3290409.

Valtonen, H. 2016. *Risk Management.* Investment Foundations Program. Chapter 18. CFA Institute. [Online] Available at www.cfainstitute.org/en/programs/investment-foundations (Accessed: December 19, 2018).

Van Belleghem, S. 2015. *When Digital Becomes Human. The Transformation of Customer Relationships.* London: Kogan Page.

Verni, K. 2015. *Practical Mindfulness. A Step-by-Step Guide.* London: DK.

Virgin Atlantic. 2022. Virgin Atlantic. Our Awards. https://corporate.virginatlantic.com/gb/en/awards.html#:~:text=Awards%202021&text=Virgin%20Atlantic%20has%20received%20a,for%20the%20 4th%20year%20running. (Accessed: October 1, 2022).

Virgin Atlantic. 2022b. Our Partners. https://flywith.virginatlantic.com/gb/en/partner-airlines.html (Accessed: October 31, 2022).

Virgin Unite. 2023. https://unite.virgin.com/our-work/ Our work (Accessed: March 1, 2023).

Vlad, C. and Bankson, R. 2022. The Toyota Way: Imitate, Improve, Innovate. Globis Insights. August 8, 2022. https://globisinsights.com/career-skills/innovation/the-toyota-way/ (Accessed: December 31, 2022).

Voehl, F. and Harrington, H. J. 2016. *Change Management. Management or It Will Manage You.* Boca Raton: CRC Press.

Von Bergen, C. W., Bressler, M. S. and Campbell, K. 2014. The Sandwich Feedback Method: Not very tasty. *Journal of Behavioral Studies in Business,* 7, 1–13.

Von Hildebrand, D. 2009. *The Nature of Love.* South Bend, IN: Saint Augustine's Press.

Von Oech, R. 2011. *A Whack on the Side of the Head, How You Can Be More Creative.* California: Menlo Park.

Voss, C. and Raz, T. 2017. *Never Split the Difference: Negotiating as If Your Life Depended on It.* New York: Random House Business.

Wagner, N. 2020. Soft Sell Advertising: What It Is, Why It Works, and How to Execute. Stven & Tate. Attraction Marketing. August 28, 2020. https://stevens-tate.com/articles/soft-sell-advertising-what-it-is-why-it-works-and-how-to-execute/ (Accessed: December 1, 2022).

Waldinger, R. and Schultz, M. 2023. *The Good Life: Lessons from the World's Longest Scientific Study of Happiness*. New York: Simon & Schuster.

Wallace, K. 2014. What Your Baby Knows Might Freak You Out. *Edition CNN*. https://edition.cnn.com/2014/02/13/living/what-babies-know-anderson-cooper-parents/index.html (Accessed: October 30, 2022).

Wallas, G. 1926. *The Art of Thought*. New York, NY: Harcourt, Brace and Company.

Walt Disney Company. 2022a. Walt Disney Company. World of Belonging. https://impact.disney.com/diversity-inclusion/ (Accessed: October 14, 2022).

Walt Disney Company. 2022b. Walt Disney Company. Charitable Giving. https://impact.disney.com/charitable-giving/ (Accessed: October 14, 2022).

Walter, D. 2005. *De-Junk Your Mind*. London: Penguin Books.

Warby Parker. 2022. Warby Parker. Buy a Pair, Give a Pair. The Whole Story Begins with You. https://www.warbyparker.com/buy-a-pair-give-a-pair (Accessed: October 14, 2022).

Ward, T. B., Smith, S. M. and Finke, R. A. 1999. *Creative Cognition*. In R. J. Sternberg (Ed.). *Handbook of Creativity*. New York: Cambridge University Press.

Warren, R. 2002. *The Purpose Driven Life. What on Earth Am I Here For?* Grand Rapids, MI: Zondervan.

Wattles, W. 2013. *The Science of Getting Rich*. Theclassics.Us.

Watts, A. 1955. *Wisdom of Insecurity. A Message for an Age of Anxiety*. New York, NY: Vintage Books.

WCED. 1987. *WCED (World Commission on Environment and Development) Our Common Future*. Oxford: Oxford University Press.

Webb, C. 2016. *How to Have a Good Day. Harness the Power of Behavioural Science to Transform Your Working Life*. London: Crown Business.

Wegmans. 2020. The Power of a Nickel. 11/19/2020. https://www.wegmans.com/news-media/articles/the-power-of-a-nickel/ (Accessed: March 23, 2023).

Weick, K. 1995. *Sensemaking in Organizations*. London: Foundation for Organizational Science.

Weiner, Y. 2017. 20 Examples of How Showing Gratitude Helped a Business. October 5, 2017. https://medium.com/thrive-global/20-examples-of-how-showing-gratitude-helped-a-business-86af0fd9e40 (Accessed: September 23, 2022).

Weinzweig, A. 2023. One Customer at a Time. Zingtrain. https://www.zingtrain.com/article/one-customer-at-a-time/ (Accessed: March 23, 2023).

Wellemin, J. 1998. *Successful Customer Care in a Week*. London: Hodder and Stoughton.

Wellington, E. 2020. 8 Companies with Exceptional Customer Service + Helpful Tips. Help Scout. September 8, 2020. https://www.helpscout.com/helpu/exceptional-customer-service-companies/ (Accessed: October 23, 2022).

Wellington, E. 2021. Customer Appreciation Ideas: 17 Ways to Thank Customers. Help Scout. February 6, 2021. https://www.helpscout.com/25-ways-to-thank-your-customers/ (Accessed: October 23, 2022).

Westjet, 2013. WestJet Christmas Miracle: Real-time Giving. 9 Dec 2013. https://www.youtube.com/watch?v=zIEIvi2MuEk (Accessed: April 21, 2023).

Whole Foods. 2022. Environmental Stewardship: Our Green Mission. https://www.wholefoodsmarket.co.uk/mission-in-action (Accessed: September 23, 2022).

Whole Planet Foundation. 2022. Become a Whole Planet Foundation Ambassador https://wholeplanetfoundation.org/get-involved/whole-foods-market-team-member-volunteer-program/ (Accessed: September 23, 2022).

Wickham, P. 2004. *Strategic Entrepreneurship*. London: Prentice Hall.

Wiest, B. 2013. *101 Essays That Will Change the Way That You Think*. Williamsburg, VA: Thought Catalog Books.

Wiley, C. 1997. What motivates employees according to over 40 years of motivation surveys. *International Journal of Manpower*, 18, 263–280. https://doi.org/10.1108/01437729710169373

Williams, A. 2015. 8 Successful People Who Use the Power of Visualization. July 8, 2015. https://www.mindbodygreen.com/articles/successful-people-who-use-the-power-of-visualization (Accessed: December 22, 2022).

Williams, A. 2022. How 5 Companies Celebrate Success. https://fullfocus.co/how-companies-celebrate/ (Accessed: December 23, 2022).

Williams Cosentino, B. 2021. How Naps Can Keep You Happy and Healthy. Landmark. April 20, 2021. https://www.landmarkhealth.org/resource/how-naps-can-keep-you-happy-and-healthy/#:~:text=Naps%20increase%20energy%2C%20improve%20reaction,and%20improve%20many%20cognitive%20abilities. (Accessed: December 3, 2022).

Williamson, M. 1996. *A Return to Love: Reflections on the Principles of a Course in Miracles.* London: Thorsons.

Wilson, M. 2021. Wegmans Food Markets Tops People's '100 Companies That Care' List — Here's Why. 9/1/2021. https://chainstoreage.com/wegmans-food-markets-tops-peoples-100-companies-care-list-heres-why (Accessed: September 23, 2022).

Wiseman, R. 2009. *59 Seconds. Think a Little, Change a Lot.* London: Macmillan.

Wiseman, R. 2013. *The As If Principle. The Radical New Approach to Changing Your Life.* New York, NY: Free Press.

Witten, D. and Rinpoche, A. T. 1999. *Enlightened Management.* VT: Park Street Press.

Wolhorn, H. 1977. *Emmet Fox Golden Keys to Successful Living and Reminiscences.* New York, NY: Harper & Row Publishers.

Wood, W. 2021. *Good Habits, Bad Habits: The Science of Making Positive Changes that Stick.* New York: Pan Books.

Wood, W., Quinn, J. M. and Kashy, D. A. 2002. Habits in everyday life: Thought, emotion, and action. *Journal of Personality and Social Psychology,* 83(6), 1281.

Wood, W. and Rünger, D. 2016. Psychology of habit. *Annual Review of Psychology,* 67, 289–314.

Wooll, M. 2022. What Is Groupthink and How Do You Avoid It? Better Up. March 31, 2022. https://www.betterup.com/blog/what-is-groupthink (Accessed: December 23, 2022).

Worline, M. C. and Dutton, J. 2017. *Awakening Compassion at Work. The Quiet Power That Elevates People and Organizations.* Oakland, CA: Berrett-Koehler.

Wrzesniewski, A. 2014. Job Crafting - Amy Wrzesniewski on Creating Meaning in Your Own Work. re:Work with Google. November 10, 2014. https://www.youtube.com/watch?v=C_igfnctYjA (Accessed: December 2, 2022).

Wrzesniewski, A. and Dutton, J. E. 2001. Crafting a job: Revisioning employees as active crafters of their work. *The Academy of Management Review,* 26, 179–201.

Yahoo. 2022. Yahoo! Careers. Worldwide Workplace. https://www.yahooinc.com/careers/ (Accessed: October 19, 2022).

Yeager, D. S., Purdie-Vaughns, V., Garcia, J., Apfel, N., Brzustoski, P., Master, A., Hessert, W. T., Williams, M. E. and Cohen, G. L. 2014. Breaking the cycle of mistrust: Wise interventions to provide critical feedback across the racial divide. *Journal of Experimental Psychology: General,* 143(2), 804–824. https://doi.org/10.1037/a0033906

Yeti. 2022. Cool Boxes. https://uk.yeti.com/collections/hard-coolers (Accessed: December 21, 2022).

Yeung, R. 2011. *I Is for Influence. New Science of Persuasion.* London: Macmillan.

Yohn, D. L. 2018. Six Surprising Facts that Explain Trader Joe's Secrets to Success. *Forbes.* June 13, 2018. https://www.forbes.com/sites/deniselyohn/2018/06/13/six-surprising-facts-that-explain-trader-joes-secrets-to-success/?sh=261664091601 (Accessed: December 19, 2022).

Yu, A., Berg, J. M. and Zlatev, J. J. 2021. Emotional acknowledgment: How verbalizing others' emotions fosters interpersonal trust. *Organizational Behavior and Human Decision Processes,* 164, 116–135.

Zak, P. 2013. *The Moral Molecule. How Trust Works.* London: Plume.

Zak, P. 2017. The Neuroscience of Trust. *Harvard Business Review.* January-February 2017. https://hbr.org/2017/01/the-neuroscience-of-trust (Accessed: December 2, 2022).

Zaki, J. 2019. *The War for Kindness. Building Empathy in a Fractured World.* London: Robinson.

Zander, R. S. and Zander, B. 2002. *The Art of Possibility. Transforming Professional and Personal Life.* New York, NY: Penguin Books.

Zappos. 2022. Meet the Zappos Family https://www.zappos.com/c/meet-zappos-family (Accessed: October 19, 2022).

Zappos Insights. 2022. Four Peer-To-Peer Ways Zappos Employees Reward Each Other. https://www.zapposinsights.com/blog/item/four-peertopeer-ways-zappos-employees-reward-each-other (Accessed: October 19, 2022).

Zappos Insights. 2023. Zappos 10 Core Values. https://www.zapposinsights.com/about/core-values (Accessed: January 19, 2023).

Zavvy. 2022. 11 Examples of Outstanding Employee Engagement Experiences. https://www.zavvy.io/blog/employee-engagement-examples (Accessed: December 1, 2022).

Zeldin, T. 2000. *Conversation. How Talk Can Change Our Lives*. London: Hiddenspring.

Zhou, J. 1998. Feedback valence, feedback style, task autonomy, and achievement orientation: Interactive effects on creative performance. *Journal of Applied Psychology*, 83, 261–276. https://doi.org/10.1037/0021-9010.83.2.261.

Ziems, M. 2017. Jeff Bezos: Three Simple Beliefs. June 8, 2017. http://the8percent.com/jeff-bezos-three-simple-beliefs/ (Accessed: October 1, 2022).

Zynga, A. 2013. The Cognitive Bias Keeping Us from Innovating. *Harvard Business Review*. June 13, 2013. https://hbr.org/2013/06/the-cognitive-bias-keeping-us-from (Accessed: October 21, 2022).

Index

Printed in the United States
by Baker & Taylor Publisher Services